Behavioral Pediatrics

Psychosocial Aspects of Child Health Care

Stanford B. Friedman, M.D.

Professor of Psychiatry and Human Development; Professor of
Pediatrics; Director, Division of Child and Adolescent Psychiatry;
Head, Behavioral Pediatrics, University of Maryland School of Medicine

Robert A. Hoekelman, M.D.

Professor and Associate Chairman, Department of Pediatrics,
University of Rochester School of Medicine and Dentistry

CALIFORNIA SCHOOL OF PROFESSIONAL PSYCHOLOGY LOS ANGELES

McGraw-Hill Book Company

New York St. Louis San Francisco Auckland Bogotá Hamburg Johannesburg
London Madrid Mexico Montreal New Delhi Panama Paris São Paulo
Singapore Sydney Tokyo Toronto

NOTICE
Medicine is an ever-changing science. As new research and clinical experience broaden our knowledge, changes in treatment and drug therapy are
required. The editors and the publisher of this work
have made every effort to ensure that the drug dosage
schedules herein are accurate and in accord with the
standards accepted at the time of publication. Readers
are advised, however, to check the product information sheet included in the package of each drug they
plan to administer to be certain that changes have
not been made in the recommended dose or in the
contraindications for administration. This recommendation is of particular importance in regard to
new or infrequently used drugs.

This book was set in Palatino by Monotype Composition
Company, Inc. The editors were Richard W. Mixter and
Henry C. De Leo; the designer was Merrill Haber; the
production supervisor was Robert A. Pirrung. The drawings
were done by J & R Services, Inc.
Von Hoffmann Press, Inc., was printer and binder.

Library of Congess Cataloging in Publication Data
Main entry under title:

Behavioral pediatrics.

    "Chapters . . . from Principles of pediatrics."
    Includes Index.
    1.   Pediatrics—Psychological aspects. 2.   Child
development. 3.   Child health services. I.   Friedman,
Stanford B. II.   Hoekelman, Robert A. III.   Principles
of pediatrics. [DNLM: 1.   Child behavior.
2.   Pediatrics.   WS105 B419]
RJ47.5.B43   618.92'89   80-11101
ISBN 0-07-022426-9

This volume is composed of selections from Principles of Pediatrics: Health Care of the Young, edited by Robert A. Hoekelman, Saul Blatman, Philip A. Brunell, Stanford B. Friedman, and Henry M. Seidel.

Contents

Part Five Psychosocial Aspects of Pediatric Care

List of Contributors

Adams, Barbara, R.N., M.S.
Assistant Professor of Nursing (Maternity) and of Pediatrics, School of Nursing, University of Rochester

Anders, Thomas F., M.D.
Associate Professor of Psychiatry and Pediatrics, Stanford University School of Medicine

Armstrong, Judith G., Ph.D.
Associate Professor of Psychology, Towson State University, Baltimore

Beardslee, William R., M.D.
Instructor in Psychiatry, Harvard Medical School; Assistant in Psychiatry, Children's Hospital Medical Center, Boston

Blatman, Saul, M.D.
Professor and Chairman, Department of Maternal and Child Health, Dartmouth Medical School

Brazelton, T. Berry, M.D.
Associate Professor of Pediatrics, Harvard Medical School; Chief, Child Development Unit, Children's Hospital Medical Center, Boston

Brown, Rowine Hayes, M.D., J.D.
Clinical Professor of Pediatrics, Abraham Lincoln School of Medicine, University of Illinois; Adjunct Professor of Law, Chicago Kent College of Law

Caldwell, Bill S., Ph.D.
Associate Professor, Child Development Division, Department of Pediatrics, University of Texas Medical Branch, Galveston

Cohen, Michael W., M.D.
Clinical Associate, Department of Pediatrics, University of Arizona Medical School, Tucson

Cone, Thomas E., Jr., M.D.
Clinical Professor of Pediatrics, Harvard Medical School; Senior Associate in Clinical Genetics and Medicine, Children's Hospital Medical Center, Boston

Davidson, Philip W., Ph.D.
Assistant Professor of Pediatrics and Psychiatry (Psychology), University of Rochester School of Medicine and Dentistry

Ey, John L., M.D.
Clinical Associate, Department of Pediatrics, University of Arizona Medical School, Tucson

Felice, Marianne E., M.D.
Medical Director, Division of Adolescent Medicine, University of California Medical Center, San Diego

Friedman, Stanford B., M.D.
Professor of Psychiatry and Human Development; Professor of Pediatrics; Director, Division of Child and Adolescent Psychiatry; Head, Behavioral Pediatrics, University of Maryland School of Medicine

Gayton, William F., Ph.D.
Associate Professor of Psychology, University of Southern Maine

Graham, David, M.D.
Assistant Professor of Pediatrics and Psychiatry, University of Maryland School of Medicine

Graubard, Allen, Ph.D.
Institute for Labor and Mental Health

Greensher, Joseph, M.D.
Associate Professor of Clinical Pediatrics, State University of New York at Stony Brook; Associate Director of Poison Control Center, Nassau County Medical Center, East Meadow, New York

Heisler, Alice B., M.D.
Assistant Professor of Pediatrics, University of Maryland School of Medicine

Hodgman, Christopher H., M.D.
Associate Professor of Psychiatry and Pediatrics, University of Rochester School of Medicine and Dentistry

Hoekelman, Robert A., M.D.
Professor and Associate Chairman, Department of Pediatrics, University of Rochester School of Medicine and Dentistry

Hofmann, Adele D., M.D.
Associate Professor of Pediatrics, New York University School of Medicine; Director Adolescent Medical Unit, Bellevue Hospital Medical Center, New York

Holter, Joanne C., M.S.W.
Assistant Professor of Pediatrics and Child Abuse Consultant, University of Maryland School of Medicine

Howell, Mary C., M.D., Ph.D.
Assistant Professor of Pediatrics, Boston University School of Medicine; Medical Director and Pediatrician, Charles Drew Family Life Center, Dorchester, Massachusetts

Hyde, James N., Jr., M.A., M.S.
Director, Division of Preventive Medicine, Massachusetts Department of Public Health

Kavanaugh, James G., Jr., M.D.
Assistant Professor of Psychiatry and Pediatrics, University of Virginia School of Medicine

Kinsbourne, Marcel B., D.M., MRCP (London)
Professor of Pediatrics and Psychology, University of Toronto; Director, Neuropsychology Research Unit, Hospital for Sick Children, Toronto

Kulig, Sharon H., Ph.D., CCC-Sp.
Private Practice of Speech-Language Pathology, Dallas, Texas

Leichtman, Sandra R., Ph.D.
Assistant Professor of Psychiatry and Pediatrics, Division of Child and Adolescent Psychiatry, Institute of Psychiatry and Human Development, University of Maryland School of Medicine

Litt, Iris F., M.D.
Associate Professor of Pediatrics, Stanford University School of Medicine; Director, Adolescent Medicine, Stanford University Medical Center

Long, Thomas J., Ed.D.
Associate Professor and Head, Program in Counseling and Guidance, Catholic University of America, Washington, D.C.

Mattsson, Ake, M.D.
Professor of Psychiatry and Pediatrics; Director, Division of Child and Adolescent Psychiatry, New York University-Bellevue Medical Center

McAnarney Elizabeth, M.D.
Associate Professor of Pediatrics, Psychiatry and Medicine; Director, Division of Biosocial Pediatrics and Adolescent Medicine, University of Rochester School of Medicine and Dentistry

McConnochie, Kenneth M., M.D.
Assistant Professor of Maternal and Child Health, Dartmouth Medical School

McKevitt, Rosemary K., R.N., Ed.D.
Associate Professor, School of Nursing, University of Texas Health Science Center at San Antonio

McKinney, Kenneth I., Jr., M.D.
Adjunct Assistant Professor of Maternal and Child Health, Dartmouth Medical School

Mofenson, Howard C., M.D.
Professor of Clinical Pediatrics, State University of New York at Stony Brook; Director Poison Control Center, Nassau County Medical Center, East Meadow, New York

Munson, Stephen W., M.D.
Assistant Professor of Psychiatry and Pediatrics, University of Rochester School of Medicine and Dentistry

Myers, Beverly A., M.D.
Assistant Professor of Psychiatry and Pediatrics, Brown University; Director, Division of Child and Adolescent Psychiatry, Rhode Island Hospital

Nader, Philip R., M.D.
Professor of Pediatrics and Preventive Medicine and Community Health, University of Texas Medical Branch

Newberger, Eli H., M.D.
Assistant Professor of Pediatrics, Harvard Medical School; Director, Family Development Study, Children's Hospital Medical Center, Boston

Parcel, Guy S., Ph.D.
Associate Professor, Department of Pediatrics, Division of School Health and Community Pediatrics, University of Texas Medical Branch, Galveston

Pless, I. Barry, M.D., F.R.C.P. (C)
Professor of Pediatrics, Epidemiology and Health; National Health Scientist; Director, Community Pediatric Research, McGill University, Montreal

Prazar, Gregory, M.D.
Pediatrician, Exeter Clinic, Exeter, New Hampshire

Richmond, Julius, M.D.
Assistant Secretary for Health and Surgeon General, Public Health Service, Department of Health, Education, and Welfare, Washington, D.C.

Rockowitz, Ruth J., M.S.W.
Social Worker, Department of Pediatrics, University of Rochester School of Medicine and Dentistry

Rogoff, Mai-Lan A., M.D.
Assistant Professor of Psychiatry, Dartmouth Medical School

Rosenfeld, Alvin A., M.D.
Assistant Professor, Department of Psychiatry and Behavioral Sciences; Director of Training in Child Psychiatry, School of Medicine, Stanford University; Fellow, Boys Town Center for Youth and Development at Stanford University

Rozycki, Darden Whelden, B.A.
Maternal and Child Health Consultant, Dartmouth Medical School; Vermont State Coordinator, International Childbirth Education Association, Norwich

Sarles, Richard M., M.D.
Associate Professor of Child Psychiatry and Pediatrics, University of Maryland School of Medicine

Satterfield, Sharon, M.D.
Director, Program in Human Sexuality; Assistant Professor, Department of Family Practice and Community Health, Assistant Professor of Child Psychiatry, University of Minnesota

Schechter, Marshall D., M.D.
Director, Irving Schwartz Institute for Children and Youth; Professor and Director, Division of Child and Adolescent Psychiatry, University of Pennsylvania School of Medicine, Philadelphia

Schmidt, William M., M.D.
Professor of Maternal and Child Health, (Emeritus), Harvard School of Public Health, Cambridge

Schonberg, S. Kenneth, M.D.
Associate Professor of Pediatrics, Albert Einstein College of Medicine of Yeshiva University; Associate Director, Division of Adolescent Medicine, Department of Pediatrics, Montefiore Hospital and Medical Center, Bronx, New York

Seidel, Henry M., M.D.
Associate Professor of Pediatrics and Associate Dean for Student Affairs, Johns Hopkins University School of Medicine; Associate Professor of Health Care Organization, Johns Hopkins University School of Hygiene and Public Health

Smoyak, Shirley A., Ph.D.
Associate Dean for Research; Graduate Director, College of Nursing, Rutgers—The State University of New Jersey

Snyder, David, M., M.D.
Clinical Assistant Professor of Pediatrics, University of California at San Francisco School of Medicine; Assistant Chief of Pediatrics, Valley Medical Center of Fresno

Starfield, Barbara, M.D., M.P.H.
Professor and Head, Health Care Organization and Joint Appointment in Pediatrics, Johns Hopkins University School of Hygiene and Public Health and School of Medicine

Stine, Oscar C., M.D., Dr. P.H.
Associate Professor of Pediatrics, University of Maryland School of Medicine; Chief, Department of Ambulatory Care, Greater Baltimore Medical Center

Sumpter, Edwin A., M.D.
Professor of Pediatrics, University of Massachusetts Medical Center

Weiner, Irving B., Ph.D.
Vice Chancellor for Academic Affairs and Professor of Psychology, University of Denver

Yogman, Michael W., M.D.
Instructor of Pediatrics, Harvard Medical School, Cambridge

Young, William W., M.D.
Assistant Professor, Department of Maternal and Child Health, Obstetrics, and Gynecology, Dartmouth Medical School

Preface

This volume is composed of selections from *Principles of Pediatrics: Health Care of the Young*, edited by Robert A. Hoekelman, Saul Blatman, Philip A. Brunell, Stanford B. Friedman, and Henry M. Seidel. From that source, those sections devoted to the psychological and social needs of children and adolescents have been included in this smaller and more focused book.

Part 1, "Comprehensive Pediatric Care," is an overview of the delivery of health care to children and adolescents. The sections range from the establishment of a data base to societal influences on health care. Above all, the topics discussed in Part 1 emphasize that the practice of pediatrics cannot be isolated from the multiple complexities of our society and organization of our health care systems.

Part 2, "Special Needs of Medically-Ill Children and Adolescents," examines some of the psychological needs of physically ill children and adolescents and of their parents. There is an emphasis on the communication process, especially as directly related to patient care.

Part 3, "Sexual Development and Pregnancy," acknowledges the special problems related to sexuality and adolescent pregnancy. It assumes that pediatrics as a discipline will continue to expand into the adolescent years, and perhaps into young adulthood in some dimensions of health care.

Part 4, "Topics In School Health," reflects the importance of school in a child's life. More specifically, the school is an ideal setting for preventive mental health, and the early identification of psychosocial problems. The multiple advantages of close collaboration between the providers of health care and school personnel are emphasized.

Part 5, "Psychosocial Aspects of Pediatric Care," includes a collection of sections that cover broad topics, such as family structure, day care, adoption, and legal issues. Other sections are devoted to specific problems related to child rearing. Lastly, common emotional disorders are discussed within a developmental context.

This book is meant to be practical and useful to the clinician. It assumes an interdisciplinary approach to meet the health needs of children and adolescents. The editors also hope that it offers some help to the providers of primary care to our youth by including information about cultural and social issues as they relate to physical and mental health.

Stanford B. Friedman
Robert A. Hoekelman

PART ONE

Comprehensive Pediatric Care

1 | Ecology of Patient Care

by Henry M. Seidel and Robert A. Hoekelman

Ecology is the study of the relation between living organisms and their environment including the sociocultural and the physical dimensions. It is notable that the word "ecology" is based on the Greek word for "house" (*oikos*). Even in its most literal sense, "house" implies a wholeness, which we try to achieve in health care.

role, it is essential that we understand the dimensions of those factors and of our potential and desired contribution. Thus, the variables which influence the course of human experience, our efforts to help during this experience, and the responses those efforts elicit in our patients constitute the ecology of health care.

THE NEED TO UNDERSTAND THE NATURE OF THE ECOLOGY OF HEALTH AND HEALTH CARE

The practice of medicine and the provision of health care require an exquisite combination of precision, purpose, and love. Competence and commitment in health professionals are necessary. However, they are not sufficient. We must be aware of the values we share with our patients, and, more than that, we must work for the development of mutual respect.

Too often, we who provide care suffer the conceit that our interventions are the major determinants of the well-being of people. It is more likely that we play a lesser role and that other determinants of behavior, emotions, and physical health are the variables which dominate.

We do want to move the patients we serve toward, or maintain them at, some *mutually* agreed and acceptable levels of behavior and function. The factors which affect the achievement of these levels are the determinants of a "quality" of life and a harmonious ecology of health. If we are to succeed as providers of health care and be satisfied with our

THE NATURE OF THE ECOLOGY OF HEALTH CARE

The gene embodies the *potential* of the individual. It exerts the prime influence on what the person is to become, on the inherent resources available to the development of the coping mechanisms necessary to the maintenance of balance and harmony with the environment, and on how that person will fare in the long run.

Each person has a *perception* of the world which has many intrinsic and extrinsic modifiers and which depends on the anatomic and physiologic receptors available to the individual. How well they work will be a principal but not the only determinant of intelligence, viewpoint, and ability to manage stimuli, feelings, and relationships with others.

There are confounding factors, ecological *perversions* which can influence the course of growth and development and which can corrupt both potential and perception. There are, for balance, ecological *potentiators* which work toward the greatest realization of potential. Much of this text is devoted to a full exploration of these potentiators and perversions.

These factors can be observed, measured, and recorded and may serve as *predictors* of the realization of the potential of a given individual. Sex, race, socioeconomic class, climate, and economic stability are but a few examples. They, along with an individual's genic endowment and perception, will provide the base from which *personality* evolves.

The individual has *parents* and a family whose contributions to the personality are so important that most of health care cannot, over time, be effectively provided without a firm understanding of those contributions. The relationship between an individual and his family is relatively fixed and less subject to modification than is the relationship of the individual to the community.

The community is the *place* where the interactions of human experience occur, constantly modified by cultural, sociologic, and economic determinants which, in turn, influence the health and well-being of the individual.

Almost everyone is at one time or another a *patient*. A few individuals learn to become *providers* of care, often as physicians, nurses, dentists, health associates, assistants, or counselors. Whether they work alone or as a team, their own personalities affect the interaction with the patient. The team's inner relationships play a major role in that interaction.

Each individual is subject to stress and to the development of problems, dependent on the outcome of the multiple interactions already indicated. These problems, in turn, become an element of the ecology of health care. It is the problem, though, which prompts the individual to seek care. The harmony and conflict of the patient and provider coming together to solve the problem contribute significantly to the achievement of a solution and to the patient's compliance with management regimens.

Some questions must then be asked. Who has the basic responsibility for health care? The patient? The provider? The family? The community? And to what degree? What is necessary to allow each individual to be successful in seeking, receiving, and responding to health care?

The attempt to understand the interdependence between the individual and the environment requires a holistic approach. To be effective we must also understand the question of responsibility for care and be willing to modify the degree of our

interventions. We must be willing to share a relationship with the patient which allows the continuing education of each of us and which allows consideration not only of biophysical but also of behavioral, psychosocial, economic, and political factors. Above all, perhaps, we must understand ourselves well so that we do not assume any degree of privilege and responsibility that is rightly the patient's. In the care of the young, this consideration is even more complex because the patient is most often accompanied by a parent or guardian.

ORDERLINESS AND ENERGY

Ecology implies a sense of order. Lehninger, a biochemist, reminds us that "living organisms create and maintain their essential orderliness at the expense of their environment which they cause to become more disordered and random." "Molecular orderliness" has a cost. It cannot arise spontaneously from disorder. Energy, derived from the environment, must be usable under the special conditions of the temperature and pressure in which the organism lives. An equivalent amount of energy must be returned to the environment in some other, less useful form. While Lehninger cites this as axiomatic in the molecular logic of living organisms, it is intriguing to consider whether the same axiomatic necessity dominates the behavioral logic of these same organisms. Is there a balance, in nature, of emotional energy? Is it renewable, reusable? For each individual, of course, there is ultimate depletion. Still, there may be more acceptable ways than we now employ to husband our physical and emotional resources. Can we, as providers of care, help the patient in this regard? If we make the attempt, to what extent do we allow the depletion of our own resources?

In any event, let us arbitrarily accept that molecular orderliness begins with the gene and, from there, further explore the ecology of health care.

The Gene

We are today at a point along the way to an unknown outcome at an unknown time of an evolutionary process which we still assume is based on natural selection. This is an evolution *from* a somewhat understood past, not *to* an understood objective. Dunn reminds us that

Both human beings and other organisms adjust to their environments as populations. The essential factor in biological adjustment is the differential representation of the variety of genotypes in successive generations. . . . In most cases the fate of the individual is not fixed in the fertilized egg, but gradually works itself out during development as one or a few pathways out of many possible ones are followed. . . . [T]he effects of the gene in the individual and in the population are not inevitably guaranteed, otherwise there would have been no evolution. . . . In man, the social and cultural milieu provides an important part of the environment in which human evolution occurs.

In other words, the presence of the gene is a necessary but not a sufficient condition.

Nevertheless, as McKusick suggests, the nature of the gene has implications not only for all aspects of the science of humankind but also for the social, political, and cultural aspects of human activity. While this may be self-evident, it does bear emphasis. Furthermore, the gene is the communicator for a succession of generations which probably began sometime after the formation of the earth, some 4800 million years ago. Homo sapiens is just about 2 million years old—or, as Lehninger puts it, a length of time, as compared with that of the existence of the earth, that is but 30 s in a 24-h day. If life began as postulated 3100 million years ago, the message of the gene has persisted and evolved over that time.

It may be that the initial life event involved the development of enzymes and a cell boundary and that the genetic system evolved later. It is more likely, however, that persistence of that primal cell required nucleic acids and a genetic system, and that nucleic acid or the so-called naked gene was the first form of life. Our present knowledge of the structure and self-replication of viruses seems to validate this. Nucleic acid molecules do carry the information necessary for their replication, and deoxyribonucleic acid (DNA) does constitute genetic material. Avery's experiment demonstrated that "the simple addition of DNA isolated from one type of bacterial cell transformed the phenotype of another strain in a heritable manner."

The gene is, then, the messenger from generation to generation. The three basic steps are replication, transcription, and translation. While we cannot strain the model too much to create analogies for human behavior, it is clear that elements of all these are essential in all satisfactory communication. To the extent that we can replicate our meanings in speech or sign, transcribe them to appropriate settings, and translate them into a language understandable to the listener, our efforts at communication may be successful. The listener, in this regard, is a receptor.

If the genetic message is to be transmitted accurately, it must be transcribed from DNA onto a transportable "device," messenger ribonucleic acid. The decoding, that is, the translation, relies also on a receptor which must be sensitized to allow the response indicated by the transmitted information. Encoding and translation require a dictionary, and the genetic "dictionary" of triplet code words for the various amino acids provides just that for the genetic message. It is appropriate to postulate similar coding in behavioral terms with a similar potential for a "dictionary." The numbers of variables seem infinite compared with those derived from the amino acids. But are they? Is it appropriate to suggest that the same sense of order dominates our psychic and social behavior?

The "View from Within"

Mountcastle has said that

Each of us lives within the universe—the prison—of his own brain. Projecting from it are millions of fragile sensory nerve fibers in groups uniquely adapted to sample the energetic states of the world around us: heat, light, force, and chemical composition. That is all we ever know of it directly; all else is logical inference. Sensory stimuli reaching us are transduced at peripheral nerve endings, and neural replicas of them are dispatched to the gray matter of the cerebral cortex. We use them to form dynamic and continually updated neural maps of our place and orientation in the external world, and of events within it. At the level of sensation, your images and my images are virtually the same, and readily identified one to another by verbal descriptions, or common reactions. Beyond that, each image is conjoined with genetic and stored experiential information that makes each of us uniquely private. From that complex integral each constructs at a higher level of perceptual experience, on my view in brain regions like those of the parietal lobe, his own, very personal view from within.

Indeed, an organic lesion in the parietal lobe will distort one's view. And, while this is not a frequent event, those who are so affected have an altered perception of the body and its relation to surrounding space, especially in stereotactic and visual exploration of the immediate extrapersonal space.

Given this and if our other neural mechanisms are intact, our sensory inputs are ultimately expressed in a perception that is subject to the infinite variety of our past genetic and experiential store of information. There is a gap which we are not yet able to define with hard neurophysiologic information. Again, Mountcastle reminds us:

> Sensations are set by the encoding functions of sensory nerve endings and by the integrating neural mechanics of the central nervous system. Afferent nerve fibers are not high fidelity recorders, for they accentuate certain stimulus features, neglect others. The central neuron is a storyteller with regard to the nerve fibers, and it is never completely trustworthy, allowing distortions of quality and measure, within a field strained by isomorphic spatial relations between "outside" and "inside."

In fact, we cannot yet delineate *precisely* how our preceptions take form. But, from infancy, we have at our disposal the inner ability, untaught by our parents, to make conclusions about our experiences and our impact on our immediate environment.

And if, in fact, our interpretations are misinterpretations and our perceptions misperceptions, as our neural connections do their work, we may make cognitive determinations which, in terms of our orientation in the extrapersonal world and in terms of our coping ability, may be inappropriate. We must try to understand this if, as care providers, we intend to intervene. This, of course, implies that our intervention might help. Pirsig reminds us of the inherent difficulty when he says:

> . . . and when you look directly at an insane man all you see is a reflection of your own knowledge that he's insane, which is not to see him at all. To see him, you must see what he saw and when you are trying to see the vision of an insane man, an oblique route is the only way to come at it. Otherwise, your own opinions block the way. . . .

Thus, patient and provider may at times be uncomfortable, vaguely ill at ease. Thus, they may both too often avoid an effort at intervention that might help.

STRANGERS IN OUR OWN HOUSE

The sense of order is nowhere more fuzzy than in our perceptions of our selves in the world and our relationships to others. Since our "view from within" is an abstraction of reality, the variations are infinite as one individual's abstraction attempts to mesh with another's or with combinations of others. There may often be a sense of unreality, of distance. We may feel as strangers in our own house.

> A physician and her husband consulted their son's pediatrician about behavior that was puzzling and somewhat disturbing to them. He was almost 10 years old, the youngest of three brothers, bright, affable, seemingly in harmony with himself, his family, and the world around him. And yet, on two or three occasions, his father had arrived home in the early evening to find him standing forlorn against the back wall of the house. They talked, sitting in the father's car, and at least twice the boy sobbed into his father's shoulder, saying, "I don't know. I feel so funny. It's like it's not real and like I'm not here and I don't know what's happening."

Does this child have a problem, or is he becoming aware and expressing for the first time the alienation and distance all of us feel in some degree and with some frequency? It is not uncommon for children and their families to seek help, asking whether a problem exists. We find, then, that we are sociobiologic creatures with a neurophysiologic armamentarium not yet precisely understood. We participate in life informed by our "view from within." That view primes our efforts to cope with "reality" and to communicate and interact with others.

THE OCCASIONAL OBSCURITY OF ORDER

We have suggested that human behavior is probably as finely ordered as organic molecular structure. Still, in behavioral terms, much more than in physical terms, there is an apparent randomness of experience. In part, this may be due to the seeming absence of a defined goal for humankind and of a common answer to questions about life and death and the future. We need to define ourselves as individuals and to find our fates. Without universally accepted direction, we make our moves based on a past which is variously understood by each of us; thus, our apparent randomness and our apparent infinity of choices.

Burgess suggests that there may be some need for "new" directions based on the idea that our anticipations of the future add a dimension which can modify what happens. Our inability to quantify the effect of such anticipation also intensifies the apparent randomness. It also reminds us that we do move through life *assuming* a future. It is the promise of this "assumptive world" that keeps us going. Sadly, when confronted with the care of the dying child, we often adopt behavior which denies for that child the possibility of this "world of the future"; we diminish the child's anticipation and increase his or her loneliness and isolation.

Health care is feasible only if it is predicated on a sense of order. Otherwise, there can be no substance to advice, counseling, and the other interventions of the health professional, since the circumstances in which the individual negotiates life are based on order.

THE NEED FOR NEGOTIATION

Negotiation is part of the process of life activity. Although we are not certain when this begins, even the fetus is in a process of anticipatory negotiation with the parents and the world around. Certainly, major negotiations take place between the child and each parent, the parents as a unit, the siblings, and the various combinations of family members. Their success requires a sense of responsibility in all participants, and the eventual results depend in large part on the ages and priorities of those involved and on the constraints imposed by the inanimate environment. The patient—the child—*viewing all this from within* may perceive that demands in a particular negotiation are too heavy, or ambiguous, or simply beyond the child's ability to respond appropriately. The provider of care must be sensitive to this interplay of perception and need in order to play a positive role as a counselor. If we are consulted because negotiations are difficult, the effort should be made to ease the burden of excessive demand, clarify expectations, and ease conflict. Certainly, the patient and the parents, the most commonly confronted "group" in pediatrics, do not always have the discipline to

structure their interactions positively; they will, therefore, often rely on a counselor.

A 17-year-old young man placed first in his senior class in high school. His parents, particularly his mother, wanted very much to have him attend Harvard. As is often the circumstance, Harvard disagreed. The young man went to Yale—suffering the persistent and thinly veiled disapproval of his mother. Five years later he was still feeling uneasy and defeated. The heavy burden put on him by his mother could not be negotiated away, and the conflict generated by his inability to meet her expectations remains unresolved.

The Inanimate Environment

A brief reminder here: The inanimate environment provides a set of constraints which may have the ultimate influence on the human condition. While we worry a good deal about our waste of resources on one hand and the relentless thrust of nature on the other, we persist in our encroachment on the limited resources available to us. A child born in 1978 will, at the age of 22 years, be one of 7 billion people on earth, which is about 3 billion more than in his year of birth. Pimentel et al., remind us that there will be a concomitant demand for food and that it is more difficult to increase food supplies than it is to control disease. This is a matter of concern if the estimate of 500 million protein-calorie malnourished people in the world in 1975 is at all correct. In the Orient about 56 g of protein per person is eaten each day, about one-seventh of it as animal protein, primarily milk. In the United States, on the other hand, 96 g of protein is eaten per person each day, two-thirds of it animal. The relation of animal protein consumption to coronary heart disease has repeatedly been suggested. It may, therefore, be fortunate that the world diet will never be able to depend in major part on animal protein. Cereals and legumes will be the staples. Still, the enormous potential dietary need (by 2135, a 173 percent increase in the demand for legumes, 200 percent for other vegetables, and 330 percent for cereals), concomitant land, water, and energy shortages, and limited crop water and limited crop responsiveness to increased fertilizer usage remind us that the ecological circumstance in which we offer child care is seriously constrained. The human "house" may be too small.

PRECISION AND PROBABILISM

It is easy, day to day, when dealing with so much that is subjective and hard to define to forget the order we assume exists. We must, therefore, attempt precision and yet remain comfortable with the frequent and often desirable need to resort to probabilism.

Numbers, used well, do help. For example, Chabot and his colleagues remind us that, in the mid-sixties in the United States, after one day of life, infant mortality increased progressively as degree of urbanization decreased; that the differences between urban and rural death rates are greatest after the first week of life; that, in all age groups at all levels of urbanization, the nonwhite is at a marked disadvantage in relation to the white infant; and that the older the infant, the greater the disadvantage for nonwhite infants in rural areas. In fact, in the years 1962 to 1967, had the white infant mortality rate prevailed in the nonwhite population, about 12,000 more nonwhite infants would have survived their first year of life in each of those years.

There are those who would say that scientific achievement is the surest approach to an improvement in an environment and a society. Others, considering these numbers, would agree with Jelliffe that there may be a need for medical scientists, including pediatricians, to escape from their conservative overly technological tunnel vision toward a more subjective, more encompassing view. Precision and passion are not mutually exclusive.

Still, if we are to make judgments, we must have predictors. We must understand as thoroughly as possible the context of the problems brought to us, and we must have reasonable approaches to solutions. Such approaches might include, in the evaluation of predictors, a strong measure of probabilism based upon clinical experience and clinical judgment.

Given this, we agree with Feinstein, who says:

All good clinicians use a distinctly clinical type of reasoning called Clinical Judgment for making decisions about prognoses and therapy of patients. We often refer to a clinician's judgment as being good or bad according to the wisdom with which these decisions are made. The reasoning in this type of clinical thinking is quite different from the reductive logic employed to establish diagnosis, etiology, or pathogenesis of a patient's disease. Clinical judgment depends not on a knowledge of causes, mechanisms or names for disease, but on a knowledge of patients. The background of clinical judgment is clinical experience: the things clinicians have learned at the bedside in the care of sick people. In acquiring this experience, every clinician has to use some sort of intellectual mechanism for organizing and remembering . . . observations.

The range of problems one is likely to encounter in pediatrics may be more limited than, for example, in family practice. But not by much. The child cannot be separated from the adult. Furthermore, problems usually require more "puzzling out" when first encountered than after referral to a consultant. The interplay of social and emotional factors may obscure the physical elements, and the patient may present too early to allow for differentiation of the diagnosis on the basis of the clinical course. Above all, in primary care the patient is seen repeatedly and with an intimacy that is not the privilege of the consultant. Thus, the observation, measurements, and recording of change over time is particularly important in pediatrics. Also, it is necessary to understand the incidence and prevalence of problems in the population served, be they physical, social, or emotional. It pays to know what's "going around."

In the long run, while probabilism implies imperfection in prediction, the rigid use of superficial objective knowledge may be a trap. The good clinician recognizes this and is sensitive to "soft" clues.

A 9-month-old baby was the last of three siblings to develop an acute gastrointestinal disturbance characterized by abdominal pain, diarrhea, vomiting, and fever. The illness of the two older siblings and of the mother lasted about 24 to 36 h. They felt better and were eating normally soon afterward. But the baby was cranky, anorexic, and still vomiting after 48 h. The pediatrician, too reliant on the too apparent, temporized during a telephone conversation. "It doesn't always last the same length of time." Restlessness and a persistent low-grade fever, however, command attention, especially in infants. The baby was finally examined. There was a palpable abdominal mass which proved to be an abscess which was walled off, the result of a perforated appendix.

Probabilism cannot and should not be avoided. It is an essence of clinical skill that is not easily acquired or applied. And it must not be confused with careless or inappropriate shortcuts in care.

The People Involved

Given these intimations of approaches to care, consider now the people involved and the nature of their involvement. For example, the potential provider of care for a 1-year-old infant with nutritional anemia may simply prescribe iron. In most instances, however, the mother's needs and feelings should be sought and attempts made to arrive at appropriate judgments, to intervene subsequently for possible improvement in the situation, and to educate.

We use the word "provider" because this person may be a family practitioner, pediatrician, nurse practitioner, nurse, or physician's assistant acting singly or as a member of a health care team. For each, there is always a range of possible approaches to the management of any given problem. And, for each, it is appropriate to add positive intervention and facilitation to the traditionally accepted task of the cure of physical disease. This requires attention to the needs of the family. As Mauksch puts it, ". . . the skill of assessing, evaluating, and assisting the needs of the family health unit require . . . a change in the total approach to health care, including . . . a different definition of relevance and significance and, above all, a change in the fundamental role of the health care practitioner. . . . To the traditional model of repair and restoration must be added the model of accommodation, facilitation, and enablement."

If this is so, then who is the patient and for whom do we advocate? The lesson of ecology is lost if we tend only the child rather than children and children rather than the family and the family rather than the community.

A 17-year-old young man is behaviorally and intellectually retarded. The public school system is unprepared in its resources and, perhaps, its inclinations to respond to his needs. His family's financial resources are limited. His inability to achieve and his social gaucheries are a source of constant distress to his mother, who is divorced, an educator, and the possessor of a doctorate, and to his 15- and 16-year-old sisters. He is hungry for affection and acceptance. He is manifestly un-

happy. His mother has shared the problems inherent in this situation with the boy's pediatrician.

Who is the patient? What should be the thrust of advocacy and intervention?

Adaptation

Survival depends on adaptation to one's milieu, and that adaptation relies in large part, once again, on an ability to negotiate. Since our interventions as health practitioners may influence negotiation, they become part of the patient's adaptive process.

Therefore, we must be aware that our behavior is modified by our experiences with the attitudes, customs, and forms of our society. It is difficult, therefore, to separate those judgments based on our "professional" perceptions from those influenced by our personal values. The mix of perceptions makes our manipulation of the adaptive process difficult. The more our value judgments dominate, the more we preach, and the less effective we are likely to be.

People who negotiate successfully are adapting. They are having relationships which, because they work, are examples of harmony. The maintenance of life by any measure demands this harmony. It is the crux of the Darwinian concept.

Weiss reminds us that, on a cellular level, the integrity of our bodies depends on the ability of the individual components down to the submicroscopic to fit together. It is particularly fascinating that the development of the embryo is a prearrangement in forward reference to the needs of the mature body. "The eye develops without seeing." What we have we have because there is already proof by past trial and error of the adaptive potential. It is more difficult, perhaps, to appreciate this in terms of our psychosocial needs than our physical needs.

The constant demand for adaptation, whether psychosocial or physical, evolves from stress and imposes stress. We may be able to respond and to survive, but there are limits. Sometimes we survive by staying and fighting, sometimes by running. Sometimes we need new enzymes for new substances, and our old enzymes, with appropriate exposure to the new substrate, change to do the work, while constantly alert for the aberrant protein. Still, not all adaptations can be valued as good even if they appear to meet the immediate needs. The development of sensitivity to penicillin is a case in point. It is not unlike a bargaining process, and sometimes the bargains that are struck are poor.

Additionally, we seek qualities in life beyond survival. They vary from individual to individual and, in the aggregate, from culture to culture, and they tell us much about why we do things. The struggle for qualities may at times, particularly in our emotional behavior, lead us from "normal" into "abnormal" behavior. A negotiation for improved quality may demand a posture which is maladaptive and thus no longer perceived as normal by those around us. We are called "neurotic." Health professionals must understand the roots of such "abnormalities." A familiar example is the child who is phobic with regard to going to school.

A 12-year-old girl, an only child, did not go to school for $2\frac{1}{2}$ weeks. Her mother, who was going to college, left home each day before the child did and came home late in the afternoon. The parents were divorced. When the school official discovered the situation, the youngster said that she needed someone "to take me all the way there and to put me through the door. It scares me to go away from home."

What absence of quality was she trying to redress? The search for an understanding of the compensation she was seeking was essential to the solution of a problem defined by her mother and the school—by society. This child's temporary adaptation is, at the least, a neurotic form of behavior. But, we cannot assume that this inappropriate bargain, in terms of reality, is any more indicative of an abnormal personality than is a good adjustment in societal terms necessarily indicative of a normal personality. The one certainty is that whatever our seeming condition, that condition is a response to hidden neurotic needs which comes to our attention as a problem only when the balance inconveniences or unsettles the family or the community. It is important, however, in assessing the individual to understand that a seeming harmony with the family and with society may not be that at all. Neurotic need, if its satisfactions serve societal ends, may not be understood as neurotic.

Intelligence, ideas, feelings, and anticipation all generate an effort for survival with quality and stimulate major conficts when there is survival without quality. Nevertheless, it is reasonable to assume that the more we know and understand, the more able we are to adapt to survival without quality even though this may cause major behavioral difficulties.

Compliance: The Individual May Behave Unpredictably

Compliance—a measure of the patient's response to our suggestions for the management of problems—gives major clues to the understanding of the individual and the family. The population can be sorted into thirds. One group will do as we suggest, one group won't, and another will think about it. While these numbers indicate the size of the problem, the predictors which will place a given patient (or patient's parent) within a given group with some certainty are unclear. Additionally, a patient's decision may be more appropriate than the physician's. There are, of course, individual determinants leading to the behavioral sorting which takes place. These may include the nature of our relationship with the patient, the degree of patient understanding of the disease, the complexity of our orders, and the patient's perceptions of the severity of the disease and idea of the worth of survival against the quality of survival. We do not yet understand how these factors balance in the ultimate decision. Meyers and his colleagues have shown, however, that with a disease like cystic fibrosis, the compliance rate is twice as high as with most other illnesses, and that this is possibly the result of the perception of the severity of the disease and the consequences of disregarding medication.

On the other hand, Gordis and his coinvestigators found that 36 percent of the children with rheumatic fever cared for in a clinic took their penicillin only one-fourth of the time or less. Their investigations suggest that this behavior may characterize those on long-term medication for chronic illness who are at the same time generally asymptomatic and functioning normally.

Extrinsic factors may also interfere with individual compliance. In a study of 300 pediatric patients with otitis media, Mattar et al. (1975a) found complete compliance in only 7.3 percent. However, pharmacists inadvertently dispensed less than the prescribed amount 15 percent of the time and labeled bottles incorrectly 3 percent of the time. Teaspoons varied in volume from 2 to 9 mL. Parents quite often had an erroneous understanding of the disease. In 36 percent of the cases, they gave fewer than the pre-scribed number of doses and in 37 percent discontinued therapy early. Conversely, with the devices of a calibrated measuring spoon, careful instruction, and a calendar for the recording of doses a test group achieved a compliance rate of 51 percent. Furthermore, a control group who went to neighborhood drugstores achieved only an 8.5 percent full compliance. Still, even though there was a higher compliance rate in the test group, why was full compliance not achieved with a short-term regimen for a clearly understood disease?

The Family: The Child Is Not an Isolate

In pediatrics, all issues are modified by the close identification of the parent and family with the child. The individual—as the example of compliance illustrates—is not an isolate.

While the term "family" suggests a broader construction, the traditional model of a mother and father and one or more children predominates. Still, "family" may be a combination of any two or more individuals, regardless of sex, age, or primary relationship. As our patients achieve adolescence, the sense of meaningful "family" may change, broaden, and reach outside the primary home. This is the most common time for loosening the initial bondings of life. Each individual, with age and experience, develops newer relationships which fashion for each a cluster of varying identities dependent on the social, cultural, and emotional context of the bonds. While procreation and the subsequent need to protect one's young are biologic mandates, sharing and the achievement of common goals are part of the "survival with quality" imperative.

Ironically, it is common in our predominant mode of care to add an immediate handicap to the tie between mother and child. The newborn nursery and the need to safeguard against the spread of infection in "modern" hospitals may impose a disruption in maternal caretaking just when attachment is beginning and most necessary. It is impossible to put a judgment on the harm—or good—we do in imposing this handicap. For it is necessary to touch and to hold the baby, to talk to the baby, and to smile at the baby, as it is to protect her from infection.

Chamberlin has shown that such "positive contacts" diminish the ultimate need for mothers to issue directives to their children and to resort to physical means to influence behavior. Praise and social conversation ultimately prove more useful. There is a basis here for anticipatory counseling and education.

Actually, too many of us are ill prepared for parenthood and for the provision of nurture in family relationships. And most of us, when we anticipate having children, worry about their health but nevertheless expect the best. If the child is ill, either at birth or later, guilt, anger, worry, and frustration all become part of the emotional mix. If the child is congenitally sick, there is grief and mourning over the healthy baby who never was. There is, in fact, an observable sequence of stages in the parental reaction—shock, denial, sadness and anger, adaptation, and reorganization—the understanding of which can be quite helpful in our efforts at positive interventions.

It is apparent, then, that the individual within a family with the greatest immediate need will govern that family's life for the moment and, perhaps, in many ways, permanently. That individual is often a sick child. Since it is impossible to live in isolation biologically or emotionally, the family constitutes an essential need. Its existence is thereby assured, and so, too, are the myriad of negotiations and bargains—and adaptations—which family life necessitates.

The Culture: Common Denominators of Behavior Are Elusive

Improved technical communication does not invalidate a point Benedict made years ago. Culturally determined behavior must not be considered by the individuals within that culture to be a common denominator for all peoples everywhere. This error is common in the thinking of those of us conditioned in an Occidental society. This kind of assumption was a contributor to the flow of events in World War II, the Korean war, and the Vietnam war. On a different level, we cling to the idea that the Oedipus complex is a normal concomitant of all human behavior. Benedict suggests that the Zuni Indians of the Southwest could not generate a behavioral field which would serve as a substrate for Oedipal or Electra feelings.

There is an ebb and flow to culturally determined behavior. Our ability to communicate, to advertise, and to influence each other is at the root. The toy fad is an example. These fads can lead to some never-before-seen and some never-to-be-seen-again maladies—frisbee finger and hula hoop hip. New styles in clothing can lead to new discomforts—sandal strap dermatitis, tight jean urethritis, and hip hugger's paresis. Changing musical and dance preferences of the young may have their side effects—hi-fi deafness, twister's knee, and strobe light seizures. Widely available taste treats provide more than pleasure and nourishment to the eager eater—pizza palate and Chinese restaurant syndrome. Emphasis on exercise and active participation in sports have produced more than physical fitness—rucksack palsy, karate myoglobinuria, and Little League elbow.

One culturally determined demographic measure is the birthrate. This rate dropped steadily in the United States after a peak in 1957. By the early 1970s, changing social attitudes, particularly with regard to the role of women and the family and shifting sexual behavior, made prediction of a rate more difficult than it had been. Clearly, many women were deferring childbearing. However, by the mid-1970s there was evidence in California that the low rate of legitimate fertility was beginning to rise and that people were having children at a somewhat older age. In a sense, they were beginning to make up for lost time. There was a concomitant but slower-paced increase in the nonmarital birthrate checked to an extent by the availability of modern contraception and legal abortion. The percentage of planned babies in the nonmarried population continues to rise along with the projected absolute numbers. This rise suggests that the reasons for nonmarital childbearing are persistent and deep-seated. Finally, the babies of the late 1950s, a large group, will be in their reproductive years by the early 1980s. Sklar and Berkov suggest that these factors and the emotional substrate which generate them will raise the crude birthrate by 9 percent and the general fertility rate by 2 percent. If the cultural option moves to earlier pregnancy than in the recent past, the implications for pediatric health care are clear. Problems will range from those inherent in the increased numbers of people to be served to the increasing tendency of the unwed adolescent to care for her own child.

The larger community, then, is a constant companion making a diverse contribution when our patients seek us out. There is a major example in that the nutrition of the individual evolves from the physical resources of the inanimate environment and the social, economic, and political behavior of the animate environment. Two circumstances are striking: The world fish catch was 22 million tons in 1950, 70 million in 1970. Suddenly, then, and without real warning, it dropped. Most experts blamed overfishing. And the land responds poorly to efforts to increase its productivity. In the United States corn belt in the early 1950s each pound of fertilizer raised corn yield by 15 to 20 pounds; in 1970, each pound strewn in the same cornfield gave only an additional 5 pounds. While the response is better in areas of the world where the land is not yet tired, the limitations in utilizing fertilizer to increase productivity are real.

The issues which affect community behavior are complex and difficult to predict. Smallpox and measles are diseases that illustrate the uncertainty. There are differences in the behavior of the two viruses and in the mode of spread of each disease. There are unascertained differences in herd immunity once widespread immunization campaigns are begun. For both, however, there are effective preventive procedures.

Following World War II smallpox disappeared in most of the world. By the mid-1970s, the last vestiges of the disease were confined to bits of Africa and the Indian subcontinent and were finally eradicated. For the first time, the unified effort of humankind resulted in the elimination of a major illness. The development of a heat-stable lyophilized vaccine was the necessary condition and the initiative of the World Health Organization in conducting widespread sustained immunization programs an additional sufficient condition. In the United States, routine vaccination of the population, vaccination of travelers, inspection of vaccination certificates of all entrants and reentrants to the country, and careful investigation with immediate isolation of all suspected cases were the bases of the elimination program. It has now become possible to eliminate routine vaccination and to save the six lives lost each year in the United States due to its complications.

Measles, on the other hand, is not eradicated in the United States or anywhere. The technical competence was available by the mid-1960s. There had been a decrease in the number of reported cases in the United States from an average of 450,000 in 1959–1964 to 22,000 in 1968. Then, by 1970 the reported number had more than doubled. In 1971 there were

75,000 cases. The disease remains because not enough children have been vaccinated. This is so because the community, in setting its priorities, has not yet decided that they should be.

The Provider: The Patient Needs Help

In 1961, White indicated that in an average month in a population of 1000 adults, 750 will experience an episode of illness and that of these, 250 will consult a physician, 9 will be hospitalized, 5 will be referred to another physician, and 1 will be referred to a university medical center. The inference was made that these figures are much the same for children since adults for the most part make the decisions for children and since economic accessibility to care for children and adolescents is adult-dominated. He has since reaffirmed figures of this order for 1970.

Thus, the patient and the provider do come together frequently to achieve wellness or to maintain wellness. The persons giving care are usually formally educated and, as we have indicated, may work alone or as members of a team. Health professionals share the common experience of specialized schooling and, in that, a particular socialization which prepares them to work with and to advocate for the child. They must understand their advocacy role if they are to provide effective care.

Reflecting this, the American Academy of Pediatrics defines pediatrics as that specialty of medicine concerned with the physical, emotional, and social health of children, beginning with conception and extending into adulthood, including advocacy in all matters affecting their welfare. Pediatric care, then, involves the provision of a broad spectrum of health services.

Advocacy may be reinforced by and, at times, confused with the apostolic mission of the health professional. Balint suggests that the

. . . apostolic mission or function means, in the first place, that every doctor has a vague, but almost unshakable idea of how a patient ought to behave when ill. Although this idea is anything but explicit and concrete, it is immensely powerful, and influences . . . practically every detail of the doctor's work with his patients. It is almost as if every doctor had revealed knowledge of what was right and what was wrong for patients to expect and to endure, and further, as if he had a sacred duty to convert to his faith all the ignorant and unbelieving among his patients.

We may react to this with some denial. Still, if advocacy is a part of our mission, we must consider the central issue: Who decides what for whom? How far can we go before we begin to impose too much of our personal value judgment on the patient? Certainly, there is a need for carefully considered restraint in this regard.

We are professionals in that we have a special knowledge, a wish to serve, colleagues with whom to serve, and the permission of our community in explicit legal terms to use our knowledge in service. We are expected to place the needs of our patients above our own personal needs; we are expected to resolve the conflicts engendered by our need to make a living and to live our personal lives in favor of the patient. In turn, we are given the privilege of defining good health practices with the expectation that our patients will respond appropriately.

There has, however, been a problem in the education of pediatricians—a gap between the function of the pediatrician in practice and the expectations generated during training. In 1975, the Committee on School Health of the American Academy of Pediatrics pointed out the variability in pediatric training programs and cited deficiencies in teaching about the care of the handicapped, the health problems of school-age children, the use of community resources, nutrition, and much more. For many years, however, there had been restless stirrings as it became evident that pediatricians worked hard, earned less than other physicians, used much of their time inappropriately on tasks which could be delegated, and employed too many care procedures which had not been validated. And, perhaps, frustrated by this and by the failure to realize their expectations of practice (the sense of being a specialist and a consultant), they on occasion became bored and lulled into making repeated errors in relatively undemanding situations.

There is no accurate documentation of the numbers who succumbed to the "disenchanted pediatrician syndrome." It is reasonable to assume, however, that appropriate training can sensitize one to the right questions to consider in the solution of patients' problems and that this alone can convert boredom to challenge. Further, an accurate definition of patient needs and of those not met can give perspective to the teamwork of diverse health professionals, each appropriately prepared to contribute uniquely to the total effort, and each able, at times, to overlap in the performance of some tasks. The pediatric nurse practitioner and the physician's associate complement, rather than supplement, the work of the pediatrician.

The exploration of educational change and team function can be facilitated by rejecting the idea that competence is necessarily related to one's professional status. It is difficult, however, in a status-oriented society, to scramble the current pecking order even if the goal is to achieve greater clarity in the definition of individual and group roles and responsibilities. Still, it would be better to define the inequality by our comparative ability to perform a given task.

Thus, the relationship among health professionals on a team offering health care is as sensitive as their relationship with the patient. If the concept of a given role, such as that of the pediatric nurse practitioner, is relatively new, the ease with which the concept becomes reality depends on the physicians' attitudes. They decide in large part how the role is developed and used, and it is probable that their decisions are, in part, based on their feelings about their own status and role, feelings which are rooted in their wish to serve the patient well. The patients' acceptance of care by pediatric nurse practitioners will be related to their interpretation of how the physician feels about that care.

Pediatricians, seeing the nurse practitioner as a surrogate in well child care (a particularly large-volume part of practice), can view that role as a direct threat to the substance of the physician's "job description" and even as an economic threat. The ultimate goal of high-quality health care for the young can suffer in the wake of this potential conflict (see Sec. 12).

The nurse practitioner must shift perceptions, too. A nurse has most often been understood as the provider of a service to and through an institution or an agency. On the other hand, a nurse practitioner provides a service directly to a person. This direct accountability to the patient is at odds with an occupational isolation of nurses which begins in the training period and which is often maintained by a rigid hierarchy within nursing and in the relation-

ship with the physician. The degree of independence implied in the practitioner's role requires some resocialization, since most nurse practitioners are unaccustomed to a collegial relationship with the physician, or sharing in decision making, or assuming responsibility for the outcome of care.

The resolution of these issues depends upon the balance of the economic, intellectual, and emotional needs of the individuals involved and on the thrust of their humanitarian impulses. The relationship with the patient provides a mechanism for enormous personal reward and, if this is not responsibly confronted, a mechanism for exploitation of the patient. A responsive patient offers a delicious "ego massage." This is fine if the gratification is mutual and if the patient's needs are well served. However, the patient may at times be manipulated inappropriately. It is not difficult to create undue dependency on the professional during the periods of vulnerability caused by illness and other stresses. Regardless, the patient is in a sense healthier when self-reliance and personal responsibility are supported. Thus, the professional who sacrifices this principle to assure personal gratification can be exploitative and, to a real extent, is immature.

If, on the other hand, the patient makes one angry, one must find out why. It may be dissatisfaction with the nature of one's work or frustration at an inability to solve many of the problems. The reason may lie within one's own life or within the immediate patient interaction with mutual perceptions of an absence of trust and a conflict of values. This requires a difficult confrontation of oneself before the anger is displaced on patients, colleagues, friends, or family. Formal or informal counseling and consultation with knowledgeable persons can help the professional in this regard. This may be necessary if the ancient teaching that one must "first of all cause no harm" is to be respected and particularly necessary if the realization occurs that too often, *more than anything,* one wants to be liked—one needs to be liked—by the patient.

The physical and demographic characteristics of the setting within which care is offered provides a substrate for the behavioral environment. The choice of a place to practice depends on a community's need, which is determined by the numbers of patients to be served and the numbers of providers already in residence. The availability of consultation and hospital services, the flexibility of emergency care, transportation availability, laboratory and medical records, and the access to a library and other continuing education services may be paramount for some. Appraisal of the requirements of one's individual and family life-styles, however, may be of greater import. While it may seem distasteful to think in terms of income and patient volume, these are dimensions which should not be ignored. It is not easy to assign a monetary value to a health care service. There is an arbitrary quality to the process which requires that the patient be familiar with the provider's rules of practice and have easy access to candid discussion about time allotments and costs. This kind of interchange can assure more open if not happier relationships.

Up to this point, we have not questioned the assumption that health care is a major societal priority. In fact, it seems to be. In 1975, there were almost 1 billion visits to physicians in the United States and more than $115 billion were spent on health care. In light of this, and considering our current concern about a life-style many consider destructive, we might invoke Mechanic's (1974) perspective:

> . . . most of the destructive health behavior patterns that we are concerned about reflect the way in which we have chosen to live as individuals and as a society. They derive from our forms of social organization and social life, and from the types of economic and social patterns that we have encouraged. Thus, to put excessive emphasis on individual responsibility for various preventive health behaviors is to misgauge the conditions from which they arise. As a society we must confront the issue of how important health maintenance is relative to other social commitments, and how far we are willing to go to promote conditions that facilitate a healthful pattern of living. There is no particular reason why health should be the highest of values or the most central of social goals. But for those persons who particularly value health and who seek to promote it, it is important to recognize the realistic constraints and opportunities for change.

Stress: Life Can Be Strenuous for the Patient and the Provider

Living and dying and the life-style to which Mechanic (1974) alludes mandate a series of challenges and changes and the need to cope with those changes. Our assumption has been that this need to cope produces stress and that stress is harmful. It is difficult, however, to define stress. Mason says:

> It is tempting to suggest that we might be better off without the term, "stress," at all, given our present crude level of insight, but perhaps the notion of a generic term which somehow ties together the threatening or taxing demands of the environment on living organisms strikes some deep, responsive chord within us which keeps alive the use of stress terminology in spite of all the confusion it creates.

The view that stress is injurious ignores its potential as a creative force and the constructive value of the individual's ability to respond and to adjust to environmental and social change. For this reason, health care should provide interventions that are positive and creative, more than compensatory.

Perhaps we should think in terms of "life events" rather than "stress." These vary and need not be hazardous. Those which are, are far more likely to force the patient to seek care. For instance, there is strong evidence that psychosocial disturbance may be temporally related to the onset of physical disease. In one study, children with juvenile rheumatoid arthritis, other patients on a general pediatric service, and others on a surgical service for appendectomy and herniorrhaphy were found to have experienced two to three times more frequent and/or more severely hazardous life events prior to the onset of their illnesses than did their healthy peers.

Perhaps ulcerative colitis is the disease entity which most clearly suggests the pathophysiologic-psychologic relation. There is a strong probability that an imbalance in this relationship at some level reflects a disturbed "key relationship," usually between mother and child, and is expressed in the combination of physiologic phenomena we call ulcerative colitis. There may well be an as yet undetermined constitutional or congenital bowel defect as one of the necessary "trigger" conditions. There is the suggestion, too, that such individuals may find in the disease a successful mechanism for coping with life events. Furthermore, there are mothers who have been kept in balance by the need to give care and who have decompensated after their children have been helped to get well.

Roghmann and Haggerty have shown that stress in their day-to-day living increases mothers' utilization of physician services for the common and frequent health complaints of their children but decreases the utilization of these services for their own health complaints—perhaps because they recognize stress as a cause of their symptoms. Acute social, emotional, and economic stressful situations have been demonstrated to be precipitating factors in injuries inflicted upon children by their abusing parents.

The circumstances which stimulate our patients to seek care may be far more subtle than this and may depend on a number of hidden variables. Care is sought when they have decided that there is a medical or health problem which needs attention. Their definition of illness, however, is in no way uniform or constant. Bona fide aches and pains generate different responses depending on how a given person perceives the advantage or disadvantage of being well and on how necessary it may be to escape the daily burden imposed by being well. This is as true for children as for adults. Society's expectations of individual behavior are particularly important. The unceasing demand for a socially acceptable level of performance may tax an individual's ability to cope. There can then be an unconscious, unpremeditated refuge in the sick role.

There is an illness behavior which is defined by the way in which we perceive, evaluate, and act upon the presence of any symptom. This behavior is modified for some by sociocultural experiences and by life events which may direct inordinate attention to minor symptoms. Thus, a mother raising children without the help of a spouse may report chronic conditions and functional disabilities more often than other people would. There are stress factors, as those in ulcerative colitis, which, given the necessary physiologic base, may be sufficient to cause illness for which care is sought, or there may be other reasons which, once a process is present, cause some people to seek care and others to demur. Those with the most hazard and the greatest tendency to *use* the sick role will seek care most often.

Of course, illness may also be perceived as a disadvantage. If the disadvantage seems too great to the potential patient, help may not be sought at all even when the illness is severe. In pediatrics, the situation may be confused by the family interaction—the basic behavior of the child overlain by the parental response. Sometimes parents delay in seeking care for children because they feel that the presence of a given illness stigmatizes the child and the family.

This is often so if there is a fear of epilepsy, mental retardation, or other chronic, handicapping conditions which the parents may feel are the result of their neglect. There are moments, too, when most parents resent their children and their responsibilities. They may even wish that they had never taken on the responsibility in the first place. A child's illness may then be viewed as a punishing fulfillment of the wish, thus reinforcing the guilt. It is safe to assume that in most circumstances there is an element of parental guilt based on an awareness of real or imagined negligence or of a real or imagined deficiency—genetic, social, or economic.

There are many objective conditions which by compromising the quality of life seem to substantiate the parents' fears. The extent of compromise may depend on race, religion, geographic location, or a host of other factors that may engender in child, parent, or both a defective image of themselves. Perhaps this interplay of stigma, poor self-concept, and guilt underlies the frequency with which patients fail to report illness or to comply with our instructions, much more than a presumed inability to understand the pathophysiologic nature of illness. In addition, we can be certain that our own behavior is perceived and interpreted by the patient and that this becomes a factor in the eventual resolution of the problem.

Death is defined as the ultimate hazard by most of us. All illness and the associated behavior is a reflection of our need to deal with this separation, with the consequent grief, and with the resolution of anger and guilt that underlies grief. Every kind of attachment must in time be broken. Therefore, that characteristic of humankind which tends toward the development of powerful interpersonal bonds is the guarantor of continuous stress. The disruption of attachment has a significant result in biologic as well as emotional terms. The parents of leukemic children, for example, can be shown to have altered rates of excretion of norepinephrine and 17-hydroxyketosteroids.

On a different but immensely important scale, the societal move from an agricultural to an urban, technical base engendered the same kinds of problems. By the mid-1970s our more mobile life-style with the constant loss and separation and the constant changing of affiliations that moving imposes added tension to attachments. As a consequence, the contribution to stability of the traditional social supports (the church, the neighborhood, and the extended family) was diminished. Therefore, as Klerman suggests, we have replaced the cognitive beliefs and charity of the church with a new secular religion, *mental health*. The extent to which we are able to cope may be reflected in the number of psychiatric care episodes, which have increased in the United States from a bit more than 1000 per 100,000 population in 1955 to 2200 per 100,000 population in 1973. It is significant that inpatient episodes remained fairly constant (850 per 100,000) and that the principle demand was on services outside the hospital. The impact, then, of these societal changes on the nature of the content of the health care of the young is profound.

Primacy: All Told, Whose Responsibility Is Health Care?

In 1975, a 20-year-old woman was sentenced to 20 years in prison in Maryland because she had punished her 2-year-old daughter for bed-wetting by placing her in a bathtub of scalding water. This obvious example of child abuse is but one of an uncounted number of circumstances in which parents' inability to adapt and to cope is reflected in the physical and emotional battering of their children. The children are deprived of the needed attachments, and their life experience begins to replicate that of their parents. Abused children are likely to become abusing parents, incapable of establishing and maintaining bonds and providing nurture. They are unable to trust proffered love. This inability, the result of absence of nurture, is often reinforced by poverty and other societal deprivations. Thus, the incidence of child abuse may be diminished by good jobs, satisfactory education, and adequate housing. These contribute more to the health of the young and, indeed, of the total community than well-trained and accessible health providers. These, then, are variables among the determinants of health which we must consider when determining where the appropriate responsibility for health and health care lies.

Lerner divides society in the United States into three levels—the poor, the working blue-collar class, and the middle class. He demonstrates a U-shaped curve for morbidity and mortality—in essence, the poorer one is or the richer one is, the more likely one is to be ill or to die earlier. In any event, the U is skewed, and the risk is clearly greatest for the poor and, particularly, for the poor young. The young among the socioeconomically advantaged do suffer less; in this group, the greater morbidity and mortality are due to the degenerative diseases of middle and later life.

The health and health care prerogatives of any individual must be constrained by the sharing of responsibility for them with the rest of society. Individual pursuit of one's own best interest may bring ruin to all. Hardin has suggested this as a human problem which has no technical solution. Metaphorically, we all share a "common" pasture. If we act selfishly to meet our individual needs, our cumulative individual decisions deplete and waste our resources. The commons and health in its broadest sense are then threatened.

Given this metaphor, worldwide malnutrition results from inappropriate use of the commons. This may be associated with retarded brain growth and mental development in the first 2 years of life. It is difficult, however, to separate the actual impact of malnutrition from other social and economic deprivations. Winick and his colleagues have shown that Korean children who have suffered early malnutrition and who are adopted into supportive homes were able to compensate for early intellectual loss. However, similar children, better fed but deprived of long-term intellectual stimulus, were unable to do so.

The commons offers an interwoven complex of resources. Its appropriate use is a key to health. This is indeed a shared responsibility. Ultimate adaptation and survival depends on a cooperative effort which requires some sacrifice of individual freedom.

There are, however, areas of health care in which primary responsibility is invested in the health professional. Certainly this includes the maintenance of high technical competence in the care and prevention of disease and, also, in the achievement of an appropriate balance of the "caring" and the "curing" functions. There must also be active concern with the social, political, and economic processes which affect the health care system within which the patient seeks care and cure. There are barriers which go beyond the behavioral and emotional which present problems for solution. Excessive cost and inadequate transportation are factors which can be as limiting as emotionally based noncompliance with "doctor's orders" and which belong on a patient's problem list along with physical ills.

The Fulfillment of Responsibility

As health providers we can make decisions appropriate to the use of health care resources only to the extent that society allows. We must give meticulous attention to those areas in which we have major control, to the environment we create with our own demeanor, and to the uses of the spaces in which we establish health care settings. Surely, all our patients are aware of what we do, but adolescents are more articulate than our younger patients in expressing their thoughts. Their candor indicates their feelings about the physical facilities and the psychological atmosphere of a hospital. Overlong and frequent hospital admissions are as threatening to them as a disease process itself. Providing attractive and human sized spaces, maintaining open and responsive attitudes, and utilizing hospitalization as a last alternative are complements to sound technical competence. Attention to the recreational, vocational, and educational needs of the young are fully as much a part of management as the determination of drug and dosage. We have at our disposal a sophisticated therapeutic armamentarium which we have used with diminishing restraint as the need to legally defend against the malpractice of omission has grown.

And yet, the pleas must be for greater restraint and discrimination. We must not forgo the sensitive appreciation of the patient's real need, and we must not place inordinate reliance on "procedures." Clinical judgment is dulled and the patient is unduly assaulted when, for example, a lumbar puncture is performed in lieu of, and not as the result of, sound probabilistic reasoning.

Occult pneumococcal septicemia is a case in point. This is not a discrete disease entity; however, the phrase itself implies that it may be. Hence, given a feverish child and a borderline leukocytosis without demonstrable locus for disease, this "entity" may well be included in a list of differential diagnostic possibilities. Then, in the face of a subjective evaluation which belies major illness in the child, and because it is relatively easy to do a venipuncture in a setting away from home, a blood culture is taken. If it is positive, a possibly unnecessary sequence of events is initiated, not the least of which is the subsequent reliance on the blood culture as the indicator of the child's clinical status rather than on careful reexploration of the history and physical examination.

The Work Is Large but Limited

The overall task for those of us who provide health care for the young is multifaceted. We are the focal point for a full range of basic health services for the well and the sick, for the most part in a variety of *primary care* ambulatory settings. We act as individuals or in groups, drawing on the skills of a variety of health professionals. And we do all this with an appreciation that our ultimate contribution to the determination of health is limited.

Consider the 273 Indian infants born in Fort Defiance, Arizona, in 1970. One half were treated by the then prevailing practices of the Indian Health Services. The other half were provided a much more aggressive follow-up with home visits, contact after missed appointments, and periodic record review to check on the achievement of health care goals. Almost all the infants had a thorough health status review at about 1 year of age. The "aggressively" treated infants had more complete immunizations, tuberculin testing, and well child visits. However, the two groups could not be distinguished significantly in terms of mortality, morbidity, hospitalization rates, number of visits for health care, and findings on physical, developmental, and laboratory examinations.

In far more primitive societies in the United States and Central America, the delivery of carefully organized primary health care has been shown to have very little influence on disease, even when well received. In these societies, the food supply, particularly the amount of protein ingested, was the larger determinant of reduced morbidity and mortality.

Overall, health care, save universal immunization, has not been demonstrated to be a positive force in changing illness rates and outcomes for more sophisticated populations. Nor has it been refuted. The lack of clear evidence in this regard can be attributed to the difficulties inherent in trying to isolate the influence of each of the components of the ecology of health care.

This is frustrating. As health care providers we cannot afford the implication of Grantland Rice's paean to process:

For when the One Great Scorer comes
  To write against your name
He marks—not that you won or lost—
  But how you played the game.

Of course we are concerned with how we "play the game." But outcomes are important. It does matter when we lose.

It is disturbing, therefore, to review the evidence and to find that there is real question as to whether or not we can win at some of the "games" we play no matter how well we perform. In addition to the absence of evidence of the real worth of health care on the outcome of medical illness, studies in related fields have shown that (1) intensive, long-term social services rendered to multiproblem families do not produce significant improvement in their social functioning, (2) nursing intervention is ineffective in improving maladaptive maternal-infant interactions among mothers deprived of affection, and (3) psychotherapy does not improve the patient's chance of recovery beyond that which might have been without any formal therapy whatsoever.

These data and opinions are distressing to those of us who have acquired the available skills judged necessary to provide health care for the young. It seems that further substantive change in our patients is beyond present reach. Some have suggested that success might be better achieved if we concentrate on team sports rather than individual events. Others say that we need to run a different race, one that requires political, educational, social, and economic prowess to win. These skills are difficult to learn and even more difficult to apply.

A more attractive view is that we only *seem* to lose. The judges may have been in error. Their measuring devices may be inaccurate, and they may be standing at the wrong finish line. Perhaps the prime criteria for success should be expressed in terms of reductions in discomfort, disability, and dissatisfaction rather than in death and disease. It may be that comforting and coping are as important as curing.

Thus, as health care providers, we must always query the nature of our contribution and our role in the ecology of the health care of the young. If we can do this with an appropriate mixture of concern, realism, and good humor, so much the better.

2 | The Data Base

by Saul Blatman

The diagnostic process in the health care of children and adolescents is dependent on an orderly, complete approach to the accumulation of a data base. The delivery of health care involves health maintenance, including early detection and prevention, and the care of the acutely or chronically ill. Information concerning the family, school, and community, and concerning the adjustment of the individual to the environment are essential ingredients of health care planning. The diagnostic process is dependent on the accumulation of a complete data base, a foundation of information, in which there is an array of facts with which the health worker must be familiar in order to plan for the patient's care.

The data base draws on information obtained directly from the child and family, and from those who may have knowledge about them, such as teachers, community workers, and others. It may be assembled in the physician's office, in the patient's home, at the child's school, at the day care center, at the camp, or wherever the child spends time. The data base should be complete, comprehensive, and reasonably and simply stated, and should serve to assemble and document information regarding the child. It should provide a balance of useful information taking into account the scientific, the sociological, and the psychological. It provides a permanent record which can be readily analyzed and when put to use saves time and energy and is not overly costly to maintain. The data base provides the first step in the provision of preventive health services for children or in the event of inability "to prevent" it should provide a means for early detection of health care problems. The data base should be arranged in such a way that it recognizes individual variations among children, those which are related to sex, age and heredity, and those which are related to environmental factors. Well-planned and coordinated approaches to health care and the avoidance of unnecessary procedures and office visits, as well as elimination of duplication of effort, are goals of a sound and carefully assembled data base. A complete and accurate data base is required for medical-legal reasons as well. And with recent government interest in standards of medical practice, there is an increasing need for the data base to be the source of documentation of quality of health care. Carefully kept records are mandatory as proof of adequacy of care.

The problem-oriented record has assumed a place of importance in record-keeping activities. The problem-oriented record focuses attention on a systematic accumulation of facts to be used in the provision of health care of an individual. It attempts to organize information around health care problems, preserves medical data, and calls upon logical thought processes in solving health care problems. Ultimately it provides a simplified method for assessing the quality of health care as it appears in the record. The problem-oriented record aims at the assembly and the logical accumulation of a data base, formulates a problem list, and then allows for a plan for the solution of each of the problems. It is then mandatory to follow up on each of the problems, calling on the data base and the plan in evaluating the completeness and appropriateness of follow-up.

In addition to the routine initial history, physical examination, laboratory work, and consultation reports when these are thought necessary, the physician must add to the data base continuously. The record must reflect the continuous care which is given by the physician and should contain a description of observations and actions by the physician and associates. Information acquired indirectly as a result of communications with others who are involved with the child must, likewise, be recorded as part of the data base. Original communications should be filed with the patient's permanent record. Many clinics now use computers for recording and storing patient information. For private practitioners this method of record-keeping is as yet uneconomical and generally unavailable.

Care should be taken to meet the needs of the patient and to be sure that the data base and problem-oriented record in themselves do not outweigh the patient's needs and direct the flow of activities which are identified as patient care. The record must at all times serve the patient and facilitate the carrying out of the health worker's responsibilities, helping to make care convenient, relatively painless, complete, and as inexpensive as possible.

The school as a location for health care for children, although not generally an important location for such activity in the United States at the present time, holds promise for the future. Even now the data base can be enriched by relevant communications between the physician and school personnel. School health records should be made available to physicians in their private office or clinic.

The "house call" as a phenomenon which provides enrichment for the assembly of the data base is used less frequently than in the past. Yet, there is no question that a home visit tells physicians much about their child patient and the child's family and living situation. Home visits by health workers other than physicians, notably by nurses and physician assistants, can provide valuable information which was previously obtained during the seemingly disappearing physician house call.

Recently the patient's record has been the subject of debate regarding its availability to the patients themselves. There are those who recommend that the record be made available to the patient for review, at least to check on inaccuracies in history recording. Going over the record with the patient might provide an opportunity for the health worker who is engaged in an educational exercise with the patient. In pediatrics, record review implies sharing the record with parents. There can be little debate regarding the need to share information from the data base with others who are concerned with the welfare of the child patient. This implies an interchange of records between schools and physicians, consultants and physicians, community agencies and physicians. Principles of confidentiality should be a consideration in providing information regarding patients and their families.

When a family leaves a physician's care because of a move to another community or for any other reason, the child's health care record should be complete and arranged in such manner as to be used easily by others who will be caring for the child. In any event, the patient's record should be aimed primarily at serving the patient and facilitating the activities of health workers.

3 | Structure of the Pediatric Record

by Kenneth McConnochie

The medical record is an important implement of the health professional. As a tool applied to health care, it is considered part of the process of promoting well-being. Though its application does not bear directly on well-being, the record might serve many objectives intermediate to this goal. The use of records has been a prominent feature of efforts to facilitate communication between professionals, to encourage diagnostic acumen, to enhance the educational process, to facilitate auditing, and to enable clinical research. Promoting adjustment, an additional objective preeminent to the health care process, has previously received relatively little attention in efforts to improve records. The focus of this chapter and the following chapter is on medical records systems as they serve each of these objectives.

Accepting the above objectives as encompassing the function of records and espousing the logic that form follows function, medical records design becomes a task of developing a structure that serves the objectives well. A basic consideration in designing the record is that performance of any implement distinctly reflects the aptitude and application of the user. The most important implication here is that no system of records will supplant skill and dedication as key determinants of quality care. Also, none of the record's functions will be fulfilled unless the structure is used appropriately; the record should facilitate adequate recording of data and should determine that data, once recorded, are organized and retrievable in a manner fostering achievement of objectives.

This view of the relationship between medical records and health care process is depicted in Fig. 3-1.

The development of the *problem-oriented system* was a major contribution to the structure of medical records. This system was designed to meet many of the objectives cited above. Components of the record discussed here reflect this system in large measure. Comments on record use as depicted in Fig. 3-1 are generally confined here to the recording process. Application is discussed in subsequent chapters.

DEVELOPING THE DATA BASE

As with the medical encounter itself, recording begins with the collection of data to form the *data base*. Implied in this term is a defined set of information appropriate in scope and adequate in quality to serve as the basis for shrewd clinical assessment.

The scope of the evaluation should reflect the nature of the presenting clinical situation. Conventional medical wisdom indicates the need for a broad, general evaluation to be the data base for several situations. These include entry of a new patient into a system for continuous care, periodic health maintenance evaluation, and diagnostic dilemmas.

A problem arises when we try to delineate the exact composition of the general evaluation. Simply to say it should be "complete" is naïve. In any of the situations above, it is appropriate to vary the composition to reflect such variables as age, sex, developmental stage, and social and geographic factors. There is no question that the general data base for a health maintenance evaluation of a 9-month-old black male in a rural area in the southern United States should be different from that for a 13-year-old white male in a Los Angeles suburb. There may be debate, however,

Figure 3-1 Medical records in practice, a systems view. The record is part of a system in which, ideally, health professionals fashion the structure in a manner which consciously addresses objectives they adopt. The implement is also designed to minimize factors limiting record use. These factors are found in the processes of recording data and applying recorded data toward achieving objectives.

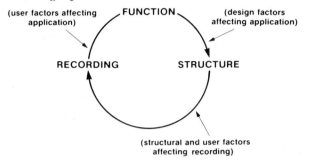

whether sickle cell disease or glucose-6-phosphate dehydrogenase deficiency screening should be part of the former evaluation and sexual history and drug use history should be part of the latter.

Principles of screening, discussed in Sec. 4, can be very helpful in resolving such issues. Acceptability, validity, and reliability of procedures, direct and indirect costs, screening time, remediability of defects sought, risks of not screening, and resources for intervention are among factors to be considered. Ideally, they are the basis for inclusion of items in the data base. Very often full application of screening principles requires studies yet to be performed. In the absence of solid data to enhance objectivity, one's best judgment must be relied upon to develop a standard data base.

In sum, items in a data base should be selected on the basis of available evidence and sound assumptions where such evidence is not available. Comments regarding development of the general data base apply equally to selection of items for inclusion in a "modified data base" as used for acute episodic problems and for chronic ongoing problems.

A standard data base is important. In its absence, there is a tendency to be inconsistent in one's approach. This is particularly the case where lack of evidence leaves room for various acceptable approaches. In this situation one's own approach is best chosen on the basis of careful reflection, not the pres-

sures and mood of the moment when a particular clinical issue is at hand. A standard data base, be it "general" or "modified," helps compensate for vagaries in human performance.

Components of the general data base include presenting concerns, identifying data, history of present illness or illnesses, past medical history, reviewing systems, family medical history, social history, physical examination, developmental assessment, and basic laboratory data. These components, constituting the traditional work-up, may be used as the format for data entry in the chart. Bits of information from each of these categories are important to most clinical situations.

Alternative formats are often more useful than this traditional format. This is particularly the case where the scope of the general data base is modified for acute problems and for management of ongoing problems. Useful modifications in format for such situations are division of data into *subjective* and *objective* categories and use of flow sheets.

When a distinction is drawn between subjective and objective data, the former is regarded as that related in an interview through a lay observer, generally the patient or the patient's parents. Observations made directly by the health professional and determinations of the clinical laboratory are considered objective.

Although emphasis on the distinction between subjective and objective data is useful, notes of caution and clarification are indicated. Assignment of historical data to the subjective category may be mistaken as an indication of lesser importance. This is a serious error; most clinical problems are assessed largely through analysis of data obtained in the interview. It is also important to recognize the arbitrary nature of the distinction. Historical data, for example, specific dates of events related by parents, may be as objective or more objective than physician observations, such as impressions of parent-child interaction.

Enabling use of flow sheets is a distinct advantage in definition of a standard data base. Though developing the prerequisite data base may be time-consuming, subsequent development of the flow sheet is relatively easy. Once developed, flow sheets should save time and reduce oversight. The process of developing a flow sheet from a data base for ongoing care of a juvenile diabetic is illustrated in Fig. 3-2.

NAME ___A. D. M.___

D.O.B. ___8 / 8 / 65___   # ___1016___

FLOW SHEET : Diabetes Mellitus—Juvenile

Data / Date Year 1976 Mo.	5/7	6/30	7/7	8/4	8/12	8/13	8/30	9/15			
SUBJECTIVE See CN			Phone	CN	CN	CN					
Daily Activity*	3	5	5	5			4	5			
Life Events		School Out New Bike Forgot Shots	Day Camp Starts	Father Lost Job	Hospital		Father New Job				
Compliance † / Health Education	3 / 5					5 / 5					
School Missed	0	0									
Illness	URI x1	0	0	0	GI	GI	◯	●			
Hypoglycemia Severity*	0	1-2+	1+	◯							
Time of Day		3⁰⁰/5	3⁰⁰ P								
Frequency	5x this week	1x									
Present Insulin AM/PM	13/5	13/5	10/4	10/4	10/4		11/5	11/5			
OBJECTIVE See Cn											
Growth‡ Weight	31.2	30.8		31.0	29.7		31.2	27			
Puberty* Stage	2										
Urines Home AC Break. G/A	1-2/0	TR-2/0	TR-1/0	TR-1/0	3/m		TR-1/0	1-2/0			
AC Lunch G/A	—	—	—	—	5/m						
AC Dinner G/A	TR-1/2/0	0-2/0 m	0-1/0	0-1/0	3/m		0-2/0	1-1/0			
HS G/A	1-1/2/0	TR-1/0	TR-2/0	1-1/0	5/L		TR-1/0	/0			
24 Hour											
Urine Office Time	10⁰⁰ P	10⁰⁰ A					11⁰⁰ A	11⁰⁰ P			
G/A	1%/0	1%/0					1/0	5/0			
ASSESSMENT See CN		CN		CN							
PLAN See CN Insulin AM/PM	13/5	10/4	10/4	10/4	Reg 8/8		11/4	11/4			
	RTC 1/mo	Call 1 wk	RTC 1/mo	RTC 1/mo	Forgot cough syr HM2		RTC 2 wk	RTC 2/mo			

CLARIFICATION:
CN   See chronologic narative
*   Definition in practice protocol book
†   Rating based on assessment of Nurse Practitioner/Health Educator according to standard protocol. Assessment documented in chronologic narative. Includes understanding and compliance with recommendations for diet; activity; insulin use; rotating injection sites; carrying food, glucagon, and identification; checking urines; and general health education material (see health maintenance objectives)
‡   See also growth chart

Figure 3-2 Flow sheet utilized in the care of a patient with juvenile diabetes mellitus.

ASSESSMENT

Analysis of the data base allows assessment of the clinical situation. This, in turn, is a prerequisite for developing plans for management. These processes are discussed in depth in sections on diagnostic acumen and effective management. Only essentials of structure are covered here.

Thorough assessment includes identification of problems and assets. Problems may be described as deviations from well-being. Assets are characteristics inherent in the clinical situation fostering successful adaptation and, ideally, return to well-being. Discerning problems and assets demands careful analysis. Several guidelines are of help in the process.

Efforts to be complete and to present a detailed picture must be tempered. Obviously, not every information bit elicited in a general evaluation need be reflected in a problem or asset. Judgments of significance are important. In problem delineation, the diagnostic principle of grouping findings according to responsible etiologic processes is a primary consideration. Detailed discussion follows in Sec. 4.

A useful classification for problems is the *International Classification for Health Problems in Primary Care.* The provider wishing to enhance uniformity of problem delineation might extract those problems from this scheme commonly encountered, thus developing a list readily available for office use.

Unlike problem definition, identification of assets does not evolve from the traditional medical focus of diagnostic reasoning. Instead, this process has grown out of efforts to improve management. Assets, as defined above, are attributes which the patient and the patient's environment bring to the clinical situation to promote well-being.

Recording of assets may not be warranted in many clinical situations. Although recognition of maternal competence is essential to a decision to manage gastroenteritis in an infant with clear fluids at home, noting her competence in the record will not often be of value to the experienced clinician having a continuous relationship with the family. It may be of value, however, when dealing with problems inherently difficult in management. This would include most chronic problems, acute problems of high morbidity and mortality, and psychosocial problems. As an example, consider high-level family functioning. As defined by Pless and his colleagues, this asset correlates well with indices of adjustment in children with chronic disorders. The presence or absence of this asset has important implications for allocation of counseling resources to a particular family. Assets must be recognized if rational plans are to be formulated.

Many providers do not generally think in terms of assets. Formal criteria are not available for help with the unfamiliar process of their identification. It begins with a search for strengths in the individual and his environment. Among areas warranting particular scrutiny are experience with past and present developmental tasks, previous responses to stress, emotional support system, life-style, family dynamics, financial and other material resources, and community health resources. Developing one's own classification for assets should involve choice of terms definable with as much objectivity as possible. Assets

are discussed more fully in Sec. 4 and, in particular, in the work of Pless and Pinkerton.

Terminology used in labeling problems and assets reflects the analytic ability of the professional. Frequent, burning urination and microscopic examination of urine showing 10 wbc's and two bacteria per high-power field may be assessed by one provider as two problems, dysuria and bacteriuria/pyuria. Another provider recognizing the high copositivity between these microscopic findings and a quantitative urine culture of 100,000 colonies will identify more precisely just one problem, urinary tract infection. Similarly, one provider for a juvenile diabetic might recognize as an asset, "gives self shots." A more sophisticated analysis might recognize this as one feature of the broader attribute, "assumes responsibility for disease management."

Terminology also reflects specificity allowed by an intellectually honest appraisal of data. Both assessments of the urinary tract problem are accurate; they are intellectually honest reflections of the data. Were someone to employ the label "cystitis," however, this would not be accurate. With the findings presented, cystitis alone may be likely, but pyelonephritis is not ruled out. It would be acceptable after identifying the problem as "UTI" to elaborate with the comment "probable cystitis." This elaboration is not necessary for adherence to the system, but it may be useful as a closer reflection of one's thinking.

PLAN

Two general types of patient management may be distinguished on the basis of whether provider role is direct or indirect. Both must be addressed for an effective approach.

The provider or the provider's designate has a direct role in plans realized by performance of procedures. This is the case when the plan is to prescribe a medication, or to perform a barium enema, an immunization, an appendectomy, or some other procedure done to a patient placed in a passive role.

Often more important to well-being is accomplishment of objectives in which the provider's role is indirect. An objective for management of juvenile diabetics is their assuming appropriate responsibility for disease management. The providers' role here may change over time in degree of activity, but it will remain indirect. They may, for example, actively promote independence at some time. It would be appropriate to reinforce the feelings expressed by young diabetics who describe their pleasure at giving themselves shots and no longer bothering to seek out mother. This may promote further appropriate responsibility. At other times this role is more passive. It may simply involve monitoring achievement of normal developmental tasks. In either situation, this role is well described by the phrase, "promoting adjustment."

Promoting adjustment includes the provider's efforts at promoting emotional change, health educa-

tion, and compliance. These three components are closely interrelated. A mother whose 2-year-old has pneumonia serves as an example. Informed of the diagnosis, her anxiety over her child's illness will be allayed only if she is educated as to significance of the diagnosis in the context of available therapy and severity of the child's condition. If so educated in an empathetic, respectful, and friendly manner, anxiety is allayed and confidence is obtained. This greatly enhances the likelihood that compliance with prescriptions and advice will be achieved. As discussed in Sec. 9, the key provider factor in this process is communication skill. Though promotion of adjust-

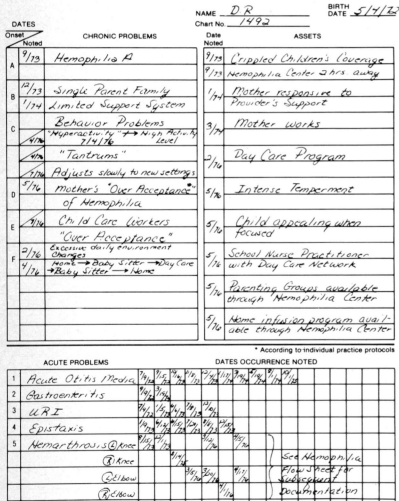

Figure 3-3 Problem and asset list for a patient with a chronic illness.

ment as in the example given does not warrant detailed recording by the experienced provider, it is worthwhile in a more complex situation to formally address each component of adjustment promotion. (See example presented in Figs. 3-3 and 3-4.)

MECHANICS OF RECORD USE

The use of records is influenced by provider factors brought to the process and by factors inherent in the form. Awareness of both provider and structural factors is important since their influences are closely interrelated. To develop a structure which facilitates recording requires a clear awareness of provider factors that influence use.

These include such factors as habits, interests, and values instilled in formal training and in later professional development. Day-to-day variations in performance reflecting changes in time pressure and demands on mental energies should not be lightly

OBJECTIVES

For the sake of brevity, some important sub-objectives for the clinical situation presented in the chronic problems and asset listing (Figure 6-3) have been left off the scheme that follows.

In addition, many specifics of management methods are not included. This is consistent with good management technique. If outcome is stated with adequate precision and achievement of this outcome represents a reasonable expectation of the resource, the manager need not seek further specificity regarding the application of the resource.

It is essential that the assessment regarding reasonable expectation be shared by the responsible resource, that is, the person who is or who operates the resource. At this point, the "resource" becomes a lower level manager. He, in turn, establishes lower level sub-objectives and, ultimately, specific methods. A useful exercise might be developing further sub-objectives assuming the role of the nurse practitioner dealing with problems and assets in this example.

SCHEME OF OBJECTIVES : (Numbers refer to objectives below. protocols referenced are not in text.)

GOAL : Child to achieve an acceptable degree of adjustment and functioning at each developmental stage.

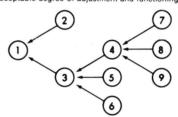

1.   To reduce the impact of hemophilia on daily functioning to the degree appropriate for the risks and physical limitations of the disease; by health and disease education, counselling, and direct medical management and other practical provisions.

2.   To promote adjustment through the provision of routine health maintenance care and supervision according to standard protocols of this practice.

3.   To reduce the physical risks and complications of hemophilia to the point that days missed from usual activity is reduced from the current level of 42 for the past 4 months to no more than 15 and 5 days respectively, for the next two four-month periods; by promoting appropriate physical activity and emotional adjustment and optimal technologic management.

4.   To enhance emotional stability to the point that physical behavior outbursts are reduced from the present average frequency of 3 episodes daily to average frequency of 0.5 episodes and 0.2 episodes daily, respectively, by the end of the next two four-month periods; by promoting activity that allows reasonable, but not excessive risks and activity, and by modifying environment as appropriate to the child's temperament.

5.   To reduce the effect of congenital factor VIII on clotting mechanism to the minimum degree achievable through currently available technology.

6.   To reduce severity of joint complications to a minimum by optimal medical management of hemarthrosis.

7.   To increase skill of child care workers in selecting appropriate activities (see criteria and suggestions provided by Hemophilia Center) and guiding child towards them to achieve outcome of Objective No. 2 through education and counselling provided by nurse practitioner. The nurse practitioner is supported in these tasks by consultation with Child Psychiatry staff at Hemophilia Center.

8.   To increase the skill of mother in selecting appropriate activities and guiding child towards them, utilizing the same resources as in Objective No. 7.

Figure 3-4 Promoting adjustment in the management of a chronic illness.

9.   To improve the "fit" between the environment and the child by reducing the frequency the child must adapt to new settings each day and promoting the ability of caretakers to ease necessary adaptations to the point that adaptations do not occassion emotional reactions; through the nurse practitioner providing education, counselling, and supervising caretakers in effective environmental manipulation and interpersonal skills.

dismissed. Supervision, especially by one's mentor during training, may be an important motivator. Audits in other settings also may be important.

Every effort should be made to develop forms which diminish time and effort required for recording and which discourage oversight in eliciting, recording, and retrieving data. Division of the record into two sections is helpful. One section contains problem and asset lists, flow sheets, and the data base. The other contains a chronologic narrative of on-going problems and new problems that develop.

The former section contains information of generic import. It warrants ready retrievability. This obviously applies to problem and asset lists. This also applies to flow sheets since they should embody plans for management of on-going problems. Health maintenance care, for example, may be considered an on-going problem and a flow sheet devised to incorporate formulated and achieved objectives for health education, screening tests, and immunizations.

To the extent that subjective and objective data can be incorporated in a check-off list or numerical rating scale, it is useful to include this in flow sheets as well. Data not so concisely represented are incorporated in the chronologic narrative. A consideration often overlooked in developing a format for the data base is the need for periodic update when continuous care is provided.

Problem lists and flow sheets should serve as an index for entries into the chronologic narrative. If this is done faithfully, there is no need for duplicate recording in flow sheets and chronologic narrative. That portion of the problem-oriented format [subjective data, objective data, assessment, plan (SOAP)] not present in one part of the chart may be cross-referenced to the section in which it is found. Very often, use of the record at follow-up visits requires only awareness of problems previously entered and provider intervention and assets brought to bear on their resolution. If this information is separated from narrative data, it is more readily retrievable. This is increasingly the case as the total number of visits increases. When information recorded only in the narrative is of particular importance to future visits, notation to refer to narrative may be made on the flow sheet.

Facilitation of recording is of particular importance in the primary care setting. The predominance of minor self-limited problems and psychosocial problems mitigates for inconsistent recording performance. Minor problems, especially when presenting in large numbers, may seem to warrant less documentation than is appropriate. Psychosocial problems may seem to demand more recording time than can be alloted. Record audits and the accompanying threat of lost hospital privileges have been strong motivating factors in hospital settings. Audits performed in ambulatory settings generally have not had such harsh penalties attached.

For the vast majority of primary care encounters, we are left with factors inherent in the individual rather than external motivators as predominant user factors. At best, the record brings to the process a design increasing efficiency and effectiveness. There are myriad mundane but important details in design which should be recognized.

Sample forms such as those included demonstrate some of these details. Others cannot be demonstrated this way. These include binding of pages to provide for ease of recording, ready addition of new forms, and maintenance of order.

4 | Use of Information from the Data Base

by Kenneth McConnochie

Platt has recently stated:

After being taught . . . not to trust any evidence except that based on measurements of physical science, the student has to find out for himself that all important decisions are in reality made, almost at an unconscious level, by that most perfect and complex of computers, the human brain . . . and the data (that he uses) are mostly not of the hard, crude type with which that simple fellow, the scientist, has to deal, but are of a much more subtle, human and interesting character, each tinted in its own colors of personality and emotion. All this the student has to discover for himself while his teachers strangely pretend to believe that the secrets of medicine are revealed only to those whose biochemical background is beyond reproach.

Recognizing the situation acknowledged in this statement is an important developmental task of the effective clinician. The process of health care decision making is rarely discussed in training programs. The experience of most prospective clinicians includes only remarks bringing to memory obscurant commentary on occult forms of art.

It is disquieting to reflect upon the limited understanding of a process ostensibly vital to our role. This discomfort reflects a reasonable assumption; greater understanding of a process contributes to improvement in its performance. Attention to the decision-making process is warranted partly on this basis. In addition, faithful documentation of decision making is also required if design of the record is to promote diagnostic acumen and effective management. Design should emphasize certain features of the process and simply accommodate others.

DIAGNOSTIC AND MANAGEMENT DECISIONS

Diagnosis

Although closely related, there are sufficient differences between diagnostic and management processes to require discussion in separate sections. The emphasis in this section is on diagnostic decisions.

Concepts which may help to improve our understanding of health care decision making have been presented by Feinstein. As he points out, fundamental to the nature of diagnostic reasoning is proceeding logically from effect to cause. Clinicians discern an effect, a manifestation of the clinical situation. They then attempt to determine the cause responsible. The process by which the responsible cause is selected from among possible candidates is the critical step in diagnostic reasoning. Ideally, this is based on a scientific understanding of pathogenesis. Often the state of medical knowledge fails us, or sufficient data on the clinical situation are not available for proceeding on this basis. In this case, choice must be based on less certain methods. Statistical information at best allows choice of the cause most likely. Also, statistics are frequently not directly applicable to the specific clinical situation at issue. Available statistics generally have been derived from populations whose characteristics only approximate those of a particular situation. The clinician must frequently resort ultimately to "judgment." This is required both to assess relevance of statistics and to make decisions in the absence of guidance from logic and/or statistics.

The "end-point" of diagnostic reasoning is an eti-

Figure 4-1 Sequential stations in the intellectual pathway of diagnostic reasoning. (*From Feinstein, A. R.: An Analysis of Diagnostic Reasoning, Yale J. Biol. Med., 46:212, 1973, with permission.*)

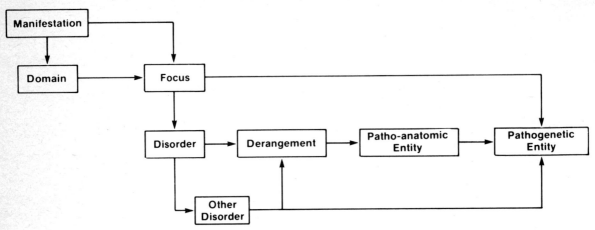

ologic or pathogenetic entity. There are several intermediate stations in the logical sequence of choices in proceeding from manifestation to etiology as presented by Feinstein; these are outlined in Fig. 4-1. In moving from station to station in this scheme, one follows the principle of "proximate cause." In practice, this sequence is appropriately interrupted at any point for therapy, therapeutic and diagnostic trials, diagnostic procedures, and other means of testing hypotheses. Indeed, such interruptions are frequently necessary for proceeding with the diagnostic process.

Structure for Diagnostic Reasoning

Understanding the diagnostic process and the strategy for progressing toward cause requires definition of concepts and terms.

The process begins with a manifestation or manifestations for which the provider seeks explanation. Manifestation is synonymous with pertinent data. It includes findings commonly termed "positive findings," "abnormalities," or "pertinent negatives." The process ends with a pathogenetic (diagnostic) entity. At best, the pathogenetic entity is sufficient to explain the manifestation. At least it provides the manifestation with a label.

A deeper look at the end-point, the pathogenetic entity, lends perspective. It is important to recognize that diagnostic entities are simply labels chosen to represent concepts. They reflect, ultimately, our current understanding and interpretation of disease processes.

There are many levels of specificity of diagnostic entities. The most elemental level is a label given the manifestation itself. Historically, disease nosology commenced with providing labels such as cyanosis, dropsy, consumption, or quinsy. The diagnosis was made simply by correctly labeling the clinical manifestation; it did not consider cause. Nosology has changed as understanding of pathogenesis has advanced. The most specific end-point is the pathogenetic entity. These represent as Feinstein points out "circumstances or agents which can cause, provoke, or predispose the development of disorders, derangements or patho-anatomic entities. Such etiologic entities include microbial, immunologic, and certain biochemical abnormalities, as well as such behavioral or psychic features as improper nutrition and emotional stress."

Whatever the clinician's level of diagnostic acumen, specificity of the process is unavoidably limited by the current state of medical knowledge. Most clinical manifestations with which the provider contends are not currently attributable to a specific pathogenetic entity. Labels of high pathogenetic specificity await elucidation of pathogenetic mechanisms. An obvious example is found in the nosology of psychosocial problems. This has advanced little beyond the stage of correct labeling for clinical observations. Correct application of labels such as autism, schizophrenia, or mental retardation does not have specific etiologic implications, although it may require highly sophisticated observation and may have important implications for therapy.

Intermediate stations in the intellectual pathway of diagnostic reasoning between manifestation and etiology (pathogenetic entity) are found in Fig. 4-1. Once recognized, a manifestation must be placed in a particular *domain*. The domain is the source of the manifestation as viewed from a structural or functional perspective. Domains can be classified into four categories: organs, regions, channels, and systems. The definition of *organs* is apparent. *Regions* are anatomically defined parts of the body such as the head, the mediastinum, the chest, or the abdomen. *Channels* are groups of structures connected in a sequence which allows for flow of materials or impulses from one to the other, such as the central nervous system, the respiratory tract, or the urinary tract. *Systems* are groups of structures that work together in performing certain functions, such as the cardiovascular system, which circulates blood; the hematopoietic system, which is responsible for components of blood and their quantity; and the entire body, which is involved as a whole in functions such as maintaining temperature.

Often a domain encompasses many structures or functions. Sometimes the particular structure or function responsible for the manifestation is but one of many within a domain. In other cases, the entire domain is responsible. The term *focus* is used to represent that portion of the domain responsible for whatever symptoms may be present.

A *disorder* is an abnormality at a focus observable by direct inspection. Disorders of structure are termed *lesions* and disorders of function, *dysfunctions*. Examination of gross anatomy determines the presence of lesions. They may be disorders of size, as in hepatomegaly; disorders of composition, such as consolidation of the lung's right middle lobe or a fistula from the esophagus to the trachea; or disorders in location, such as shift in the mediastinum or depression of the diaphragms. Dysfunctions are gross abnormalities of amount, quality, or direction of function. In tachycardia the heart rate is too fast; in anemia the amount of circulating red blood cells is too little; and in hemolysis the rate of red blood cell destruction is too great. In achalasia the quality of esophageal muscle function is abnormal in coordination and tone; in renal failure the regulatory function

of the kidneys is grossly abnormal. In mitral regurgitation there is some flow of blood in an abnormal direction; in hydrocephalus the flow of cerebral spinal fluid may be obstructed.

A *derangement* is a general pathologic process causing the gross abnormality recognized as the disorder. The basis for distinguishing between derangements and disorders is that the former requires microscopic or chemical examination as opposed to the gross examination sufficient for determining the presence of disorders. Inflammation, infarction, neoplasia, trauma, fibrosis, congenital anomaly, and some biochemical abnormalities are considered derangements. Neoplasia or congenital obstruction of the aquaduct of Sylvius are derangements which might account for the disorder hydrocephalus. In G-6-P-D deficiency the biochemical abnormality of red blood cells deficient in glucose-6-phosphate dehydrogenase is a derangement making them susceptible to the disorder hemolysis.

A *pathoanatomic* entity is defined as an abnormality specific in location and morphology that may lead to or constitute a derangement and/or disorder. Meningitis is a pathoanatomic entity localized in the meninges and consisting of the pathologic process of inflammation. There are several disorders in meningeal function consequent to the derangement which may be important to diagnosis or management, including decreased rate of absorption of cerebrospinal fluid contributing to increased intracranial pressure.

The last and most specific diagnostic terms are pathogenetic or etiologic entities, defined above. Isolation of the organism *Hemophilus influenzae* would be accepted as identification of the etiologic agent.

Diagnostic Reasoning

The overview of diagnostic reasoning presented above requires amplification. The order of stations in the scheme is determined by the principle of *proximate cause*. For example, the cause immediately underlying a manifestation is a disorder. In turn, underlying each disorder or group of disorders is a general pathologic process, a derangement. The derangement or the pathologic entity of still further specificity may or may not be identifiable.

At each subsequent station there may be several apparent candidates for the proximate cause in question. At initial stations, the location of the cause, the domain and focus, is selected rather than a cause itself. The critical step in diagnostic reasoning is selection of the responsible cause from among those tentatively considered. Selection of causes or their location should be based on precise understanding of gross and microscopic anatomy, physiology, and mechanisms involved in their abnormalities.

Careful reflection quickly reveals the limited specificity and precision with which "modern medicine" provides a diagnosis for most manifestations confronting the primary care provider. In the scheme presented, one frequently does not get more specific than the level of disorder. It is also very common in managing a situation to find medical knowledge insufficient for proceeding on a scientific basis. Logical reasoning can no longer be applied in isolation of other methods at this point. Statistical methods must then be used in conjunction with logic.

There are fundamental differences between statistical methods and logical reasoning. Logically, a major decision is broken down into several sequential intermediate decisions. Clinical data and scientifically established concepts are brought to bear on each intermediate decision until it can be made with certainty. Sometimes, however, they enable "ruling out" several causes initially considered, but leave more than one possibility remaining. It is then appropriate to apply statistical methods. If used correctly, this allows choice of most likely cause though not certain attribution of cause. Relative probabilities thus obtained enable development of subsequent management plans. These may include therapy and/or obtaining additional data.

Although therapeutic decisions will subsequently be discussed more fully, comments made here regarding use of logic, statistics, and "judgment" apply equally to both therapeutic and data-gathering decisions. Understanding the role of statistics requires knowledge of their several limitations.

Statistical methods do not seek to explain manifestations directly; they do not seek proximate cause. There is consequently the risk of obtaining the answer to a question different from that actually posed. They frequently only determine associated factors. Associated factors may or may not be linked causally to the manifestation. Therapy based on epidemiologic studies may be totally misdirected. It may, in fact, be directed at another manifestation, not a cause.

Inherent in statistics is a rate of error. Decisions based on "statistical significance" of P values of 0.05 will be wrong in 1 of 20 cases. This is often acceptable in focusing data gathering. It is frequently unacceptable for therapeutic decisions, however. Unusual clinical situations such as asymptomatic disease and multiple concurrent diseases, for example, cannot be dealt with by statistical methods.

An often overlooked hazard is assessing a particular situation on the basis of statistics derived from a population not sufficiently similar. Consider the management of a focal seizure with fever in a 2-year-old with a history of birth trauma. Knowledge of seizure pathogenesis would dictate that statistics based on children with simple febrile convulsions would have limited applicability to management of this child. Logic must be used to determine whether the population from which statistics were derived is sufficiently similar to make statistics applicable to the particular clinical situation.

Logic should be used in choosing the subject of statistical study as well as applicability of a particular study. Logic dictates that analysis of costs and benefits of a particular procedure requires identical considerations to those employed in optimal selection of routine screening procedures.

There are major differences, of course, in the setting between evaluation of an apparently well person and one who is ill. In performing procedures on a well person, many would argue there is a greater ethical imperative to meet screening criteria. It is, of course, more likely that assessment of the ill person is a prerequisite to intervention, perhaps immediate intervention. Although these considerations may greatly influence the weight attached to individual criteria, they do not require introduction of new criteria.

Just as statistical methods are called upon when decision making cannot proceed on the basis of logical reasoning alone, logic must prevail in application of statistics. The two are complementary.

Both in assessing applicability of statistics and in cost/benefit analysis, logic and statistics alone are inadequate for consideration of some factors important in many clinical situations. Often this is partly due to lack of medical concepts and data. In this case, one's decision is necessarily based on judgment.

In other cases, one's decision is due to deficiencies inherent in medical concepts and data. Early in this century, Peabody had these deficiencies in mind in stating "treatment of a disease may be entirely impersonal; the care of a patient must be completely personal." Consider assessment of the personal significance to a disabled child and the child's family of a therapeutic procedure in which both the risks and the potential benefit are great. It is exceedingly presumptuous to "judge" in this case. According to Engel this sort of assessment should be made on the basis of a personal relationship in which the clinician has made "a personal, moral and ethical commitment." Extraordinary communication skill is often required in facilitating the patient's recognition of preference and in sensing the patient's acceptance of a particular alternative as the preferred one. Although progress has been made in defining and teaching communication skills, to a great extent this involves elements of artistry. It draws heavily on human qualities innate to the provider. With relative precision, Rogers defined these qualities as "accurate empathy," "genuineness," and "unconditional positive regard." With equal accuracy, Peabody stated, "The secret of the care of the patient is in caring for the patient." Although in general discussion this process is subsumed in the term "judgment," this is in many ways an inappropriate convenience.

Management

Fundamental to rational management strategy is precise definition of objectives and clear formulation of plans. Plans should relate specifically to objectives. Selection of objectives is consequently a prerequisite to developing plans. Once objectives are selected, formulation of plans involves assessing the likelihood that a particular therapeutic modality (cause) will produce the desired result (effect).

Developing Management Strategy

A goal applicable to management of all clinical situations and perhaps encompassing all other goals and objectives is *successful adaptation of the patient*. This goal, however, is only slightly more tangible than those implied in a traditional matrimonial toast ("happiness"). Its accomplishment is not more measurable nor does the goal itself provide guidance regarding methods of achievement. These features of tangibility can be attained only if the goal is defined in operational terms.

Finding operational, measurable terms is the purpose of defining objectives. Defining objectives proceeds logically from effect to cause. A desired change is perceived (effect) and a scheme (cause) for attaining this change is developed. In terms of management concepts, effect as used here approximates "goal," "main objective," and "outcome." Cause approximates concepts of "subobjectives," "procedures," and "resources" (Subry).

Amplification of these concepts is needed. All components of well-formulated objectives are subsumed in answers to the questions "what" and "when." "What" includes outcome to be achieved and also resources to be expended. Resource statements ideally include specifics regarding people, equipment, and cost per unit of outcome produced. Outcome statements specify a single result to be attained. This will be a change in status or prevention of change as in prevention of further deterioration in a chronic disorder.

In patient care, dealing with global outcomes such as adjustment requires identification of lesser outcomes linked to adjustment through logic, statistical methods, and judgment. Those processes, discussed above under diagnosis, are equally applicable here. Outcomes must be increasingly refined to the point that their achievement is represented as objectives whose attainment implies appropriate expectations of resources available or anticipated.

The "resource" responsible for achieving the outcome allows further characterization of objectives. If primary responsibility is that of the provider, it is a *procedure objective*. If the responsibility falls naturally to the patient, it is a *product objective*. Semantic games with the concept of adjustment serve to illustrate differences. The phrase "to promote better adjustment" serves as a statement of procedure objective. It accurately describes the provider's indirect role. "To achieve better adjustment" serves as a statement of product objective. Though the providers may be active in promoting adjustment, ultimate responsibility for success in attainment is not theirs.

The second question to be answered in statements of objectives, "when," obviously includes specifics of projected time required for accomplishment.

Questions of "why" and "how" have not been considered. The answer to the former question should be found in the scheme that has linked main objectives to lesser objectives, in the reasoning that has linked effect to cause.

The answer to the question "how" is not sought directly in formulating individual objectives either. In refining objectives, however, one should eventually come upon outcomes whose achievement represents reasonable expectations of available resources. At this point, method is determined.

Selection of Resources

In terms of health care process, selection of a resource or method which can be expected to produce the desired change is selection of an appropriate therapeutic modality. At each intermediate-level objective, the provider examines available therapeutic resources to assess their ability to produce the change. One focuses on a cause (the resource) to assess its ability to produce effect (the outcome). In reasoning from cause to effect (once again logic), statistics and judgment are employed. Cost/benefit analysis is inherent in the statement of objective, since the resource statement includes cost per unit of outcome. Adequate specificity or tangibility of the objective has been achieved when available therapy can be anticipated to produce the desired effect.

THE DIAGNOSTIC PROCESS AND RECORD SYSTEMS

Most patient management is based not on awareness of the underlying etiologic entity or entities, but on knowledge of a pathologic entity of intermediate specificity. By accommodating this reality, the *problem-oriented record* contributes substantially to the ease of documenting decisions and perhaps to an understanding of decision making as well. The great utility of intermediate-level entities is not commonly appreciated. In addition to advantages of a problem-structured record, there are potential disadvantages which should be recognized.

The "problem list" is a list of pathologic entities of varying specificity, some unrelated and some related. Different intermediate-level entities are incorporated in a single problem or single more specific entity according to the process outlined in the section on diagnostic reasoning (above). Accordingly, problem definition is an intellectually honest process reflecting the accuracy and precision afforded by available clinical data, current medical concepts,

and acumen of the clinician. Only when problems are defined and revised to become more specific on the basis of substantiating data is this process progress. Otherwise clinicians delude themselves and their patients and increase chances of harming rather than benefiting.

The accurately defined problem of intermediate-level diagnostic specificity has many uses. It serves as a branch point at which hypotheses are focused and tested, both by diagnostic procedures and by therapeutic trials. Testing becomes more efficient as diagnostic reasoning allows focusing on possible diagnostic entities and assigning a tentative order of likelihood. As a result of hypothesis testing at a particular intermediate level, direction of diagnostic reasoning at subsequent levels is determined. Diagnostic entities of lesser specificity may be clustered at intermediate stations of greater specificity or they may be maintained in separate paths of reasoning. At many intermediate levels of specificity, the problem may be the focus of therapy. This is particularly common at the disorder and derangement level. Frequently one terminates diagnostic pursuit to determine the pathogenic entity at an intermediate level not because immediacy of the situation requires it, not because medical concepts or data are limiting, but because optimal management may proceed without it.

There are potential disadvantages to a problem-structured record related to the fact that it separates components of the clinical situation and emphasizes problems. It is appropriate here to discuss the influence this may have on medical decision making.

Because this structure facilitates dealing with separate components, it may discourage efforts to integrate and synthesize. Such a tendency toward diagnostic slothfulness may be counteracted, however, by recognizing the level of diagnostic specificity of the problem label. Gross errors of omission may be avoided, for example, if one recognizes in dealing with neonatal jaundice that the jaundice is simply a manifestation.

Even when specificity of components is acknowledged in management, there are difficulties inherent in dealing with separate components, particularly if the components recognized are only "problems." One advantage attributed to the problem-structured record has been discouraging oversight. This is true, but only to the extent that information is embodied in the problem list. Overlooking certain kinds of information actually may be encouraged in a record structured only on the basis of problems. This is partly because of relative ease of access of the problem list and partly because inherent in the structure is relegation of other information to secondary status. According to "problem-oriented" convention, important concerns not linked with previously defined problems require entry as new problems. There is laudable reluctance to conform with this faithfully. An intense temperament may contribute to problems for a child's caretakers, but as Thomas, Chess, and Birch state, one is reluctant to label this innate characteristic as a problem of the child (see Fig. 3-3). Also, much information equally pertinent to patient management as the problem list is not about problems, semantic gymnastics not withstanding. Resources for managing problems are equally important to recognize as the problems themselves.

Another deficiency inherent in the problem-oriented structure lies in implications for health care objectives. If a provider's orientation toward the patient is based on the problem list alone, the objective implied would seem to be total resolution of problems. Unfortunately, reality suggests this objective is not often met. More realistic expectations of today's providers are still found in the anonymous statement made long ago, "To cure sometimes, to relieve often, to comfort always." The only objective implied in the problem-oriented structure is one achieved only sometimes. This is inherently frustrating. Providing comfort, an objective always within sight, is totally neglected. Similarly, one would assume from the problem-structured record that well-being is defined as a problem list devoid of problems. This seems a bit narrow.

Although compensating for these structural deficiencies should not be difficult for the cognizant professional, these features of the problem-structured record may be misleading to the preoccupied or to the neophyte. Deficiencies may be mitigated by appropriate use of additional information-system structure, the asset line, and the objective list suggested by McNabb. Discussion of these structures follows.

MANAGEMENT STRATEGY AND RECORD SYSTEMS

Pless and Pinkerton state, "Therapeutic intervention, if it is to succeed, must take cognizance of all five determinants (of intervention), the illness itself and its particular features, the attributes of the child,

the characteristics of his family, the resources of the physician, and the milieu of the community."

In the context of management concepts previously discussed, the determinants outlined have potential as resources (with the exception of the illness itself) for accomplishing some change in status. It is hoped that characteristics of the child, family, physician, and community are assets aiding in achieving some improvement. Partly reflecting this positive thinking and partly to counterbalance the emphasis inherent in the "problem" list, attributes of such resources are listed in an "asset" list. It is suggested the convention be adopted that important attributes of these determinants not clearly constituting problems be incorporated in this list. Admittedly, this sometimes may require bending one's concept of asset.

With status of resources assessed and incorporated in the asset list, one may proceed with appropriate setting of objectives and determination of methods. In more familiar terms, only when the clinical situation is fully assessed may reasonable plans and estimate of prognosis be made. Chamberlin has noted inadequate evaluations of children in which social data in charts were deficient. The reader is referred to Pless and Pinkerton for documentation of significance of psychosocial attributes in prognosis and treatment.

The value of addressing objectives is fully appreciated in dealing with difficult management problems such as chronic disease and major psychosocial problems. Confronted by such situations, the clinician may feel similar to mariners not knowing their course. For this condition, there is no favorable wind. Setting of objectives breaks big problems down into manageable components and, in so doing, provides direction. In developing management strategy, the desired change is broken down into components which contribute sequentially and/or concurrently. Component changes contribute sequentially if one is a prerequisite to another in series. They contribute concurrently if joint contribution is necessary or enhances likelihood that change will be accomplished.

With management thus schematicized, progress can be documented with relative clarity. Progress, however small, may be extremely significant to a child with a disabling condition and to the child's caretakers. If viewed in the context of the entire problem, the significance of a small change may be lost. If viewed in the context of a scheme of carefully linked subobjectives, its true significance may be appreciated.

If objectives and assets are recognized, one is less likely to manage individual problems in a manner incongruent with the patient's best interest. Assets are resources inherent in the clinical situation that are frequently of greater importance to a patient's well-being than direct therapeutic modalities such as medication. The provider should be aware of assets as characteristics to be nurtured and reinforced. Above all, nothing should be done to diminish their impact. If plans are developed on the basis of management concepts, assets will be related directly to desired outcomes. Lesser objectives will be related necessarily to greater objectives and ultimately to the best interest of the child.

Contributions to the concept of well-being are particularly relevant to definition of health care objectives. Havighurst has outlined developmental tasks for different age ranges. Their accomplishment seems relevant to the adjustment of a child whether the child is essentially well or chronically ill. The role of the health professional in promoting their accomplishment has recently been acknowledged by Breslow and Somers in a proposed "Lifetime Health Monitoring Program." Pinkerton and Weaver developed an "acceptance" rating for childhood asthmatics and their families which seems to reflect adjustment. The overaccepting asthmatic child, for example, is immature and physically self-indulgent and limits activity beyond that point made necessary by the actual physical disability.

Application to Practice

Documenting decisions for every individual clinical situation on the basis of schemes outlined would quickly become an exercise in management and library technology rather than in patient care. The individual provider must exercise reasonable judgment in their application. These schemes are most appropriately employed in the development of standard protocols for an approach to clinical situations frequently encountered, such as well-child care or obesity in adolescence and/or the difficult-to-manage hemophiliac child with a high activity level (see Figs. 3-3 and 3-4). Whether or not documentation of their use aids one's approach to a particular situation, they provide a structure for one's thoughts in this approach.

Pless and Pinkerton place health care plans into three broad categories: education, counseling, and practical provisions. The health professional's role is obviously concrete and direct (see discussion of "Plan" in Sec. 3) only in a small percentage of these plans. It is very easy to overlook other types of plans. Perhaps the most valuable element of structure introduced is the objective statement in its requirement for answers to the questions "who" and "when." This elicits a commitment that is hard to overlook.

THE RECORD AS A COMMUNICATION TOOL

This section examines the medical record as a communication medium serving objectives of particular relevance to on-going primary care practice. It is important to consider strengths and limitations of this medium. There are few studies, unfortunately, to substantiate impressions.

The record serves communication between professionals in different organizations and within the same practice. It also facilitates recall for the professional between one point in time and another. It is, consequently, an implement called upon to promote continuity of approach and coordination of care. In addition, it is virtually the only potential source of documentation, short of tape-recorded encounters, for audits of health care performance. Primary care research is also a potential use of the record. Although it will not be discussed here, the professional must also recognize the record as a document for medical-legal, insurance, and other administrative purposes.

In studies in which the record rather than the provider was the element of continuity examined, continuity has been shown to be associated with better provider knowledge of patients' problems, better satisfaction of both patients and providers, better compliance, and lower rates of illness, laboratory tests, and hospitalization. It is presumed that retrieval of information is essential to the record's contribution to these outcomes. For those designing and using record systems, questioning proceeds to what features of record-system structure facilitate retrieval of information important to continuity. The significance of such queries is emphasized by studies documenting frequent nonrecognition of recorded information regarding problems, diagnostic tests, and referrals. The contribution of the record to continuity-related outcomes might be substantially greater if oversight were not so prevalent.

Among a limited number of studies of medical records, the only record-system components scrutinized for associations with continuity have been components of the conventional problem-oriented system. In one study, Simborg and his colleagues found that problems listed in a problem list in the front of the chart had a follow-up rate at subsequent visits higher than those not listed. The "problem-oriented" encounter note in the chronologic section, however, did not influence follow-up.

Other studies of interest focus on content rather than specific structural components and relate to outcomes other than continuity. Failure of physicians to identify the concerns of patients, a failure that is common, is associated with patients' decreased satisfaction and compliance. Studies of records have shown an association between more complete recording and improved recognition of problems and better compliance with instructions. Zuckerman and co-workers compared tape recordings of encounters with information in the record and with patients' understanding of diagnosis and plan. When diagnosis and names, dosage, and purpose of medications were written in the chart, they found patients had greater awareness and understanding of them. Such patient knowledge correlates with increased compliance and satisfaction (see also Sec. 10).

Mechanisms determining associations between recording and findings discussed are of great interest. The key issue is whether some feature of the record is causally related to findings or whether observations on records only represent additional manifestations of the true determinant(s) of findings. According to Zuckerman, "The act of committing something to writing compels the practitioner to be specific about his recommendation, and that this specificity, when conveyed to the patient, allows the patient to express concerns which otherwise would result in lack of understanding or failure to carry out instructions." While this speculation relates to understanding and compliance, implications about the record as a written medium of communication are of generic relevance. It is reasonable to assume that committing something to writing promotes more appropriate health care. The process of writing brings into operation feedback mechanisms at that moment. It consequently may make careful reflection

more likely. It seems unlikely that this feedback would do more than enhance specificity, however.

Specificity of care is desirable, of course, but the general nature of content is at least equally important. Documentation may play a role here. It allows subsequent feedback which, in some settings, has been shown to influence content of care. (Record audit is discussed below.) Records also have been shown to exceed physician recall as the source of some types of information about patients' disabilities. It also seems possible that content of a patient encounter is influenced by structure of the record. Substantiation of this notion includes only the study of the problem list discussed above. Perhaps lists of problems, assets, and objectives provide a structure for reasoning which promotes appropriate content of care. In the management of a particular clinical situation, however, they are undoubtedly of lesser importance than the aptitude and application of the health professional.

Use of Records to Monitor Health Care

Although records represent a practicable means of auditing health care, there are limitations inherent in their use for this purpose. If health care procedures are to be monitored, performance of procedures must be adequately reflected in documentation.

In terms of previous discussion on management strategy, this means that auditing health care resources requires documentation of patient outcomes or product. In turn, outcomes must be attributable to resources on the basis of logical reasoning and statistical methods. For purposes of a scientifically pure assessment, judgment is unacceptable for attribution of cause. In order to find measurable outcomes, objectives must be increasingly refined. As discussed in the section on management, this is also necessary for establishing a link between greater and lesser outcomes. Instruments presently available may be inadequate for measuring "global" outcomes but satisfactory for measuring lesser but still important outcomes.

Several authors have noted that documentation is particularly inadequate for the purpose of auditing content of care falling into the categories of health education and counseling. There is concern that a general emphasis on measuring health care performance will consequently result in the emphasis of readily measurable outcomes. These result largely from "practical provisions" as defined by Pless and

Pinkerton. If this results in a relative deemphasis on health education and counseling, audit procedures may have a significant detrimental influence on health care.

Use of Records in Primary Care Research

Limited understanding of health and disease is apparent when disease concepts are placed in the perspective of diagnostic reasoning schemes presented. Our understanding frequently does not go beyond intermediate levels of diagnostic specificity. Even when we do identify an etiologic agent, there are generally other etiologic factors needed to account for a particular clinical situation. Why, for example, if 40 percent of 4-year-olds harbor *D. pneumoniae* in their throats does a particular child develop pneumonia from this agent. One wonders what specific immunologic, nutritional, psychosomatic, and/or microbial factors are involved.

Limited understanding of health care intervention is also apparent, particularly when management is placed in the perspective of a scheme of health-oriented objectives. In some ways, understanding of intervention is more limited than understanding of disease causation.

In the face of such limited understanding it is disquieting to note the persisting pertinence of Daniel Drake's comments in the early nineteenth century. He noted, "The student is liable to have his mind bent upon practical matters, long before he is able to comprehend them; as a result his attention is diverted from elementary studies and a foundation is laid for empiricism. Of the different modes of generating quacks, this is the most prolific; and as they bear the external marks of legitimacy, they are the most pernicious to society." Health professionals, of course, remain students long after credentials are awarded.

These generalities apply more greatly to primary care than other levels of care. It is particularly important that reliable, valid data be obtained regarding problems commonly presenting. Such studies would develop a currently deficient scientific base. They would have potentially great implications for health care practice, organization, and economics.

Few examples of studies utilizing records from primary care practice settings have been published to date, despite such great need. In order to perform such studies, a practicable method of retrieving desired data is required.

A great stumbling block to use of records for research is the need for consistent, precise labeling. Meeting this need is difficult, in part, because current practice as well as medical heritage is replete with diagnostic entities for which current convention accepts multiple labels. To compound this problem, the change in medical concepts over time determines that labels applied at one time will subsequently be imprecise. Still further difficulty results from inaccurate and inconsistent data collection and application of criteria for diagnostic labeling. Dealing with these difficulties represents a formidable yet attainable objective.

5 | Current Morbidity and Mortality among the Young

by I. Barry Pless

INTRODUCTION

The major causes of death, disease, and disability among children and adolescents comprise the focal point of the combined efforts of all those working in the field of child health. Simply put, our goal is to prevent whatever might conceivably be preventable, both with respect to the disease itself and its consequences, and to limit disability that results from that which cannot be prevented. Logic requires that to do either task effectively efforts must be concentrated not only where the problems are greatest, but also where current knowledge and techniques are likely to be most beneficial. This in turn requires that we have a reasonably accurate understanding of the larger picture of health and disease in our communities and in the nation as a whole, as well as an appreciation of those areas in which the work of pediatricians has had the greatest impact. Accordingly, in the first part of this chapter we shall examine basic statistics regarding morbidity and mortality in childhood from a number of viewpoints. Each of these should help the practitioner to view his own role in this broad perspective.

The first viewpoint examines the general pattern of morbidity and mortality over time. Such trends may be applied as a basis for predicting patterns of child health and health care in the future. While these figures are only meaningful when they come from large-scale studies, the general picture is unlikely to vary greatly in individual communities. A second perspective is gained by comparing one country with another. It must be appreciated that the outstanding causes of illness and death differ greatly between, for example, the United States and Guatemala. In large measure these differences reflect major variations in the social and economic composition of the countries, but they are also a function of important differences in how health care is organized and delivered. Readers who make such comparisons must consider carefully all the reasons for these variations. A third level is that which reflects differences between regions within a particular country. In this case, the United States is taken as an example to illustrate the importance of socioeconomic and racial factors which clearly influence the rates of disease in different regions. Finally, the picture will be presented from the perspective of primary care practitioners. By noting differences between their own experiences and those reported by others, the physician may be able to judge the extent to which their own practice is unusual and to seek explanations for the differences found.

Before sailing forth into these potentially confusing waters dotted with rates of death and disease, a few general observations may assist the readers and encourage them to continue to the end of the voyage. The first is a reminder of the difference between prevalence and incidence—a distinction that is of great importance but often overlooked. *Prevalence* is the proportion of persons in a population who have a specific disease at any particular time, whereas *incidence* is the proportion who develop new cases of the disease over any given period of time. Both are expressed only in relation to those who are potentially at risk for the disorder. Thus, for example, we do not include both sexes in the denominator when we present figures on circumcisions or teenage pregnancies! Most of the rates presented here will be prevalence rates, especially in the case of chronic diseases. These will usually be expressed as rates per thousand children under age 18 years.

Mortality statistics, on the other hand, are often presented as rates per hundred thousand, in view of their much lower frequency of occurrence.

Crude rates, as a rule, tell us little about the true distribution of events in a particular population or group. To be accurate, they must be "standardized" to allow for differences in age and sex distribution in different populations, countries, or settings. This correction process usually involves one of several statistical maneuvers whereby, for example, the populations being studied are compared with or matched against a standard population.

Most physicians or other primary health care providers cannot be expected to be interested in a presentation of statistics or other data describing the current status of morbidity and mortality of children without some encouragement and incentives. For the most part, clinicians deal with individual patients or small groups of patients and are rarely able or have reason to examine their work in relation to other groups of the community as a whole, or to view it as part of a large picture of health in their county, state, or province. Nevertheless, such statistics can provide a framework and background for assessing one's practice and for predicting trends which may affect the pattern of work in the future.

It may be helpful to bear in mind that an average physician's practice consists of approximately two to three thousand patients. The composition of a typical practice changes at the rate of about 10 percent a year because of losses and additions. The losses are due to children who move away or who become too old, whereas the additions reflect a combination of new arrivals and new births. As a result over an average 10-year period, a physician with a well-established practice will see about 4000 to 5000 different children. Accordingly, a statistic relating, for example, to the prevalence of asthma of approximately 30:1000 indicates that at any given time a doctor should expect to have about 60 children with this disorder under his care. Practitioners with many more or many fewer may ask themselves why this is so. On the other hand, the doctor may conceivably go for much longer than 10 years before he encounters his first case of mongolism in a newborn—a disorder with an incidence of about 1 in 700 live births.

Figures describing rates of occurrence of events like birth and death among children are often referred to as "vital statistics." The pediatrician is most likely to appreciate these in graphic form where certain trends are clearly evident. These statistics help to predict future developments which may affect the volume or "demand" side of practice.

For example, the striking decline in birthrate for both white and nonwhite children, which began around 1955, still continues (Fig. 5-1). In 1960, the U.S. birthrate per 1000 population was about 24 for the country as a whole. By 1970, it had fallen to 18, and by 1974 when it reached the rate of 15 per 1000, for the first time it began to level off. There is much uncertainty about future trends, but some demographers predict rates for the year 1980 below 14 per 1000, a figure which approaches the crude death rate and thereby results in zero growth of the population.

Birthrates in other countries are also generally on the decline with a few important exceptions. Within the United States alone there are wide differences, with Maryland having the lowest rate (11.4) and Utah the highest (26.1) during 1974. For pediatricians some of the consequences of this trend seem clear: the supply of newborns is diminishing and more of their total effort may have to be diverted to other areas. The implications of the trend have been examined in greater detail, both in relation to the absolute and relative size of the child population on the one hand, and to the increase in the number of pediatric beds and pediatric manpower on the other.

In this connection it is important to note that, although the fertility rate had fallen by nearly 50 percent between 1957 and 1974, there is an increasing number of women approaching childbearing age as a

Figure 5-1 Birthrate in the United States, 1940–1975.

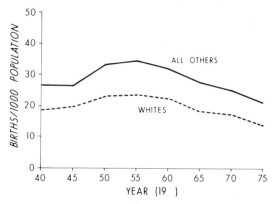

result of the postwar "baby boom." Thus, the leveling off may be a reflection of this balancing effect and the anticipated zero population growth may not occur in the near future as some have predicted. Against this, the growing number of legal abortions must also be taken into account, particularly if it has a substantial impact on births to unmarried adolescents. Several studies of the effect of abortion-law reform on birth patterns have pointed to the falling number of low-birth-weight and premature babies. This, combined with generally improved care in nurseries, has probably had a significant impact on infant mortality and on the quality of surviving infants. The net effect may be to reduce appreciably the incidence of handicaps secondary to births factors. And this too, in the long run, will influence pediatric practice.

LEADING CAUSES OF DEATH, DISEASE, AND DISABILITY

For most physicians, the death of a patient is fortunately a rare event. It is the prevention of premature death that must be the first priority of all pediatricians. To consider the causes of death in each age group during childhood is more than a mere intellectual exercise. As shall be discussed in detail later, the the commonest cause of death in all ages beyond the first year of life is accidents. Yet the proportion of time devoted toward attempts at the prevention of accidents in childhood is strikingly less than that devoted to the care of most minor illnesses!

Considering first, causes of death in children who have survived past their first birthday, apart from accidents which lead the list in each age group, there have been remarkably few changes over time. In the preschool years, accidents are followed by infectious diseases, congenital malformations, and neoplasms (Table 5-1). The order is altered for children ages 5 to 14 years (neoplasms preceding infectious diseases and congenital malformations). In the late teens, ages 15 to 19 years, homicide and suicide are of great importance, followed again by deaths from various neoplasms.

It is clear from these figures that apart from possible breakthroughs in the treatment of children with infectious diseases, the most promising areas for improving mortality rates in childhood lie in the prevention of accidents and possibly, too, in a better

understanding of the social and psychologic factors that lead to the high rates of homicide and suicide among adolescents.

In infancy, the picture has changed dramatically. It is here in the first year that almost one-half of all deaths up to age 18 are found!

During this single year of life the most striking differences among countries and between races are found over time. In general, there has been a steady decline in infant mortality in the United States which reached "a record low" of 16.1/1000 live births in 1975 (Fig. 5-2). While this still places the United States well below the "top ten" of countries ranked according to their infant mortality rates, it does represent a major achievement. Only 10 years earlier the United States figure was 24.7/1000, 33 percent higher!

Examined in a broader time frame the balance sheet of accomplishments and shortcomings becomes even clearer. Deaths under 1 year per 1000 live births dropped from over 40 in 1940 to less than 20 in 1970. Most of this decline took place after 1955. Between 1964 and 1974, the fall in infant deaths dropped from 24.8 to 16.5. This impressive achievement appears to have been due primarily to improvements in the therapy of perinatal illnesses, particularly asphyxia, immaturity, and respiratory and gastrointestinal causes.

Thus the general trend for mortality at all ages has been one of steady improvement, but the pattern is uneven—striking in some areas, disappointing in others. As has been shown, neonatal mortality has been greatly improved, as have deaths from most of the infectious diseases in childhood. But since the great fall in mortality between 1932 and 1952, there has been little change in death rates due to pneumonia and bronchitis in most countries. A similar pattern applies to meningitis. In contrast, deaths from congenital abnormalities have remained virtually unchanged since 1932—the rates persistently hovering around 400 per million children between birth and 14 years. A few exceptions such as spina bifida are noteworthy, but surprisingly perhaps, the outlook for congenital heart disease has remained stable—around 150 per million—probably because improved technology has resulted chiefly in the postponement of death, from infancy to a later period in childhood. Another area where little improvement is seen is in accidents, although it must be acknowledged that, with the increasing hazards of modern society, better medical services can probably be cred-

Table 5-1

Major Causes of Death[a] by Age: United States 1975

Cause of Death	Age (years)					Total Number[b] of Deaths
	<1	1–4	5–14	15–24	0–24	
Accidents (E800–E949)[c]	43.3 (4)[f]	28.2 (1)	18.1 (1)	60.3 (1)	38.3 (1)	35,880
Neonatal conditions: birth injuries anoxia, etc. (760–778)	863.4 (1)	0.1	. . .	. . .	28.4 (2)	26,600
Congenital anomalies (740–759)	278.7 (2)	8.9 (3)	2.0 (3)	1.6	11.9 (3)	11,120
Infectious illnesses[d] (000–136, 320, 466, 470–474, 480–486, 590)	161.6 (3)	9.0 (2)	2.0 (3)	3.0	8.6 (4)	8080
Homocide (E960–E978)	5.8	2.5	1.0	13.7 (2)	6.8 (5)	6350
Neoplasms, malignant and benign (140–239)	6.0	5.9 (4)	5.1 (2)	7.1 (4)	6.1	5700
Suicide (E950–E959)	. . .	. . .	0.5	11.8 (3)	5.2	4910
Cardiovascular diseases (390–448)	26.4 (5)	2.6 (5)	1.5 (5)	4.4 (5)	3.7	3470
Gastrointestinal diseases (531–575)	17.1	0.5	0.2	0.8	1.1	990
Anemias (280–285)	1.5	0.5	0.3	0.4	0.4	380
Respiratory diseases (490–493)	3.2	0.5	0.2	0.3	0.4	360
Nephritis and nephrosis (580–584)	0.6	0.1	0.2	0.3	0.2	230
Diabetes mellitus (250)	0.2	0.1	0.1	0.4	0.2	220
Nutritional deficiencies (260–269)	3.4	0.1	. . .	0.1	0.2	160
Complications of pregnancy and childbirth (630–678)	. . .	. . .	. . .	0.4	0.2	160
All other diseases (residual)	60.6	7.7	3.4	8.0	7.8	7330
Ill-defined conditions (780–796)	166.3	2.7	0.7	3.8	7.7	7250
All other external causes (E980–E999)	3.1	1.1	0.3	2.5	1.4	1350
Total	1641.0	70.8	35.7	118.9	128.8	120,600
Estimated number of persons (in millions)	3.08	12.79	37.75	39.98	93.60	
Number of deaths	50,525[e]	9060	13,479	47,545	120,609	

[a] Rates per 100,000 estimated population in specified age group.

[b] Number rounded to nearest ten.

[c] Numbers in parentheses indicate specific illnesses according to the International Classification of Diseases, Adopted 1965.

[d] All infectious illnesses including those related to specific organ systems, e.g. diarrheal diseases, pneumonia, meningitis and pyelonephritis.

[e] 36,416 (72%) of these deaths occurred during the neonatal period (1st 28 days of life). Since there were 3,144,198 live births during 1975, this represents a neonatal mortality rate of 11.6 per 1000 live births.

[f] Numbers in parentheses indicate the rank order for the five leading causes of death in each age group.

Source: Adapted from data presented in National Center for Health Statistics Monthly Vital Statistics Reports (Volume 25, No. 10, December 30, 1976 and Volume 25, No. 11, February 11, 1977).

ited with preventing what might otherwise have been an increase. Finally, one puzzling situation (which may reflect an epidemiologic quirk attributable to changes in reporting procedures) is the apparent increase in the rate of deaths from malignant conditions. This could, of course, be due to an actual rise in the rate of malignancies themselves, or to a worsening of their prognosis for unknown reasons in spite of therapeutic advances.

A comparison between causes of death in the

Figure 5-2 Infant mortality rate in the United States, 1940–1975.

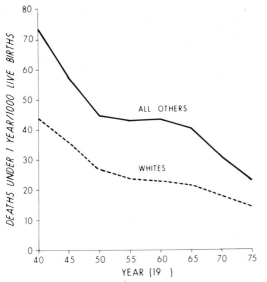

Of continuing interest and the source of much heated debate is the position of the United States relative to other countries. On the one hand, in contrast to most Latin American countries where rates range from 45 to 80, the United States looks very good. But credit must also be given to nations like Cuba which, through a concentrated effort, succeeded in cutting its infant mortality rate almost in half in 7 years! It is, however, the other side of the coin that troubles many American health care workers most—the fact that the United States continues to rank far below the leaders: Sweden, Finland, Denmark, Norway, and Japan. In 1974, each of these had rates below 11/1000; and in 1975 the rate for Sweden was an incredible 8.3/1000.

When such "league tables" listing infant mortality by country are given, the objection is frequently raised that such comparisons are unfair or meaningless. The strongest arguments are directed toward differences in the composition of the societies being compared. To meet this problem, at least in part, Wallace and Goldstein compared death rates for whites only in Sweden and the United States and noted that the striking differences still persist. Although there are obviously other important social differences between the two countries, some factors accounting for the Scandinavian successes relate to their network of maternal health centers, improved nutrition, regionalization of perinatal services, existence of neonatal transport services, and absence of the stigma attached to illegitimacy. Some observers, noting the low census figures for Swedish intensive care nurseries, attribute their low infant mortality figures to reductions in high-risk pregnancies (particularly in teenagers), realized through ready access to contraceptives and abortions.

It is particularly in infant mortality that the direct effect of improvements in health care can best be demonstrated. Several studies suggest what can be achieved both at the national level through the all-out efforts of countries like France and Japan, as well as at the local level as the result of comprehensive neighborhood health programs in low-income populations. Even in rural areas, declines in infant mortality appear to have resulted from specific efforts directed at improved perinatal care alone. In an analysis of differentials by degree of urbanization, it has been found that, in general, increasing urbanization is associated with decreased infant mortality. Better medical care, higher income, better education,

United States and its neighbor, Mexico, for children of all ages, clearly illustrates the important differences between "developed" and "developing" societies. Of the top five causes in the United States (prematurity and other diseases of early infancy, birth injury and asphyxia, congenital abnormalities, accidents, and pneumonia) only one, accidents, is commonly regarded as preventable. By contrast, in Mexico the leading causes include pneumonia, diseases of early infancy, gastroenteritis, infections in the newborn, bronchitis, and measles—most of which can and should be eliminated!

Within the United States the outlook for nonwhites continues to be significantly poorer than for whites, although the gap is narrowing. Thus, in 1974 the infant mortality rate for whites was 14.8 compared with 24.9 for "all others," whereas in 1964 the difference was much larger—21.6 versus 41.1/1000. It seems clear, therefore, that differences in the socioeconomic composition of regions (reflected in racial composition), as well as differences in their medical care, account for much of the persistent discrepancy between, for example, the Pacific states, with a rate of 13.9, compared with most Southern states where rates vary between 17 and 21. While this record seems impressive by comparison with other countries, the contrasts given are reminders of how much room for improvement still remains.

and improved nutrition all appear to contribute to this finding.

There can be no doubt that the simplest explanation for most of the differentials observed between or within countries is the powerful effect of social class—a concept which incorporates most of these variables. What is strange and puzzling is to find this effect persisting in spite of determined efforts to eliminate or, at least, to minimize it. In the government White Paper that introduced the National Health Service into Britain, one of the fundamental principles was "to divorce the care of health from questions of personal means or other factors irrelevant to it." This meant "completely free access to medical care services by all who wanted to use them." It was reasoned, quite logically it seems, that to the extent that social class is equated with income and the quality of medical care that this could purchase, the effect of this dramatic social reform would in time be to reduce social class differentials associated with death and disease. Yet in Scotland, as in many other countries as recently as the sixties, there still exists a strong (possibly greater) relationship between infant mortality and social class. Rates in classes I and II in 1970 were around 12/1000 whereas in classes IV and V they were 22 and 32, respectively.[1] Why this is so is a complex, intriguing, and frustrating question for social scientists, epidemiologists, and above all, for those responsible for formulating health policy.

Many observers have been troubled by the possibility that efforts directed at the salvage of sick newborns might result in increasing the burden to society through the care of more handicapped survivors. Several recent reports, however, suggest that quite the reverse may be the case; that is, that there is a decreasing incidence of sequelae among low-birth-weight infants who have received improved neonatal care. In particular, it has been noted in Sweden that there has been a decrease in the incidence of cerebral palsy from 2.2/1000 for the

period from 1954 to 1958 to 1.3/1000 from 1967 to 1970. The results are far from conclusive, but they do provide grounds for optimism that continued efforts in this area will be rewarded.

One manifestation of infant death has in recent years received increasing attention by clinicians, although it has long been of great interest to epidemiologists. Several studies suggest a fairly consistent incidence of sudden infant death syndrome (SIDS) of about 3/1000 live births. Although the relationship with sleep appears clear, other theories underlying the cause of this distressing phenomenon range widely. They include deficits in temperature control, chronic hypoxia, disturbed cardiopulmonary control mechanisms, milk hypersensitivity, and nontraumatic dislocation of the atlas. If the amount of interest currently being expressed in the investigation of this mysterious syndrome is any reflection of the likelihood of payoff, promising results should be within reach.

Another area of growing interest for which there is less optimism is the number of deaths, injury, and deprivation due to child abuse and neglect. It is impossible to place any accurate figure on the actual number of deaths attributed to this cause, but at least there is a decreasing likelihood that it will be confused with SIDS. In the past, parents who experienced SIDS were frequently charged with child abuse, neglect, or homicide, and the ordeal of appearing before judge and jury added needlessly to their personal tragedy. With better awareness of the syndrome, which may account for as much as 10 percent of all deaths in the first year, this possibility is greatly diminished. Moreover, there is recent evidence to suggest that, with more careful observation of the mother during pregnancy, at the time of delivery, and during the very early weeks of infancy, a constellation of risk factors may be identifiable that could lead to the prevention of this calamity.

Finally, a major cause of morbidity as well as mortality for both mother and child is the epidemic of teenage pregnancies, particularly among those under age 15. The figure for pregnancies in this age group has nearly doubled since 1960! The ratio of all illegitimate births (births out of wedlock) per 1000 live births is the substrate from which this problem emerges. For all births to teenage mothers, legitimate or not, the trend shows a gradual rise from 40/1000 in 1940 to 53/1000 in 1960. It then rose steeply and doubled within the next 10 years. In the years since

---

[1]Social class status in Great Britain is determined by placing the family in one of five categories according to the father's occupation: I, members of the professions and senior industrial and business executives; II, lesser business executives, school teachers, and higher clerical workers; III, skilled artisans and lesser clerical workers; IV, semiskilled workers; and V, unskilled workers. (See F. J. W. Miller et al.: *Growing Up in Newcastle Upon Tyne*, London: Oxford, 1960, pp. 5–8.)

1970 when the rate was 107/1000, it has continued to climb steadily. The present situation is one where approximately one in ten teenagers become pregnant each year, so that one-fifth of all United States births are now in this age bracket. Age-specific birthrates per 1000 women aged 14 to 17 years were 27.2 in 1968, 30.6 in 1973, and 29.8 in 1974. The suggested decline is attributed to increased numbers of abortions. In 1974, about 27 percent of pregnancies in girls under 19 years were terminated through abortion, comprising about one-third of all legal abortions.

MORBIDITY AND DISABILITY

Practitioners and epidemiologists both are keenly aware of the need to distinguish between morbidity and disability. Children frequently experience an illness (or an episode of morbidity) which is not accompanied by any significant indication of disability. Those with colds, for example, may attend school and play actively, and it is not uncommon to see children with a limb in a plaster cast participating in vigorous athletics! For practical purposes, days in bed, days off from school, and days of reduced or limited activities are the best measures of significant disability. From the family's viewpoint and in a broader sense from that of society as well, it is disability, not illness as such, that is of greatest concern. For the harassed pediatrician, however, an episode of illness for which medical advice is sought, whether over the telephone or in the office, is a more meaningful measure of the burden placed on his or her time and energies. Accordingly, this section will describe the causes and distribution of both morbidity and disability.

Ogden Nash has defined the family as "a unit composed not only of children, but of men, women, the occasional animal, and the common cold." The latter is clearly the dominant illness of childhood and occupies a disproportionate share of the doctor's time and skill in view of its usually self-limited nature. Indeed the majority of morbidity among children is attributable to minor infections, usually involving the upper respiratory or gastrointestinal tract. Together these account for more than 60 percent of all acute illness. The average child has between one and two "colds" per year, and one-third of all children have at least one episode of some other

infection annually. What is striking is that an equal proportion, one in three, has at least one accident each year, about 3 percent of which are severe enough to require hospitalization.

Finally, to complete this picture, it should be recognized that approximately one child in ten will develop a chronic physical illness by age 15, at least 5 percent have emotional problems, and roughly the same proportion are handicapped because of low intelligence. A precise figure for the constellation of problems encompassed by the rubric "learning disorder" is impossible to give. The range could extend from 3 to 23 percent!

This panoramic view needs to be examined in greater detail to enable it to be of value for the physician in practice. In the sections that follow, data will be presented based on the results of population studies which enable us to visualize what lies beneath the tip of the iceberg of disease which comes to the doctor's attention. They will also be presented from results obtained from analyses of actual practices.

Population-based Morbidity

Based on the household surveys of the National Center for Health Statistics, six out of ten acute conditions are due to respiratory illnesses, another 10 percent are due to infectious and parasitic disease, 10 percent are due to injuries, and 4 percent to digestive system conditions.

Chronic conditions affect children less often, and the rate of occurrence is usually expressed as the prevalence per 1000 children under 17 years. Various allergic disorders dominate the picture (between 90 and 100/1000), followed by other respiratory conditions (50 to 60/1000), locomotor, such as orthopedic and paralytic disorders (about 23/1000), and disorders of speech, hearing, and vision which, combined, affect between 17 and 28/1000—the higher figure being that for boys. Skin infections and diseases affect 15/1000; digestive system disorders, between 8 and 13/1000 (again boys are more frequently affected). Lastly, mental and nervous disorders involve 6 to 7/1000.

While such illnesses represent much of the work of everyday practice, there is little that can be done to prevent the majority of them. By contrast, the infectious disorders of childhood present a different challenge. It is particularly over the last quarter century that the decline in incidence of infectious diseases in the United States has been so impressive. This followed the development of effective vaccines and represented one of the major triumphs of modern public health. The practicing community has played a major role in this accomplishment, but in the last few years a decline in levels of immunization has resulted in an alarming situation. Table 5-2 shows the number of reported cases of diphtheria, pertussis, tetanus, polio, and measles (rubeola) for the period from 1950 to 1975, and illustrates the reason for the growing concern. Although the figures are actual cases and not rates, and therefore do not reflect changes in the population (and further they are not restricted to children), they nonetheless are a good indication of the problem. There were over 600 more cases of pertussis in 1974 than in 1973, and whereas there were only 152 cases of diphtheria in 1972, there were 307 in 1975!

Clearly, the situation has not yet materialized completely. Nevertheless, the fall in immunization levels heralds trouble ahead. Some estimates suggest that about one-third of those under age 15 are not protected against polio. Most emergency rooms report a striking increase in measles. In 1974 there were about 22,000 cases, 25,000 in 1975, and 40,000 were projected for 1976! Similarly, in 1975, there were 8 reported cases of paralytic polio, and in 1977 there were 17!

Several detailed studies provide one explanation for these disturbing events. A survey of 3-year-olds in Quebec showed a range from 58 to 80 percent completely protected by DPT inoculations, depending on the region. Within regions the success rate is directly related to social class. In a large-scale American study, the figures for all children ages 1 to 4 are as follows: rubella, 60 percent; measles, 65 percent; diphtheria, pertussis, and tetanus, 36 percent; polio, 63 percent. More important are the trends: In 1964, 79 percent of the 1- to 4-year-old group had three or more doses of polio vaccine, whereas in 1973 this had fallen to 60 percent.

Commenting on these figures, Merrit Low, president of the American Academy of Pediatrics, stated,

> Many countries do better, some do worse; but we should be nearer the top. We must focus on the obvious lacks even as we prepare for the new threats. Community efforts, outreach and special local programs are really needed. The private and public sectors must participate together.

These exhortations get to the heart of the problem. In many communities it is not clear whether it is the responsibility of public health officials or of private doctors to ensure that complete immunization is provided for *all* children. It seems apparent that if the private sector does not fulfill its responsibilities adequately, health departments have no option but to move in and do so themselves. Obviously, cooperation is preferable to competition in this important area.

Table 5-2

Reported Cases of Specific Communicable Diseases in the United States, 1950–1975

Year	Number of Cases				
	Diptheria	Pertussis	Tetanus	Polio	Measles
1950	5796	120,718	486	33,300	320,000
1955	1984	62,786	462	28,985	610,000
1960	918	14,809	368	3190	441,703
1965	164	6799	300	72	261,904
1970	435	4249	148	33	47,351
1971	215	3036	116	21	75,290
1972	152	3287	128	31	32,275
1973	228	1759	101	8	26,690
1974	272	2402	101	7	22,094
1975	307	1738	102	8	24,374
Change 1974–1975	+13%	−28%	+1%	+14%	+10%

Source: Data obtained from the National Center for Health Statistics and represent minimal numbers because of underreporting through the National Morbidity Reporting System.

Population-based morbidity figures, both acute and chronic, are reflected in hospital admissions. There are approximately 8100 admissions per 100,000 children annually in Scotland compared with 5000 in the United States. Admission rates and the reasons for admission vary greatly according to age and sex. An analysis in one region of Quebec by age, sex, and cause reveals a consistent dominance of boys in most categories of illness among those under 10 years, with only a suggestion of the reverse in the older age bracket. In the preschool group respiratory, infective, and neurological disorders dominate; among 5- to 14-year-olds, gastrointestinal disorders and accidents occupy the second and third positions, while for the older teens the order is changed, with accidents leading the list.

In smaller, local studies, the picture is similar, although differences in methodology and definitions make the results difficult to compare. For example, in the Rochester, New York studies, questions about acute illness in the preceding 2 weeks were accompanied by a request for a rating by the parent of the child's general health. Somewhat more parents in the Rochester sample rated their child's health as "fair to poor" compared with a national sample (8 percent versus 5 percent). The prevalence of any illness in the preceding 2-week period overall was around 20 percent, with rates being higher for whites than blacks and bearing a slight relationship to income. As mentioned previously, not all children for whom an illness was reported were kept at home because of it, nor were all who remained at home kept in bed.

A somewhat similar community survey of a sample of 1032 children in Montreal showed that about 30 percent of children had a minor illness in the 4 weeks preceding the interview, and about 15 percent had seen a doctor in the past 2 weeks. A more detailed analysis of rates of some of the conditions reported over 12 months is shown in Table 5-3. These figures are subdivided by the age of the child, the sex, and the average income of all families living in the same census tract. Several interesting differences are seen: In the preschool-age group in the 12 months preceding the interview, about 25 percent of children suffered from tonsillitis, about one in five reported diarrhea, and 16 percent had a "skin problem." The same three symptoms were most frequent in the next age group (6 to 10 years), whereas among adolescents, tonsillitis was followed by skin and vision problems, and 10 percent reported emotional difficulties. Several symptoms are reported in direct relation to income; for example, diarrhea, skin problems, and accidents, while others are related inversely, for example, emotional difficulties, measles, and mumps. Tonsillitis was reported more often for girls than for boys, whereas accidents were much more frequent among boys.

Studies of chronic illness at the community level also reveal quite consistent patterns. In the Rochester

Table 5-3

Common Symptoms of Morbidity Over a 12-Month Period in 1032 Children by Age, Income, and Sex (Montreal, 1975)

| | Percentages | | | | | | | |
| | Age (years) | | | Income ($) | | | Sex | |
Symptom	0–5 (N = 232)	6–10 (N = 243)	11–17 (N = 557)	<$8250 (N = 333)	$8,250/ 11,500 (N = 394)	>$11,500 (N = 305)	Boys (N = 558)	Girls (N = 474)
Tonsillitis	25.5	34.2	22.3	23.2	27.2	26.9	23.3	28.7
Diarrhea	21.1	16.0	9.5	11.1	14.0	16.1	14.7	12.5
Skin problem	16.0	8.9	14.2	10.2	14.6	15.1	12.5	14.3
Accident	6.0	6.2	9.0	6.3	8.4	8.2	10.8	4.0
Vision	1.7	4.1	14.0	11.5	5.6	10.2	8.3	9.5
Emotional	3.0	6.9	10.6	9.9	7.5	6.6	7.7	8.4
Bronchitis	6.5	8.3	6.1	7.6	8.1	4.9	7.7	5.5
Asthma	5.2	4.9	4.3	3.6	6.3	3.6	5.7	3.4
Discharging ear	7.6	6.9	3.4	5.4	4.3	7.3	5.0	5.5
Measles	4.7	3.7	0.7	4.2	1.8	1.0	2.7	1.9
Chickenpox	4.3	5.0	0.5	2.7	1.5	3.3	1.6	3.4
Mumps	2.2	6.6	1.8	5.7	2.5	0.7	2.9	3.2

studies, 209 of the 1520 children studied (about 13 percent) had one or more chronic disorders. The largest group was those involving the respiratory system (38 percent), particularly asthma and other allergies, followed by disorders of the nervous system and sensory organs (20 percent). Most of these conditions appeared to result in little significant disability—only about 21 percent of the total were judged to be moderate or severe.

In the Isle of Wight survey in England, the total prevalence of physical disorders among the 3271 children who were 10 to 12 years old was 57/1000. Here again allergic disorders dominated, with neurological conditions, such as epilepsy and cerebral palsy, following.

It should be noted that virtually all the indications of health described in this section are affected in greater or lesser degree by such major social factors as sex, race, and income. For example, in a study conducted in North Carolina during 1973, the number of acute conditions for children under 17 years of age was reported to be 254 per 1000. The figure is substantially higher for whites than nonwhites; among whites it is slightly higher for boys than for girls; and it is directly related to income; that is, the higher the income the greater the proportion of acute conditions reported.

Practice-based Morbidity

Studies describing the profile of illness seen in practice and the activities of the physicians treating them began appearing in the literature as long ago as 1934 with the report authored by C. Aldrich. A second important landmark was the self-description by Boulware in 1958, followed by those of Jacobziner and his colleagues in 1962, and Breese and his colleagues in 1966. Some brief excerpts from the latter will be used to illustrate morbidity as seen by what may be regarded as a typical, small group practice in the mid-sixties. This will be contrasted with the collective results obtained from the National Ambulatory Medical Care Survey (NAMCS) and those obtained from the National Disease and Therapeutic Index (NDTI).

The report by Breese was, interestingly, a "by-product" of their famous streptococcal studies (an outstanding example of the valuable contributions that can be made by active practitioners who are willing to invest time and effort in research). The results are based on all patient visits during 48 study days (2613 patients). In this section we will focus only on aspects of morbidity rather than any of the results describing utilization of services. As found in many other studies, 40 percent of visits were for "routine" well-child examinations. Of the 60 percent that were illness visits, 73 percent were due to acute infections, especially viral respiratory illnesses. Of the noninfectious diseases, allergies accounted for 4 percent of the total, injuries for 4 percent, and all other disorders (neurologic, cardiac, or metabolic conditions) for only about 3 percent. (As an aside it is noteworthy that by the age of 5 to 6 years 15 percent had had their tonsils removed, and by age 11 to 12 the figure was 40 percent!)

Of children seen in hospital, the principal purpose was to visit healthy newborns (83 percent). Visits to sick children were divided among sick newborns, for example, prematures (6 percent) and a variety of illnesses in older children, such as croup, gastroenteritis, meningitis, pyelitis, and several others due chiefly to infections.

The general picture is similar to that provided by Bergman et al. in their "time motion" study of four solo practitioners, based on 5 nonsuccessive days of observation each, and also that of Hessel and Haggerty, based on interviews with 19 practitioners, combined with 3 days of recorded observations. Bergman's study has the advantage of giving the percentage of time dealing with each area of morbidity. Between 15 and 30 percent of office time was spent treating respiratory illnesses, with the remainder of problems—accidents, behavioral, skin, allergy, and other poorly defined syndromes requiring about 5 percent each. There were some important variations from one practitioner to another, but the patterns clearly illustrate how rarely the more complex, challenging chronic disorders are seen in everyday practice. Hessel and Haggerty's results emphasize this point, showing that overall 2.4 percent of all patients were seen for chronic diseases and on the average only about one-third of office time was devoted to the diagnosis and treatment of sick children.

These findings are reflected on a larger scale in the results of the National Disease and Therapeutic Index, a continuous study of private medical care based on a 1 percent sample of pediatricians (and other specialists) who report all visits over a random 48-h period. Again it is clear that two categories dominate: newborn and well-child care (36 percent) and respiratory and other infections (27 percent). Of all patients seen, 4 percent had allergic disorders, the same proportion had accidents.

The wide array of other illnesses of childhood comprise less than one-third of all visits. The NAMCS, carried out in 1975 by the National Center for Health Statistics, concluded:

The most common symptomatic complaints concerned fever, respiratory ailments and earache; these problems accounted for 27% of all visits to pediatricians. An unusually high proportion of the physician's office activity centered on nonsymptomatic problems—chiefly routine examinations. One of every three visits involved a well-patient examination.

In Sec. 7, Tables 7-4 and 7-5 show two sets of NAMCS results—one based on problems, complaints, or symptoms presented to primary care pediatricians, and the other based on "official" diagnosis categories (adapted from the International Classification of Diseases). Together they describe most of the spectrum of pediatric practice in the United States in 1975. Of interest is the fact that only 10.4 percent of all visits to pediatricians during that year were for problems judged to be "serious or very serious." This, combined with the relatively small proportion of diagnoses in the "all other" category, suggests the extent to which the morbidity seen in present-day pediatric practice in the United States is essentially primary, as opposed to consultative care.

An interesting contrast may be seen from an analysis of the work of general practitioners in the English Stoke-on-Trent study and that of consultant pediatricians in outpatient departments in the southeastern region of Scotland. In the case of the former, the pattern of diagnoses is remarkably similar to that just described for American pediatricians. Colds, bronchitis, inoculations, and minor injuries dominate in each age group. In the latter, where pediatricians serve almost exclusively as consultants to general practitioners, a much different picture emerges. About one child in six (exclusive of newborns) in the region is seen annually in a hospital outpatient department. (Some indication of the distribution of responsibilities is given by the following: on an average day in the United Kingdom, there

are an estimated 240 hospital admissions for children under 15 years, 500 outpatient hospital attendances, and 8600 general practitioner consultations.) Thus pediatricians see less than 8 percent of all child-doctor encounters—"less than," because some outpatient departments and hospital admissions are to surgeons and other specialists. Accordingly, in *this* setting, more than half of the pediatrician's work involves the diagnosis and treatment of the major illnesses toward which most training is oriented.

It is interesting to speculate on the extent to which the picture of "office morbidity" has changed over time. Few comparable data are available but it would appear from the preceding that office practice in most communities has become, if anything, increasingly focused on well-child care and the care of minor infectious illnesses. Part of the explanation may lie with the growth of pediatric subspecialties, and the understandable inclination of the generalist to refer many of the more complex, low incidence disorders to colleagues with apparently greater knowledge and skills. Some of the explanation may also be due to the "loss" of many older patients to those in internal medicine. This is supported by the finding that only 15 percent of pediatric office visits are made by patients over the age of 10 years.

Variations according to country are chiefly explained, as was noted above, by the role pediatricians play; that is, whether they function chiefly in a consultant or primary care capacity. Apart from North America where most pediatricians in office practice provide primary care, the pattern of morbidity seen by pediatricians in most other countries is similar to that described for Britain. Within the United States there are some minor variations, depending on the ratio of pediatricians to general practitioners in the region. Thus, for example, children with otitis media are more likely to be seen by pediatricians in the South and East than they are in the Midwest or West. But this is misleading, since it says nothing about possible variations in actual morbidity in the population. To the extent that diseases are associated with geography, poverty, or race, such variations are easily understood. For other disorders, such as accidents, however, there is no simple explanation for some of the striking differences found. Data on hospitalization due to accidents among children in the province of Quebec suggest differences as great as threefold from one region to another. In the age group 5 to 9 years, rates per

1000 for boys ranged from 6.5 to 14.0 depending on the region, and in the next age group the range extended from 4.7 to 15.8 per 1000. Mortality rates for accidents which parallel these figures suggest that important environmental factors, such as weather, roads, traffic patterns, and proximity to emergency care, are involved in the frequency and outcome of accidents in childhood.

Clearly the most important factors responsible for differences in morbidity, apart from those already cited, are age and sex. Disorders of the respiratory tract followed by infections of all kinds lead the list for hospitalizations in the preschool group. Among adolescents, gastrointestinal disorders dominate and are accompanied by interesting if only partially understood differences according to sex. Girls are consistently hospitalized more often than boys for these disorders (a relative risk of 1.2:1), whereas for accidents, the rates for boys exceed those for girls at all ages. The risk ratio increases markedly with each successive age—rising from 1.3:1 to 3.0:1 in those over 10 years of age. There are few other categories where sex differences are as striking. This apparently greater "accident proneness" of boys remains puzzling in these days of growing sex equality and an apparent diminution of earlier sex-related patterns of behavior.

Some of the differences in the profile of illnesses treated in practice is undoubtedly a reflection of fee schedules and other financial incentives or disincentives that influence physician decision making. A list of the fifteen most frequent surgical procedures for which payments were made in Quebec during a single year shows suturing in the lead, followed by tonsillectomies. The other major categories of interest to those in primary care are the large numbers of meatotomies, myringotomies, and foreign-body removals. Many of these are done in private offices or clinics. In contrast, many fewer dollars are spent to reimburse doctors for the time spent in counseling, whether for behavioral or school problems, or in the care of children with chronic disorders.

These Canadian observations are based on large enough numbers to be easily generalized to other locales. While of limited interest to those in primary care who do not give care to children in hospitals, they offer a rough indication of the more serious conditions encountered in everyday practice. At the same time, they provide tantalizing, potentially valuable clues for epidemiologists searching for a better understanding of the causes of childhood illness. Although they may not be directly applicable to the United States, they are of special interest because they reflect a pattern of illness that prevails after the introduction of comprehensive national health insurance, covering both hospital and private-office care.

Some of the effects of this major breakthrough on care patterns have been carefully documented in several reports. It is of importance for readers in the United States to consider these changes in relation to a report from the National Center for Health Statistics, which describes the extent of hospital and surgical insurance coverage as of 1974. For those under age 17 years, 73.8 percent had hospital insurance. But this figure is directly proportional to family income, rising from 22.8 percent for those with annual incomes under $3000 to 91.3 percent for those with incomes above $15,000. Rates also varied by race and region, with children in the South being least well covered—67.6 percent versus 80.6 percent of those in the North Central region. In light of the anticipated introduction of some form of national health insurance for children, it will be of great interest to see the extent to which patterns of morbidity in practice are changed.

Disability

As stated earlier in this chapter, the reflection of morbidity that matters most is the extent of disability it produces. Unlike disease, there is no generally accepted way of assessing degrees of disability. Consequently, several different indicators are generally used which, when taken together, provide a reasonable description of the extent and manner in which illness takes its toll. Common to most indicators is the concept of functional impairment as reflected in alterations in normal activities. Thus *disability* is defined by the National Center for Health Statistics as a "general term used to describe any temporary or long-term reduction of a person's activity as a result of an acute or chronic condition." For measurement purposes, questions are asked about a particular day which is then classified as one which may or may not be one of restricted activity, that is, one during which the child cuts down on his usual activities for the whole of that day because of an illness or an injury.

As pediatricians will readily appreciate, "usual

activities" are dependent on age, and to complicate matters, many children's illnesses are episodic, for example, asthma and epilepsy. Thus, even with a chronic disorder, levels of disability may vary greatly from one day to the next. The problem becomes particularly difficult if one is asked to make an overall judgment about disability for such children. To further confuse matters, parents of children whose activities are normally restricted because of a handicap may fail to distinguish between what is "usual" for their child as opposed to the normal range of activities of the child's healthy peers. According to the National Center for Health Statistics, "Persons who have permanently reduced their usual activities because of a chronic condition might not report any restricted activity days during a two week period. Therefore, absence of restricted activity days does not imply normal health." The best that can be done in most instances is to take a population approach and to hope that by selecting a representative sample of days, this will provide a reasonable cross section of the true picture at that time.

Table 5-4 shows a number of commonly used indicators of disability. The principal dimension is based upon parents' responses to the presence or absence of limitations in activities during the 2 weeks preceding the interview. A distinction is made according to the extent to which illness or injury prevents the child from carrying on the *major* activity typical of that age group, for example, ordinary play with other children or school attendance; those which only *limit* the amount or kind of major activity performed; and those with other limitations, such as in athletics or extracurricular activities. As Table 5-4 shows, at any given time, over 95 percent of all children under 17 years of age are not disabled in any way. About 2 percent each have mild and moderate limitations and 0.2 percent are severely disabled. With increasing degrees of limitation, there are proportionately more days of restricted activity per child per year (from 25 to 58 days), and similarly there are increasing numbers of days during which the child "stays in bed for all or most of the day because of specific illness or injury." As would be expected, the proportion of children who are admitted to hospital and the length of hospital stay are also proportional to the level of disability, as is the number of physician visits per year.

For the nation as a whole, an average child loses 5.6 days of school per year, and the total of school days lost per 100 children per year is 486. Most of this is due to respiratory disorders (61 percent). Other infections account for 16 percent and injuries for about 9 percent. As might be expected, boys miss somewhat more school than do girls—the difference being accounted for chiefly by accidents.

Comparisons with other countries are difficult, because different definitions of disability are usually used. One important exception is provided by the results of an international study reported by Kohn and White. Morbidity and the use of health services are described for twelve study areas in seven different countries, using identical methods and definitions. In the population under age 15 years, prevalence of "complete health" was 463 per 1000—defined as the absence of all morbidity indicators of any kind. For all study areas combined, 239 out of 1000

Table 5-4

Indicators of Disability among Children (National Health Survey, United States, 1974)

	Mild (limited, but not in major activity)	Moderate (limited in amount or kind of major activity)	Severe (unable to carry on major activity)
Percentage of all children under 17 years of age	1.8	1.7	0.2
Days of restricted activity per child per year	25.2	38.4	58.5
Days of bed disability per child per year	9.5	14.3	. . .
Percentage with one or more short-stay hospital episodes per year	10.9	16.1	50.4
Average length of hospital stay (days)	. . .	5.3	30.5
Number of physician visits per child per year	8.0	11.6	14.5

persons under 15 years were rated as "functionally healthy." This meant that there was no evidence of social dysfunction in these children within the 2 weeks preceding the interview, but there was a chronic condition *without* disability and/or they received the lowest grade on one or more health indicators (including, for example, morbid conditions, anxiety, dental state, vision, and physician utilization). About 35 out of 1000 children had an illness with morbidity rated as being of "high severity."

This morbidity index measured the extent to which the respondent was "bothered" about his health, or "whether it hurt," or caused pain, worry, or concern when the underlying problem was at its worst. Some interesting differences were found: In contrast to the median figure of 35 out of 1000 children with high severity morbidity during the 2-week reporting period, the rates for Helsinki and Liverpool were much lower (19 and 14, respectively) whereas those of Lodz (Poland) and Banat (Yugoslavia) were much higher (50 and 46, respectively). On the utilization side, rates of physician contact within 2 weeks for those with perceived morbidity of high severity, ranged from a low of 529 out of 1000 in Helsinki to a high of 933 out of 1000 in Liverpool.

These figures represent a minute portion of the elaborate information obtained from this ambitious, large-scale international study. By themselves they shed little light on the complex set of factors which interact to influence the use of health services in different settings. They do, however, help us appreciate some dimensions of the problem, its importance in the development of theoretical models and in actual practice, and the extent of the limitations in our understanding of the behavioral and social factors which influence patterns of use.

USE OF HEALTH SERVICES AND PATTERNS OF PRACTICE

Based on a recent Academy of Pediatrics report, the average member in general pediatric practice works 58 hours per week and personally sees about 27 patients a day. Most patients are seen without referrals, which is not surprising since less than 6 percent of practicing pediatricians are in subspecialties. About one-third are in the suburbs and less than 9 percent in rural areas. School problems represent the activity in which there has been the most notable increase in the past 5 years, followed by allergies, hospital care

of newborns and other sick children, and counseling. Nevertheless, more than one-quarter of the average member's time is still spent on health supervision of preschool children, although one-third of the respondents also reported providing care to adolescents over 18 years old.

More elaborate studies of the use of health services are of increasing importance in a society which lacks any coherent system of national health care. For the clinician, however, the questions of interest are "who visits, when, and how often?" Although these are essentially the same questions that investigators ask, one difference is that for the latter they are posed relative to larger segments of the population and, more importantly, in relation to the further question, "Why?" Under what circumstances do people seek medical care? What are the triggers for action, the barriers against, or the facilitators of "appropriate" utilization? Included in the latter is a general interest in the circumstances of payment or the way health care is organized which may influence the use of services.

Answers to these questions are of great importance for those responsible for the development of health care programs, whether at a local or national level. For their counterparts in the clinical setting, they are also of interest and may even be of diagnostic significance. Numerous studies have shown that when the physician asks himself (or better, asks his patient), "Why have you come to see me *now*?" he may obtain important clues that help formulate a correct diagnosis.

It has long been known to medical sociologists that patients with the same symptoms of equal severity elect to seek medical attention, if at all, at different points in time. This pattern has been observed with sufficient regularity to have led to the development of theoretical models of health utilization which allow a seemingly random set of events to obtain some order.

The general model used to explain utilization is one which takes account of both the "natural system" and its interrelationships to medical morbidity and the "social system" and its interrelationships to disturbances in social roles, that is, to ill health which is a manifestation of disturbance of social states. Each, in turn, is related to perceived disharmony or morbidity which, when combined with what have been termed individual "predisposing" and "enabling" factors lead to the use of those health services which are available to the individual. The enabling factors are usually conceptualized in terms of "cost" (in relation to convenience, opportunity, and finances), whereas the former or predisposing factors comprise a broad range of sociocultural influences, for example, the belief that the perceived symptom is serious or that medical care is appropriate and will be of some help. At present, little can be done to influence these beliefs, whereas much can and has been done to affect some of the cost factors that affect how health services are utilized.

In the previously described international study, a detailed statistical analysis provided indications of some of the factors that determine the "who," "when," and "how often" of child health care in the twelve settings studied. As has been pointed out repeatedly, utilization by children, especially in the preschool-age group, is strongly affected by the relatively high proportion of well-child visits. On the average 138/1000 children under 15 years had a physician contact in the preceding 2 weeks, with the median number of contacts being 1.4 per child. The proportion was lowest in Grande Prairie, Alberta (94/1000), and highest in Buenos Aires (201/1000). Over a 12-month period the median rate was 724/1000, with much less variation between locales. For children, most were face-to-face visits, although in general the telephone plays an important role, particularly among doctors in the United States and Canada.

There was also a striking difference in the rates of providing prescriptions or medicines, ranging from 788/1000 in Buenos Aires to 331/1000 in Vermont! By contrast, Vermont had the highest rate of injections or immunizations (424/1000) and Fraser (British Columbia), the lowest, 83/1000. For "routine" physical examinations there were also significant variations, with Helsinki having the highest rates (within a 12-month period), namely, 745/1000, compared with the lowest of 176/1000 in Buenos Aires.

It is clear from the results that perceived morbidity bears a strong relationship to utilization, and that the combined presence of acute and chronic conditions has the strongest effect of all. The perceived severity of the illness is also of great importance. Contacts rise from 332/1000 for children with morbidity of "no severity" to 745/1000 for those with morbidity of "high severity."

In summary, this elaborate analysis provides limited support for the theoretical model in which mor-

bidity, predisposing and enabling factors are held to predict utilization. In it the role of *cost* is placed in a broader perspective. Nevertheless, it is still of great interest to health providers and particularly to those who pay the bills (whether they be patients themselves, insurance companies, or the government) to know whether making health care more accessible will significantly increase the cost of providing it. The answer to a certain extent is obvious, but perhaps less so than many might think. Data from various studies do not agree on the degree to which costs, either those directly related to payment or those indirectly related, provide barriers to utilization. Recent results (from work in Rochester, New York) suggest that there may be a limit to the extent to which utilization is increased *even if* such barriers are removed entirely. This has also been born out in observations made in Quebec.

Regardless, one task of individual clinicians, as well as that of health planners, is to ensure that some form of health care is equitably available to the majority of the population. The removal of *obvious* barriers and the foreknowledge of the effect this may have in various circumstances is essential information for all concerned. It is equally important to recognize that there are many other factors that influence utilization. Clinicians are aware that frequently subtle cues serve to trigger the decision by a patient to obtain medical advice. In recent years, there has been a growing body of literature to illustrate, often in theoretical terms, ways in which different population subgroups respond to symptoms in relation to utilization. Thus assertions are made about the presumed salience of ethnic background, race, religion, and a host of other social and demographic characteristics which are assumed to influence health or illness behavior. Although the theoretical arguments for the importance of these factors is strong, relatively little empirical evidence has been available with which to test these hypotheses. This is particularly so in the case of children, since most earlier work had been restricted to adults. It is only recently that data relating exclusively to utilization by children have been available to shed some light on the question.

A detailed analysis of three models of medical care utilization (those of Andersen, Suchman, and Rosenstock), using mothers' accounts about the use of ambulatory services, provides limited support for some of the salient features in each model. Thus, there is evidence that attitudes such as "medical orientation" and "skepticism" influence use, but only mildly; that, along the lines suggested by Rosenstock, in addition to background factors (such as perceived benefits, barriers, and readiness), utilization is precipitated by specific "cues and triggers." Again, however, the correlations are relatively low. In the Andersen model, where the family becomes the unit of analysis and a wider range of factors are considered, correlates are found with such variables as age of child, marital status of mother, maternal education and race, parental occupation, number of children, access to care, and use of services in the past year.

What is most clear from this analysis is that different explanations apply to short-term (2 weeks) and long-term utilization. Further, it appears that different forces are at work to explain use of preventive and curative services. The results also suggest that a clinically useful approach must also take into account the role of perceived "stress" as a trigger or cue for action. There is persuasive evidence that the mother's perception of stress on the preceding day increases the probability of contacting a doctor about an illness by about 50 percent. The likely explanation involves both increasing anxiety and a lessening in the family's ability to cope by nonmedical means. It suggests, therefore, that a rigid appointment system may act as a barrier to appropriate use of medical care. Finally, the results indicate that some illness behavior is "impulsive," not planned, particularly in the short term.

These findings are supported by studies which show that, among low-income mothers, "health beliefs interact with situational demands and constraints in relation to actions taken in the face of health threats." By contrast, the use of preventive services for children has been shown to be positively influenced by membership in a prepaid insurance group plan, as well as by such variables as family size, age of child, and education of parents.

Although at first glance the emphasis placed upon stress-induced utilization may seem surprising, many clinicians will recognize the phenomenon in other forms. The presence of stress due to causes other than illness is frequently a decisive factor in determining the tolerance a parent may have for a given symptom in a child. For example, a child with a chronic cough may be treated at home for weeks and is only brought to the physician when the mother's perceived level of stress is heightened, for example, because of an argument with her husband. This process may be sufficiently subtle and difficult to identify so that it will not become apparent unless the physician asks the important question: "Why have you brought this child to see me *today*?" In other words, the parent may not appreciate the mechanisms involved, since he or she has, in effect, reacted to internal cues and triggers rather than to those which are external and hence more easily identified.

Roghmann's work distinguishes between acute and chronic stress because each has a different level of importance in influencing the use of health services. Families in poverty live with one kind of chronic stress day after day. It has been suggested that such families are "crisis-oriented"; it is only when a symptom reaches an extreme level of severity that the decision is made to seek medical advice. From the pediatrician's point of view this is obviously an unsatisfactory way of dealing with illness. It stands to reason that neglect of an important symptom (whether the explanation is ignorance of its significance or economic barriers) may influence the likelihood of its cure. Accordingly, much effort has been invested in trying to determine the extent to which this assumption truly applies.

It is not surprising therefore that so many studies emphasize the overriding importance of social class in influencing not only morbidity and mortality, but the use of medical services as well. As pointed out in several other sections of this text, the link between health care and health outcome is not as great or as direct as many people assume. Nor, however, in our view is it as small as some have suggested. The point made by many epidemiologists is frequently misinterpreted or even misrepresented. They do not argue that medical care has *no* influence on the health of children (or adults) as a whole, but rather that it may be *less* important in determining health than other factors such as those commonly used to categorize persons as to "class."

It is apparent that the effects of social class, whether assessed by income, education, occupation, or all three, are classic examples of a conundrum that has long plagued epidemiologists: Does class influence health outcomes directly, as for example, in the case of low income leading to poor nutrition and hence disease, or indirectly, by affecting the utilization of services which, in turn, may influence the effects of disease?

Examples of the basic association between health care and socioeconomic variables still abound. Schaefer and Hughes studied 258 families 12 and 18 months after the birth of a child. They showed a strong relationship between maternal education and levels of birth control, prenatal care, and child care. The latter included such indicators as checkups 1 to 2 months after birth, immunizations, routine care visits, breast-feeding, long-term illness, and hospital admissions.

The pervasiveness of social class isolated from the confounding issues relating to cost of care are best seen in countries like Britain where the National Health Service has been in operation for a long while. The landmark Newcastle Thousand Family studies, which began in 1947; the three major national cohort studies (1946, 1958, and 1972); and the Isle of Wight Survey, all combine to present convincing evidence of how much the numerous correlates of social class influence the health of children. Not only, as has been seen, is infant mortality directly related, but class has also been shown to have statistically significant correlations with perinatal deaths (for example, 19.9 in class I versus 42.2 in class V), height and weight at ages 3 and 15 years, staphylococcal disease, and illegitimacy—to name but a few.

Numerous reports show how these income-related problems may be ameliorated by various efforts to reduce barriers to accessibility. In one experiment low-income families who were provided with a model of care similar to that given in a middle-class group practice were benefited in numerous ways. By comparison with a control group who received episodic care, the experimental group had fewer hospitalizations, fewer operations, fewer illness visits, more health supervision visits, more preventive services, and reported greater satisfaction. All this was obtained at a lower cost than that incurred by the controls. Similar benefits have been described for those who have received care at well-organized neighborhood health centers.

More radical changes in other countries have yielded equivalent results. After the introduction of universal health insurance in Quebec, lower income families reported increases in early prenatal care, postpartum checkups, and postnatal examinations of infants, along with increases in the percentage of those consulting doctors for symptoms related to measles, tonsillitis, diarrhea, and vomiting.

CURRENT PUBLIC HEALTH PROBLEMS

Modern epidemiology concerns itself with much more than the study of the incidence of infectious diseases. It is, properly speaking, the study of health and disease in populations, and its goals are many. For some it is still best applied in "the search for causes." Indeed many important discoveries have resulted from the efforts of epidemiologists in their quest for etiologic factors that contribute to disease and ultimately to its prevention or cure. But increasingly other goals have become of equal importance: the identification of syndromes, completing the clinical picture, understanding how health services operate, and establishing those circumstances under which services work most effectively.

To this end much of the work of those in community pediatrics has involved evaluation studies—both at the clinical level, as in the case of trials of new drugs or other methods of treatment, and at the program level. Attempts in recent years have been made to assess such programs as neighborhood health centers, those for children and youth (C and Y Projects), or to establish the efficacy of others directed at mental health and school health.

From all of this has come a better definition of current public health issues. Several investigators have shown that apart from the outstanding problems posed by "traditional" causes of illness, such as malignant conditions or accidents, a new pattern of morbidity has arisen which pediatricians must recognize and be prepared to deal with. Whether these are "public health" problems or those of the individual practitioner is a matter of opinion and may increasingly be the subject of heated debate in the near future. Much depends on the attitudes, training, and style of practice of future generations of pediatricians, family doctors, and their associates in nursing. Ours is a pluralistic system of health care, in sharp contrast to the approach of many other countries. In it the role of public health is poorly defined. In many respects it may be viewed as a "last-ditch" strategy, one restricted to filling in the gaps where the private sector has failed.

To illustrate this point, consider the question of immunizations. Most doctors in private practice do not view their responsibility as extending to an obligation to ensure that *all* children in their practice are adequately immunized. They may do so for those who arrive in their offices according to recommended schedules, or who come as a result of an illness. But there are few situations where records are kept in such a way that they can, and are, periodically and systematically reviewed and attempts made to reach out to those who have fallen behind. Few communities have attempted to evolve a cooperative system whereby immunizations are regularly reported to health department officials whose resources could be used to keep track of children whose immunization is incomplete. Under such circumstances it is reasonable for health departments to argue that a better job may be done by traditional "mass" public health strategies, for example, through well-baby clinics or the schools.

For other examples of the "new morbidity," which includes such areas as school problems, behavior problems, screening, or other preventive procedures, the same argument may hold. If the private sector cannot accept responsibility for these problems, someone else must. Either new specialists (or subspecialists) will emerge, or community health programs will evolve in an attempt to fill the vacuum.

The argument for adopting "community strategies" for such problems is strengthened by the realization that much of the new morbidity is characterized by a complex set of interacting forces. The problems are not simply "medical" in the sense that a single etiologic factor is predominant (it rarely is, even in the old morbidity), nor are these problems amenable to single or simple forms of treatment. Many, if not most of these new patterns of illness (which are not really new, simply, newly appreciated), involve simultaneously and equally dysfunction in the child, his family, and the community. Biological, psychological, and sociological forces are clearly at work in most school and behavioral problems. Together, these alone account for at least 5 percent of all children visiting pediatricians' offices.

Even in the case of chronic physical disorders, which affect about 10 percent of children, the management problems that must be addressed more comprehensively if secondary psychosocial handicap is to be prevented, involve much more than simply providing adequate treatment of the disease. They require equal attention to the family and the community, to the home and the school, and to the child and his peers. In an attempt to deal appropriately with this challenge, the "team approach" has become popular. Social workers, psychologists, nurses, family counsellors, dietitians, disease special-

ists, teachers, health aides, and others may all be called upon to help "manage" a single patient! Whether this approach will prove more successful than the solo efforts of the sensitive primary physician with the necessary time and training, remains an open question.

Perhaps the greatest challenge among the many that comprise the new morbidity is the area that is the least new of all—the challenge of prevention. In June 1974, the American Academy of Pediatrics Committee on Standards published a revised schedule for preventive child health care. In doing so they recognized "the primary importance of upgrading the health care of many children who have not received health supervision comparable with that given by practicing pediatricians." In addition, they were responding to legislative requirements (for example, Title XIX) and other anticipated changes in financing care. More importantly, they were reaffirming a conviction "that preventive pediatrics is the core of quality medical care for children. It is the sound basis on which the opportunities of each child for optimal physical, intellectual and emotional growth and development are built."

Our colleagues in epidemiology have recently completed a careful reassessment of the whole spectrum of preventive medicine. They propose a rationale for the application of current knowledge toward prevention through a set of "packages" of preventive medical services, one for each age-sex group. For example, for the school-age child, a minimum of two health supervision visits are recommended for healthy children—one at age 8 to 9 and one at age 13 to 14 years. At these times, chiefly through the use of such procedures as immunization, diagnosis, therapy, and counseling, primary and secondary prevention of many conditions could, theoretically, be accomplished, for example, maladjustment, smoking, caries, malnutrition, accidents, communicable diseases, venereal disease, and unwanted pregnancies. Few of the techniques or procedures are alien to the average pediatrician, although the skills and strategies involved in effective counseling undoubtedly require further elaboration. The main problem, however, does not lie in the tools, but in the organizational context in which they must be applied. The concepts of screening and high-risk groups require more scrutiny. There remain too the important questions of how these packages may be implemented effectively, how certain procedures can be done in most practice settings, how to evaluate the effects and the role of governmental efforts as a whole, especially toward targeting efforts on earlier age groups. There is, above all a question of how to centralize organization and financing to influence the provision of preventive services.

Ironically, the ultimate obstacle to accomplishing many of the objectives involved in the new morbidity may be the astonishing neglect of the most important determinant of the child's health and health care—the family. Although much lip service is paid by academics about the need to know more about families, most physicians remain surprisingly ignorant of many of the most fundamental structural and functional aspects of families of children they treat. In his introduction to a recent monograph on the subject, the late Professor John Cassel wrote

> While theories largely derived from psychiatry, psychology and sociology abound as to the nature of these processes, there have been few empirical studies attempting to confirm, reject or define these theories and bring together the evidence in a systematic and cohesive manner that can find a useful place in practice.

Many sets of findings have been elaborated by Cassel into a general theoretical approach which has stimulated much of the most promising work in this area of investigation. In general terms, the theory that has guided these studies has been

> . . . that susceptibility to a wide variety of diseases and disorders (including somatic as well as emotional and behavioral disorders) is influenced by a combination of exposure to psychosocial stressful situations and the protection afforded against these situations by adequate social supports.

Most practitioners will immediately recognize that, in the case of a child, the family can play either role: It may constitute the psychosocial stress that results in dysfunction, or it may provide the needed social support when other forms of stress, such as illness, affect the child.

In the studies reported in the monograph by Kaplan and Cassel, Prendergast shows the association between parent-child relationships and such health-related behaviors as physician visits, illness episodes, and accidents which caused restricted activity. The "children" in this study were of high school age. In earlier studies by the same author, similar associations are found with marihuana and alcohol use and abuse among the same teenagers. Clearly psychosocial stress plays an important role, both in the illness and in utilization. Nicholls reports relationships between various complications of pregnancy (for example, low birth weight, previous abortion, stillbirth, or early neonatal death) and stressful life events before and during pregnancy, combined with diminished psychosocial assets. Finally, Boardman and his coworkers show a clear association between "family competence" and school absence due to illness.

All of these studies were inspired directly or indirectly by Cassel's earlier work showing the manner in which social disorganization increases susceptibility to many disease states. In commenting on these studies, Kaplan suggests that "the epidemiology of the future will concern itself with the parent-child relationship and its health consequences." Indeed it will and must if it is to provide for the busy clinician the kind of knowledge and tools he needs to play a truly effective role in controlling much of the morbidity and mortality, new and old, of childhood.

6 | Factors Influencing Child Health

by Henry M. Seidel

WHAT IS HEALTH?

Health has a subjective quality which makes precise definition elusive. One must then consider the many factors that influence health in order to achieve a practical working definition. Such a definition will probably be different for each of us, since individual value judgments and the collective preferences of society play a big role. It will also evolve, changing often during the course of a career, responding variously to expectations that are age-dependent. The unifying forces for most people are the fact of death as the basic condition of life and the high value put on feeling "healthy" during life. Any effort to define health or, at least, to reach some agreement on the factors which contribute to it implies that we think we have some control over those factors.

Therefore, at the outset, a caveat is in order. Darwin suggested that evolution was determined for the large part by a process of positive natural selection. However, he and those who followed him studied phenotypes. Now that we are able to learn much more about the processes of change at the molecular level, we have a strong suspicion, based on what happens inside the gene, that adaptation and survival based on darwinian selection may, at least, have to share a role in evolution with random chance. This is difficult for those of us who depend upon order and structure in our thinking. Nevertheless, there is a possibility that the genetic variation within species may be adaptively neutral and that the variability depends on mutational pressure and random gene frequency drift. These questions are being constructively argued by the population geneticists. There is an implicit concern, however, that the well-being we value is so much dependent on chance that control of our health is even more limited than we had suspected.

Furthermore, none of the factors which influence health are independent. When we speak of health, we imply an entity which has an apparent unity, a unity which may involve more than the World Health Organization's concept of "a state of complete physical, mental, and social well-being." Perhaps we can agree with Galen (A.D. circa 130 to 200) that a definition would be absurd if precise and settle for the idea that "that condition in which we do not suffer pain, and are not impeded in the activities of life, we call health; and if anyone wishes to call it by any other name he will accomplish nothing more by this than those who call life perpetual suffering." Galen would exclude from ill health conditions such as aging which are "in accordance with nature." Indeed, is all that is not health disease, or is all that is not disease health? Is death the ultimate in poor health or does it have a more sublime connotation? We are confronted with an interweaving infinity.

Nevertheless, we can *try* to isolate some of the parts. Those we select are determined by our contemporary values and culture. There would certainly be variance from place to place and time to time. We are helped, perhaps, by our somewhat improved ability in recent decades to measure and to record those aspects of our experience which we accept as indicators of health. Still, we do not do it exceptionally well, either within or among nations. Since there is no consistency of record-keeping or consistency of judgment from place to place, the major question of the reliability of numbers when applied on a worldwide scale remains. Internationally, we have not achieved a common understanding of health, of the related needs, or of how to plan for their satisfaction. Moreover, on a national scale, it is most disturbing that the 1976 report of the Macy Foundation Commission on Physicians for the Future reminds us that the United States has not yet developed a mechanism for a valid assessment.

SOCIETY'S PRIORITY FOR THE CHILD

Galen wrote on the health of the very young. He particularly noted aspects of their growth and development. However, organized concern about the health care of the young is a relatively recent development, certainly less than a century old in the United States. We began to give somewhat greater attention to the child when the infant mortality rate was more than four times its present level. As recently as 1915, 10 percent of all newborns did not reach their first birthday.

This sluggish approach has abundant historical precedent. In fact, until very recently, the child has been exploited, very much the chattel of the parent, lacking full assurance of legal recognition of the rights of an individual. The Constitution of the United States has not guaranteed, for example, that a child has the right to representation, to a trial by jury, or to due process under the law. The health of the young has been compromised by this second-class status.

A subtle example of these traditional attitudes is evident in adoption practices in the United States. Adoption is based on the ancient Roman ideal of imitating nature. Originally, we tried to match children to their adoptive parents by religion and complexion. This effort, of course, denied the child's individuality and the reality that adoption cannot simulate the biologic course. It reinforced the traditional priority which put the needs of the adult ahead of those of the child. However, there have been several positive changes in adoption practices in the past 15 years. Recently, for example, there has been an increased effort on the part of the adopted to learn their biologic identities when they reach majority. This move represents an effort to break from the past and to serve the social, emotional, and health needs of these children and young adults. The law, however, is still restrictive, tending to conceal the facts of biologic identity, thus serving first the presumed needs of both adoptive and biologic parents. Certainly, positive change would not deny the rights of any group. Rather, it must seek an assurance of equal concern for the needs of all. We know that adoption does not compromise a child's ability to achieve the full potential of physical and intellectual growth. It is a matter of concern that we persist with legal practices which may obstruct emotional fulfillment.

WHICH FACTORS INFLUENCE HEALTH?

The original intent for this chapter had been to organize the factors that influence health according to seven themes, *biomedical, social, political, economic, educational, organizational,* and *professional sociological.* Lalonde, attempting the same kind of generalization, commented that two approaches might be taken: a look at the past with retrospective note of changes in the nature and incidence of sickness and death, or a look at the present as it is made evident in statistics on illness and death and in a concomitant effort to establish underlying causes. He invokes McKeown (1972) who, using the historical approach, had concluded that "in order of importance the major contributions to improvement in England and Wales were from limitation of family size (a behavioral change), increase in food supplies and a healthier physical environment (environmental influences), and specific preventive and therapeutic measures." Having thus cited the *behavioral* and *environmental influences,* McKeown goes on to say that "it is to these same influences that we must look . . . for further advance." These, and continuing *expansion of our knowledge of human biology,* Lalonde concludes, are the pathways to the understanding and to the consequent manipulations that might lead to better health. Finally, reflecting on the fact that economically deprived segments of the Canadian population, including its native peoples, contribute disproportionately to the infant mortality rate in Canada and, further, that there is geographic and specialty disproportion in the distribution of physicians in Canada, Lalonde, aware of these readily evident barriers to accessibility to care, concludes that *the organization of health services* presents as a fourth contributing pathway.

Unfortunately, in spite of our need to better understand the effects of this organization, it has been extraordinarily difficult to measure the impact of medical care on the health of people, to relate the process of care to the outcome we can observe in the patient. For example, there has been considerable argument about the effectiveness of *primary* pediatric care as compared to *episodic* care. Alpert and his colleagues studied the question carefully. They found that continuous care for low-income inner-city families *appeared* to decrease hospitalization, operations, illnesses, and appointment-breaking and that increasing the numbers of health supervision visits and preventive services increased patient satisfaction. In addition, these changes, overall, were accomplished at a cost lower than that of episodic care. On the other hand, patient morbidity was not altered. Studies such as these are limited and cannot be overinterpreted. However, they must give us pause and they can provide a base on which to discuss an appropriate mechanism for health care delivery. At the moment, there are no certain societal definitions of an appropriate health care delivery mechanism. It may well be that the value judgment of society will opt, in the long run, for episodic care and good accessibility to care as defined by the patient. This may not make possible the achievement of the frequently stated objective of constructive prevention, of so-called health maintenance. It may, however, demonstrate that ready accessibility is *the* prime factor in assuring desired medical care outcomes (see Sec. 7).

THE HEALTH FIELD CONCEPT

In any event, four themes provide a basis for consideration of health in general and, for our needs, of the health of the young: *human biology, environment, life-style,* and *health care organization.* This is the health field concept first proposed by LaFramboise.

There are those, however, who claim but one essential factor—economics. They believe that the economic imperative underlies our decision making in all areas and that is the one, strong, compelling force. Certainly, using LaFramboise's formulation, this is readily apparent in health care organization, life-style, and environment. May it not also be so in human biology as we decide the areas for study when we allocate our resources to those who investigate

and expand our biological knowledge? What are the economic determinants in this process?

If the neoclassical economist is right, the apparent power of the economic determinant has contributed to the evolution of a life-style which despoils our animate and inanimate environment and, as Schumacher puts it, "mutilates man." This is almost as terrifying to contemplate as the fact that two influenza viruses may infect a human cell simultaneously and that they can combine and recombine with each other in previously unexperienced ways *ad infinitum.* Certainly, if the recombination permits viability and replication of that cell, there are here elements of a randomized jigsaw puzzle which seem to put us in the mode of forever chasing, but never achieving, a degree of mastery over an infinity of threats to health.

Nevertheless, we choose that model which includes economics and the fortuitous behavior of nature within the themes of LaFramboise. This seems a more useful structure, certainly more heartening, and no less likely to be appropriate for our purposes.

Indeed, all of these factors defy absolute categorization. Having created some boxes for the sake of making a point, let us recognize their artificiality and let us not strain to keep them separate and neat. All the factors flow and meld—those alluded to and many the reader might care to add—in a number of combinations reminiscent of the potential of the RNA viruses.

LIFE-STYLE AND MONEY

We cannot deny the economic forces. Our resources are finite and there are significant indicators in the way we choose to allocate them.

For example, our expenditures for health in the decade 1965 to 1975 increased at a rate of 10 percent per year or more. In addition, in 1965, health costs, $38.9 billion, were 5.9 percent of the gross national product. By 1975, this figure had risen to more than $115 billion, 8.3 percent of the gross national product (GNP).

These expenditures reflect literally billions of separate health sector transactions: the payment of fees to physicians and dentists; drug purchases; hospitalization; costs of x-ray and laboratory tests; and residence in extended care facilities among many others. In large part, these costs represent a payment for reactive medical care rather than for preventive health care. There is evidence, too, that there is an age differential in the way we spend our money. The very young and the very old seek health care more often and thus commit larger sums of money to this care than do the intervening age groups. Those who are older, however, have better insurance coverage and, therefore, better accessibility to care in economic terms.

A disturbing figure, the result of complex social, political, educational, and economic factors, is the percentage of total federal expenditures for health that are dedicated primarily to satisfying the unmet needs of the young. In the mid-1970s, the combined expenditures of local, state, and federal government for their health care did not exceed the total expenditures of the American citizenry for pet food. By 1975, 10 cents of every federal health dollar was spent on services for children. Just 15 years earlier the figure was 50 cents. Essentially, since 1960, the absolute numbers of dollars dedicated to children had remained substantially the same, and there had been a dramatic fall in the percentage of the total expenditure.

Why? People under 19 years of age comprise almost 49 percent of the population of the United States; people over 65, almost 10 percent of the population. And yet, the marked discrepancy in dollars spent exists.

One might reason that there is a significant difference in the content of care in the two age groups. Indeed, there is. Chronic illness is a characteristic of old age. On the other hand, children under 4 years have almost four acute illnesses a year; persons 65 or older, just a bit more than one a year. It is legitimate to wonder if the variation in content of care justifies the discrepancy evident in the 5 cents spent per child and adolescent as compared to the 78 cents spent per senior citizen. It is necessary, therefore, to compare the powerful political lobby active on behalf of the aged with the lesser effort on behalf of children. Children do not vote.

There is no assurance, however, that more money will assure an improvement in the morbidity and mortality of the young. Abelson reminds us that increased expenditures are encouraged by a health care system which utilizes third party payers in the mode common in the United States. A demand for care which is generated by both the provider *and*

the patient is facilitated. This is not the consumer-demand model which dominates, for example, the automobile industry. Unmindful of the old tenet that there is no such thing as a free sandwich, people will seek treatment, even major invasive surgery and diagnostic manipulation, on the basis of inadequate symptoms. Physicians need to practice defensive medicine in an unfavorable malpractice milieu, ordering more tests and procedures than they otherwise might—all this with both the lay and the professional assumption that there is somehow a correlation between better health and greater expenditure. In fact, life expectancy reached a plateau in the United States in 1954. The already cited dramatic increase in health care expenditures since that time has not caused a favorable shift from that plateau. The United States mortality rate for each age under 75 years remains higher than that of England or Sweden.

This seems to confirm Fuchs's statement that

Once basic levels of medical sophistication, personnel, and facilities become available, additional inputs of medical care do not have much effect. In other words, the total contribution of modern medical care to life expectancy is large, but over the considerable range of variation in the quantity of care observed in developed countries, the marginal contribution is small.

Certainly, a certain minimum level of income is important, But, there is not now and there may never have been a direct relationship between life expectancy, per capita income, and per capita health care expenditures. Our "style" of life is of apparent importance.

Beyond Money

Clearly, then, there is an impact on health outcome which is determined by other factors which either order or intimidate our priorities. This is evident in the experiences of infancy and of adolescence. The almost total dependency of the infant requires the family structure we have developed and to which we cling. In fact, the newborn's ability to survive in the United States has improved dramatically in this century, from mortality rates in excess of 29:1000 live births in 1915 to 15:1000 live births in 1974. We are often reminded, however, that the rates in many other countries are lower, notably those in Scandinavia, Holland, Australia, New Zealand, and Japan. And we rationalize that the heterogeneity of our population, the diversity of our environment, our size, and our economic complexity are contributing factors. Certainly, our biomedical sophistication has not dealt with these factors. More black babies than white babies die. Mothers continue to smoke and compromise their fetuses. The acting-out pregnant adolescent continues to eat and to live in such a way that the potential of the infant is compromised by the greater likelihood of prematurity and of slowed cognitive development.

A major behavioral change in the United States has been the great increase in the numbers of working mothers. About one-quarter of American children under 3 years of age are involved. They need surrogate daytime care. Perhaps 10 percent of them are placed in group day-care centers. It has been shown that psychological health may not be adversely affected by such care. However, Doyle has clearly demonstrated the increased incidence of physical illness in the very young in such settings. The risk is greater in the very young.

Adolescents, on the other hand, do not get as physically sick as often as the other young, but their health does become impaired and they do die. Fuchs offers the jarring reminder that accidents and suicide are the prime reasons for death and, further, that there is a significant sex-related differential. The male youth dies more often and more violently than does the female, and the rates for both are increasing.

Such facts suggest that we are not yet, in the 1970s, prepared to exercise the individual and collective discipline which can serve the objective of good health and long life. While we appear to accept the responsibility of role models for our young whether we be parents or health professionals, there is evidence that we yield to the indulgence of the moment and repress the abstraction of future illness.

The Vagaries of Life-Style

Somers notes that the 18,032 young Americans, 15 to 24 years of age, who died in auto accidents, the 5182 who were murdered, and the 4098 who committed suicide in 1973 to 1974 contributed to a death rate for this age group which was 19 percent higher than in 1960 to 1961. This change was almost entirely due to violence. Further, deaths from homicide in the period 1956 to 1976 increased principally in

the ages 1 to 4. She suggests that we are a "culture of violence" and that television with its commitment to entertainment by displays of violence is a major contributing factor. Admittedly, this concept is difficult to validate. Still, this suggests a circumstance in which the professional may reach beyond the confines of the clinic and the consultation room to become involved in the affairs of the larger community and to take an active role, attempting to influence those aspects of life-style which appear to diminish the positive health status of our children and youth. It has been said by the Chinese that one is only partially a physician if one is invested *solely* in the care of individuals, that to be a "real" physician one must be concerned, too, with groups, with populations. Certainly, it is quite true that other professionals are concerned that pediatricians do not move into the community with ease, join school boards, serve on advisory committees, testify with alacrity in courts of law. This reluctance to participate, justifiable or not, is perceived with a jaundiced eye by colleagues who must also serve children. Louise Raggio, formerly head of the Family Law Section of the American Bar Association, very much committed to the solution of the legal problems of the young, said in 1975, "This foot dragging of doctors is forever a burr under my saddle." Clearly, however, active involvement *as a citizen* forces the exercise of personal value judgment and some confusion in role as one shifts between the stances of individual care provider and community participant.

There is a danger, too, in such action if, as individuals or in groups, we lose sight of the requirement that we consider the overall needs of the young in context. Unfortunately, when we aggregate in groups—of pediatricians, of parents, of foundations providing funds—we tend to abandon the holistic view and to adopt smaller, more manageable goals which, while important, tend to give skewed attention to an assortment of priorities which, overall, may not be appropriately ordered. For example, we would probably all agree that it is well to have dealt with the threat of poliomyelitis. However, are we assured that the dedication of our resources to the solution of particular problems is ordered by a thoughtful decision-making process or by the singular attention of an articulate, aggressive few who dominate the process in order to serve the demands of their individual need. Why, indeed, does a Jerry Lewis commit himself to the problems of muscular dystrophy to the exclusion of other equally demanding circumstances? If, in the long run, groups of parents or foundations are governed by such singular attention, the long-run impact on the health of the young will of course be evident. But we must ask if this approach is appropriate. We must also consider the impact of the ambivalence of organizations of pediatricians which find it difficult to distinguish between service to the needs of the young and to the defense of the role of the pediatrician in a changing health care system. Foundations and parent and professional groups have done great good. The lingering question asks whether the contribution might not have been greater.

There are, in addition, poorly understood life-style paradoxes. For example, Rowe and his colleagues suggest that poverty protects against dental caries. They found that, by the age of 14, children from families whose per capita income was $1000 or lower had significantly lower caries rates than those from families with an income of $2000 per capita and up. This "protective" effect of lower income seems especially apparent in blacks. The explanation is not at all certain since there were no data available in this study to substantiate conclusively that increased frequency of food intake or greater sucrose consumption might be responsible for the differences observed. In any event, our assumptions in this regard might have been quite the opposite.

Another life-style paradox is inherent in the conflict evolving from our devotion to the automobile. Accidents are the leading cause of death in children after the age of 1 year, and automobiles cause more of these deaths than all else combined. Indeed, at all age groups, the leading causes of death are life-style–related; driving, eating, drinking, smoking. Still, individually or collectively, we do not take adequate measures to ensure greater safety for the young. It is still necessary, as Heagarty indicates, to search for the means to educate the patient and to discover the therapeutic manipulations of behavior so that the potential for meaningful life of all the young is improved. There is evidence that descriptive literature, counseling, particularly during the prenatal period, the use of film, and live demonstrations of the use of car seats can all influence parents positively in this regard. There is also evidence that pediatricians, if reminded by their professional organizations or by drug salespeople, will more often counsel their patients in this regard. However, we

have no assurance that these stimuli are sustained, that there is meaningful prolonged change in behavior, or that, by these mechanisms, accident rates are diminished. However, there has been some suggestion that the life-style change caused by presumed gasoline shortage and increased cost—the reluctant slowdown to 55 mph—may have some benefit. Our knowledge concerning behavioral change and the possible contribution of the health professionals in this regard is, in any event, still limited. We need considerable multidisciplinary investigative effort in order to clarify the circumstance.

HUMAN BIOLOGY AND THE BIOMEDICAL INFLUENCE

Our increasing biomedical sophistication is not paralleled by our ability to make health and medical care services available to everyone. Americans do expect that high-quality medical care can and should be readily accessible and that biomedical discoveries can be quickly and efficiently translated into improved service. They are not sensitive to the gap that exists between available knowledge and the availability of full service and to the fact that social and political considerations take precedence over the satisfaction of need. The constant changes in our individual and collective value judgments which affect our life-style and our ability to set collective priorities often preclude the expenditure of our resources in what might seem to be a more rational way. Thus, we may choose to explore biomedical areas that are more politically convenient than they are appropriate, for example, to the needs of children. Legislators may choose to allocate dollars to those studies which are of more immediate personal concern to them.

Still, there is an abundance of examples which assure that our biomedical knowledge has had an overall positive impact on child health. Regardless, if the first precept of medicine is *primum non nocere*, one must constrain enthusiasm.

Favus and his colleagues offer a reason. The first warnings came at mid-century that children who had received prior irradiation for thymic enlargement had an increased risk of the development of thyroid carcinoma later in childhood or adolescence. As the confirmatory studies proliferated, the use of external radiation declined. And, by the 1960s, there were fewer childhood thyroid neoplasms. Many of the children exposed to irradiation for thymic enlargement or tonsillar and/or adenoidal enlargement are now adults. Favus studied 1056 people who were treated during the 1940s and 1950s. Palpable nodular thyroid disease was found in 16.5 percent, nonpalpable lesions were detected in 10.7 percent—an overall rate of 27.2 percent. Of the 180 patients operated on for these lesions, 33 percent had thyroid cancer. For some of the patients, the risk became apparent as long as 35 years after original therapy. These results, highly statistically significant, are an example of our unfortunate tendency to use too soon management regimens which have not had controlled clinical trials and a period of judicious caution in which to consider their potentially inappropriate outcomes.

This same study reminds us, in another way, of other gaps in care. The ability of examiners to detect thyroid abnormalities, particularly nodules, was influenced by their knowledge of scintigram results. Without such knowledge, nodules were palpated in 141 subjects by one or more examiners. Given a review of the scintigram, repalpation increased this number to 174! And, further, nonnodular abnormalities were found in an additional 15 patients.

This variation within and between human observers is well known and, of course, has profound impact on health.

A 17-day first born male has projectile vomiting, post-prandial, readily visible peristalsis, and evidence of dehydration and weight loss. The pediatrician cannot feel a pyloric tumor but, because of the grouping of signs and symptoms, consults with a surgeon. The consultant feels one! Then, on reexamination, the pediatrician concurs. The baby is brought to operation. Pyloric stenosis is not found. The baby, fortunately, does well postoperatively and recovers with the help of medical management of an acute gastroenteritis.

LIMITATIONS OF BIOMEDICAL KNOWLEDGE

The potential of a swine influenza epidemic in 1976 generated a response which was based on the growth of our knowledge and technical capability and a greater confidence in our ability to predict the behavior of pathogenic organisms. It also emphasized our limitations. There was circumstantial evidence that the swine influenza virus had been responsible

for the tragic pandemic of 1918. While there were many who argued that a repetition of 1918 was unpredictable and that the availability of antibiotics would reduce fatality from secondary bacterial pneumonia, there were others who asserted that the clinical course in 1918 was far too brief to allow implementation of adequate therapy. Our presumed technical ability to develop, test, and administer a vaccine to millions of citizens in a few months was a major determinant in the decision to vaccinate a large part of the nation.

After that decision, careful epidemiologic study showed an epidemic probability of 0.10 with the costs of purchase and administration of the vaccine at 50 cents per person. It was also found that the younger one was the less likely one was to be protected by the immunization, and the more likely one was to have a reaction to the shots. It was not possible to develop a better vaccine which contained effective neuraminidase, a component which, in an appropriate medium, stimulates those antibodies which interfere with a virus's ability to multiply and spread through the body. There was also predictive evidence that the likelihood of an epidemic caused by the A Victoria strain of virus was perhaps four times greater. Overall, care had to be exercised with those who were sensitive to egg white, who were pregnant, and who had severe intercurrent disease. Fortunately, the past experience of children in such epidemics was relatively mild. Unless they were otherwise ill, they tended to be less seriously affected than older folk.

Withal, biomedical competence—great but limited—a human reluctance to risk a decision to hold back, and the political behavior of an incumbent president during an election year mandated the effort. It was possible to rationalize that it might be cost effective if we restricted the target group by and large to adults and if more than 59 percent of them took the immunization. High-risk groups, particularly the ill and the aged, would receive a vaccine which combined the swine (New Jersey) and A Victoria strain. All told, this was a major and unsuccessful program which drained our limited resources in an inappropriate way and which certainly, once again, diminished our ability to provide for the needs of children in other ways.

Perhaps, however, the need to correlate our technical biomedical expertise with appropriate behavior is most evident in our care of the premature infant. Aranda and his colleagues estimate that a 1500 g newborn in North America is exposed to about 20 prescribed drugs between conception and discharge from the nursery, 10 on the average via the placenta or breast milk, the rest as part of post-natal nursery routines, and as specific prescriptions for the individual infant's needs. There is also an unmeasurable contribution from over-the-counter medications, alcohol, nicotine, caffeine, and the industrial chemicals affecting the mother and fetus.

Furthermore, Miller and his colleagues showed that the frequency of low-birth-weight infants was highest in the lowest socioeconomic class and that this frequency did not depend on the numbers of mothers with medical problems or complications of pregnancy so much as it did on low-maternal-weight gain during the gestation, smoking, use of inappropriate drugs, and the refusal of prenatal care. Our ability to assess the full impact is hindered by the separation in time from early gestation to adult life and the difficulty in relating outcomes over that time to these events. There is little doubt, however, that the provider's use of drugs does lead to important episodes of toxicity in all newborns, particularly in the premature, and that social class and maternal behavior increase the numbers of low-birth-weight infants, thus depleting resources and compromising our technical competence.

There is irony in our limited knowledge. It would be impossible now to withhold dietary treatment from an infant with phenylketonuria. We know that the future of these infants is modified by their pre-treatment blood levels of phenylalanine and that their risk of retardation increases with the level. Thus, it may be possible to withhold the phenylalanine restrictive diet from a person with a relatively low level and still avoid retardation. However, such a female child, might, as an adult, have a retarded child, or, on the average, two. Certainly, women with elevated phenylalanine levels who are not treated and not retarded have children who are *not* phenyl-ketonuric and who are retarded. If, on the other hand, the future mother is treated in infancy, it is not known whether the benefit of early treatment will be sustained in her pregnancies and yield a normal child or whether the diet can be introduced at the time of pregnancy with a favorable outcome. Holtzman suggests that the aborted retardation of the mother might be offset in the future with the unfortunate affliction of her children.

Biomedical Expertise and the Future

In 1976, two United States senators and a biologist at the California Institute of Technology had this interchange concerning experimentation and recombinant DNA:

Senator Kennedy: Do you agree that in terms of magnitude this is of as great significance as the splitting of the atom?

Mr. Sinsheimer: What this technology does is to make available to us the complete gene pool of evolution. We can take the genes of one organism and recombine them with those of others in any manner we wish. To my mind this accomplishment is as significant as the splitting of the atom.

Senator Schweiker: Are you saying that all that has gone before, we now have the power to change in some way . . . the evolutionary process?

Mr. Sinsheimer: Yes!

Our discussion to this point has already suggested the mixed forces that influence health and the limitations put on our scientific and technical expertise by our behavior. One can agree with Sinsheimer that our knowledge of the atom and the gene give us a power we do not fully understand and that there is nothing in history to assure us that our finite wisdom and the nature of our social institutions are sufficient to preclude folly. The meaning of health!?

ENVIRONMENT

We seem to do irreparable damage to our environment continually. As Wolman puts it,

In the millennia of earth's history, man has had only a brief life-span. In that short time he has been an endangered species, a beneficiary of nature's largesse, and a predator. Within the limits of a rigid ecologic ethic it is difficult for him, as a reasoning animal, to steer a middle course between the. . .hazards of these opposing forces.

The examples of sewage disposal, chemical pollution, smoke, and undisciplined use of natural resources abound.

Less evident, but quite important, are some of the environments we construct. The children's hospital is an example. These were built to respond to a requirement to treat the sick young. They were not planned to serve their psychological needs. As Field states,

. . . and no wonder, with the dead weight of hospital tradition in the driver's seat, with the huge investment in facilities, with manufacturing, professional, and service know-how all geared to curative medicine. In this sense, the hospital has unwittingly become one of the major impediments to redirecting our knowledge and capacities into innovative channels. Here lies the basic mismatch between the institutions and the changing system of health care delivery.

Field is properly worried about "the negative impact on children of the linear rows of rooms with a corridor on one side and windows relating to nothing in particular on the other." The qualitative impact of hospitalization itself is an influence on the health experience and outcome. In the effort to modify this experience so that it more nearly meets the psychosocial needs considered important in our present value judgment, might we not construct settings in which children can relate better to the space *immediately* around them. Beds might be located so that the child can see the activity of people, close to interactions that can compel their attention and lessen the boredom of immobility. They ought to be able to see and talk to their peers and they should be able to create a warm and comforting play space about themselves. Of course, the type of illness, the need for greater tactile stimulus in the younger child, and the constant presence of a parent may present constraints. An illness may require isolation. The younger child cannot initiate the gratification of tactile need. And the parent needs emotional and physical space, too. Regardless, these inside spaces can be modified so that they are more flexible and, thus, more responsive to the individual child's need.

The Misuse of the Environment

Lead poisoning, for example, is the result of our misuse of the environment. We have known about this since antiquity. The Greeks understood the hazard of making wine in lead pots. Lead can be absorbed by breathing, swallowing, or through the skin. It is present in our drinking water, canned fruits, toothpaste, putty, newsprint, and paint. It persists in deteriorated housing, where the poor still live and where their children nibble at the painted chips of frayed wallpaper and crumbling plaster. A few such chips may contain 100 mg of lead, more than 200 times a safe daily intake. In fact, young children remain the principal victims of an unnecessary disease. Efforts to pass and implement laws which will constrain the owners of such housing are variably successful. Since the courts are overburdened, the legal system is more malleable for those who have economic access to a lawyer and who would avoid the necessary expenditure to repair the housing. After all, the margin of profit in deteriorated housing would be reduced or eliminated by the cost of these repairs.

In Baltimore, Maryland, in early 1976, one landlord had notice of 87 violations of the city housing code. These notices, although 1 year old, had not been pursued because the city's budget was ordered by a priority which did not allow for the necessary follow-up inspections and criminal prosecution. The violations, by mid 1976, go unanswered. The landlord continues to collect his rent. Children live in the houses.

Lead is but one example. The major crops in the Mississippi delta are cotton, soybeans, and rice. Pregnant women there have levels of residues of chlorinated hydrocarbon insecticides in their serum which are comparable to those found in occupationally exposed men. The cord blood of their offspring have significant residue levels. These are higher in blacks and in mothers who live in rural areas where exposure is more intense. Since there are no signs or symptoms in the newborn that give evidence of acute chlorinated hydrocarbon poisoning, we do not yet know the possible extent of the impact of such levels on the lives of those newborns. We have too seldom done the prospective controlled studies which can relate this early life event to adult experience. This is necessary since, during the period of D'Ercole's study, in spite of diminished use of DDT, over 90 percent of the mothers, 84 percent of the black newborns, and 45 percent of the white newborns demonstrated evidence of recent DDT exposure.

This is particularly vexing in view of Walsh's charge that

Existing food quality standards and the quality standards imposed by growers' cooperatives achieve high cosmetic standards at the cost of unnecessarily heavy use of insecticides. . . the standards restrict the volume of produce reaching the market, thus raising prices and benefiting growers more than consumers.

The suggestion here is that this particular environmental contamination stems from a life-style—stimulated desire for "unblemished tomatoes and flawless oranges," pretty to look at but expensive and no more nourishing.

The Potential of the Environment

Meier suggests that there will be a time when the world will reach a steady state because there are no present alternatives to cities and, as now conceptualized, the world will consist of cities. If a livable, workable, steady state is to be achieved in those cities, there must be a limit on human fertility. We must save energy; we must use water appropriately; we must use food well and reuse our waste food well; we must construct a social system which provides satisfaction and reward in a setting of human congestion. Cities as we have known them do not do these things well. The injudicious use of the automobile, for example, is a serious threat to our available resources. An integral part of our life-style, it compromises our living space, fosters spreading road systems easily clogged by breakdown and accident, as much hindrance as help to our ability to move about. Could a stable world permit the proliferation of the automobile or, considering the Western-type American bathroom, the luxury of flowing water for bathing and for flushing?

In 1970, enough of our energy resources were used to temperature-control a typical detached house in one large American city to require an annual payment of $840.00. By 1975, the cost was nearly double. The physical environment we build can drain our energy and our dollar resources. The implied potential waste suggests a need for savings, the possibility of smaller houses, fewer detached houses, thicker walls, more insulation, fewer windows, and, ultimately, better workmanship. There might be better control of air movement between floors, fewer open stairwells, fewer split-level designs. As a con-

sequence, there might be better thermal comfort and greater acoustical privacy. The sun might be better used with the technical capability currently possible and, in warmer climates, even water might be heated by the sun. If an appropriate steady state is to be achieved, the impact on our lives within the home and among our homes as they become smaller, quieter, and closer together, is quite evident. Architectural planning with accountability to our needs to conserve will have a psychosocial impact which may well alter the emotional state of individuals and groups of individuals.

The Inseparability of Factors

Teachers are the prime observers of children during much of their growth and developmental experience. Day by day, the teacher has the opportunity to be sensitive to possible deviations from the norm, to ask relevant questions, and to thereby play an important role in the prevention, diagnosis, and management of childhood disease and behavioral problems. The teacher functions within the school, an architectural and social entity—an environment—which attempts to adapt to the prevailing judgment of society.

Unfortunately, the professional educational process does not satisfactorily offer that content which will prepare the teacher for observation of the normal child and for observation and participation in the management of the abnormal child. Also, a basic unfortunate assumption of primary education in the United States has been that all children at the age of 6 can be boxed in a classroom, literally and figuratively, ready to learn reading, writing, and arithmetic. Certainly, there is some recognition of the variability of children in the development of open-space schooling, self-paced learning, and other attempts to modify the rigidity of the traditional classroom. The problem, of course, is that any single effort in one school does not adapt well to the need for structure in many children and the ability of others to tolerate absence of structure. Thus, any structure—from the traditional to the perhaps illusionary freedom of "open space"—is still a structure and a constraint on at least some of the children within it. Given this, the American school of the 1970s is uncertain and is staffed by teachers who are uncertain about their evaluations of their seemingly normal pupils, and who are even more perplexed by their physically, emotionally, and mentally handicapped pupils. There is currently an argument concerning a choice between isolation of the handicapped in homogeneous classrooms or schools or their inclusion in the "mainstream" of the regular school. This argument reflects the paucity of our real knowledge and understanding. Our high societal value of education combined with the experimental mode of much of what we do—experiment without real controls—puts the children in a compromised position which influences their emotional and behavioral health.

Valletuti, however, argues persuasively that much can be done in that the teacher has a real role in prevention and in the diagnosis and management of students with medical problems. An adequately prepared and sensitive teacher can detect hearing, vision, and nutritional disorders, in fact, a host of problems. To this point, teachers have been educated as programmers, generating and applying the materials and methods of pedagogy. There has not been a similar appropriate emphasis on evaluation and diagnosis. The cookbook approach to teaching, that is, curriculum guides, prepackaged programs and materials, and the grade, age, and intelligence levels, and sex preference categorization of materials and subject matter, all mitigate against this assessment of the individual. Certainly, the group expectation intimidates the individual need and often makes a sham of presumed individualized instruction.

Valletuti suggests the development of educational programs using a diagnostic paradigm involving

. . .three separate, but interdependent aspects: (1) Educational evaluation for programming purposes and for developing strategies for classroom organization and behavioral management; (2) a diagnostic awareness of underlying and perhaps reversible medical causes for which treatment may be obtained; and (3) an appreciation for the special methods of instruction and management needed to meet the educational needs of students with medical conditions.

Let us, in this context, consider for a moment the influence on the total health outcome of a hospitalized child—sick, separated from home and school, a member of a material, competitive culture which gives major importance to education. Many adults admitted to a hospital are excused from work, have sick leave, and are not asked to make up the time. Not so the child. When the young go back to work— to school—the rest of the class has gone on its way. The individual in this circumstance must convalesce and catch up, too. The depth of impact varies, of course, but the quality of life for each is to some extent soiled. To that extent, health is impaired.

In fact, current value systems do put a high priority on superior intelligence and the fullest exploitation of that intelligence with early and intensive efforts to foster cognitive development. Fisch and his co-workers (1976a) studied 7-year-old children with superior intelligence prospectively and compared them with children of average and low intelligence. They take note of the argument concerning the impact of birth order on intellectual and motor performance. It had been reported that the first-born infant is likely to be more advanced in motor performance at an early age because of the presumably increased parent-child interaction and stimulation the first-born experiences. However, others have found no such differences related to birth order. Fisch suggests that there is a favorable correlation with smaller family size and longer intervals between siblings. In addition, while it is difficult to isolate the factors, children with high intelligence scores do tend to come from homes in which the social and economic level is *above average* and in which parents have had 4 to 5 years *more* schooling than the average for the United States. In fact, a combination of the social and economic factors and the *mother's* educational level appears to be the best predictor of superior intelligence in children at age 7. Given this value judgment of society that superior intelligence is an advantage and that this can affect health positively, education is important.

The French philosopher Rousseau knew this 200 years ago. His book, *Emile*, considers approaches to the education of children and suggests that they should be allowed a setting in which they may act as children in due proportion to their age and to their ability; be taught to see and to hear and to try so that they may be explorers; be encouraged to develop personal standards to which they might adhere rather than a rigid dependence upon the approval of others; be allowed a full exercise of their common sense and encouraged to provide the development of an ability to reason rather than a rigid dependence upon memory. And, Rousseau affirms, they should be encouraged to value the body and its usage.

All told, the numbers we have accumulated tell us more about the physical health and growth and development of our children than about their intellectual development, educational attainment, and emotional state. Certainly, we are aware of very little about comparative change over time, and we have a minimum of documentation about the psychological well-being of children and about change in their social and emotional status over time. Zill and Brehm remind us that it is almost impossible to get definitive evidence about educational progress, that there are no well-validated instruments to measure the more subjective characteristics of health, and that, therefore, any indication of long-range change is difficult. We are able to count the numbers of times a child is seen in a psychiatric facility, but we do not know how to assess the meaning of this usage. It may be related to a real increase in emotional disturbance or simply to an increased acceptance of the concept of consultation and care in this particular area. As Zill states, "We can't resolve issues such as this or clarify the meaning of administrative statistics without survey-based data on the incidence and prevalence of childhood problems in the general population." In fact, our ability to explore these more subjective areas is limited, and our understanding of the full impact on the health of the young is thus constrained. We can assert their importance. We cannot quantitate the impact.

THE LIMITATIONS

There are serious gaps in our understanding. Also, given an unlikely societal behavioral change which might make it easier to define our priorities and objectives and to work out ways to achieve them, we will probably continue for a while on a plateau of relatively exquisite biomedical and technical sophistication and of relatively crude control of the lifestyle, environmental, and economic forces. Indeed, the consequent inconsistencies have led to the thoughtful suggestion that we slow the pace of our biomedical training. Sinsheimer clearly felt this need in his concern over the work with recombinant DNA. There is no substantial evidence that he has been heard.

Also, there are limitations to the potential for the

exploitation of our present knowledge. For example, the fact that American children have achieved greater height than their parents for more than a century is generally regarded as good, an indication of health. However, by the 1970s, it did seem that the genetic potential had been substantially realized and that the likelihood of increasing height and relative weight in the subsequent century was much less. In 1876, the average height was 5 ft 6 in. By 1976, the average 18-year-old male was over 5 ft 9 in tall; the average 18-year-old female, just about 5 ft $4\frac{1}{2}$ in, with significant leveling in the decades of the sixties and the seventies. The contribution of biomedical, social, political, and economic forces is evident, and the possible constraints on the *full* realization of the genetic potential equally evident.

An important area of ambiguous understanding involves the group of children who do not perform in school or at home at the level which society dictates. They are often too active, too distractible, too impulsive. They may have very soft neurologic indicators of developmental delay. There is some evidence that some of them may have had a clinically inapparent viral infection, particularly perinatally. There has been other evidence that these signs and symptoms are associated with the ingestion of salicylates, and of common food additives. Obviously, this is a circumstance in which many of the factors which influence health intermingle. Feingold advocates a presumably palliative diet which is too eagerly accepted by lay persons and professionals alike. The clinically controlled studies that might provide appropriate answers in such a circumstance are too often incomplete or not done. There is a gap here which demands caution.

Or consider that food is a major link among the factors which define health. What, for example, is the relationship of cholesterol and coronary heart disease? There are a number of epidemiologic, retrospective, cross-cultural, and pathophysiologic studies which attempt to establish the relationship. Much of the evidence is circumstantial. Should we modify our children's diet? As Berwick puts it, "Data on pediatric intervention programs, because of the pace of the disease processes, would take decades to gather—straining our pocketbooks and our patience, and confounding results with peculiar trends." The implications for life-style, cost, and the ability of the health professional to exercise judgment before fact are clear. The limits of our ability to manipulate most of the forces of health are evident. Certainly, therefore, any progress in the manipulative exercise requires the inclusion of the patient as a full partner. Obviously, we must recognize that "decision making with imperfect information" is the province of an entire community, not the privilege of the more technically competent segment.

SUMMARY

The discussion of some of the variables that influence human health constantly suggests the subjective, ubiquitous, and uncertain area that relates to the "human factor." This rubric includes the variety in attitude, need, and value judgment which, in the decisions based on that variety, will influence the course of health. In the end, the external forces of nature may prevail. But there is no specific evidence to suggest that that need be or that the mind of man will not sustain the struggle. This much is certain: the mind *and* the heart of humankind are in full play, with all the wisdom and folly that that implies. Their interactions will continue to alter the potential for health, whether it be, to some, the destructive bent of the spoilage of our water and land or, perhaps, the promise inherent in the splendid symbiosis of a man and his cello.

It is wise to consider Dubos's admonition that utopian goals are, in fact, at odds with human experience.

While it may be comforting to imagine a life free of stresses and strains in a carefree world, this will remain an idle dream. Man cannot hope to find another Paradise on earth because Paradise is a static concept while human life is a dynamic process. Man could escape danger only by renouncing adventure, by abandoning that which has given to the human condition its unique character and genius among the rest of the living things. Since the days of the cave man, the earth has never been a Garden of Eden, but a valley of decision where resilience is essential to survival. The earth is not a resting place. Man has elected to fight, not necessarily for himself, but for a process of emotional, intellectual, and ethical growth that goes on forever. To grow in the midst of dangers is the fate of the human race, because it is the law of the spirit.

Herein, the principal factor that influences health.

THE HEALTH OF THE HEALTH PROFESSIONAL

A final consideration: How healthy must one feel in order to work acceptably as a care provider? The particular expertise of the health professional does suggest a special responsibility. This is not a new thought.

Abraham Jacobi, as much as anyone a founder of pediatrics, observed that

The young are the future makers and owners of the world. Their physical, intellectual, and moral condition will decide whether the globe will be more Cossack or more republican, more criminal or more righteous. For their education and training and capabilities, the physician, mainly the pediatrist, as the representative of medical science and art, should become responsible. . .to him belongs the watchful care of the production and distribution of foods. . . . He has to guard the school period from sanitary and educational points of view, for heart and muscle and brain are of equal value. It is in infancy and childhood, before the dangerous period of puberty sets in, that the character is formed, altruism inculcated, or criminality fostered. . . . In the near or dim future, the pediatrist, the physician, is to sit in and control school boards, health departments, and legislatures. He is the legitimate adviser of the judge and jury, and a seat for the physician in the councils of the republic is what the people have a right to demand . . . mainly to the young even amongst us I should say, do not forget your obligations as citizens. When we are told by Lombroso that there is no room in politics for an honest man, I tell you it is time for the physician to participate in politics, never to miss any of his public duties, and thereby make it what sometimes it is reputed not to be in modern life—honorable. A life spent in the service of mankind, be our sphere large or narrow, is well spent. And never stop working. Great results demand great exertions, possibly sacrifices. After all, whether everything in science and politics that now is our ideal will be accomplished, while we live or after we shall be gone, we shall still leave to our progeny new problems.

Jacobi's prescription for the health of the health professional was written in 1904. It is too sexist for current needs and it may arrogate too much to the physician. In reality, however, the pediatrician, male or female, has not often enough given active attention to Jacobi's injunctions—a concern still in the 1970s, another factor influencing the health of the young. Pediatric education has offered a content inadequate to sensitize the young student to these considerations (see Sec. 7). The socialization process of the health professional, with the influence of status and income, has not reinforced the need—thus, again, the gap between education and reality. Of all the factors which influence health, this may be the one which is most susceptible to the attention of the care provider.

7 Health Care Delivery System: Organization, Control, Costs, and Effectiveness

by Barbara Starfield

ORGANIZATION OF CHILD HEALTH SERVICES

When trends towards specialization spread throughout the profession of medicine, pediatrics emerged as a separate entity; the American Academy of Pediatrics (AAP) was formed in 1930. By the early 1970s, there were about 20,000 physicians who called themselves pediatricians and almost 1000 subspecialists in pediatrics (that is, pediatric allergists, pediatric cardiologists). With a population of 69 to 70 million children in the United States, it is clear that many receive care from physicians who do not limit their practices to pediatrics. In fact, more children are cared for by physicians who do not designate themselves as pediatricians than by physicians who do. In the United States, many children are seen by generalists (general practitioners or family physicians), who provide care to both children and adults. For the country as a whole, there are about two pediatricians for every five generalists.

Where and how do those physicians who care for children work? The vast majority work in private offices where they practice as individuals, charging a fee for each visit made by their patients. Table 7-1 shows that 91 percent of pediatricians and 98 percent of generalists spend most of their time in patient care. But only 66 percent of these pediatricians practice from private offices, whereas 88 percent of generalists do so. Particularly in localities where the physician/population ratio is low, local agencies, often tax-supported, have assumed much of the burden of providing services. During the 1960s, the federally funded "war on poverty" supported the development of maternity and infant care centers, comprehensive children's clinics, and neighborhood health centers which have survived into the 1970s. Many of these are sponsored by local health departments; some are organized by community agencies, often under community (nonprofessional) control. Table 7-2 indicates the approximate number of children served by these organizations. In addition, well-infant and well-child care facilities organized by public health agencies in local health department facilities and schools provide an unknown amount of service, primarily to children in poor families.

The plethora of types of facilities and the lack of coordination among them make the American health care system extraordinarily fragmented. The remainder of this section deals with some of the main types of organizations providing services to children in the United States. The types to be discussed are the independent office practice, prepaid group practice, tax-supported direct service programs, and hospital-based services.

Table 7-1

Number of Physicians in the United States by Specialty and Activity, Dec. 31, 1974

		Patient Care					Other Professional Activity			
		Total	Office-based	Hospital-based			Medical Teaching	Administration	Research	Other
				Intern	Resident	Physician's Staff				
Total number of physicians	379,748*	301,238	205,955	11,288	47,734	36,261	6464	11,739	8159	2666
General practice	53,997	52,932	47,436	0	2427	3069	155	593	102	215
Pediatrics	20,682†	18,842	12,008	905	3825	2104	571	680	485	104
All other physicians	305,069	229,464	146,511	10,383	41,482	31,088	5738	10,466	7572	2347

* Includes 49,482 physicians (21,614 inactive, 20,343 not classified, and 7525 addresses unknown) who are not distributed across table.

† Does not include the pediatric subspecialties of allergy, cardiology, or psychiatry.

Source: Adapted from Center for Health Services Research and Development, Gene Roback (Res. Assoc.): *Physician Distribution and Medical Licensure in the U.S., 1974.* Copyrighted 1975, and reprinted by permission of the American Medical Association.

Table 7-2
Extent of Coverage of Population with Selected Comprehensive Care Programs

Program	Total Population	High Priority Population	Population Presently Served	Year	Number of Programs
Children and youth projects	77,000,000	15,400,000	487,000	June 1972	76
				1973	56
Maternity and infant care projects:					
Maternity	3,500,000	700,000*	140,000 (est.)		
Infant	3,500,000	700,000*	47,000		
Official crippled children	11,116,000†		500,000	FY 1972	54
Mental retardation:	5,400,000‡		71,182	FY 1972	177
University affiliated facilities (UAF)			Approx. 16,000	FY 1971	21
Community clinics			60,859	FY 1971	156
Head Start:	3,500,000	700,000		FY 1972	
Full year			269,500		1605
Summer			86,400		434
Neighborhood health centers:					
Total			330,000	FY 1973	113
Children			115,500		

* There are other high-risk groups, using criteria other than income.

† C. G. Schiffer and E. P. Hunt: *Illness Among Children,* Washington: U.S. Government Printing Office, 1963.

‡ President's Panel on Mental Retardation: *A Proposed Program for National Action to Combat Mental Retardation,* Washington, 1962.

Sources: D. A. Trauger, Special communication to the authors, Jan 2, 1974, for all sections of table except (1) Head Start data from Head Start Office, (2) Mental retardation data from Mr. Rudolf P. Hermuth.

Above adapted from: H. M. Wallace: *Health Care of Mothers and Children in National Health Service,* Cambridge, Mass.: Ballinger Publishing, 1975, p. 317. Reprinted with permission.

Organizational Arrangements

Independent Office Practice

Most medical care for children is provided by physicians who charge a fee for each service and who work in private offices. Recent national data indicate that 41 percent of all private office visits by patients under 15 years of age were to pediatricians, 36 percent to generalists, and 23 percent to other types of physicians.

Little is known about the office organization of physicians who see children. However, the AAP has sponsored surveys of its own members (which comprise about 60 percent of pediatricians, all of whom are board certified). According to a survey done by the AAP, most of its members locate their offices in middle-class residential neighborhoods, while slightly fewer are in business districts. Only 8 percent practice in poor residential neighborhoods. Just under one-third of these office-based pediatricians employ no nurses. Group practices were significantly more likely than solo practices to employ both highly trained office staff and to have specialized laboratory technicians and equipment.

Most pediatricians (73 percent) had no x-ray facility in their offices. Those who had x-ray facilities used them primarily for simple chest and bone x-rays; one-third did intravenous pyelograms (IVPs) and fluoroscopies. Only 80 percent of the physicians included visual screening tests in periodic health examinations; 72 percent performed developmental screening; and 60 percent conducted audiologic screening. Table 7-3 describes the kind of laboratory tests which are (or are not) provided by the physicians. Despite the heavy emphasis in training programs for learning these procedures, the great majority of pediatricians never again perform differential white counts, sedimentation rates, urine cultures, or spinal cell counts.

The proportion of practitioners who work alone has been significantly reduced over the past 25 years. In 1949, about 80 percent of private pediatricians were in solo practice and 17 percent in some other

Table 7-3

Type of Laboratory Test Provided by Respondent
Pediatricians in Their Offices (351)

Laboratory Test	Provided	Not Provided
Urinalysis	309	42
Hemoglobin, hematocrit	277	74
White blood count	185	166
Urine culture	138	213
Erythrocyte sedimentation rate	133	218
Differential blood count	131	190
Spinal fluid cell count	29	322
Mono slide test	119	232
PBI	52	299
Blood serology	46	305

Source: The Council on Pediatric Practice: *Lengthening Shadows,* Evanston: American Academy of Pediatrics, 1971, p. 95.

form of private practice; by the early 1970s, 45 percent of board-certified pediatricians were in solo practice. Of those who worked with others, 17 percent worked with one associate, 25 percent worked in a group of pediatricians, and another 12 percent worked in a multiple-specialty group. One-third of the groups had been established in the previous 5 years (after 1965).

Prepaid Group Practice

Group practice is an increasingly popular recourse for practitioners who seek to economize on expensive office equipment and technology; group practice also enables practitioners to share on-call hours at night, on weekends, and on holidays. Although the extent to which partnerships and informal small groups influence the nature of care given to patients is unknown, there have been several studies which indicate that those group practices which assume financial liability for their care by pre-budgeting (prepaid group practice) provide more efficient and probably more effective care to patients. In these groups, patients enroll either individually or as members of their employer's health plan, and the premiums which cover the costs of their care are paid in advance. Each physician is paid a predetermined salary so that an individual physician's income does not depend upon the number of services provided, as is the case in fee-for-service practice. Enrollees of prepaid group practices find access to care easier than people who are not

part of such plans. Although enrollees of prepaid groups tend to visit physicians more often, their rates of hospitalization are much lower than users of other types of services. This is due primarily to lower rates of hospitalization for common respiratory conditions and minor surgical conditions. Drug costs are also reduced. These two factors are responsible for lower costs of care for individuals in such plans than is the case for individuals or families who pay fee-for-service (whether the payment is out of pocket or channeled through an insurance company) to an individual physician or one who works in a fee-for-service group. Delay in seeking care is reduced for enrollees of prepaid group practice and the care provided, both preventive and corrective, is of generally higher quality in prepaid group practices than in other organizational arrangements. The prevalence of health conditions known to be susceptible to influence by medical care, such as prematurity, is reduced in populations covered by prepaid group practices. These and other findings indicate that the circumstances under which physicians work have more of an influence on the nature of the care they give than the details of their training or their qualifications.

Despite the advantages to patients of prepaid group practice, physicians have not flocked to this form of practice; in 1970, only 2 percent of them were employed in such practices. As a result, the federal government, which has been assuming an increasingly large share of the costs of medical care, has encouraged the development of organizational forms which are based on prepayment. In 1972, the HMO (Health Maintenance Organization) Act was passed, which recognized two major forms. The first is the prepaid group practice just discussed. The second is the medical foundation to which individuals prepay a sum of money and which in turn reimburses physicians a negotiated fee for each visit and procedure. Because the total amount of money each year is fixed, the physicians who belong to the foundation must accept lower fees toward the end of the year if the funds become depleted. This arrangement is generally believed to keep utilization and medical costs from soaring, as tends to occur with usual fee-for-service arrangements. Moreover, most foundations assume responsibility for monitoring the quality of care, particularly the types and amounts of diagnostic and therapeutic procedures used in the care of patients.

Tax-supported Direct Service Programs

In 1932, the Commission on the Costs of Medical Care recommended prepaid group practice as an appropriate organizational form for services in the United States. The major medical societies opposed the suggestion, and it was not implemented. As the Great Depression of the 1930s deepened, the need for social welfare became clearly evident. Legislation to implement national health insurance was believed not to be politically feasible because of the opposition of the strong medical societies. A compromise position was taken by Title V of the Social Security Act of 1936, which was intended to improve the health of mothers and children by providing support to states to extend and improve related health services. It was this program which was responsible for initiating the substantial involvement of state and local health departments in some aspects of the delivery of health care.

Health Department Programs Health departments provide a sizable proportion of preventive and case-finding services, particularly in rural and urban areas where the number of nongovernmental physicians is inadequate. About half of the health departments are under county jurisdiction, 14 percent under city departments (New England states and the Southern and Western Mountain states have a higher proportion of these), another 15 percent combining a city and a county, 9 percent a town, and the rest covering larger areas.

The five most common child health programs sponsored by health departments, in decreasing order of the frequency with which health departments name them, are: immunization, maternal and child health, family planning, school health, and ambulatory medical care.

About half of the states require some immunizations as a prerequisite for school attendance, and the remainder delegate immunization authority to local boards of education and health. Many states also require a physical examination prior to school entry. Forty-two states allow for some kind of school screening or examination for children. Eleven of these require only limited screening procedures (usually vision and hearing); most, however, also require a general physical examination at least once during school. Many of these services have been provided in schools for many years, particularly in areas where families cannot afford them or where the

children do not otherwise receive them. Funds for new programs have been derived from taxation and are administered by local departments of education or health.

In 1968, slightly over one-third of the public primary and secondary schools reported the availability of a physician. Physicians were half as likely to be available in schools located in large metropolitan areas than in areas outside large metropolitan areas. Among the schools where physicians were available, one-third responded that the physician was "resident in the school" and the rest responded that they were on demand to the school with some waiting time required for services. There are about 1400 full-time physician equivalents working in the public elementary and secondary schools, about $\frac{1}{14}$ the number of all office-based children's physicians. In fact, school health activities are much more likely to be conducted by nurses than by physicians.

The traditional preventive health orientation of health departments was reflected in the low rank given to direct provision of ambulatory medical services, which are seen by most as outside departmental purview: half of the departments do not engage in any form of medical care for illness. Furthermore, estimated total expenditures for all of these health department programs for children amount to less than $10 per child receiving services per year.

For communities lacking sufficient numbers of physicians, these deficits in "public health" programs became untenable during the 1960s when the civil rights and antipoverty movements drew attention to great gaps in the provision of health services. Several laws passed from 1963 to 1967 enabled the development of new health care units in economically deprived areas.

Neighborhood Health Centers and Project Head Start The first major health legislation directed at fighting the war on poverty was the Economic Opportunity Act of 1964, which created the Office of Economic Opportunity (OEO) as a separate agency in the federal government, directly responsible to the Secretary of Health, Education, and Welfare. Of the six principal activities, two were most significant: the neighborhood health centers (NHC) and Project Head Start.

Neighborhood Health Centers The funding and organization of these health centers largely bypassed established channels of organization and financing at the state and local government level. Participation by the community itself in the planning and operations was an integral part of the program. The centers are aimed at low-income persons of all ages, with special emphasis on the young and the old. Only 13 percent are operated by health departments. The remainder is funded by direct federal grants to nongovernmental community agencies. About two-tenths of 1 percent of children in the country receive care in these centers.

The 113 centers themselves vary greatly in size. The three largest each have 20,000 or more registrants, while about three-fourths of the NHCs have less than 10,000 registrants each. As the average private pediatric solo practice has about 1000 to 3000 patients, the number of children in a neighborhood health center of average size is one to three times the number in the average pediatric practice.

With the demise of the OEO in 1973, administration of the neighborhood health center program was transferred to the Bureau of Community Health Services of the Health Services Administration. As a result, its separate identity was lost and there was greatly reduced attention to its unique features, particularly the large role of the local community in the operations of the centers.

Project Head Start Project Head Start is the name given to the Child Development Program initiated by the Office of Economic Opportunity (OEO), but now administered by the Office of Child Development (OCD). It was conceived and developed in 1965 and was based on a concept of providing children from disadvantaged backgrounds and their families with an experience that would allow them to enter a learning setting with a "head start" comparable to their classmates. The program was considered to be a family development, as well as a child development, program and required, in addition to educational and child development components, a full health program, social services, psychological services, nutritional services, and parent participation. The original plan was to enroll some 70,000 children in the summer of 1965, but the community response to request for proposals was so dramatic that by the end of the first summer 550,000 children were enrolled.

The program is restricted to children between the ages of 3 and 6 from families who fall below the poverty levels as defined by the OEO. At its peak there were 2500 full-year and summer programs, with a total enrollment of over 750,000 children. Budgetary restrictions led to a reduction in both the number of programs and number of children; only 356,000 children were served in 1973. Programs are administered locally by community action agencies, which conduct a variety of community programs for low-income groups, or by single-purpose agencies concerned entirely with the operation of a Head Start program. A substantial number of the programs are delegated by the community action agencies to local school districts or other existing community agencies. Programs are funded 80 percent through federal money and 20 percent through local contributions and are reviewed by local community boards, state offices, and federal regional offices.

Programs Resulting from the Social Security Amendments

The second major piece of health legislation in the 1960s was the Social Security Amendments of 1963. This act contained several sections destined to have a significant impact on health care delivery. Title XIX (Medicaid) of this act provided a means of payment for medical care through tax dollars for those who could not afford to pay for it. It was intended that medical care be provided through existing organizational arrangements, primarily independent office practices.

Medicaid and EPSDT Children and youth represent more than 50 percent of the group eligible for Medicaid, but the program has not yet been successful in effectively reaching many of the children in greatest need. Unfortunately, most state welfare systems have exhibited an inability to administer adequately health care programs of this complexity and magnitude. In addition, the virtual absence of standards of care, a failure to give appropriate emphasis to preventive services, and the fact that, in the face of state budget crises (all too common in recent years), state legislatures sometimes exhibit an unwillingness to provide adequate funds have been important limiting factors to the success of the projects.

In an attempt to bring needed medical care to children who were not receiving it, all state agencies responsible for administration of Medicaid programs were required, effective July 1969, to provide acceptable evidence of their intent to move toward development of statewide screening and case-finding programs aimed at early recognition and prompt treatment of chronic illnesses and handicapping conditions in those under age 21. Children are to be surveyed periodically "to be sure there are no hidden problems, that the medical significance of any symptom is known, that evidence of neglect and/or child abuse is identified, and that necessary preventive and remedial measures are being taken." The early and periodic screening, diagnosis, and treatment (EPSDT) program was designed to accomplish this.

To implement this requirement, the Title XIX agency must have agreements with state and local crippled children's agencies that share responsibility for the early identification of individuals under age 21 in need of health care services and with other official and voluntary agencies having responsibility for child services, such as state health departments. It is important to recognize that EPSDT was not conceived as a means of ongoing health supervision and child health care, but rather as an attempt to screen periodically for manifest health defects.

Health Components of the Elementary and Secondary Education Act (ESEA) In April of 1965, the Elementary and Secondary Education Act was signed into law. Title I of this act contained a provision for "financial assistance to local educational agencies. . . to meet the special educational needs of educationally deprived children." Federal guidelines for approval of applications stipulated that health services be made available either through Title I funds or through other available funds and services. Although complete data are not available, most of the expenditures have been for screening and detection of health defects, sometimes followed by referral to clinics and practitioners for further evaluation and treatment, and some projects have included remedial dental treatment.

Title V Amendments: Children-and-Youth Projects and Maternal and Infant Care Projects The Title V Amendments were directed primarily at children. These Amendments, passed at various times from 1963 to 1967, were directed toward providing adequate care for low-income pregnant women and their infants (the MIC or Maternity and Infant Care program), at providing family planning services to women of low income for whom "the postponement of pregnancy might be desirable," and at providing

comprehensive health services for children in low-income families (C and Y or Children-and-Youth projects). The latter were perhaps the most innovative of the federally funded programs up to that time for at least two reasons. First, it was required that eligibility be defined by residence in a specified geographic area, rather than according to the income of the family or the preexistence of particular health needs. Second, care was to be comprehensive, including prevention and health promotion as well as treatment services. The projects were funded largely (75 percent) by federal funds and 25 percent by state funds, involving about one-half a million children residing in low-income areas. Many of the projects also have a dental care component. Over 75 percent of the centers are open 5 or more days per week for complete services; only 15 are open for emergency care or partial care on a 24-h basis.

The size of the programs varies widely, covering from 1000 to 40,000 children. Total costs are about $130 per child per year.

About one-third of the C and Y projects are sponsored by health departments, one-third by medical schools, and one-third by teaching hospitals. Twenty out of twenty-two projects sponsored by teaching hospitals are located in the central city. There is more variability of location among the health department–sponsored programs than those sponsored by either teaching hospitals or medical schools. The central city projects are somewhat larger than the other programs because of concentration of eligible children. In general, medical school–affiliated projects and teaching hospitals serve a higher proportion of their eligible target population than do health department–affiliated projects.

The MIC projects were initiated to combat infant mortality in high-risk areas (primarily areas of urban poverty), and eligibility is essentially determined by low income. Comprehensive medical, nutritional, and dental services to mothers are offered, and there is active outreach to draw eligible women into the project early in pregnancy. About 141,000 women and 47,000 infants are served by 56 MIC projects. Program costs are about $470 per client. This is a significantly higher cost per participant than for the C and Y programs, largely because of complete coverage for hospitalization, delivery, and postpartum care for mothers with infants at high risk. One may ask if the differences in organization (salaried personnel, greater variety of personnel) and the absence of patient fees in these tax-supported programs which deliver comprehensive care are associated with better care as compared with traditional private practice. Although this is largely unknown, a few studies indicate that care is at least of equal quality to that in other facilities. Moreover, there is evidence that accessibility and continuity of care are markedly improved and that those who receive care in these projects are well satisfied. In this sense, they might have served as a prototype for more widespread developments in the future. However, despite the importance of the C and Y, MIC, and neighborhood health center projects to those who have received care from them, the program was never sufficiently widespread to cover a significant proportion of the needy population. Moreover, by the mid-1970s there was already evidence that the federal government was reducing its commitment to them.

In view of the limited national scope of the innovative C and Y and MIC projects, most of the financial outlays of governmental agencies go to programs which provide only certain aspects of child health care rather than comprehensive services. Even Title V of the Social Security Amendments of 1965, some provisions of which were aimed at providing comprehensive health services to needy individuals, had the effect of making more money available to health departments for traditional health department functions. In 1973, over $400 million were spent on Title V programs for maternal and child health services. Of this, 37 percent went to traditional health department programs, 37 percent to crippled children's services, and only 27 percent to the innovative maternity and infant care and children and youth projects.

Highest benefit levels appear to have been for vision screening, which in 1974 was performed for almost 9 million children. But estimates of the impact of federal funds must be separated from estimates of program impact. The actual growth from 1960 to 1972 in numbers of children receiving the services enumerated is not especially great—11 percent in the area of vision testing, for instance—suggesting that the new source of federal reimbursement is being used to substitute for state and local money more often than it is being used to extend services to children previously without them. Overall, the number of children receiving benefits may actually be declining, as reflected in reductions in school health screening programs and immunizations. Moreover,

although total federal outlays for the maternal and child health program are large, the number of children actually receiving benefits remains a relatively small proportion—certainly no more than 15 percent—of children in the neonate to 18-year-age group.

Hospital-based Services

In 1970, at least one in eight physician visits for persons under age 21 were to hospital clinics and emergency rooms. The proportion of visits occurring in these facilities is increasing, particularly for children in the youngest age groups. Furthermore, in the central cities of the United States, about 18 percent of all children's visits and 36 percent of indigent children's visits are to hospital clinics and emergency rooms. Despite the initiation of various innovative community-based services and practice arrangements such as the neighborhood health centers and the C and Y projects, care provided by hospital-based personnel continues to grow relative to these new types of programs. Although there have been numerous studies done in individual outpatient departments of teaching hospitals, little is known about the amount, scope, or type of care provided in these facilities across the nation. An unknown proportion, but undoubtedly most of the medical services in these facilities, are provided by physicians in training, who rotate through outpatient departments as part of their postgraduate learning experience. This hospital-based sector remains the "hidden system" of care, particularly prevalent in central city areas near teaching hospitals, by which many children receive most if not all of their health services.

Scope of Pediatric Practice

Until recently no one knew what kinds of services were being provided by the nation's practitioners. As a result of the mushrooming costs of health care, more and more people are asking for documentation. What is the money buying, and is its purchase resulting in improved health? Although sporadic studies of individual practices had appeared in the 1930s, nothing in the way of national data existed until the development by the National Center for Health Statistics (Department of Health, Education, and Welfare) of the National Ambulatory Medical Care Survey (NAMCS) in 1969. This is an ongoing systematic survey of office-based practice only and does not yet include hospital outpatient departments or tax-supported direct service programs. During 1974 there were approximately 634,073,000 visits to offices of all physicians within the scope of the NAMCS. In volume of visits, pediatricians ranked third among all the specialties. With their 51,885,000 patient encounters, pediatricians were exceeded only by the two other primary care providers (general and/or family physicians and internists). For the 26 percent of the nation's population who were under the age of 15 years, pediatricians were the leading providers of office-based ambulatory care.

Table 7-4 lists, in order of frequency, the 10 most common problems, complaints, or symptoms that pediatricians in office practice encountered. These 10 problems accounted for two-thirds of all visits to pediatricians.

Table 7-5 presents data on the diagnoses most frequently made in ambulatory visits to the pediatrician.

Table 7-6 contains information about treatments or services provided by the pediatrician during the office visit. In general, the pediatrician tended to exceed the average for all physicians in the proportion of visits that involve laboratory procedures, immunization, and—by a substantial margin—routine examinations and counseling. Pediatricians fell below the overall average in the proportion of visits that involve x-rays, office surgery, or drug therapy.

In 54 percent of visits, specific follow-up is planned (Table 7-7), and one in thirty-five visits results in a referral. These data indicate that the need to provide continuity to integrate care over several visits, both to the same physician and to others to whom the child may be referred, is a major challenge in primary care.

Prospects for Change in Organization of Services

All children are supposed to have a "medical home" which provides continuity and integration of care over a period of time. The preceding discussion demonstrates the diversity of organizational arrangements with which the United States population contends. Even for individual children who identify a "regular source of care," there is indication that this source of care does not always provide all of the required services, nor does it always serve to integrate the services which the child received elsewhere. About one in five children who have a physician whom they identify as their "regular source of care" actually go to another physician when they have a need for medical care. Moreover, physicians in primary care facilities frequently fail to recognize both the fact of visits elsewhere and what occurred elsewhere, despite the fact that this may significantly influence the patient's response to subsequent care.

This fragmentation and lack of coordination of care

Table 7-4
Number, Percent, and Cumulative Percent of Office Visits to Pediatricians by the Most Common Patient Problems, Complaints, or Symptoms: United States, 1975.

Rank	Most Common Patient Problems, Complaints, or Symptoms	Code Number	Number of Visits (in thousands)	Percent of Visits	Cumulative Percent
1	Well-baby exam	906	6233	13.4	13.4
2	General medical exam	900	4687	10.0	23.4
3	Cough	311	3425	7.3	30.7
4	Fever	002	3170	6.8	37.5
5	Visit for medication	910	2859	6.1	43.6
6	Throat soreness	520	2439	5.2	48.8
7	Earache	735	2001	4.3	53.1
8	Allergic skin reaction	112	1662	3.6	56.7
9	Cold	312	1464	3.1	59.8
10	Required physical exam	901	974	2.1	61.9

Note: Symptom titles and code numbers come from a symptom classification developed for use in the National Ambulatory Medical Care Survey.

Source: National Center for Health Statistics: "Office Visits to the Pediatrician," National Ambulatory Medical Care Survey, 1975. (Mimeographed.)

Table 7-5

Number, Percent, and Cumulative Percent of Office Visits to Pediatricians by the Most Frequent Diagnoses Rendered by the Physician: United States, 1975.

Rank	Most Frequent Diagnoses	Code Number	Number of Visits (in thousands)	Percent of Visits	Cumulative Percent
1	Medical or special examination (chiefly well-baby and child care)	Y00	12,462	26.7	26.7
2	Otitis media: no mention of mastoiditis	381	3795	8.1	34.8
3	Acute upper respiratory infection of multiple or unspecified sites	465	2944	6.3	41.1
4	Acute pharyngitis	462	1839	3.9	45.0
5	Bronchitis, unqualified	490	1731	3.7	48.7
6	Prophylactic inoculation and vaccination	Y02	1667	3.6	52.3
7	Eczema and dermatitis	692	1577	3.4	55.7
8	Acute tonsillitis	463	1477	3.2	58.9
9	Hayfever	507	981	2.1	61.0
10	Medical and surgical aftercare	Y10	841	1.8	62.8
11	Streptococcal sore throat and scarlet fever	034	771	1.7	64.5

Note: Diagnoses and code numbers are extracted from the Eighth Revision, International Classification of Diseases (ICDA). Adapted for Use in the United States, 1965.

Source: National Center for Health Statistics: "Office Visits to the Pediatrician," National Ambulatory Medical Care Survey, 1975. (Mimeographed.)

is a major challenge to a health care system. If practitioners, health programs, and health institutions continue to function as separate and uncoordinated agencies, and if individuals continue to seek care from as many sources as they choose, the likelihood of duplication of services will result in ever-increasing costs of care without commensurate gains. In fact, effectiveness is likely to decrease as patients are given conflicting advice and therapies from different practitioners. It seems likely that the United States will be forced by circumstances to adopt some degree of regionalization of health services as has been done in most of the developed world. Under regionalization, services are organized according to the degree to which they are needed. Those services which are required by large proportions of the population or those with great frequency are provided on local or community levels easily accessible to the population. These are called primary health services. Primary health services must be highly accessible. The experience of several prepaid group practices which, by definition, provide care for a defined population, is useful in determining how many

physicians may be required to assure accessibility to primary care services. In general, 1 physician for each 3000 children has been found satisfactory.

Physicians in primary care (all family physicians and most pediatricians and internists) must assume responsibility for providing a broad spectrum of care (both preventive and curative) over a period of time, and for coordinating all of the care which patients receive, including that from specialists. Should primary care physicians require advice with difficult cases, patients are referred for consultation to secondary health facilities, which are more centralized than the primary care services, and are usually located in community hospitals. Those patients who require care for complicated and unusual illnesses are referred to tertiary medical centers, which are even more centralized and carry out training and research functions as well. These tertiary care centers provide services requiring a high degree of technical expertise on referral from primary or secondary health centers. Expensive equipment required to support such specialty services will be located only in tertiary centers—and not in every health center

Table 7-6

Number and Percent Distribution of Office Visits to
Pediatricians by Treatments Ordered or Provided;
United States, 1975

Diagnostic or Therapeutic Services Ordered or Provided	Number of Visits (in thousands)	Percent Distribution
Diagnostic Services		
Limited history/exam	19,136	41.0
General history/exam	15,612	33.4
Clinical lab tests	10,442	22.4
Blood pressure check	3612	7.7
Vision test	1955	4.2
X-ray	1933	4.1
Hearing test	1277	2.7
Therapeutic Services		
Drug prescribed	19,234	41.2
Immunization or desensitization	10,693	22.9
Medical counselling	7322	15.7
Injection	4340	9.3
Office surgery	1482	3.2
None	1339	2.9

Source: National Center for Health Statistics: "Office
Visits to the Pediatrician," National Ambulatory Medical Care Survey, 1975. (Mimeographed.)

which desires it and can obtain money to purchase
it (as is the case currently).

The passage of the National Health Planning and
Resources Development Act of 1974 may ultimately
facilitate regionalization. The legislation has two
principal parts. The first, a new Title XV in the Public
Health Service Act, revises existing health planning
programs, all of which expired June 30, 1974. The
second, a new Title XVI in the same act, revises existing programs for the construction and modernization
of health care facilities. Title XVI also provides funds
to new health-systems agencies for their use in the
development of health resources which will implement their plans.

Under this law, a network of new health-systems
agencies (HSAs) are to prepare and implement plans
to improve the health of residents, to increase the
accessibility, acceptability, continuity, and quality
of health services, to restrain costs, and to prevent
unnecessary duplication of services in their area.
This requires the collection of data, establishment of
goals, and coordination of activities with a variety of
other types of agencies. Another major responsibility
is the review for approval or disapproval of all appli-

cations for federal funds for health programs within
the area. Although the wording of the legislation
suggests that significant changes might occur in the
organization of health services as a result of the law,
only time will tell whether the HSAs will have sufficient control over the training and deployment of
resources to accomplish their aims. The issue of
control is discussed in the next section.

CONTROL

Early attempts at control over the profession of medicine took two forms. The English model relied upon
the institutions of learning (mainly the hospitals) to
certify practitioners whom they would train. In the
French and German models, adopted by the United
States, individuals were licensed by the state after
passing an examination. In the United States, the individual states have always retained jurisdiction over
entry into professions, and the obtaining of a license
to practice medicine has proved to be rather easy for
graduates of United States medical schools. In the
nineteenth century, there were a large number of
medical schools, most of them operated for profit,
and matriculation was rather routine.

The ready obtainability of a state license led to
an abundance of physicians in this country. By 1910,
there were as many as 1.9 physicians per 1000 population (2.5/1000 in the cities). Business was highly
competitive, causing great concern on the part of the
few physicians who had received scientific training

Table 7-7

Number and Percent Distribution of Office Visits to
Pediatricians by Disposition of the Patient: United
States, 1975

Disposition of Patient	Number of Visits (in thousands)	Percent Distribution
No follow-up planned	11,005	23.6
Return at specified time	20,795	44.5
Return if needed	11,015	23.6
Telephone follow-up planned	4597	9.9
Referred to other physician/agency	1365	2.9

Source: National Center for Health Statistics: "Office
Visits to the Pediatrician," National Abulatory Medical Care Survey, 1975. (Mimeographed.)

in the prestigious medical centers in Europe. These physicians, the medical "establishment" of the time, comprised the membership of the fledgling American Medical Association. They were instrumental in the decision of the Carnegie Foundation to fund a study of medical education in the first decade of the twentieth century. This study culminated in the Flexner report of 1910, which recommended that entry into the profession be restricted to those who already had exposure to a broad liberal arts education. A trend which had already begun now accelerated; proprietary medical schools, which were in financial distress due to the large number of competitors, closed in increasing numbers because they were unable to compete for the reduced number of students who could qualify for admission. The costs of medical education increased markedly; prospective physicians had to pay for an undergraduate (college) education as well as the high medical school tuition. Medicine rapidly became a profession in which students from the upper social classes were heavily overrepresented.

The medical profession has always claimed responsibility for regulating entry into its ranks. The assumption of autonomy and control over itself is said to be one of the characteristics of a profession. Its social status and influence have enabled it to regulate entry into the profession as well as to set the standards of practice. This is true historically, and continues to be a feature of current attempts to assure the quality of care. Although state boards have the legal authority to dispense licenses to practice, this authority is in all states delegated to the profession, which in turn nominates the candidates who will be appointed by the state authority. Standards for health facilities, as well as for individual practitioners, are determined by the profession which also monitors adherence to them. Thus, medical schools are accredited by the Liaison Committee on Medical Education which is composed of representatives of the American Medical Association and of the Association of American Medical Colleges. To be accredited, hospitals must receive approval from the Joint Commission on Accreditation of Hospitals, a council made up of representatives of the American Medical Association, the American Hospital Association, the American College of Surgeons, and the American College of Physicians. Accreditation, both of hospitals and medical schools, is essential to the financial viability of all institutions. Most "third"

party payers (the government and insurance companies) which reimburse hospitals or contribute to the support of medical schools require them to be accredited as a condition for payment.

Until recently, the instruments of control have been addressed to the structure of the profession and its institutions. For example, individuals must only demonstrate that they graduated from medical school and can achieve a passing grade on an examination developed by the profession itself, either in the state (state licensing exams) or nationally (National Board of Medical Examiners or "Flex" examination). There is no requirement that prospective physicians demonstrate competence under the conditions of actual practice, either when they enter the profession or subsequently. Medical schools qualify for accreditation by demonstrating to the Liaison Committee a "sound educational program." The Liaison Committee ascribes four "inherent responsibilities" to a medical school:

1 The opportunity to acquire a sound basic education in medicine and to foster the development of lifelong habits of scholarship and service

2 The advancement of knowledge through research

3 The development of graduate education to produce practitioners, teachers, and investigators, both through clinical residency programs and advanced degree programs in the basic medical sciences

4 Participation in continuing education aimed at maintaining and improving the competence of those professionals engaged in caring for patients

Hospitals qualify for accreditation primarily by demonstrating to the satisfaction of the Joint Commission that their physical facilities are adequate; that certain services are available (for example, dietetic, nursing, medical records); that there is an organized medical staff; that only members of this staff have the privilege of admitting patients; and that these members assume the responsibility for the care of admitted patients.

This emphasis on "credentialing" and accrediting is increasingly recognized as inadequate. Licensing of personnel on the basis of passing grades in medical school and passing a state or national examination in a field where knowledge is accumulating at a rate which makes what is learned in medical school obsolete within a few years, can no longer suffice or assure that physicians will remain well qualified to practice medicine. Moreover, although knowledge is a necessary condition of adequate practice, it is insufficient. To be effective, knowledge must be applied appropriately and with compassion. Similarly, although adequate facilities and safe equipment within the hospital are important, they alone do not guarantee high standards of practice. Despite a few isolated attempts from within the profession to encourage systematic reviews of the professional activities of physicians (efforts dating back to the second decade of this century), the profession itself has failed to initiate activities which would assure medical care of high quality. With but a few exceptions in certain individual hospitals and among a few physicians, it required the passage of federal legislation to stimulate the profession to take stock of itself. This legislation became inevitable when the government assumed responsibility for paying for most of the care of the elderly and indigent. As medical costs rose, legislators asked whether benefits from these increasingly expensive services were commensurate with the increase in costs. Review of medical activities in hospitals was the first to be proposed, largely because hospital costs assume a disproportionate share of the health care dollar. Legislation passed in 1972 [the Professional Standards Review Organization (PSRO) Act] required that hospital admissions of patients covered by governmental payments be reviewed for justifiability, and that hospitals periodically designate individual diagnoses for which all medical records of patients with the diagnosis would be audited to determine the adequacy of care. These requirements, while opposed by many physicians, have stimulated the profession to specify standards for care for common problems causing hospitalization. Most usually, these standards are set by "experts" (often physicians in teaching institutions) who meet until a consensus is reached on a certain number of criteria of care. These are called *normative* criteria. Alternatively, care provided to samples of patients in a local area may be examined and standards set on the basis of procedures usually found to be performed; the resulting criteria are called *empirical* criteria. Although the PSRO Act requires that peer review of activities in ambulatory care eventually be instituted, it is unlikely that the profession will develop the means to undertake this on a wide scale. Moreover, there is no evidence that peer review is successful, either in

preventing poor physicians from continuing to practice or in upgrading the overall level of performance of the profession, because the legal means to remove a practitioner's license or to prohibit many practices are lacking.

In view of the failure of the medical profession to develop effective self-policing, what alternatives are there to control a system which commands an ever-increasing proportion of national expenditures without demonstrating any consequent improvement in the health of the population?

Alternative 1 Inter- and intraprofessional accountability. Studies have shown that the organization within which physicians practice is a greater influence on the quality of practice than the individual characteristics of the physician. Team practice, in which nurses and community health workers share responsibility for certain aspects of care with the physician, is likely to result both in greater recognition of patients' problems and more likelihood that they will be addressed by the physician. Prepaid group practices in which several physicians share fiscal accountability in their practices is also likely to result in greater consideration of the necessity and justifiability of professional actions.

Alternative 2 Greater assumption of responsibility by individual practitioners for their actions. Under the current system patients who fail to obtain relief of their complaints often seek subsequent care elsewhere, and thus physicians do not observe the ineffectiveness of their ministrations.

Most physicians do not assume responsibility for follow-up of their patients in the event that the patient does not voluntarily return for care. As the costs of care become an increasing concern of third party payers (government, insurance companies, employers), duplication of services as reflected in visits to different providers of care for the same problem will become evident. As a result, physicians may be encouraged to assume greater responsibility for episodes of care rather than just for individual visits made by patients. This is likely to make physicians more aware of deficiencies that may exist in their performance.

Alternative 3 The historical prerogative of professional self-control may be abrogated by the movement toward consumer involvement, control, and ownership of health facilities. Physicians and consumers are known to differ in the priority they place on the various aspects of health care. The effect of assumption of decision making by non-professional community members in the health field is largely unexplored, but increasing interest among consumers in moving in this direction suggests that this may be an important avenue of control in the future.

There are few places in the world where physicians are as autonomous as in the United States. Although in most nations it is common for the state to delegate certifying power of physicians to professional organizations, there are few places (and none in the more highly developed countries) where the profession is able to exert such control over the organization of practice, the means of reimbursement, and the choice of location where the physician works. For example, despite the outlay of $1.9 billion in public funds between 1966 and 1971 to increase the supply of physicians, with a consequent 16 percent increase in the number of medical schools and the addition of 48,000 physicians nationally, the number of physicians in rural areas increased by only 3785. Moreover, whereas the specialties gained 15,200 physicians, the number of family practitioners decreased by 13,500. Of the 48,000 new physicians, only one-third went into direct patient care. But this situation is changing rapidly in the United States. In 1973, legislation which encouraged the formation of prepaid group practices (the Health Maintenance Act) was passed. National health insurance, with its inevitable controls to prevent unrestrained use of services, is actively debated and seems likely of eventual passage. Professional review of the quality of care, at least of diagnostic and therapeutic maneuvers for certain diagnoses, is already mandated by the PSRO Act. The Health Professions Education Act of 1976 was designed to influence the types of physicians who are trained. Denial of federal funds to medical schools which do not have postgraduate training programs in family-oriented practice will certainly cause changes in the curricula in many if not all schools. Incentives in the form of scholarships during medical school to trainees who agree to set up practice in medically underserved areas after their training were provided in the National Health Services Legislation of 1975 and extended in the 1976 legislation.

Only four critical areas are likely to remain firmly under the control of the profession. The first concerns the selection of candidates for the profession. Ever since the Flexner report, the upper social classes have been overrepresented, compared with their proportion in the general population, in the profession of medicine. The high and rising cost of medical education is a powerful deterrent to applications from students in families who cannot afford the financial cost. Even for applicants, those from families with lower incomes have less chance of being accepted than those from wealthier families. Standards for entry are set by governing boards and admissions committees of the medical schools, and these work against the lower-income groups. Such control, with its consequent effect of minimizing representation of the lower classes among physicians, is unlikely to be wrested from the profession without a major social change.

The second concerns the location of practice. In many countries with national health insurance, physicians are not reimbursed for their services if they locate their practices in areas which already have a sufficient number of physicians. None of the proposals for national health insurance in the United States contain such a provision, and there is little likelihood on the horizon of such control over place of practice.

The third area likely to remain in the professional domain concerns the disciplining of physicians. In some countries, the dissatisfaction and complaints of patients may be addressed to governmental agencies which consider them and recommend sanctions (usually financial) against the physician. As mentioned earlier, the medical profession in the United States has been rather impotent in disciplining its members in any meaningful way, as there is no way short of revoking a license (which is hardly ever done) to impose sanctions. To date, both professional and legislative bodies have failed to come to grips with this issue.

The fourth area which is likely to remain in the hands of the profession concerns control over the technical aspects of medical care. Physicians have reserved to themselves the right to define the quality of care, although the rest of the population may set different priorities as to what is important to them. The last section of this chapter deals with this issue.

COSTS OF CHILD HEALTH CARE

Part of the explanation for the diversity of organizational arrangements of care discussed earlier in this chapter results from the diversity of sources of funding of health services. Historically, the poor, if they were cared for at all, were cared for by charity. Even today, the "two-class" system of medical care persists in the mode of funding, much of which is also reflected in the different types of organization which are available to the poor and the nonpoor.

Costs of care are paid either directly (fee-for-service) through purchase of private insurance or by paying taxes to support governmental insurance or direct service programs. Most physicians and hospitals are paid directly by patients, insurance companies, or governmental agencies, although some physicians work for salary. In some other countries, such as Great Britain, physicians are paid a prearranged sum of money ("capitation") for a certain number of identified individuals (a "panel") over a period of time (usually a year). Few if any physicians in the United States are paid directly by capitation, but it is not uncommon for some organizations (such as group practices) to negotiate a capitation from insurance companies or governmental agencies for a certain number of individuals. The group budgets according to money received, and the physicians are generally paid a salary rather than a capitation.

Table 7-8 indicates the various ways of reimbursing health care providers. There are no data to indicate either the absolute or relative frequency of the combinations of payment by patients and payment to physicians, but the out-of-pocket or private insurance/fee-for-service combinations are by far the most common. For most individuals, the type of financing arrangement varies with the type of service provided. For example, even though many people have health insurance (either because they purchased it or are covered through plans provided by their employers or trade unions) their health insurance policies are likely to cover only certain services.

Data from the 1972 Health Interview Survey indicate that approximately 75 percent of children under 17 years of age have insurance for hospitalization. The proportion of the population covered varies markedly, according to family income and color. Only 30 percent of the children in families with less than $5000 income have hospital insurance as compared with 92 percent of those in families with over $10,000. Only 30 percent of children under 17 years have insurance covering visits to physicians; for those in families with incomes under $5000, only 7 percent have such coverage.

Much of the cost of care for the indigent child is paid for directly by the government. This tax-supported contribution to the funding of care for children is composed of two parts: the direct services to mothers and children (discussed earlier under "Organizational Arrangements") and payment

Table 7-8

Ways in Which Medical Care Fees Are Paid and Received

Payment by Patients	Payment to the Physician		
	Fee-for-Service	Capitation	Salary
Out of pocket	Most services in ambulatory settings and some services provided in hospital.	No examples available	Services in most hospital outpatient departments
Through private insurance	Some services in ambulatory settings + most services provided in hospital.	A few prepaid group practices	Most prepaid group practices
Through general taxes	Medicaid (Title XIX)	Some groups of physicians providing care to indigent patients with financing by state-administered tax funds	Direct governmental programs (veterans, government-supported health centers)
Through federal insurance programs	Medicare (Title XVIII) for those over age 65	No examples available	Some prepaid group practices

schemes (largely Medicaid) which are channeled through the "private" health care system. All states were required to have a Medicaid program in operation by 1971 or forfeit the federal funds previously available to them as medical assistance for the indigent. As a first step, state plans were expected to provide certain basic services on a uniform basis to all recipients of cash assistance under the federally aided programs of Aid to the Blind, Old Age Assistance, Aid to the Permanently and Totally Disabled, and Aid to Families with Dependent Children. States could then proceed, at their own pace, to progressively extend eligibility and services to other groups until complete coverage of the indigent was achieved by 1975.

The Medicaid program is a federal-state enterprise. Each state drafts a medical assistance program and assumes responsibility for its administration. In most states, this responsibility has been assigned to the welfare or social services department. The federal government, through the Department of Health, Education, and Welfare (DHEW), approves state plans, sets policies and standards, provides consultative services, and supplies a major share of the costs, from 50 percent in states with the highest per capita income to 83 percent in states with the lowest per capita income. The Secretary of DHEW is provided with guidance in administration of the Medicaid program by the Medical Assistance Advisory Council whose 21 members include both providers and recipients of care. The same arrangement is duplicated at the state level.

The five basic services provided include inpatient and outpatient hospital services, physicians' services (in the office or elsewhere), laboratory and x-ray services, and nursing-home care for people over 21. States were encouraged to extend the scope of services beyond the basic five and to provide dental care services, family planning services, drugs, and prosthetic devices.

State Medicaid programs are required to include children under 21 whose parents are unable to afford the expense of needed health care. Some programs include the "medically needy" (that is, financial eligibility for medical assistance at a level exceeding those established under the state's plan for recipients of financial maintenance assistance but insufficient to meet the costs of medical care). The states must establish standards to determine the eligibility of this group. State standards for both income and resources are subject to federal policies and guidelines. However, income ceilings are often set too low to offer a realistic definition of those who indeed cannot afford medical care. There are therefore many individuals in the "gray" area who neither qualify for governmental help nor can afford to purchase their own insurance. Table 7-9 indicates some of the reasons for lack of insurance; inability to afford

Table 7-9

Number and Percent Distribution of Persons Under 65 Years with No Health Insurance by Reason for Having No Coverage, According to Family Income: United States, 1968

Family Income	Number of Persons with No Coverage (in thousands)	Total	Reason for Having No Coverage					
			Cannot Afford Insurance	Other Type of Aid Available†	Insurance Not Available or Not Obtainable	Do Not Believe in Insurance or Have Good Health	Other	Unknown
All incomes*	36,224	100.0	41.0	17.1	5.1	5.2	24.3	7.3
Less than $3000	10,163	100.0	56.0	11.9	3.1	3.2	19.7	6.0
$3000– $4999	8771	100.0	47.9	16.1	4.5	3.2	21.7	6.6
$5000– $6999	7167	100.0	35.9	20.1	6.2	6.1	24.1	7.7
$7000– $9999	4202	100.0	27.7	21.8	9.0	7.1	27.9	6.4
$10,000–$14,999	2760	100.0	16.0	26.1	7.9	8.7	35.2	6.3
$15,000 or more	1175	100.0	9.0	22.5	5.2	13.5	37.3	12.7

* Includes persons with unknown family income.

† Included are public assistance or public welfare, VA hospitals, Uniformed Services Dependents Medical Care Program, crippled children's programs.

Source: NCHS, HIS Series 10, #66.

it is a relatively greater reason for children in families with low income than it is for adults in such families. Low income weighs more heavily on insurance coverage of children than on coverage of adults. When family funds are meager, they must be rationed; illness in low-income adults, particularly if they are employed, has greater economic consequences than is the case for illness in children.

Direct payments by patients under age 65 dropped from two-thirds of the total health care dollar in 1950 to one-third by 1975. During that same period, the share paid by private health insurance increased from 9 percent to 35 percent, and that paid by the government increased from 20 percent to almost 30 percent. (The remainder was paid by charitable organizations.) Although comparable figures for children alone are not available, the proportion of expenditures which are paid directly, rather than through insurance, government, or philanthropy, is greater for children than for young or middle-aged adults.

In fiscal 1973, $80 billion were spent for personal health care. Only 15.4 percent of this was spent on persons under 19 years, even though persons in this age group comprise about 35 percent of the popula-

tion. About one-third of the expenditures for children was paid to hospitals for inpatient care; another third was for physician services. Private sources provided 71 percent, and public funds provided 29 percent. Two-thirds of the public funds were spent by the federal government and one-third by states (Table 7-10). Public assistance payments under Medicaid accounted for 38 percent, military dependents' medical care programs for 25 percent, and general hospital and medical care programs for 16 percent. Maternal and child health care programs, school health, medical vocational rehabilitation, and OEO programs (mainly neighborhood health centers) accounted for the remainder of public fund expenditures.

Medical expenditures have been increasing over the past several decades. The average expenditure for medical care for children under 19 years of age rose from $111 in 1969 to $212 in 1975, a far greater increase than could be accounted for by inflation alone. Table 7-11 shows that hospital costs have been increasing as a proportion of health care expenditures, despite evidence that the health needs of children are primarily increasing in the nonhospital sector.

Table 7-10

Personal Health Expenditures by Category of Expenditure: Percentage from Private, Federal, and State and Local Sources, 1973

	All Ages				Under Age 19 Only			
			Public				Public	
	Total	Private	Federal	State and Local	Total	Private	Federal	State and Local
Amount (millions of $)	80,048	49,713	21,105	10,230	12,367	8792	2137	1439
Percentage		62	25	13		71	17	12

	Amount (millions of $)	Percentage by Source			Amount (millions of $)	Percentage by Source		
Expenditures for:								
Hospital care	36,200	47	35	18	3765	50	32	18
Physician services	18,040	78	17	6	3938	88	8	4
Drug and drug sundries	8780	92	4	4	1713	94	4	2
Dentist services	5385	95	3	2	1199	91	5	4
All other*	11,643	48	34	18	1752	41	29	30

* Includes other professional services such as physical therapy; prostheses such as eyeglasses and similar services and appliances.

Source: Adapted from *Social Security Bulletin*, vol. 37, no. 5, May 1974.

Table 7-11

Expenditures for Personal Health Services, United States, 1969–1975

| | Per Capita Expenditures | | | | | |
| | All Ages | | | Under Age 19 | | |
	1969	1974	1975	1969	1974	1975
Total	$256	$420	$476	$111	$183	$212
Hospital care	110	190	215	27	61	71
Physicians' services	58	88	102	37	57	70
All other	88	142	159	47	65	71

Source: *Social Security Bulletin,* vol. 38, no. 6, June 1975; *Social Security Bulletin,* vol. 39, no. 6, June 1976; *Research and Statistics Note (DHEW),* October 23, 1970.

The persistent increases in the costs of care are responsible for much congressional interest in national health insurance. However, questions about whether its administration should reside with governmental agencies or be delegated to private insurance companies, and the scope of the benefits to be included have been insurmountable stumbling blocks to the passage of national health insurance legislation.

EFFECTIVENESS OF CARE

As the section in this chapter on "Control" has indicated, the medical profession has been unable to assure that high standards of care are maintained in actual practice. Although all practitioners must demonstrate at least a minimum amount of theoretical knowledge as a condition of licensure before they enter practice, the relationship between performance in these tests and subsequent quality of practice has never been demonstrated. Even the procedure by which physicians become certified as "specialists" is a dubious assurance of high quality. Prerequisite to certification as a specialist (pediatrician, internist, surgeon, and the like) is completion of a required number of years of postgraduate residency in a specialty and passage of a test designed by "specialty boards" made up of physicians who are members of self-constituted specialty societies. About 60 percent of physicians who limit their practice to pediatrics have taken and passed this examination, thereby acquiring "certification." Some studies have shown that length of postgraduate residency is associated with better quality of care in practice and also with the satisfaction of patients with the care. But other

evidence indicates that the organization of practice (group practice, teaching-hospital practice) is more important as a determinant of the quality of practice than board certification. In fact, board certification itself appears to have no relationship to quality of practice. Moreover, some studies show that patients are more satisfied with the care received from physicians who are not board certified, indicating that, at the very least, the process of certification fails to tap some dimensions which are considered, at least by patients, to represent "quality" of care. Continuing education requirements and periodic recertification procedures imposed by professional organizations are unlikely to improve the situation unless the model of quality of care on which the original educational and certification procedures are based is broadened.

Improving Health and Well-being

The significant declines in mortality over the last century can be attributed more to improvements in public health efforts than to specific technologic advances applied to individual patients. The discovery of antibiotics is the only scientific advance applied to individual patients which has had a major impact in improving length of life, and even here, the predominant effect seems to have been to reduce deaths from acute infectious complications of chronic illness in the elderly. The marked improvement in life expectancy over the last century is a result primarily of lowered infant mortality. This, however, can hardly be attributed to conventional health services. The infant mortality rate began to decline long before specific medical interventions were imposed and was a result of general improvements in sanitation, hygiene, and feeding practices.

Perhaps reduction of mortality is too great an expectation for personal health services. Rather, some say that the measure of the system would be a reduction in the occurrence of disease and its manifestations. But even here, it is unclear that physicians make a critical difference. Certainly the introduction of immunization has been responsible for large declines in the incidence of diphtheria, tetanus, pertussis, poliomyelitis, rubeola, and rubella. But, once again, it is the public health sector rather than the practice of individual physicians which has been responsible. Federal funds to support immunizations have been crucial to the effectiveness of these programs; attempts to reduce or eliminate the input of money have led to reduction in the completeness of immunization and to epidemics of some of the diseases among children, particularly the poor.

The impact which health services can be expected to have, even under the best of circumstances, is limited by the role of other influential forces. Figure 7-1 shows that at least four factors determine the state of health of individuals. Genetic constitution is the basic determinant. People differ in their predisposition to specific illnesses and in their response to treatment of these illnesses, largely because of differences in their genotype. Probably the second most important determinant of an individual's state of health is the social and physical environment.

Where we live, how we live, the food available to us, and the stresses which are imposed upon us by our social system all have their impact on how healthy we are and how well we resist insults to our health. Children are particularly vulnerable to the effects of the physical and social environment because they are even less able to select their surroundings and exposures than are adults. Third is the role which individuals themselves play. Although young children are less likely to determine their life patterns than adults (whose smoking, drinking, eating, and driving behavior are major underlying causes of death), the patterns set for them by their parents influence not only how ill health is dealt with in childhood, but also how well they are taught behavior destined to have a major impact on their health in later life. The final and probably least critical determinant of health, except in unusual situations, is the provision of medical services. The following discussion will show why this is so and what might be done to enhance the contribution which these services make to health.

Who Defines What "Good Care" Is?

Consumers of health services and providers differ on the priorities which they place on the three main elements of care. Accessibility to medical care has been shown to be of prime importance to consumers. If there are no services available when they are needed, it makes no difference what their potential quality is. Costs are the second most important concern of patients. In contrast, neither access nor cost are considered appropriate subjects in medical school curricula.

Medical curricula focus almost exclusively on training practitioners to make a diagnosis; to support this diagnosis with appropriate information from the history, physical examination, and laboratory findings; and to institute treatment appropriate to the diagnosis. The nature of most educational settings (university-based, research-oriented, generally highly specialized faculty) is responsible for important limitations in the nature of medical training. These are as follows:

1   The focus of the educational process is largely on the biochemical and biophysical bases of disease processes. The first 2 years of most medical schools are almost completely devoted to under-

Figure 7-1

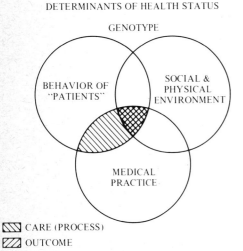

DETERMINANTS OF HEALTH STATUS

GENOTYPE

BEHAVIOR OF "PATIENTS"

SOCIAL & PHYSICAL ENVIRONMENT

MEDICAL PRACTICE

▨ CARE (PROCESS)

▨ OUTCOME

standing the biomedical causes of disease. In contrast, relatively little attention is devoted to understanding the social and psychological causes of ill health, despite every indication that social, environmental, and behavioral phenomena are major determinants of disease.

2 The emphasis of the diagnostic process is on assigning single causes for disease and on arriving at a single diagnosis. While this has been appropriate in the past, it is more appropriate today to consider multiple causes for a disease. Moreover, one disease is often complicated and modified by the presence of another.

3 Students are not sufficiently exposed to the concept of human variability. They are taught how diseases *usually* manifest themselves and what therapies *usually* are appropriate, but have little exposure to the epidemiologic aspects of illness—that is, the range of expression of illness in the population.

4 Students' exposure to illness is short-term. Their education, composed of blocks of time in various specialties, ill prepares them to assume responsibility for patients over long periods of time, as will be required in their subsequent practice of medicine.

5 Students learn about illnesses either through reading about them or by participating in the care of ill patients. In both instances, knowledge is derived primarily from experiences with patients at university-affiliated hospitals. Patients appearing for care at such institutions are not representative of the population as a whole, or even of the patients with whom the student as a practitioner will subsequently meet.

In the education of physicians, *quality* of care, including techniques of diagnosis and therapy, is virtually the only concern. With this limited concept of quality, it might be expected that at least diagnosis and therapy would be optimal in clinical practice. This, unfortunately, is not the case as the following situations indicate.

Many well-accepted diagnostic strategies are of unproved usefulness, and some are harmful. For example, studies have shown that patterns of laboratory use may bear little or no relation to the needs of the patient. The extent of error, both in clinical observations and in laboratory findings, appears largely unrecognized by physicians.

Many commonly applied therapeutic maneuvers are of unproved usefulness and may be dangerous. For example, several studies demonstrate that surgical rates in the United States are much greater than in other developed countries, in the absence of any demonstrable difference in need for surgery as defined by prevalence of disease or illness. Even within the United States, the number of admissions to hospital and rates of surgical procedures vary markedly from area to area, being largest in those areas with the greatest availability of surgical manpower, and are unrelated to differences in medical need.

Another example relates to the misuse of drug therapy. For many physicians, representatives of drug manufacturers are the primary source of information on new drugs. Several surveys have shown a widespread lack of appreciation for the dangers of many of them and a large number of errors in their prescribing.

Even when diagnostic and therapeutic interventions can be shown to be appropriate and of demonstrated efficacy, their application does not necessarily produce the desired outcome. This is because adequate diagnosis and therapy, while necessary conditions for care of high quality, are by themselves insufficient. The treatment of illness and the maintenance of health also require the active participation of the patients and potential patients, and a social and physical environment which is supportive, as Fig. 7-1 shows. The very best quality of care, defined as efficacious diagnosis and treatment, will fail to achieve its effect if (1) those who require it and can benefit from it do not appear for care, (2) if they fail to accept and understand it, and (3) if there is unwillingness to comply with the prescribed therapy (see Fig. 7-2).

For these reasons, it has been suggested that the professional definition of quality of care be broadened from its concentration on diagnostic and therapeutic strategies to include two additional facets of medical practice: problem recognition and follow-up and reassessment.

Problem Recognition The application of diagnostic or therapeutic strategies requires first that problems, or potential problems, be recognized. Where this process has been examined, the evidence indicates that the existence of many types of health problems is often overlooked.

Physicians are consistently poorer at recognizing

Figure 7-2   Process of pediatric care.

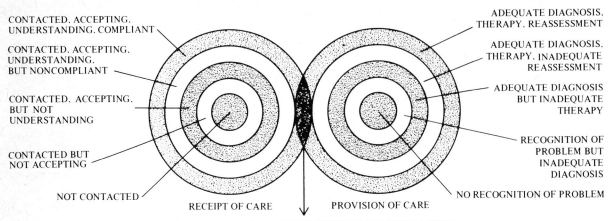

CONTACTED, ACCEPTING,
UNDERSTANDING, COMPLIANT

CONTACTED, ACCEPTING,
UNDERSTANDING,
BUT NONCOMPLIANT

CONTACTED, ACCEPTING,
BUT NOT
UNDERSTANDING

CONTACTED BUT
NOT ACCEPTING

NOT CONTACTED

ADEQUATE DIAGNOSIS,
THERAPY, REASSESSMENT

ADEQUATE DIAGNOSIS,
THERAPY, INADEQUATE
REASSESSMENT

ADEQUATE DIAGNOSIS
BUT INADEQUATE
THERAPY

RECOGNITION OF
PROBLEM BUT
INADEQUATE
DIAGNOSIS

NO RECOGNITION OF PROBLEM

RECEIPT OF CARE   PROVISION OF CARE

EFFECTIVE PEDIATRIC CARE FOR EPISODES OF MEDICAL NEED

the existence of significant behavior problems and social factors related to illness than they are at recognizing problems with obvious biophysiologic or anatomic manifestations. But even organic problems may be neglected. Many children (and adults, too) can be shown to have health conditions which fail to be followed up by their physicians, even when information about them was available. Failure to recognize the problems which patients bring to physicians is a serious defect in the provision of health services, as it has been shown that this failure is associated both with decreased satisfaction of patients and their failure to follow medical advice. Without recognition of the full range of patient's problems, no diagnostic strategy or therapeutic intervention can be fully effective.

Problem recognition also extends to prevention of disease. One type of prevention, *primary prevention,* is traditional to pediatricians. It consists of recognizing susceptibility to disease and applying measures to prevent it from occurring. Immunizations are the most obvious and simple example of primary prevention. But prevention goes far beyond this. Sometimes, only certain people are at risk of acquiring disease later on in life; pediatricians must direct efforts at discovering who these people are and at keeping them under surveillance. This is known as *secondary prevention.* As social, environmental, and behavioral factors become recognized as important antecedents of many chronic illnesses, pediatricians will become more involved in activities directed toward preventing them. Up to now, secondary pre-

vention has not been a common feature of pediatric practice and, where identification of children at risk *has* taken place, it generally has been at the initiative of governmental and social agencies. Examples of such efforts are hearing and vision screening in schools, special screening programs for specific diseases in special populations (sickle cell anemia, Tay-Sachs disease), and state-mandated neonatal screening for inherited metabolic disorders, such as phenylketonuria. Experiences with these programs and with general screening programs such as EPSDT for indigent children indicate that failure to follow up defects discovered by the screening is a serious problem which largely negates any potential benefit of the screening program. If abnormal screening does not uniformly result in diagnosis and remediation, there is little justification for the screening program. Ultimately, pediatricians must assume responsibility for coordinating all of the care of children, including primary prevention and secondary prevention, as well as treatment of manifest illness.

Follow-Up and Reassessment   In order to assure that diagnostic procedures and instituted therapy are adequate, patients must be followed to determine if problems are resolving as expected.

Medical textbooks and teachings rarely contain information which would help the practitioner to define appropriate intervals for reassessing particular health problems. Such information would have to come from careful studies of the natural history of patients' problems, with and without intervention, and such studies are rare. Moreover, little is known about the extent to which practitioners do follow up on problems which they treat. Where the issue has been examined, it has been found that failure to follow up on treated patients results in unresolved health problems for patients. At the very least, this produces a highly inefficient health care system; care is paid for but no benefit is gained. At the most, it will ultimately lead to societal demands for more accountability of the profession. As has been shown earlier in this chapter under the heading "Control," such demands are already being initiated.

Outcome of Care

This chapter has, up to this point, examined issues relating to the *structure* and *process* of medical care. Manpower, facilities, accessibility, and costs reflect the structure, or form, of health services. The process of care has been addressed in the discussion of quality which involves the recognition of patients' problems, further data gathering to arrive at a medical diagnosis, the institution of therapy, and reassessment to assure optimum response to therapy. As has been shown, patients also contribute to the process of care by their decisions to seek or not seek it (*utilization*), to accept or not accept it, and to understand it and comply with recommendations. The third means by which care may be evaluated is based upon the attainment of goals, or outcomes. Outcomes may be divided into four categories: mortality rates, morbidity, disability, and other measures.

Mortality Rates

Until recently, benefits of health care have been judged almost solely by trends in death rates. Deaths are uniformly registered and therefore available and easily tabulated. But after infancy, deaths in childhood are so relatively infrequent that they are a very insensitive indicator of the value of medical interventions. Unfortunately, death is the only indicator which is routinely obtainable.

Morbidity

Morbidity (sickness, illness, injury) is obtainable only for those few conditions for which reporting is mandated by law because of their potential public health impact (contagiousness). Some examples are rubella, rubeola, and hepatitis. As Sec. 5 has shown, these causes of morbidity comprise a very small proportion of the health problems of children. Whereas national health surveys, whether they are household surveys or surveys of practitioners' offices, provide some data on the prevalence of other child health conditions, they are not sufficient as sources of information about the impact of health activities because of the following reasons: (1) They are national in scope and hence insensitive to small variations in health practices or health status; (2) they do not permit discrimination between socio-environmental and medical influences on health; and (3) they do not make it possible to link either the cause of disease or its course to interventions by health practitioners, either for individual patients or for populations.

Disability

The ongoing household survey administered by the National Center for Health Statistics of the U.S. DHEW obtains information about disability from a sample of the population. Disability is ascertained by asking questions regarding limitations of mobility, restrictions of usual daily activity, and confinement to bed. Limitation of mobility is relatively uncommon in children and signals rather severe disability when it occurs. Normal daily activity is difficult to define for children, particularly for the very young. Confinement to bed is also not very satisfactory as a measure of disability in childhood because children are not frequently confined to bed even when ill. Because of the inadequacy of these measures, some investigators have proposed collecting data on symptoms such as eating and sleeping disturbances and irritability, which are nonspecific reflections of most illnesses. Knowledge about the existence of these symptoms improves our ability to obtain information on the presence of illness, particularly in young children, but is not yet in wide use.

Other Measures of Health

Increasing complexity of society is reflected in increasing complexity of disease. The unifactorial etiology of disease served us well in the past, but diseases and their causes are no longer simple. In all likelihood, the vast majority of diseases are not single entities at all, but rather symptom complexes which are caused by interactions among genetic predispositions, socioenvironmental influences, and patterns of personal behavior. Health status is a far more complex concept than we have imagined. It seems likely that in the near future attempts will be made to measure the effectiveness of health care not only by death rates, morbidity rates, and disability rates, but also by evidence that individuals are more or less comfortable, more or less satisfied with their health, more or less able to achieve their physical and intellectual potential, and more or less able to cope effectively with physical, emotional, and social stresses of modern living. The pediatric practitioner of the future will be confronted more with these new concepts of disease and health than with the acute illnesses which have preoccupied the child health doctor of the past.

It seems likely that physicians of the future will be encouraged, and perhaps even required, to keep certain types of data about the children in their practices. A recent conference of experts has recommended such data sets for hospitals to use for each patient admitted; this set has been accepted by the National Committee for Health Statistics and is likely to be mandated in all facilities receiving public funds (and most do, either as direct reimbursement for services or as grants for buildings or programs). A subsequent conference adopted a minimal set for ambulatory care. This includes registration data (patient identification number, name, address, birth date, sex, race, marital status) and encounter data (facility identification number, provider identification number, patient identification number, source of payment, date of encounter, patient's purpose for visit, physician diagnosis, diagnostic and management procedures, and disposition).

The adoption of this or a similar system for collecting information in a standardized way will facilitate the understanding of health and disease processes and the role which medical care plays in influencing them.

8 | Prospects for Change in the Health Care of the Young

by Robert A. Hoekelman

A review of the content of this textbook, particularly this first part, "Comprehensive Pediatric Care," provides an overview and considerable depth of discussion in most areas of how the health of the young and health care delivery to the young was and is. In this chapter some indication of what needs to be done, what can be done, and what will be done to improve the health of the young and its delivery will be considered.

There is no doubt that those who are concerned with the delivery of child health care face serious difficulties in finding the resources and mechanisms to ensure that all children in need of preventive, maintenance, and curative services receive them. No matter how the pediatric health care pie is sliced, as it presently exists, all the appetites will not be satisfied. This is true for those who seek these services and more so for the greater numbers who are in need, yet do not recognize that need or have the resources to seek the appropriate care.

Any review of health care needs and prospects for meeting them demands an assessment of the services that are required, how these can be organized and delivered effectively and efficiently, who will deliver these services, and how they can be prepared to do so.

Traditionally, primary care pediatricians have conducted high-volume practices in solo or small partnership arrangements. They have provided preventive services and health maintenance supervision, and have managed acute minor illnesses on an ambulatory basis. Only a small part of their efforts,

however, have been spent in the diagnosis and treatment of serious illness in the hospital, for which most of their postgraduate training prepared them. These problems have increasingly been referred to subspecialty pediatricians, located in large medical centers, because primary care pediatricians have not had the time to deal with them or their knowledge and skills in the management of severe illness have atrophied from disuse.

Most pediatricians learn to do what they do through on-the-job experience rather than through formal training. To many, the content of private practice comes somewhat as a surprise. Some pediatricians are not satisfied with this role and turn to subspecialty training and practice, but most adjust quickly and find primary care practice extremely rewarding.

There are, however, forces coming to bear on the future of primary pediatric practice over which the individual physician has little or no control: (1) The incidence of serious disease in childhood is decreasing due to public and individual preventive health measures; therefore, the number of these illnesses occurring in a single practice is diminishing. (2) The reproductive behavior of the population is changing. The use of contraceptive devices and the liberalization of abortion laws have significantly decreased the birthrates, particularly in the populations served by most pediatricians. Infant mortality, prematurity, and morbidity have diminished as well, and regionalization of perinatal care has transferred, or will transfer, the management of most high-risk newborn infants from the primary care pediatrician to neonatologists in regional centers.   (3) The rapid increase in medical knowledge and technology has produced methods of treatment for many childhood diseases that can only be provided in large institutions by specialists who devote most of their efforts to these problems. The primary care physician cannot morally or ethically elect to continue to care for these patients.   (4) Other professionals have demonstrated their ability to provide competently much of the care currently undertaken by the practicing pediatrician. Increasing numbers of family practitioners, pediatric nurse practitioners, and physician's assistants are being prepared to provide those services, working both with, and independent of, the pediatrician.   (5) Private practice is moving toward consumer control. Demands will be made on the practitioner to institute new organizational and financial arrangements in the provision of primary care. Issues of availability, acceptability, accountability, and efficacy of the care provided will need to be dealt with by each practitioner.

These forces need not be viewed negatively. They can be used by pediatric practitioners as a means of improving the health care available to children. Pediatric practice will need to be reorganized to meet the needs of all children, not just those who seek care. Care must also become more continuous and comprehensive, and must be coordinated with the health-related needs of children that are met by others. Pediatricians will have to relate to broader issues that affect the health of children within the family structure, within the community, and within the greater environment.

The list of issues, long neglected, is extensive and includes specific problems within the broad areas of education (attaining full intellectual potential), communication (understanding and being understood), socialization (behaving appropriately with others), and normalization (functioning within acceptable limits) for both well and ill children. Efforts to deal with these issues effectively will need to be directed through the community. The prospect for success in effecting improvement in the health of children is probably greater moving along this avenue than that of providing individual health care. It is clear that the practicing pediatrician cannot accomplish these goals without working collaboratively with other professionals within and without his or her practice setting.

This change in the complexion of primary care practice will require changes in our system of undergraduate and graduate medical education. The curriculum must be altered to include educational objectives commensurate with the activities of primary care physicians, and to exclude those objectives that are no longer pertinent to practice. Early tracking of students who plan to enter primary care versus those who plan on subspecialty practice will be required, and interdisciplinary education with other professionals who will be working collaboratively with physicians in team-oriented care will need to be instituted. In addition, the milieu in which medical education takes place must be supportive to the broadened concept of the practice of primary care.

Primary care has finally been defined to the satisfaction of almost everyone, and educational programs to prepare physicians to provide primary care to children have begun to emerge in response to reason, demand, and dictum. Questions now arise as to who should provide the bulk of that care and how it can best be organized to ensure that the health care needs of all our children are met. The politics of primary pediatric care begin to occupy more of our thought and discussion.

Dodds has reviewed the politics involved at all levels of pediatric care, but speaks mostly to the conflicts that exist between general practitioners and pediatricians in the delivery of primary care. The Institute of Medicine has recently embarked on a study to assist in the development of a cohesive health manpower policy for primary care based upon (1) a policy determination of what functions should be served by the primary care system, and   (2) the specification of what roles should be played by various categories of health care personnel in the delivery of primary care services. Two of the policy questions that will be addressed are whether primary care practice should be restricted to specially trained "primary care physicians" and what type(s) of physician manpower model(s) should be developed and supported to provide primary care services. The results of this study, due in 1978, will shape the future development of manpower resources for primary care.

In the meantime, and most certainly thereafter, these issues will be debated. White and Haggerty, who agree on most things, are at opposite poles concerning physician manpower for primary care. White's view is that "we need to strengthen internal medicine and pediatrics, supported by psychiatry and obstetrics, in their concern for the provision of family-centered primary care and forget about the all-purpose family physician," while Haggerty believes that "if the final purpose of the medical school is to help meet the medical care needs of the people, education for family practice must be an integral part of the curriculum."

In considering these positions, it is helpful to review the available evidence concerning primary pediatric practice as it is currently conducted. The National Ambulatory Medical Care Survey indicates that 121 million visits were made to physicians' offices by patients under 15 years of age during 1974. Of these, 42 percent involved pediatricians, 36 percent family practitioners, and 22 percent other medical and surgical specialists. Since a reasonable number of the visits to pediatricians must have been for consultation and subspecialty care and very few, if any, of the visits to family practitioners were of this nature, the distribution of visits for primary care pruposes between pediatricians and family practitioners would have been fairly equal.

These figures speak only to those primary care needs that are being addressed and do not include those that for economic, educational, or physician accessibility reasons remain unaddressed. We are not providing to all our children the levels of care deemed appropriate by the American Academy of Pediatrics. Miller states that "preventive services which should be routine for every child are maintained at marginal levels at best, and at grossly unsatisfactory levels for the disadvantaged." Results of studies of the levels of child health care achieved for specific population groups demonstrate that for most children we fall far short of our goals in terms of levels of well-child care provided and immunizations administered. One of the qualities of primary care held to be important is that of continuity of care by a single physician. Andersen and his coworkers report that in 1970 only 25 percent of poor children had a private physician responsible for their care and 20 percent had no identified regular source of care.

One of the reasons for our poor performance is the economic barrier that prevents access to primary care services despite federal- and state-financed health care programs. Wallace and Goldstein have reported that the extent of coverage for payment of health care for children and youths, even those in high-priority groups, is still very restricted. When the economic barrier is removed, as with the implementation of the medicaid program, utilization of health services by populations not in the habit of seeking other than emergency care lags considerably. This phenomenom is a reflection of the need to remove the educational barrier which interferes with adequate utilization of primary care services as well as the financial barrier. We must convince parents of the need to obtain preventive and curative health care for their children through primary educational efforts and with outreach, "search-and-find" programs.

Most important to the discussions of who should provide primary care to children is the issue of accessibility in terms of the number and distribution of physicians. Although the doctor-shortage debate continues with a variety of ways of addressing the question, the most important consideration in pediatrics is the number of children not receiving accepted levels of care.

The prospects for improvement in physician accessibility for primary care of children are not great. Although the number of pediatricians is predicted to increase from 18,820 in 1970 to 32,150 in 1980 and to 47,830 in 1990, the number of general practitioners will fall from 57,950 in 1970 to 53,750 in 1980 and to 49,140 in 1990. Even though this represents an increase of over 20,000 potential primary care practitioners for children (76,770 to 96,970), and the percentage of general practitioners certified by the American Board of Family Practice will increase from 3 to 25 percent, the ratio of pediatricians and general practitioners per 100,000 population will actually fall from 37.6 in 1970 to 34.5 in 1990.

These data lead one to conclude that access to quality primary care provided by pediatricians for all the children in our nation is not obtainable. This realization, however, should not deter us from setting a goal of access to quality primary care for all our children, utilizing family practitioners and other health professionals (pediatric nurse practitioners and child health associates) working in concert with pediatricians.

There is no need to argue the quality issue. Family medicine educators point out that their residency programs concentrate on teaching primary care and family-focused continuity of care, while most pediatric residency programs do not. A family medicine residency provides 3 years of education in the approach to patient problem solving based upon the same physiologic principles utilized by pediatricians and internists. Swisher has estimated a 70 percent overlap in attitudes, values, and styles of utilizing medical skills between family medicine residents and pediatric and internal medicine residents, which is perhaps greater in dealing with primary care problems. Pediatricians are involved in training family medicine residents in their block assignments to inpatient units (minimally 4 months), in pediatric electives (up to 3 months), and throughout their 3 years of training in continuity patient care experiences. These efforts would be ludicrous if pediatricians were to adopt an ambivalent attitude toward the worth of primary care delivered to children by family practitioners. This is especailly true since there are no data to show that pediatricians do a better job in deliverying primary care to children than do family practitioners. Pediatricians must nevertheless maintain their leadership roles in the delivery of health care to the young and develop partnerships with family practitioners and others if they are to succeed in meeting all the needs.

Pediatrics initially was concerned only with recovery from disease and disability. At the beginning of the twentieth century prevention of disease and disability became an activity of equal importance, and at mid-century pediatrics began to focus upon ways and means by which individuals could be assisted in reaching their full potential in all spheres. This last activity requires collaboration with other health and nonhealth professionals and a greater involvement in the sociopolitical arena in an attempt to influence those educational, economic, and life-style factors that contribute so significantly to the potential of children.

A holistic approach to the health of children, their families, and members of their community is receiving considerable attention from some child health care workers. Holistic medicine implies utilization of old and new alternative approaches to health care, including psychotherapy, biofeedback and autogenic techniques, forms of massage (acupressure and polarity therapy), meditative disciplines (transcendental meditation and yoga), awareness experiences (EST and Arica training), nutritional therapies, modified Eastern martial arts (T'ai Ch'i and aikido), visual arts, music and dance, and application of other types of health practices such as chiropractic, Chinese acupuncture, and Latino hot-cold systems. Organized medicine and most of its membership currently reject these approaches to health care, but significant numbers of people have turned and are turning to them as an adjunct or an alternative to traditional care, usually before seeking formal contact with the medical care system. Fink refers to this early involvement with formal and informal nonmedical health systems as *preprimary care* and considers it a form of self-care in which decisions concerning one's own health are made without physician involvement. Faced with the impossible task of meeting the illness and health needs and demands of our population, physicians should familiarize themselves with these alternative forms of health care so that they can better advise their patients on their appropriate and inappropriate use and, where applicable, utilize them to enhance their patients' well-being.

The problems presented to the health professions in devising a system of health care delivery to meet the needs of the young are formidable and represent a challenge that will tax the resources of those professionals. The solutions to those problems and the decisions regarding their adoption will not be made by physicians exclusively. Their degree of input into the decision making will depend upon their involvement with what, to them, may seem peripheral matters, but to the public and their representatives are crucial concerns. The health of the young will be best ensured and maintained through the cooperative and collaborative efforts of everyone.

REFERENCES

Ecology of Patient Care

Adair, J., and Deuschle, K. W.: *The People's Health: Medicine and Anthropology in a Navajo Community*, New York: Appleton Century Crofts, 1970.

The assumptive world, *N. Engl. J. Med.*, February 1967. (Editorial.)

Balint, M.: *The Doctor, His Patient, and the Illness*, rev. ed., New York: International Universities Press, 1972.

Benedict, R.: *Patterns of Culture*, Boston: Houghton Mifflin, 1934.

Berelson, B., and Steiner, G.: *Human Behavior*, New York: Harcourt, Brace & World, 1964.

Berkmann, P.: Spouseless motherhood, psychological stress and physical morbidity, *J. Health Soc. Behav.*, **10**:323, 1969.

Brown, L. R.: The world food prospect, *Science*, **190**:1053, 1975.

Burgers, J. M.: Causality and anticipation, *Science*, **189**:194, 1975.

Chabot, M. J., Garfinkel, J., and Pratt, M. W.: Urbanization and differentials in white and non-white infant mortality, *Pediatrics*, **56**:777, 1975.

Chamberlin, R. W.: Parental use of "positive contact" in child rearing: Its relationship to child behavior patterns and other variables, *Pediatrics*, **56**:768, 1975.

Coe, R. M., and Wesson, A. F.: *Sociology of Medicine*, New York: McGraw-Hill, 1970.

Committee on Long Range Planning, American Academy of Pediatrics, James E. Strain, Chairman, June 1975.

Drotar, D., Buskiewicz, A., Irvin, N., Kennell, J., and Klaus, M.: The adaptation of parents to the birth of an infant with congenial malformation: A hypothetical model, *Pediatrics*, **56**:710, 1975.

Dunn, L. C.: Introductory remarks, culture and society, *Health Ann. N.Y. Acad. Sci.*, **84**:787, 1960.

Eisenberg, L.: Psychiatric intervention, *Sci. Am.* **229**:79, 1973.

Feinstein, A.: *Clinical Judgment*, Baltimore: Williams & Wilkins, 1967.

Finch, S. M., and Hess, J. H.: Ulcerative colitis in children, *Am. J. Psychiatry*, **118**:819, 1962.

Gordis, L., Markowitz, M., and Lilienfeld, A. M.,: Studies in the epidemiology and prevention of pheumatic fever: IV. A quantitative determination of compliance in children on oral penicillin prophylaxis, *Pediatrics*, **43**:173, 1969.

Hardin, G.: The tragedy of the commons, *Science*, **162**:1243, 1968.

Heissel, J. S., Ream, G. Rappaport, M., and Coddington, R. D.: The significance of life events as contributory factors in the diseases of children: III. A study of pediatric patients, *J. Pediatr.*, **83**:119, 1973.

Jelliffe, D. B.: Letter to the editor, *Pediatrics*, **56**:837, 1975.

Klerman, G.: Symposium at Columbia, Md., Oct. 12, 1975.

Lane, J. M., Millar, J. D., and Neff, J. M.: Smallpox and smallpox vacination policy, *Annu. Rev. Med.*, **22**:251, 1971.

Lehninger, A. L.: *The Molecular Basis of Cell Structure and Function*, New York: Worth, 1972.

Lerner, M.: "Social Differences in Physical Health," in J. Kosa and I. Zola (eds.), *Poverty and Health: A Sociological Analysis*, Harvard, Cambridge, Mass.: 1975.

Lusted, L. B.: Decision in medicine, *N. Engl. J. Med.* **293**:254, 1975.

McDermott, W., Deuschle, K., and Barnett, C.: Health care experiment at many farms, *Science*, **175**:23, 1972.

McKinlay, J. B.: Some approaches and problems in the study of the use of services: An overview, *J. Health Soc. Behav.*, **13:**115, 1972.

McKinlay, J. B., and Dutton, D. B.: "Social-Psychological Factors Affecting Health Service Utilization," in S. W. Mushkin (ed.), *Consumer Incentives for Health Care*, New York: Milbank Memorial Fund, 1974.

McKusick, V.: *Human Genetics*, Englewood Cliffs, N.J.: Prentice-Hall, 1969.

McWhinney, I. R.: Problem solving and decision making in primary medical practice, *Proc. R. Soc. Med.* vol. 65, November 1972.

Marigold, L., and Lovejoy, F. H., Jr.,: Adolescent attitudes in a general pediatric hospital, *Am. J. Dis. Child.*, **129:**1046, 1975.

Mason, J. W.: A historical view of the stress field, *J. Hum. Stress*, **1:**22, 1975.

Mattar, M. S., Markello, J., and Yaffee, S. J.: Pharmaceutical factors affecting pediatric compliance, *Pediatrics*, **55:**101, 1975*a*.

Mattar, M. S., Markello, J., and Yaffee, S. J.: Inadequacies in the pharmacologic management of ambulatory children, *J. Pediatr.*, **87:**137, 1975*b*.

Mauksch, H. O.: A social science basis for conceptualizing child health, *Soc. Sci. Med.*, **8:**521, 1974.

Mechanic, D., and Volkart, E.: Stress: Illness behavior and the sick role, *Am. Sociol. Rev.*, **26:**51, 1961.

Mechanic, D.: *Medical Sociology: A Selective View*, New York: Free Press, and Toronto: Collier-Macmillan Canada, 1968.

Mechanic D.: *Politics, Medicine, and Social Science*, New York: Wiley, 1974.

Meyers, A., Dolan, T. F., Jr., and Mueller, D.: Compliance and self medication in cystic fibrosis, *Am. J. Dis. Child.*, **129:**1011, 1975.

Mountcastle, V. B.: The view from within: Pathways to the study of perception, *Johns Hopkins Med. J.*, **136:**109, 1975.

Pimental, D., Dritschild, W., Krummel, J., and Kutzman, J.: Energy and land: Constraints in food protein production, *Science*, **190:**754, 1975.

Pirsig, R. M.: *Zen and the Art of Motorcycle Maintenance*, New York: Bantam, 1974.

Porter, C.: *Maladaptive Mothering Patterns: Nursing Interventions*, American Nurses' Association Clinical Sessions, Proceedings, 1972.

Rogers, K. D., Ernst, R., Shulman, I., and Reisinger, K. S.: Effectiveness of aggressive follow-up on Navajo infant health and medical care use, *Pediatrics*, **53:**721, 1974.

Roghmann, K. J., and Haggerty, R. J.: Daily stress, illness and the use of health services in young families, *Pediatr. Res.*, **7:**520, 1973.

Saunders, L.: *The Changing Role of Nurses in Issues in Nursing: Bonnie Bullough and Verne Bullough*, New York: Springer, 1966.

Schreiber, H. A.: On the failure to eradicate measles, *N. Engl. J. Med.*, Apr. 4, 1974, p. 804.

Scrimshaw, N. S., Guzman, M., Flores, M., and Gordon, J.: Nutrition and infection field studies, Guatemalan villages, 1959–64: V. Disease incidence among preschool children under natural village conditions, with improved diet, and with medical and public health service, *Arch. Environ. Health*, **16:**223, 1968.

Sklar, J. and Berkov, B.: The American birth rate: Evidence of a coming rise, *Science*, **189:**693, 1975.

Solnit, A. J., and Stark, M. H.: Mourning and the birth of a defective child, *Psychol. Stud. Child.*, **16:**523, 1961.

Weiss, P.: "The Biological Basis of Adaptation," in J. Romano (ed.), *Adaptation*, Ithaca, N.Y.: Cornell University Press, 1949.

White, K. L., Williams, T. F., and Greenberg, B. G.: The ecology of medical care, *N. Engl. J. Med.*, **265:**885, 1961.

White, K. L.: Life and death and medicine, *Sci. Am.*, **229:**23, 1973.

Wilson, E. O.: *Sociobiology: The New Synthesis*, Cambridge, Mass.: Harvard/Belknap, 1975.

Winick, M., Meyer, K. K., and Harris, R. C.,: Malnutrition and environmental enrichment by early adoption, *Science*, **190:**1173, 1975.

Wolff, P. H.: Mother-infant interactions in the first year, *N. Engl. J. Med.*, **295:**999, 1976.

Structure of the Pediatric Record

International Classification for Health Problems in Primary Care. American Hospital Association, Chicago, 1975.

Haggerty, R., Roghmann, K., and Pless, I. B.: *Child Health in the Community*, New York: Wiley, 1975.

Pless, I. B., and Pinkerton, P.: *Chronic Childhood Disorder—Promoting Patterns of Adjustment*, Kimpton, distr. by Year Book Med. Publ., Chicago, 1975.

Sacks, T. G., and Abramson, J. H.: Screening tests for bacteriuria, JAMA, **201:**79, 1967.

Weed, L. L.: *Medical records, medical education and patient care*, Cleveland: Press of Case Western Reserve University, 1969.

Use of the Information from the Data Base

Becker, M. H., Drachman, R. H., and Kirscht, J. P.: A field experiment to evaluate various outcomes of continuity of physician care, *Am. J. Pub Health*, **64:**1062, 1974.

Breslow, L., and Somers, A. R.: The lifetime health-monitoring program, a practical approach to preventive medicine, *N. Engl. J. Med.*, **296:**601, 1977.

Brook, R. H.: Quality—Can we measure it? *N. Engl. J. Med.*, **296:**170, 1977.

Brook, R. H., Davies-Avery, A., Greenfield, S., et al.: Quality of Medical Care Assessment Using Outcome Measures, Santa Monica: R-2021/1-3-HEW, Rand Corp., 1976.

Chamberlin, R.: Social data in evaluation of the pediatric patient: deficits in outpatient records, *J Pediatr.*, **78:**111, 1971.

Drake, D.: "Practical Essays on Medical Education." Quoted in *Familiar Medical Quotations*, Strauss, M. B. (ed.), Boston: Little, Brown and Co., 1968, p. 143.

Engel, G. L.: Enduring attributes of medicine relevant for the education of the physician, *Ann. Int. Med.*, **78:**587, 1973.

Farley, E. S., Jr., et al.: An integrated system for the recording and retrieval of medical data in a primary care setting. 1, 2. *J. Fam. Pract.*, **1:**44, 1974.

Feinstein, A. R.: An analysis of diagnostic reasoning. I. The domains and disorders of clinical macrobiology, *Yale J. Biol. Med.*, **46:**212, 1973. II. The strategy of intermediate decisions, *Yale J. Biol. Med.*, **46:**264, 1973.

Francis, V., Korsch, B. M., and Morris, M. J.: Gaps in doctor-patient communication, *N. Engl. J. Med.*, **280:**535, 1969.

Havighurst, R. J.: *Developmental Tasks and Education*, New York: McKay, 1972.

Heagarty, M. C., and Robertson, L. S.: Salve doctors and free doctors—a participant observer study of the physician-patient relation in a low-income comprehensive-care program, *N. Engl. J. Med.*, **284:**636, 1971.

Hulka, B. S., Kupper, L. L., Casset, J. C., et al.: Practice characteristics and quality of primary medical care: the doctor-patient relationship, *Med. Care*, **13:**808, 1975.

International Classification of Health Problems in Primary Care. Developed by the Classification Committee of the World Organization of National Colleges, Academies, and Academic Associations of General Practitioners/Family Physicians, Chicago: Am. Hosp. Assn., 1975.

Katz, M. M., Cole, J. O., and Lowery, H. A.: Studies of the diagnostic process: the influence of symptom perception, past experience, and ethnic background on diagnostic decisions, *Am. J. Psychiatr.*, **125:**109, 1969.

Linn, B. S., Linn, M. W., Greenwald, S. R., and Gurel, L.: Validity of impairment ratings made from medical records and from personal knowledge, *Med. Care*, **12:**363, 1974.

McNabb, N.: *The Goal-oriented Record* (unpublished manuscript), Rochester, New York: Monroe Developmental Center, 1975.

Martin, D.: "The Disposition of Patients from a Consultant General Medical Clinic: Result of a Controlled Evaluation of an Administrative Procedure." In White, K. L. (ed.), *Medical Care Research*, Oxford: Pergamon Press, 1965, p. 113.

Peabody, F. W.: The care of the patient, *J.A.M.A.*, **88:**877, 1972.

Perrin, J. M., Charney, E., MacWhinney, J. B., Jr., et al.: Sulfisoxazole as chemoprophylaxis for recurrent otitis media. A double blind crossover study in a pediatric practice, *N. Engl. J. Med.*, **291:**664, 1974.

Pinkerton, P., and Weaver, C. M.: "Childhood Asthma." In *Modern Trends in Psychosomatic Medicine*, 2d Series, London: Butterworth, 1970.

Platt, R.: Quoted in Strauss, M. B. (ed.), *Familiar Medical Quotations*, Boston: Little Brown and Co., 1968, p. 143.

Pless, I. B., and Pinkerton, P.: *Chronic Childhood Disorder—Promoting Patterns of Adjustment*, Kimpton, distributed by Year Book Med. Publ., Chicago, 1975.

Rogers, C. R.: The necessary and sufficient conditions of therapeutic personality change, *J. Consult. Psychol.*, **21:**95, 1957.

Simborg, D. W., et al.: Information factors affecting problem follow-up in ambulatory care, *Med. Care*, **14:**848, 1976.

Starfield, B. H., et al.: Continuity and coordination in primary care: their achievement and utility, *Med. Care*, **14:**625, 1976.

Starfield, B. H., and Borkowf, S.: Physicians' recognition of complaints made by parents about their children's health, *Pediatrics*, **43**:168, 1969.

Starfield, B. H., and Schaff, D.: Effectiveness of pediatric care: the relationship between processes and outcome, *Pediatrics*, **49**:547, 1972.

Subry, R.: *Results Management*, Applied Management Corporation, Denver, undated publication.

Thomas, A., Chess, S., Birch, H. G.: *Temperament and Behavioral Disorders in Children*, New York: New York Press, 1968.

Thompson, H. E., and Osborne, C. E.: Office records in the evaluation of quality of care, *Med. Care*, **14**:294, 1976.

Traux, C. B., and Carkhuff, R. R.: *Toward Effective Counseling and Psychotherapy: Training and Practice*, Chicago: Aldive, 1967.

Weed, L. L.: *Medical Records, Medical Education and Patient Care*, Cleveland: Press of Case Western Reserve University, 1969.

Zuckerman, A. E., et al.: Validating the content of pediatric outpatient medical records by means of tape-recording doctor-patient encounters, *Pediatrics*, **56**:407, 1975.

Current Morbidity and Mortality Among the Young

Aldrich, C. A.: The composition of private pediatric practice, *Amer. J. Dis. Child.*, **47**:1051, 1934.

Alpert, J. J., Robertson, L. S., Koza, J., Heagarty, M., and Haggerty, R. J.: Delivery of health care for children: Report of an experiment, *Pediatrics*, **57**:917, 1976.

Anderson, R. A.: *Behavioral Model of Families' Use of Health Services*, Chicago: Center for Health Administration Studies, Research Series, 1968.

Bergman, A. B., Dassel, S. W., and Wedgwood, R. J.: Time-motion study of practicing pediatricians, *Pediatrics*, **38**:254, 1966.

Breese, B. B., Disney, F. A., and Talpey, W.: The nature of small group practice, *Pediatrics*, **38**:264, 1966.

Breslow, L., et al.: *Preventive Medicine USA: Theory, Practice and Application of Prevention in Personal Health Services*, New York: PRODIST, 1976.

Boulware, J. R.: The composition of private pediatric practice in a small community in the south of the United States, *Pediatrics*, **22**:548, 1958.

Chabot, A.: Improved infant mortality rates in a population served by a comprehensive neighborhood health program, *Pediatrics*, **47**:989, 1971.

Chabot, M. J., Garfinkel, J., and Pratt, M. W.: Urbanization and differentials in white and non-white infant mortality, *Pediatrics*, **56**:777, 1975.

Forfar, J. O., and Arneil, G.: *Textbook of Paediatrics*, Edinburgh: Churchill Livingston, 1973.

Frappier-Davignon, L., Quevillon, M., and St. Pierre, J.: Etude de l'imunité des enfants de trois ans dans la province de Quebec, *L'Union Médicale du Canada*, **104**:1386, 1975.

Gorwitz, K., and Smith, D. C.: Some implications of declining birth rates for pediatrics, *Pediatrics*, **56**:592, 1975.

Hagberg, B., Hagberg, G., and Olow, J.: The changing panorama of cerebral palsy in Sweden, 1954–1970: I. Analysis of general changes, *Acta Paediatr. Scand.*, **64:**187, 1975.

Haggerty, R. J., Roghmann, K. J., Charney, E., and Klein, M.: "The Rochester Neighborhood Health Center" in R. J. Haggerty, K. J. Roghmann, and I. B. Pless (eds.): *Child Health and the Community*, New York: Wiley, 1975.

Hein, H. A., Christopher, M. C., and Ferguson, N. N.: Rural perinatology, *Pediatrics*, **55:**769, 1975.

Hessel, S. J., and Haggerty, R. J.: General pediatrics: A study of practice in the mid-sixties, *J. Pediatr.*, **73:**271, 1968.

Jacobziner, J., Rich, H., and Merchant, R.: Pediatric care in private practice, *J.A.M.A.*, **182:**986, 1962.

Kaplan, B. H., and Cassel, J. C.: *Family and Health: An Epidemiological Approach*, Chapel Hill: University of North Carolina Press, 1975.

Kohn, R., and White, K.: *Health Care: An International Study*, London: Oxford University Press, 1976.

Low, M. B., Presidential address—1976: Whither pediatrics, *Pediatrics*, **59:**499, 1977.

McDonald, A. D., McDonald, J. C., Salter, V., and Enterline, P.: Effects of Quebec Medicare on physician consultation for selected symptoms, *N. Engl. J. Med.*, **291:**649, 1974.

Miller, F. J. W., Dourt, S., Walton, W., and Knox, E. G.: "The Picture of Illness in the First Five Years" in *Growing Up in Newcastle Upon Tyne*, London: Oxford University Press, 1960.

Miller, F. J. W.: Childhood morbidity and mortality in Newcastle upon Tyne: A further report on the Thousand Family Study, *N. Engl. J. Med.*, **275:**683, 1966.

Pless, I. B.: The changing face of primary pediatrics, *Pediatr. Clin. North Am.*, **21:**1, 1974.

Pless, I. B., and Satterwhite, B.: "Chronic Illness," in R. J. Haggerty, K. J. Roghmann, and I. B. Pless (eds.): *Child Health in the Community*, New York: Wiley, 1975, p. 78.

Roghmann, K. J.: "The Utilization of Health Services," in R. J. Haggerty, K. J. Roghmann, and I. B. Pless (eds.): *Child Health and the Community*, New York: Wiley, 1975, p. 169.

Roghmann, K. J.: "Models of Health and Illness Behavior," in R. J. Haggerty, K. J. Roghmann, and I. B. Pless (eds.): *Child Health and the Community*, New York: Wiley, 1975, p. 119.

Roghmann, K. J. and Haggerty, R. J.: "The Stress Model for Illness Behavior," in R. J. Haggerty, K. J. Roghmann, and I. B. Pless (eds.): *Child Health and the Community*, New York: Wiley, 1975, p. 142.

Rosenbloom, A. L., and Ongley, J. P.: Who provides what services to children in private medical practice? *Am. J. Dis. Child.*, **127:**357, 1974.

Rosenstock, I. M.: Why people use health services, *Milbank Memorial Fund Quarterly*, Part 2, **44:**94, 1966.

Rutter, M., Tizard, J., and Whitmore, K.: *Education, Health and Behavior*, London: Longmans, 1970.

Schaefer, E. J., and Hughes, J. R.: Socioeconomic factors and maternal and child health care, *Med. Care,* **14:**535, 1976.

Siemiatycki, J.: *Evaluation of Survey Strategies,* unpublished doctoral thesis, Montreal: McGill University, 1976.

Suchman, E. A.: Social patterns of illness and medical care, *Journal of Health and Human Behavior,* **6:**2, 1965.

Wallace, H. M., and Goldstein, H.: The status of infant mortality in Sweden and the United States, *Pediatrics,* **87:**995, 1975.

Factors Influencing Child Health

Abelson, P. A.: Cost-effective health care, *Science,* **192:**424, 1976.

Alpert, J. J., Robertson, L. S., Cosa, J., Heagarty, M. C., and Haggerty, R. J.: Delivery of health care for children: Report of an experiment, *Pediatrics,* **67:**917, 1976.

Aranda, J. V., Cohen, S., and Neims, A. H.: Drug utilization in a newborn intensive care unit, *Pediatrics,* **89:**315, 1976.

Berwick, D. M.: The endurance of uncertainty, *Pediatrics,* **58:**148, 1976.

Boffey, P.: Swine flu vaccine: A component is missing, *Science,* **193:**1224, 1976.

Brockington, F.: *World Health,* 3d ed., Edinburgh: Churchill Livingstone, 1975.

Centennial Symposium on Human Genetics and Development, *Johns Hopkins Med. J.,* **138:**233, 1976.

Connors, C. K., Goyette, C. H., Southwick, D. C., Lees, J. M., and Andrulonis, P. A.: Food additives and hyperkinesis: A controlled double blind experiment, *Pediatrics,* **58:**154, 1976.

Culliton, B. J.: Biomedical training: Time for a slowdown, *Science,* **193:**747, 1976.

D'Ercole, J. A., Arthur, R. D., Cain, J. D., and Barrentine, B. S.: Insecticide exposure of mothers and newborns in a rural agricultural area, *Pediatrics,* **57:**869, 1976.

Donabedian, A., Axelrod, S. J., Swearingen, C., and Jameson, J.: *Medical Care Chart Book,* 5th ed., Ann Arbor: University of Michigan, 1972.

Doyle, A.: Incidence of illness in early group and family day care, *Pediatrics,* **58:**607, 1976.

Dubos, R.: *Mirage of Health,* Garden City, N.Y.: Doubleday/Anchor, 1959.

Favus, M. J., Schneider, A. B., Stachura, M. E., Arnold, J. E., Ryo, U. Y., Pinsky, S. M., Colman, M., Arnold, M. J., and Frohman, J. A.: Thyroid cancer occurring as a late consequence of head and neck irradiation: Evaluation of 1056 patients, *N. Engl. J. Med.,* **294:**1019, 1976.

Feingold, B. B.: *Introduction to Clinical Allergy,* Springfield, Ill.: Charles C Thomas, 1973.

Field, H. H.: "Environmental Design Implications of a Changing Health Care System," in W. H. Ittelson (ed.): *Environment and Cognition,* New York: Seminar Press, 1973.

Fisch, R. O., Bilek, M. K., Horrobin, J. M., and Chang, P. N.: Children with superior intelligence at 7 years of age, *Am. J. Dis. Child.,* **130:**41, 1976a.

Fisch, R. O., Bilek, M. K., Deinard, A. S., and Chang, P.: Growth, behaviorial, and psychological measurements of adopted children: The influences of genetic and socioeconomic factors in a prospective study, *J. Pediatr.*, **89:**494, 1976*b*.

Fuchs, V.: *Who Shall Live?: Health, Economics, and Social Choice*, New York: Basic Books, 1974.

Heagarty, M. C.: Life-style change: A difficult challenge, *Pediatrics*, **58:**314, 1976.

"HEW News (12/1/75) Quotes," *Pediatrics*, **58:**183, 1976.

Holtzman, N. A., Batshaw, M. L., and Valle, D. L.: "Genetic Aspects of Human Nutrition," in R. S. Goodhart and M. E. Shils (eds.): *Modern Nutrition in Health and Disease*, Philadelphia: Lea and Febiger, (in press).

Jacobi, A.: History of pediatrics and its relations to other sciences and arts, *Arch. Pediatr.*, **21:**801, 1904.

LaFramboise, H. L.: Health policy: Breaking it down into more manageable segments, *J. Can. Med. Asso.*, **108:**388, 1973.

Lalonde, M.: *A New Perspective on the Health of Canadians: A Working Document*, Ottawa: Information Canada, 1975.

McKeown, T.: *A Historical Appraisal of the Medical Task in Medical History and Medical Care*, Oxford: Oxford University Press, 1971.

McKeown, T.: An interpretation of the modern rise in population in Europe, *Popul. Stud.*, **XXVII:**345, 1972.

Meier, R. L.: A stable urban eco system, *Science*, **192:**4, 1976.

Miller, H. C., Hassanein, K., Chin, T. D. Y., and Hensleigh, P.: Socioeconomic factors in relation to fetal growth in white infants, *J. Pediatr.*, **89:**638, 1976.

Report of the Macy Foundation Commission on Physicians for the Future, New York: Josiah Macy, Jr., Foundation, 1976.

Rowe, N. H., Garn, S. M., Clark, D. C., and Guire, J. E.: The effect of age, sex, race, and economic status on dental caries experience of the permanent dentition, *Pediatrics*, **57:**457, 1976.

Sayre, J. W.: Children and child care in the United States: Some historical perspectives, *Am. J. Dis. Child.*, **130:**693, 1976.

Schoenbaum, S. C., McNeil, B. J., and Kauet, J.: The swine influenza decision, *N. Engl. J. Med.*, **295:**759, 1976.

Schumacher, E. F.: *Small Is Beautiful: Economics As If People Mattered*, New York: Harper & Row, 1973.

Snell, J. E., Ackenbach, P. R., and Peterson, S. R.: Energy conservation in new housing design, *Science*, **192:**1305, 1976.

Somers, A. R.: Violence, television, and the health of American youth, *N. Engl. J. Med.*, **294:**811, 1976.

Triseliotis, J.: *Search of Origins*, Boston: Beacon Press, 1973.

Valletuti, P. J.: "The Teacher's Role in the Diagnosis and Management of Students with Medical Problems," in R. A. Haslam and P. J. Valletutti (eds.): *Medical Problems in the Classroom: The Teacher's Role in Diagnosis and Management*, Baltimore: University Park Press, 1975, chap. 1.

Wade, N.: Recombinant DNA: A critic questions the right to free inquiry, *Science*, **194:**303, 1976.

Walsh, J.: Cosmetic standards: Are pesticides overused for appearance's sake? *Science,* **193:**744, 1976.

Wegman, M. E.: "Child Health and a Changing World," in J. A. Askin, R. E. Cooke, and J. A. Haller, Jr. (eds.): *Symposium on the Child,* Baltimore: Johns Hopkins Press, 1967.

Wegman, M. E.: Annual summary of vital statistics—1974, *Pediatrics,* **56:**960, 1976.

Weinstein, L.: Influenza—1918: A revisit? *N. Engl. J. Med.,* **294:**1058, 1976.

Wolman, A.: Ecologic dilemmas, *Science,* **193:**740, 1976.

Zill, N., and Brehm, O. G.: *Childhood Social Indicators,* New York: Report of Foundation of Child Development, 1975.

The Health Care Delivery System: Organization, Control, Costs, and Effectiveness

Childrens Defense Fund: *Doctors and Dollars Are Not Enough.* Washington: Washington Research Project, 1976.

Donabedian, A.: An evaluation of prepaid group practice. *Inquiry,* **VI:**3, 1969.

Davis, K., and Carney, M.: *Medical Care for Mothers and Children: The Title V Maternal and Child Health Program.* Washington: Brookings Institution, December 1974.

Harvard Child Health Project: *Toward a Primary Medical Care System Response to Children's Needs,* 3 vol., Cambridge, Mass.: Ballinger Publishing, 1977.

Prospects for Change in the Health Care of the Young

Alpert, J. J., and Charney, E.: *The Education of Physicians for Primary Care,* DHEW Publication (HRA) 74-3113, 1973.

Andersen, R., et al.: *Health Services Use: National Trends and Variations,* DHEW, 1972.

The Development of an Integrated Policy for Primary Care, Washington, D.C.: Institute of Medicine, National Academy of Sciences, 1976.

Dodds, R. W.: A framework for political mapping of conflict in organized medicine—especially pediatrics, *Med. Care,* **27:**1035, 1970.

Fink, D.: Holistic health: Implications for health planning, *Am. J. Health Planning,* **1:**23, 1976.

Haggerty, R. J.: The role of the university in education for family practice, *New Physician,* **18:**45, 1969.

Haggerty, R. J.: The boundaries of health care, *Pharos,* **35:**106, 1972.

Hansen, M. F., and Reeb, K. G.: An educational program for primary care, *J. Med. Educ.,* **45:**1001, 1970.

Hoekelman, R. A., et al.: Changing roles and relationships in the provision of child health care, *Am. J. Dis. Child.,* **127:**537, 1974.

Miller, C. A.: Health care of children and youth in America, *Am. J. Public Health,* **65:**353, 1975.

National Ambulatory Medical Care Survey: National Center for Health Statistics, 1974.

Roghmann, K. J., Haggerty, R. J., and Lorenz, R.: Anticipated and actual effects of medicaid on the medical care pattern of children, *N. Engl. J. Med.,* **285:**1053, 1971.

Silver, H. K., and McAtee, P. R.: A descriptive definition of the scope and content of primary health care, *Pediatrics,* **56:**957, 1975.

The Supply of Health Manpower, DHEW Publication (HRA) 75-38, 1974.

Swisher, S.: Oral communication, June 11, 1976.

Wallace, H. M., and Goldstein, H.: Child health care in the United States: Expenditures and extent of coverage with selected comprehensive services, *Pediatrics,* **55:**176, 1975.

White, K. L.: Medical care for children, *Am. J. Dis. Child.,* **116:**458, 1968.

PART TWO

Special Needs of Medically Ill Children and Adolescents

9 | Discussion of Diagnostic Findings

by Ruth Rockowitz, Philip W. Davidson, and Robert A. Hoekelman

One important goal of any diagnostic procedure is to facilitate choice of treatment and shed light on the prognosis. An extremely important component of this goal is conveying this information to the parents or advocates of the child, or to the child. In most clinical circumstances where the illness is minor or carries an excellent prognosis, such information is presented in a straightforward statement by the diagnostician to the patient or the advocates.

However, in some special circumstances, when dealing with gravely ill, severely handicapped, mentally retarded, learning disabled, or emotionally disturbed children, the situation becomes far more complex for clinicians, patients, and parents. In these special cases, the interpretive presentation must become a part of a broader counseling session which deals with feelings and emotions, as well as facts, in order to assure understanding of the information being shared.

This section will focus on the process of information sharing with parents or patient as an extension of the diagnostic process itself. This demands an equal degree of skill and precision and is necessary to increase the prospects for compliance with the proper treatment for the child. A set of basic principles for such counseling and a general outline that the clinician can follow will also be presented.

The goal of the interpretation of diagnostic findings is more than merely announcing technical information. The real objective of providing that information involves establishing a partnership between the provider and parents that will enhance the parents' capacity to respond appropriately to their child's illness and to comply with the recommended treatment. There is no one blueprint for building this very important relationship; however, interpretation of the physician's findings to parents, without unnecessary delay, is an essential part of case management, as is the need to pay attention to the family's expectations and questions initially and over time.

Kirkpatrick and his colleagues provide an in-depth analysis of the development of trust and the complicated trust-doubt-anger triangle which presents when parents are confronted with distressing information. This triangle may be further complicated when clinicians become frustrated by their inability to cure or "save" the child, when they know there are no local resources to deal with the child's problem, or when the parents ask questions they cannot answer.

A professional-parent relationship based upon the posture, "I have the information and I know what's best for your child," represents a basic misinterpretation of the kind of relationship between parent and clinician that is necessary when information about a complex and threatening illness has to be shared. Whereas diagnosis and treatment are biomedical, psychosocial, or educational matters, their presentation to parents is decidedly nonmedical—such presentation is itself a psychosocial process of interpersonal communication. It is inappropriate to assume that simply "having the information" or knowledge about "what's best" for the child is a sufficient condition for communicating diagnostic, therapeutic, and prognostic information to the parents.

To open a communication system effectively, clinicians must assure a two-way flow of information between parents and themselves; simply telling parents the facts of an evaluation does not guarantee that they hear or understand. Clinicians must communicate with the parents and the parents with them for an understanding to be achieved. Such a communication system can be described in general terms, but its effective implementation depends on careful individual planning and a reasonable investment of time.

Table 9-1 outlines a method for conducting an interpretive conference. The format outlines four major steps, each with equal importance, that are essential to an effective outcome. It is applicable for use when the child is evaluated by the clinician alone (physician, nurse, psychologist, social worker, educational specialist) or when several professionals have been involved in the diagnostic evaluation as members of an interdisciplinary team.

Preparation

Certain planning activities must be accomplished before the interpretive conference takes place to assure that the conference will achieve its purpose. The conference should occur as soon as possible after the examination and testing of the patient. The clinician(s) conducting the interpretive conference is best prepared, both emotionally and cognitively, immediately after the last visit or staffing conference, and parents are anxious to hear information about the outcome of the evaluation as soon as possible.

Should more than one professional be involved in the interpretive conference, the basic issue should be to assure that maximum communication will be established between parent and professionals while adequate professional expertise is available to ensure that most parental questions can be effectively answered. With certain conditions, such as mental retardation and learning or emotional disorders, the physician may not be included in the conference or may not be the primary spokesperson. In these circumstances, the psychologist, the special educator, or the social work clinician might ideally serve that role.

There are, of course, instances where the physician is viewed by the parents as an authority figure. The implication of this perception is that the creditability of a team that does not include the physician may be impaired. On the other hand, the physician need not automatically be cast in the role of leader at an interpretive conference unless the bulk of the information to be discussed is biomedical. In no case should the interpretation of technical material to parents be left in the hands of nonprofessionals or professionals whose lack of expertise will allow for parental misunderstanding. Also, the information should not be revealed by someone who did not participate in the diagnostic workup.

Once the team members have been selected, they should caucus long enough to organize the presentation of the conference, following the outline in Table 9-1. This planning session should allow enough time to assure that all the team members agree on the major information to be shared with the parents and that certain discipline-specific terminology is understood by all. Team members should also select a leader who will accept the role of actively structuring the interpretive conference. This is of paramount importance since organization of the conference is the key to satisfactory communication. The leader's responsibility is to control the flow of information both from professionals to parents and vice versa. Without such control, the conference will have only a minimal chance of establishing two-way communication. Control implies not just organization, but also a certain empathic sensitivity for the parents' feelings and reactions, so that emotional highs and lows can

Table 9-1
Interpretive Conference Format Outline

I   Entry pattern
   A Review of evaluation procedures conducted
   B Parents' and child's perceptions
   C Restatement of parental concerns
      1 Main worry
      2 Additional concerns
II   Presentation of findings
   A Encapsulation: brief overview
   B Reaction by parents and patient
   C Detailed findings
      1 Normal test results
        a Reactions
      2 Abnormal test results
        a Reactions
III Recommendations—only after time has been allowed for reactions
   A Restatement of concerns with both parents
   B Recommendations—one at a time
   C Reactions after each recommendation
   D Sharing with the child
IV   Summary
   A Repetition of findings, in varied wording if possible
   B Restatement by parents or patient
   C Planning for future contacts

---

be adequately recognized, permitted, and dealt with without disrupting the purpose of the conference.

The clinician planning to present the information alone should also plan the presentation ahead of time, following the same procedures recommended for the team. This is especially important for individual presentations since the individual has a more difficult task of control than does the group once the conference has begun. Under this circumstance the physician must continuously play the role of spokesperson, without having the flexibility of listening to another professional present information while organizing his or her own thoughts or "picking up" on others' lost points.

Conduct of Conference

Entry Pattern

The beginning of the interview often sets the tone for what follows. It is assumed that prior planning has included those physical requirements which create an empathetic climate, privacy, and freedom from interruption.

A review of what has been done diagnostically should be shared with a minimum of technical jargon so that parents will not be intimidated when asked to discuss their "main worry." During such a discussion a "hidden agenda" often surfaces, related either to the cause of the problem or to the problem itself. Therefore, before bringing the information to the parents, the parents' perception of the child and the child's current situation should be sought. For example, one might ask both parents, "How do you see your Mary's problem today?" Even if both parents have accompanied their child throughout the evaluation, each may have different knowledge about, and reactions to, what is happening. This is also an appropriate time to ask what they have been already told of their child's condition by others.

Presentation of Findings

Dwelling on technical data that do little to enhance the parents' understanding of their child's disorder accomplishes nothing and may interfere with establishment of good professional-parent communication. Presentation of such data only serves to confuse, rather than clarify, the parents' concerns. Especially when several different tests have been done in a lengthy, technical evaluation, it is helpful to parents to understand that the data presented are a summary compiled from the results of all those tests.

Some parents need a name for their child's illness or problem. There is a place for certain terminology in providing a technical name in order to avoid the use of a label such as epilepsy, learning disability, or mental retardation. If labels have not already been used, they may well be in the future by others. Most parents want honesty in an interpretive session and will resent ambiguous assurances which border on deception. For example, if a child has leukemia, the parents should be told that that is the diagnosis rather than given vague terms, such as blood dyscrasia or bone marrow dysfunction, to explain their child's illness.

Focusing on the parents' own perceptions of their child should be practiced when explaining findings, particularly as they may relate to their experiences with other children. Age or grade equivalents rather than ratio scores seem to be useful tools when it is necessary to convey the presence of developmental delay or immaturity. For example, one might say, "Your daughter seems in many ways to behave more like a 10-year-old than a 15-year-old," instead of, "Your daughter has an IQ of 55," or "Susan can read single words as well as most of the children in her fifth grade class, but she has difficulty storing and then applying her math facts. In math, she works more like a first grader," instead of, "Susan's test scores show scatter."

It is often said that after the parents hear the bad news, they hear very little else. For this reason, the actual presentation of findings should begin with areas of strength or normality. Abnormal findings, stated frankly but gently, should be restated more than once using different words to convey the same findings. Indeed, Gesell in emphasizing the relationship between empathy and honesty has stated: "No one can impart a grave diagnosis properly who cannot imagine the nature of the sorrow involved." Parental reaction to diagnosis of the problem should be encouraged and their feelings, once given, should be accepted, including the anger that is often directed at the clinician. Responses expressing shock, guilt, bereavement, and inadequacy are frequently seen in various intensities and combinations. Communication at this level is also influenced by sociocultural and educational level differences between the professional and the parents.

Recommendations

Specific information should be shared at a pace that can be handled emotionally and cognitively. Parents seldom feel comfortable asking for clarification of jargon, but if they are asked to restate their "main worry" and other worries, the recommendations can be made meaningful and relevant. Parents usually find it helpful when they receive recommendations that include, among other things, communication with other parents with a similar problem and referral elsewhere for help.

Recommendations are not complete until interpreter and both parents are able to reach a decision about what will be communicated to the child and who will do it. Parents' wishes, and the cognitive and emotional development of the child, are important considerations in deciding this very important issue.

Summary

After recommendations have been shared and before termination of the session, findings should be highlighted once again. One successful method for obtaining feedback is to ask parents to restate what they heard and what decisions were made. This method provides the professional with the parents' perception and understanding of the problem and allows for further clarification of the explanation if necessary.

Often more than one interpretive session is indicated. This can be further confirmed by arranging for parents to contact the clinician by telephone (at a definite time) when they have had time to think about, and react to, the information that was shared or when further questions and concerns arise. The session should be terminated only after the clinician has stated a willingness and ability to participate in a therapeutic alliance with the parents.

Discussion of diagnostic findings is a dynamic process that is an initial step in building a therapeutic milieu. The model presented here organizes a typically complex, often unwieldy, process which can easily end in a disastrous interaction between the professional and the parents and decrease chances for successful therapeutic intervention with the patient. If the clinical findings, diagnosis, and prognosis are clearly presented during the conference, the maintenance of two-way communication will be facilitated since both the professional and the parents can identify the limits of the situation and focus on the problems that can be dealt with successfully. This method of imparting information allows the professional to better relate to the parents and the parents to relate better to the professional, to facilitate immediate and future communication and compliance with recommendations made.

10 | Compliance with Recommendations

by John L. Ey

Compliance does not lend itself to easy definition. Even now it does not have a separate heading in the *Index Medicus*. While the terms "cooperative behavior," "med-errors," "defaulters," "dropouts," "adherence," and "therapeutic alliance" are employed to describe this aspect of medicine, "compliance" is still the most commonly used word. Sackett defines compliance as "the extent to which the patient's behavior coincides with the clinical prescription, regardless of how the latter is generated." Charney defines it by asking a simple question, "Has the patient followed the medical advice?"

Much effort has been made in developing, testing, and proving the effectiveness of drugs. Their clinical success depends ultimately on whether they are properly administered. Physician training emphasizes careful history taking, a thorough physical examination, and an accurate diagnosis and treatment. The prescription, which should represent the important final step of this process, is often not taken. Hippocrates warned us, "The physician must not only be prepared to do what is right himself, but also to make the patient, attendants, and externals cooperate." To achieve this, we must recognize and seek ways to deal with the problem of noncompliance. Frequently the physician is unaware of the problem.

Sackett and Haynes' book is an invaluable guide on compliance. They reviewed many studies on this subject and developed rigorous criteria in evaluating compliance studies. This section will concentrate primarily on the pediatric studies that deal with this problem.

General Overview

Compliant patients can be divided into roughly three groups: one-third take their medicine fully, one-third not at all, and the remaining third only partially. A large number of studies have examined a variety of demographic variables which affect compliance, such as age, education, sex, socioeconomic status, and race. With only a few exceptions, these factors have not been helpful indicators of noncompliance. However, we can make a few generalizations. Private patients have a better compliance rate than clinic patients. Acutely ill patients do better than chronically ill ones, but the change in compliance in the acutely ill may drop dramatically in the course of a few days. Patients with symptoms are more likely to take their medicine, while those with complex regimens of three or more medicines more frequently fail to comply. On the positive side, a stable family, a warm, long-standing relationship with the physician, and a recognition of the seriousness of the illness on the patient's or parents' part all appear to help in achieving compliance. Haynes, in 1976, compiled a list of "confirmed" noncompliance factors (see Table 10-1).

To fully recognize the merits of each study on compliance, one may utilize the criteria developed by Sackett and Haynes. These include the following methodologic standards:

1 Study design (randomized trial versus descriptive)

2 Selection and specification of the study sample (multipopulation sample versus a single clinic sample)

Table 10-1
"Confirmed" Factors Associated with Noncompliance

Factor Category	Specific Factors
Disease	Psychiatric diagnosis
Regimen	Complexity
	Degree of behavioral change
	Duration
Therapeutic source	Inefficient and inconvenient clinics
Patient-therapist interaction	Inadequate supervision
	Patient dissatisfaction
Patient	Inappropriate health beliefs
	Previous or present noncompliance with other regimens
	Family instability

Source: R. B. Haynes, "A Critical Review of the 'Determinants' of Patient Compliance with Therapeutic Regimens," in D. L. Sackett and R. B. Haynes, *Compliance with Therapeutic Regimens,* Baltimore: Johns Hopkins, 1976.

3 Specification of the illness or conditions (replicable diagnostic criteria versus none)

4 Description of the therapeutic regimen (complete description versus none)

5 Definition of compliance (replicable definition versus none)

6 Compliance measures (objective direct measures versus subjective measures)

By using their point scores in evaluating compliance studies, one can recognize those studies which are well designed and those which are not.

Keeping these criteria in mind, we will review the compliance problem in terms of its incidence, the possible risk factors involved, its variance in acute and chronic illness, its predictability, and those techniques which may enable one to detect "takers" and "nontakers."

Incidence of Compliance

Recent reviews have shown that complete failure to take medication occurs in between one quarter and one half of all outpatients. In one study, only 18 percent of patients in a clinic population completed a 10-day course of penicillin, while another, conducted in private practice settings, showed that 56 percent did so. Other studies have shown a much higher rate of compliance, but most of these have used indirect methods to determine this.

Etiology

One must ask why so many patients fail to follow the physician's instructions and what factors can be used to separate those who will take their medicine from those who will not. Risk factors have some bearing upon noncompliance. Patient age has not shown close correlation with compliance. Only 7 of 37 studies that Sackett reviewed showed that the young were more compliant than the old. No consistent difference in compliance was found between the sexes. Socioeconomic status, level of education, religion, and race did not prove to be good predictors of the compliant person. Family studies have not shown any consistent pattern except that large, disorganized families are more likely to fail to follow instructions.

Others have shown that if the mother feels the illness is serious, the child is more likely to be a "taker." To date, no study has shown higher compliance when the physician alone felt the illness was serious.

In the case of oral penicillin prophylaxis for rheumatic fever, certain risk factors can be identified as relating to noncompliance. Thus, noncompliance is more likely in females, in adolescents, in large sibships, when hospitalization is not required, when there is no restriction of activity, and when patients are unaccompanied by their parents at clinic visits. Gordis demonstrated that the probability of noncompliance was 90 percent when four or more of these factors were present. This information can be used to determine priorities for alternate approaches to management, such as using benzathine penicillin for both treatment and prophylaxis.

Mohler demonstrated that patients failed to take their full course of penicillin for an acute streptococcal tonsillitis because they felt well (37 percent), they were careless (27 percent), they had insufficient money to purchase the medication (17 percent), they refused to swallow tablets (11 percent), and they misunderstood the instructions (8 percent).

Compliance Studies

Studies on compliance in the pediatric age group can be divided into those which address acute illness, those which address chronic illnesses, and those concerned with prophylaxis. Charney studied three private practices in Rochester, New York, to see how well patients completed a 10-day course of penicillin for streptococcal tonsillitis and otitis media. The study was strengthened by its use of direct urine testing for penicillin rather than relying upon parent interviews or pill counting. Preliminary testing did not reveal any increased compliance by using the urine measurement method. Children with tonsillitis completed the full course more frequently (66 percent) than those with otitis media (51 percent). His study examined a large number of disease, drug, patient, family, and physician factors, but defined only four features which could be used to differentiate "takers" from "nontakers." These were (1) the mother's perception of how serious the illness was, (2) whether the patient was seen by his or her regular doctor rather than a substitute, (3) how long the patient had been cared for by the physician, and (4) certain personality characteristics of the mother relating to responsibility and clear thinking as perceived by the doctor.

Korsch studied the outcome of visits for acute illnesses to a pediatric emergency room. She found that 42 percent of the parents carried out all the doctor's advice, while 11 percent failed completely. Compliance was more favorable when the mother was satisfied with the visit.

Gordis, Markowitz, and Lilienfeld, in reporting on secondary prophylaxis in rheumatic fever, stressed the problem of continued compliance in taking medicine for chronic childhood illnesses. In assessing oral penicillin taking at home, they compared the use of interviews versus serial urine testing as measures of compliance and found that mothers and their children who claimed compliance consistently overstated the amount of penicillin taken. On the other hand, admitted noncompliers and poor compliers did better than they claimed.

Gordis asked why patients did not follow medical advice. His results suggested increased compliance when there is a need to hospitalize, when there is a need to restrict activity, and when a confirmed diagnosis of rheumatic heart disease is made. Other studies show that recognition of the seriousness of the illness is associated with increased compliance. Paradoxically, Gordis found that 73 percent of the noncompliers' parents believed another attack of rheumatic fever was possible in contrast to 58 percent of the compliers' parents. Possibly, the noncompliers were more concerned about a repeat illness because they knew that their children were not taking their medicines.

Physician Prediction of Compliance

Charney found that the physician's ability in predicting patient compliance is no more reliable than mere chance. He did show, however, that physicians could identify certain characteristics of the compliant children's mothers. An adjective checklist completed by the physicians to describe the mothers found such terms as "responsible," "organized," "efficient," and "clear thinking" to be significantly correlated with the "takers." Mushlin examined the ability of residents in internal medicine to predict patients' compliance in keeping appointments and taking medicine. Their predictions concerning follow-up appointments were better than chance, while for medication compliance, they were correct less than one-half of the time. Physicians were unable to predict noncompliance in three-fourths of the patients. These studies suggest that the physician has great difficulty in knowing who will or will not follow directions.

Methods of Measurement

Since we are limited in our ability to predict compliance, we need to rely on some means for measuring it accurately. Current techniques of measurement can facilitate the recognition of compliance and whether or not a sufficient amount of drug is being taken. Gordis gives us a listing of direct and indirect measures of compliance in Table 10-2.

Measuring antibiotic in the urine by the inhibition of the bacteria *Sarcina lutea* has been shown to be an accurate assay of penicillin intake with a high sensitivity and specificity. Similarly, serum levels of theophylline, diphenylhydantoin, and phenobarbital can help confirm compliance. Indirect techniques such as medicine measurement (pill counts) may not be reliable (see Table 10-3). Future compliance studies must be longitudinal and include direct measurements of medicine taking to provide an accurate assessment. The physician should consider these direct measurements before stopping or changing a medication. Once there is confirmation that the drug is being taken, the physician needs to retest this over time. These direct measurements will become more available, less expensive, and less cumbersome, providing the physician with a useful tool in patient management.

Table 10-2
Direct and Indirect Measures of Compliance

Direct Measures
1 Blood levels of
  a Medication
  b Metabolite
  c Marker
2 Urinary excretion of
  a Medication
  b Metabolite
  c Marker

Indirect Measures
1 Therapeutic or preventive outcome
2 "Impression" of physician (predictability)
3 Patient interview
4 Filling of prescription
5 Pill-count
6 Metabolic consequence of taking a specific drug*

*Directly measurable effects of the drug, such as the serum potassium levels in hypertensive patients taking thiazides, rather than the therapeutic outcome, that is, a reduction in blood pressure.
Source: L. Gordis, "Methodologic Issues in the Measurement of Patient Compliance," in D. L. Sackett and R. B. Haynes, *Compliance with Therapeutic Regimens,* Baltimore: Johns Hopkins, 1976.

Doctor-Patient Relationship

Korsch and Francis have examined doctor-patient relationships by video-taping patient interviews. They discovered that those mothers expressing the greatest satisfaction with their visit had the highest compliance rate. Failure to relieve the mother's anxiety or to answer her concerns can lead to noncompliance. Time spent in the interview process was not a major factor. Open-ended questions, the elimination of medical jargon, and the recognition of the mother as an individual help to establish a successful visit. Charney found that if the patient was seen by his or her own physician instead of a substitute, a higher compliance rate occurred. This suggests that a warm doctor-patient relationship sometimes fails to carry over to a medical partner. Charney advises us that "thus far we have been more concerned to measure the warmth of the patient (degrees centigrade) than the warmth of the doctor (degrees empathy)." If a warm relationship and consideration of the mother's concerns are not accomplished, Yudkin's "second diagnosis," the real reason for the visit, is often missed.

To evaluate the relationships among comprehensive care, continuity of care, and compliance, Gordis and Markowitz evaluated two groups of patients: (1) newborns of adolescent mothers and (2) rheumatic fever patients. In the first part of the study a team consisting of a pediatrician, nurse, and social worker was available for complete care in comparison with matched controls who sought care wherever they could find it. A number of health care variables were examined. Only the level of polio immunization showed significant improvement in the study group. There was no difference in the morbidity or mortality of the two groups. In the second portion of the study two physicians provided complete continuous medical care for a group of rheumatic fever patients. The matched controls were seen in a specialty clinic solely for their rheumatic fever problems. Figure 10-1 demonstrates that after being followed for 1 year both groups showed a rise in noncompliance. Although reason dictates that continuity of care should increase compliance, this has not always been shown to be the case.

Methods Used to Improve Compliance

Several studies have demonstrated ways to improve compliance in appointment keeping, treatment for acute illness, and treatment for chronic illness.

Broken appointments are a significant problem and affect the use of personnel, physicians' time, costs, and of course, patient care. This problem has been especially prominent in clinic populations. One

Table 10-3
Comparison of Compliance Estimated by Urine Test and Pill-Count in Children Prescribed 10 Days of Penicillin

	Percent Complying	
On Day	Urine Test	Pill-Count
3	46	44
6	31	29
9	8	18

Source: L. Gordis, "Methodologic Issues in the Measurement of Patient Compliance," in D. L. Sackett and R. B. Haynes, *Compliance with Therapeutic Regimens,* Baltimore: Johns Hopkins, 1976. Adapted from A. B. Bergman and R. J. Werner, Failure of children to receive penicillin by mouth, *N. Engl. J. Med.* **268:**1334, 1963.

Figure 10-1 A comparison of percent of noncompliance in the continuous care group ($n = 39$) and the specialty clinic group ($n = 38$) before and after the study period. (From L. Gordis and M. Markowitz, Evaluation of the effectiveness of comprehensive and continuous pediatric care, *Pediatrics,* **48:**766, 1971.)

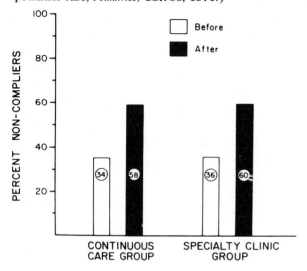

Table 10-4

Keep Rate by Reminder Groups*

Group†	Number of Appointments	Keep Rate, %
No card sent	228	48
Card A (date, time)	216	67
Card B (date, time, doctor/ nurse, reason)	219	61
Cards A and B combined	435	64

* Keep rate = kept plus canceled appointments, divided by kept plus canceled plus broken appointments.

† Difference between control group and group receiving cards is significant ($x^2 = 16.92$; $p < 0.001$). Difference between card A and card B is not significant.

Source: L. F. Nazarian, et al., Effect of a mailed appointment reminder on appointment keeping, *Pediatrics,* **53:**349, 1974.

neighborhood health center used mailed reminder cards for patients scheduled for return appointments 12 days to 8 weeks following their initial visit. Two types of reminder cards were used: one simply gave the date and time of the appointment; the other listed the time, the date, the reason for the visit, and the name of the provider the patient was to see. The cards were sent 1 week before the scheduled visit. Patients who received either type of reminder showed a significant improvement in attendance rates compared with patients who received no card (see Table 10-5).

In examining the purpose of these appointments, it was found that well-baby visits and follow-up of acute noninfectious illnesses were most significantly improved in appointment keeping.

While these studies are encouraging, there are still large numbers of appointment failures. These failures include children with serious illnesses needing close follow-up such as severe anemia, lead poisoning, failure to thrive, and child abuse. In New Haven, Connecticut, medical student outreach workers were used to contact patients with extremely low (39 percent) keep rates. The student personally visited the patients, arranged their appointments,

and helped to solve baby-sitting and transportation problems. These efforts increased the keep rate for these patients to 95 percent.

Improved compliance for acute illness treatment with short-term antibiotic regimens has been demonstrated with the use of some unique reminders. These include a clock depicted on the medicine bottle label indicating the times the medication is to be taken and a very large, brightly colored sticker placed on the refrigerator or medicine cabinet door stating the dose and time instructions. Each of these reminders was prepared by the pharmacist, who had determined beforehand that the medication schedule was convenient for the family. For the clock and sticker groups a significant rise in compliance was seen (see Table 10-5). Children showed more im-

Table 10-5

Effectiveness of Compliance Reminders

Amount of Medication Taken	Control		Clock		Sticker	
	No.	%	No.	%	No.	%
70% or more	15	28	24	53	37	62
Less than 70%	38	72	21	47	23	38

Control versus clock: $x^2 = 5.4$; $p < .025$
Control versus sticker: $x^2 = 11.3$; $p < .005$

Source: J. Lima, et al., Compliance with short term antimicrobial therapy: Some techniques that help, *Pediatrics,* **57:**383, 1976.

Figure 10-2 Hypothesized model for predicting and explaining compliance behavior. (From M. H. Becker, "Socio-behavioral Determinants of Compliance," in D. L. Sackett and R. B. Haynes, *Compliance with Therapeutic Regimens,* Baltimore: Johns Hopkins, 1976.)

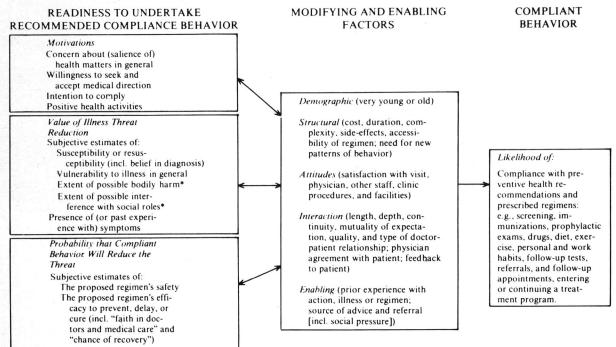

provement in compliance than did adult patients. The pharmacist was mentioned most often as the source of information on how to take the medicine. This study suggests that while these reminders appear to be helpful, the extra time spent by the pharmacist may have been equally valuable.

Compliance in the treatment of chronic illness is, perhaps, the most difficult problem the primary care physician is called upon to manage. Seizure disorders, asthma, and cystic fibrosis are chronic pediatric disorders the primary care physician will need to address. Blood levels of theophylline, diphenylhydantoin, and phenobarbital and antibiotic excretion in the urine are direct measurements to compliance that can be useful in monitoring the treatment of these disorders.

In a recent study of theophylline levels in asthmatics, it was demonstrated that saliva levels of theophylline correlated closely with blood serum levels. In a preliminary study it was found that only

11 percent of 43 patients achieved therapeutic theophylline levels in saliva, while 23 percent had no detectable theophylline. In a subsequent group of patients, physicians were more directive in giving therapeutic instructions and parents were made aware that compliance was being measured. Under these circumstances, 42 percent achieved therapeutic saliva levels, while only 6 percent had none, and the median level for the group increased. Thus, careful instructions given the patient or parent by the physician may well improve compliance.

Seizure control has been aided with determinations of serum phenobarbital and diphenylhydantoin levels. One study found that only 25 percent of 30 children tested had adequate anticonvulsant levels of these drugs. A program designed to test serum levels frequently and to provide closer supervision improved the compliance rate to 85 percent.

Not all patients with chronic illnesses are poor compliers. One study of cystic fibrosis patients found an 80 percent compliance in the use of antibiotics. This suggests that the patient's or the parent's recognition of the severity of the disease was realistic. However, 39 percent of these patients were found to have taken antibiotics when they had not been prescribed. Thus, one must be concerned with overmedication as well as with compliance.

The Health Belief Model

The health belief model is somewhat complex, but has proved of value in understanding compliance. The model separates those factors which are influential in the readiness of a patient to undertake compliant behavior, those which are modifying and enabling factors, and the end points of compliant behavior (see Fig. 10-2). Becker and his colleagues have tested this model in a pediatric clinic for children with otitis media. This guide was able to identify characteristics of compliant mothers, such as concern about their child's illness, their recognition of its seriousness, and their awareness of ways to improve their child's general health.

This model could be used to develop a questionnaire to identify those patients in need of help in compliance. More studies of this model of patients of different populations in differing conditions are needed.

In planning treatment of patients, physicians need to consider all aspects of compliance. Several methods designed to increase compliance may be used with reasonable expectations of improvement; however, the most important factor operative in increasing compliant behavior is the establishment of a warm, open communication between the physician and the patient. Recognizing this, the physician or other health care provider must take every step to ensure that such a relationship is established.

11 | The Acutely Ill Child

by Marianne Felice

Great strides have been made in the prevention, diagnosis, and treatment of childhood illnesses in the past fifty years, but children continue to become ill. Illnesses today are different, however, from those of past years and to a great extent represent chronic illnesses that in the past were fatal. Hence, the sick child and his family continue to consume major fractions of the pediatrician's time, talents, and energy although his specific knowledge and skills should reflect the changing patterns of childhood health and disease.

A discussion of the management of the ill child must encompass a variety of topics including the degree and duration of illness, issues of hospitalization and the medical delivery system, family support systems, the emotional components of physical illness, and, finally, the problem of the dying child.

THE ACUTELY ILL CHILD AT HOME

Whenever possible, the ill child should be treated at home surrounded by a familiar environment and tended by a responsible, caring adult who knows him well. Fortunately, this is the *usual* case, rather than the exception, since most youngsters are only mildly to moderately ill for a brief period and have their parents, extended family members, or reliable, familiar baby-sitters available to them. However, the pediatrician should not always presume this adult attendance exists. In deciding to treat a child at home, the physician should specifically seek the answers to the following questions: Who will assume responsibility for the child while he is ill? Is a telephone easily available? Are medical facilities reasonably nearby? Above all, do the parents understand the nature of the child's illness and the instructions which have been given? The answer to the last question should be verified by having one or both parents repeat the instructions to the physician.

Fathers should be encouraged to have a more active participation in their children's health care. Often, mothers assume full responsibility for the children's health, and fathers are ignored so that they cannot support either the mother or the child. This leaves the mother in the difficult position not only of tending to the child but of having to repeat the physician's explanations and directions to her husband, a situation which is often the source of misunderstanding, misinterpretation, and resentment for both parents. When a child has a significant illness, the pediatrician should encourage both parents to bring the child to the physician whenever possible, and the physician should relate directions and explanations to both parents simultaneously. In this way, parents can share the task of caring for their sick child and support one another.

Treating an ill child at home is an opportune time for the pediatrician to teach parents about medications. If a prescription is written, the physician should explain the name of the drug, why it is being given, and the common side effects that should be anticipated. Antibiotic prescriptions frequently result in low compliance; parents begin to give antibiotics and then stop giving the medication when the child starts to feel better, usually after 24 to 48 h of treatment. Parents may need to be told that many types of infections require a full course of antibiotic therapy. When a medication is discontinued by a physician before all the pills, capsules, or liquid are finished, the parents should be advised about what to do with the unused portion. For example, those medications which decompose with time, such as tetracycline, should be discarded, but other medications, such as antihistamines, may be used again at a later date. Parents should be reminded to store medications safely. Parents also should be taught which over-the-counter drugs they should have available, such as baby aspirin and ipecac syrup, and instructions should be given about using them. Physicians may also educate parents by teaching them the proper administration of medications. The familiar "1 teaspoon four times a day" results in varied quantities of medicine from one home to the next if careful directions are not given. Some parents may need practical hints for aiding a child to take an unpalatable medicine, for example, crushing an aspirin in applesauce.

In most families, there is a tradition of myths and home remedies for common acute illnesses, and parents will often turn to these ideas when their children are ill. Again, this is the opportune time for parent education. For example, in talking to the parent of the child with an upper respiratory tract infection, it is often appropriate to explain that the youngster did *not* "catch cold" by not wearing his galoshes in the rain. In explaining the management of fever, a physician may wish to emphasize certain *do nots* in an effort to dispel misconceptions: *Do not* give enemas to bring down fever; *do not* give cold baths to bring down fever. Some myths and home remedies are peculiar to certain communities and cultures, and each pediatrician should try to be familiar with the traditions of the locality (see Sec. 7).

In this age of widespread immunization programs, issues of contagion are often neglected. Parents should be informed of the infectious nature of certain childhood illnesses in order to protect other siblings, pregnant female relatives, and the elderly. The most common examples are protecting pregnant relatives from German measles or protecting those on steriods or immunosuppressive drugs from children with chickenpox.

Children acutely ill at home often pose problems for the parents caring for them. A mother is usually unaccustomed to seeing her normally active toddler listless and resting. She may feel compelled to entertain the child without realizing that the child may have a need for rest and is not in the mood for entertainment or love. On the other hand, many parents may try to restrain a child and insist on bed rest when the child feels well enough to play. Parents need to be reminded that children gauge their own activity level when they are ill. Parents also have a tendency to overfeed children, particularly when they are sick, and must be reassured that if a child drinks appropriate fluids, this is sufficient during a brief illness.

Parents understandably become quite anxious when their children are ill, and this anxiety may result in frequent telephone calls to the pediatrician. The physician may perceive such calls as unneeded and annoying without appreciating how frightened parents may be. New parents particularly require support during children's illnesses, and the pediatrician should patiently teach the parents when it is appropriate to call and when it is not. Pediatricians should not frighten parents into *not* calling and reporting on their children's progress. When a physician decides to treat a child at home, arrangements should be made for follow-up, either in terms of a telephone conversation or another office visit, and the importance of such follow-up visits should be well explained to the parent.

HOSPITALIZATION OF THE ACUTELY ILL CHILD: INDICATIONS FOR HOSPITALIZATION

It is not always feasible or safe to treat an acutely ill child at home; hospitalization may become necessary. *Whom* to hospitalize and *when* to hospitalize are not always clear-cut issues. Children critically or seriously ill are obvious candidates for inpatient care. Children *not* seriously ill also must be considered for hospitalization if the home environment is such that the child will not receive adequate care. Some hospitalizations, however, can be averted by tapping available community resources such as public health nurses, homemaker services, and medical home care programs. This not only may be far more economical, but also allows the child and parents to remain in their home environment.

In teaching hospitals, children with unusual diseases may at times be admitted to the hospital as teaching cases. At times, this results in a child's receiving expensive services and laboratory tests. Even though such a child usually receives good medical care, physicians should carefully weigh the advantages of medical research and medical education against the psychologic trauma of an unnecessary hospitalization for a youngster and the added expense to parents.

It is sometimes necessary to hospitalize children for appropriate diagnostic work-ups. Most diagnostic procedures can be accomplished on an outpatient basis, and should be done in this way as often as possible. Occasionally, a child requires numerous or complicated tests or clinical observation, and it may be more efficient to admit him for a few days for evaluation. When this occurs, the pediatrician should schedule the admission carefully, utilizing as few hospital days as possible, for example, by postponing an admission from Friday to Monday if none or only a few tests can be performed over the weekend.

Some children require elective surgical procedures. In recent years the literature has reflected an emphasis on the timing of these procedures. This emphasis on timing has been based on the observation that between the ages of 4 and 7, children seem to be dramatically concerned about body integrity.

Psychiatrists refer to this as *mutilation anxiety*, or *castration anxiety*. Some authorities have recommended that elective surgery *not* be done during those years of psychosocial development. In actual clinical practice, however, it is usually not feasible to postpone surgical procedures for 3 or 4 years. An alternative approach is to delay surgery only long enough to explain to the child what is going to happen to him. This should be done gradually with age-appropriate language, and the parents should be utilized as the primary supportive resources.

Unfortunately, children are sometimes admitted to the hospital primarily for the convenience of the physician. After receiving a late call from the parents, the pediatrician typically has the child admitted in the middle of the night and attended by a pediatric house staff on call, thus avoiding having to examine the child at that time. The pediatrician should look into the "real" reason for ordering the hospitalization and avoid doing so for personal convenience.

12 | Care of the Child in the Hospital

by Marianne Felice and Stanford B. Friedman

When a child is admitted to the hospital, the child and the family become enmeshed in an unfamiliar and often frightening web known as the *medical delivery system.* To the lay person, hospital activities are unpredictable, and there is a loss of control over the immediate environment. In this milieu, both the child and parents may express their fear in several ways. The child may cry, be "uncooperative." The child is afraid of being separated from his parents, afraid of pain, afraid of the strange environment and strange people, and afraid of the unknown. Parents may become hostile or agitated or constantly question the health team. They realize that their child's care is being usurped from them, and they are afraid that they no longer can care for or protect *their* child. They too are afraid of the strange people and the unknown environment. Usually, there are no facilities for parents on the pediatric floor, and often not even a waiting area.

The supportive role of the parents in helping a child to get well must be emphasized, and the parents should be assured that they are needed and welcomed on the pediatric floor. In the maze of hospital personnel who encounter the youngster, the parents should have one person consistently available with whom they can communicate and from whom they can expect answers concerning their child's care. This person is usually the primary care physician. The primary care physician should report at least daily to the parents, and more often if the child is critically ill. Whenever possible, information should be given to both parents at the same time. They then have the opportunity to ask questions, and neither parent is required to interpret the physician's remarks to the other.

In this age of specialization, it is common for a youngster to have one or even multiple consultants during hospitalization. It is vital that the child and the parents be notified that a consultation has been requested and the reason for it be explained. Communication between the pediatrician and the consultant should be made clear before the consultant sees the child so that the parents do not receive conflicting or confusing reports from more than one person. The following case vignette is illustrative of confusion around the process of consultation.

Gary was a 10-year-old obese white male child admitted to the hospital for a diagnostic work-up of recent onset of "spells" consisting of his becoming dizzy and falling down. The degree of consciousness after each episode was unclear. On the day of hospital admission, the child appeared to vacillate between near coma with insensitivity to pain to aggressive fighting behavior. Physical examination disclosed no abnormal finding. All studies were negative except an equivocal EEG. Neurologic consultation was requested without the child's or parents' knowledge. The neurologist told the mother that the child probably had a form of seizure disorder and that medication would be recommended to the pediatrician.

The nurses noted that the child seemed quiet and did not play with other children, and a child psychiatry consultation was requested. Because the pediatrician feared the mother would object to psychiatry, she was told simply that "another doctor" would be talking to her son. The psychiatrist arrived on the ward and introduced himself to the mother as a psychiatrist. The mother said she was confused. While the psychiatrist talked to Gary, the mother was told to wait in the hall until the psychiatrist's interview was over. A few minutes later, the mother went to the nurses' station and demanded to see her son's pediatrician, who was paged but did not answer. The child psychiatrist returned to the mother and said that Gary appeared to be depressed and that he would return the following day to take the boy to the playroom to complete the evaluation. The mother began shouting at the nurses about the quality of care in the hospital.

This case vignette illustrates the importance of good communication between the primary physician and the consultants. Such problems can be easily avoided if the primary physician and the consultant speak together prior to the consultant's seeing the patient to decide who discusses the consultant's findings with the child and/or the family (see Fig. 12-1).

Just as it is important to communicate with parents, it is important to communicate with the child, no matter what the child's age. This communication may sometimes take the form of actions rather than words. For example, it is more comforting to a toddler to be *held* for reassurance than to hear *words* of reassurance. In speaking to a child, it is important for the pediatrician to remember to sit down and be on the child's eye level. It is also important to use age-appropriate words when speaking to a child in order to ensure that the child understands what is to be done and to allow an opportunity to ask questions. Procedures should be explained to youngsters, and it is important to be honest. For example, if a child is to have blood drawn and asks if it will hurt, admit that it will hurt for a few moments. In this manner, the youngster learns to trust hospital personnel. All painful procedures should be performed as quickly and gently as possible. In some institutions it is appropriate to have a special treatment room in which a child receives all painful procedures so that the ward or hospital room is not associated with the unpleasant experience.

It is common practice in teaching hospitals to have all medical students rotate through the pediatric service. All students, regardless of their career interests, are then taught pediatric procedures such as starting IVs, drawing blood, and performing spinal taps and bone marrow aspirations by practicing on young patients. This may result in unnecessary pain for a child. These procedures must be learned, of course, by students interested in pediatrics, but they will have ample opportunity to learn these tasks as first-year house officers. We should reevaluate our pediatric teaching programs and consider whether *all* students need to master pediatric procedures at the expense of infants and children, and their parents.

Children having surgery should have the surgical procedure explained to them. It is sometimes appropriate to explain surgical procedures with the use of dolls, by having the physician place a bandage on the doll similar to the future bandage of the patient. They should be told where they will be when they awaken and who will be there. If a child is expected to be returned to an intensive care unit after major surgery, the intensive care nurses should visit the child prior to the surgery.

In preparation for anesthesia, the child should be forewarned about the anesthesia mask and the odor of the gas. Many physicians find that the presence of parents during induction and recovery phases of anesthesia helps to alleviate much fear and fantasy for both parents and child.

It is generally accepted that children admitted to hospitals are best placed on pediatric units especially designed for children and staffed by personnel trained to care for children. In large children's centers, children may be assigned to wards by age and type of medical problem. In community hospitals, children are usually assigned to wards by age alone, and in smaller hospitals all ages may be assigned to one pediatric ward. Any of these arrangements are appropriate. In many hospitals, there are no facilities for adolescent patients, and teenagers are admitted to the adult wards. For a few older adolescents, those near adulthood, this may be acceptable, but for younger and some older adolescents, such an arrangement may be detrimental to their care. Whenever possible, adolescents should be placed together in a setting designed for their needs.

Figure 12-1 Relationship between the primary care physician and all consultants.

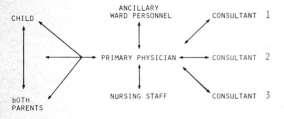

For young children particularly, separation from their parents is a painful experience. In these instances, rooming-in policies are strongly recommended until the child adjusts to the hospitalization. The question of visiting hours and who may visit are important issues in pediatrics. Policies regarding these questions should be made on the basis of what is best for the child and the family, and not what is most convenient for the hospital personnel.

The question is often raised whether or not it is more beneficial for a child to have a private room or be with other children. Certainly, this issue must be individualized for every patient and weighed in accordance with the patient's needs and illness. Parents often have fantasies that their child will receive better care if placed in a private room, and *if* this is not true, it should be communicated to the parents. As a general rule, children should have as much contact with other children as is medically feasible.

Upon hospitalization, children often regress in development. A common example is a regression in toilet training. Parents need reassurance that this phenomenon may occur because of the strange and frightening hospital environment. Neither children nor adolescents are accustomed to medical terminology to describe urination and defecation, and they may hesitate to express these needs to nurses. Parents are of invaluable assistance in clarifying these terms. It is also important to respect a child's or adolescent's need for privacy in completing his toilette, in dressing or undressing, or when being examined. Hospital personnel are sometimes unintentionally insensitive to a child's embarrassment, and may neglect to pull curtains around the bed when the child is undressing or to draw a sheet over the naked genitals when the abdomen is being examined in full view from the hall.

Although isolation may be a medical necessity, pediatric personnel must remember that it does affect the child. Children in isolation receive fewer visits from the nurses, may rarely see their physician, and spend less time with their parents. When someone does come into the room, the visitor is gowned and often masked. This is frightening, stressful, and depressing. One such youngster portrayed his feelings in a drawing (see Fig. 12-2). Isolation should be for as brief a time as medically feasible, and the physician in charge of the patient should ensure that all steps have been completed to abort unnecessary

Figure 12-2   Drawing by a 13-year-old boy in isolation.

isolation days, for example, proper cultures obtained and culture reports checked frequently.

When a child is hospitalized, siblings should not be neglected by the parents. Some children resent the attention being paid to the hospitalized child and will begin to misbehave at home. Other children, particularly those of school age, will be confused by their brother's or sister's absence from home and may even fantasize that they caused the hospitalization in some way. Parents may need to be reminded that *all* the children should be informed of their sibling's hospitalization and told the reason for the hospitalization. It sometimes helps the children at home to feel included and needed if they each have a special chore to do for the hospitalized youngster, for example, feed the patient's goldfish or paint a picture to decorate the hospital stand. Whenever practical, the hospitalized and nonhospitalized siblings should speak by phone, and be encouraged to visit the hospital. Siblings told that the hospitalized child has a minor problem (anemia, the "flu") when indeed the medical situation is serious or potentially fatal may be psychologically vulnerable in later life when they develop these same "minor" medical problems.

A major component of a child's life is school. School-age children admitted to the hospital miss their usual classroom instruction. Obviously, children critically or seriously ill canot be expected to study, but children convalescing should be given as

Table 12-1
Rights and Responsibilities of Patients,
Parents, and Hospital Staff Members

1 Patients should receive medical care without regard to age, sex, religion, race, social class, economic status, diagnosis, or language barrier.
2 Access to hospital personnel and medical resources is on the basis of medical need, promptly met, with the understanding that some patients, because of the seriousness of their condition, may require priority.
3 Patients, parents, and hospital staff members should be treated with politeness and respect, including the use of names and courtesy titles in addressing one another.
4 Patients and parents have the right to have the names and roles of all persons concerned with their care explained to them.
5 The treatment of all patients should respect their privacy, subject only to whatever unavoidable limitations exist because of space.
6 All patients or parents should have full access to information concerning their condition, their treatment, and administrative and financial policies affecting them. They should be involved wherever possible in all decisions relating to their care and should understand their responsibility to be as informative as possible to all concerned with their care.
7 Confidentiality of information is a patient and parent privilege. Access to such information is only for the personnel involved in care unless patient or parent explicit consent is given. Physicians and nurses learn from the careful observation and care of their patients, and the patient and parent can assist in providing them fully with all medical information. It should be understood that a patient's record may be used by the medical center faculty for clinical research and teaching with full protection of the patient's confidentiality and identity.
8 Patients and parents should receive from the medical staff the information necessary to give informed consent prior to the start of any nonemergency treatment or procedure involving surgery or significant diagnostic procedure. The informed consent should include the specific procedure or treatment, the reasons for the procedure, the reasonably foreseeable discomforts and risks, and some indication of medically significant alternatives.
9 The patient or parent may refuse treatment to the extent permitted by law and should be informed of the medical consequences of this action.
10 When a hospital serves as a teaching as well as patient care institution, students and other personnel in training are inevitably directly involved with patient care. Patients and/or parents should recognize their opportunity and responsibility to share in the teaching function as well as in receiving the medical benefits of treatment of a teaching hospital. At the same time, the staff must recognize the need to inform and obtain consent from patients or parents for their participation in special teaching exercises.
11 Patients or their parents are occasionally requested to participate in clinical investigation. Before this can be done, studies are carefully reviewed by experts for safety, comfort, and scientific value and by a special Committee on Investigation Involving Human Subjects. In addition, the patients' and/or parents' consent for this participation must be obtained after the nature and risks have been clearly explained to them, and they may withdraw from any investigation without prejudice to the medical care given.
12 Patients and parents also have the responsibility to respect the rights and comforts of other patients in the hospital, particularly in regard to privacy, noise, and confidentiality.

Source: Adapted from the University of Rochester Strong Memorial Hospital Medical Center statement on patient rights and responsibilities, Nov. 24, 1975.

much schooling as possible in order to prevent their falling too far behind their peers. If a child is hospitalized for a short time (for instance, 7 to 10 days), the parents can serve as liaison between the classroom and the child and work with the child's teacher to ensure that the youngster will keep abreast of classes. Children whose anticipated hospitalization is for a longer length of time should receive instruction through the school system for a hospital or home tutor as soon as possible. In many school systems, hospital instruction cannot be requested until the child has been out of school for 6 weeks or more. This is too long a time period for a child to be missing schoolwork, and whenever possible, the physician should protest such a policy.

Another valuable component to any child's life is *play.* For the hospitalized child, also, play is important, and most pediatric floors are well-stocked with age-appropriate toys and games. A structured activities program is now a common feature on most pediatric wards and is known by various names in different hospitals: Child Life Program, Play Program, or Children's Activities. Physicians should make use of a Child Life Program in caring for their patients and welcome the observations made of the child at play. Such observations can often add insight into a child's progress or lack of progress in the hospital. Children should be encouraged to act out or "draw out" their feelings about their illness or hospitalization. When structured activities are planned, as many children as possible should participate. Youngsters with intravenous lines should have the tubing anchored in such a way that ambulation is possible. Children in traction or on bed rest can often have their beds moved to the playroom so that they too can take part in the activities.

It is appropriate that some children receive leave, or passes, while they are recuperating from a long illness in the hospital. Pediatric health care personnel sometimes neglect the importance of children's attending significant and meaningful events in their lives, such as a school event or a family celebration. Often a child can be allowed to leave the hospital for a couple of hours without detriment to his health care. This is particularly true for the adolescent struggling to maintain peer group acceptance during the illness. Hospitalization then should not totally prevent a youngster who is ambulatory from participating in a major event in his or her life.

Patients, parents, and members of a hospital staff are partners in the healing process. Each has rights and responsibilities (see Table 12-1). The primary care physician, as the patient's advocate and a member of the hospital staff, should ensure that all concerned understand and respect these rights and responsibilities.

INDICATIONS FOR DISCHARGE FROM THE HOSPITAL

It is sometimes as difficult to decide when to discharge children from the hospital as it is to decide when to admit them. Children should not be kept in the hospital for unnecessary lengths of time, but what constitutes an unnecessary length of time is not always clear. Fortunately, most children are admitted for a given symptom, diagnosed, treated, and sent home within a brief period. Some children require extended convalescence with a minimum of nursing care. For these children, alternatives to traditional hospitalization should be sought, such as convalescent homes for children, chronic illness hospitals, and visiting nurse programs. If parents are expected to perform nursing tasks for the child at home, such as injections, gavage, or dressing changes, they should be *gradually* taught the procedure, and the child should be discharged only when the parent and physician both feel comfortable that proper care can be given at home. Again, public health nurses can be of invaluable assistance in helping such families. Often, children are admitted to the hospital with suspected primary psychosocial problems, such as child abuse. In these cases, social work consultation should be requested as early as possible so that the child will not spend extra days in the hospital while such a consultation and disposition are implemented. Pediatric health personnel must be innovative and imaginative to minimize the length of hospitalization and encourage comprehensive rehabilitation of the child.

13 | The Chronically Ill Child

by Marianne Felice and Stanford B. Friedman

Chronically ill children pose multiple problems for pediatric health personnel. Sometimes these youngsters have complex medical problems and, thus, require the services of multiple physicians or clinics. These children may have significant psychosocial problems concomitant with their illness or as a result of their illness. They often require frequent checkups and characteristically have thick, illegible medical records. Their families require much support, understanding, and guidance concerning the child's disease and its effect on the total family. And, lastly, children with chronic disease evoke a vast array of feelings in the staff members who work with them. These feelings are often ignored, suppressed, or displaced.

EFFECT OF CHRONIC ILLNESS ON DEVELOPMENT

How a chronic illness influences a child's development is contingent upon several questions: Was the child born with the illness? Is the illness an inherited disorder? Is the illness an acquired disease? How old was the child when the illness was acquired or when the disease was diagnosed? The importance of these questions relates to the fact that children begin to develop a body image as they grow, even in infancy. Five-month-old infants explore their own bodies, their fingers, their toes, their genitals, their faces, and incorporate their findings into developing images of themselves. By the age of 2 or 3 years, these youngsters have some concept of their own bodies that they identify as "mine." If, in their explorations, they discover that an arm or a leg is absent or that they have some other abnormality, they incorporate

that abnormality into their self-image. Later, at the age of 3 to 5, they begin to compare their body with other children's bodies. It is then that they recognize that they are different from other children. The child growing up with an abnormality generally appears to be better adjusted and more accepting of a self-image than the child who acquires a disability during later years.

After children with a chronic illness or physical deformity have accepted their self-image, they must learn to cope with peer acceptance. Young children are quite adaptive and generally will play to the best of their abilities with other children in spite of their deformities. Although youngsters can be cruel and tease one another about their differences, usually children accept other children, particularly if the disabled children accept themselves. Parents, however, often become anxious about their deformed or chronically ill children's being in the presence of normal children and may try to shield them from their peer groups. Physicians should give reassurance and support to such parents so that the child is able to relate to a normal peer group.

Children with disabilities that are visible often receive more attention and support then children who have "hidden" disabilities. For example, the child with rheumatoid arthritis with visibly swollen joints and difficulty in movement will often evoke much positive support from the family, teachers, and friends. On the other hand, the child with juvenile diabetes, whose disability is not visible, will often not receive similar support.

A major problem for children with chronic illnesses is the difficulty that physicians and parents have in allowing them to develop independence. Parents have a tendency to overprotect their handicapped child, and physicians contribute to that overprotec-tiveness by emphasizing restrictions. It is helpful to both parent and child if the physician lists those activities the child *can* do as well as those activities the child *cannot* do.

In treating chronically ill children over several years, it is appropriate for the physician to give attention to vocational planning for the youngster, either personally or through staff members. Each child should be encouraged to develop socially and intellectually as completely as possible, but it is also necessary for the physician to recognize a child's limitations and then encourage realistic aspirations.

One problem peculiar to pediatricians is the reluc-tance to terminate the doctor-patient relationship when the youngsters reach adulthood. This is par-ticularly true if the pediatrician has followed a child from infancy. Whenever possible, chronically ill children, upon reaching adulthood, should be trans-ferred to internists or family practice physicians. The child or adolescent should be gradually prepared for this change over several visits. Such a transfer serves to support a youngster's striving for adult independence.

THE EFFECT OF CHRONIC ILLNESS ON THE FAMILY

The parents of chronically ill children often feel guilty about their child's illness. If a child has an inherited disorder, both parents may scrutinize their family backgrounds to see how the disease was inherited. If the illness is acquired, the parents may feel that they did not adequately "protect" the child from getting the disease. If an infant is born with a congenital but not inherited disorder, the mother may become ob-sessed about her prenatal activities and wonder if some action of hers caused the disorder.

Guilt often leads to anger (see Fig. 13-1). Guilt feelings cause discomfort, and the parent becomes angry at feeling uncomfortable. The anger may be manifested in many ways. Parents often become angry with the physician who initially diagnoses the child's illness, with one another, with themselves, and even with the afflicted child.

Invariably, the marital relationship between par-ents of a chronically ill child either remarkably im-proves or drastically disintegrates shortly after the diagnosis is made. Being told that one's youngster has a chronic illness is a crisis and imposes a stress

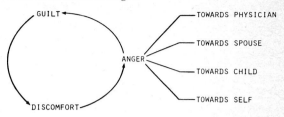

Figure 13-1 Parental guilt over a child's chronic ill-ness often leads to anger.

on most marital relationships. If the marital relation-ship is stable and the parents are mutually support-ive, the marital bonds grow strong. If the marital relationship is unstable, the child's illness serves as a final stress that may sever marital ties.

The cost to the family of having a child with a chronic illness may be astounding, and the parents will often need help in finding financial aid. Most families are not able alone to carry the financial burden of their child's illness, but may be too proud to ask for help. Physicians should be sensitive to these needs and offer their help or the services of their staff whenever possible.

The cost to society too of a child who is chronically ill is immeasurable. These children often require expensive medications, repeated hospitalizations, and sometimes long-term institutional care. Often the physician can be valuable in educating the local community concerning chronic illnesses and in working with various agencies to improve their services to chronically ill children and their families.

The siblings of children with chronic illness de-serve some attention. Siblings often worry about whether or not they will have the same disease if it is a congenital or inherited disorder. If it *is* an inherited disorder and they have been spared, they will often feel guilty. If it is an acquired disease, these children may have magical thoughts or fantasies that it is something that their brother or sister did to deserve the illness. Often in sibling rivalry a child may wish that the brother or sister were dead. When that brother or sister acquires an illness, the sibling may then feel tremendous guilt and responsibility for having brought on the illness. The primary physician caring for the child with a chronic illness should always inquire as to the health, well-being, and psychological state of the youngster's siblings and may be able to provide insight to the parents con-cerning the siblings' behavior.

THE MEDICAL DELIVERY SYSTEM

Children with chronic illnesses often receive fragmented health care. Frequently, a primary physician suspects an illness and then requests a consultation at a children's hospital. The child is swept up into a children's service, a work-up is completed, and a diagnosis made. The child is then assigned to a specialty clinic, returning regularly for care. Usually, this clinic is attended by full-time staff specialists, but the child is seen at each visit by a different house staff member who does not know or recognize either the child or the family. What the primary physician who originally referred the child has contributed is often ignored.

There may be a controversy over whether a child with a chronic illness should receive care from specialty clinics or from a primary care physician. All aspects of this issue should be examined. Often a child can be seen once or twice a year at the specialty clinic and have other checkups through the regular pediatrician. If communication is good between the specialist and the primary care physician, this is a suitable arrangement. During adolescence, children with chronic illnesses often continue to be seen in pediatric clinics where they feel uncomfortable, and their dependency is reinforced. Whenever possible, adolescents should be seen in an adolescent setting. If this is not possible, it is sometimes appropriate to have adolescents seen in adult medical groups if those physicians are sensitive to the issues of development.

When to hospitalize the chronically ill child is a difficult question to answer. Usually parents are able to cope with innumerable medical problems at home simply through years of experience. Hospitalization often takes on special meaning to the child who is a regular visitor to the physician or hospital and who may view hospitalization as followed by death if the reasons for hospitalization are not carefully explained.

It is important that pediatricians and their staff be aware of their own emotional responses to the chronically ill child. This child, more than any other youngster, is able to evoke mixed feelings and frustration in the staff. The staff members are often angry while caring for the child. They are frustrated because their patient does not get better. Often, chronically ill children involve several consultants. Each consultant may give different messages to the child and the family. Complicated cases, especially if the child is mentally retarded, are often rejected by all members of the medical delivery system. When such children are hospitalized, they and their families frequently spend much time in the admissions office while house officers and administrative clerks decide "where the child belongs." The 15-year-old mentally retarded cerebral palsy patient may be rejected by the staff responsible for adolescent care because the patient looks like an 8-year-old, and rejected by the ward for school-age children because the child "is really an adolescent."

COUNSELING

Chronically ill children and adolescents and their parents need opportunities to receive counseling. Most often, parents need this help early in the disease, shortly after the diagnosis is made. Youngsters most often need this assistance as they approach adolescence. Not all parents nor all youngsters will *require* counseling, but all chronically ill children and their parents should be given this option.

Usually, the counseling can be provided by a sensitive and understanding physician willing to take time with these families. Social workers and psychologists are also capable of handling these problems, and can work closely with the physician caring for the child. For adolescents, a group of youngsters with similar problems may meet regularly with an interested physician or staff member to share their common problems. In many areas, parents of chronically ill children band together as groups to offer support to one another.

The number of children with chronic illnesses is rapidly increasing as advances in technology have enabled physicians to change the natural history of many diseases. However, this results in some new problems. For example, prior to the era of antibiotics, children with cystic fibrosis usually died before adolescence. Now they frequently live to young adulthood. As adolescents, they are usually dependent upon several medications simultaneously and may resent this dependence. Boys with cystic fibrosis are sterile. Adolescent girls with cystic fibrosis must grapple with their fears of having children when their own life expectancy is so uncertain. Now physicians must focus upon the psychosocial and psychosexual problems related to these issues of sterility and pregnancy.

THE ROLE OF THE SCHOOL

An important component of any child's life is school. Children with chronic illnesses frequently are absent from school because of their illness, clinic or physician visits, or hospitalization. Absence from school should be kept to a minimum. In some communities, children with chronic diseases attend special schools, particularly when the youngster is visibly handicapped. However, many children with chronic illnesses, particularly those whose illnesses are not visible (such as diabetes or asthma), attend regular schools. The school should be made aware of medical problems of a child. Sometimes teachers can be quite helpful as objective observers of a child's condition. When medications are changed, teachers can be instructed to look for untoward side effects. With the parents' and child's permission, a physician may contact the school and notify the teacher or principal or school nurse of changes in a youngster's illness. Often, parents prefer to make this communication themselves. Sometimes teachers are not medically knowledgeable, and may welcome information the medical profession can give them about a youngster in their classroom. In this way, the school system and the medical system can work collaboratively to best benefit a given youngster.

14 | The Dying Child

by Marianne Felice and Stanford B. Friedman

DEVELOPMENTAL ASPECTS OF DEATH

To manage the dying child properly, it is important that the physician recognize that children have different concepts concerning death depending on age and stage of development. The very young child, the preschooler, has a very limited concept concerning death. By age 3 to 6 years, youngsters generally have had some contact with death; that is, a pet may have died, or a grandparent. These young children are thought to consider death a reversible phenomenon. This concept of reversibility is often demonstrated for the modern child in movies and television. For example, it is common to see a cartoon character flattened like a pancake with a steamroller and the next moment up and about and racing down the road. Such activity is completely plausible in the mind of the preschooler.

By school age, the youngster often views death as a prolongation of sleep. Dead people's eyes are closed, and they look as if they are sleeping and hence must be asleep; they simply do not wake up. This concept of death as sleep is generally present in the young school-age child of about 6 to 8 years. After accepting the concept of reversibility, these children who view death as a prolongation of sleep generally ask such questions as: "What happens when you die and you get put in the ground?" "Who does Jackie play with?" "Doesn't he need some cookies and milk?" "Won't he get cold?" "Isn't it dark down there?" "How can somebody be in the ground and heaven at the same time?" Later around age 8 to 10 years, the youngster may personify death, usually as a monster who sneaks in during the night and kills the living.

This fantasy is often "substantiated" by cinema and television.

Somewhere in adolescence, usually by midadolescence, the teenager is able to abstract the concept of death as an irreversible phenomenon. This may occur at the same time that most adolescents begin to deal with various philosophies, such as the purpose of life, the meaning of existence. Sometime in late adolescence or early adulthood, most people begin to grapple with the concept of their own death.

Children, as well as adults, have fears concerning death. Frequently, physicians do not address the fears as the young patient sees them. Dying children, whose concept of death is poorly defined, are concerned that while they are dying their parents will leave them alone; this is the fear of abandonment. The child who is terminally ill and has experienced innumerable medical tests and studies is usually more afraid of bodily harm than of the abstraction known as death. How much children know about their own impending death has not as yet been well studied.

A comparative study between chronically ill children who were not terminally ill and leukemic children who were terminally ill but in remission revealed much higher anxiety levels in the leukemic children. Such a study suggests that school-age children are more aware of the seriousness of their illnesses than physicians have previously believed.

In managing the dying child, one must be aware that besides the normal developmental concepts of death, a child is affected by other experiences with death. That is, siblings, parents, and grandparents may have died. How those deaths were handled by the family may be reflected in the dying child's behavior. The child who has seen a torturous death in a very sick grandparent or sibling may be more frightened of the pain or bodily harm in dying than of death itself. Children from religious families also will be influenced by the religious attitude toward death in the family.

THE FAMILY OF THE DYING CHILD

Parents of terminally ill children have typical reactions to the information that their child has a fatal illness. Parents generally receive the news of the diagnosis with an initial feeling of disbelief and shock. This feeling of disbelief may not necessarily be intellectual denial. The parents usually can intellectually accept the diagnosis but not experience the full emotional impact. Parents may desire a second opinion, as a result of some degree of denial or hope that the diagnosis is incorrect. Parents can be warned ahead of time that these feelings may occur. This initial stage of disbelief may take days or several weeks to subside.

After the parents have experienced the feelings of disbelief and shock, they frequently experience anger, and the anger may be directed toward the physician who made the diagnosis, toward the staff caring for the child, toward one another, and, of course, toward themselves for not having protected their child from contracting the terminal illness. After anger, parents may experience the "bargaining" stage in which they ask themselves: "If I give up such and such, perhaps my child will be cured." After bargaining, parents generally feel depressed, and then perhaps begin to deal with their feelings about the illness. Some parents experience anticipatory grieving and actually grieve over the loss while their child is still alive. This is particularly true in leukemic children at the terminal stages of the disease.

As part of their anticipatory grieving some parents have experienced what has been described as the "Lazarus syndrome." A child is expected to die and is quite ill, and the parents actually grieve as if the death had already taken place, psychologically preparing themselves for it. The child then recovers as if risen from the dead. The parents are not always psychologically equipped to deal with the child who recovers. The physician can be of assistance in helping the parents deal with their feelings at this time.

The marital relationship of parents of a terminally ill or dying child is often stressed. It is typical in our culture for the husband to support his wife early in the course of their child's illness, and for the first few days the father frequently makes the important family decisions, allowing his wife to experience more emotion than he does. In fact, the husband may truly *feel* the impact of the diagnosis only some days or weeks following the time when his wife no longer needs such intensive support. Mutual support of the parents is extremely important for the child, for the parents themselves, and for the other siblings. When children are hospitalized, mothers generally are more comfortable in caring for them than fathers are. Because of this, and for work reasons, fathers may spend significantly less time with the child on the ward and not have much contact with the physician. This places the mother in a role of translator of the physician's words to the father. It is important, whenever possible, that the physician give information concerning the child's condition to both parents, preferably at the same time. Sometimes mothers may completely take over the role of caring for the dying child, and the father may feel excluded from his wife's world. This too can be circumvented by the physician's making a positive effort to communicate to *both* parents.

The siblings of the dying child are often ignored by the parents and the physician. What and how to tell siblings must take into account their ages, development, and past experiences. Siblings should be told that their brother or sister is dying in words and a manner comfortable for the family. Siblings should be made to feel that they are still part of the family and that they can be of help in dealing with this family crisis. If the siblings are old enough, issues such as heredity or contagion should be brought up in order to reassure them that they themselves do not have the same illness.

The parents also may ask for help in coping with extended family members, that is, with what to tell grandparents, aunts, and uncles. What information parents give depends upon the relationship and the closeness that the family members feel. However, it is important that all family members be told the same thing so that they do not hear conflicting information. Parents also should be warned that extended family members and/or neighbors may unintentionally add more stress to their lives. For example, relatives may make such statements as "Johnny can't have leukemia—he looks too healthy," or they may send newspaper and magazine articles which seem to contradict what the physician has told them. Well-meaning grandparents or relatives may not allow the parents a normal life when the child is terminally ill or shortly after the child's death. They may make such statements as "How can you have a party when one of your children is dying?" or "How can you go away on a trip when your son just passed away a few months ago?" If parents are forewarned of some of these situations, they may be better equipped to deal with them.

The role of religion in dealing with a dying child must also be considered. Ministers, priests, and rabbis can be of great help to parents and the dying child, and religious families will contact their pastors and ask for help. In some hospitals, there is a ministry devoted to dying patients and their families, and even though they may not be of the same faith as the family, they may be of invaluable help to them.

Most studies and written discussions to date have been with parents of children whose deaths followed a terminal illness. Parents who lose a child suddenly or unexpectedly may not respond to the child's death in the same manner as the parents who have had time to prepare themselves psychologically for the loss. The former often have feelings of disbelief which may last for several weeks. Some authors have noted that the parents may deny the death of the child for some time and commonly dream of the deceased youngster. It appears that parents who endure the sudden, unexpected loss of a child experience intense, disruptive, and at times almost intolerable grief reactions.

Death by accident deserves special attention in that the parents or an older sibling may feel directly responsible for the fate of the child. The resulting guilt may be persistent, particularly if in reality the accident might have been prevented by better judgment or supervision by the parent or sibling responsible for the child's safety. Guilt arising under such circumstances is usually not resolved by the usual grief process.

THE MEDICAL DELIVERY SYSTEM

It is important that open communication be maintained among the staff members caring for the dying child so that it can be determined ahead of time whose responsibility it will be to tell the parents that the child is dying or has died. When a child has multiple consultants, the physician with the closest rapport with the family and the child should inform the parents of the death. Preferably, this responsibility should be shouldered by the primary physician and not left to an unfamiliar intern in the middle of the night.

How to tell parents that the child has died is another issue of concern. In talking about the diagnosis of terminal illness or death, there is a need for privacy between the parents and the physician. This is generally acknowledged by most physicians, and yet it repeatedly happens that parents are told about the diagnosis or the death in the hallways and in the presence of other people. Sitting down with the parents, rather than standing, promotes a feeling in parents that the physician is not eager to leave as soon as possible.

In talking to the parents about the terminal illness or about their child's impending death, it is important that explanations to the parents be kept as simple as possible. Parents often complain that they do not understand the medical situation. What they primarily want is only enough information to comprehend the situation, to understand the recommendations of the physician, and to know what is expected of them as parents.

The parents should be spoken to every day, and often the same information should be repeated several times. They may not "hear" what the physician says the first time, and may need frequently repeated explanations. The various details of the illness should be conveyed in a series of discussions rather than having one explanation all at once. It is at these times that parents can be given anticipatory guidance about the questions they will be asked by relatives and friends, and can be forewarned to anticipate feelings in themselves such as wanting to shift to a different hospital or a different physician. Then, when they actually have the feelings, they are relieved to know that their physician had expected them to.

The staff caring for a dying child is often depressed. The morale of the nurses, house staff, and medical students is important. Upon losing a child, all the staff members may experience feelings of failure and loss, and it is often desirable for the staff to meet together to discuss a child's death as soon as possible after the death has taken place. Blame should not be placed by one group of professionals upon another. Rather, a supportive attitude should be maintained by those in charge. Staff members in intensive care nurseries and other intensive care units are particularly susceptible to feelings of depression and issues of low morale. To be constantly in the presence of severely ill children, coping with the reactions of strained parents, is a stressful situation, and the programs of such units should always include outlets for emotional release and a means for discussion of the feelings concerning the death of infants and youngsters.

Whenever it is medically appropriate, permission for a postmortem should be obtained. This request should come from the physician having the closest rapport with the family, and responsibility for obtaining the postmortem should not be shoved from attending physician to house staff to student. Ideally, it would be best not to ask for the autopsy at the same time that one is informing the parents that their child has just expired. Unfortunately, the postmortem must be done within a brief time, and this may be the only chance that the physician has to ask the parents. He should be as frank as possible, explaining the reasons for the postmortem and reassuring the parents that mutilation and maiming will not result.

FOLLOWING DEATH

It is advisable that the physician contact the parents about 6 weeks after the child's death and offer to talk with them. At this time, parents have an opportunity to ask the physician those questions that they did not ask previously. Parents often relive the illness and ask old questions again. This assures them that their understanding of the child's disease was correct. As one mother said: "Talking later put a period on the whole episode." The physician also has the opportunity to see how the parents and siblings are adjusting and to give them information concerning the postmortem examination. Such actions assure the parents that the physician still cares about *them* and their adaptation to the stress of the child's death.

It is normal for a family to grieve after a child has died, and the physician should be supportive of the grief reaction. Lindemann has described the acute process of mourning in much detail; striking features of acute grief include frequent sighing respirations, waves of somatic distress, exhaustion, and digestive symptoms. The period of mourning cannot be sharply defined, and there are marked differences among individuals. In general, however, feelings related to the loss are intense for 3 to 6 months following the death of a child. Birthdays, the date of the child's death, and holiday seasons all may remind parents of their loss and even many years later be associated with renewed periods of grieving. However, in the normal mourning process parents return more or less to their previous level of psychological and social functioning approximately 4 to 6 months after the child's death.

After parents have lost a child through death, they may wonder whether or not they should have another child. After talking the situation over with the parents, the physician generally can recommend that they have another child, but the physician should also forewarn the parents that the new baby is not to be a replacement of the former child. A phenomenon known as the *replacement child syndrome* occasionally takes place in which parents attempt to have another child as soon as possible after the death of a child and to make the new child into the one who has died. In some extreme cases, the same name is given to the second child. A sensitive physician who maintains contact with the parents can help them avoid this potential problem, helping them realize that no child can truly replace another and can be emotionally damaged in the attempt.

It is difficult and painful for all to deal with dying children. The parents of these children need support from the physician during the terminal illness as well as after the death has occurred, and, as mentioned earlier, pediatric staff members, particularly nurses and house staff, need opportunities to express their feelings of failure and loss when an infant or child dies.

REFERENCES

Discussion of Diagnostic Findings

Balint, M.: *The Doctor and His Patient and the Illness*, New York: International University Press, 1957.

Battle, C. U.: The Role of the pediatrician as ombudsman in the health care of the young handicapped child, *Pediatrics*, **50**:6, 916, December 1972.

Bryan, T.: Peer popularity of learning disabled children, *J. Learning Disabilities*, **7**(10): 621, December 1974.

Colley, T. E.: Interpretation of psychological test data to children, *Mental Retardation*, **11**(1): 28, February 1973.

Doleys, D., Cartelli, L., and Doser, J.: Comparison of patterns of mother-child interactions, *J. Learning Disabilities*, **9**(6): 371, June/July 1976.

Gayton, W. F., and Walker, L.: Down's syndrome—informing the parents. A study of parental preferences, *Am. J. Dis. Child*, **127**:510, April 1974.

Gesell, A., and Armatruda, C.: "Parent Counseling in Developmental Disabilities," in H. Knobloch and B. Pasamanick (eds.), *Developmental Diagnosis*, Hagerstown, Md.: Harper & Row, pp. 359–361, 1974.

Johnson, C., and Prinz, R.: Hyperactivity is in the eyes of the beholder, *Clin. Pediatr.*, **15**(3): 222, March 1976.

Kirkpatrick, K., Hoffman, I., and Futterman, E. H.: Dilemma of trust relationship between medical care givers and parents of fatally ill children, *Pediatrics*, **54**:169, August 1974.

Korsh, B., Gozzi, E. K., et al.: Doctor/patient interaction and patient satisfaction, *Pediatrics*, **42**:855, November 1968.

Lewis, M., and Lewis, D. O.: Pediatric management of psychological crisis, *Curr. Probl. Pediatr.*, **3**:1, October 1973.

MacKeith, R.: The feelings and behavior of parents of handicapped children, *J. Developmental Med. Child Neurol.*, **15**:524, 1973.

Morgan, S. B.: Team interpretation of mental retardation to parents, *Ment. Retard.*, 10, June 1973.

Zborowski, M.: "Cultural Components in Responses to Pain," in S. Stein and R. Cloward (eds.), *Social Perspectives on Behavior*, New York: Free Press, pp. 145–156, 1958.

Compliance With Recommendations

Anderson, F. P., Rowe, D. S., Dean, V. C., and Arbissen, A.: An approach to the problem of noncompliance in the pediatric outpatient clinic, *Am. J. Dis. Child.*, **122**:142, 1971.

Becker, M., Drachman, R., and Kirscht, J.: Predicting mothers' compliance with pediatric regimens, *J. Pediatr.*, **81**:843, 1972.

Becker, M. H., Drachman, R., and Kirscht, J. P. A new approach to explaining sick role behavior in low income populations, *Am. J. Public Health*, **64**: 205, 1974.

Becker, M. H., and Maiman, L. A.: Sociobehavioral determinants of compliance with health and medical care recommendations, *Med. Care*, **13**:10, 1975.

Charney, E.: Patient-doctor communication, *Pediatr. Clin. North Am.*, **19**:263, 1972.

Charney, E.: Compliance and prescribance, *Am. J. Dis. Child.*, **129**:1009, 1975.

Charney, E., et al.: How well do patients take oral penicillin? A collaborative study in private practice, *Pediatrics,* **40:**188, 1967.

Emey, R. D., and Goldstein, E. O.: Compliance of chronic asthmatics with oral administration of theophylline as measured by serum and salivary levels, *Pediatrics,* **57:**513, 1971.

Francis, V., Korsch, B., and Morris, M. J.: Gaps in doctor-patient communication, *N. Engl. J. Med.,* **280:**535, 1969.

Gordis, L.: Effectiveness of comprehensive care programs in preventing rheumatic fever, *N. Engl. J. Med.,* **289:**331, 1973.

Gordis, L., et al.: Why patients don't follow medical advice: A study of children on long-term antistreptococcal prophylaxis, *J. Pediatr.,* **75:**957, 1969.

Gordis, L., and Markowitz, M.: Evaluation of the effectiveness of comprehensive and continuous pediatric care, *Pediatrics,* **48:**766, 1971.

Gordis, L., Markowitz, M., and Lilienfield, A.: The inaccuracy in using interviews to estimate patient reliability in taking medication at home, *Med. Care,* **7:**49, 1965.

Korsch, B. M., Gozzi, E. K., and Francis, V.: Gaps in doctor-patient communication, *Pediatrics,* **42:**855, 1968.

Korsch, B., and Negrete, V. F.: Doctor-patient communication, *Sci. Am.,* **227:**66, 1972.

Mohler, D.: Studies in the home treatment of streptococcal disease. Failure of patients to take penicillin by mouth as prescribed, *N. Engl. J. Med.,* **252:**116, 1955.

Mushlin, A.: Diagnosing potential noncompliance, *Arch. Int. Med.,* **137:**318, 1977.

Sackett, D. L., and Haynes, R. B.: *Compliance with Therapeutic Regimens,* Baltimore: Johns Hopkins, 1976.

Yudkin, S.: Six children with coughs, *Lancet,* Sept. 9, 1961, pp. 561–563.

The Acutely Ill Child

Green, M., and Haggerty, R. J.: *Ambulatory Pediatrics,* Philadelphia: Saunders, 1968.

Care of the Child in the Hospital

Mason, E. A.: The hospitalized child: His emotional needs, *N. Engl. J. Med.,* **272:**406, 1965.

North, A. F., Jr.: When should a child be in the hospital? *Pediatrics,* **57:**540, 1976.

The Chronically Ill Child

Leichtman, S. R., and Friedman, S. B.: Social and psychological development of adolescents and the relationship to chronic illness, *Med. Clin. North Am.,* **59:**1319, 1975.

Moore, T. D. (ed.): *Care of Children with Chronic Illness,* Report of the 67th Conference on Pediatric Research, Columbus, Ohio, 1975.

Pless, I. B., Satterwhite, B., and Van Vechten, D.: Chronic illness in childhood: A regional survey in care, *Pediatrics,* **58:**37, 1976.

Steinhaver, P. D.: Psychological aspects of chronic illness, *Pediatr. Clin. North Am.,* **21:**825, 1974.

The Dying Child

Engel, G. L.: Is grief a disease? *Psychosom. Med.,* **23:**18, 1961.

Fischoff, J., and O'Brien, N.: After the child dies, *J. Pediatr.,* **88:**140, 1976.

Friedman, S. B.: "Psychological Issues in Caring for the Fatally Ill Child," in M. M. Vuksanovic (ed.), *Clinical Pediatric Oncology,* Mt. Kisco, New York: Futura, 1972.

Friedman, S. B.: Psychological aspects of unexpected death in infants and children, *Pediatr. Clin. North Am.,* **21:**103, 1974.

Hankoff, L. D.: Adolescence and the crisis of dying, *Adolescence,* **10:**373, 1975.

Kirkpatric, J., Hoffman, I., and Futterman, E. H.: Dilemma of trust: Relationship between medical care givers and parents of fatally ill children, *Pediatrics,* **54:**169, 1974.

Kubler-Ross, E.: *On Death and Dying,* New York: Macmillan, 1969.

Lindemann, E.: Symptomatology and management of acute grief, *Am. J. Psychiatry,* **101:**141, 1944.

Nagy, M. H.: "The Child's View of Death,"in H. Feifel (ed.), *The Meaning of Death,* New York: McGraw-Hill, 1959.

Spinetta, J. J., and Maloney, L. J.: Death anxiety in the outpatient leukemic child, *Pediatrics,* **56:**1034, 1975.

Szybist, C.: *The Subsequent Child,* U.S. Department of Health, Education, and Welfare, Health Services Administration, Bureau of Community Health Services, Rockville, Md.

PART THREE

Sexual Development and Pregnancy

15 | Development of Sexual Identity

by Judith Armstrong

"Gender identity" is the term generally used to refer to one's sense of being male or female and the behavior which corresponds to this inner assurance. Psychological differences and similarities between the sexes are, in every sense of the word, a "hot" issue, and it is common to see articles which are polemic on the subject of biology and destiny. Actually, it is only in the past decade that one finds careful and sophisticated observational studies on the origin and development of sexual roles, and with this, a questioning of either-or concepts such as heredity versus learning or nature versus nurture. We are, from the beginning of life, influenced by our body and by our experiences. Moreover, the effects of learning that occurs at critical stages (for example, nurturance or neglect in infancy) can be even more resistant to change than biological characteristics (one has a *choice* to use one's physical apparatus of impregnation or childbearing). This is why the developmental approach, which studies the interaction of an individual with experience over time, gives the best picture of the origins of normal and abnormal gender identity.

Two important points must be made before looking at the data. From the first fundamental questions asked, such as, "Are girls more passive than boys?" or "Are boys more active than girls?" one becomes entangled in culture-linked semantic stereotypes. Is a child who visually investigates the surroundings while sitting behaving passively or engaging in a type of activity? Are children who manipulate adults into getting something for them being passive or active? And is a child who lashes out after being taunted by a peer actively or passively responding to the situation? Clearly, it is important to avoid global expressions which conceal and confuse a variety of behaviors. Yet even with the most careful of definitions, a second trap appears when one attempts to interpret individual behavior on the basis of group averages. If it is found that boys are more aggressive than girls, does it mean that a girl who enjoys fighting is abnormal and exhibiting gender confusion? Research evidence gives a clear "no." For every characteristic studied, differences between individuals of the same sex are as great as differences between the sexes. Thus it would be misleading to consider the sex differences in behavior which will be presented as models of sexual appropriateness or to use them as definitive criteria of normality or disturbance in a particular patient.

Determinants of Gender Identity

The most complex and comprehensive treatment of the origins of gender identity is found in psychoanalytic theory. Freud's primary assumption that human beings share characteristics of both sexes has been confirmed by recent hormonal research, and his assertion that sexual sensations are vital experiences in childhood is supported by observational data. Freud also postulated that the child enters a stage of intense cognitive and emotional awareness of sex differences at about the age of 4 and begins then to behave seductively toward the parent of the opposite sex. At the resolution of this stage the child, now about 7 years old, consolidates a gender identity through identification with the same-sex parent, thus sharing in the power and possessions of that parent while avoiding the punishment due to a rival.

One major obstacle to the acceptance of this hypothesis is an observation that plagues learning theories of gender identity as well: Children conceptualize and behave in terms of their own ideas of masculinity or femininity considerably before age 4, indeed prior to the development of stable internal intellectual processes and in the absence of any clear-cut social reinforcement. Evidence obtained from hermaphrodites as well as from the play content of normal children indicates that awareness of gender identity begins as early as 18 months and is differentiated by about 5 years of age. Obviously, this means that we know little about the mechanisms that control normal gender development. However, there is suggestive evidence from primate studies that the infant's affectional tie to mother is essential for the development of heterosexual interest, while normal sex-role learning requires the presence of both a same-sex (identification) model and an opposite-sex model with whom the child can compare and contrast sex-appropriate behaviors. This means that boys and girls require close relationships with both a mother figure and a father figure to ensure normal development of gender identity. In later childhood, peer interaction may be of primary importance in furthering gender differentiation. Not only do children practice increasingly complex set-role behaviors through social play, but sex play itself is a common outgrowth of the child's enthusiastic curiosity about all aspects of human functioning. Again, studies of primate behavior point to the necessity of peer play for the development of normal sexual behavior in adulthood. Without peer play, patterns of adult sexual activity are significantly altered.

Gender Identity

Sex Differences

Observational studies point to contrasts in the behavior of male and female infants which have implications for gender differences seen later in childhood. Newborn males are less well developed neurologically than females, one consequence being that they are often awake and crying in the first weeks of life. Although these characteristics allow for intense mother-child contact, it is an interaction of a potentially frustrating kind, while the more smoothly functioning female infant is easier to comfort than the male. Indeed, by the time the child is 3 months old, mothers interact less frequently with male infants than with female. It is possible that the above pattern forms a prototype for the differing role of socialization in males and females; in males the force of social pressure is toward control of behavior, in females, toward comfort. Indeed, female infants are more verbal and less emotionally labile than males, while boys from an early age and despite considerable punishment, show more aggression than girls. While such factors could account for the greater independence and rebelliousness seen in adult males and the greater conformity and acceptance of the status quo traditionally associated with females, care should be taken to attribute such differences to biological bases.

From the first hours of life, parents relate to the male or female child within the framework of their own expectations of gender-appropriate behavior. Boys are handled more roughly than girls and given more physical punishment—conditions that could easily reinforce aggressive behaviors. Female infants are indeed more verbal than male infants, but mothers also talk to them more. Thus, by the time children are 5 years old, their gender identity has felt the considerable effects of both biology and society.

The school-age child, while possessing a stable concept of its own gender, requires the presence of both mother and father to aid development of appropriate sex-typed behavior. The importance of the father-son relationship is especially critical at this time and absence of a father figure has been associated with poor peer relationships and slowed intellectual development in males. It is during the school years, with the apparently spontaneous appearance of sex-segregated peer groups, that play and intellectual styles specific to the gender become clearly evident. However, recent research in schools indicates that some aspects of sex-stereotyped play are unconsciously fostered by teachers, who praise children for playing with sex-typed toys and punish children who try to join play groups of the opposite sex. On the other hand, in spite of the fact that fighting is punished by adults, boys remain intensely interested in matters of dominance, while this is not a focus of all-girl play. When the play groups are mixed, boys retain their dominance rivalry but girls do not allow the boys to dominate them. In the area of intellectual interests, grade school girls continue to show superior verbal ability, while boys tend to excel in visual-spatial and mathematical abilities.

However, it is not until late adolescence that major intellectual and emotional differences between the sexes emerge. Now girls, who were formerly equal to boys on measures of IQ, self-esteem, and achievement motivation, become less confident, may show an IQ loss, and report feeling less control over their own fates than boys. While such behavior is in keeping with traditional sex roles, there is evidence that a self-image of inadequacy not only lessens intellectual growth, it also interferes with the woman's caretaking ability. Thus, neither traditional nor modern roles are served by this loss of self-esteem.

Perhaps mental health professionals are influenced by this dilemma when they judge typically masculine attributes (such as assertiveness and independence) as characteristics of the psychologically mature person while viewing feminine characteristics (such as emotional excitability and concern about appearance) as immature and neurotic. In other words, the "typically feminine" woman is well adjusted for a woman, but emotionally disturbed for an adult.

While social pressure toward conformity with expected gender behavior is strongly applied to females in late adolescence, it is the male who feels the firm hand of socialization throughout childhood. Most notable, while there is no particular stigma attached to a girl who is a tomboy, behaviors that are considered "sissylike" in a boy are severely punished by family and peers. There is simply less chance for a boy to express feminine aspects of his personality than for a girl to show her male attributes.

The more rigid sexual stereotyping of the boy may be a significant factor in the overrepresentation of males in all categories of emotional disturbance. In other words, the more stringent the sexual stereotype, the more likely the growing individual is to be caught in the trap of cultural repression and contradiction and the more significant the psychological stress. Circumstances which widen sex-role prerogatives, such as being a member of an intact family with a working mother, have favorable effects upon the child' intellectual and emotional development. In fact, cross sex identification, where the child identifies with characteristics of both mother and father, has been associated with creativity in adulthood.

Sex Similarities

It is in considering parallels between the sexes that the distorting lens of social and linguistic stereotypes is most clearly apparent. Research creates contradictory findings dependent upon the definition of a term, and the best clinical judgments "forget" behaviors which do not conform to the rule. There are a number of areas in which, according to the majority of research, boys and girls are similar—similar in spite of casual observations and confirmed opinions to the contrary. To wit:

Girls and boys are equally sociable and suggestible. Both sexes are similarly involved with peers, prone to imitate adults, and prone to be manipulated by social pressure.

Boys and girls are equally independent and active. Neither sex is more dependent on mothers. There are no consistent differences in activity levels in male and female infants, and both sexes show similar interest in developing their own activities and exploring new situations.

During grade school years confidence, motivation to achieve success, and ability to use analytic reasoning are found in equal measure in the sexes.

Given the overriding similarities between boys and girls in behavior and self-concept and the fact that the majority of attributes we traditionally think of as masculine and feminine do not make their appearance until late adolescence, a number of researchers have proposed that the social learning which triggers these differences comes not from parents, who have had their primary influence in early childhood, but from the expert purveyors of cultural standards, such as teachers, counselors, TV, and doctors.

Abnormal Development of Gender Identity

While the focus of this section is normal sexual development, it is also apparent that the onslaught of research, coupled with our recent cultural blurring of sexual roles, may leave the clinician in considerable confusion about recognizing the signs of truly deviant gender identity. There are few certainties which remain. Many childhood indications of gender identity instability are normal and bear no relationship to later sexual behavior. These include:

1 The expressed desire of a preschool girl to possess a penis or of a preschool boy to have breasts and a baby. Jealousy of the prerogatives of the opposite sex is a common topic for young children who are beginning to be proudly aware of their abilities and reluctantly apprised of limitations.

2 Many children through the age of 5 tend to classify adults as "grownups" without differentiating them into male and female. They may not be aware that boys grow into men and girls into women. It is not unusual, therefore, for young children, nourished after all on tales of toads transmogrifying into princes, to express the belief that they can grow up to be either sex if they so choose.

3 Transient homosexual love interests are common in late childhood and early adolescence, especially when sexes are segregated (such as in many summer camps), and may simply be an important first step toward sexual self-discovery. It is important, therefore, that the family not classify an otherwise normal child as "homosexual" since the label itself may be integrated by the child into his or her own developing self-concept and produce a homosexual gender identity where one was not imperative.

There are also several childhood behaviors which do relate to deviant gender identity in adulthood. These include:

1 The syndrome of the "sissy," that is, the effeminate boy who expresses a strong wish to become the opposite sex, attempts to dress in girls' clothing, and prefers girls' activities and companionship. Such reactions are associated with gender transposition in adulthood. The syndrome of "tomboyism" in girls is not related to later homosexuality or transsexual behavior unless associated with a dogmatic aversion to all aspects of femininity coupled with a strong stated desire to become a boy.

2 Homosexual behavior in late adolescence may be associated with homosexual preference in adulthood. Here a careful history of the patient and exploration of the incident is essential before reaching any conclusions.

3 While there is no evidence of hormonal or genetic factors in most cases of gender identity deviance, family interactions often play a crucial role in their etiology. Confused and contradictory identification models are often presented in homes where the child's same-sex parent is ashamed of his or her own sexual identity or where the absence of one parent and excessive closeness with the other encourages gender ambiguity.

Obviously, children who show clear signs of gender transposition require family as well as individual counseling. Simplistic suggestions, such as demanding that children dress in sexually appropriate clothing or depriving them of particular toys, only intensify children's defiance and worsen the problem. Perhaps the most anguishing point for those involved with such children is the realization that what is gender identity deviant for the culture may be natural and essential for an individual, so that flexibility of role options and acceptance of personal differences may be the best prevention of emotional disorder.

16 | Sexual Attitudes and Behaviors

by Mai-Lan Rogoff

The development of sexual behavior and sexual identity is a topic of more than passing interest to most parents. Sexual development and, later, adult sexual behavior are significantly affected by parental attitudes towards sexuality, which influence information and attitudes transmitted to the child. Sexuality is not only a physiologic response, but a complex mixture of physical capabilities, technical expertise, self-image, and interpersonal communication as well. Communication during the sexual experience is both verbal and nonverbal, the latter being often more direct than verbal communication, but also more easily misunderstood. Sexuality can communicate a range of feelings from love and respect through disinterest to wounding and hurting, with the miscommunication often occurring through lack of understanding or a different cultural background, rather than through an intent to hurt. It is important that the pediatrician have some understanding of the adult human sexual response, its changes during pregnancy, and some of the common problems regarding development of sexuality and sexual identity. This section will discuss conclusions which may be drawn from current studies and also mention those important areas about which very little is presently known.

Sexual Physiology

Sexual physiology has probably best been studied by Masters and Johnson who published their report *Human Sexual Response* in 1966. In their study of 350 male and 230 female volunteers, the researchers used various modes of stimulation: masturbation, intercourse, fantasy, and artificial coital devices with recording equipment. They divided the sexual response cycle in the normal adult into four phases: excitement, plateau, orgasm, and resolution. Genital and extragenital components were noted for each of these phases. Excitement in both men and women is marked by nipple erection (more inconsistent in men), a sex flush starting in the epigastrium and spreading to the upper trunk and face, and an increase in voluntary muscle tension. There is venous engorgement causing increased breast size, enlargement and a color change of the labia minora, enlargement of the clitoris in women, and an easily reversible erection of the penis in men. In addition, during excitement in the woman there is lubrication of the vagina by transudation through the vaginal walls, expansion and distension of the vaginal barrel, and elevation of the cervix with a change in the angle of the uterus. In men the testes begin to elevate and the scrotal skin thickens. During plateau, often described as a sensation of impending orgasm, there is: continued increase in venous engorgement and voluntary muscle tension with the development of an "orgasmic platform" in the outer third of the vagina; full elevation of the uterus and cervix forming a vaginal "tent"; development of a "wine red" color of the labia minora and retraction of the clitoris under its hood in women; and further enlargement of the penis, coronal ridge, and testes in men, with a Cowper's gland emission (which may contain sperm) occurring during this phase. During orgasm in both men and women there is loss of voluntary control with spasm of striated muscles, involuntary contractions of the rectum, and 0.8-s interval contractions of the vaginal platform in women and the penile urethra in men. There are also uncoordinated uterine contractions in the nonpregnant woman which become more coordinated and regular as pregnancy progresses. In both sexes, hyperventilation up to 40 breaths per minute, tachycardia up to 180 beats per minute, and blood pressure elevations of up to 30 to 80 mmHg systolic and 20 to 40 mmHg diastolic have been reported. The resolution phase in both men and women is marked by detumescence, a return to a prestimulation state, and generalized perspiration. There are many idiosyncratic reactions as well: desire to urinate or defecate, to be held, to roll over and go to sleep, or to have a cigarette.

The physiologic sexual response cycle is dependent on the integrity of many systems, including local genital anatomy, peripheral neurology, sympathetic and parasympathetic nerve trunks, endocrine systems, cardiovascular and sensory systems, and the central nervous system. The sex drive appears to be primarily androgen-dependent in both men and women. In the brain this is by androgen effect on the anterior hypothalamic and preoptic areas. Androgens also facilitate cord reflexes and have a direct effect on local genital anatomy.

Sexual Behavior

Sexual attitudes and practices in humans are affected by the cultural environment with its differing expectations, freedoms, and taboos. These differences affect attitudes toward masturbation, premarital and extramarital sexual contacts, experimentation with methods of sexual stimulation such as oral-genital sex or different coital positions, and attitudes towards homosexuality. Cultural anthropologists have described systems of sexual permissiveness and sexual taboos in non-Western societies quite different from those of Western societies, yet apparently productive of no more psychological conflict. Discrepancies between values and behaviors wherever they occur result in conflict and negative consequences.

In contemporary American society, a changing pattern of sexual values and behaviors appears to be taking place. Sexual attitudes and practices vary with age, sex, socioeconomic class, education, and other variables, which result in the production of subcultures. The Kinsey Institute, in its studies on human sexual behavior, described some of these differences. Prepubertal sex play was reported to be very common, although few episodes of erotic arousal were reported. Girls tended to have brief periods of play in childhood, with a decrease in incidence as adolescence approaches, whereas boys tended to have a more or less continuous increase toward adolescence. By adulthood, 92 percent of the men and 58 percent of the women reported masturbation to orgasm, with the frequency peaking at adolescence in men; in contrast women experienced a rise in frequency toward adulthood. Women's masturbatory fantasies, when present, tended to be more similar to their own real-life situations than those of men. Women who had early masturbatory experiences to orgasm tended to be more sexually active as adults and to experience a higher rate of orgasm in marital intercourse than women who had little or no masturbatory experience. Premarital activity varied depending on education. Ninety-eight percent of men and 38 percent of women with less than an eighth-grade education had premarital intercourse by age 20, compared with only 68 percent of men and 17 percent of women with some college education. Education also affected the frequency of experimentation with positions, oral-genital sex, etc., with those having more education having more variety in their sexual experiences. Morton Hunt, in his recent study *Sexual Behavior in the Seventies,* based on a sample of 2026 adults, found a somewhat changing pattern of sexual attitudes and practices in the intervening 30 years. He found a dramatic increase in the incidence of premarital sexual experiences, especially in women, among whom 66 percent of the sample between the ages of 16 and 25 had had some premarital sexual experience. The incidence of extramarital sex had not increased among men; by age 45, about half the men in both Kinsey's and Hunt's samples had had some extramarital contact. The incidence of extramarital sex also remained the same among married women between 25 to 40 (18 percent); however, 24 percent of women in the 18- to 25-year-old age group had experienced extramarital sex, as compared with 18 percent of Kinsey's sample. Hunt's data also indicate that different sexual practices, such as oral sex, are increasing in the population, with the increase being most dramatic among those with less education. The sociologic data thus show a range of attitudes and practices.

During pregnancy, modifications in sexual behavior occur based on both physiologic and psychologic change. Humans are among the very few animals which continue to practice copulation during pregnancy. Most of the studies of changes in human sexual behavior during pregnancy have found a general decrease in interest and activity despite this tendency to continue some sexual relationships. The decrease appears more marked in primiparas than in multiparas. Medical advice, fears of hurting the fetus, and loss of sexual interest were all given as reasons for practicing continence. A variety of reactions to the decrease of sexual interest and desire have been noted, ranging from frustration and resentment to what was termed "a bland, almost indifferent, acceptance." Most of the husbands seemed to accept the decrease in activity as a temporarily necessary change in their relationship, and some noted that when the baby began to move, the introduction of a third human being began to disturb their ability to be sexually intimate.

One concern of pregnant women who engage in intercourse is that intercourse itself or orgasm may precipitate labor. However, no increased incidence of premature delivery in women who engage in sexual activity up to the week prior to parturition has been reported. Birth weight, precipitation of labor, and Apgar score are independent of frequency of sexual relationships or orgasm. There are, however, uterine contractions during orgasm which become more coordinated as pregnancy progresses. Therefore, intercourse and orgasm need not be prohibited in normal pregnancies, but may need to be limited in women who have a history of prematurity or who are experiencing complications of pregnancy.

The meaning of pregnancy to expectant mothers and fathers is a question which has been approached by several psychoanalytic writers. Pregnancy is generally understood by analytic writers as a turning point in life marked by increased conflict which, under favorable conditions, can result in psychological growth and maturity. Pregnancy also marks a "point of no return," the realization of which is often frightening to prospective parents. The first task of the pregnant woman is that of coping with the alteration in her self-image as her body undergoes physical changes. Around the fifth month, quickening makes evident the fact that the baby is a different being from the mother who must then learn to adapt to this new physical presence, as well as to the continuing change in her own sense of self. During this time previous conflicts and good feelings toward the pregnant woman's own mother often emerge together with earlier attitudes, wishes, and

patterns of behavior. This period usually ends with the establishment of a new equilibrium in the mother-daughter relationship. Fathers generally also need to adjust to the presence of a third human being, a feeling of exclusion during the pregnancy, and an anticipated exclusion after delivery. Both parents will be adjusting to the increased feelings of responsibility and to the change from a "couple" to a "family."

Following parturition, the rapidity and intensity of the return of sexual interest seem to vary. Resumption of activity appears to be related to the husband's attitude, the woman's physical condition before and after pregnancy, and whether or not she is nursing.

Sexual Development

The newborn male infant is physiologically capable of penile erection, as for example in response to a full bladder, and the female infant of vaginal lubrication—both apparently on the basis of reflex. By the end of the first year of life, some form of genital play can be observed in both male and female infants. The genital manipulation occurring around 16 months in both sexes is noted to be accompanied by distinct signs of pleasure such as giggling and smiling, which do not characterize the earlier casual genital play. Male children continue to engage in this genital manipulation and also develop increasing curiosity about their fathers' genitals and a fascination with the process of urination. In female children, direct genital manipulation is often abandoned in favor of indirect means of stimulation such as sitting on a rocking horse, thigh pressure, or rubbing against the crossed leg of a familiar adult. While engaged in this sort of behavior the child tends to acquire a mesmerized look with withdrawal of attention from the outside world.

The fascination with parental genitalia and with the process of urination occurs in both male and female children after a year and a half of age. This seems to be part of the normal exploration of the environment and, if treated as such by the parent, will probably not result in trauma to the child. Little boys may play with their urinary stream, comparing the trajectory to that of other little boys or making patterns with other males; little girls, in attempting to emulate this practice, will experience some frustration. Girls will often ask their parents why it is that father or brother are physically different. Maintenance of an attitude of "different but equal" and encouragement of the little girl's feeling that she is whole, complete, and quite acceptable as she is will minimize any sense of loss or inferiority engendered by realization of the difference between the sexes.

Touching and holding of the infant has been shown to be an extremely important factor in the development of normal social and sexual behavior. In human infants there is need for physical and emotional attention. Infants who are either separated from their mothers between the ages of 6 to 15 months or who experience depriving mothers undergo a syndrome of "anaclitic depression" characterized by apathy, poor feeding, poor weight gain, minimal interpersonal responses, increased susceptibility to infections, lower IQ, and delayed growth milestones, as well as decreased general and self-sexual exploration. They sometimes engage in prolonged periods of masturbation with vigorous rocking and head-banging. Depression in childhood can also decrease sexual exploration with peers and thus retard another facet of the child's socialization. It is interesting that petting behavior, stroking, hugging, rocking, and playing with nipples commonly occur in the child under 3 years of age and again in the adolescent and adult as a part of sexual play.

As children grow and continue to explore both their environment and the limits of parental tolerance, parents become concerned with nudity, self-exposure, and masturbation on the part of their children. While masturbation is a normal part of growth, excessive masturbation may be used by the overly anxious child for release of anxiety. In this instance, conflict in the family as well as hyperactivity or other psychological disturbances in the child may be contributing to the child's constant masturbation. Children engaged in trying to establish their autonomy from their parents may repeat behaviors such as self-exposure or masturbation if it becomes evident that this behavior is upsetting to the parents. Much attention is given to the genital area around the age of 2 and 3 years through toilet training, and the association of this area with "dirty behavior" may add to the child's conception of his genital area as being "dirty."

There is some conflict among sex educators as to the effect of parental nudity on the young child, especially when the child begins to ask questions about the anatomic difference between the sexes.

The effect of parental nudity seems to be related to the content of its communication. If the parent is acting very seductively toward the child and especially if there is conflict between the parents, then the nudity may contribute to the seductiveness and serve to increase the child's confusion about his or her role in the family. If nudity is simply an accepted part of family life, the child will accept it as such. Children often observe their parents' genitalia while parents are in the bathroom, and if this does not arouse anxiety in the parent and questions are answered factually and within the child's capability of understanding, this information will simply be added to the child's growing fund of information about the world. This same attitude is useful in dealing with questions about the child's origins. If answers are not given but covert glances suggest to the child that there is hidden information, then the child's imagination will fill in the blanks, sometimes with frightening fantasies. An overly complete answer which goes beyond the child's ability to understand may also result in fears. Exploration of the child's fantasies and correction of misconceptions while offering simple explanations with details given only in response to questions seem to be most useful.

The state of the parental relationship seems to affect the response of the child to parental nudity, climbing into the parental bed, and even to observation of the parents having intercourse. If the parental relationship is undergoing difficulty or if the parents are separated, there is more chance that nudity or sharing the bed will be perceived as confusingly erotic to the child. The effect of children's witnessing the parents engaged in sexual intercourse also is dependent on its context. Freud first mentions a presumed traumatic effect of watching the "primal scene" in 1896. Most subsequent Western studies on the influence of the observations have focused on their contribution to severe behavior problems. Viewing the parents having intercourse may influence masturbation fantasies and psychosexual development. Children will try to relate any new experience to experiences which they already understand, and this may make a child interpret the biting and moaning of intercourse as aggressive, with violence being done, usually to the mother. Viewing the primal scene may thus be somewhat confusing to the child, but it is not necessarily traumatic. There are certainly many cultures in which it is not customary or possible for the parents to have a bedroom that is entirely separate, and although some measure of privacy is usually attempted, this is not always possible. Again, the effect of viewing the act of intercourse itself seems related to the attitudes and circumstances under which the child has been allowed to watch.

Sexual Identity

Sexual identity, which is a basic personality feature, is influenced by parental attitudes as well as by genetic endorsement (see Sec. 15). The core morphologic identity or basic sense of maleness versus femaleness is established by the end of the first 2 years of life. Sex role behavior is then acquired, and finally sexual partner orientation is established. There is some evidence that sexual differentiation begins to be established while the child is still in utero through exposure to hormones or possibly even to stress. In female rhesus monkeys, an increase in masculine behavior occurs with prenatal exposure to androgens, but there is no effect if the exposure is given postnatally. Actual changes in morphology toward maleness resulting from perinatal androgen exposure have been reported in a number of species, including humans. Conversely, if effective androgen usage is blocked in genetic males, there are changes in morphology toward being female. There seem to be certain critical periods in which this effect is most likely to take place. The area most affected by the presence or absence of androgens appears to be the hypothalamus, in which ultramicroscopic structural sex differences have been reported.

The adrenogenital syndrome provides a naturally occurring situation in humans in which excessive androgen is present perinatally. Several studies have found that girls with adrenogenital syndrome tend to be tomboys, tend to prefer boys for peer contact, and are less interested in playing with dolls, but not to the degree of being considered abnormal or of developing transsexual or homosexual behavior. They are, however, statistically different in their tomboyish behavior from a matched group of "normal" unrelated girls, from a sample of unaffected female siblings, and from their mothers, suggesting that the difference is due to the excess of androgen. Other studies have noted an above-average IQ in girls with adrenogenital syndrome, but, since their IQ is not different from the IQ of their parents or unaf-

fected siblings, this does not appear to be a result of androgen effect. Boys given estrogen as part of therapy for diabetes tend to engage in less rough-and-tumble play and to be less aggressive and athletic although not overtly feminine. The effects of chronic illness on these behaviors must be considered, but nevertheless, these observations suggest that socially recognized "male" and "female" behaviors may be influenced by the amount of circulating hormone.

Once infants begin their extrauterine existence, they are subject to cultural influences. The relative importance of underlying biologic differences versus social learning in sex role differentiation is presently being examined in several fields, including psychology, ethology, and anthropology, as well as medicine. Several studies have shown some behavioral male/female differences even in the newborn. Male infants tend to have greater muscular strength, a higher threshold to jet air stimulation, and lower basal skin conductance, as well as slower speech development and less ability to be toilet trained. Sex of the infant also generates a differential parental reaction. Mothers, for example, differ in the amount of stimulation given (more stimulation given to the females) and in the toys offered to the child as a function of the perceived sex of the infant. Some of these differences may encourage exploratory behavior and aggression in boys and may lead to the frequent finding in psychiatric clinics that boys are seen more often than girls for problems involving lack of control. It may also be that boys are responding to a socially imposed sex role stereotype which dictates aggressiveness and restricts expression of feelings. Children seem to have a fairly well developed sense of sex role expectation by the age of 5 or 6, and boys continue to be seen by their 9- and 10-year-old peers as more aggressive and antisocial than girls. Both boys and girls seem to share common expectations in regard to sex-appropriate behavior. Children from lower socioeconomic class families tend to conform more closely to traditional sex role stereotypes than middle-class children. This may reflect a different style of child raising as well as values and beliefs held by the parents.

The boy who does not conform to these sex role stereotypes is likely to experience ostracism by his peers, be labeled a sissy, and turn toward the girls for peer contacts where he may be more accepted. This will then further change the feedback to him from his peers and increase the deviation of his development from normal. Being called a tomboy does not carry the degree of social censure of being called a sissy, perhaps because of the differential value given to male and female characteristics by our society. This may allow the tomboyish girl to have a more normal peer development than the boy who does not conform to sex role expectations. Early intervention, between the ages of 5 and 12, may help the effeminate boy to reintegrate into his peer group. Treatment consists mainly of engaging the boy in activities which are more stereotypically neutral and in helping him to find a less aggressive group of boys with whom to associate. It is necessary to involve the parents in this therapy. Social ostracism, in most cases, is sufficiently unpleasant to warrant early treatment of these boys. Treatment after puberty is much less successful in changing sex role orientation.

Sexual behavior and self-concept as a sexual being play a far-reaching role in human adaptation, from the sex act itself to social status and attitudes taken in adult life. Many of the traditional concepts of male and female behavior are presently being challenged. Men are becoming more aware of women's potential for sexual enjoyment and are feeling more responsible for providing it. This, as well as the feeling of loss of the traditional male-dominant position, can be very threatening to both partners and can lead to feelings of inadequacy and, at times, to dissolution of the relationship. The more positive view is that a new equilibrium is being reached, in which men and women again see themselves as "helpmates" and in which they can encourage the growth of their children toward loving and responsible sexuality.

17 | Contraception

by Kenneth L. McKinney

Physicians providing medical care to adolescents have a unique opportunity, indeed an obligation, to provide these patients with information about reproductive physiology and human sexuality.

By the time they graduate from high school a significant number of teenagers are sexually experienced (as many as 40 percent of females and 70 percent of males). Between 25 and 30 percent of women seeking abortion are age 19 or under. In this group less than 20 percent used contraception consistently. It has been estimated that nearly 3 million women ages 15 to 19 are in need of family planning services (see Sec. 65 and 66).

It is apparent that there is a need for contraception among teenagers and equally apparent that they are not obtaining these services. Many lack any knowledge about contraceptive methods or their availability. Some have misconceptions about their own sexuality and the effect of contraception on it. For others there is embarrassment in seeking contraception as it implies planned sexual activity. Among one group of teenagers seeking abortion, between 6 and 9 percent wanted to become pregnant at the time of conception. Feelings of inadequacy or poor self-image, such as "I can't get pregnant" or "I can't get her pregnant," may account for nonuse in about 30 percent. Finally, teenaged women with plans for further education use contraception more frequently than do those without such plans.

There has been a great deal of discussion about whether or not provision of contraception advice promotes or increases sexual activity. Some physicians cite this as a reason for not providing contraception for teenage single patients or discussing sexuality with them. While the vast majority of those seeking contraception are sexually active and will continue whether or not contraception is provided, there will be a smaller group who really do not wish to continue a sexual relationship, but are so controlled by their peer group that stopping is impossible without support from someone such as the physician. There is also a small group not yet sexually active who are under tremendous peer pressure to begin. Failure to understand and discuss the adolescent patient's needs, or worse, the delivery of a moralizing lecture without listening to the patient, will turn all these groups away from proper medical care and will force those with some misgivings into continuing or new sexual relationships.

The ideal contraceptive should be totally effective, completely safe, ensure complete return to the preexisting fertility potential upon discontinuation, esthetically pleasing, temporally unrelated to intercourse, and easy to use. Since there is no ideal contraceptive method, physician and patient must arrive at a compromise which best suits the patient's needs. Answering the following questions may help in the selection process:

Does the patient have any medical problems which contraindicate the use of a method?

How much protection does the patient need?

What would the patient do in the event of a method failure?

Does the patient have any personal feelings about a method which preclude its use?

Does the physician feel any method is undesirable in terms of patient continuation?

Oral Contraceptives

A complete history should be taken and a thorough physical examination performed. Laboratory work should include a CBC, urinalysis, pap smear, and rubella titer. A history or physical examination suggesting prenatal diethylstilbestrol (DES) exposure necessitates proper evaluation or referral to a gynecologist knowledgeable about the problem and having the ability to perform colposcopy. This should be done before a contraceptive method is prescribed.

Availability of synthetic estrogen and progestins and the discovery that cyclic administration of a combination of these compounds inhibits ovulation led, in 1956, to clinical trials of "the pill" in Puerto Rico. Oral contraceptives were originally marketed as either sequential type, consisting of 15 or 16 estrogen pills followed by 6 or 7 estrogen-progestin pills, or a combination type, consisting of 20 or 21 estrogen-progestin pills. Sequentials are no longer marketed, so the following discussion will concern the combination type and the "mini-pill" or progestin-only pill.

The typical combination pill is administered cyclically for 21 days, followed by a 7-day break or rest period during which no hormonal pills are taken. Pills are packaged in 21-pill packs, which consist of 21 active ingredient pills, or 28-pill packs, which consist of 21 active ingredient pills and 7 inert pills or, in some cases, iron pills. Some patients find the 28-pill pack more convenient, since they take a pill every day, while others consider its use an insult to their intelligence. To begin the first cycle of oral contraceptives an arbitrary starting time is selected which will guarantee protection in the first cycle. It must first be ascertained, however, that the patient is not pregnant. The most common technique is to begin taking the pill on day 5 of a menstrual cycle. If the patient would like to avoid periods on weekends she may begin on the first Sunday after the beginning of a period. After completing a 21-pill pack the patient takes no pill for 7 days and then begins a new cycle. In this way she will always begin a new pill pack on the same day of the week. In general, withdrawal bleeding begins about 2 to 3 days after the last active ingredient pill is taken, and the period will last 4 to 5 days. It is important that the patient understands that most women experience some change in their periods while on the pill. Most find that the period is shorter and lighter. Indeed, some may have a light flow for only a day or so.

There are over 20 combination pills manufactured today. They consist of one of two estrogens, either ethinyl estradiol or mestranol, and any one of nine progestins. While manufacturers may promote their product based on the potency of the estrogen or progestin found in animal studies, there appears to be no advantage of one ingredient over another at this time.

Administration of the combination pill results in the inhibition of ovulation in most cycles. This effect is brought about by the suppression for FSH and LH production. It appears that ovulation rarely occurs, and in this case the contraceptive effectiveness is probably related to thick cervical mucus which impedes sperm transport and endometrial alteration which inhibits implantation. The combination pill is nearly 100 percent effective with a failure rate of about 1 pregnancy per 1000 women users per year. The progestin-only or mini-pill is administered continuously. It does not work by inhibiting ovulation, but rather by endometrial alteration and cervical mucus changes. The failure rate is 25 to 35 per 1000 women per year. This relatively high failure rate plus irregular and unpredictable vaginal bleeding makes its use limited.   *Contraindications to the use of the pill* include thrombophlebitis, thromboembolic disorders, cerebral vascular disease, coronary artery occlusion, or a past history of those conditions. In addition, markedly impaired liver function, known or suspected estrogen-dependent neoplasm, known or suspected breast cancer, undiagnosed abnormal reproductive tract bleeding, and known or suspected pregnancy are contraindications to the use of the pill.

As noted above, there are over 20 combination pills available from which the physician may choose. There appears to be good evidence in both retrospective and prospective studies that pills containing 50 μg or less of estrogen reduce the risk for developing thromboembolic problems. The patient must be counseled about bothersome side effects and more serious complications.

Side Effects

Breast tenderness and, rarely, breast enlargement (and even more rarely, decrease in breast size) may be noted, especially during the first few cycles with pills containing higher doses of estrogen. The problem usually disappears or may only be noted for the first few days of each new pill cycle.

Nausea and *vomiting* may occur in the first few cycles, but usually disappear and are more common with the higher-dose pills. They may be overcome by taking the pill at bedtime or with a meal.

Breakthrough bleeding is probably the most common side effect, especially in the first two to three cycles. It is more common with those pills having smaller amounts of estrogen (50 μg or less) and will usually disappear spontaneously. Patients should be advised that breakthrough bleeding in the first few cycles is common; thus will result in higher patient continuation rates. Heavy breakthrough bleeding may be controlled by administration of estrogen (20 μg ethinyl estradiol daily for 5 to 10 days) or by taking two contraceptive pills daily for the rest of the cycle. The latter method is less effective. Persistent breakthrough bleeding should be evaluated thoroughly by a gynecologist.

Weight gain may occur in some patients for one of three reasons. It may occur because of fluid retention. In this case the patient may notice a cyclic pattern to the change. It may occur because of appetite stimulation by the progestin, or it may relate to increased food intake unrelated to pill use.

Depression has been reported in some women using oral contraceptives. Before discontinuation of the pill, other causes of depression must be sought and, if not found, another method of contraception should be considered.

Other rare side effects include skin rashes; change in eyeball configuration, making it difficult to wear contact lenses; increased cervical mucus production with resulting discharge; and pigments of the skin of the face, especially in women who have dark complexions, who have a history of similar changes during pregnancy, or who have excessive exposure to the sun.

There may be a decrease in carbohydrate tolerance in some patients. Prediabetic and diabetic patients should have blood glucose levels monitored while they are taking oral contraceptives.

Women who use the pill are likely to have less premenstrual symptoms, menometrorrhagia, dysmenorrhea, benign ovarian cysts, benign breast disease, acne, and iron deficiency anemia.

Significant Complications

There is a significant increase in the incidence of thrombophlebitis, pulmonary embolism, and cerebrovascular disease in pill users. Women using the pill are at a five- to tenfold greater risk for these events than nonusers. There is also a threefold increase in the incidence of myocardial infarction in users between the ages of 30 and 39 years and a fivefold increase in those who are older.

Cholelithiasis, cholecystitis, and hypertension occur more frquently in users of the pill than in nonusers. However, some women with essential hypertension have experienced a decrease in blood pressure when placed on oral contraceptives, suggesting that essential hypertension may not be an absolute contraindication to using the pill. There may be a relationship between the use of oral contraceptives and the development of benign liver adenomas. Administration of estrogen and progestins to pregnant women may also have adverse effects on their infants.

Patients must feel free to contact their physician should any bothersome signs or symptoms develop. They must understand the risk of fetal abnormalities following hormone exposure, so that, if a period is missed, pills will be discontinued unless pregnancy termination would be the option selected for dealing with contraceptive failure. Patients must be encouraged not to stop the pill for a presumed problem without confirming the need for discontinuation with the physician. In one study 5 percent of patients seeking abortions had been pill users who discontinued their use for a "problem" which, in the opinion of the reviewing physician, did not necessitate discontinuation.

Although there has been concern about infertility in patients after discontinuing oral contraceptives, it appears that the incidence of both amenorrhea and infertility is similar for non-pill users and post-pill users.

Once started on oral contraceptives, patients should be seen annually for complete evaluation and at 6-month intervals for a blood pressure check and history taking. There is no evidence that the patient needs to "take a rest" from the pill at any given interval. Finally, it is essential that the physician prescribing oral contraceptives stay abreast of current developments which may alter patient follow-up prescribing practices.

The data shown in Table 17-1 may help to put the risk of pill taking in proper perspective.

Table 17-1
Mortality per 100,000 Women per Year as it Relates to Contraceptive Method, Abortion, and Pregnancy

Method	Deaths without Abortion			Deaths with Abortion		
	Pregnancy Related	Method Related	Total	Abortion Related	Method Related	Total
Pill	0.00	3.00	3.00	0.00	3.00	3.00
IUD	0.44	0.30	0.74	0.07	0.30	0.37
Mechanical	2.50	0.00	2.50	0.42	0.00	0.42
None	12.00	0.00	12.00	1.92	0.00	1.92

Intrauterine Devices (IUDs)

Ernest Gräfenberg developed an IUD which he used successfully in his patients in the early 1930s. However, it was not until the early 1960s that IUDs became accepted as a reasonable method of contraception. Devices currently marketed are made from an inert flexible plastic compound, are radiopaque, and return to their original shape after a short period of deformity. A monofilament thread is attached to one end. Some devices are wrapped with copper wire (Cu 7, Copper T) or contain a small amount of progesterone (Progestasert), while the most widely used (Lippes loop, Saf-T-Coil) are plain plastic.

The IUD offers a highly effective method of contraception. The failure rate ranges from 1 to 3 pregnancies per 100 women per year.

The mechanism of action of intrauterine devices is not fully understood. Alterations of the endometrium to prevent implantation, altered tubal motility, and alteration of intrauterine secretions which destroy sperm and/or the fertilized egg have been suggested as the mechanism. Addition of copper wire results in inhibition of progestational proliferation, while addition of progesterone release continuously results in progestational changes in the endometrium, which may inhibit implantation.

Contraindications

Contraindications to the use of an IUD are acute or chronic pelvic inflammatory disease, known or suspected pregnancy, undiagnosed abnormal reproductive tract bleeding, hypermenorrhea, dysmenorrhea, and congenital uterine anomalies or distortion of the uterine cavity by leiomyomas.

Side Effects

Women wearing intrauterine devices tend to have an increase in length of menstrual periods and amount of blood loss. There may be the onset of cramps in women who had never experienced them before. Generally, women who have not required medication for dysmenorrhea will not require any if they wear an IUD, nor will women who use an analgesic require stronger medication. Many women will experience breakthrough bleeding after IUD insertion. Most will establish their own bleeding pattern by the third or fourth cycle following insertion. Once this pattern has been established, patients must be instructed that *any further change in their bleeding pattern must be looked upon as a complication* and reported to the physician immediately.

Complications

Perforation occurs about 1 time in 2500 insertions. It usually occurs at the time of insertion. If the device is pushed partway through the uterine wall, however, it may take months to work its way into the abdominal cavity. To avoid perforation, a number of steps must be taken. The patient must be examined carefully so that the exact position of the uterus is noted. After painting the cervix with an appropriate antiseptic solution, the cervix is held with a tenaculum or allis clamp to stabilize it. The uterine cavity is then measured with a uterine sound. In doing this, one frequently finds unusual curves or deviations in the cervical canal. Traction on the tenaculum will help to straighten the canal, making passage of the device easier. The device with its inserter is placed to the fundal depth measured with the uterine sound, and the inserter is withdrawn leaving the device in the uterus. Immediately following insertion, the patient is taught to feel the thread which protrudes from the cervix. She should then check for its presence weekly during the first three cycles following insertion and monthly thereafter. If she cannot feel the thread, she must be evaluated for possible expulsion or perforation. Insertion during or just at the end of a period may be easier because of a certain amount of cervical dilation. Postpartum or postabortal insertion should be delayed until the uterus is well involuted.

Pelvic inflammatory disease occurs in 1 to 5 percent of women wearing IUDs. It may occur at any time after insertion, but is more common following menstruation. The onset of symptoms is often insidious. Foul vaginal discharge, breakthrough bleeding, vague lower abdominal pain or low backache, dyspareunia, hypermenorrhea, low-grade fever, or a general feeling of ill health may signal the onset of pelvic inflammatory disease. The patient must understand this and contact the physician immediately should these symptoms occur, so that proper evaluation and treatment can be instituted. After appropriate cultures have been obtained, the IUD should be removed and antibiotic therapy started.

Pregnancy may occur with the IUD in place. If the device is left in place, the incidence of spontaneous abortion is nearly 50 percent. If it is removed during the first trimester of pregnancy, the incidence of spontaneous abortion drops to 30 percent. There is also evidence of a high rate of sepsis in those who do abort. Patients must understand this risk so that the device can be removed immediately should pregnancy occur.

Loss of the IUD will be suspected by the patient when she cannot feel the string. Usually the device has merely moved within the uterine cavity. After ascertaining that the patient is not pregnant, the device can be located with a uterine sound or small curette and its tail pulled back through the cervical canal. If this does not work, an x-ray using radiopaque dye or a metal sound to define the uterine cavity must be taken. If the device is in the uterus, it can usually be removed under fluroscopy. If it is outside the uterus it must, of course, be removed. If silent expulsion has occurred, a new device can be inserted at the time of the next period. Should the patient be pregnant, with the device in the uterus and the string not visable, she must be counseled regarding the risks so that a decision can be made to either continue the pregnancy or terminate it.

Patient Follow-up

Once the device has been inserted, the patient should be reexamined in 6 weeks. If her examination is normal, the instructions given at the time of insertion should be reemphasized. Thereafter, annual examination is sufficient.

Device Selection

A number of intrauterine devices are available (Fig. 17-1). The rates of pregnancy, expulsion, medical removal, and continuation provided by each manufacturer are quite similar.

There appears to be a relationship between device size and failure rate for the plain devices. The larger ones have lower failure rates, but may not be as well tolerated, especially by nulligravid patients. The smaller size of the copper-wrapped and hormone-containing devices may be an advantage to the nulligravid patient. The higher cost, need for change (Cu 7 at 2 years, Progestasert at 1 year) and lack of knowledge regarding long-term effects of copper and progesterone may be considered disadvantages. Plain devices need be removed only for complications or patient desire.

Diaphragm

The diaphragm is a relatively inexpensive and simple method of contraception. It consists of a circular spring covered by a dome of soft, thin rubber. Sizes vary from 60 to 90 mm. A spermicidal jelly or cream is placed in the dome and the diaphragm inserted into the vagina before intercourse. The failure rate is given at 5 to 7 pregnancies per 100 women per year, although recent data from Planned Parenthood indicate a failure rate in the range of 2 to 3 pregnancies per 100 women per year. Success is dependent on proper fitting and patient motivation. A properly fitted diaphragm fits snugly behind the pubic bone, covers the cervix, fills the space behind the cervix, and cannot be "felt" once it is in place. After the proper size is selected, the patient should insert the diaphragm herself and be reexamined by the physician, so that both will know she can insert it properly (see Fig. 17-2). The patient should also practice removing the diaphragm before leaving the doctor's office, so that she knows she can do this properly. The following points require emphasis.

Figure 17-1 Contraceptive devices in common use.

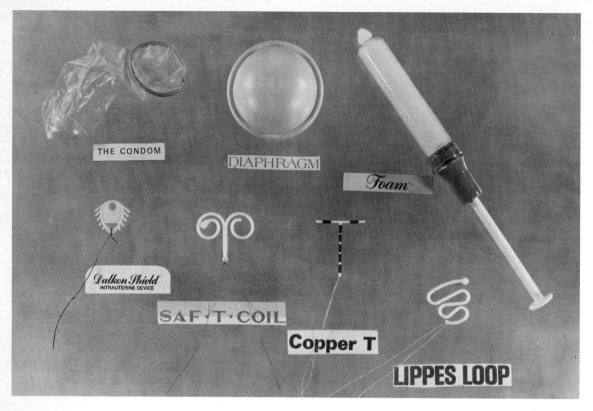

The diaphragm must be used every time she has intercourse.

The diaphragm may be inserted up to 2 h before intercourse and must be left in place for 6 h after intercourse.

One to two teaspoons of spermicide must be placed in the dome of the diaphragm.

If more than 2 h elapses before intercourse, more spermicide must be placed in the vagina.

If she has intercourse again before the 6-h period has elapsed, the diaphragm must be left in place and more spermicide placed in the vagina.

If, for any reason, she loses weight in excess of 10 lb, she should have the diaphragm size checked to ensure that it still fits properly.

She should inspect the diaphragm occasionally for breaks in the rubber dome.

Side effects are rare and may occur in the patient who is allergic to either the rubber in the diaphragm or to one of the chemical ingredients in the spermicide.

Some women who were diethylstilbestrol-exposed have narrowing of the upper vagina and cannot be properly fitted. Women with uterine prolapse or a large cystocele or rectocele may likewise be difficult or impossible to fit.

Condoms

Condoms were originally made from animal intestine, but today are usually made from rubber. They are relatively inexpensive, safe, and easy to obtain. Used properly, the failure rate is 3 to 7 pregnancies per 100 women per year.

The condom should be unrolled onto the erect penis before any penile-vaginal contact, since there is sometimes discharge of fluid containing sperm from the penis prior to ejaculation. The distal portion of the condom should be deflated and left free as

Figure 17-2 Self-examination of diaphragm position.

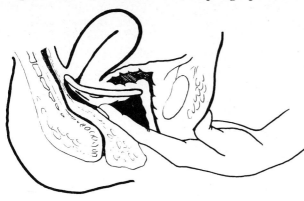

a receptacle for the ejaculate. Some men and women complain of decreased sensation or burning sensation from decreased lubrication. The use of vaginal spermicide or K-Y jelly may overcome this problem. Common Vaseline (petroleum jelly) should not be used since it contains ingredients that may cause rubber to disintegrate. After ejaculation and *before* erection subsides, the penis should be removed from the vagina with the proximal end of the condom held firmly to prevent slippage and spilling of semen.

Vaginal Creams, Jellies, and Foams

Vaginal spermicides are easy to use, widely available, and, aside from rare allergic reactions causing vaginal irritation, have no side effects. The disadvantage is a high failure rate of 12 to 15 pregnancies per 100 women per year. If used in combination with condoms, the failure rate is 2 to 5 pregnancies. The foam type probably provides the best protection. A vaginal insertion device allows introduction of the foam in the upper vagina anterior to the cervix. It should be inserted at least 30 min before intercourse. If intercourse is repeated, another applicator full of the compound must be used.

The Rhythm Method

Eliminating sperm-ova contact will prevent pregnancy. Therefore, if one knows the life-span of egg and sperm and the exact time of ovulation and absolutely avoids intercourse during the ovulatory phase of the menstrual cycle, pregnancy should not occur. The variability of each of these factors gives the rhythm method a failure rate of 15 to 25 pregnancies per 100 women per year. To calculate the "unsafe" period the woman records the length of six to eight consecutive cycles. Subtracting 18 days from the length of the shortest cycle gives the first "unsafe" day. Subtracting 11 days from the longest cycle gives the last "unsafe" day. Because cycle length may vary over long periods of time, the calculation of the unsafe period must be based on the most recent six to eight cycles.

Coitus Interruptus

Coitus interruption or withdrawal is probably the oldest method of contraception and is still used widely. It has no serious side effects, but does have a high failure rate of 20 to 30 pregnancies per 100 women per year. Many people find it less than satisfactory because their concentration on the method makes it difficult to enjoy their sexual feelings.

Postcoital Methods

Administration of diethylstilbestrol (DES) (25 mg twice daily) or ethinyl estradiol (5 mg daily), or conjugate equine estrogen (30 mg daily), beginning within 72 h of unprotected intercourse for 5 days, appears to be a highly effective method of contraception. Kuchera followed 1000 women who were treated in this way with DES. With no treatment the estimated number of pregnancies should have been 100, but none occurred in patients using diethylstilbestrol. Thus, the "morning-after" pill appears to be effective. However, the patient must be made aware of the risk of fetal anomalies and carcinoma of the vagina in female offspring which follow exposure to these compounds, and of the need to ensure that she is not already pregnant before they are used.

Table 17-2
Fertility Rates for Various Methods of Contraception

Method	Pregnancies/100 Women per Year
Pill	0.1
IUD	1–3
Diaphragm	2–7
Condom	3–7
Foam	12–15
Rhythm	15–25
Withdrawal	20–30

There is also an increased risk for ecotopic pregnancy because of a delay in transport of the fertilized egg along the fallopian tube. Fortunately, this is rare.

Summary

There are methods currently available to control rates of reproduction which vary in their effectiveness even when properly applied. Table 17-2 summarizes the fertility rates, in terms of pregnancies per 100 sexually active women per year, experienced with each method discussed here. These should be compared with an annual fertility rate of 80 for each 100 sexually active women who use no methods of contraception whatsoever.

Abortion is an alternative to contraception and a means for managing contraceptive failure for those who do not wish to have children. Because of the higher risks involved with abortion compared to other methods of population control, it cannot be accepted as an alternative to contraception. However, when performed under proper circumstances, abortion carries far less risk to the mother than does completion of pregnancy. Table 17-1 demonstrates the relative risks of various methods of contraception, abortions performed legally, and pregnancy in terms of mortality. Comparable figures for morbidity are not available, but can be presumed to be of the same magnitude.

It is evident that while all methods currently available have certain limitations, modifications of existing methods or development of entirely new ones will be necessary to achieve the ideal. The following are in various stages of development and may be available in the next 8 to 10 years: implants which release a low dose of contraceptive steroid, a steroid-releasing diaphragm or ring, sperm suppression using oral or injectable steroids in males, and an injectable long-acting compound for women.

18 | Personal Adaptations to Pregnancy

by Darden Whelden Rozycki

Implicit in the title of this chapter is concern for the fetus and the physiologic processes occurring within the mother's body. Equally as important for the physician to consider are the personal adaptations of the pregnant woman. Swartz and Swartz stated, "At any time from conception to adulthood the child is the product of a fixed genetic endowment acted upon by the environment." They suggest that during pregnancy the mother's physiology acts as the primary environmental influence on the fetus and placenta. Others have qualified this statement to some extent by correlating the expectant mother's emotions with the subsequent emotionality of her child, and with a predisposition toward colic in the neonatal period. Future studies may demonstrate other correlations between a woman's emotions and the personality of her newborn, but at this point it can be concluded that, in comparison to maternal physiology, the pregnant woman's "beliefs, thoughts, attitudes, and behaviors toward the unborn child exert little direct effect on the child's survival, course and well being. However, with few exceptions, at the moment of birth these two factors undergo a dramatic shift in importance. Parental behaviors and attitudes assume an overwhelmingly more important role than maternal physiology in the child's ultimate survival and well-being."

Brazelton acknowledges that no long-term studies have supported his conviction that "the essence of a child's well-being, both emotional and physical, is dependent on the tone of the mother-father-child relationship." Yet many physicians who are either presently involved in short-term research projects or who have had years of experience in private practice anticipate that this will prove to be a valid assumption.

It is therefore becoming increasingly common for physicians to arrange a pediatric prenatal visit with the expectant couples for whose children they will be caring. This contact serves a number of purposes. First, it allows the physician to define a data base before examination of the newborn in the hospital. Second, it allows the pediatrician to assume an active role as advocate for the fetus. Third, the pediatric prenatal appointment facilitates a smooth transition from obstetric management to pediatric management for both the physicians and the family. A fourth benefit becomes evident when one accepts the trend in general pediatrics away from caring specifically for infant and childhood diseases and toward caring for the child in the context of the family. The appointment will broaden the perspective of the physician, providing him or her with more information about the family. The final advantage to this appointment is documented by studies which have shown the beneficial effects of early assessment and intervention. Klaus, Kennel, and their colleagues have detailed the maternal-newborn bonding process. Brazelton has used his Neonatal Behavioral Assessment Scale not only to chart a newborn's capabilities of responding to the environment, but also to facilitate understanding and acceptance by parents of their child. Kempe has suggested that prenatal, perinatal, and postnatal observations of a mother and father can make possible the early identification of families who may manifest child-abusive tendencies, and that active intervention through the provision of extra services may decrease the risk of deviant child-rearing behavior. Bibring and Valenstein, and Caplan, have found that the special state of disequilibrium which is prevalent during pregnancy makes the expectant mother more receptive to guiding influences than she is during less emotional, more stable periods of her life.

It is often the case that prenatal appointments provide the adult woman's first exposure to a comprehensive medical care system. It seems reasonable for physicians to join with other health care agents in an effort to potentiate the physiologic care given by offering concern and support for the psychological adjustments involved. To do justice to this task, an understanding of the dynamics of "the childbearing year" is essential.

Pregnancy As a Growth Crisis

Pregnancy has been viewed from different perspectives. Caplan regarded it as "a period of increased susceptibility to crisis." Bibring and Valenstein considered it "a normal life crisis," where that term is meant to imply "a time-limited disturbance of the equilibrium . . . precipitated by biological and psychological stress." They further stated that the "crisis is gradually supplanted by a different state of functioning, by a different adaptation from what had prevailed before the crisis." The Colmans referred to pregnancy as "an altered state of consciousness," a state which lasts over a prolonged period of time. Physicians should be aware of the crisis nature of pregnancy as well as the degree to which the pregnant mother has accepted the challenge to grow and mature.

Developmental Tasks of Pregnancy

It is stated that a pregnant woman has four developmental tasks facing her. It is important for the physician to determine how she is coping with these tasks because, as Clark asserts, when these "critical tasks are resolved, the woman completes pregnancy with growth, self-esteem, and autonomy." Clark continues by listing the tasks as (1) pregnancy validation, (2) fetal embodiment, (3) fetal distinction, and (4) role transition. Although a woman may deal with two tasks concurrently, each one can and should be differentiated from the others.

Pregnancy validation involves accepting the existence of the pregnancy, which often motivates the woman to seek medical confirmation of her suspected gravid state. Fetal embodiment requires that the expectant mother "incorporate the fetus into her body image" (Colman and Colman). Dealing with these two tasks may precipitate withdrawn, introspective behavior. The woman contemplates the implications of pregnancy and begins to create an image of herself as a mother. This requires that she assess her relationship with her own mother, which in turn may cause complex feelings of conflict, guilt, and fear of inadequacy.

The third task, fetal distinction, is often resolved at the time of quickening or perhaps during a prenatal appointment when the woman hears her baby's heartbeat on the Doptone. At this point she is made aware of the fact that the baby is an individual in its own right, dependent upon her but distinct from her. She will usually exhibit less introspective behavior and become more interested in her environment, but with a new perspective: "How will the baby fit in?"

The fourth developmental task of pregnancy, role distinction, implies that the woman must recognize that the fetus will be relinquished in order for the baby to be born, and that she must, on the day of birth, assume active responsibility as a mother. In working toward the resolution of this final task, a woman must deal with her expectations and fears about both the birth process and about her new role.

Characteristics of the Expectant Mother

How a woman approaches and completes her developmental tasks depends to some degree upon the unique and time-limited personality traits which will manifest themselves during her pregnancy. When Bibring and colleagues studied the implications of pregnancy, they found "a surprising number of young women who were originally diagnosed as being substantially disturbed, or even considered to be what we call borderline or incipient psychotic individuals." They further discovered that after birth the disturbed state usually subsided, either spontaneously or with limited professional therapy. Knowledge about these special adaptive characteristics of pregnant women can benefit both the physician and patient.

The most obvious emotional manifestation of pregnancy is reflected by sudden and unexplainable mood swings. This lability is further augmented by the fact that pregnant women are more intensely emotional than nonpregnant women. They are extremely sensitive, often irritable, and may demonstrate inability to tolerate frustration. Feelings of ambivalence coupled with emotional instability lead those dealing with them to conclude that they are unpredictable. Communication is further complicated by an expectant mother's seeming vagueness and the difficulty which she sometimes has in remembering simple instructions or daily commitments. These traits are possibly the result of the passivity and increased introversion manifested throughout the last two trimesters of pregnancy. Levine and Caplan suggest that this "field contraction" allows the woman to resolve internal and previously suppressed conflicts which rise to the surface of consciousness during the childbearing year.

Anxiety and tension are often expressed by pregnant women. Their concerns generally center around childbirth, pain, and loss of control; their baby's health and the possibility of mental or physical defects; and their ability to mother. These fears can increase the woman's sense of vulnerability, which in turn accentuates her inclination toward dependency on those around her. The expectant mother needs to be reassured that her reactions, some of which may be totally alien to her, are acceptable and normal.

Characteristics of the Expectant Father

In our culture, the role of the expectant father is not clearly defined. Research is only now beginning into his developmental tasks and the special personality traits which he may assume.

Primitive cultures often prescribe certain rituals for the man to follow during his wife's pregnancy and birth experience. Trethowan discusses these "couvade" practices, such as physical symptoms of pregnancy appearing in the husband, and the Colmans suggest that these practices may be relevant to all men: at the same time that they allow a man to share the childbearing year with his wife and help him to actively evolve into a parent, they provide an outlet for any possible envy that he might have for his wife's unique creative capacity.

There is no doubt that pregnancy has deep implications for a man. He must create a new role for himself, and he must often accomplish this at a time when his relationship with his wife is unstable, when demands are being placed upon him which he may feel incapable of fulfilling. If he is expected to assume an active parenting role after his baby's birth, it seems reasonable that he should be given psychological support during the transition period of his wife's pregnancy.

Factors Affecting a Woman's Attitudes toward Pregnancy

There are many factors which influence a woman's ability to cope with her pregnancy and to solve the developmental tasks involved. A brief overview of these general factors will be presented to aid physicians with their interpretations of concerns that may be expressed at the pediatric prenatal appointment. Suggestions of questions which they might ask during this visit will be given in order to guide physicians toward more personalized, comprehensive care.

Personality Characteristics

The age, level of maturity, psychosexual development, pain tolerance levels, self-esteem, and normal methods of dealing with crises all contribute to a woman's success in coping with her pregnancy in a positive manner. A variety of contraceptive methods and the availability of legalized abortion have encouraged the new trend in the middle and upper classes toward establishing oneself in a career, fulfilling one's intellectual needs, and then beginning a family. This in turn has resulted in increasing numbers of "elderly primigravidas," whose concerns often differ markedly from the concerns discussed by expectant mothers in their twenties or from the special problems presented by teenage primigravidas. How comfortable a woman is with her sexual identity may be reflected in such diverse ways as expression of embarrassment by the evident product of her sexual involvement or pride in her fertility. Her attitude toward the actual birth, the decision of whether to be awake and participating or asleep and unaware, will also be affected by her psychosexual development. Pain tolerance levels are important to consider, not only in reference to labor and birth, but also during pregnancy, when a woman may endure varying degrees of discomfort. And finally, a woman's self-esteem and previous experiences of successfully or unsuccessfully resolving crises in her life offer her means of dealing with her present continuing state of crisis. During the prenatal visit, observations may be made about the personalities of the expectant mother and father. Because the couple may initially feel hesitant about sharing their feelings and fears, it is important that all questions be open-ended and nonjudgmental. For example, in order to assess the couple's coping mechanisms which not only play an important role during pregnancy, but which will contribute to the successful resolution of the postpartum period, the physician might say, "Pregnancy is considered by some to be a time of stress; have you two found this to be true for you?"

Physiological Changes

Pregnancy necessitates adjustment to a variety of physiologic phenomena. Day by day, for 9 months, women must contend with the altered biologic functioning of their bodies. Not only are subtle and unrecognized shifts in hormone levels occurring, and the body's internal tissues swelling and distending, all of which may take place without the conscious awareness of the pregnant woman, but there is a dramatic change in physical shape, which is a fact that few expectant mothers can ignore. Thus, during pregnancy, women are confronted with their unique biologic role. How a woman regards the changes occurring in her body may both affect and reflect her attitudes toward pregnancy. Reactions to such "minor complications" as morning sickness, tender nipples, engorged vulva, fatigue, or even compulsive eating habits can vary from resentment of the pregnancy through acceptable irritation to pride and pleasure at those indications that she is indeed gravid. Generally, by the time of the pediatric prenatal visit, she has resolved the ambivalence that these early discomforts may have caused or heightened, but a whole new set of physical challenges are presenting themselves. The answer to such a simple question as "How do you feel about your new shape?" will often indicate, directly or implicitly, how the woman feels about the baby and her impending role as a mother.

Cultural Factors

In America today several pressures are being applied to women in an attempt to alter attitudes and patterns of the past. The literature of Zero Population Growth, the increasing concern about ecological issues, the desire for increased leisure time, and inflation have combined to cause the fertility rate to drop from the record high of 3.76 children per woman in 1957 to a low of 1.75 in 1976. Yet our welfare system still encourages poor women to procreate in order to better support themselves. The women's liberation movement has encouraged all members of society to recognize the choices available to them: to marry, to be single, to involve oneself in a career, to remain childless, to bear children at any age from 20 to 40, and to raise children with or without a partner. These possibilities potentially allow a woman to do as she wishes, although in individual cases she may interpret this freedom as a restriction, or may feel inadequate or inferior if her goal is to be a wife and mother. Just as this woman needs support in her desires and plans, so does the woman who has chosen, or is forced by financial considerations, to be a working mother. Other pressures that exert a more subtle influence are the result of attitudes reflected by advertisements. In magazines and on television the idealized American female is pictured as slender and agile.

Specific cultural pressures need not be discerned at a pediatric prenatal meeting. They will gradually manifest themselves over the following months and years.

Social Factors

An expectant mother's relationships with her extended family and her friends alter during pregnancy, and the degree of support and encouragement which she receives has a direct effect upon her attitudes toward her condition. Many women become intensely involved with their mothers as they attempt to sort out their goals for themselves as prospective parents. Their new role will essentially transform them into equals with their mothers and mothers-in-law, a fact which they or the expectant grandparents sometimes find difficult to accept. A woman's relationships with her siblings may demand her attention, and she may solve old rivalries during her pregnancy. If a woman's friends are unsupportive of her gravid state, she may experience prolonged ambivalence herself. Perhaps she will feel it necessary to nurture new friendships. The amount of support that is surrounding a woman can be determined at a pediatric prenatal interview by a direct question, "Do you feel well supported during this pregnancy?"

Relationships with the Expectant Father and Members of the Immediate Family

The adjustments which must be made within the immediate family during pregnancy are considerable. According to Duvall, the developmental tasks include:

1 Reorganizing house arrangements to provide for the expectant baby.

2 Developing new patterns for earning and spending income.

3 Reevaluating procedures for determining who does what and where authority rests.

4 Adapting patterns of sexual relationships during pregnancy.

5 Expanding communication system of present and anticipated emotional constellation.

6 Reorienting relationships with relatives.

7 Adapting relationships with friends and associates and altering community activities to meet the reality of pregnancy.

8 Acquiring knowledge about and planning for the specifics of pregnancy, childbirth, and parenthood.

9 Testing and maintaining a workable philosophy of life.

It should be remembered that the expectant mother's adaptation varies depending upon her stage of pregnancy, and that her family's attitudes toward her will be affected accordingly.

How the expectant father reacts to pregnancy has important implications for the pregnant woman's adjustment. Therefore, the husband, or partner, should be asked to come to the pediatric prenatal appointment. Whether he is anxious about increased financial burdens, decreased sexual activity, passive or dependent characteristics suddenly exhibited by his wife, the sex of the baby, or his parenting ability, his concerns should be understood and supported in order that he may better understand and support his wife. The expectant couple should be encouraged "to be sensitive to one another's needs . . . to share experiences, to help the other cope with the unfamiliar or frightening, [thereby encouraging] . . . growth in each individual and in the couple, growth enough to support the infant they both will care for in the future" (Colman and Colman).

Relationship with Health Care Providers

An unfortunate development is presently emerging in regard to health care: as physicians and medical technology gain increasing power over disease and death, many of the consumers who will benefit from these developments are becoming alienated from the traditional medical care system. This fact is perhaps most evident in the field of women's health. The authors of two popular books, *Our Bodies, Ourselves* and *Immaculate Deception*, were motivated to publish because of experiences with "doctors who were condescending, paternalistic, judgmental and non-informative," and because of a sense of frustration with "impersonal and technological intervention in the birth process." It is essential that health care professionals regard this alienation of a portion of the populace as a serious problem. Because the child-bearing year may mark the adult woman's entry into the medical system, it is imperative that special efforts be made at this time to educate, understand, and support each woman as an individual. The home birth movement is gaining articulate adherents each day, and the implications of their rejection of the traditional health care system should be recognized, and corrective measures within that system should be taken. The fact that most hospital staffs *do* care must be demonstrated. Showing concern for the psychological adaptations necessitated by pregnancy can be a first step.

19 | The Setting of Birth

by William W. Young

The transcendent objectives of obstetrics are that every pregnancy culminate in a healthy mother and that every child be physically, mentally, and emotionally "well-born." In North America the hospital has evolved as the setting which offers the best opportunity to achieve these objectives.

Babies have, of course, been born in every imaginable situation. Controversy exists today regarding the optimum setting for childbirth. The Bongo woman in Fig. 19-1 endured the natural process of birth alone in the jungle. However, due to the high rate of pregnancy wastage under natural conditions, few would advocate a return to primitive birthing customs. In developing countries where most deliveries occur in homes—and away from so-called medical interference, both infant and maternal mortality are dramatically high—300 to 500 maternal deaths per 100,000 deliveries versus 12.8 per 100,000 recently in the United States. The home "sitting setting" shown in Fig. 19-2 depicts female and male midwives of the 1800s "standing by" a woman in childbirth. Death and disease were still commonplace. Physicians and midwives blamed one another for maternal deaths. The physicians said the midwives lacked training; the midwives said the physicians lacked skill. There was a certain amount of truth in both of these accusations.

Improvement in maternal and perinatal outcome followed the introduction of asepsis, antibiotics, and transfusion, plus antenatal and intrapartum care by qualified well-trained birth attendants. In North America these have been provided through hospital-based maternal-newborn care. In Europe and Scandinavia, carefully monitored systems for handling normal low-risk deliveries in homelike birth centers and at home have evolved and have many

respected advocates. At present a small vocal movement against hospital-based maternity care is occurring in North America. Objections are raised to the treatment of birth as a disorder, disease, or potential crisis in the modern hospital. The hospital is viewed as an expensive, inhuman, technological "jungle" in which birth is impersonal and dangerous for mother and child. In objection to this, some families are electing to deliver at home. Other families deliver at home because high-quality home delivery services have been developed and are the most available in the area (for example, Frontier Nursing Service and Canadian Arctic Settlement Nurses). Birthing centers near but separate from hospitals have also been established to provide maternity care more acceptable to some patient consumers than hospital care. In the Netherlands where one-third of deliveries occur at home, expectant families are carefully screened for 100 contraindications to home delivery and 10 percent of laboring patients are transferred with intrapartum complications to the hospital. Their excellent maternal and perinatal mortality rates indicate that good results can be obtained in carefully screened and monitored populations. Cooperation between domiciliary and other services is essential.

That the setting in which a child is born should be safe for mother and baby stands unchallenged; advocates for hospital-based and other settings for childbirth all agree. The ends are clear, but the means remain controversial. Since the return of home delivery unmonitored and outside the existing system raises the specter of increased maternal and perinatal mortality, obstetricians and pediatricians are trying to make hospital delivery as acceptable and pleasant as possible. Flexibility and responsiveness to patient

Figure 19-1 Bongo woman during delivery.

Figure 19-2 Pennsylvania birth scene, 1776. (*Reproduced with permission from M. Matthews: Birth of a Nation: 1976. Contemporary Ob/Gyn, 7:92, 1976.*)

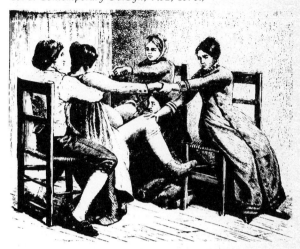

needs will be keys to mutually satisfactory solutions. Toward this end, family-centered maternal-newborn care in hospital is being encouraged.

It is hoped the implementation of a family-centered philosophy and care within innovative and safe hospital settings will actively provide the public with the services they need, request, and demand and make it unnecessary for them to seek unconvential facilities for childbirth.

FAMILY-CENTERED MATERNITY/ NEWBORN CARE

Family-centered maternity/newborn care can be defined as the delivery of safe, quality health care while recognizing, focusing on, and adapting to the physical, economic, and psychosocial needs of the consumer patient, her family, and her newborn. The emphasis is on the provision of safe maternity/newborn health care with the minimal disruption of the family unit while maintaining safety.

Childbearing is recognized as a developmental opportunity and/or possibly a situational crisis, during which the family benefits from the supporting solidarity of being together. It is hoped that the family-centered philosophy can assist families to cope, adjust, and achieve their own goals within the concept of a high level of wellness, and within the context of the cultural atmosphere of their choosing.

The provision of maternity/newborn care requires a team effort of obstetricians, pediatricians, family physicians, certified nurse-midwives, nurse practitioners, and the public. The composition of the team as well as the needs of the public may vary from location to location. The hospital itself should meet the published standards for obstetric services, midwifery services, and neonatal services.

Included in the concept is an emphasis upon preparation and education of families and staff to increase their awareness of the responsibility they share toward ensuring a healthy outcome for mother and child. Classes serve as specific preparation for pregnancy, labor, delivery, and newborn care. The public and providers also utilize this opportunity to match expectations and achieve mutual goals from the childbirth experience. Within the maternity/newborn unit, fathers or other supporting individuals should be welcome to remain with the mother throughout the birth process. Interaction immediately after birth is encouraged.

A combination labor and delivery room or "birthing room" is an excellent setting for normal spontaneous vaginal deliveries that does not disrupt the family contact. A homelike atmosphere, with open visiting arrangements and comfortable attractive furnishings, is possible. The family birth experience should continue into the immediate postdelivery period. When all is well, mother and infant may recover in common, accompanied by their supporting family and assisted by the maternity/newborn personnel. Equipment and personnel for emergencies, both maternal and fetal, must be available. Standard separate labor and delivery rooms should likewise be available and flexible to safely satisfy individual patient requests. The nursery should allow flexible rooming-in. The maximum desired maternal/infant contact should be possible.

The physician responsible for newborn care must remember that he or she is the baby's advocate. Provision for an adequate delivery and neonatal care setting is part of that advocacy. There is some evidence to support the concept that, toward the latter part of pregnancy, the emotional state of a mother, and perhaps the father as well, is directed toward the immediate, impending events of labor and delivery and the parental involvement in those events. Early in pregnancy, emotions and attitudes are more fetally oriented. In modifying or agreeing to alternative delivery settings, the advocate for the soon-to-be-born baby must not lose sight of basic and objective infant needs.

For example, the Committee on the Fetus and Newborn of the American Academy of Pediatrics has provided recommendations for standards for hospital care of newborns. A resuscitation island, an area set aside for providing care for the baby at birth, is urged for each delivery area. The further delivery areas are removed from the nursery, the greater the need for support equipment at the site of delivery. In the average hospital, resuscitation equipment is located in the labor and delivery room and longer-term support equipment in the nursery. In an alternative setting for delivery, especially one physically removed from standard obstetrical suites and the nursery, it may be more difficult to ensure that all the needs for a difficult delivery are at hand. Fortunately, newborn adjustment to extrauterine existence is a normal process, as are labor and delivery, and severe complications of labor and delivery are unusual. When deliveries take place at home the birth attendants must provide all the equipment and expertise. An unexpected emergency, such as neonatal asphyxia, demands extra attention which may not be available. To some, the hospital is a foreboding, cold, uncomfortable place and not like their home. They object to giving birth in that setting. However, in most facilities, provision of essential services in more desirable surroundings is quite feasible. The future will undoubtedly see changes in the birth setting.

20 | Education for Childbirth

by Darden Whelden Rozycki

Birth is the pivotal point of our existence. Because of the investment that all cultures have in procreation, both men and women have accumulated information about childbirth by the time they reach puberty. This knowledge, whether it is based on myths or scientific facts, has a demonstrable effect upon their actual experiences with birth.

In America today, a dramatic shift in attitudes toward birth is occurring. Less than two decades ago, most expectant mothers seemed grateful for the medication that put them to sleep for the delivery of their child, and most of their husbands appeared satisfied with a passive role. Because of the rapid spread of a grassroots consumer movement since the early 1960s, however, it must be concluded that many American couples actually desired the opportunity to participate actively in childbirth. Leading health care professionals involved themselves in this movement at its inception, but much of the pressure for changes in traditional maternity practices was initially applied by consumers. Expectant parents organized childbirth preparation groups and hired teachers to educate them; expectant parents petitioned hospitals asking for permission to have fathers present in the delivery room; and expectant parents persuaded physicians of the benefits of rooming-in.

The credibility of this movement is now established. Physicians, nurses, and other health care providers are enthusiastically implementing family-centered maternity care in hospitals around the country, and, with consumers, are joining such organizations as the International Childbirth Education Association. The growth of this organization since its founding in 1960 indicates the spiralling interest in childbirth education and family-centered mater-

nity care. It was begun by seven groups and eleven individual members, increased in size to include 3600 members in 1972, and by 1977 listed over 11,000 members throughout the United States, Canada, and 20 foreign countries. This increased interest by both professionals and consumers in childbirth is also reflected in the number and diversity of available books and the number of magazine and journal articles being written about this subject. Even movies and prime-time television programs have realistically depicted birth.

The reawakening to the possible values of active involvement throughout the childbearing year has allowed expectant couples to evaluate various opportunities available to them, and to consciously or unconsciously choose the degree of participation with which they are most comfortable. They may decide to limit their knowledge about birth to information gathered from family, friends, obstetrical assistants, and their physicians. They may attend general prenatal or childbirth classes offered by their hospital, their physician, a local mothers' group, a childbirth education association, or an independent teacher.

A variety of approaches to childbirth are chosen by pregnant women, ranging from an individual's desire to be "knocked out" to the wish to participate and share the experience with those whom she loves. The attitude of each woman reflects her expectations and should be respected and dealt with honestly, because it is she who will determine, with the help of the medical professionals, the expectant father, the extended family, and friends, how she will approach birth.

For those women and men who choose to take formal childbirth education classes, several methods are taught throughout the country. Despite the use of different techniques, their basic goals are similar. The primary aim of these classes is usually to make the transition from pregnancy through childbirth into parenthood a positive and healthy experience for the parents and the baby.

Actual class content varies considerably depending upon the method and the teacher. The psychoprophylactic (Lamaze) method, or variations of it, is the most popular in America, and a number of studies have been published which document its benefits. Lamaze series usually involve 12 to 16 h of class preparation and require further hours of reading and practice at home. The class format provides time for both lecture and discussion periods as well as for the use of audio-visual materials. Information is given about the anatomy of reproduction, fetal development, nutrition, and psychological adaptations to pregnancy. The physiological and emotional characteristics of labor are dealt with in depth. Because most childbirth educators believe that it is their responsibility to expose expectant parents to available alternatives, hospital procedures and analgesia and anesthesia are also discussed. Often a tour of the hospital obstetrical facilities is made. It is felt that this allows the couples to choose wisely the ways in which they wish to participate. They are encouraged to set goals for themselves, and teachers usually try not to impose their philosophies or prejudices upon them. Due to the rising percentage of caesarean births, this topic is covered in many classes. In an 8-week course, discussion time is also devoted to the adjustments of the postpartum period, breast-feeding, newborn care, and family planning.

Education about these varied subjects serves a number of purposes. First, the couples are given the opportunity to regard birth from both a broad and specific, pivotal perspective. Second, they are made aware of the importance of caring for their health, and are exposed to the idea that they can help influence certain physiological processes. Third, they are encouraged to confront negative feelings and superstitions about the perinatal period and substitute facts in their place. These three aspects combine to help block the fear-tension-pain cycle which has been described as a cause of discomfort in childbirth.

To help eliminate other causes of pain, couples are taught limbering exercises, relaxation skills, and breathing techniques. The limbering exercises, which include learning control of the pelvic floor muscles, improve a woman's general physical condition and strengthen the muscles which are under the most strain in pregnancy and during labor and birth. Learning how to relax enables the woman to interrupt the tension-pain process. The breathing techniques, which are designed specifically to be coordinated with contractions, allow the woman to concentrate on an activity other than the contractions of the uterus.

To date the studies which have been published on the theoretical benefits of childbirth education classes are either inconclusive or contradict one another. The only valid claim is that the need for analgesia and/or anesthesia is reduced. Regardless of the scientific basis for participation in these classes most couples who enroll in them express positive feelings about the preparation which they receive. Overall, couples who attend these classes, as well as their health care providers, generally agree that they provide additional, albeit undocumented, benefits.

The fact that these classes are geared not simply to the expectant mother but to the father of the baby as well is important. This provides the woman with a continuum of support throughout the pregnancy, the birth, and the postpartum period. It also allows the father to assume an active role during the birth of his child. It has been hypothesized that his involvement in the preparation and actual birth process facilitates paternal-newborn bonding. It should be noted that in those situations when an expectant father does not accompany the woman to classes or to the hospital, it may be helpful for the expectant mother to bring a supportive person of her choice.

One of the most important aspects of childbirth education classes is the rapport that grows among the participants over the 6- to 8-week period. Communication among members of the group is fostered by class discussion, and the personal friendships and support that develop usually continue into the postpartum adjustment period and often over an extended time.

Another benefit of these classes is derived from the fact that couples learn to think of themselves as members of the obstetrical team. Their rights as patients and their roles are defined. Concurrently, the role that the hospital staff will assume is explained so that expectant parents understand that each role is meant to complement the other, that birth is a cooperative effort. By encouraging couples to assume their share of responsibility for their prenatal care and during the birth process, it is felt that a beneficial contribution is made toward the formation of the family.

REFERENCES

Development of Sexual Identity

Broverman, I. K., Broverman, D. M., Clarkson, F. E., Rosenkrantz, P. S., and Vogel, S. R.: Sex role stereotypes and clinical judgments in mental health, *J. Consult. Clin. Psychol.*, **34**:1, 1970.

Green, R.: *Sexual Identity Conflict in Children and Adults*, New York: Basic Books, 1974.

Howell, M.: The effects of maternal employment of the child, *Pediatrics*, **52**:327, 1973.

Maccoby, E., and Jaclin, C.: *The Psychology of Sex Differences*, Stanford, Calif.: Stanford, 1974.

Money, J., and Higham, E.: "Juvenile Gender Identity: Differentiation and Transposition in Child Personality and Psychopathology," in Davids (ed.), *Child Personality and Psychopathology: Current Topics*, vol. 3, New York: Wiley, 1976.

Sexual Attitudes and Behaviors

Bibring, G., Dwyer, T. F., and Huntington, D. C.: A study of the psychological processes in pregnancy and of the earliest mother/child relationship, *Psychoanalytic Study of the Child*, **16**:9, 1961.

Falicov, C. J.: Sexual adjustment during first pregnancy and post partum, *Am. J. Obstet. Gynecol.*, **117**:991, 1973.

Hunt, M.: *Sexual Behavior in the Seventies*, Chicago: Playboy Press, 1972.

Kinsey, A. C., Pomeroy, W. B., Martin, C.E., and Gebhard, P. H.: *Sexual Behavior in the Human Male*, Philadelphia: Saunders, 1948.

Kinsey, A. C., Pomeroy, W. B., Martin, C. E., and Gebhard, P. H.: *Sexual Behavior in the Human Female*, Philadelphia: Saunders, 1953.

Lee, C., and Steward, R. S.: *Sex Differences: Cultural and Developmental Dimensions*, New York: Urizen Books, 1976.

Maccoby, E. E., and Jacklin, C. N.: *The Psychology of Sex Differences*, Stanford University Press, 1974. (Also an excellent reference book on sex differences.)

Masters, W. H., and Johnson, V. E.: *Human Sexual Response*, Boston: Little, Brown, 1966.

Contraception

Blye, R. P.: The use of estrogens as postcoital contraceptive agents, *Am. J. Obstet. Gynecol.*, **116**:1044, 1973.

Janerich, D. T., Piper, J. M., and Glebatis, D. M.: Oral contraceptives and congenital limb reduction defects, *N. Engl. J. Med.*, **291**:697, 1974.

Kuchera, L.: The morning after pill, *J.A.M.A.*, **224:**1038, 1973.

Royal College of General Practitioners: *Oral Contraceptives and Health*, New York: Pitman Publishing Co., 1974.

Shah, F., Zelnick, M., and Kantner, S. F.: Unprotected intercourse among unwed teenagers, *Family Planning Perspectives*, **7:**39, 1975.

Speroff, L.: Which birth control pill should be prescribed, *Fertility and Sterility*, **27:**997, 1976.

Tietze, C.: Mortality with contraception and induced abortion, *Studies in Family Planning*, **45:**6, 1969.

Tietze, C., Bongaeerts, J., and Schearer, B.: Mortality associated with the control of fertility, *Family Planning Perspectives*, **8:**6, 1976.

Zelnick, M., and Kantner, J. F.: The resolution of teenage first pregnancies, *Family Planning Perspectives*, **6:**74, 1974.

Personal Adaptations to Pregnancy

Arms, S.: *Immaculate Deception*, Boston, Houghton Mifflin, 1975.

Bibring, G. L., and Valenstein, A. F.: Psychological aspects of pregnancy, *Clin. Obstet. Gynecol.*, **19:**357, 1976.

Boston Women's Health Collective: *Our Bodies, Ourselves: A Book by and for Women*, New York: Simon and Schuster, 1976.

Brazelton, T. B.: Anticipatory guidance, *Pediatr. Clin. N. Am.*, **22:**533, 1975.

Caplan, G.: Psychological aspects of maternity care, *Am. J. Public Health*, **47:**25, 1957.

Clark, A. L., and Alfonso, D. D. (eds.): *Childbearing: A Nursing Perspective*, Philadelphia: Davis, 1976.

Colman, A. D., and Colman, L. L.: *Pregnancy: The Psychological Experience*, New York: Herder and Herder, 1971.

Colman, A. D., and Colman, L. L.: Pregnancy as an altered state of consciousness, *Birth and the Family Journal*, **1:**7, 1973.

Duvall, E.: *Family Development*, Philadelphia: J. B. Lippincott, 1962.

International Childbirth Education Association, P.O. Box 20852, Milwaukee, 53220.

Kempe, C. H.: Approaches to preventing child abuse, *Am. J. Dis. Child.*, **130:**941, 1976.

Klaus, M. H., and Kennell, J. H.: *Maternal-Infant Bonding: The Impact of Early Separation or Loss on Family Development*, St. Louis: Mosby, 1976.

Levine, N.: A conceptual model for obstetric nursing, *J. Obstet. Gynecolog. Neonatal Nursing*, **5:**9, 1976.

Menninger, W. W.: "Caring" as part of health care quality, *J.A.M.A.*, **234:**836, 1975.

Nadelson, C.: "Normal" and "special" aspects of pregnancy, *Obstet. Gynecol.*, **41:**611, 1973.

Newton, N.: *Maternal Emotions: A Study of Women's Feelings toward Menstruation, Pregnancy, Childbirth, Breast Feeding, Infant Care, and Other Aspects of Their Femininity*, New York: Hoeber, 1955.

Swartz, W. H., and Swartz, J. V.: Family centered maternity care, its relationship to perinatal regionalization and neonatal intensive care, *Clin. Perinatol.*, **3**:431, 1976.

Trethowan, W. H.: "The Couvade Syndrome," in Howells, J. G.: *Modern Perspectives in Psycho-Obstetrics*, New York: Brunner/Mazel, 1972.

Education for Childbirth

Bean, C. A.: *Methods of Childbirth: A Complete Guide to Childbirth Classes and Maternity Care*, Garden City, N.Y.: Doubleday, 1972.

Bing, E.: *Six Practical Lessons for an Easier Childbirth*, New York: Grosset and Dunlap, 1967.

Doering, S. G., and Entwisle, D. R.: Preparation during pregnancy and ability to cope with labor and delivery, *Am. J. Orthopsychiatry*, **45**:825, 1975.

International Childbirth Education Association, P. O. Box 20852, Milwaukee, Wisconsin 53220.

Stevens, R. J.: Psychological strategies for management of pain in prepared childbirth. I: A review of the research, *Birth of the Family J.*, **3**:157, 1976–77.

Tanzer, D.: *Why Natural Childbirth? A Psychologist's Report on the Benefits to Mothers, Fathers and Babies*, Garden City, N.Y.: Doubleday, 1972.

PART FOUR

Topics in School Health

21 | Introduction to School Health

by Philip R. Nader

Definitions of School Health

Almost every school in the nation has some notion of what is included in the term "school health." Yet, many educators and health care providers have diverse ideas and priorities for a school health program's goals. In order to successfully accomplish them, agreement must be reached on a definition of school health by all those concerned.

The health program in a school was traditionally considered to comprise health services (often limited to services provided by nursing and medical staff), health education (often limited to curricular health instruction), and health environment (often limited to physical environment and safety).

More recently, the health program may be considered part of all aspects of the total school program which might influence or be influenced by a child's health. In this sense it then includes services not only from health and health-related personnel such as physicians, nurses, social workers, psychologists, aides, and volunteers but also from educational and counseling personnel. In this broader definition all school staff have a responsibility and a recognized role.

This chapter will first examine common clinical and developmental issues and problems faced by the school-age child and his family. Then, the purposes and methods of relating primary health care providers to schools will be examined.

22 | School Learning Problems and Developmental Differences

by Marcel Kinsbourne

This complex problem area is of growing concern to parents, educators, and physicians. This portion of the chapter covers issues of prediction, evaluation of "readiness" skills, evaluation of language development, the investigations required to assess children presenting with school learning problems, and the management of such problems. After general guidelines, specific details are presented which emphasize the activities appropriate for primary health care providers.

School Failure

A child's failure to achieve in school results from a failed interaction between the school system and the child. The primary source of the failure may lie on either side. The classroom may be overcrowded, or the teaching may be incompetent or cast in a pattern culturally alien to the child. The child may have missed school because of illness or frequent changes of residence, may not be adequately attending to the instruction on account of an emotional block or attentional lapses, or may find the material unintelligible as presented.

Under the heading of learning disability are those failures of school-child interaction due to a misfit between the child's learning requirements and the learning experience customary in the child's classroom. Of those, there is a subset in which the child's learning requirements differ from the norm for reasons related to brain maturation. This consequently affects the child's behavioral development. This child lacks the attentional skills or cognitive

reading readiness skills, or both, which most children have at the time of school entry.

Prediction

The scholastic underachievement due to learning disability usually comes unexpectedly and surprises both the parents and the teacher. In fact, this ingredient of surprise has an important effect on the quality of the human reactions that follow the failure once it becomes manifest. In many instances, the surprise is understandable and hard to forestall. After all, schools generally begin to teach children to read at the age of 6 precisely because before that age most children have not acquired the appropriate readiness skills by virtue of spontaneous brain maturation. If such readiness skills are lacking in a child who is only 4 or 5 years old, how can this be interpreted? Such skills would not, after all, necessarily be expected to be present in a child of that age, and the absence of reading readiness skills at that age by no means predicts their continued unavailability at a later date. If antecedents of these readiness skills in younger children were identified and could be measured, early prediction would become possible. To date this has not been achieved. Existing early screening instruments lack the necessary degree of reliability and validity, and important inferences cannot be made from a history of early setbacks, such as prenatal, perinatal, or postnatal adversities of an infectious, traumatic, or nutritional type. Naturally, children who have undergone such experiences are more at risk of subsequent learning failures than are other children; yet most of them nevertheless do *not* show such failures. A premature prediction of a learning failure based on such probabilistic grounds is quite likely to generate the failure it predicts on the basis of self-fulfilling prophecy by inculcating adverse expectations in the minds of the adults that surround the child and thus creating learning problems which otherwise would not have existed.

There are, however, two situations in which a school problem can be forecast with some degree of reliability. If a child develops language skills noticeably more slowly than is usual, then there is a realistic possibility that the delay of language development will continue in the form of a relative verbal immaturity and make it difficult for the child to mobilize the verbal skills called for by beginning reading instruction at the usual age. It then becomes important to follow language progress and formally assess the verbal skills of this child at the moment of decision about entry into grade 1. If the child's skills are still substantially behind age expectation at that time, then it would be wise at the very least to hold up school entry for a year.

The other telltale omen of later school failure is the presence of hyperactive-impulsive behavior in the younger child. Such babies may be unduly active, colicky, and sleepless. The infant who has learned to walk may be unusually curious and take more than the usual number of risks. In preschool, these children may already be found to be inconstant in attention, to be more than usually demanding of the ministrations of instructors, and to find it difficult to relate on a continued basis without conflict with the other children. These behavior patterns warn of later difficulties in concentration on school material, and such difficulties should be forestalled by appropriate measures.

Diagnosis

Clinical Picture The diagnosis of learning disability takes place in two successive steps: First, it is determined whether the school failure is indeed based on selectively inadequate or immature readiness or whether other factors may account for the problem. Wechsler intelligence testing yields a "mental age," and scholastic achievement testing documents a significant lag of reading and/or spelling age behind mental age (according to various definitions, a minimum disparity varying from 1 to 2 years is

required, the latter figure being more commonly used for the older children). The definition rules out mental retardation, in which mental and achievement age would be more on a par with each other. The testing will reveal social, economic, and cultural factors that militate against literacy, and interviews with the child and family will reveal instances in which an emotional disorder is probably primary. It may be difficult to distinguish emotional disorders in the older children, who may manifest the emotional repercussions of protracted failure and in whom the early signs of the disorder, whether prior to, coincidental with, or attributable to the school failure, may be hard to ascertain in retrospect. The additional burden of a bilingual education may account for underachievement in normal but not verbally gifted children.

Finally, no one of the above factors may in itself be deemed sufficient to induce school failure, but they may do so in combination. For instance, a child of dull-normal intelligence who by virtue of birth date is enrolled relatively early and who happens also to be emotionally immature and dependent may fail for a combination of reasons rather than a single reason, and such a child may not be properly termed *learning-disabled.*

If the child's school failure cannot be accounted for in terms of emotional blocks or adverse environmental circumstances, then it must stem from some disparity between the level of development of the child's school-relevant cognitive skills and the level which is prerequisite for purposes of learning from that child's classroom instruction. This disparity, in the case of reading and writing, could be located within the child's repertoire of basic visual skills: Is the child sufficiently well able to break up word sounds into their constituent speech sounds and recombine them from these (as required for purposes of phonics instruction)? Maybe such children are insufficiently able to associate the visual information with the auditory, or, again, perhaps their basic linguistic skills, with regard to both vocabulary and syntax, are unexpectedly limited so that they are in the position of being expected to learn to read words that they do not understand or to comprehend printed paragraphs that they would not understand if these were read to them aloud.

The above are all shortcomings within the sphere of "information processing." In contrast, some children fail although they do possess the requisite readiness skills. They do so because of an inability to maintain concentration on the task. These children, customarily labeled *hyperactive,* show a characteristically deviant pattern of behavior both in and outside the classroom. They are best described as *impulsive* and *distractible,* and these attributes of their thinking determine a life-style which has an unfavorable impact both on the classroom situation and the wider world outside. They act impulsively and at times recklessly upon the physical environment, exploring with insatiable curiosity even under hazardous circumstances. This naturally leads to frequent admissions to outpatient facilities on account of injuries and toxic ingestions, particularly in the younger children. They are comparably impulsive in making decisions for problem solving and so come up with quick and faulty answers in the classroom.

If they are overtly more distractible than impulsive, their minds wander prematurely from the topic to return only after some delay, during which time they may have half-forgotten their imperfectly conceived decision. Similar problems beset their social relationships with parents, teachers, siblings, and peers. These children are sociable and eager to make friends, but they approach the process of relating in the same inpulsive and impetuous fashion that characterizes their actions with physical objects. Thus, they fail to go through the customary courtship rituals and intrude themselves upon social situations when a more cautious approach is conventional. They are often rejected and notoriously prone to failure in maintaining friendships. Ultimately, they often retreat to relating virtually exclusively with younger children who are willing to accept their dictatorial ways.

Investigation   This falls into four categories. The first two, achievement and psychometric testing, define the problem and confirm that a learning disability exists. It is most timesaving for all concerned if these items of information are available to the primary case worker before the situation is scrutinized in detail. The third and fourth categories, analysis of error patterns and readiness testing, constitute the psychoeducational work-up for which referral to a qualified professional (educational psychologist and/or remedial educator) is needed. By and large, the standard instruments in these two categories are of little use.

1 Achievement testing: These instruments yield a *reading age, writing age,* and *arithmetic age* with reference to age-related national norms. They document that significant underachievement is in fact present with reference to the child's chronological age. The many acceptable instruments include the Wide Range Achievement Spache, Californian, and Metropolitan Readiness Tests.

2 Psychometric evaluation: This establishes a mental age for the child. It now becomes possible to distinguish those children who are underachieving with respect to mental as well as chronological age from those whose underachievement is illusory because of mental subnormality which would necessarily result in slower-than-normal educational progress. The test profile may also reveal a selective intellectual weakness, for instance, specifically for verbal items, which could have a bearing on the origins of the educational pattern. Finally, the psychologist will make potentially revealing observations about the child's task orientation, strategies, and task-related efforts: Is he competitive or defeatist, impulsive or compulsive, anxious, depressed, or blandly denying difficulty?

Relevant tests include the age-appropriate Wechsler instrument (WPPSI, WISC, WAIS), Porteus Maze Test, Goodenough Draw-a-Person, and Token Test.

3 Profile of error types:

  a Which type of mistake is most prevalent? Does the child substitute wrong letters or use the correct letters in the wrong sequence? Reverse letters or letter sequences? Produce misshappen letters? Impulsively guess at words on the basis of initial letters? Compulsively and laboriously sound out every word?

  b Which type of reading instruction gives the child trouble? Does the child have difficulty in summing up the visual memory that is called for by the whole-word (look-say) approach? Have trouble learning the regularities of spelling utilized by the linguistic approach? Find it impossible to analyze word sounds into constituent speech sounds as done in the phonics approach?

4 Developmental (readiness) profile: Can the child

selectively attend to the various aspects of a stimulus or display individually? Does the child search through them completely? Search through them systematically? Search through them economically (nonredundantly)? This information is elicited by a variety of tests of detection, matching, and reproduction.

Some investigations are often suggested by others; however, they should not be done routinely, but only for specific indications (Table 22-1). Optometric and labyrinthine testing are *never* indicated by the presence of a learning disability.

Management

In the management of learning disability, the role of the primary care provider may be restricted to that of specialist-consultant, or the role of coordinator of the overall investigation may be assumed. Depending on the scope of interests and training of the primary care provider, this role may be that of specialist, or that responsibility may be shared with a child neurologist.

As specialist, the primary care provider can:

Rule out alternative diagnoses (such as progressive cerebral degeneration, status petit mal).

Establish the need for ancillary investigation (such as audiometry).

Identify the cause of sensorimotor complaints relevant to school performance (such as clumsiness).

Determine whether the learning difficulty is associated with signs of disordered (hard signs) or delayed (soft signs) neurologic development.

Identify disorders of higher mental function that require medical management (such as hyperactivity-stimulant therapy) and supervise the management.

Hypothesize the pathogenesis of the disability (genetic, perinatal trauma).

Explain to parents the practical irrelevance of the preceding hypotheses.

Counteract pressures on parents to resort to crank remedial programs based on unsubstantiated neurologizing.

Table 22-1

Nonroutine Investigations for Learning Problems

Investigation	Indication
Audiometry	If there is evidence or suspicion of deafness or a delay in language development.
Speech pathology evaluation	If there is evidence of deficiency in spoken language skills.
Neurologic investigations	Skull x-ray, electroencephalography, brain scan; only if there is evidence of progressive or stable brain disease (epilepsy, cerebral degeneration, arrested hydrocephalus) in addition to the learning disability. The learning disability in itself is *not* evidence for any of these diagnoses.
Psychiatric or behavioral assessment	If the child: 1 Has a primary emotional problem (neurotic, characterologic, etc.). 2 Shows more than the expected adverse emotional reaction to his school failure. 3 Is caught up in disturbed family dynamics.

In learning disabilities the only justification for a diagnostic effort is that it enables the clinician to choose appropriately between alternative management options. The only acceptable evidence that the clinical decision was correct resides in the success of the educational and/or pharmacologic regimen that is instituted. If the rate of acquisition of academic skill is not accelerated, then the educational prescription was wrong. If the child's impulsive and distractible style of problem solving and relating is not corrected ("normalized"), stimulant therapy as given was not correct (either because the child's problem was not, in fact, stimulant-responsive or because the drug dosage and scheduling were faulty).

Clinicians will never achieve infallibility in either of these areas, not only because of the limitations in our understanding of learning disability, but also because of potentially intractable aspects of the environment (rigid, overdemanding or anxious, overprotective parents, gimmick-ridden educational methods, emotional resistances to the consistent use of psychoactive drugs). They will, however, have contributed to the limits of their ability if as coordinators, they attend to the following principles:

1 Establishing the child's learning requirements:
  a Achievement level (in terms of grade equivalent).
  b Selective strengths and weaknesses at that level (for example, whole-word versus phonics).
2 Establishing and meeting adjunct needs:
  a Individualization of instruction.
  b Control of level of surrounding activity.
  c Supportive pharmacotherapy.
  d Supportive psychotherapy (child and family).
3 Instruction in school that is in accord with these general principles:
  a Didactic
    (1) Teach at educational (not chronological or mental age) level.
    (2) Make implicit links in explanation explicit.
    (3) Check understanding and retention of each point before moving on to the next point.
    (4) Minimize potentially distracting displays.
    (5) Let learning time be self-paced.
  b Motivational
    (1) Should be based on teacher-student relationship (avoid distracting physical motivators).

    (2) Compare child's progress to child's own previous achievement level (not that of other children).
    (3) Interperse difficult tasks with success episodes (tasks the child can master).
4 Avoid speculative methods (any procedure that relates hypothetically, rather than logically, to the educational goal).
  a Enrichment—where it floods rather than specifically focuses attention of the child.
  b Multisensory approach—where it simultaneously bombards rather than supports selective attention.
  c Physical education—when it purports to accelerate brain maturation (as opposed to raising feelings of personal competence).
  d Laterality manipulation—when it purports to change the lateralization of higher mental function.
  e Nutritional fads (inclusive, such as megavitamins, or exclusive, such as additives and preservatives, except when an additive-reduced diet can objectively be shown to ameliorate hyperactive behavior).

23 | School Readiness and the Primary Care Provider

by Bill S. Caldwell

Primary care physicians are often the most critical persons concerned with school readiness because they are the first professionals who see a preschool-age child. They have the opportunity of securing key data in evaluating readiness.

Primary care providers may be called upon to perform a physical examination for meeting school entry requirements. If the providers respond with only a cursory physical exam and nothing more, they are missing an opportunity to have a significant voice in the overall planning for the child. If the school conceives of readiness in terms of a score on a standardized readiness test and if the primary care provider thinks of readiness in terms only of physical clearance, then the child with special needs may be lost in the gray areas which have been the concern of neither.

Definition of Readiness

Readiness is a term used frequently by educators and other early childhood workers. One hears of readiness tests, readiness tasks, and readiness skills. The terms imply that children are being examined to determine whether they are ready for something and that their status will be measured against a fixed goal. Usually, this goal is entry into school.

The skilled provider of primary care will conceptualize school readiness in broad terms which include the exceptional child as well as the typical child and which take into account all the variables which influence school progress. Readiness is not equated with fixed standards of performance for all children. Many handicapped children will never reach fixed criteria, and normal children will vary greatly in their abilities to handle readiness tasks. Thus, it is as important to think in terms of whether parents and the school are ready for the child as it is to think of a child's being ready for school. Many children are ready for school who do not meet fixed criteria, whether these are set by group norms, developmental specialists, or curriculum guides. The physician should be keenly aware of the rate at which a child is developing, the child's level of functioning, the demands which the parents impose, and the expectations the local school has for beginning pupils. School readiness, therefore, should mean the degree of "fit" between the variables which characterize the child and family and those which characterize the school system (Fig. 23-1).

Assessment of School Readiness

Since preschool children cannot read and do not engage in most types of abstract thinking, assessment for school readiness by the physician is not a matter of merely determining whether a child can pass a given test. All phases of screening, testing, and evaluating data critically depend on a solid knowledge of how and why children grow and develop. The norms for typical children based on studies over a period of years should become as fixed in the physician's memory as certain other bits of knowledge which are used daily.

No test, no assessment technique, no short-term observation can replace a carefully elicited, closely analyzed history. A test score is a sample of behavior on a given day for certain specified tasks. A good history, by contrast, adds perspective, time, and breadth in determining school readiness. The history taken in preparation for discussing with the parents their child's school readiness should include ques-

Figure 23-1 School readiness variables which characterize the child and family and those which characterize the school that must be weighed in assessing whether or not a given child is ready to begin school.

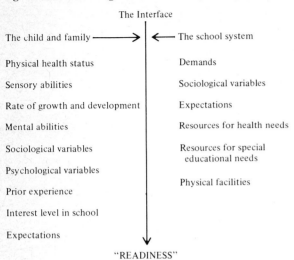

The Interface

The child and family ———→ ←—— The school system

The child and family	The school system
Physical health status	Demands
Sensory abilities	Sociological variables
Rate of growth and development	Expectations
Mental abilities	Resources for health needs
Sociological variables	Resources for special educational needs
Psychological variables	Physical facilities
Prior experience	
Interest level in school	
Expectations	

"READINESS"

tions relative to knowledge and skills which are considered to be usually present by the schools in the community in which the child lives. If possible, both parents should be involved in a child's evaluation for readiness. The physician may use a published parent questionnaire or may devise one in order to facilitate the history-taking process.

The history should include not only the usual questions concerning developmental stages, illnesses, accidents, and hospitalizations, but also questions concerning the child's cognitive development. The physician should attempt to elicit from the parent the way in which the child approaches a problem, how defeat is handled in attempts to learn, whether the child imitates others in solving new situations, whether curiosity is displayed, the extent of exposure to and participation in reading activities, and manifestations of imagination. Many physicians find that a standardized measurement such as that provided by the Vineland Scale of Adaptive Behavior is a good framework for information gathering supplemented by additional questions. Other excellent examples of questionnaires include those developed by Bettye Caldwell and Hilda Knobloch.

As the history is taken, the physician must be alert to inconsistent data and must be exacting in securing information from the parents, not only as to whether a child *can* perform a certain task but *how* the task is performed, the ease with which it is accomplished, and whether this skill is an isolated skill or part of a continuing activity. One child may with much effort be able to cut with a pair of scissors when asked to do so and given paper and scissors. A second child may pick up a pair of scissors while making something, use the scissors appropriately, and proceed with the job at hand. Parental response to questions can help the physician distinguish between these two types of children.

In securing a history from a parent it is advisable to ask the parent to describe the child's behavior and accomplishments rather than to make evaluative statements of what the behavior means. It is better to ask, "What happens when Steven is with his friends?" than to ask, "Does Steven get along with other children?" In the latter case a simple "yes" leaves little room for further discussion. The skillful physician uses many questions which require descriptions of behavior: "Tell me, how does . . .?"; "Describe Mary Lou's afternoons when . . ."; "And then what happens?"; and "What would Jerry do if . . .?"

A useful technique in gathering data about a child and his place in a family is to say to the parent, "What words would you use to describe . . .?" Additional information can be obtained by extensions of this question: "And what words would describe his [mental abilities, physical health, relationships with others] . . .?" Information can also be obtained by asking, "Do you think Jimmy is more like you or your wife [husband]?" Follow the response with "Why?" if necessary.

As the physician gains knowledge about the child, the parents' readiness for their child's entry into school is also assessed. The physician finds out, by direct questioning, if necessary, the parents' expectations for their child, their concepts of the child's school and what it can provide, and the degree to which they believe their child will adjust to and succeed in school in terms of academic progress and psychosocial adjustment.

When a careful history has been obtained, the physician has learned about some of the child's personal characteristics, likes and dislikes, and strengths and weaknesses, and is ready to examine the child. With many children it is best to carry out the "games" of developmental or readiness testing first, leaving the physical examination until last.

It is certainly appropriate for primary care physicians to use developmental and readiness tests, provided they understand the tests' weaknesses or restrictions for their use. The best readiness assessment will be carried out by the physician who is most knowledgeable about specific age-appropriate behaviors. A collection of such behaviors taken from the most popular tests for young children include age-appropriate abilities at 2, 3, 4, 5, and 6 years (Table 23-1).

The primary care physician does not need to become a psychologist but does need to know how to administer simple screening tests. If skilled in the use of the Denver Developmental Screening Test, the Draw-a-Person Test, Drawing Geometric Figures, and the Peabody Picture Vocabulary Test, the physician will secure an immense amount of data. Each of these tests should be used in a standardized way and scored by an exact method. It is largely a waste of time to use such tests unless they are administered correctly and the results used appropriately. Any screening test is simply a sample of behavior. A physician can develop a repertoire of test items which is used objectively to evaluate a child's cognitive abilities.

Table 23-1
Appropriate Abilities at Various Ages

Two years:
  Walks downstairs alone, holding rail, both feet on each step.
  Imitates vertical line.
  Identifies self in mirror.
  Lifts and drinks from cup.
  Uses "me," "you," refers to self by name.
  Follows simple instructions.
Three years:
  Picks longer of two lines.
  Can point to teeth and chin on request.
  Cuts with scissors.
  Makes three-cube pyramid in approximately 15 s.
  Copies a circle.
  Jumps with two feet together.
  Identifies six body parts, pointing at pictures.
Four years:
  Goes up and down stairs one foot per step.
  Copies cross.
  Washes hands unaided.
  When shown two circles, can tell "How many?"
  Completes "A hat goes on your head, shoes go on your _____."
  Can button.
  Cares for self at toilet.
Five years:
  Dresses self except tying shoes.
  Copies square.
  Can count six objects when asked, "How many?"
  Can answer "Why do we have horses, books, clocks, eyes, ears?"
  Can tell "What is a chair made of?"; "A dress?"; "Shoes?"
Six years:
  Tells how crayon and pencil are same and different.
  Can tell how many pieces "if something is cut in half."
  Can tell difference between common objects; dog and bird, shirt and coat, milk and water.
  Can complete "A lemon is sour; sugar is _____."
  Can tell what a forest is made of.

Interpretation of Readiness

In assessing school readiness, the primary care provider is concerned with a child's physical, mental, and psychosocial characteristics. Data are used from an expanded history, from indications of functional levels given by developmental and readiness tests, and from data emerging from a thorough physical examination. Such a battery of assessment techniques is time-consuming, but it should be remembered that the child is entering a critical time of his life. The degree to which the physician can develop an accurate profile of the "whole child" may determine success or failure in school.

Perhaps the greatest danger in assessing school readiness is a tendency to overinterpret findings. Readiness is affected by some physical and mental variables whose characteristics allow us to predict whether they will or will not continue to influence the individual. This is true with certain sensory deficits and certain metabolic and genetic conditions. However, when a person is assessing cognitive abilities and personality variables, only the novice or fool will make definite predictions.

In most instances the physician, in describing the child, should include strengths and deficits in terms of age-related behavior. For example, "Mary has no physical deficits; she has the knowledge, skills, and emotional behavior of most children her age. Her ability to handle paper-and-pencil tasks seems more like that of a 4-year-old." The physician should not be content to make a few check marks on a sheet of paper to indicate readiness status. The child should be described to the parents as evaluated, and this should be compared with the parents' own description and their expectations of the child.

Referral for Readiness Evaluation

If the primary care provider cannot reach a decision relative to a child's physical, mental, and psychosocial status, then a consultation or referral should be considered. First a decision must be made as to whether the primary care provider should continue the overall management of this child. Information from a consultant may be needed before making this decision. Parents should be told exactly why a consultation or referral is appropriate. If this is not done, sometimes a misconception of the severity of the problem is unknowingly implanted, and the parents react to the child in an adverse manner.

When the advice of another professional is being sought, it is helpful if one gives the following information: specific reason why the consultation is requested, exact questions which are to be answered, and how the information obtained will be used. Criteria for referral are not finite and specific. In general, however, a primary care provider should refer for consultation if:

1 He has questions regarding the sensory status of the child.
2 He discovers a physical defect which is unfamiliar to him or one which requires special treatment
3 There is evidence the child is 25 percent or more behind in relation to age-appropriate skills and knowledge, that is, if the child's age and corresponding performance level are as follows:

Chronological Age, Years	Performance Level
6	4 yr.–6 mo. or less
5	3 yr.–9 mo. or less
4	3 yr. or less
3	2 yr.–3 mo. or less

4 The child has a physical, mental, or emotional handicap which will require the services of a specialist (physical therapist, speech therapist, psychologist, special educator).

The primary care provider in most instances will provide continuing care for a child. Information obtained from consultations should, therefore, be integrated with other data so that the parents will receive an understandable explanation of their child's status. It may be necessary to reinterpret what has been told the parents by someone else. All of this explanation is a highly important part of school readiness visits to the primary care provider.

By using information concerning a child, by using knowledge of local school programs, and by using acquaintance with resources available, the primary care provider will to a large degree determine whether the parents understand the concept of readiness and act accordingly to this understanding. A broader concept of school readiness, greater attention to the many areas which determine readiness, and more judicial use of consultants and referral sources would ensure a good start for more children when they enter school.

24 | School Readiness: Screening for Speech and Language Disorders

by Sharon G. Kulig

Assessment of childrens' readiness for school must include consideration of their ability to make use of what is seen and heard and their ability to make themselves understood. Reading, writing, and arithmetic are complex communicative behaviors, and the student's language development is the foundation upon which these skills are based. Recent estimates suggest that as many as 1 out of every 10 Americans may exhibit a disorder of speech, language, or hearing. Primary care providers should undertake screening for speech and language problems as a maintenance procedure. A listing of possible problem areas to be considered in the speech and language screening of children aged 6 months to 6 years is presented in Table 24-1.

Adequate hearing acuity is a basic requirement for the acquisition of speech and language skills. No child is too young or too uncooperative to be referred for audiologic evaluation. Audiometric evaluation should be arranged by the primary health care provider prior to or in conjunction with any speech pathology consultation.

The language, rhythm of speech, articulation, structure, and function of the speaking mechanism, and voice of children aged 31 months and older can be screened for disorders by non-speech pathologists. One standardized approach to screening children for speech and language disorders is The Physician's Developmental Quick Screen for Speech Disorders, or the PDQ. This 5-min screening test, designed for use by non-speech pathologists, considers disorders of language, the rhythm of speech, articulation, the speaking mechanism, and voice. There are 10 single-page, age-graded forms of the PDQ. Each form contains age norms and instructions for administration and scoring. One of these, appro-

Table 24-1
Areas to be Considered in the Speech and Language Screening of Children Aged 6 Months to 6 Years

Areas to be Screened for Possible Disorder	Chronological Ages When Screening Should Be Undertaken, Months									
	6–12	13–18	19–24	25–30	31–36	37–42	43–48	49–54	55–60	61–72
Language	Yes	Yes	Yes	Yes	Yes	Yes	Yes	Yes	Yes	Yes
Rhythm of speech	No	No	Yes	Yes	Yes	Yes	Yes	Yes	Yes	Yes
Articulation	No	No	No	No	Yes	Yes	Yes	Yes	Yes	Yes
Speaking mechanism	Yes	Yes	Yes	Yes	Yes	Yes	Yes	Yes	Yes	Yes
Voice	Yes	Yes	Yes	Yes	Yes	Yes	Yes	Yes	Yes	Yes

priate for use with children 43 to 48 months of age, is illustrated in Fig. 24-1.

Language

Delayed or disordered language might involve difficulties with the reception or expression of verbal messages. Language problems can be manifested, for example, by sentence structure, grammar, vocabulary, or sentence length which are inappropriate for a youngster's chronological age. Both receptive and

expressive language skills, however, must be considered. For example, the first language item (Fig. 24-1) is concerned with the child's ability to follow directions involving prepositions. Stimulus materials needed, test procedures to be followed, and anticipated subject behavior in response to this test item are outlined as follows:

Materials needed: Small toys or other manipulable objects familiar to the child (such as a pencil and a cup).

PHYSICIAN'S DEVELOPMENTAL QUICK SCREEN FOR SPEECH DISORDERS (PDQ)
Experimental Edition

FORM 7 To be used with patients from **43 to 48 months** of age. Copyright © 1973 by Sharon G. Kulig, Ph.D. and Kathryn A. Baker, M.A., Child Development Division, Department of Pediatrics, University of Texas Medical Branch, Galveston. The reproduction of any part of this form by mimeograph, hectograph, xerox or in any other way, whether the reproductions are sold or are furnished free for use, is a violation of the copyright law.

PATIENT'S NAME _____ SEX _____ DATE _____

IDENTIFICATION NO. _____ EXAMINER: _____

DATE OF BIRTH: _____ CURRENT AGE _____ (mos.)

I. LANGUAGE
Directions: Indicate with a checkmark if the patient performs or does not perform the behavior indicated. **Parental report** may be used in lieu of direct observation but should be noted.
Yes No
( ) ( ) Is successful when asked to follow directions involving some prepositions (e.g. "Put the penny in the cup....", "Put the penny under the chair", "Put the penny on the desk")
( ) ( ) Responds successfully when asked his name (first and last, e.g., "What is your name?" "Johnny what?")
( ) ( ) Plurals usually appear in his speech.
( ) ( ) Past tenses usually appear in his speech.
( ) ( ) Tells of daily activities and experiences.
(If patient failed ANY of the above, he fails this section of the screening test.)
SCORE   Pass   Fail   (circle one)

II. RHYTHM OF SPEECH
(Note: Disregard this section unless the parent "volunteers" information that the child may be "stuttering".)
If parental concern about the child's "rhythm of speech" is expressed, check here _____.
Proceed with the remaining sections of the test. At the conclusion of your screening examination, counsel with the parent as per the Rhythm of Speech section supplemental to this form.

III. ARTICULATION
Directions: Have the child imitate your production of each of the following words, **watching** as well as **listening** to his production. Circle any word in which the underlined sound is mispronounced or absent. Record the number of circled words from each word group in the indicated space. Important: Remember to watch the child as he imitates your models.

No. of words   Word Group
circled
_____   1. no   money   pin
_____   2. happy   beehive
_____   3. walk   away
_____   4. pie   puppy   nap
_____   5. man   mommy   game

Yes No
( ) ( )   The patient's parent asserts that the child's speech is intelligible to listeners unfamiliar with the child's speech patterns. (The patient fails this section of the test if two or more words of ANY word group are circled; or, if his parent answers that the child's speech is not intelligible to listeners who are unfamiliar with the child's speech patterns.)
SCORE   Pass   Fail   (circle one)

IV. SPEAKING MECHANISM
Yes No
( ) ( )   I believe that the patient's speaking ability is compromised by the structure or function of his speaking mechanism (palatal, breathing, tongue problems, etc. suspected).
(If the answer to the above question is yes, the patient fails this section of the screening test.)
SCORE   Pass   Fail   (circle one)

V. VOICE
Directions: Based on parental history or your observations of the patient's voice as he verbalized during your administration of the Language and Articulation sections of the screening test, indicate by a checkmark your description of the patient's voice. If more speech sampling is desired, engage the patient in conversation, e.g., What did you have for lunch today? Where's daddy? Did you watch T.V. last night?...What did you see?
1. Typical Quality   normal _____ hoarse _____ (in absence of URI)*
                        chronic history of hoarseness _____
                        hypernasal (sounds as though he's "talking through his nose") _____
                        hyponasal (sounds as though he "has a cold" in absence of such findings) _____
2. Typical Pitch   normal _____ significantly low _____ significantly high _____
3. Typical Loudness   normal _____ significantly weak _____ significantly loud _____
(If patient exhibits a significant voice deviation, he fails this section of the screening test.)
SCORE   Pass   Fail   (circle one)

*If the patient presently exhibits a URI, a statement regarding typical voice quality must be deferred

Form 7 (43 - 48 months)

SUMMARY OF RESULTS

If patient has failed ANY of the above sections, he should be referred to a speech pathologist for further evaluation.

Referred to: _____ Date: _____

Referred for further evaluation of: Language _____ Rhythm of Speech _____ Articulation _____ Speaking Mechanism _____ Voice _____

Figure 24-1

Test procedure: Hand the pencil to the child and say, "Put the pencil on the chair." After the child succeeds (or fails) at completing this task, say, "Put the pencil in the cup." The child might also be instructed to "Put the pencil under the chair." (Do not, of course, accompany your instructions with gestures.)

Child should: Demonstrate the child's understanding of at least two prepositions (on, in, under, in front of, beside, or behind, for example) by correctly completing instructions such as the above. Parental report that such behavior is typical of the child would also satisfy requirements for passing this item.

Rhythm of Speech

The second section (Fig. 24-1) deals with the patient's fluency, or rhythm of speech. It is not unusual for parents of children younger than 4 years to volunteer concern that their child might be stuttering. Unwarranted anxiety can be lessened by advising parents that repeating and hesitating during speech is usually not symptomatic of true stuttering in children younger than 4 years.

Families should be cautioned against labeling their child a stutterer. They should be asked to discourage any interrupting of the child while he is talking, albeit nonfluently. Parents need to understand that one does not help any youngster by guessing at or supplying words on which he is nonfluent. Certainly pressuring a child to "Hurry up and tell Grandma hello on the telephone" or "Tell the nice lady how old you are" should be avoided. Comments such as "Slow down and start over," "Stop and start over," or "Take a deep breath and start over" may inadvertently teach the child to fear and ultimately to avoid speaking situations. Parents help most effectively by being relaxed and patient listeners.

The family then is assured that the period of normal nonfluency is one of those times when "doing nothing is doing something." They are told that normal nonfluency in a child younger than 4 years can usually be safely regarded as yet another stage in growing up. Should parental concern persist despite such counseling, the health care provider should make arrangements for the parents to consult a speech pathologist. Although it has long been recognized that repetitions and hesitations normally characterize the speech of children between 18

months and 4 years of age, the likelihood of their developing true stuttering tends to increase with advancing chronological age. For this reason, a speech pathologist should be consulted without delay by the primary health care provider whenever concern about stuttering is noted in relation to children 4 years of age and older. The speech clinician will in turn evaluate the case to determine the presence of true stuttering.

Articulation

Children's variations in articulation or sound production must always be viewed in light of the normal development sequence. The health care provider monitors the 43- to 48-month-old patient's production of five consonant sounds (Fig. 24-1). Each of these sounds is tested in the beginning, middle, and end positions of key words by asking the child to imitate the examiner's production of each test word. As the child repeats a word, the examiner is careful to watch as well as listen to the child's production. Any word in which a test sound is mispronounced or absent is simply circled. The patient fails this section of the test if two or more words of any word group are circled.

In considering a child's articulation, one must also consider the child's intelligibility in conversational speech. It is generally recognized, for example, that as much as 90 percent of the 3-year-old's speech should be understandable even to strangers. Children over 3 whose conversational speech is not readily intelligible should be referred to speech pathologists for further evaluation.

Speaking Mechanism

A patient's speaking ability may be compromised by the structure or function of his speaking mechanism. Palates may be cleft; they may be of inadequate length or immobile. Lingual frenula may be restrictive, though this does not occur frequently. Some considerations in evaluating the possible restrictiveness of a patient's lingual frenulum or the structural or functional inadequacy of the soft palate are illustrated in Table 24-2. It should be stressed that speech pathologists tend to adopt a conservative stance when considering the relation between articulation disorders and the status of the peripheral speaking mechanism. It has been suggested, for example, that an examiner is more likely to err in blaming a defect

Table 24-2

Considerations in Evaluating the Adequacy of the Peripheral Speaking Mechanism for Speech

1 Lingual frenulum

Yes   No

( )   ( )   Difficulty touching the ridge behind the upper front teeth with the tongue tip or inability to extend the tongue between the upper and lower front teeth and past the lips.

Note: The child who adequately produces the t, n, and d sounds is usually not an appropriate candidate for a frenulum release ("tongue clipping") procedure.

2 Soft palate

Yes   No

( )   ( )   The palate does not move equally vigorously on both sides when the patient is instructed to say "ah."

( )   ( )   The palate does not appear to reach all the way to the back of the throat when the patient is instructed to vigorously say "ah."

( )   ( )   The uvula is cleft.

( )   ( )   There is a change in the coloring of the mucus membrane of the palate outlining a submucus cleft.

Note: Gently palpating the palate or shining a light through the nostrils while looking at the palate should assist in confirming the presence or absence of a submucus cleft.

Abnormalities in the length, mobility, or configuration of the palate are often accompanied by a voice which sounds "too nasal" or by escape of air from the nostrils during speech.

Note: If the answer to any of the above questions is yes, the patient fails the Speaking Mechanism section of the screening test on the basis of questionable tongue mobility or suspected palatal difficulty.

The above specialized format is offered for study by those examiners concerned with the possible restrictiveness of the lingual frenulum or the structural or functional inadequacy of the soft palate (insofar as this can be evaluated by peroral inspection).

upon oral structure than in attributing it to some other cause. For this reason, diagnoses of structural causation should be made with great caution.

Voice

Screening of voice involves the child's typical vocal quality, pitch, and intensity (loudness). Voice deviations can involve abnormalities of quality such as hoarseness, which in children is often associated with vocal cord nodules. One study of hoarse school-age children, for example, revealed vocal cord nodules to be present in 57 percent of those subjects who were referred to otolaryngologists for further evaluation. Another quality deviation, hypernasality, is suggestive of palatal deviations, while a breathy voice quality can be indicative of vocal fold paralysis. A voice that is inappropriately loud or soft may signal the presence of significant hearing loss; abnormalities of vocal pitch on the other hand can accompany endocrinologic disturbances or suggest the presence of laryngeal web. It is understood that non-speech pathologists do not typically posses knowledge or experience with screening children for voice disorders. However, research suggests that requiring non-speech pathologists simply to "think about" (perhaps for the first time) the pitch, intensity, and quality of children's voices results in the decision to refer to speech pathologists children possessing voice deviations which might not otherwise have been identified. Examiners should defer screening patients exhibiting "colds" for voice disorders until upper respiratory symptoms are resolved.

The PDQ, then, is one instrument intended to assist primary care providers in identifying children in need of additional evaluation by a speech pathologist. Validation work to date has produced good preliminary results. Levine has reviewed other screening test instruments related to the office assessment of language development by physicians. The REEL scale, or Receptive-Expressive Language Scale, the Communicative Evaluation Chart from Infancy to Five Years, the Verbal Language Development Scale, and the Denver Articulation Screening Exam are also screening tests which consider communication abilities of children.

It does little good to screen for speech and language disorders unless follow-up allows for additional evaluation and therapy when a need for these is indicated. The American Speech and Hearing Association annually publishes a directory which lists geographic locations of speech pathologists and audiologists, their educational backgrounds, areas of certification, and current employment settings. Health care providers might also contact state speech and hearing associations, university speech and hearing clinics, and public school districts in order to identify certified communicative disorder specialists practicing in their area.

25 | Dealing with Common Classroom Behavior Problems

by Thomas J. Long

Classroom behavior problems can include aggressive behavior, anxiety, daydreaming, adverse eating habits, hyperkinesis, hypochondriasis, imaginary playmates, lying, masturbation, nail biting, stealing, temper tantrums, thumb sucking, and withdrawal. Not all classroom behavior problems come to the attention of the physician with equal frequency. Some, such as hypochondriasis, common among adolescents and adults, are rare among young children. Others, such as depression as manifested in adults, rarely occur in preadolescent children. This section will focus on the identification and collaborative management of three common classroom behavior patterns: hyperactivity, aggressive-resistant behavior, and inhibited-withdrawn behavior.

Hyperactivity

One of the most frequent behavior problems brought to the attention of the pediatrician is hyperactivity. Its incidence is estimated at 5 percent of all primary school children. It is a complaint with which all pediatricians, child psychologists, and family practitioners will inevitably be required to cope. Since it is a behavioral syndrome, it is appropriately diagnosed only by observation of the child's behavior (psychologic or neurologic test patterns are no more than suggestive). There is an extensive body of research literature which indicates the need for collaboration between professionals not only in the management but also in the diagnosis of the syndrome.

According to the U.S. Department of Health, Education, and Welfare (HEW), the term *minimal brain dysfunction syndrome* (MBD) refers "to children of near average, average or above average intelligence with certain learning or behavioral disabilities ranging from mild to severe, which are associated with deviations of function of the central nervous system. These deviations may manifest themselves by various combinations of impairment in perception, conceptualization, language, memory, and control of attention, impulse or motor function." Furthermore, the HEW Task Force found the following MBD characteristics most often cited: (1) hyperactivity, (2) perceptual motor impairments, (3) emotional lability, (4) general coordination deficits, (5) disorders of attention (short attention span, distractability, perseveration), (6) impulsiveness, (7) disorders of memory and thinking, (8) specific learning disabilities (reading, arithmetic, writing, spelling), (9) disorders of speech and hearing, and (10) equivocal neurologic signs and electroencephalographic irregularities. Minimal brain dysfunction syndrome is commonly referred to as *hyperkinesis,* or *hyperactivity,* a term we here prefer since it generally avoids the vague implication that the hyperactive child has some malfunctioning of the brain. Children who manifest the condition are generally neurologically intact, at least by any currently available testing methods.

Connors has devised a rating scale (Table 25-1) which serves as a useful diagnostic tool for identifying the hyperactive child. The items of this scale serve as a brief delineation of the main characteristics of the syndrome. It is possible to get a preliminary definite description of a child as hyperactive when these behaviors are so outstanding that the child cannot function on an age-appropriate level.

The child's short attention span, distractability, and easy frustration interfere seriously with learning, so that these children with near-normal or better intelligence function in school well below their abil-

ity. The impulsiveness, temper tantrums, and general restlessness interfere with both peer and adult relationships. The result is a child often friendless, usually unhappy, doing poorly in school, and subject to constant reprimands from both teachers and parents. Such a child can prevent an entire classroom from functioning smoothly.

In the diagnosis of hyperactivity there are two elements, history and behavioral observation, which are of prime importance. Other diagnostic procedures are ancillary, often helping to preclude other undetected problems. Vision and hearing tests

Table 25-1
Conners Abbreviated Rating Scale

Child's name _____

Completed on _____ by _____
                  (date)   (name)

Instructions: Please consider the last month only in filling out the checklist. Check the appropriate column for each item, "Not at All," "Just a Little," "Pretty Much," or "Very Much," which best describes your assessment of the child. Please complete all 10 items.

Observation	Degree of Activity			
	Not at All	Just a Little	Pretty Much	Very Much
1 Restless or overactive				
2 Excitable, impulsive				
3 Disturbs other children				
4 Fails to finish things he starts, short attention span				
5 Constantly fidgeting				
6 Inattentive, easily distracted				
7 Demands must be met immediately—easily frustrated				
8 Cries often and easily				
9 Mood changes quickly and drastically				
10 Temper outbursts, explosive and unpredictable behavior				

Source: Adapted by C. K. Conners from his article "A teacher rating scale for use in drug studies with children," *Am. J. Psychiatry,* 126:884–888, 1969, and reproduced with permission.

should be routinely available before further evaluations are undertaken. There are no confirmed laboratory tests for hyperactivity. A number of suspected hyperactive children will have diffusely abnormal electroencephalograms, but these should be obtained only to detect a seizure pattern suggested by history.

The importance of a detailed history results from the fact that the majority of hyperactive children behave differently in different settings. These children are most severely stressed when they are expected to stay on a task over relatively prolonged periods and particularly in a situation where there are multiple stimuli. The average classroom fits these conditions perfectly. In the classroom, the hyperactive child may be in perpetual motion. These same children in the physician's office often behave in a very controlled manner. Physicians considering medical treatment for only those children who are obviously hyperactive during an office or clinic visit may be missing a substantial number of children with this syndrome who might benefit from psychoactive medication.

The parent is usually the best source for the patient's long-term history. Teachers, however, have demonstrated remarkable sensitivity for systematic observation of the suspected hyperactive child's behavior. Parents appear to lack this sensitivity, or perhaps the home environment substantially reduces the stress imposed on these children so that the degree of restless behavior is reduced. Parents may also simply become inured to the child's behavior and, consequently, be less aware of its deviant degree. In any case, the physician should immediately solicit the help of the classroom teacher for the purpose of obtaining an observation of the child's behavior and a current nonhome history when the presenting complaint is hyperactivity or a learning difficulty not accounted for by reason of retardation. Use of the Conners scale (Table 25-1) or a similar one, incorporated in a request for a detailed description of behavior at school, should be part of the regular diagnostic procedure of any health care provider assessing this complaint.

Primary care providers should routinely solicit information from the classroom teacher for all their school-age patients. This might be done for all at the end of each student's first year of each major school change (to elementary, middle, and high school), but teacher information should certainly be sought for those evidencing classroom behavior or learning difficulties as soon as the problem is brought to attention.

While Wender contends that most extrahistorical information is of limited value diagnostically and therapeutically in cases of suspected hyperactivity, pediatricians would be lax should they not carry out the usual physical and neurologic examinations and, as their suspicion for a positive diagnosis mounts, seek appropriate laboratory tests and psychologic examinations. The latter might often be done through the psychology service of the child's school and will be most useful to the physician if a sense of trust for the services provided by the school system has previously been developed.

Management

In the treatment of hyperactivity, the only intervention with a solid body of research data demonstrating efficacy is the administration of stimulant drugs, notably methylphenidate. (Tranquilizers slow down hyperkinetic children more predictably than the sympathomimetic amines, but the quality of the resulting behavior is seldom as good.) It has been found that stimulant medications at low doses enhance the performance of hyperactive children in comparison to placebo; further, that medium to high doses lead to less enhancement or actual detriment in performance of the child. These findings led Sprague and Sleator to postulate a dose-response curve that shows peak enhancement on methylphenidate at 0.3 mg/kg body weight and a decline at higher doses.

An even more interesting aspect of dose-response studies is the comparison of the learning performance curve with the one obtained from teacher ratings of the child's social behavior in the classroom. While the learning curve peaks at the low dose previously mentioned, the social behavior curve peaks at a much higher point (0.7 to 1.0 mg methylphenidate per kg body weight). Thus, a physician seeking primarily to optimize the behavior of the child in school on the basis of teacher reports would be likely to prescribe a dose of medication well above the point of peak enhancement of learning. There might be times, however, when enhancement of social behavior aspects are to be desired even in the face of some lessening of learning performance.

Classroom teachers are again helpful when the decision has been made to attempt drug management of hyperactivity. Not only can they assist in considering the variables impacting on level of dosage, as when a child on the verge of being expelled because of deviant social behavior should receive medication at a higher dosage than a hyperactive child not in such danger, but also they are the most sensitive monitors to even minor variations in drug dosage. Effective treatment of school children with learning and/or behavior disorders includes reports from the teacher on treatment effects. The teacher is the laboratory for the schoolchild with learning and/or behavior problems. Teachers, with few exceptions, are eager to share information with the physician. Primary care providers must play an active role in setting up channels of communication with the school for this purpose.

A certain percentage of hyperactive children are not helped by stimulant medication, perhaps 20 percent under controlled conditions. Certain environmental impingements might be controlled in order to diminish the stimulus overload hyperactive children might encounter, as well as help them learn appropriate social behavior despite their handicap. Physicians should be familiar with elementary child management techniques which, while no panacea for hyperactivity, certainly can have positive, if nonspecific, effects. Parents too should be familiar with good child-rearing practices. If the family situation serves only to exacerbate the child's difficulty, the physician might well consider family counseling or referral to optimize whatever positive effect the family has on the child.

Family counseling is an adjunct treatment for the hyperactive child. Once it is accepted as such, the primary care provider will maintain responsibility for the child after referral. It is not reasonable to expect from the family counselor evidence of impossible behavior changes in the child, but an increase of stability in child-rearing practices as a result of the referral might be legitimately hoped for. Support from the primary care provider may be required in order to have families attempt new behaviors which they find difficult.

In addition to the above, parent discussion groups, psychotherapy for the child, revised educational practice, and remediation or counseling and support for teachers can all have a positive effect on the hyperactive child. There are helpful books available for parents and teachers of the hyperactive child such as that of Stewart and Olds. These often contain a catalog of methods for helping the child to like himself, establishing a healthy home atmosphere, and teaching the child to behave.

Aggressive-Resistant Behavior

Normal aggression stems from a child's need to feel important and to control others. Children also use aggression in an effort to let it be known that they are persons in their own right. However, the child who is constantly aggressive is motivated by factors other than a natural desire to be recognized and to control.

A child might be mildly aggressive by being negative or disobedient. Stronger aggressive behavior includes lying or stealing. Extreme aggression involves revenge and harm to others. It is usually physical in nature: fighting and cruelty, destruction of property, vandalism, or fire setting; but when these acts are restricted, it might be evidenced through words or glances.

Excessive aggression is often caused by the child's reaction to parental overindulgence or the overprotection associated with parental rejection or the child's reaction to unfair or severe punishment.

How to handle a child's aggressive behavior is not an uncommon question. The most straightforward answer is that such behavior is to be immediately terminated when it endangers the child or others or threatens serious damage to property. Mishandling the child causes aggressive behavior to continue. Permitting aggressive reactions in children to gain advantages for them simply reinforces the undesirable behavior and can produce unnecessary anxiety in them. Unchecked aggressive behavior in children, especially when directed against themselves or a loved one, can produce the fear in the children that there is no limit to the extent of their destructive ability.

In assessing the normality or abnormality of aggressive behavior the following should be considered: (1) the frequency and duration of the occurrence, (2) the circumstances eliciting the behavior, (3) its appropriateness for the situation, (4) the form of the behavior, and (5) the object against which the aggression is directed. As with hyperactivity, both the parent and the teacher can be of great help in assisting the physician in an appropriate diagnosis of the degree of severity of the problem. It is most helpful to have descriptions of the circumstances surrounding the episodes of aggression against which to apply the preceding considerations. Acting-out behavior is almost always an interactive process, and situational descriptions can help in understanding second-party contributions to such behavior.

Parents and teachers sometimes establish patterns of undesirable behavior by unwittingly rewarding it. A child who is behaving well may never be noticed but may be quickly scolded when acting out. The child, preferring negative attention to no attention, learns to continue the behavior for which some attention is obtained. A physician coming to understand the interactive elements of a child's acting out might gain a clue as to how a change might best be managed.

Acting-out behavior is best corrected by implementing a reward system for desired behavior rather than punishing the undesirable behavior. Punishment, itself aggressive, has the usual consequence of causing the child to inhibit the unwanted behavior in the face of the punisher without causing the child to adopt appropriate behavior.

Secondly, a system of well-planned rules and regulations are necessary for appropriate behavior control. A good rule must (1) serve a useful purpose, (2) be understandable, (3) be applicable to behavior that is under the child's control, (4) be enforceable, and (5) have a stated consequence if violated. Rules must be applied to clear-cut situations, times, and places.

A consistent program of reinforcement of desired behavior matched with control of unacceptable behavior, without reinforcing it, and a clear set of rules will be most favorable for behavior improvement over time. For such a program to operate effectively, the help of the adults with whom the child spends the major portion of the day is imperative. Teachers are generally well-educated in principles of behavior modification and/or contingency management. Teachers may also help in managing the child at school and working with the parent for home management. It may be useful to invite the teacher to sit in on a meeting with the physician and the child's parents in order to coordinate remedial activities. A coordinated approach will go a long way in assisting children to gain control over their own behavior. Physicians should request follow-up data for their files after an appropriate time interval following initiation of treatment.

Inhibited-Withdrawn Behavior

Withdrawal reactions range from mild and occasional shyness to continued avoidance of contact with others. Shyness is not in and of itself pathologic. Follow-up studies of shy children have demonstrated that the shy child, though tending to continue to be shy during adulthood, did not necessarily manifest adult symptoms of maladjustment. When shy children became adults, they tended to select occupations which offered security and shelter and to marry more outgoing partners, but given an opportunity to develop in their own style they seemed to evidence very satisfactory adult adjustment.

Withdrawal reactions can also be expressions of a child's feelings of helplessness and a protective way of avoiding situations which might lead to disparagement or demand effort. Such reactions are also self-punitive, since they sustain immaturity and provide no resolution of the child's difficulties.

Signs of withdrawal reactions include excessive crying, isolation, fear, absence of distress or anxiety when threatened with loss of love, and interrupted sleep, nightmares, or sleepwalking following what might be considered a well-controlled demeanor during the day.

Withdrawn children might be quiet, obedient, undemanding, considered "good" and, as a consequence, not be the subject of teachers' complaints. This is a population, whether complained about or not, with which the physician should be concerned. It is especially with this category of child that regular descriptive reports of child behavior accumulated at some central location might help in early identification of a problem. Babies who seem not to protest against unfavorable circumstances might fail to do so as a result of damage to the central nervous system. A psychotic child or one with severe auditory processing problems might be recognized by symptoms of isolation, innappropriate affect, uncommon reactions to common stimuli, or extreme difficulty in communication.

With school-age children, especially those who have a history of good adjustment, perhaps with evidence of overconformity and perfectionism, the onset of a serious pathologic disorder might be gradual, showing a progressive loss of interest in people and normal pursuits. Excessive preoccupation with certain abstract subjects and a marked drop in school performance may also be noted.

The shy child who is also evidencing some difficulties in learning, who repeatedly avoids situations which are "upsetting," who demonstrates few interests, and who garners few friends might be helped in school by a program geared to elevate self-confidence. Work graduated to assure repeated success in school, establishing forums in which the child can experience positive peer interactions, or refraining from harshness are all useful ways for the teacher to assist the mildly withdrawn child.

When withdrawal is a major symptom, a referral to a mental health specialist should be accompanied by some specific behavioral observations. These observations should be elicited from parents and school personnel. They should be made over a period of time, covering many settings and be as detailed as possible. Every effort will be made to determine whether the withdrawn behavior is situation-specific or diffuse. Behavioral observations made exclusively in the office cannot be considered sufficient data.

As children give evidence of more severe withdrawal reactions, the help of a mental health specialist is called for. Therapeutic treatment, whether carried out by a psychiatrist, psychologist, or social worker, will generally focus on the family. Therapy with children generally attempts to facilitate their learning to accept and express their emotions in the presence of an understanding adult while the offending environment is realigned. Treatment of the severely withdrawn child has often meant hospitalization and long-term therapy.

26 | School Absenteeism

by Philip R. Nader

Very little is written on the subject of school absenteeism patterns. It is a complex phenomenon which tends to be rather stable for a given child, and is influenced by many factors including the prevalence of illness, parental and home influences, and probably school and educational situations as well.

Absenteeism has been noted to be higher in lower socioeconomic classes, in children whose parents are under stress, have a chronic illness, have been recently hospitalized, have lower educational expectations, and are worried about their child's health. It is lower among children of well-to-do families, who live in less crowded conditions, and in those children who "like" school.

The relation of absenteeism to actual school performance and achievement has received surprisingly little attention. The most that can be said at present is that except for the higher socioeconomic classes, excessive school absence is most likely associated with poorer educational achievement, less participation in school activities, higher high school dropout rates, and higher rejection rates by the military services.

The relation of absenteeism to health also has not been extensively examined. Children are usually absent from school for "medical" reasons, such as illness or symptoms of illness. It has been estimated that about 75 percent of absences are accounted for in this way. Nonmedical reasons include illness in the home, going on trips with parents, oversleeping, inclement weather, and inappropriate clothing. However, there is some indication that children excessively absent for medical reasons are also excessively absent for nonmedical reasons.

Observations in the literature raise some interesting questions about the relation between absence and the presence of symptoms and/or the identification of a health problem by a school health service. Excessively absent sixth graders had in one study more symptoms of a psychosomatic nature than did a group of otherwise similar students with a low absentee rate. In a large prospective study of absenteeism among first and third graders, a high-absentee group had more contacts with the school nurse than did a low-absentee group. These studies might tend to indicate some relation between absence and being referred for a health problem by the school health service. In one study of high school students, a high absentee rate did not lead to identification of students with significant health problems. Another study noted no effect on school absenteeism among children registered for "comprehensive health care" at a Boston Neighborhood Health Center. In an unpublished study in Galveston, Texas, there was an indication that absence might be increased for lower socioeconomic students having to go to the clinic for a medical problem during the school day while more affluent students requiring a visit to the doctor or dentist went after school and, therefore, did not lose school time in order to have a health problem attended to.

School absence patterns still represent an area not fully investigated in the field of school health.

27 | Psychogenic Somatic Complaints

by David Graham

Every day thousands of childen in school complain of various maladies and symptoms largely determined by psychologic factors. These can be termed *psychogenic somatic complaints*. In order to understand the diagnosis and appropriate management of these symptoms, this broad category can be further divided into three subcategories which reflect the processes involved in symptom formation. These are (1) psychophysiologic, (2) conversion, and (3) malingering.

Psychophysiologic Symptoms

Psychologic processes often influence the course of illnesses and symptoms. Such processes are termed *psychophysiologic*. Bronchial asthma is an example of an illness which is frequently influenced by emotional factors. In some asthmatic children, emotional stress is known to precipitate bouts of wheezing. For instance, one fifth-grade boy with a history of asthma developed an attack the morning of a class play in which all the participants were to wear makeup including lipstick. His association of lipstick with a feminine identification was so disturbing that he vocalized his wishes not to be in the play. When these went unheeded, an asthmatic attack was precipitated.

Conversion Symptoms

Engel defines the process of conversion as "a psychic mechanism whereby an idea, fantasy or wish is expressed in bodily rather than verbal terms and is experienced by the patient as a physical rather than a mental symptom." The presence of a conversion symptom, therefore, represents an attempt to reduce anxiety caused by psychologic conflict. With the reduction of anxiety, the person achieves the *primary gain*. A *secondary gain* from a conversion symptom is achieved to the extent that the person successfully copes with whatever environmental situation produced the psychologic conflict. Often, the secondary gain may result in a great deal of attention and concern from significant adults. For example, a girl is known to hyperventilate and occasionally faint whenever she approaches a particular boy in the hallway in school. It is discovered that the boy has made some unsolicited, aggressive sexual advances toward her. Each time that she hyperventilates, the girl is taken to the health room, where she remains to rest. This girl has successfully coped with her environment by being taken to the health room whenever she begins to hyperventilate. She not only leaves the situation that has caused the anxiety but also gains much attention. These are considered secondary gains. The secondary gain acts as a reward for the behavior and serves to potentiate the conversion symptoms. Although any bodily symptom may be involved in a conversion process, common complaints noted among adolescents are abdominal pain, dizziness, headaches, and hyperventilation. While no published information is available as to how often conversion symptoms occur within schools, headaches and abdominal pains have often been noted as reasons for schoolchildren's visits to the school nurse.

Malingering

Malingering is a third category of psychogenic somatic complaints. This is the process of fabricating a bodily complaint in order to accomplish a specific goal. Adults quickly emphasize that the goal is to deceive and, therefore, view the malingerer negatively. However, in children it is important to focus on the reason for the malingering rather than on the actual deception. In school settings, the specific goal is usually to have a "ticket of admission" to the health suite or a "ticket of exit" from the classroom.

To a child, the health room may offer a respite from a stressful school situation, and it may provide a friendly, supportive atmosphere where one can confide or seek advice. However, a child usually believes that a somatic complaint is needed to gain access. If the child does not happen to have a symptom, one may be fabricated. A typical example is a child who is depressed and wants to talk with someone. Although the school may provide mental health staff in the form of guidance counselors or pupil personnel workers, children may view them as part of the educational establishment and may be reluctant to confide in them for fear all information will enter their school record. The health room staff may be perceived as extraeducational by students and, therefore, a safer place to seek advice and divulge feelings.

If the fabricated complaint is viewed only as an attempt of the child to avoid something, then the negative connotation of malingering is applied to the child. Instead, the cause of the child's feelings of avoidance should be sought. For example, a child with an undiagnosed learning disability may try to avoid failure in class by going to the health room when a particular subject is taught. A child who is teased for being poorly coordinated may try to avoid gym class. A child who is bullied by a peer during lunch may feign abdominal pain each lunch period.

Incidence of Psychogenic Somatic Complaints among Schoolchildren

There are no studies that give direct evidence of the incidence of psychogenic somatic complaints in school populations. However, there are some data inferring that such complaints are not uncommon.

The most common complaints presenting to school nurses—headaches, gastrointestinal symptoms, and dysmenorrhea—have been found to have a significant psychogenic component. In a study of visits to an elementary school nurse, Van Arsdell found that trauma accounted for half the visits; headaches, 4 percent; emotional reasons, 3 percent; and gastrointestinal symptoms, 9 percent. The remainder included other medical and dental symptoms. In a study of presumably normal high school students, Rogers found headaches and dysmenorrhea were the most common complaints while gastrointestinal symptoms ranked as the fifth most common complaint. A recent unpublished survey of 54 Baltimore city elementary and secondary school nurses indicated that abdominal pain and headaches were the most common complaints reported by children coming to the health room.

Recurrent abdominal pain is common in a childhood population. Apley and MacKeith found that it occurred in 9.5 percent of boys and 12.3 percent of girls. Investigation of 100 cases revealed only 8 percent had a definable organic cause. In a study of 80 children consecutively referred to a hospital with headaches, a convincing physical cause was found in only 4, and in 75 percent there was evidence of emotional stress.

Predisposing Factors in the Development of Psychogenic Somatic Symptoms

As a child grows, numerous situations which are emotionally stressful arise and make the child vulnerable to psychogenic somatic symptoms. The child entering school for the first time, in nursery school, kindergarten, or first grade, must learn to cope with separation from the family. Separation is a developmental situation which can cause significant stress. Children who fail to adjust well to separation from their mothers may display school phobic patterns. Complaints of numerous somatic symptoms both before and after arriving at school are characteristic of these children. Although often a form of malingering, both psychophysiologic complaints and conversion may also be operating. The child's goal is to remain with or return to the mother.

Beginning in elementary school and extending into high school, a low self-esteem may predispose a child to psychogenic somatic symptom formation. Peer acceptance is of major importance to the elementary school child. Chronic rejection by peers leads to a sense of poor self-esteem. It is not unusual for a child to complain of headaches or abdominal pain following an incident involving peer rejection.

Underachievement and learning disorders often result in psychogenic somatic complaints. This may also be related to peer rejection. When children recognize that they cannot do as well as their peers in class, feelings of inferiority soon lead to lowered self-esteem. Inability to feel successful at school apparently makes a child vulnerable to psychogenic somatic symptoms at all ages. Rogers and Reese came to the conclusion that at the secondary school level "while [the] presenting physical complaints usually were medically insignificant, the association of high frequency [of somatic complaints] with low academic status, a tendency toward poor participation in school activities, high drop out rate and frequent absence—especially associated with truancy—marked the frequent health room visitor as a person not succeeding in various areas of life activity."

With the onset of puberty, adolescents become more aware of their own bodies, especially of how they think they might appear to others. Elkind describes this characteristic egocentrism of the adolescent as "the belief that others are preoccupied with his appearance and behavior." Young adolescents are able to conceptualize the thoughts of other people but are often unable to differentiate between what others are thinking about and their own mental images. Therefore, they may attribute their own mental preoccupations to others. Young adolescents who are concerned about whether their own development is "normal" may think that everyone is looking at them with the same questions in mind. This is evident in junior and senior high school gym classes, where often there is embarrassment for those who mature or who fear that they are maturing "too early" or "too late." Gym locker rooms and showers offer little privacy. This is especially true for boys, who usually must use common showers without separate stalls or curtains. Although shower curtains are usually provided for girls, privacy for changing into gym clothes frequently is absent. Breast and genital exposure is almost assured. In early junior and senior high school, when adolescent sexual development may vary greatly, students are prone to compare their own sexual maturation with that of others. Finding a discrepancy, the question "Am I normal?" follows. Concern with body image, egocentric thinking, and questions about the normality of

their own sexual development can easily make some adolescents susceptible to significant stress in gym locker rooms and showers. Using a somatic complaint to get out of gym class often provides necessary temporary relief for such an anxious adolescent.

Another instance in which the egocentrism of adolescence predisposes to psychogenic somatic complaints is seen in some girls during menarche or subsequent menstrual periods. It is not uncommon for the menstruating adolescent to think that everyone is aware of her menstruation. She may become preoccupied with fears of staining clothes, blood running down her legs, or bad ordors. To what extent such fears contribute to dysmenorrhea is unknown. However, anxiety and worry have been reported as contributing factors in the etiology of dysmenorrhea.

Management

Communication with school personnel is essential in diagnosing and managing children with psychogenic somatic complaints which occur in the school. Not only does the nurse or physician need information, but frequently it is necessary to modify the school situation in order to decrease or eliminate the child's symptoms. Communication can be in the form of a conference at the school or telephone conversations with appropriate school personnel. In some cases it is possible for the school nurse to gather much of the information. The nurse can also act as an intermediary in following up on management plans with school personnel. In illness such as asthma, it may be necessary for the school to make some provision to administer medicine to the child. Although this seems simple enough, many schools do not have a nurse available. School administrators are frequently reluctant to take the responsibility for giving a medication. It becomes necessary for the physician to impress upon the school administration the consequences for a child unable to receive the medication, namely, that there will be more frequent absences from school due to illness.

When treating children who have conversion symptoms, counseling school and health room personnel to reduce the secondary gain to the student is important. Thus, the adolescent who has headaches diagnosed as conversion should not be sent by the teacher to the nurse at the first sign of a headache. In fact, the symptoms should be ignored or minimized.

To accomplish this will necessitate much support via frequent contacts with the teacher and other involved school staff members.

The child fabricating somatic complaints in order to gain entrance to the health room requires a different approach. To dismiss the child's complaints as being dishonest, foolish, or manipulative is to ignore the possibility of significant stress in the child's school life. Instead, investigation should be made into the reasons for malingering. This often necessitates obtaining information from the teacher, principal, guidance counselor, or other school staff members in addition to the routine family history.

Since much of the physician's or nurse's effectiveness in detecting and managing schoolchildren with psychogenic somatic symptoms depends on communication with school personnel, facilitation of these contacts should have favorable results. Establishing a positive working relationship with the principal in the school is the first step in accomplishing this. In most schools the principal is responsible for all the programs within the school. Therefore, either the principal or some delegated person should be kept informed about a child's status. In addition, recommendations for major changes in an educational program for a child should generally first be discussed with the principal. The next step in facilitating communication is arranging to contact the child's teacher. Solicitation of the teacher's ideas and attitudes about the child serve both to provide information and to enlist support in classroom management. Frequent short follow-up contacts with the teacher provide opportunities to modify the teacher's approach to the child. These contacts also let the teacher know that there is someone to call upon when problems arise with the child.

Some schools have pupil personnel workers or guidance counselors who have had training in behavioral and mental health problems. These professionals may be able to offer counseling to children in the school setting. Practicing physicians should view these school-based personnel as potential resources in the management of psychogenic somatic complaints of children.

28 | School Phobia

by Philip R. Nader

School phobia does not mean a "fear" of school. The term applies to variable symptoms of anxiety in a school-age child who is excessively absent from school. It also differs from truancy in which the child is neither at home nor at school. Many interacting factors can result in school phobia. In the preadolescent school-age child, the major psychologic factor is an interdependency between a parent and the child. "The umbilical cord pulls at both ends" was Eisenberg's analogy.

Many astute clinicians and school nurses are quickly alert to tendencies in parents and children toward overprotection and overresponse to minor illness which may result in excessive school absence. When the parent or child is made aware of this situation, it improves. Such instances represent the mild end of the spectrum of school phobia. Most published follow-up studies of school phobia are biased due to the severity of problems referred to child study centers or to psychiatrists. All follow-up studies of younger children with school phobia show more positive results in overall adjustment than do those of older children and adolescents referred for school phobia.

Primary care providers are often required to recognize and treat this problem. They are also in a key position to prevent the development of a school phobia pattern. This is very important because the problem is almost never easily or quickly handled if it is already well-established.

Prevention of School Phobia

The primary care provider will need to be alert to family or life situations in which school phobia might develop. These can include a child perceived as "delicate," or vulnerable; a chronically ill child; or a child who was born prematurely or who had serious or frequent illnesses as an infant. Others might include an observed overprotective parent–child interaction pattern, parental illness, hospitalization, death, separation, divorce, or other family crisis. An appropriate schedule for the development of child independence is suggested by Schmitt: ". . . being left alone by six months of age with adults other than the parents; being left with a sitter during waking hours by age two years; leaving the child in places other than at home by three years."

The primary care provider may also help to prevent school phobia in children by working as a school consultant. By alerting local school officials to the loss of student attendance and revenues, interest will be focused on this problem. A regular and periodic review of school absence data including total days absent and pattern of instances of absence should permit early identification of children developing a school phobia picture. The primary care provider can support school personnel in doing as much as they can before calling on outside help, since often it is the school itself that has the practical benefit of resolving the problem early. Other preventive activities based in the school include discussions and meetings for groups of parents of kindergarten children who have had older siblings with excessive absenteeism. The topics would range from "usual and expected separation difficulties" to "common illnesses caught at school and how to manage them" to "the importance and salience of school attendance." For "hard core" families, more in-depth assessment of the family problems would be required in order to effectively intervene. The primary care provider could assist school personnel in outlining such in-depth assessment procedures.

Detection of School Phobia

The presentation of this problem may be a direct complaint from the parent or school that the child will not go to school. More frequently, a variety of psychosomatic complaints are present. Organic symptoms of an acute or chronic organic illness may also exist with parental or other adult reaction leading to excessive or unwarranted school absence. The truism "It has to be thought of before a diagnosis can be made" is applicable in school phobia.

Confirmation of School Phobia Symptoms

Called "the great imitator" by Schmidt, a multiplicity of signs and symptoms of school phobia may be present. The following have been described: insomnia or excessive sleeping and "tiredness"; pallor; recurrent sore throats; "sinus"; hyperventilation; cough; palpitation; chest pain; abdominal pains; headaches; vomiting; diarrhea; dysmenorrhea; bone and joint pains; and syncope. In other words, the complaints do not suggest the diagnosis.

The child may be of either sex, and the problem is present in all socioeconomic strata. No specific intelligence characteristics have been ruled out, but such children are often described as "good students" and bright or average in their school abilities.

The aforementioned bond between mother and child may be heard in the mother's comment: "*We* didn't feel good today so *we* didn't go to school." When a child stays at home with Mother during the school day, there seems to be little realization on Mother's part of how allowing or encouraging this promotes dependency. Such a communication pattern between child and parent rightfully should raise the question of why this situation exists and should lead to an assessment of family communication styles.

Since almost all school phobia is a family problem, the primary care provider should be aware of three common patterns of communication found in families with school phobia: (1) Both parents are overconcerned and basically unaware of their contribution to the problem—these situations are often amenable to short-term counseling; (2) the mother (usually) is overprotective, but the father disagrees completely and is vocal about it—the child responds by being exceptionally manipulative (this situation is likely to respond more quickly to counseling than the third pattern); and (3) the mother is extremely overinvolved, even talking for the child, and the father is absent or might as well be (having absented himself).

The family communication patterns should be actively assessed. How do the parents see the problem? What happens every morning? Is one or the other parent inadvertently giving a message that it's all right to stay home from school? ("You don't feel like going to school, do you?") The child's perception of, and likes and dislikes about, school and other significant areas of the child's life should be explored with the child.

Information obtained directly from the school will include data on previous attendance, performance, peer acceptance, or any realistic reasons why the child might fear school (bullies or extortion). Beware the pitfall of a parental suggestion of changing schools or teachers or even realistic reasons why the child might fear going to school. These reasons, while perhaps significant, are usually not a sufficient cause of school phobia.

A complete and thorough physical assessment with appropriate laboratory examination is indicated along with a complete description of negative findings delivered to the parent and child. This should not be omitted even if the primary care provider is virtually certain of the absence of undetected serious organic disease. Unnecessary laboratory tests not only are costly but serve to reinforce doubts as to the real nature of the problem.

Management

Management will not be successful unless parents, child, school, and all who are involved are taken into account in an active treatment plan. Successful management requires the primary care provider to clearly identify both short- and long-term goals. These goals dictate the treatment plan. Follow-up should be designed to assess the efficacy of the treatment plan and to revise it or consider referral.

Short-term goals for the treatment of school phobia almost always center on plans to interrupt the pattern of behavior which is resulting in school nonattendance. Returning the child to school, therefore, is the major short-term goal. Long-term goals include a gradual reduction in the child's anxiety, an improved self-image, resolution of a precipitating family crisis, and improved overall child functioning and family communication patterns.

Implementing the Treatment Plan

In approaching the child, it is important that the veracity of the child's complaints be recognized ("The stomachache really hurts"). Now, however, "everyone" has decided it will eventually get better, and "everyone" has decided that no matter how difficult it will be, the child will return to school. If the parents succeed in returning the child to school at the next possible time, the child's anxiety may initially increase but soon will recede because the more regular the attendance, the more the child's participation in school life will gradually increase. In follow-up it may be necessary to anticipate possible future difficulties (for example, change to a larger junior high school). Counseling, allowing the child to express some concerns, may smooth later transition crises.

In approaching the family, the primary care provider will emphasize finding out how the family will work together to solve the problem (getting the child back to school). The primary care provider must avoid taking sides against one or another of the parents, and recognize and keep in check any angry feelings toward the "offending" parent. The ease with which parents are able to recognize the problem and their role in its resolution can predict immediate success and the lack of need for a referral. However, often the primary care provider will have to deal repeatedly with parental doubts and fears and be firm about the diagnosis and management plan. The parents should be engaged in a discussion of how they can interrupt the child's pattern of behavior. Simple advice giving regarding normal child rearing and limit setting may be all that is required. In approaching the school, the most valuable piece of information needed is that the child is free from any unrecognized serious medical problem. Most teachers, counselors, and nurses can be supportive and firm if they have this reassurance. Ongoing communication is essential, not only to assess the success of management, but also to minimize the resocialization trauma unavoidable after prolonged school absence. Use of school resources for support and further evaluation of any existing academic or social problems may be required to return the child to optimal functioning.

Indications and Procedures for Referral

In the preadolescent school phobia, referral may be required, but this is usually because more severe family or marital problems are interfering with a successful resolution of the problem. Referral of a child with adolescent school phobia is almost always made because of a more serious psychopathologic condition in the child (depression or schizophrenia).

Widely divergent parental opinions which seem unresolvable in a reasonable period after initial counseling will require referral to some type of family counseling service.

Referral resources are determined by geographic, financial, and interpersonal trust factors. The family will require a great deal of support and confidence that their problem can be solved with the appropriate help. Direct communication between the primary care provider and the source of referral (private psychiatrist, child development or mental health clinic, social worker, psychologist, family service agency) is mandatory until it is definitely known that the family has been seen and treatment initiated. Someone must keep in contact with the family and school at least until the child is attending school on a regular basis.

29 | Chronically Handicapped Children in School

by Beverly Myers

A chronic illness or handicap may be defined as a condition that affects one or more organ systems and persists for many months or perhaps a lifetime. It has been estimated that up to 20 percent of children in the United States have some form of handicap (Table 29-1). One well-done study has estimated a prevalence of 5.7 percent in children of chronic physical disorders including asthma, epilepsy, cerebral palsy, and heart disease, and 6.6 percent for those with psychiatric illness. (This does not include the large number with visual or speech impairments.) Fortunately, there are now fewer children whose chronic disorders are so seriously incapacitating as to require long-term hospitalization or maintenance at a separate school facility. The majority of such children can function in a normal school setting.

While the treatment of acute disease primarily involves physicians and nurses, the management of a child with a chronic illness or handicap necessarily entails others who come in contact with him in his daily life. For this reason, parents and school personnel become partners with the health professionals in fostering the optimal physical, intellectual, psychologic, and social development of each handicapped child. Close cooperation between school, home, and the physician's office is essential if we are to seek to deal with the increased vulnerability to social and emotional maladjustment that has been noted in children with chronic health problems. Understanding the relationships among viewpoints and experiences of chronically handicapped children, their parents, their teachers, and their physicians will form the basis of the management of a number of special circumstances required by such children in school.

The Child

Society has powerful influences on the behavior of its members who are deviant. This particularly applies to the child who is different because of a chronic illness or handicap. The child's self-esteem is heavily influenced by the family's and the school's attitudes toward him. Continuously negative or unrealistically optimistic reactions or overly high or excessively low expectations may lead to significant difficulties. Thus, parents, teachers, and peers may have a positive *or* negative influence on a child's adaptation.

Other influences on a child's reaction to a chronic illness or handicap include the age at onset, the nature of the illness, and the presence of disfigurement. A congenitally deformed child who has never known normality would appear to have different expectations than the child who acquires a deformity later and constantly expects to be returned to his prior state. A young preschooler will react to the changes in the parents' handling or to the separation brought about by hospitalization. The school-age child is more aware of the handicap or illness itself, which may worry and depress him. Preoccupation with body image and a need for peer acceptance may underlie the adolescent's denial of concern.

Children with central nervous system defects are more vulnerable to maladaptive behavior than those with other physical handicaps. The child with a fatal illness or progressive degenerative disorder will usually be under greater stress than children with other

Table 29-1

Estimated Number of Handicapped Children Served* and Unserved by Type of Handicap

Condition	Total Handicapped Children Served and Unserved,† 1974–1975	Percent Served
Total age 0–19	7,886,000	50
Total age 6–19	6,699,000	55
Total age 0–5	1,187,000	22
Speech-impaired	2,293,000	81
Mentally retarded	1,507,000	83
Learning-disabled	1,966,000	12
Emotionally disturbed	1,310,000	18
Crippled and otherwise health-impaired	328,000	72
Deaf	49,000	71
Hard of hearing	328,000	18
Visually handicapped	66,000	59
Deaf-blind and otherwise multihandicapped	40,000	33

* Estimated total numbers of handicapped children served—obtained from State Education Agencies (SEA) (fall and winter, 1975). Information by type of handicap was not available and is projected from data provided by SEA for school year 1972–1973.

† Total number of handicapped children ages 0 to 19 years provided on basis of estimate obtained from various sources, including national agencies and organizations and state and local directors of special education. According to these sources, the incidence levels by types of handicap are as follows: speech-impaired, 3.5%; mentally retarded, 2.3%; learning-disabled, 3.0%; emotionally disturbed, 2.0%; crippled and otherwise health-impaired, 0.5%; deaf, 0.08%; hard of hearing 0.5%; visually handicapped, 0.1%; deaf-blind and otherwise multi-handicapped, 0.06%. The total number of handicapped children in the above categories represents 12.035% of all school-age children 6 to 19 and 6.018% of all children 0 to 5 years. The population figures to which the incidence rates were applied were obtained from the Bureau of the Census and reflect the population as of July 1, 1974.

Source: From Committee on School Health: *School Health: A Guide for Health Professionals,* Evanston, Ill.: American Academy of Pediatrics, 1977.

chronic disorders. Hereditary disorders and physical disfigurement each have special meaning and stress for the child and his family.

A child's reactions to the stress of a chronic illness may manifest in a number of ways. Some children consider their illness a punishment for misdeeds, while others may blame their defect or their hospitalizations on their parents, who seem to be abandoning them. A prevailing fear of new situations or of failure may inhibit many children. One may observe varying combinations of denial, rebellion, depression, anxiety, immaturity, overdependence, excessive independence, passive resignation, or mature acceptance, depending on the many influences on a child.

The Parents

A chronic illness in a child poses somewhat different stresses on his parents than does an acute illness. An acute episode's frightening experiences usually recede in memory, but a chronic illness cannot readily be forgotten. Parents experience several stages of reactions to the discovery that their child has a chronic abnormality. The initial stage of shock and numbness gradually gives way to a long-term struggle to master the stressful facts. Parents continually seek to explain why the problem occurred and what can be done to cure it even when there may be no answers. One may note defense mechanisms (such as denial, rationalization, projection, intellectualization) which are cognitive distortions of reality and serve a homeostatic purpose. Many feelings are aroused: chronic grief or sorrow for the loss of a normal child, anger at others who have not done enough, guilt at their own possible or real responsibility, and shame that this should occur to their child. Such emotions and defense mechanisms are inevitable, but may change with the years as some degree of mastery and acceptance of a difficult situation becomes possible.

These reactions will disrupt child rearing: Parents may become overprotective, so that their indulgence fosters excessive dependency. Disciplining a handicapped child may be so unacceptable that the child never learns standards of behavior expected from his peers. Overprotection may also lead to unnecessary restrictions on a child's activities and experiences. On the other hand, some parents set up excessive demands to demonstrate that the handicap does not make any difference, even when it does—and these children may become prey to depression as they fail to live up to their parents' expectations. It is indeed difficult for parents to arrive at appropriate expectations and limits for their handicapped child. Inconsistent efforts at child rearing reflect their sense of confusion, inadequacy, ambivalence, and uncertainty.

Professionals and teachers dealing with the parents of a handicapped child must be sensitive to and tolerant of such parental reactions. Excessive parental anger at a teacher or physician may be more easily tolerated when these frustrations are understood. With patience for distorted parental attitudes and gentle explanations of reality, a professional may enable parents to recognize and modify their inappropriate handling of their child.

The Teacher

Like parents, teachers may feel inadequate in handling a child with a disorder they do not understand. Such a child may provoke in the teacher many of the reactions described in parents. To cope with their discomfort they may prefer to have others teach the child, thus avoiding the stress. Medical personnel can be of great help to the teacher and, thus, enable a child to remain in a classroom where his development can be fostered. By presenting factual information about the illness, suggesting modifications in classroom routine, and giving support by showing

continuing interest and availability, the medical personnel can enable the teacher to feel more comfortable in handling the challenge of a different child, the challenge to learn about a physical disorder, the challenge to foster a child's emotional growth, and the challenge to help other children accept individual differences and even defects.

Exposure to the same social influences in a normal classroom that nonhandicapped children experience may well be an important influence on a handicapped child's development. Separate classrooms and special schools isolate handicapped children and may foster yet even more socially deviant behavior. Thus, it would appear preferable to include handicapped children, where possible, within normal classrooms so as to encourage greater social competence. To accomplish this, a teacher will need much support from medical and special education personnel. So, for example, a teacher's gentle but firm guiding support and interest can enable fearful children to enter new situations and to discover that they will not fail all the time. The teacher can also enable the class to discover that the handicapped children have assets of their own, and are worthwhile as friends. Thus, a teacher's role in fostering social competence in the handicapped child demands the professional's support.

The Primary Health Care Provider

Managing a chronic illness poses challenges for medical professionals as well. The pressures to cure patients rather than to care for them is a reflection of the physician's desire for omnipotence. It is important for medical professionals to be aware of their own attitudes toward the chronically ill, for cognitive distortions of reality (defense mechanisms such as denial) and strong feelings (anger) may get in the way of appropriate management—and the chronically ill child deserves competent, sensitive, and appropriate management.

There are times when a consultant may take on the task of providing ongoing medical management and communication with school personnel. The primary care provider may, however, take on one or both of these tasks. By the development of a supportive relationship and a periodic review of a child's health status, the primary care provider can come to know the child and the child's family and communicate this knowledge to the school when needed. Sometimes this may mean being the mediator between the parents and school personnel by interpreting parental reactions.

It is obvious that good communication between medical personnel caring for children and those who are involved with teaching them at school is valuable. The professional must not forget the importance of obtaining written parental consent for transmission of written information to the school, and parental knowledge of verbal physician-teacher communications helps foster cooperation among those involved. If possible, letting a child know of such communication may help the child feel more like a participant and less the helpless victim.

What information should be transmitted? The following are some suggested guidelines. Of course, use of language comprehensible to the teacher is essential for good cooperation.

1 The nature of the disorder. This includes the diagnosis with some description of the presenting symptoms and a general idea about prognosis. It is important to clarify for school personnel what the parents and child understand about the problem, since a teacher might inadvertently communicate information in a way that might be frightening or harmful.

2 Modifications in classroom routine. These include reduction of activities where excessive fatigue may be a problem (as in cardiac disorder), avoidance of some activities which are dangerous or impossible (as with gym in some orthopedic disorders), tolerance for slow performance (for example, in the child with cerebral palsy), and appropriate seating placement (as for the child with hearing loss).

3 Emergency problems that may arise and steps to take to deal with them. The classic example is, of course, epilepsy, where guidelines are needed for handling a generalized seizure. Bleeding problems in hemophilia are another example. Specific information about whom to contact and where to take the child if an emergency arises may be needed.

4 Decisions regarding class placement. Discussions with the principal, the special education personnel, the school nurse, and the teacher may be necessary in order to decide what type of class placement is needed for a child.

a Homebound teaching for certain children is necessary when a child is immobilized in casts, too tired to tolerate a full day (for example, in chronic renal disease), or too much at risk of acquiring contagious illness (such as for the child with leukemia).

b Separate schools do exist for children with mental retardation, visual or hearing impairments, chronic illness, and orthopedic handicaps. While many children with such handicaps can and should be handled within a regular classroom whenever possible, some children do present sufficient individual needs that separate school (or class) placement is appropriate. The final decision should be a joint one made by the school, parents, and medical personnel.

c Separate class placement may be indicated for some children with severe learning or behavioral problems which can be better handled in a self-contained, special education classroom, while others can be included in a regular classroom with periodic resource-room help.

5 Medications required during school. Written consent from parents and written directions from the physician are usually required, and the school nurse is responsible for dispensing the medication.

Special Circumstances

The Child with a Fatal Illness Cystic fibrosis, muscular dystrophy, and leukemia are disorders with an ultimately fatal outcome that a teacher may very well encounter. It is indeed a painful experience for all concerned and one that demands all the resources (both internal and external) that parents, teachers, and physicians can command, so that each can continue to function without overwhelming distress. The goal for all concerned is to enable a fatally ill child to enjoy his life as long as possible—a period that may last many years. Expectation should be as close to normal as possible. Such children require support but not indulgence. A listening and interested person without excessive cheerfulness can do much to make each day worthwhile. Nevertheless, one may see periods of anxiety, depression, regression, increased dependency, apathy, restlessness, and uncooperative behavior—states which demand acceptance, patience, and understanding. The teacher, like the physician, may well feel the desire to flee when confronted with a child with a fatal illness. Yet, if able to avoid overidentifying or becoming paralyzed with despair, the teacher can do much to make attending school a beneficial experience, when fears of pain, death, or hospitalization can be temporarily forgotten. Children with long-term fatal illnesses need hope even if this is only the knowledge that those around them (parents, teachers, physicians) will not abandon them. Medical personnel's support of teachers and parents may enable each to continue to relate warmly to these children.

Physical Disability Cerebral palsy, limb deficiencies, and other orthopedic handicaps may be severe enough to require special school (or class) placement, but often such children can be handled in the regular class with some modifications. While physical distortions may alienate or frighten some children, the visible, definable defect may be less anxiety-provoking to the handicapped child than the invisible (such as a cardiac defect).

As noted above, children with central nervous defects such as cerebral palsy would appear to be more vulnerable to behavioral and emotional disorders than those with orthopedic handicaps not involving the brain. Yet it is the same familial stresses that lead to psychiatric disorder in both groups. Thus, attentiveness to and intervention in familial stresses such as maternal mental health problems, marital conflicts, and disorganized homes may aid the chronically handicapped to cope with both these family stresses and those which the handicap itself creates.

Chronic Illness Epilepsy and heart diseases, as invisible handicaps, may provoke many fears in children who have difficulty conceptualizing their problem. Sometimes pictures and diagrams may help, and continuing explanations as a child matures will be important. Parents and teachers have great difficulty determining what is appropriate activity for the chronically ill child. Some children will push themselves to the point of excessive fatigue and may need to be encouraged to relax. Perhaps the more common problem is the child who uses somatic complaints or fatigue to get out of unpleasant or unwelcome demands. Determining appropriate expectations and making these explicit to parents, teachers, and children may prevent such problems as the "cardiac cripple" who really has the capacity to carry out all activities.

Disfiguring Handicaps Scars from burns, congenital facial deformities, and skin diseases pose real threats to children and those around them. The tendency for withdrawal in such children is real, and they may need ongoing individual support to face the stares from an alien world.

Sensory Handicaps Impairment in vision and hearing, if severe enough, may require special class placement. These disorders, especially hearing loss, do isolate such children from their peers, and disturbances in personality development may result. The appropriate recognition of visual handicap or of hearing loss (in the child with language delay) is essential to proper educational management and may prevent compounding behavioral problems.

Conclusion

Children with chronic handicaps should have the opportunity to mature to their best physical and mental capabilities. Relationships with society via family, peers, teachers, and physicians may be beneficial or detrimental to functioning as an adult. The professional's skillful use of factual knowledge and sensitivity to personal attitudes may aid the chronically handicapped child and family. Cooperation between parents, physicians, allied health personnel, and educators is essential in fostering optimal growth for each handicapped child in school.

30 | Roles and Responsibilities of the Physician

by Philip R. Nader

The previous section of this part has dealt with specific developmental or clinical problems in relation to the school-age child. Over and over again, interaction and communication between the health care provider, the school, and the home were emphasized. In order for these three to interact to benefit the child, intervention is required. The physician, or primary health care provider, is the necessary ingredient to catalyze such efforts. Others' efforts will also be required, but without support and action from physicians it is unlikely that much in the way of cooperative programs between health and education will be achieved.

Physicians potentially have numerous roles and interests in schools—as parents, as school board members, as community leaders, and as providers of care to children. Some may also develop formal full- or part-time consulting arrangements with schools for sports or athletic programs, and as physician consultants to school districts, nurses, and health educators. As the compulsory education law broadens to include younger and older groups as well as the severely physically and mentally handicapped, physicians will play mandated roles in assessment and school placement of such individuals.

Training does not routinely equip a physician to consult or work with a school, but the physician trained in child health brings deep knowledge of and experience with child development, dealing with families, and follow-up case management skills which are valuable in a school setting. These same skills which equip physicians for a unique role with an individual patient or family may work against them when they encounter another area such as the school. Here, one is not necessarily asked for an opinion, and if one is offered, it is not necessarily accepted. Thus, one often becomes an educator and persuader rather than a final decision maker. Teamwork in which one is not captain of the team is not always an easy task for a physician.

Increasing numbers of residencies, fellowships, and medical schools are beginning to offer exposure to school health, but most physicians have little prepractice experience. The interested physician will become equipped by reading and by consulting with others who are experienced. A willingness to get involved and time for mutual trust to develop are prerequisites for successful school consultation. However, these are necessary but not sufficient activities. Physicians should be informed about community resources and those of the school system, the major child health needs, and community concerns. They should learn who are the key personnel and what the crucial administrative relationships are, and have some notion of what a school health program might include.

31 | The School Institution

by Allen Graubard

The American public school system is a massive enterprise, encompassing over 45 million elementary and secondary school students, with more than 2 million instructional staff people. (About 90 percent of school-age youth attend public schools.) Different from most other countries, which have centralized federal control of the schools, the United States system is organized according to the principle of local control. There are thousands of local school districts, each raising its own funds through local taxation (supplemented by state and federal subsidies). School committees or boards of education, either elected or appointed, are the official policy-making bodies for these local school districts. The day-to-day workings of the schools are directed by a full-time staff official such as a superintendent, with what can be an extensive bureaucracy including assistant superintendents, supervisors, principals, and assistant principals.

The Stereotype "Traditional" School

From the early part of this century on, the form of public schooling became fixed, especially in urban areas. Schools often meant large buildings housing several hundred or even several thousand students in one school, often moving in different "ability streams." Classrooms contained 30 to 40 students sitting at desks arranged in rows and taught by properly credentialed teachers. Silence in the classroom, unless talking and movement are permitted by the teacher, has generally been the rule; and "conduct" and discipline are prime concerns for many teachers and administrators. Motivation to learn is mainly a matter of external pressure exerted through the system of grading and threats of punishment. Students compete for good marks and are constantly told how important it is to get these marks, often because of future rewards such as prizes, scholarships, and opportunity to gain educational credentials which will make possible more prestigious and higher-paying jobs in the adult world.

Reaction to the Stereotype Periodically, wide-ranging critiques of the public school system and its methods, attitudes, and values have appeared, the most well-known being the "progressive education" idea associated in this country with the name of John Dewey during the early decades of this century. Although progressive education ideas received much discussion in teachers' colleges and in books and magazines, there was little penetration of its philosophy and methods into the great majority of American public schools.

The 1960s saw a revival of many of the ideas associated with the spirit of progressive education, deepened by the widespread critique of dominant American institutions and values that characterized the social movements of that decade. These ideas gained a wide audience through the very popular writings of radical critics of the educational system. Examples include A. S. Neill, founder of the most well-known libertarian "free school," Summerhill; John Holt, author of *How Children Fail*; and Paul Goodman, whose *Compulsory Miseducation* is one of the most succinct and convincing statements of the contemporary version of the progressive critique.

The "Alternative School" Concept

The concrete manifestation of this growing spirit of opposition is what is variously called the *free school movement* or, more generally, *alternative schools*. The free school movement had two distinct sources, one pedagogic and the other political. The political source involved a question of community control of education. Out of this source came the community schools, small community-controlled schools, often, in urban communities run by blacks mainly for black youth, using methods and curricula which enhanced individual and group self-images.

The pedagogic source of the movement was the newly reformulated progressive education idea, emphasizing freedom as a key pedagogic principle. The basic ideas of the free, or alternative, school (although there is much variation in their style and content) are that young people learn best when they are given freedom, when they are not directed or coerced in their learning experiences. This often means small classes, informally taught, sometimes by voluneers; few or no requirements; sometimes limited resources; friendly relations between teachers and students; democratic governance procedures in the school; and community learning opportunities.

Influence of the Alternative School on the Traditional School System

Over the past 10 years, several hundred nonpublic free schools were started. They were usually very small, averaging less than 50 students per school, and they were almost always very poor. Many of the schools lasted less than 3 or 4 years. The idea gained support, and alternative schools were established as part of public school systems. Some received support from the federal government and private foundations. The number of public alternative schools has grown steadily over the past few years. Besides these thousand or so public alternative schools there are also many examples of *open classrooms* for younger students, more electives, minicourses, and *modular scheduling* for secondary students. Other new approaches include *humanistic education* and a number of educational curricula in affective as well as cognitive areas. Many of the ideas of the free school have had effect even beyond the actual alternative schools. This can be seen in the growing student choice in curriculum, student initiative in courses, and the modification of authoritarian discipline procedures.

32 | School Health Program Goals

by Philip R. Nader

A unique and essential ingredient is often overlooked in planning and operating school health programs. It is the interaction among three groups—the child and the family, school personnel and the education system, and health care providers in the systems of health care delivery. Each group has different perceptions, priorities, and values which impinge on and influence the child's health and development. These differences form barriers that frequently keep the groups from interacting effectively. They also present a challenge to develop ways to enhance the interaction of these groups in working toward the total health of the child.

School health is the naturally occurring arena where these three groups come together. Examination of their interaction and their perceptions, priorities, and values in relation to health is a prerequisite for approaching the development of a school health program.

The Home and the Family

Constraints Placed on Children The target of most school health efforts is children who, for the most part, remain passive recipients of program activities. Both the school and home groups place this constraint on children. Health care providers often reinforce this passive role and rely on mothers to initiate and maintain desired behaviors for their children. The opportunity for children to practice skills in relation to their own health could be present and reinforced in the school setting. The family, however, remains the major unit that provides the social learning that will lead to independent or self-directed health-related behavior.

School health programs should help children be-

come active participants and decision makers regarding their own health care. More knowledge is needed about children's concepts and perceptions of health and illness. Also, we need to find ways of helping children learn how to promote and maintain their own health. The school remains that institution in society charged with instruction of children. Information is gradually accumulating which indicates that developing health concepts and behaviors are related both to the child's cognitive development and to social learning. The extent of the constraint placed on children in relation to health decision making is most pronounced when high school students are permitted to drive a car but need special permission to go to the school nurse. This is one constraint that school health programs could plan to overcome.

Family Stress and Child Health Mechanic studied the health and illness behaviors of 350 mother-child pairs in fourth graders and eighth graders. While the overall results indicate little maternal influence in determining children's patterns of illness behavior, it was found that family stress made mothers more likely to report their own and their children's symptoms. They also were more likely to contact the physician concerning their children's health. The combined work of Roghmann and Haggerty and others documents the influence of family stress and coping patterns. Stress was found to increase health care utilization via that portion of the health care system which is more responsive to access demands, namely, phone calls and emergency room visits. The family stress surrounding a chronically ill child is increased by lack of knowledge. For asthma, Pless found that the better the parents' knowledge and understanding of the child's illness, the better the child's adjustment: "Only 27% of children whose parents had 'excellent' knowledge of their illnesses had low adjustment scores, compared to 43% of those with parents having 'poor' understanding."

A school health program with planned appropriate outreach and parental involvement could respond more quickly to families' and children's stress. Also, over an extended period of time it may be possible to alter the coping styles and strengths which families and children have available to deal with stress when it inevitably appears.

The School

Adult Attitudes and Expectations   Adult attitudes and beliefs directly impinge on the children who are the recipients of school programs. Both parent-child and teacher-child interactions are based on knowledge, beliefs, and experiences which often do not allow them to respond most effectively to children's health or developmental needs. Previous experiences with health care systems may cause inappropriate fear, lack of understanding, and unrealistic expectations of the seemingly magical intervention of the health professionals. Common examples include concern on the part of teachers about showing moving pictures to epileptic students for fear of precipitating a seizure, ascribing chewing on pencils and other forms of pica to mineral or other dietary deficiencies, and excessive attention to children subject to attacks of "asthma." Other unrealistic expectations commonly encountered include the value of a "brain wave" or "medication" in solving a difficult behavioral and educational problem.

School health programs have an obligation to attempt to overcome these knowledge and attitudinal barriers through education. Teachers are generally enthusiastically receptive to joint "in-service" efforts on some of these health-related areas if administrators can be convinced of their value over more "pressing" educational priorities. The support of concerned community parents can be critical in establishing the priority for such teacher seminars. Parents may also be valuable in securing health care professionals from the community to be resources for such seminars. Health care providers will gain insight into the problems faced by educators through mutual participation in health-related seminars.

Priority for Health in Education   Health education and promotion of health often have low priorities in the educational curriculum. Seminars such as the ones mentioned above may stimulate interest. Another avenue may be to develop health education programs outside the formal curriculum which are specifically focused on children having specialized educational needs or those who have consequences of a health or developmental problem. Examples include children with physical handicaps or chronic illnesses. Outcomes should be predicted and measured: improved educational performance; better social adjustment and improved school attendance for the child; better understanding of the nature of the problem; and improved coping skills for the child, his parents, and his teachers. School health programming that takes into account the needs of each system has a better chance of overcoming the inherent obstacles previously mentioned.

The Health Care System

The "New Morbidity"   For today's school-age children and adolescents the "new morbidity" and major unmet health needs are dental, emotional, and learning problems; making decisions about sexual behavior; problems associated with alcohol and drug use; and coping with chronic handicapping conditions. These clearly stand out as striking even in areas where more traditional health problems are prevalent. It becomes necessary, therefore, to develop school health programs and activities with these health problem needs in mind. However, health care providers (as well as parents and teachers) are handicapped by their lack of knowledge and experience in dealing with these health concerns. Difficulties may also result from working in an environment which traditionally has emphasized disease and episodic illness care more often than health maintenance, comprehensive primary health, or preventive medicine. The disease orientation and training often found in health care providers may ill equip them to learn firsthand the numerous physical health and mental health problems which are to be found undetected and untreated in a community. This environment also inhibits the development of health care providers' roles in prevention and early detection of these problems.

Preventive School Health It has been suggested that a modification of Caplan's preventative health model be adapted by primary health care providers working collaboratively with school systems. Primary preventive activities are those which improve the school environment. Secondary preventive activities are those which relate to early detection of conditions inimical to a child's sound physical, social, or educational growth. Tertiary preventive activities are case-patient-family–oriented. They aim to rehabilitate existing problems and reach the optimal level of function for a given handicapping condition.

For example, a practicing pediatrician in a group practice caring for the majority of students in schools in a given geographic area is retained by that district as a school medical consultant. In the area of primary prevention a portion of the physician's time is spent in in-service sessions with teachers on developmental variation normally observed in young elementary school children. This service improves the general milieu of the school environment, and teachers gain self-confidence in that normal variation may be observed without unnecessary labeling of children as "deviant" or "problematic." This interaction also benefits the physician who desires an opportunity to practice preventive medicine and sees serving as a school consultant as potentially affecting a large number of children influenced by a small group of teachers, compared with the relatively small number of children on whom the physician could have an impact in the office one-to-one setting.

In secondary and tertiary areas, health care providers, by interacting with school personnel concerned with pupil learning and/or adjustment problems, have their horizons widened. They find out important information related to the future health or development of patients which might not otherwise have been brought to attention by the parent. School personnel, through this kind of interaction, will also benefit by not feeling isolated in attempting to deal with the problems and by having support from a professional who may be highly respected by parents.

In all areas, the family and child should benefit from the increased communication that would naturally occur among concerned professionals.

Access to Health Care Adequate access to health care requires joint efforts between the home, the source of care, and the school. When health care systems are not utilized, providers often may blame "poor" attitudes on the part of the family or lack of motivation or knowledge without paying enough attention to issues of trust, confidence, and priorities which individuals must consider and decide on before participating in curative or preventive health services. The school health service offers an obvious setting to assist in this process of providing smooth and adequate access to health care. A school health program has the opportunity for interaction with the child in the role of student rather than patient. This is especially attractive to many who view school health as a possible vehicle for overcoming some of the actual or perceived barriers which block adequate access to a health care system. This may necessitate going beyond usual home visiting following a written notification to a parent of a child's health problem. It may even entail, in some instances, placing direct services (such as a dental clinic) in the school. Access may be enhanced by providing school health nurses with more skills in problem assessment and management (for example, school nurse practitioners). It may also include providing outreach workers who can become familiar with both families and services. It may also mean developing more formal relations between individual schools and specific sources of health care for children, and more adequately training physicians to handle school health consultative services.

The following general goals are suggested for groups considering establishing a modification of community school health programs.

A school health program should provide ways to enhance the health and learning environment of children:

Through protection against disease and disability and through guidance for optimum health (primary prevention).

Through early identification of health problems and remediation to limit them (secondary prevention).

Through prevention of complications and through rehabilitation when health problems are fixed (tertiary prevention).

A school health program should provide a bridge between school health services and health care providers in a community:

By utilizing a simple referral procedure between the school and the health care provider.

By maintaining, improving, or developing communication between school personnel and health care providers.

By utilizing, improving, or developing adequate communication between the home, school, and the health care systems in the community.

A school health program should assist children and their parents to become more responsible and assertive about their health:

By determining critical skills for different developmental age groups and specific skills for groups of children with special health needs.

By designing learning activities, including content and process, to facilitate the development of specific skills.

By providing opportunities for the practice of the particular skills.

A school health program should utilize health resources effectively and efficiently in enhancing the health and learning environment of children:

Through teaming.

Through consultation.

Through training programs.

By sharing responsibilities in the school with the health care provider.

By sharing responsibilities in the school with the home.

A school health program should periodically assess the effectiveness of health services provided in the school and in the community:

Through the collection of data to determine the type of program change or implementation that is needed (needs assessment).

Through the description of roles and processes involved in the implementation of program activities.

Through the comparison of stated objectives and outcome of the program activities.

33 | Nursing Roles in School Health

by Rosemary McKevitt

It is often the school nurse who is the key health professional involved in implementing a school health service. This is a responsibility requiring the ability to work collaboratively with children and their families, school administrators, teachers and other school personnel, school physicians, other physician health care providers, and community agencies.

School Nurse Activities

General and specific child health information required by state laws or school district routine is requested from parents upon the child's entry into school and updated periodically so that any special health needs may be identified. The nurse works closely with teachers of children with chronic conditions to ensure the teachers' understanding of the nature of the condition including any emergency care procedures which may be indicated and the child's capabilities as well as limitations which have relevance to the school program. In addition, the nurse works with the child's primary care provider to convey relevant information about the child's behavior in school. The nurse is generally a part of the school team which considers special educational placement for children with learning or behavioral difficulties. In this capacity, the nurse contributes relevant health data and participates with other members of the interdisciplinary team in planning a program suited to the child's needs.

Health promotion and early identification of health problems are a major portion of the nurse's work. The nurse is responsible for planning systematic health appraisal of all schoolchildren, although some of the specific activities may be delegated to other personnel. Screening programs for vision and hearing problems are routinely conducted at specified grade levels along with other selected assessment procedures. When health problems are identified, a referral process is initiated which involves counseling with the student and the family about the nature of the problem, the necessity of further care, and the health resources available to take care of the problem. If the family has no ongoing source of primary care, the nurse can assist the family in obtaining regular access to the health care system. With parental consent, the nurse and the child's health care provider may discuss the nature of the health problem and exchange information which relates both to the child's health care and to the educational program. The school ordinarily requests some response from the health care provider with respect to the problem the school has recognized. This is particularly essential when the proper management of the problem requires school involvement in providing data (as in the case of children with learning problems) or when the health problem may affect the child's school program. Even children under treatment for relatively short-term health problems, a fracture or middle ear infection, for example, often need temporary modifications of their educational programs such as provision for facilitating mobility or special seating in the classroom. The nurse can be a helpful liaison when familiar with the school and the child's educational program and when able to speak the educator's vernacular as well as the language of the health professions.

The school nurse often becomes involved in a variety of individual and group health education activities. Virtually every contact with a student is an opportunity for incidental teaching or health counseling. Children who seek minor first aid learn how to provide this care for themselves next time; the teenager who anxiously seeks information for "a friend who thinks she's pregnant" is given opportunity to talk and is encouraged to think through possible personal concerns. Special programs may be developed in the school for students with similar health needs. For example, several students interested in losing weight may meet with the nurse to discuss the various dietary, exercise, and emotional factors involved and to provide mutual encouragement in following their health adviser's recommendations.

During the school years, youngsters gradually assume increasing responsibility for their own health maintenance and health care. The nurse is in a prime position to facilitate this process by discussing with students relevant data about health, helping them to clarify alternatives, and reinforcing sound health-related decisions. For example, a nurse practitioner who finds no objective data indicating a need for medical evaluation of a student who complains of frequent headaches may provide the student with information about headaches in general and specific data about the student's physical health derived from a problem-related physical assessment. The nurse may encourage the student to keep track of when the headaches occur, to look for patterns, and then to consider possible reasons for the problem and what might be done about it. In this manner, students learn active problem solving related to their health and assume responsibility commensurate with their age and ability. Follow-up with such students would entail helping them evaluate the effectiveness of their plans and reinforcing appropriate health behavior.

Emergency care is often viewed as a high-priority need by the school. Policies and procedures are developed by the school nursing staff, administration, and medical consultants. While many school nurses are directly involved in providing emergency care, particularly in the more serious situations, most supervise first-aid responsibilities of other school staff. On occasion, a specially trained paraprofessional worker assumes this responsibility under the nurse's supervision. Often the nurse becomes involved in in-service education for school personnel on the assumption that all adults in the school should be knowledgeable about emergency care. Prevention of many emergency situations can be accomplished through analysis of previous accident data, observa-

tion for health and safety hazards in the school environment, and careful policy making related to appropriate protective equipment for students involved in laboratory, workshop, and athletic activities.

Factors Influencing Role Implementation

The school nurse's role varies somewhat from school to school for a variety of reasons, some of which relate to administrative or organizational structure. Nurses may be employed either by boards of education or by local health departments. If employed by the school system, the nurse generally has only school nursing responsibilities. If employed by the health department, the nurse's school-related activities may constitute only part of a total community nursing role because the nurse provides nursing service to all age groups within a specified geographic district and may also have responsibility for health department clinics and other activities. In the latter instance, assigning school health activities high priority within a context of other, sometimes more immediate, community health needs has proved problematic to some nurses. Others have found the position of accountability to both community health agency and school system to be troublesome. Generally, the pupil load, or ratio of students to nurses, tends to be higher when the nurse is employed by the health department.

The nurse's role may reflect a unique response to differing role expectations. As one school nurse wrote, "School nursing is a varying combination of what an administrator wants, teachers expect, students need, parents demand, the community is accustomed to, the situation requires, and the nurse, herself, believes." Role conflict may easily develop as the nurse attempts to integrate diverse expectations into a meaningful whole and establish reasonable priorities.

The educational preparation and experiential background of nurses exert major influence on how they interpret the school nurse role. Nurses who work in schools may have had from 2 to 5 years of basic nursing education. About 7 percent have master's degrees. Some have had specific academic course work related to school nursing; many have not. A few have completed school nurse practitioner or pediatric nurse practitioner programs; most have not. Some have had previous experience in community nursing or in an ambulatory pediatric care setting; others have had little experience except in acute care or in inpatient institutions or, perhaps, have not worked in nursing for several years. Some state education departments set minimum educational requirements and certify nurses for working in school, in a manner similar to teacher certification. In other areas, each school district sets its own criteria.

The Expanded Role of the Nurse in the School

In recent years, considerable interest has been directed toward the expanded role of the nurse in various settings. Designated by such titles as *nurse practitioner* or *nurse associate*, the expanded role generally involves learning skills which enable the nurse to provide more comprehensive health care. The notion of the nurse practitioner in the school setting was a natural extension of the pediatric nurse practitioner role in other ambulatory child health care settings in which the nurse practitioner, working with a pediatrician colleague, assumes a primary care role, providing comprehensive well child care, managing minor health problems, and making initial assessments of more serious acute and chronic conditions. Nurse practitioner or nurse associate programs vary but usually consist of a minimum of 4 months of intensive study, including both theory and practice, and a preceptorship with a practicing physician.

The nurse practitioner in an expanded school nurse role has a larger repertoire of assessment skills to utilize in evaluating children's health status. Beginning with a health history obtained in interviews with the child and the family, the nurse practitioner develops a complete data base utilizing school sources of information such as the child's teacher, as well as the family. The nurse practitioner is equipped to conduct a complete physical examination including the neurologic component, appropriate developmental screening, and, in some schools, selected laboratory tests. On the basis of the findings, appropriate intervention is planned with the child and the family. Specific health education and guidance are major tools of the nurse practitioner. If referral outside the school is indicated, a report of the nurse practitioner's findings assists in the further management of the problem. On occasion, a more limited problem-oriented assessment may be appropriate for triage of students who seek the help of the

nurse practitioner during the course of an average school day.

As expansion of the role of the nurse entails the acquisition of new assessment techniques, basic knowledge of child development and common health problems of children and adolescents is also broadened. Nurse practitioners, or nurse associates, who work in the schools should have specific educational experiences to prepare them for initial evaluation of behavioral and learning problems. Practice skills such as interviewing and health counseling are sharpened and integrated into the nurse's role. Role reorientation is an important component of the expanded nurse role, with emphasis on an interdependent, collaborative relationship with physicians and a generally more assertive approach in assuming responsibility for primary health care.

Implementing an Expanded School Nurse Role

Teaming is particularly important in the implementation of the expanded nurse role in the school. Unless trained paraprofessionals are available to assume some of the more routine activities such as emergency care, clerical activities, and some screening procedures, nurses may not have enough time to fulfill an expanded role. A physician consultant is essential to provide backup for and to collaborate with the nurse practitioner; the physician and nurse practitioner team can provide comprehensive primary health care to a segment of the school population who have no other source of primary care. In most communities, delivery of primary health care takes place predominantly outside the school in health offices and agencies. In this case, the nurse practitioner and physician team is instrumental in providing a link with the primary care system within the community. An example might be the management of a child who has a learning problem. The nurse practitioner initially gathers relevant health data, perhaps conferring with the physician consultant on questionable findings. Both the nurse practitioner and the medical consultant may be involved in a conference with the child's teacher, school psychologist, principal, special education consultant, parent, and school social worker. After all relevant data are presented about the child's behavior at school and at home, alternatives related to the child's program are considered. If the child has a primary health care provider outside the school, this provider may be included in the team conference. In the event that this is not feasible or when the child's pattern of utilization has been transient or episodic, the medical consultant needs to communicate to the child's physician the nature of the school's concern and the possible alternatives and resources within and outside the school which offer promise of aid to the child and the family. The nurse practitioner may facilitate the continuing exchange of information relating to both the educational and medical management of the child's problem. Working in collaboration with the physician, the nurse practitioner may also provide health counseling to the child and family to enhance their understanding of the problem and promote their active involvement in both the medical and educational plan.

Developing the Expanded Nurse Role

If some support and interest is evident within the community, school, and health care establishment, careful attention must then be devoted to developing a systematic plan for school nurse role expansion. As in the implementation of any change, continued involvement of those concerned is essential. Discus-

sions among nurses, school administrators, other members of the school staff, and members of the medical community can help to identify resources, anticipate problems, and promote realistic expectations. A carefully phased plan is important, one which includes provision for the training of paraprofessional workers as well as of the nursing staff, for using a medical consultant, and possibly for the use of pilot schools. Continued interest and assistance from consumer groups and periodic reviews of progress facilitate a program of evolutionary change.

The school nurse or nurse practitioner is often the health care professional who has the greatest opportunity to interact with those areas of a child's life which most profoundly affect health: the family, the school, and the health care system. A child goes to school as a pupil, and the family expects the child to be taught; a child goes to a pediatrician as a patient, and the family expects the child to receive medical care. At the present time, the success of health professionals in the schools is generally predicated on the degree to which they make their knowledge and skills relevant within the context of an educational system.

34 | School Health Education

by Guy S. Parcel

Public health measures and medical advances such as immunizations, sanitation, and antibiotics have made considerable contribution to altering the nature of major health problems. What people do for themselves about their health may be more important than what others do for them. The increased awareness of the limitations of the curative aspects of health care has placed greater emphasis on the importance of health maintenance and preventive medicine. Through the years, the process of health education has been used to assist people in preventing illness and maintaining certain levels of "wellness." The underlying assumption has been that an informed public and knowledgeable individuals are better prepared to make decisions that will promote health rather than contribute to the development of an illness or a health-related problem.

Within this framework school health education has become particularly attractive for several reasons: Almost all children go to school and while in school constitute a captive audience. Since schools have become the major institution for learning, schools have been suggested as the logical place for children to learn about health and to develop the abilities that are needed to make effective decisions about health-related behavior. That schools can meet this objective has yet to be demonstrated. As the search for improving the effectiveness of school health education continues, there is an increasing awareness that success must involve a cooperative effort between educational personnel and child health care personnel. For example, the pediatrician has a knowledge of child health and child development in much greater depth than most educational personnel in the schools. On the other hand, the educational personnel will probably have more refined and effective skills in teaching and an opportunity to reach more children than the pediatrician. The child health care professional has an essential role and an important contribution to make in school health education programs.

Since most health care providers have limited contact and experience in working with schools and probably were last in a school as a student or parent, the following background information concerning school health education may be helpful. The inclusion of the area of health education as part of the instructional program in schools is by no means a new concept. Traditionally, health education has been found within the school program in two distinct areas: Through the involvement of a school nurse or school physician, health education activities have been included as a part of health services. The school nurse, while doing screening for vision and hearing, may individually or in groups discuss with the children the purpose and meaning of doing the screening and the importance of health care related to sight and hearing conservation. As another example, the school nurse may go into the classroom and give the students instruction related to particular health behavior such as dental health (brushing teeth) or nutrition (eating right). When health instruction is incorporated into the regular teaching of the classroom teacher or by special health education teachers, it is referred to as *curricular health education.* Within this latter area, either health education is integrated into the classroom curriculum, or it is established as a separate curriculum within the total instructional program of the school.

Early approaches to curriculum development in health education were primarily centered around dealing with some type of crisis health problem. In the 1950s, it was recognized that the abuse of alcohol had become a serious health and social problem. In an attempt to find a solution to this problem, schools were called upon to provide instruction pointing out the dangers and health hazards associated with consuming alcohol. The assumption was that if students knew about these dangers and were told about the health hazards, they would not get into trouble with alcohol abuse. Some states went so far as to have laws requiring public schools to provide instruction in alcohol abuse prevention. Schools all over the country responded to this apparent health problem and began providing instruction concerning alcohol abuse. However, it soon became very clear that this type of instruction did little to alter the drinking patterns of American youth.

It has been demonstrated that even when information is most effectively taught, it does not necessarily lead to a change in behavior. The failure of drug education programs in the late 1960s and early 1970s helped considerably to demonstrate the weaknesses of health education programs that are primarily based on a cognitive approach. Many drug education programs were developed that effectively taught the pharmacologic aspects of drug abuse, legal penalities, and the physical risks of taking certain drugs. When these programs were evaluated, it was found that knowledge about drugs and the dangers involved in drug use did not significantly influence drug-taking behavior.

The failure of drug education programs reinforced what many educators had been suggesting for years—that health behavior is related not only to knowledge but to other factors such as attitudes and feelings associated with particular forms of health behavior. It also became more apparent that health-related problems could not be effectively dealt with on a crisis basis. If health problems are to be prevented through education, a means of dealing with these problems must be developed long before they reach a crisis state.

Recent developments in teaching methods have focused on the learners' attitudes and feelings. This type of teaching is frequently referred to as *affective education*. Teaching in this area is related more to social learning than to cognitive learning of facts and concepts. Some of the more recent programs developed in drug education actually have very little to do with information about drugs. Instead these programs focus on helping the child develop a better understanding of self, interrelationships with other people, and, for older children, a clarification of values. These types of programs hypothesize that children who feel good about themselves, who can develop effective relationships with other people, and who have a clear understanding of what is important to them are going to be less likely to get into problems related to the abuse of drugs.

Numerous techniques have been developed for teaching in the area of affective education. Many of these techniques are based on group processes and facilitating self-awareness. When dealing with children's attitudes, feelings, and values, the teaching process requires someone with skill who will help the child learn but at the same time protect the child from unnecessary and excessive emotional stress. This has been one of the major problems in the area of affective education. When new methods come along, people tend to jump on the bandwagon, including those who have inadequate preparation for using these methods. College courses, in-service training, and continuing education are essential for preparing teachers to use affective education successfully.

Most educators would agree that affective education is critical in helping children develop the abilities to assume responsibility for their own health behavior. It is important that children learn how to make decisions and how to solve problems. A strictly cognitive approach to health education seems to offer some potential in helping children cope more effectively. What is needed in the planning and conducting of health education programs is an integration of both cognitive and affective learning.

Approach Based on Skills

A skills approach to health education can provide a framework for integrating cognitive and affective learning. The underlying assumption of the approach is that *competence* is the primary outcome of health education. If one is competent, then one will be able to assume responsibility for one's own health which will include self-directing one's behavior and being able to make appropriate use of available health resources. Skills form the building blocks of competence. Thus, the focus of a health education program is to work toward the development of specific skills. For example, the decision of junior high school students to smoke is probably more a function of skills related to self-understanding, dealing with peer pressure, and decision making than to an understanding of the dangers of smoking.

Application to the Curriculum for All Children The skills approach requires identification of skills, consideration of content and process necessary to develop the identified skills, and the provision of opportunities to practice these skills. A general skill such as the ability to communicate feelings may apply to a specific desired behavioral outcome. For example, a health education activity for kindergarten children could be directed toward enabling children to tell adults different feelings they have when they think they might be sick. The content (what children need to learn) and the process (how they will learn) are then designed to be incorporated into the kindergarten curriculum to promote the development of this specific skill.

If skills are to be successfully developed, they need to be appropriate for the level of cognitive develop-

ment as well as social development. The very young schoolchild has limited ability to develop reasoning skills and relates concepts of health and illness more directly to actual experiences of illness. As children develop, they are better able to associate causation with specific states of health and illness. It is not until children reach higher levels of development that they are able to deal with abstractions and more complex value issues. A health education curriculum should be designed so that learning activities are directed toward simple and basic skills in the early grades and move toward more complex skills in the higher grades. For an outline of recommended steps for the development of a health education curriculum, refer to Table 34-1.

Application to Noncurricular Areas of School Activities In the schools, there will be groups of children who have specific health problems and special educational needs that will not be met

Table 34-1

Four Steps for the Development of Health Education Curriculum

---

Step 1 Assessment of needs and resources
a Determine children's illness experiences.
b Study children's concepts of health and illness.
c Determine teachers' and parents' perceptions of children's health needs.
d Determine teachers' and parents' attitudes toward health education.
e Determine teachers' and parents' willingness to become involved in health education activities and programs.
f Determine nature and extent of current health education activities in the school curriculum.
g Identify persons willing to assume leadership roles and responsibilities for coordination.

Step 2 Program planning and curriculum development
a Select persons for the planning and development group.
b Organize and schedule planning and development activities.
c Present and clarify philosophical and theoretical frameworks for the health education programs.
d Review selected literature and written curricula from other sources.
e State program goals in terms of skills that are to be developed by the children.
f State specific behavioral objectives considered important in the development of each skill.
g Review and evaluate available teaching methods, teaching aids, and student materials relating to the stated objectives.

h Design learning activities and instructional materials to help students master stated objectives.
i Field-test learning activities, make preliminary evaluation, and revise as necessary.
j Present program to parents and school personnel.

Step 3 Teacher preparation
a Identify teacher competencies and in-service training objectives necessary for carrying out the health education program.
b Identify persons responsible for specific areas of in-service training and scheduled training activities.
c Conduct in-service training and monitor the results of each activity.
d Evaluate the effectiveness of in-service training.

Step 4 Program implementation and evaluation
a Schedule sequence of learning activities for the health education program.
b Collect and analyze preprogram data.
c Conduct program monitoring students' progress in mastering objectives leading to the development of skills.
d Provide continuous consultation and assistance for teachers.
e Organize parent groups and coordinate parent education activities with classroom learning activities.
f Coordinate health services and pupil services to provide additional resources for children needing individualized attention.
g Collect and analyze postprogram data and determine implications for revision of the health education program.

through the health education curriculum. Once a means of identifying these children can be established, they can constitute target groups for which the school health programs can develop special educational activities designed to help develop specific skills. A few examples of possible target groups are children with asthma, pregnant teenagers, children with seizure disorders, students who want to quit smoking, children very deficient in interpersonal skills, and students with problems related to drug or alcohol abuse.

As an example of an application of the skills approach for a target group, a health education program could be designed to complement the health care of children with asthma. The goal of such a program would be to develop lifetime skills in the management of asthma. The school nurse could serve as the primary coordinator of learning activities in the school and could meet with the asthmatic children on a regular basis to help the children understand the nature of asthma and principles of management. In addition to providing information, the group meetings for parents could be designed to help them explore their knowledge, concerns, and problems associated with asthma as well as their interactions with their children.

Physician's Role in School Health Education

The goal of health education is to assist individuals in developing skills that will enable them to self-direct their health behavior and make appropriate use of health care resources. If this goal is to be achieved through a school health program, it will require a cooperative effort by health care personnel and educational personnel. It is unlikely that any one discipline by itself will be able to accomplish such a formidable task. The physician plays a key role. In both curricular and noncurricular health education activities, the physician can contribute to school health education in five distinct ways: (1) by helping to plan health education activities by reviewing content and process for accuracy and age appropriateness, (2) by actually conducting health education activities for children and parents through the school program, (3) by assisting with the training of personnel involved in health education, (4) by assisting with the collection of data to evaluate the outcomes of health education activities, and (5) by providing encouragement and support for giving a high prior-

ity to school health education activities within a community. Specific ways in which a physician may contribute will be discussed for curricular and noncurricular areas.

Curricular Areas   In developing a health education curriculum, the physician can play a very important role in identifying the health concerns related to particular age groups. On a daily basis, the physicians see adults and children of different ages for various illnesses as well as for health maintenance. The physician is aware of the health concerns and needs expressed by the patients. These concerns and needs can be identified and interpreted for the educational personnel in planning health education activities. With the physician's help, critical skills can be identified for the various age groups. Once these skills are identified, learning activities can be developed to assist children in attaining these skills. Physicians involved in child health care in particular will have a unique knowledge about health care needs according to children's developmental levels.

Health professionals need to become involved with in-service training programs in health education. Through their training and experience, physicians are specialists in various aspects of health, illness, and child development. They can assist teachers in understanding normal processes of child development and assist them in identifying the developmental needs of children. The teachers are required to deal with a very broad spectrum of information related to health behavior. It is difficult for teachers to keep informed of current knowledge in all these areas. The physician can be especially helpful in upgrading and improving teachers' knowledge within specific health areas and can suggest resources for additional information. There is almost always a gap between information generated by the health sciences and the information available for use in instructional programs. The physician may serve in an important role in narrowing this gap.

Physicians may be called on to serve as guest lecturers in classrooms. When a classroom teacher is faced with dealing with complicated or sensitive material, the physician is often asked to come into the classroom to talk to students. The easiest way for physicians to handle such a request is simply to come into the classroom and do the best that they can under the circumstances. However, there are some obvious drawbacks to this approach. The physician may not be prepared to present the material at a level appropriate for the students. Also, the physician's time will be limited, and therefore only a small number of students can benefit from the physician's talk. A better approach would be for the physician to work with the teacher to identify more specifically the skills and information that students need to learn. The physician and teacher working together can apply the knowledge of the physician to a particular teaching situation and then plan for an ongoing program that can be presented by the teacher and carried on even at times when the physician cannot be present. In this way, a larger number of students can benefit from the physician's contribution over a longer period of time.

Teaching, like the practice of medicine, is an art and requires a certain set of skills, especially communication skills. A good physician is not necessarily a good teacher. When getting into teaching through health education activities, it is important for the physician to communicate effectively. Talking with children is different from talking with adults.

Vocabulary is often a major problem. One should avoid terms or concepts that are inappropriate for the developmental level of the child. The appropriate level can be determined primarily by using a questioning approach rather than a telling approach. "Why do doctors give shots?" rather than "Doctors give shots because. . . ." Using questions has three major advantages: (1) The level of conceptualization can be determined; (2) the degree of understanding can be evaluated; and (3) the children can learn from each other.

Learning can be facilitated by helping children with the self-discovery of concepts. This is done by the continuous asking of questions and reinforcement of correct answers.

Doctor: How does a condom work to prevent pregnancy?
Student: It keeps the sperm from coming out.
Doctor: Not exactly. The sperm comes out, but what does the condom really do to the sperm?
Student: Keeps it from reaching the egg.
Doctor: That's right! That's a very good answer. If the condom is used right, it can keep the sperm from reaching the egg. Now what do we mean by "if it is used right"?

Clarifying responses and clarifying questions can also be used to facilitate learning. "When you say that premarital sex is bad, do you mean that some people think it is wrong to have sexual intercourse before marriage?" "How do you feel about that?" It is often just as important to help the students to clarify feelings as to give them correct information.

The amount of time, effort, and resources devoted to the school health education curriculum will depend on how much priority a school district gives to health education. When it comes to health, it is obvious that physicians carry considerable influence and prestige in a community. The physician's continuous encouragement and support is essential to gain the necessary resources for doing an effective job in health education. This can be accomplished by making time available to school board members and administrators to encourage a high priority for the school health education curriculum.

Noncurricular Areas Physicians have awareness and knowledge of major health problems of children within a community. They can assist schools in selecting appropriate groups of children who can benefit from specific health education programs. This might include screening programs to identify children with particular problems or working with other physicians practicing in the community to bring together parents and children who have particular health problems. Physicians are more likely to have ongoing contacts with parents and can be in a position to encourage parents to participate in health education programs. The physician may also assist in interpreting the objectives and values of health education programs for particular groups.

School health education programs can offer the physician an opportunity to reach larger numbers of children with particular health problems. In a busy practice it is very difficult to devote sufficient time to giving health education on a one-to-one basis. However, by getting children and their families together, it may be possible to utilize blocks of time to meet the health education needs for a larger number of children and their families. By working as a member of a team including educational personnel as well as other health professionals, the physician can meet with children and parents to deal with the particular health concerns of a special group. For example, it would be very difficult for a physician in practice on a one-to-one basis to devote sufficient time to help adolescents deal with the implications of teenage pregnancy. However, by meeting with pregnant teenagers as a group, it might be possible to help adolescents deal more effectively with the experience that they are going through as well as to assist them in developing the parenting skills and child health care skills that they will need in the very near future.

Health education programs for target groups should result in improving the health of the children or improving the ability of the families to cope with a particular health problem. The physicians who see the children or the families as part of their routine health care are in a position to evaluate the effectiveness of such programs. The physician can assist the schools in determining whether or not the programs are producing the desired results. Are the children improving in health, or are the families coping more effectively with a particular health problem?

The concept of peer counseling has been gaining interest for the adolescent age group. Adolescents with particular health problems or concerns are getting together to attempt to deal with these problems through peer support. This approach has particularly grown out of drug education. Physicians can play a very helpful role in a community in helping these groups get together to plan for their particular counseling or educational activities. Adolescents doing the counseling will need specific information relating to the problem that they are dealing with as well as skills in counseling. It is important for these peer counselors to be able to recognize their limitations and to be able to refer and use outside consultants. Physicians can help adolescents find referral sources as well as serve as consultants to the group. The concept of peers helping each other on the surface appears to be very attractive; however, it is essential that they do have professional backup. This is an important role for the physician. For example, peer counseling has been established in some communities for contraception and abortion referral. A physician can work with such groups to provide them with the necessary knowledge and can help the groups link with appropriate sources within the community.

As with health education curriculum areas, the physician plays an important role as a resource for in-service training for school personnel involved in health education in noncurricular areas. Actual conduct of health education programs may involve social workers, psychologists, teachers, counselors, and other educational personnel. The background and training of these professionals may be limited in regard to specific health problems. The physician can work with these groups to expand and update their knowledge in particular health areas.

Crisis approaches to health education appear to have only very limited success. Unlike illness care that can intervene at particular defined occurrences of ill health, preventive medicine and health maintenance is an ongoing lifetime process. It must begin with very young children and be carried on through adulthood, building skills that will enable people to assume greater responsibility for their own health. The one thing that most children have in common is that they attend schools. It therefore seems obvious that if there is to be an impact on the quality of life through improved health behavior, the school health program offers one critical interface for health care providers, educators, and families to work together to meet the health needs of the children.

35 | Getting Started in School Health

by Guy S. Parcel and Philip R. Nader

Not all physicians can or will become involved in school health. Those who do will do so in a variety of ways and to different degrees. There is no single model. Involvement will depend on interest, available time, and receptivity of the school personnel. Getting started is probably the most difficult task.

Some time commitment will be necessary. Since most health care providers are unable to devote large blocks of time without compensation, a few hours a week may have to be sacrificed to initiate interest before a formal relationship can be worked out.

One possible starting point is to talk to parents and schoolchildren. The physician probably has more direct contact with children and their parents than any other professional. Find out from patients and parents what they perceive as important health education and health service activities. What activities are they already participating in within school programs? How do they perceive the value of these activities? What additional activities do they think the schools should be conducting?

Next, make a visit to the schools to get a good data base on what is actually going on. Avoid the role of the medical expert. Express a sincere interest in learning about the school's interests and activities concerned with health. A key administrator is often a good entry point into the system. This could be a health education coordinator (if there is one), a curriculum coordinator, a nursing services coordinator, or the superintendent. Express your shared interest in child development and child health. Ask if you can have an opportunity to talk to teachers, nurses, and students and to observe health education and service activities.

When making a visit to a school, the key person to make contact with first is always the school principal. Some principals will be very interested in helping you get around to visit people in the school, and some principals will be so puzzled by why a physician would visit a school that they will not know how to go about helping you. Regardless of the reception by the principal, *never* go into a school without a contact with the principal.

Informal conversations with the teachers are sometimes more successful than organized planned meetings. Keep in mind that extra meetings are usually not very popular with teachers after they have spent a full day working with children. The teachers' lounge and the cafeteria offer an excellent opportunity to talk with teachers. Conversation over a cup of coffee can give you a better atmosphere to learn about health-related activities and the teacher's perception of the children's health needs.

The school nurse is a key member of the school health team. As soon as possible make a visit to the health clinic and *listen* to the nurse's views and knowledge of health-related activities and needs. Don't get locked into the confines of the clinic. There are other members of the health team. Talk to the school psychologist, counselor, and special education teachers. They are good resources for learning about the types of problems that occur in that particular school.

At this point you may see obvious opportunities to help with health services and education programs or have some good suggestions as to what could be done. Wait. First attempt to find out what school personnel perceive as an important area that you can provide some assistance. Do what you can to help meet their needs even if it may not be highest on your list of priorities. Maybe it is as simple as helping to get parents to turn out for a PTA meeting. It is a service for the school, and they will be able to see evidence of your interest in meeting their needs.

When that is accomplished, you are in the system and now in a better position to work as a team member to more formally develop, plan, and conduct health-related activities.

REFERENCES

School Learning Problems and Developmental Differences, School Readiness, and Classroom Behavior Problems

Caldwell, B. M.: *Cooperative Preschool Inventory*, rev. ed., Berkeley, Calif.: Educational Testing Services, 1970.

Clements, S. D.: *Minimal Brain Dysfunction in Children: Terminology and Identification*, NINDB monograph 3, U.S. Department of Health, Education, and Welfare, 1966.

Connors, C. K.: A teacher rating scale for use in drug studies with children, *Am. J. Psychiatry*, **126**:884–888, 1969.

Johnson, D., and Myklebust, H.: *Learning Disabilities: Educational Principles and Practices*, New York: Grune & Stratton, 1967.

Kinsbourne, M.: School problems, *Pediatrics*, **52**:5, November 1973.

Kinsbourne, M. and Caplan, P.: *Children's Learning and Attention Problems*. Boston: Little, Brown, 1969.

Kulig, S. G., Baker, K. A., and Levine, H. G.: Screening for speech and language disorders: A training program for physicians and allied health professionals, *J. Am. Speech Hearing Assoc.*, **17**:8, 507–512, 1975.

Psychological Corporation: Vineland Social Maturity Scale, rev. ed., New York: Dell. (Order from the Psychological Corporation, New York.)

Rutter, M., Tizard, J., and Whitmore, K. *Education Health and Behavior*, p. 197, London: Longmans, 1970.

Sleator, E. K., and Von Neumann, A.: Methylphenidate in the treatment of hyperkinetic children, *Clin. Pediatr.*, **13**:19–24, 1974.

Sprague, R. L., and Sleator, E. K.: What is the proper dose of stimulant drugs in children? *Int. J. Ment. Health*, **4**:75–104, 1975.

Stewart, M. A., and Olds, S. W.: *Raising a Hyperactive Child*, New York: Harper & Row, 1973.

Swanson, J. M., and Kinsbourne, M.: "Artificial Colors and Hyperactive Behavior," in R. Knights and D. Bakker (eds.), *Treatment of Hyperactive and Learning Disordered Children*, Baltimore: University Park Press.

Thorpe, H. S., and Werner, E. E.: Developmental screening of preschool children: A critical review of inventories used in health and educational programs, *Pediatrics*, **53**:3, 1974.

Verville, E.: *Behavior Problems of Children*, Philadelphia: Saunders, 1967.

Wender, P. H.: *Minimal Brain Dysfunction in Children*, New York: Wiley, 1971.

West, R., Kennedy, L., and Carr, A.: *Rehabilitation of Speech*, rev. ed., New York: Harper & Row, 1947.

Absenteeism, Psychogenic Somatic Complaints, and School Phobia

Apley, J., and MacKeith, R.: *The Child and His Symptoms*, 2d ed., Philadelphia: Davis, 1968.

Barcai, A.: Attendance, achievement and social class: The differential impact upon social achievements in different social classes, *Acta Paediopsychiatr. (Basel)*, **38:**153–159, 1973.

Coolidge, J. C., Brodie, R. D., and Feeney, B.: A ten-year follow-up study of sixty-six school phobia children, *Am. J. Orthopsychiatry*, **34:**675, 1964.

Douglass, J. W. R., and Ross, J. M.: The effects of absence in primary school performance, *Br. J. Educ. Psychol.*, **35:**28–40, 1965.

Eisenberg, L.: School phobia: A study in the communication of anxiety, *Am. J. Psychiatry*, **114:**712, 1958.

Elkind, D.: *Children and Adolescents*, New York: Oxford Univ. Press, 1970.

Engel, G. L.: "Conversion Symptoms," in C. M. McBryde and R. S. Blacklow (eds.), *Signs and Symptoms: Applied Physiology and Clinical Interpretation*, Philadelphia: Lippincott, 1970.

Friedman, S. B.: Conversion symptoms in adolescents, *Pediatr. Clin. North Am.*, **20:**873, 1973.

Gallagher, J., Roswell, H., Felix, P., and Garell, D. C.: *Medical Care of the Adolescent*, 3d ed., New York: Appleton Century Crofts, 1976. (Distributed by Prentice-Hall, Englewood Cliffs, N.J.)

Nader, P. R., Bullock, D., and Caldwell, B.: School phobia: Symposium on behavioral pediatrics, *Pediatr. Clin. North Am.*, **22:**3, 1975.

Rogers, K. D., and Reese, G.: Health studies: Presumably normal high school students, *Am. J. Dis. Child.*, **109:**28, 1965.

Schmidt, B.: School phobia—the great imitator: A pediatrician's viewpoint, *Pediatrics*, **48:**433, 1971.

Van Arsdell, W. R., Roghmann, K. J., and Nader, P. R.: Visits to an elementary school nurse, *School Health*, **42:**142, 1972.

The Chronically Handicapped Child in School

Graham, P., and Rutter, M.: Organic brain dysfunction and child psychiatric disorder, *Br. Med. J.*, September 21, 1968.

Green, M. "The Care of the Child with a Long-Term Life Threatening Illness," in Green and Haggerty (ed.), *Ambulatory Pediatrics*, Philadelphia: Saunders, 1968.

Haslam, R., and Valletutti, P.: *Medical Problems in the Classroom: The Teacher's Role in Diagnosis and Management*, Baltimore: University Park Press, 1975.

Miller, L.: Toward a greater understanding of the parents of the mentally retarded child, *J. Pediatr.*, **73:**699–705, 1968.

Pless, I. B., and Roghmann, K. J.: Chronic illness and its consequences: Observations based on three epidemiologic surveys. *J. Pediatr.* **79:**351, 1971.

Richardson, S.: *Attitudes and Behaviors toward the Handicapped*, presentation at Conference on Psychological and Social Implications of Developmental Disabilities, Johns Hopkins Medical Institution, Mar. 1, 1976.

Rutter, M., Tizard, J., and Whitmore, K.: *Education, Health and Behavior*, London: Longmans, 1970.

Solnit, A. J., and Stark, M. H.: Mourning and the birth of a defective child, *Psychoanal. Study Child*, **16**:523, 1961.

The School Institution

Featherstone, J.: *Schools Where Children Learn*, New York: Liveright, 1971. (Distributed by Norton, New York.)

Goodman, P.: *Compulsory Miseducation*, Westminster, Md.; Vintage Books, Random House, 1964.

Graubard, A.: *Free the Children: Radical Reform and the Free School Movement*, Westminster, Md.: Vintage Books, Random House, 1974.

Holt, J.: *How Children Fail*, New York: Dell, 1970.

School Health Program Goals

Caplan, G.: *Principles of Preventative Psychiatry*, New York: Basic Books, 1964.

Mechanic, D.: Influences on children's health attitudes and behavior, *Pediatrics*, **33**:3, 1966.

Nader, P. R.: The school health service: Making primary care effective, *Pediatr. Clin. North Am.*, **21**:1, 1974.

Nader, P. R., Emmel, A., and Charney, E.: The school health service: A new model, *Pediatrics*, **49**:6, 805, 1972.

Roghmann, K., and Haggerty, R. J.: "The Stress Model for Illness Behavior," in R. J. Haggery, K. J. Roghmann, and I. B. Pless (eds.), *Child Health and the Community*, Wiley, 1975, pp. 142–156.

Senn, M. J.: The role, prerequisites and training of the school physician, *Pediatr. Clin. North Am.*, **12**:4, 1039, 1965.

Van Arsdell, W. R., Roghmann, K. J., and Nader, P. R.: Visits to an elementary school nurse, *School Health*, **42**:142, 1972.

Nursing Roles in School Health

American Nurses' Association and the American School Health Association: *Recommendation on Educational Preparation and Definition of the Expanded Role and Functions of the School Nurse Practitioner*, New York: American Nurses' Association, 1973.

Bellaire, J. M.: School nurse practitioner program, *Am. J. Nurs.*, **71**:2192, 1971.

Conrad, J.: The high school nurse as a pediatric nurse practitioner, *Pediatr. Nurs.*, November 1975, p. 15.

Guidelines for the School Nurse in the School Health Program, Kent, Ohio: American School Health Association, 1974.

School Health Education

Dobbs, J. M., and Kirscht, J. P.: Internal control and the taking of influenza shots, *Psychol. Reps.*, **28**:959–962, 1971.

Gochman, D. S.: Children's perceptions of vulnerability to illness and accidents, *HSMHA Health Rep.*, **86**:3, 247–252, 1971a.

Gochman, D. S.: Some correlates of children's health beliefs and potential health behavior, *J. Health Soc. Behav.*, **12:**2, 148–154, 1971*b*.

Gochman, D. S., Bagramian, R. A., and Sheiham, A.: Consistency in children's perceptions of vulnerability to health problems, *Health Serv. Rep.*, **87:**3, 282–288, 1972.

Kasl, S., and Cobb, S.: Health behavior, illness behavior and sick role behavior, *Arch. Environ. Health*, **12:**246, 531–541, 1966.

Marshall, C. L., Hassanein, K. M., Hassanein, R. S., and Paul, C. L.: Attitudes toward health among children of different races and socioeconomic status, *Pediatrics*, **46:**3, 422–426, 1970.

Palmer, B., and Lewis, C.: *Children's Concepts of Health and Illness*, presentation at Fifth Annual Conference on Piaget, UCLA, January 1975.

Parcel, G. S.: Skills approach to health education: A framework for integrating cognitive and affective learning, *J. School Health*, **46:**403–406, 1976.

PART FIVE

Psychosocial Aspects of Pediatric Care

36 | Mental Health of the Young: An Overview

by Julius B. Richmond and William R. Beardslee

Recent changes in the nature of pediatric practice have given the understanding of child mental health increased importance both in the training of pediatricians and in their clinical practice. Advances in the development of preventive and therapeutic agents over the last 40 years have brought about major reductions in infant mortality and childhood morbidity and mortality. No longer is the practicing pediatrician's time consumed by rickets, scurvy, poliomyelitis, mumps, measles, and diarrhea. Rather, more time and energy are focused on the prevention of disease and the care of children with chronic disorders, including developmental disabilities.

In addition, the past decade has been characterized by the increasing awareness by organized consumers of the desirability of high-quality child health and child care services. There have been growing pressures from communities for improved child health services. This has been reflected in the development of such programs as Head Start, maternal and infant care, children and youth programs, and early periodic screening, diagnosis, treatment (EPSDT) for Medicaid-eligible children. The new approaches to more comprehensive services for the handicapped also reflect intensified community sophistication.

The increasing interest in child health will undoubtedly result in an effort to reorganize services and to generate local initiatives to reflect local needs and priorities. The emphasis will be increasingly on the enhancement of health and the prevention of disease. Thus, competence in the assessment and guidance of growth and development needs to be part of the clinical skill of the pediatrician.

Finally, advances in knowledge of child development, gained through the in-depth study of healthy children as well as through observations of deviations or delays in development, have provided the pediatrician with the conceptual framework to effectively deal with the mental health needs of children.

The cultural and psychological background of the family warrants special attention in understanding the mental health needs of children. The emotional climate in which a child is reared is a reflection of the personality development of parents or parent-substitutes. It is important, therefore, that the pediatrician know something of the developmental background of each parent and the immediate environmental factors operative in the child's life. As children have different roles within different families, it is important for the pediatrician to know how the child fits into the family constellation. Just as the structure and function of a baby have determinants which antedate birth, the practices and attitudes which determine how the child will be cared for have comparable antecedents. The pediatrician may develop an understanding of these during the prenatal period or after birth as he or she comes to know the life of the family unit.

The pediatrician may regard the family as carrying the "chromosomes" which perpetuate the culture and which form the cornerstone of emotional development. Cultural influences may be likened to a mainstream with many tributaries. Each varies from time to time in depth, rate of flow, and course; the mainstream is modified by its tributaries, but also exerts an influence upon them.

In the United States many variations exist in cultural patterns relating to childbearing attitudes and practices. These are determined in part by geographic, religious, educational, social, and economic backgrounds. Thus in some communities a great premium is placed upon the birth of a boy as the first child. Certainly religious backgrounds tend to influence the size of families. Higher educational backgrounds among parents have been correlated with a later childbearing age and with limitation in the size of families.

The relative rapidity of social movement in the United States has tended to create confusion among young parents as to basic group identification. Increasing educational opportunities have tended to make for social movement upward for many young parents. It is helpful for the pediatrician to know how much they identify with the old and how much with the new social grouping and its culture. Either of these identifications (usually some of both) involves some reintegration on the part of the parents which may require professional assistance.

Moreover, changes in the structure of the American family have led to a large increase in the number of single-parent families and to a marked decrease in the availability of the extended family for assistance in child care. Therefore, parents are relying more and more heavily on pediatricians for guidance.

The pediatrician should learn to match his or her cultural background with its attitudes toward childbearing and child rearing against the variety of cultural backgrounds of parents who come seeking advice. It becomes easier to understand as a consequence that there is no "right" attitude or "right" practice. For one family and its objectives certain practices may be adequate, but fail in another. Thus the pediatrician can be helpful by being objective rather than judgmental in viewing the family. This requires the capacity to observe and to listen and as a consequence to understand.

The pediatrician tends to develop an objective attitude by remembering that it is the culture, and not the physician, that within certain limits determines what is mental health. For example, Erikson and others have appropriately pointed out that children brought up in one American Indian culture might not be considered adequate to the developmental tasks of another if transplanted to another tribe living in a different climate and with significantly different cultural demands as a result. Many similar cross-cultural comparisons can be made. Although the pediatrician generally deals with more subtle contrasts, they are nevertheless real and significant for each family. In a country made up of people of such varied origins and with so much educational, social, economic, and geographic movement, it is unlikely that any stable tradition of child-rearing practices will emerge in the next several decades. The objective in each instance, therefore, is to help *each* family attain *its* goal in child rearing in *its* unique but most effective manner.

To assist in reaching this goal, the pediatrician must have a firm command of the body of knowledge of child development. Within the cognitive sphere, Piaget's work provides the most useful framework with its emphasis on the child's actions as necessary for the acquisition of knowledge, and on the predictable sequence of stages through which a child passes in developing intelligence. B. F. Skinner's work in the area of behavior modification and its applications has proved valuable both in helping children to learn and in providing a way to manage difficult or troublesome symptoms. Several workers in the area of early infant and child behavior, among them Chess, Thomas, and Birch, have helped to focus attention on the importance of the very early period of the child's life.

The work of Erik Erikson probably provides the best integrative framework through which pediatricians can understand the different factors in the mental health of the child and can best plan for their patients. Erikson stresses the importance of all three major factors—biological, intrapsychic and cultural—in the child's mental health. He sees the child as going through a series of stages in development and for each stage formulates the essential task or critical area to be mastered. Thus, as one example, for the very young infant, the dilemma is basic trust versus mistrust, and firm patterns for the solution of this dilemma must be successfully established for the infant to develop in a healthy way. As another example, for the adolescent, the dilemma is identity versus role diffusion. Youths in this stage must make sense of their own physical endowments, past experience, and present opportunities in a way that allows them to function in the world and have a sense of certainty about themselves. Specifically, youths must come to grips with three areas: (1) relationships to others, both sexual and nonsexual, (2) independence from family, and (3) choice of work or career. Familiarity with each stage, both with its task and with the signs of its successful resolution, provides the pediatrician with the organizing principle of the child's mental health.

Schools, families, child care centers, and hospitals are all concerned with the mental health of the child. The pediatrician, whose role is integrative, can combine medical findings, observations of the child and the family, and perceptions of the large cultural influences to best evaluate the mental health needs of children and to care for them. Such an evaluation is a vital part of the comprehensive pediatric evaluation of the child. Such evaluations provide the basis for helping parents become more effective in the rearing of their children.

37 | Changing Patterns of Family Structure

by Shirley A. Smoyak

Although the main concern of pediatricians is infants and children, they cannot be diagnosed and treated effectively and efficiently unless their chief socializers, their parents, are considered. Parents not only contribute tendencies and characteristics to their offspring by their combined gene offerings, but they continue to influence growth and development by daily messages to their children, subtle and otherwise, about the world in general and their own family (its norms, values, and expectations) in particular. Children have always grown up in families. There are, however, some major differences in how children were raised historically and how they are reared now.

Because most of us have experienced childhood and adolescence in some type of family setting, and because most of us, as adults, create families of our own, the temptation is very great to view our own experience as normal and usual. This ethnocentric tendency leads to assumptions that the familiar must be the correct or the right way and that other styles or patterns at best are strange, and at worst are wrong or bad.

Privacy about matters of family life has produced what sociologists call pluralistic ignorance. Each of us knows what goes on in our own bedrooms and how we handle a sassy 2-year-old at bedtime, but we really don't know how the neighbors do it. Systematic, rigorous research on the intimacies of family life is in its infancy.

This chapter will provide an overview of changing patterns of family structure. It will attempt to explode some cherished myths about what "The American Family" is, in order to provide a more realistic basis

for the clinician as he or she confronts a sick, injured, or well child in a practice setting. Marriage, as a normative institution, has certainly lost its take-for-granted and couple-for-life qualities. Families, however, while changing in structure and variety are here to stay.

Family Origins

There is great difficulty in tracing patterns or structures in families historically for two major reasons. The first is that upper-class or high-status families are grossly overrepresented in the literature. The second is that until the last 50 years or so, writers tended to describe families as they *should* be, rather than as they really were. This led to what William J. Goode has so aptly labeled "the classical extended family of Western nostalgia." In fact, some accounts of colonial families in America are so wrapped in nostalgia that the reader comes to the conclusion that those times were not so rough at all (and if they were, the close, warm family ties made it "all better").

The exact nature of the family structure and relationships of primitive man and woman is shrouded in various levels of conjecture and scientific guesswork. Since recorded history, no fixed pattern across cultures has been found. Culture, not biology, determines rules of organization within families. In most primitive, nomadic, communal societies, family descent was reckoned through mothers (possibly because maternity, in contrast to paternity, could be verified). Clans were consequently organized along matrilineal lines. Roughly 5000 years ago, when the development of agriculture changed so drastically how people lived and organized themselves, patrilineal lineage emerged. As the concept of private property developed, the transfer of this property from father to son became an important socioeconomic factor.

Historically, family units were such that all the work of survival was located within their boundaries. Functions such as educating the young, assuring safety from invaders, praying to a God or superior being, and providing nurturance, clothing, and shelter for each member were done within the family. Every family textbook includes a discussion of the "erosion of family functions," and it has been quite popular from time to time to predict the eventual demise of the family as we know it, since all the reasons for its being exist no longer. There have been several varieties of social organization which deemphasized or practically eliminated the idea of family; none has survived. The fact is that although there is no general societal law that people must live in families after childhood, most do.

Historians of the family, notably Phillipe Aries, have taught us that much of what we take as familiar and commonplace is a relatively recent invention. Childhood as a concept to us is real; Aries's argument is that it did not exist before the Middle Ages. In medieval days, as soon as a child could live without the constant attention of a mother or mother-surrogate, it was accorded adult status. This was not because adults then were unusually cruel or uncaring, but rather because the lack of awareness of childhood was very functional. The reason for infants not counting was very grim statistics; the odds against survival were very high. Therefore, parents protected themselves by not investing love or affective ties to an infant until they were sure it would survive. Much of what families used to do for survival within their own units is now accomplished outside the home (work, education, religion, social control). The family, however, is still primarily responsible for socializing children and for providing affective support or psychological refueling for its adult members.

Culture determines how children are socialized and prepared for adult roles. In the past, their sex and order of birth determined what they would do. Today, the dramatic shift is toward opening the range of possibilities for careers or occupations and life-styles.

Confusion of "Marriage" with "Family"

Prophets of doom for the family frequently make their predictions on the basis of a confusion of terms. They equate "marriage" with "family" and then go on to reason that since divorces are more likely to occur and that single-parent families are on the rise, families are approaching extinction.

A family is not necessarily a husband and wife, as father and mother, living with their offspring. The term "family" includes one-parent varieties (adoptive and biological), parent(s) and grandparent(s) together in one household or close by, older sibling caring for younger ones without a parent present, or complex patterns of several nonrelated adults living in a family community.

Doomsayers see the trend toward decreasing numbers of children as foretelling extinction of the family. Their optimistic counterparts see the same data in a hopeful light, viewing this as an opportunity to improve the quality of life generally.

Types of Family Structure

Change from Extended to Nuclear Units

The acknowledged authority in the field of historical analysis of the family is William Goode. Having surveyed worldwide data, he concludes that in every country where there is modernization, industrialization, and urbanization, traditional family patterns undergo a shift from large, extended networks to small units which he names *conjugal*. The large networks have a great deal of variability in their structure—some patrilineal, other matrilineal; some including aunts, uncles, and cousins, others not; some continuing to see the oldest marital pair as the authority/decision makers, others giving that status to the oldest son at some point; some living under one roof, others occupying separate sleeping units but sharing one communal area; and so on and on. The nuclear or conjugal units have much less variability. Their ties (both affective and economic) to the larger kin network all but disappear.

The element of free choice of partner based on love appears and becomes a norm. Dowry and bride-price are viewed as archaic. Cousins are less likely to marry each other. There is a decreasing authority of parents over children and husbands over wives. Equality between the sexes emerges as an idea if not a reality, with the legal system reflecting this by equal inheritance of children.

"The American Family"

Everyone knows (even non-Americans) what "The American Family" is. It is a white, middle-class mother and father living together in a suburban home with their boy child and girl child (an optional third child of either sex). The father leaves for work daily and is successful at his career (if not, his wife's duty is to help him forget this at night); the mother makes the house into a home and provides the psychosocial glue for everyone (her psychological reinforcers are the achievements of others). Its members are happy, harmonious, together and help the economy greatly by being consumers.

This very pleasant stereotype excludes more than half the population in the United States today. It is a tribute to American advertising to realize how pervasive this "ideal type" picture has become, although census data provide contradictory evidence. The federal government believes the stereotype, too; for example, one must be a "deviant" (husbandless) in order to receive welfare support, and day care continues to be a grossly underfunded area. Although the old, familiar male-breadwinner, female-homemaker model nuclear family is disappearing, laws at federal, state, and local levels still reflect the old assumptions about how families ought to live.

While a nuclear unit may be able to function as a well-oiled system when times are not rough, hard times produce serious stress and strain on the members. If they have only themselves to rely upon (economically, affectively, psychologically), then at any point when one member is not functioning at par, the total system suffers. A father out of work for prolonged periods becomes a disaster. A mother with a major illness puts the family into a turmoil. Even minor crises can become major events when there are not sufficient hands to help. When there are preschool children in the unit, every move the family makes must be seriously considered. When there is not a friendly aunt or grandparent about, "Is this trip necessary?" becomes a constant question. Minor illnesses of children, especially in a chain variety, produce major fatigue of mothers.

A pediatrician not aware of the family—its structure, stresses, and strains—in which the child resides will assume that directions given will be carried out. Judicious inquiry and listening will provide impor-

tant data about what parents can and cannot carry out in the area of care at home. For example, recommending isolation of a child who lives in a one-bedroom apartment with two other siblings is absurd.

Questions are now being raised over the division of labor in families, producing additional stress. At first glance, in every society, it seems that physical or sexual difference is the determinant of who does what kind of work. On closer inspection, it is obvious that culture, not biology, is the determinant.

Social definitions are the key to understanding how the work is assigned. Today, there is very little work which cannot be handled equally well by either men or women (including flying airplanes, teaching statistics, managing the stock market, and performing surgery). Who does what work is being renegotiated within families and in the larger society. The new view is that women are no better (or worse) prepared to care for children than are men, just as they are no better (or less) able to handle jobs previously considered men's only.

Physical strength is no longer the crucial factor in determining how work is allocated, but it is still a great factor in determining power relationships within families. The exact dimensions of how superior physical strength of males relates to psychological dominance over females is not known. The shifting of earning power within families, with women contributing equal or more dollars to the family kitty, may be attenuated in its influence over the power balance because of this physical strength issue.

In the past, women could not vote, sue, or own property or real estate. In fact, it was extremely hard for a woman to leave the home at all without being charged with abandoning her domicile. Things are certainly much better today, but the internal matters of power politics of husbands and wives have yet to be resolved.

Love as a necessary ingredient in marriage (viewed by some as necessary and sufficient) is an American invention. In most of history, love occurred outside of, not within, marriage (see Chaucer, Shakespeare). Love in marriage was considered a strange phenomenon indeed. Only Americans have accorded such high value to love in, and for, marriage. In nuclear units, this focus on love produces high expectations and frequent disappointments.

Fathers, both in nuclear units and in other arrangements, have come under scrutiny previously reserved for mothers only. They are now expected to be more involved in all aspects of child rearing. Tenderness is no longer reserved for special, private moments, but is expected of men as a generalized stance toward their families.

There may be a real danger to the careers of fathers who elect to be humanistic and greatly involved in the rearing of their children. Infants and children can be so fascinating and time-consuming that the occupations and careers of fathers may be seriously neglected. It is well-known that scientists, artists, discoverers, composers, and explorers have often protected themselves either by not marrying at all or by postponing having children or leaving their care to women.

Taking care of children is an "expanded role" for men. Not all are up to it. In recent years, there have been instances where men have been awarded the custody of their children in divorce; earlier, this was an unheard-of arrangement.

One-Parent Families

One-parent families are formed in various ways. A single parent may find himself or herself alone with children because of the death of a spouse or because of separation, divorce, or desertion. So far, children born out of wedlock tend to live with their mothers or are placed for adoption or foster care. There are a few, poorly documented instances where the father has laid claim to the child, and this may become an increasing possibility.

Single-parent families are no longer "mother-only" families. Previously, it was fashionable in the literature to consider the effects of absent fathers on the growth and development and sexual adjustment of children. There has not been a consideration of what the effects of absent mother might be.

Recently, one-parent families have been formed by adoption. Previously, most states awarded children to couples only, with much consideration of their stability and likelihood to remain together. Now single people, both men and women, are adopting children of all ages. Usually "hard-to-place" or older children are considered for such adoptions.

Single parents do find pleasure, rewards, and a sense of contributing to humanity. On the other hand, they sometimes experience even more severe stress and strain than nuclear families because of societal prejudice and misunderstandings and a lack of resources during illnesses and various crises. Single parents are sometimes refused renting arrangements by landlords. Their parenting obligations are usually seen as handicaps by employers. They are likely to experience social isolation and loneliness to a greater degree than their single friends without children. Becoming a parent puts one into an entirely different social milieu.

More so than in families with two or more adults present, these parents very often experience an overwhelming sense of total responsibility. There is no spouse to arouse in the middle of the night when the infant awakes for the third time. There is no validator there to assure that a decision is "o.k." There is no one to turn to when the adolescent fires a barrage of "mismanagement" accusations. Hence, pediatricians may find that they are called upon more frequently to play the role of validator. In a busy pediatric practice, it would be wise to delegate much of this function of "parenting consultant" to the pediatric nurse practitioner. There is one advantage to being a single parent—that of being in total charge of making the parenting rules and carrying them out. With one adult only, there is no need to resolve conflicts over the style or method of child rearing. When single parents marry or decide to join a multiple-parent living arrangement, they have difficulty arriving at a consensus over division of labor and making decisions about child-rearing styles and rules. "Yours, mine, and ours" is not so happily managed in real life as it is on television. Here again, pediatricians or pediatric nurse practitioners are useful as consultants.

Alternative Family Structures

Foster families have been the socializing agents for children in many societies. This became a more popular pattern when large, extended family networks were replaced by nuclear units. Grandparents, and aunts and uncles, became less likely to take on the total responsibility for child care when the biological parents could not or did not. The state's right to remove a child from his or her natural parents is an unresolved issue. On the one hand, opinion is that the child should be left with the natural parents and that they should be given the resources (dollars or therapy) by governments in order to be better parents. On the other hand, opinion is that pressured or ill (physically or mentally) or incompetent parents can only do harm and that therefore the child should be placed under foster care. To date, there are no well-done studies of outcomes to say definitively which approach is best. What is known is that child abuse is more likely to occur when parents feel they cannot cope.

Whether to remove the child or to help parents to cope is frequently a difficult decision to make, with the child at society's mercy. Frequently, judges call upon pediatricians to provide a professional view of the family's strengths and weaknesses.

Before the modern-day types of communes, the two best-known alternative patterns were the Oneida experiment and the Israeli kibbutz. Both had similarities to the communes of the sixties and seventies; they were formed as an alternative to what was perceived as dehumanizing industrialization and urbanization, and they self-consciously developed new rules of organization for their members.

The contemporary communal movement sees as its goal combining the presumable warm and supportive group life of the extended family with a greater degree of personal freedom than is possible in traditional middle-class family life. Their naïveté about human relationships is both encouraging and frightening. Conflict is handled by assuming it will not occur and is not necessary. While certain American Indian tribes have lived and do live in a spirit of noncompetition and little conflict, it is doubtful that people in their late teens and twenties can throw their socialization to the wind and manage such an idyllic, conflict-free life.

The communal attempts have not been evaluated fairly. Their failure in each instance (Russia, Israel, America) was explainable to some degree by the fact that they were not simply a change in family structure, but a change in the total politics of government. If adequate controls on the political aspect of the commune could be managed, a more scientific test of their viability would be possible. Even the present hippie, rural groups are political protests, although not so well organized as the ones in the last century.

The planned-for utopian or egalitarian milieu of the communes has not come to pass in most instances. While the first members very self-consciously divide the labor in a nonsexist fashion, with both men and women participating in agriculture, child care, household management, and the like, a gradual erosion of the ideal, with sexism and old forms of the male-female games comes creeping in. In the United States, the most radical experiment with sexual norms was in the Oneida community in New York. That group practiced total economic communism and group sexual access (any man and woman could have sexual relations if they were mutually agreeable). It didn't work. But there is no definitive answer to the question of whether the reason was economic or sexual. The question of whether "coupling" is a human need is unresolved. Another question is: How does a community of rebels replace itself? Weber has shown that innovative organizations inevitably succumb to bureaucratization. Whether family rebels succumb to traditionalism is another question. The Shaker community replaced itself by attracting more Shakers, but eventually lost to the larger environment.

Some of the communes of the last decade and this one are less than total communities. To the degree that the larger society's media reaches the commune's children, and in some instances, where public schools are used, the communal socialization will be less than complete. A next generation of mixed types should appear.

For the most part, whatever the family's style of child rearing has been and whatever the family structure is, children turn out, at least by their adulthood, to hold the norms and values of their parents. There are a few exceptions. Families which are both very rigid in their day-to-day rules and their religious beliefs produce adult-children who are far more liberal (even to the point of social deviance). This happens more often when the family's norms do not match the small society in which they live. On the other hand, very loose, "normless," agnostic families produce traditionalists. It appears that there is a "happy medium" toward which a next generation gravitates when reared at either end of a traditional-liberal continuum.

School-Age Parents

Every year the United States records nearly one-half million births to school-age parents. Of these parents, about one-half are married at the time of the birth; the divorce rate for this group is four times higher than the national average. Parents in this group tend to use naïve solutions to child-rearing problems. They have high energy to cope with the demands of infants and toddlers, but their judgment concerning matters of safety, general nutrition and health, and particularly fostering the autonomy of their offspring is wanting. This trend will produce "family maps" of higher family disorganization and difficulties with conflict resolution within the systems.

Homosexuals as Parents

Some people today would consider two same-sexed adults as a family, with or without children present. Homosexuals, male and female, have demanded to be seen as fit parents. So far, one or the other has applied as a single parent for adoption. As of 1976 no instance had been recorded of a pair seeking adoption and being successful with the request. When one partner in a heterosexual pair decides to "come out" as a homosexual, it is the "straight" partner who is awarded custody of the children. There are a few instances where a courtroom bargain is made between the divorcing pair; for example, a homosexual mother may be awarded the children if she stays closeted.

A Remaining Family Function: Socialization

Americans are the greatest consumers in the world of advice on children. Who is right about which advice is a matter which can only be answered from theory, or accidental experiments in child rearing. True experiments in child rearing, for obvious reasons, are almost never attempted. A cautious conclusion which may be derived, considering the complexity of the problem in judging which experiences have which effects on children, is "that we now at least know what are some of the worst ways of rearing a child, but we are much less sure of how to do it well" (Goode).

Fifty years ago, no profession identified as one of its functions "how to teach parents to be parents." Parents were supposed to know—either intuitively or because they learned it from their own growing up in large, extended families. Today, advice, counseling, and teaching about parenting is considered to be part of the work of pediatricians, nurses, child study specialists, and behavior modifiers. Courses on effective parenting can be found in curricula in high schools and graduate schools. "Socialization failure" is a fairly common diagnosis today. When a child behaves badly in the classroom or resists going to school, the tendency now is to treat this as a system difficulty and to use a range of strategies to involve the parents in some type of parenting program. The thrust of some of these programs is helping parents to accept their role with less anxiety and guilt (the parent-effectiveness approach); others focus more directly on improving specific parenting skills (the parent-responsiveness trend); still others prescribe family therapy, assuming that if disturbing relationships in the total family system were not intervening, the parents could go on with their work.

Children do not become normal adults unless nurtured in some type of close, continuing social unit, where norms are clearly set, where self-esteem is fostered, and where separateness-connectedness issues are worked on openly and directly. The most important work of parents as socializing agents is to get each succeeding generation to want to go on. Parents, in one way or another, have to accomplish getting their children "hooked" on the idea of continuity. Simply put, they have to make it pleasant to be alive and, further, to suggest that one's "debt" for such pleasure is to pass it on to the next person or generation. Warmth and tenderness must be experienced before they can be valued and shared with others. Too many people have had traumatic experiences with love turned to hate, warmth to cold, and tenderness to hostility. They fear being vulnerable and fear trusting others.

The largest order of parenting is to protect children from distrust and hostility and to predispose them to enjoy working and appreciating tenderness. In other words, parents must convince children that they live in a just world. Otherwise, "behaving," achieving, going on would make no sense. Young children believe in "immanent justice"; some outgrow this belief quickly, while others never do.

The implications of the belief in a just world, for various age groups, is undergoing study by several psychologists. "It might be argued that were it not for their faith that good deeds will be rewarded and transgressions punished, people would be unwilling to undertake socially beneficial activities, whether these be spending long years in school or obeying traffic laws. There may be particular situations in which the belief in a just world is especially functional. The dying patient . . . may derive much-needed comfort . . ." (Rubin).

In the case of illness or injury of a child, the pediatrician should make it a point to determine how this event is perceived by the child (how it is explained to him or her by the parents). Parents may be bearing unnecessary or inappropriate guilt. Children may be needlessly laying blame on their own heads. Blame assignment has serious long-range effects on self-esteem.

More children today are being reared in an androgynous fashion; they are being invited to explore the dimensions of experience previously totally sex-linked. Boys in nursery school diaper baby dolls; boys in junior high school enroll in cooking courses. Girls in nursery school play with dump trucks; girls in junior high take woodworking. Gym classes are no longer sex-segregated; each child performs according to physical potential. Doomsayers see this as producing mass confusion over sex identity in the next generation. Optimists rejoice at the opening up of more fully humane persons.

Consideration is being given to providing experiences for children in heterogeneous age groupings. The dysfunctionality of being with only one age group continuously has been documented. Foster grandparents are now popular. Most metropolitan areas have "big sister" or "big brother" programs for lonely or troubled youngsters.

The Future

The family is an integral subsystem in the larger societal order. Predicting its future cannot be done without considering shifts in all of society. The dimensions of the effect of the women's movement on marriage and the family cannot yet be reckoned with any degree of accuracy. It appears, however, that the largest effect will be on the socialization process.

Considering recent trends and the numerous surveys and studies recently reported, the following future directions for American families seem highly plausible:

1 There will be increasing value placed on humanity (human potential, tenderness and warmth, interpersonal needs) rather than on materialism. The gross national product will lose its luster and power to produce particular mercenary actions.

2 The trend toward decreasing numbers of children per family will continue. This will produce greater intensity in parent-child relationships and an even greater use of professionals as parenting advisers. The move will be toward artificial extended families, with couples and their children grouping together for support. Neighborhoods will be reinvented (community centers are their precursor).

3 The previous obsession with defining "masculine" and "feminine" will disappear. The new concern will be the dimensions of humanity.

4 The new American ideal—strength without domination—will gain impetus and influence in determining family values and life-styles.

5 The challenge for pediatricians, in this new day, will be to keep abreast of changes in family patterns and dynamics and to use this knowledge in providing humanistic and enlightened patient care. The expanded dimension of practice will include the consultant role in the area of parenting problems. This role will be shared with pediatric nurse practitioners in various practice settings.

38 | The Health Needs of Parents

by Henry M. Seidel

The health needs of parents, like those of children, are grounded on physical, social, and emotional determinants. Because the basic advocacy of the pediatric practitioner is that of the child, we do not, as a rule, see the parent as an independent entity with needs and an experience which may not include the child as a prime factor. In fact, however, there is real fascination in understanding the differing characteristics of the various groupings possible within a family.

For example, given a family of three—mother, father, and child—the various "units" include each of them as individuals, the group of three, and the three dyads, mother-father, mother-child, father-child—a total of seven combinations. Thus, a family of four would have 13 such units. The characteristic of a given unit varies with an infinite subtlety dependent on the particular combination and the basis of the interaction in which it may be involved at any given time. Thus, appropriate care of the child requires an understanding of the parent and of that parent's own health needs.

While those needs include the physical, social, and emotional, we are most likely to become involved with the latter. Health professionals, in fact, within their individual practices and in a broader public arena, have often presumed to act as "experts" in suggesting "principles" to parents regarding their relationship with their children and the mode and manner of their individual life-styles. The net effect of this overabundance of advice in recent decades has been a diminution in the confidence of parents, a loss of ability to resort to common sense, and a consequent breach in composure and naturalness. The sense of direction that one might have had is often confused by the dizzying impact of the audio-visual media and the disruption in the role of the extended family in the last half of the twentieth century.

The care of children might be improved if we took greater advantage, as a society, of the resources inherent in the intelligence, humor, and judgment of parents. And, if we are to presume to advise parents, we must work to exploit just these resources, putting aside value judgment and the occasional impulse to preach. Perhaps our contribution to the health needs of parents can, more than anything, be to make available an objective listening ear and to give the opportunity to work together to achieve a balanced viewpoint.

There is a problem in determining the extent to which we should become involved with the health needs of parents. Should pediatric practitioners, for example, take care of the sore throat of a child, but not of that child's parent? Is it appropriate, when both are in our offices, to send the older person off to another setting at the cost of convenience, dollars, and delay?

Much of the response will depend on a variety of concerns:

1 An objective assessment of one's own experience and competency. There may be much in primary care which requires a technical sophistication which we cannot invoke with appropriate confidence. On the other hand, one often possesses the relevant skills. Certainly, one is much more likely to treat the familiar condition.

2 The circumstance of the particular family and the individual parent's access to care. The burdens of additional cost or an unreasonable wait for care elsewhere should be alleviated if possible. Often, transportation may be a problem.

3 The equipment and the physical setting available. One is not apt to diagnose and treat a vaginal discharge in a parent if the appropriate adult examining table is not at hand.

4 The practitioner's concern over the possibility of a malpractice action. There is often a fear that the risk is greater if the boundaries of one's specialty are crossed.

Obviously, it is practical to limit one's involvement to those aspects which are of immediate relevance to the child. Nevertheless, there is a gray area in which there is an unspoken constraint on going beyond the limits of one's *certified* area of competence. While a valid and explicit reason is the objective of high-quality care, there is also the emotionally charged and implicit one that, as the economic pie has been apportioned to the various health care specialities, this quasi-formal arrangement must be respected. Thus, one is left to judge the potential patient's need and to decide accordingly.

There are specific instances in which this judgment is easier:

1 The Adolescent Parent

The adolescent parent has an imposed set of needs which requires total care from an individual with a perspective on the young. A poignant example is the teenage, unmarried mother who elects to raise her child and who conceptualizes and treats that child as a "baby doll." The professional can provide a sensitive understanding of the interdependencies of that dyad, a ready availability both to the mother when she needs reassurance about her own self-worth when it is challenged by a "baby doll" who inevitably does not behave perfectly and to the baby when there is need to modify the frustrated actions and attitudes of a child-parent.

2 The Abused Parent of the Battered Child

The origins of child abuse are set most often in the socially disorganized childhood experience of the parent. A successful manipulation of this shattering circumstance, if the objective of a functional stability in a *preserved* family unit is to be met, is the inclusion of the parent within the *caring* and, to the extent of competence, the curing efforts of the professional involved. The parent, as much as possible, should be "gathered in" rather than "referred out." Fragmen-

tation of service to the individuals concerned, with the consequent requirement of a difficult-to-achieve sensitive communication among too many persons, can only endanger the potential of successful outcomes.

3 The Parents of the Relatively New Firstborn

Anticipatory guidance is a major responsibility and reflects a common need in parents, a need of which they may not be acutely aware. For example, the emotionally nourishing interdependence of the male-female dyad prior to the birth of a child may easily be threatened by that new child in a circumstance in which care is left to the mother and in which she may then have diminishing ability to give attention to the care and feeding of the father. Resentment and a strain on the bonding between the parents may develop. It is not necessary to render a judgment on the allocation of presumed male-female tasks within a family in order to sensitize the actors to the need for *their* attention to the germinal problems.

4 The Sick or Potentially Sick Parent with a Major Diagnostic Clue in the Observable Circumstance of the Child

There are numerous instances in which we can extend our caring and curing to parents as a result of our involvement with the child. Depression in the parent is a good example. If depression can be described as an inner feeling of helplessness resulting from a wide gap between one's perception of who one is and of who one ought to be, then it is easy to conceptualize the stress imposed by child rearing and the role of the pediatric professional in reacting sensitively to parental symptoms like anorexia, fatigue, crying spells, or insomnia—all symptoms of depression.

While the day of the house call is largely past, it is still possible in the office or clinic setting to sense the presence of *alcoholism* or *inappropriate dependency* on drugs. In addition, illness detected in the child should kindle thought and attention to a related circumstance in the parent. Obviously, for genetically determined disease, there must be access to genetic counseling—and to discussions attentive to the resolution of parental guilt. In fact, the awareness of the potential of parental guilt must be a common denominator in the development of a management plan for all childhood illness. An expression of physical abnormality in the child should initiate appropriate screening for a similar expression in the parent. Obvious examples, both genetic and environmental, are tuberculosis, venereal disease, streptococcal disease, lead poisoning, and hearing loss. The less obvious circumstance includes the increased susceptibility to major psychic disturbance in the relatives of children with phenylketonuria and the increased likelihood of glucose 6–phosphate dehydrogenase deficiency in a family where an index finding appears in a child.

Conclusion

These responsibilities, then, are numerous and recur with high frequency with relationship to needs of both the body and the psyche. The degree of need and of consequent professional involvement may result in a judgment based not only on the variables already discussed, but also, finally, on an assessment of the psychosocial competence of the parent involved. The parent-child relationship may abet or obstruct this effort. In fact, there may at times be a competition for our loyalties in fulfilling responsibility. In such an event, it is likely that most practitioners will choose in favor of the child. However, lest this be given too simplistic an interpretation, it is well to consider the development of a therapeutic plan for the child born with a meningomyelocele, or the content of testimony in a divorce action when the law provides a requirement for legal representation for each adult, but not for the child, when the rights to trial by jury and to due process are not extended to children in our society. There is a point then when, if for no other reasons than the requirement of technical skills or of the priorities of advocacy, the pediatric practitioner must refer the parent and so involve the expertise of the full health care team.

39 | Employed Mothers

by Mary Howell

Pediatricians and pediatric educators have tended to assume that the child-patient's mother is "at home." Our traditional picture of family structure—and the life experience of most physicians—includes a father in paid employment and a mother who works in her home for no pay.

In fact, in 1975, nearly half (47.4 percent) of all U.S. mothers were in paid employment. That figure includes 54.8 percent of all mothers whose children were between the ages of 6 and 18, and 38.9 percent of all mothers with at least one child under the age of 6. Among single-parent mothers, 55 percent of those with preschool children and 66 percent of those with children 6 to 18 were in paid employment.

Many of our traditional assumptions about the three-way relationship between pediatrician, mother, and child-patient need therefore to be re-evaluated. For instance, mothers who are in paid employment are not sitting at home waiting for return telephone calls from medical personnel. Some cannot even receive incoming personal calls at their places of employment and need immediate help and advice whenever they are able to place a call to a clinic.

Such mothers share the care of their children with at least one other person—another adult in the home or in some away-from-home child care arrangement. Instructions for follow-up care for illness or guidance through developmental hurdles need to be communicated in such a way that all responsible for the care of the child can coordinate their efforts.

Employed mothers may not be able to bring the child for illness care or for health supervision at usual clinic hours. Unless evening or weekend hours are offered, the employed mother may need to send her child for visits accompanied by someone other than

herself. Yet she must be assumed to be responsible for medical expenses for her children and needs to be informed in advance about the costs of visits and drugs.

Careful review of the research literature indicates that the children of employed mothers, as a group, do not differ from the children of nonemployed mothers in many significant respects. Studies that sought to find the "damage" done to children as a consequence of maternal employment often confounded associated variables—such as poverty—with maternal employment itself. Children whose mothers have been paid workers are less likely to hold extreme beliefs about sex-role dysjunction; that is, they are more likely than the children of non-employed mothers to view their own sex as capable of, and competent in, qualities traditionally assigned to the opposite sex, such as instrumental achievement (a stereotypic "male" trait) and emotional sensitivity (a stereotypic "female" trait).

Because the well-being of children, both with regard to sickness and with regard to developmental progress, is strongly dependent on the well-being of their adult caretakers, it is useful to review some of the sources of stress for mothers in paid employment:

Money

Most employed mothers take and keep paid jobs because their families need their contributions to family income. Among husband-wife families, in 1974, only 4 percent had incomes below $5000 when both adults were in paid employment, whereas 13 percent fell below this "poverty" level when the wife earned no income. The median contribution to family income made by employed wives was one-fourth, in

1974; when the wife was employed full time year round, her median contribution was two-fifths.

Women head one in eight U.S. families. Of these women 54 percent are paid workers outside their homes. Nearly two-thirds of these workers are the only earners in their families, and one-third of them have incomes below the "poverty" level.

The discrepancies between men's earnings and women's earnings reflect long-standing discrimination against women with regard to education and training, employment and advancement opportunities, and salaries. In 1974, in each of the various major occupation groups, women's earnings ranged between 41 and 66 percent of those of men in comparable work. Much of this differential remains after adjustment for education and work experience. Employed minority women earn only 54 percent of the earnings of white men, with a median income in 1974 of $6611.

Time

Most employed mothers also work a second full-time job, that of homemaker. While all need some arrangement for supplementary child care while they are out of their homes, few have any substantial amount of supplementary assistance for general household maintenance and must do that work before and after going out to their paid jobs. In addition, employed mothers are very concerned that they spend as much time with their children as possible and that time spent with children be in positive and mutually gratifying interaction.

Employed mothers report that they have little *personal* time—for social contacts, community-building activities, and solitary pursuits. Many also remark that unless fathers and older children assume their own responsibilities with regard to maintenance of the common household, the standard of neatness and order in the home is almost inevitably lower than the mother wishes. Time pressures can be a real source of unease for employed mothers, so that unforeseen time costs—such as an illness—can throw a usually well-organized household into a turmoil.

On the other hand, in households in which all family members contribute a fair share toward mutual caretaking, the burdens of time and energy associated with the mother's income are distributed. Some also report an appreciation of closeness and

unity of purpose when responsibilities for income earning and household maintenance are thus shared.

Child Care

Finding and paying for supplementary child care services are major problems for all employed mothers, whatever their incomes and occupations. The most common arrangement is to seek this help from other family members or near kin. Much of the for-hire child care available to mothers is less than optimal; this is especially likely to be true in for-profit child care centers.

Only about 15 percent of children needing supplementary child care—which is, of course, a larger group than just the children of employed mothers—can find places in centers for group care. Even in group care, and even with the minimal salaries now customarily paid to child care workers, centers with adequate standards for healthy child development must charge in the area of $50 per child per week. Clearly, few families can bear these costs without subsidy.

Networks of neighborhood child care offer many advantages for the families of employed mothers. Most families report that they prefer child care services located in their home neighborhoods. Unfortunately, most families can afford to pay little—and most at-home mothers dare not charge reasonable fees for their work—so that these informal arrangements are often highly unstable and break down under stress. Our public policies have been remarkably backward, compared with those of other industrialized nations, with regard to supplementary child care services for the families of employed mothers.

Mothering Self-Esteem

The most consistent finding from research on the families of employed mothers is that children thrive or struggle in relation to their mother's sense of personal well-being and self-esteem. Mothers report that they enjoy parenting, and feel that they do it well, when they are at ease about the course of their own lives. Specifically, employed mothers who want to be employed, and at-home mothers who do not want to be employed, are higher in "mothering self-esteem" than mothers who are at home but wish they had paid jobs, and employed mothers who wish they were at home.

Guilt and worry about the welfare of their children can add a significant burden for employed mothers. Such guilt and worry are often engendered and magnified by medical professionals who are unfamiliar with the research literature and subtly accuse or threaten employed mothers with consequent "trouble" in their children's lives.

The sum of self-esteem that a mother finds in her paid job depends on many factors. She may derive a great deal of satisfaction from her contribution to family income; from work-related skills, friends, and interests; and from appreciation shown at her work place for her efforts and accomplishments. If, on the other hand, she is underemployed, ill paid, or discriminated against in hiring, salary, training, and promotion; if she is unable to find and afford stable and high-quality child care; and if she bears the entire burden of household maintenance for all the members of her family, then she may feel caught between resentment and her family's need for her income. When her own sense of well-being and self-esteem is so stressed, her mothering capacities and reserves are also likely to be pressed to their limit.

40 | Day Care and Preschool Programs

by William R. Beardslee and Julius B. Richmond

There have been major changes in the structure of the American family which give day care and preschool programs growing importance in the life and growth of the young child. As a consequence, the issues of day care and preschool programs are coming increasingly to the attention of pediatricians. There are more requests by parents for such programs for their children than ever before. Unfortunately, the need for adequate facilities far outstrips the available resources. In 1974, the Department of Health, Education, and Welfare reported about 1.3 million children in all licensed day care centers, Head Start programs, and approved family day care homes compared with a total of 19.5 million children under age 6 in the United States, of whom about 7 million live in families in which the mother works.

Day care and preschool programs are designed to help families rear their children. This discussion will be limited to those defined as *developmental* day care or preschool programs. This eliminates a consideration of *custodial* programs, as, in general, these programs are substandard and do not serve the best interests of children and parents. There is sufficient knowledge concerning desirable environments for children to justify this elimination of custodial care.

A developmental day care or preschool program is one which provides care to the child during the day; is not located in the home of origin; is comprehensive in its approach, including attention to the physical, cognitive, and emotional development of the child; and provides for a significant involvement of the parents in the program. The financial support for a day care center or preschool program of education may come from government, from private philanthropic organizations, from the collection of fees from parents, or from a combination of these three. By general usage, day care refers to care for the child from 0 to 3 years of age, and preschool to care for the child from 3 to 6 years. Although the developmental needs of children vary according to their age, day care and preschool programs will be discussed together. The issues facing the pediatrician are similar across the age range, and the pediatrician's concern is not primarily with the details of the curricula of the centers, but with their appropriateness and the quality of care.

Until recently, day care and preschool programs had tended to be custodial. In 1854, the first nursery was established in the United States by a philanthropic woman's organization to care for the children of poor working mothers. After the Civil War, public taxes financed kindergartens and day nurseries to take care of the children of war widows looking for work. The federal government provided day care centers for children in World War I, during the Depression, and in World War II. When World War II ended, these centers closed, with the exception of those in California. These centers were primarily custodial, and arose from the demand of women in the labor force, rather than from a primary desire to meet the needs of the child.

It was not until the 1960s with the funding of Head Start and then through the Great Society program that the federal government again became active in care for young children. The pattern of government involvement in day care and preschool education in the United States is in curious contrast to that of many other countries as diverse as Israel, Denmark, and Hungary in which day care and preschool programs are more generally available to families. The centers form an integral part of the health care and education systems of these countries, although, certainly, there are major differences in the ways these programs are run.

Recent changes in the structure of the American family, as documented by Bronfenbrenner, indicate the increasing importance that such programs have in the present and will have in the future:

One third of all married women with children under 6 were working in 1974, and 3 out of 10 married women with children under 3 were working in 1975. There is a trend for the younger mother under 25 to return to work rather than the older mother.

One out of every 8 infants under 3 was living in a single parent family in 1974. Ninety percent of the single parent families are not part of an extended family network, and 54 percent of those mothers with children under 6 are working.

Single parent families occur in a much higher frequency in lower income groups. Sixty-seven percent of families with incomes under $4,000 a year have only one parent, and single parenthood is especially prevalent for young families.

The "illegitimacy ratio" (illegitimate births per 1,000 live babies born) has risen from 35 to 130 in the last quarter century. The number of teenagers having children is rapidly increasing, and illegitimacy is highest among teenagers.

As the possibility of adequate care within the family for the young child is being increasingly limited, and as the trends in family structure indicate, families are seeking alternatives.

Pediatricians are involved with day care centers and preschool programs at every level of their functioning. The pediatrician is usually consulted by parents about placing a child in a day care or preschool program. Through a comprehensive approach to the child, which integrates knowledge of the biology of health, disease, and development, awareness of emotional needs, and an understanding of the family and the larger social context, the pediatrician is in a favorable position to provide guidance. In addition to working with the individual family, many pediatricians provide screening examinations for the early detection of developmental deviations and illness to children in centers, and specific advice to centers about the control of infectious disease, nutrition, safety, and the like. More broadly, many pediatricians serve as consultants to programs, facilitating the psychosocial development of the children through guidance to the staff about the structure, curriculum, and administrative organization of the centers. Finally, pediatricians are involved in establishing the standards by which a day care or preschool program should be run and in insisting on adherence to these standards in their operation.

Discussions with parents about day care or preschool programs provide pediatricians with an excellent opportunity to share their approach to the child with the parents. A relaxed, full discussion is important to the pediatrician's future rapport and relationship with the parents. The pediatrician should review what is known about the effects of day care and preschool programs and should provide the parents with a chance to voice their feelings and questions. Such a discussion can help parents learn how to conceptualize the needs of their children which are relevant not just to a decision about a preschool program, but to many other decisions parents will make concerning child rearing.

It is useful to place such a discussion squarely in the context of the child's general developmental needs. The pediatrician should be aware of mother-child bonding and attachment and separation as key issues. It is worthwhile to review with the parents the child's needs for love and support in human interactions; regularity and predictability in the environment; adequate nutrition; and a setting that is physically safe and cognitively stimulating and that encourages exploration and mastery. Parents should consider these needs as they evaluate day care centers or other alternatives.

When a family has decided to place a child in a day care program, it is important for the pediatrician to discuss the separation of parent and child and the feelings that surround it. For many children, going to a day care center will be their first major separation from the family. Parents may fear that they soon will be replaced in the child's affection. Although the evidence does not support this conclusion, parents should be aware that the child may show some signs of anxiety. Parents may have difficulty in letting the child go and may need help and support. In a well-conducted day care or preschool program, the professional staff is generally very helpful in facilitating this process of separation for both parent and child. In general, it is supportive to parents to point out that most parents and children can use the help of professionals in the day care and preschool center who can observe the child and give guidance to the family.

In deciding which program to choose, parents should be encouraged to visit and observe various centers. In communities where there are no choices of centers, the judgment must be made whether the only available center is a *developmental* day care center. As noted, once a child is enrolled, it is appropriate and helpful for the parents to be actively involved in the program.

Parents often ask whether there is an increased risk of illness in children who attend day care or preschool programs. Although there may be an increased risk of some minor illness, especially to younger children, there is no evidence to suggest that such a risk is a contraindication to day care or that children cannot be safely cared for from a medical standpoint in a day care or preschool program.

A key question in the parents' minds is: Is day care or preschool education safe, or is placing a child in day care likely to harm the child? Naturally, a specific answer to a question from a specific parent is possible only after complete evaluation of the child and the family. In general, it is fair to conclude that the evidence does not indicate that high-quality, developmental day care or preschool education programs are harmful. Moreover, there is evidence that for many children such an experience is very beneficial.

After a major review of the studies of the effects on children of having mothers who work, Rutter concludes that such children are not more likely to become psychologically ill or delinquent. He also reports that there is no evidence that the children have difficulties because of being cared for by several mother figures as long as the care is good. Finally, he asserts that there are no data in support of the view that day nurseries inevitably cause psychological damage. In the past, considerable professional concern has been expressed about these matters, because of some of the evidence from studies of custodial centers.

Bronfenbrenner has recently examined the carefully controlled studies that compare good day care with good care at home. He reports that the studies show that no significant differential effects on IQ occur (although there was not much evidence of a sustained longitudinal nature). The existing evidence did not justify regarding day care as an emotionally harmful experience. Bronfenbrenner also stresses that more research is needed.

It is important to bear in mind that these studies compared two high-quality kinds of care. Many homes because of economic and/or other adversity do not offer the possibility of high-quality care during the day. Moreover, many children, because of their special needs, can especially benefit from day care and preschool programs.

Here it is useful to review what experience with disadvantage children has compelled us to learn. Without any sort of enrichment program, a general downward drift in developmental performance is seen over a period of years in children of low-income families (although this does not apply, of course, to every single child in the situation). It is this trend that Head Start and other early childhood day care and preschool programs have sought to reverse.

There is a sound conceptual and empirical base for trying to reverse this developmental decline. The conceptual base is that the environment does have considerable impact on later development. Empirical data demonstrate that enrichment programs such as Head Start do make a significant difference and that the developmental quotient of children can be significantly raised through such programs. Moreover, it is clear that not just children from disadvantaged areas, but also those with special handicaps such as mental retardation, sensory deficits, or cerebral palsy do benefit significantly. Although there have been some conflicting studies on how long-lasting the IQ gains that children make in Head Start and similar programs are, it is now clear that permanent gains are made by many children in these programs. The importance of the parents' involvement in day care and preschool programs is emphasized by a review of the longitudinal evaluation of preschool programs. It has been demonstrated in several studies that intervention with the parent and child together had major impact on the child, leading to substantial, lasting gains, and that in addition there were benefits for other children in the family and for the parent who was involved. Finally, Head Start and other similar programs have benefited their participants in many ways beyond those measured by cognitive testing. Early detection and treatment of illness, more adequate nutrition, and general gains in emotional well-being and motivation for learning are but three examples. Further, there is evidence that the presence of the centers themselves has had beneficial effects on the communities in which they are located.

It is useful for pediatricians to visit centers and observe their workings. Many pediatricians work as consultants to such centers. The American Academy of Pediatrics has published sets of recommendations for day care centers and preschool programs which are relevant for pediatricians, especially in their role as consultants. The recommendations detail how to review the administrative organization of the center, its programs, and the health needs of the children in terms of both screening and on-going care. The Department of Health, Education, and Welfare has a resource guide available which is also useful in advising centers.

In assessing the quality of care in day care or preschool programs, the pediatrician should pay special attention to the ratio of staff to children enrolled, to the professional training and orientation of the staff, and to understanding the typical daily experience for a child in the center. In many ways, the most rewarding part of involvement with a day care center is actually being there while it is in operation. A well-run day care center is an excellent place to observe healthy children at different ages and stages of development. Working with a day care center can be an important part of the training of pediatricians because it affords them a unique opportunity to observe children not under the stress of illness or hospitalization. It is a refreshing challenge and a rewarding involvement for busy practitioners, allowing them to have a significant impact on the growth and development of children. Especially with the changes in family structure, the day care center can be, and often is, a vital center in any community; it can provide help to families with handicapped children; and it may be the beginning of a way out of the cycle of poverty and despair that has limited so many of our young children in low-income neighborhoods in the past. Involvement with it allows pediatricians to be active in helping to bring about a creative solution to the problems posed by the evolving changes in family structure.

41 | Marital Discord and Divorce

by Rowine Hayes Brown

Introduction

Divorce is becoming increasingly popular in the United States. Our divorce rate is currently the highest in the Western world. If the present trend continues, it is now anticipated that half of all marriages will ultimately end in divorce. There are also numerous incompatible couples who continue to reside together in a hostile, combative atmosphere because of religious dogma, economic restrictions, and fallacious reasoning that marital discord is less harmful to the children's development than separation and divorce.

The significant change affecting children is the dramatic increase in the number of single-parent families. In 1975, it was reported that there were more than 9 million children living with divorced parents, and probably 20 million children living with a divorced, separated, or deserted parent. For children born in the 1970s, it has been predicted that two out of five children will live for some period with a single parent.

Past research has shown that a conflict-ridden intact family may be more harmful than divorce for family members. Divorce can be a positive and liberating solution to certain family problems, but it can also be a time of crisis, resulting in stress, conflict, and trauma for the adults and their children. However, most divorce research has failed to measure in any precise manner the effect of divorce. The recent research by Hetherington is one of the first studies to concentrate on the entire family system. It makes an in-depth analysis of changes in family interaction and functioning in the 2 years following divorce. Of the families studied, there were none in which at least one family member did not report distress or exhibit disrupted behavior; poor parenting was apparent in most cases during the 2 years following divorce.

In all social strata of our society, it is assumed that children need healthy relationships with both parents for normal emotional and physical development. Children who undergo the trauma of parental conflict, separation, and loss may react with emotional, behavioral, or somatic symptoms. Pediatricians need to be knowledgeable about the effects of marital discord and divorce upon children to accurately diagnose, manage, and treat their presenting complaints.

Effects on the Child

Children of all ages are affected by disruptions of harmony in the home. The presence of two parents in the home does not necessarily guarantee happiness or a climate where children can mature and develop to their full potential. The parents should contain their hostility in the presence of their children. Although difficult to do, they should outwardly treat each other with respect and expect their children to show respect for both parents. Quarreling between parents may make the home an unhappier place than it would be with one parent.

If the parents can handle their divorce in an intelligent manner, they will be able to save their children from some of the potential trauma. Children should be informed as soon as the parents reach a decision to divorce. Knowledge of the impending divorce will upset them, but they will be less disturbed than if they are kept uninformed.

Initially, young children are apt to be more severely

affected than older children, but may make better future adjustments. They may be too young to comprehend explanations the parents give concerning the reasons for divorcing, but are still influenced by the parental fighting. Older children are deeply concerned about the implications of divorce. If the parents involve the children in their arguments and expect them to choose sides, the children will become enmeshed in their parents' problems and blame themselves for the family strife. Following the divorce, the children can be expected to experience feelings of guilt, anger, anxiety, and depression.

When the mothers have experienced the divorce as very traumatic, the children will suffer greater effects from the divorce than otherwise. In Goode's study of divorced mothers, the majority felt that their children had better lives as children of divorced parents than they would have had as children experiencing marital discord. Addeo postulated that youngsters of divorce living with one parent do not fare any worse in the long run than progeny of an uninterrupted marriage. Another study reported that as a group, adolescents in divorced homes showed less psychosomatic illness, less delinquent behavior, and better adjustment to the parents than children in unhappy intact families.

The Hetherington study found that the first year of the divorce was a period of poor parenting and maximum negative behavior by the children; after 2 years, there was marked recovery and constructive adaptation for both parents and children. Initially, divorced parents relate to their children by making fewer maturity demands, communicating ineffectively, being less affectionate, and showing marked inconsistency in discipline. Divorced parents, particularly mothers, experience difficulties interacting with their sons, which may explain why previous studies have found the effects of divorce more severe and enduring for boys than for girls. The parents often experience a lack of control over their children. The mothers try to be more restrictive and use authoritarian control, which the children often ignore or resist. The absent fathers, desiring their contacts with their children to be happy, usually relate by being extremely permissive. Eventually, to everyone's benefit, the fathers' indulgent behavior decreases, and the mothers' child-rearing practices become more effective. During this period of adjustment, the parents may be victimized by their children. The children are more likely to oppose their mothers and comply with their fathers. The boys tend to be more opposi-

tional and aggressive, and the girls more whining, complaining, and demanding.

Divorce can be disruptive to the emotional and sexual development of children. Children form strong emotional attachments to those who care for them. Separation from persons upon whom the children are emotionally dependent has been found to be deeply disturbing and may interfere later with their interpersonal relationships. According to psychoanalytical theory, adjustment in adulthood depends upon the success with which young children pattern themselves after their parents, particularly the parent of the same sex. Children learn adult roles by identifying with their parents. When boys are brought up in homes without male models, they may experience difficulty in establishing their male identification. Divorced mothers may further damage their sons by pushing them into assuming the overwhelming adult role of "man of the house."

Children often feel stigmatized by the divorce of their parents. If they come from a cultural or religious background in which divorce is uncommon, they will be more seriously affected. Children need to establish and maintain good relationships with their peers. However, children of divorce feel different from their peers. Afraid of being ostracized or ridiculed, the children may refuse to talk about the divorce. Children suffer more severe consequences when they are forced to move to new neighborhoods and may be faced with loss of familiar ties to friends and classmates.

When the divorced parent providing the primary child care is able to remain at home and continue former activities, some of the negative effects of the divorce may be diminished. However, during the first year of divorce, the parents experience considerable difficulties in running an organized household with established eating and sleeping routines. Divorced parents, coping with significantly less contact with adults, experience intense feelings of loneliness and often feel trapped in their children's world. Even their socializing attempts are hampered by the limited recreational opportunities for single parents.

Other major problems faced by divorced parents are economic and occupational difficulties. Although it often is assumed that the care of the children will be provided by the parents in the home, the parents may be forced to seek employment to augment the family income. Arrangements must be made for the care of the children by relatives, babysitters, nurseries, or day care centers. Thus, the impact of the economic position of the divorced parents may unfavorably influence the children's adjustment. Young children may respond to their working parents with symptoms of separation trauma. Older children may experience feelings of rejection and resent the working parents' social contacts. School children also may feel embarrassed if the family financial situation prohibits their full participation in the activities and lifestyle of their peer group.

Symptoms and Developmental Disorders

Children may display emotional and behavioral symptoms in response to marital discord and divorce. Young children may react with crying spells, resistance to toilet training, eating and sleeping disturbances, and temper tantrums and may lose previously achieved developmental milestones. School-age children may become anxious, indifferent, angry, depressed, and guilt-ridden; may regress to earlier behavior, such as thumb sucking; may experience night terrors and general fearfulness; may develop learning problems; may become agressive toward other children; may "act up" in school, at home, or in the neighborhood; and may commit antisocial acts, such as stealing or vandalism. Adolescents may become depressed if they view the divorce as rejection and may develop intense guilt feelings if they blame themselves for the family breakup. They may react by displaying disruptive behaviors at home, in school, or in the neighborhood and may commit angry rebellious acts, such as truancy, running away, and delinquency.

Any one of a number of common psychosomatic symptoms and syndromes may develop in the children. Some of these pertain to the gastrointestinal tract and include nausea, vomiting, anorexia, constipation, vague abdominal pains, or in some instances, more serious difficulties, such as gastric ulcers or ulcerative colitis. Some children have developed an excessive appetite leading to obesity, and others have displayed pica, anorexia nervosa, psychogenic vomiting, or encopresis; any of these conditions may be difficult to treat or are even refractory to treatment. The children may be further affected when neglected by mothers who are experiencing psychosomatic illnesses arising from the marital stress.

Custody and Visitation Rights

Historically, custody is almost always (86 percent of the time) awarded to the mother, particularly when the involved children are infants; this has been true even when the mother has not been the "innocent party." Such awards of custody are ordinarily made under the assumption that the mother will stay at home and take care of the children. However, in many instances where child support and alimony payments are inadequate, the mother joins the work force to supplement her income and makes arrangements for child care. Today, more fathers are fighting for and winning custody of their children and making similar child care arrangements.

The courts have long used the guideline of the "best interests of the child" when deciding the awarding of custody. Criticism of this policy is frequently heard today from assertions that in the majority of custody hearings, the children are not represented by their own counsel and are seldom involved in the decision which will affect the rest of their lives. Advocates of the rights of children now propose that no hearing or order concerning the custody, care, or property of minor children should be commenced or made by the court unless the minor is represented in court by an attorney to protect the minor's best interest. Goldstein suggests that the best guideline in deciding placement for the child would be that which is "least detrimental" among the available alternatives. In application of such a yardstick, the court would need to check out any inherent detriments in any placement being considered.

Children should have a voice or personal representation in the custody proceedings, and their preference should be considered, although it should not always be determinative. Even though the child may be as young as 4 or 5 years of age, consideration of his or her wishes works out more satisfactorily for both the child and parents. The custody decree arrangements can affect the child's adjustment to the divorce and separation. It is difficult for a child to relate positively to both parents if they are not communicating with each other. The unplanned shifting of the child back and forth between the parents may lead to feelings of instability and tension. When custody is awarded to the mother, children may feel rejected if they never see their father. In instances where regular visitation plans are worked out between the parents and the child, the relationship between the child and the absent parent is improved and the arrangement is more satisfying for everyone.

A common complication of a divorce is continued fighting between the parents over custody and visitation rights. Children may be expected to ally themselves with one parent, thus augmenting the tension already present. Experts in the area of divorce are deliberating various custody and visitation arrangements to find the alternatives least detrimental to the welfare of the child.

The Role of the Pediatrician

Even though the period leading up to a divorce may be difficult to detect, the pediatrician should be cognizant of subtle manifestations and become involved as soon as he or she becomes aware of serious marital discord. Although knowledge of the mother, who brings the child to the office, will ordinarily be greater than knowledge of the father, the pediatrician should establish close rapport with the child and both parents.

Because the pediatrician usually possesses much relevant information concerning the child since birth, and is aware of the family situation, his or her counsel will be sought and accepted. The parents may request their pediatrician's opinion concerning the effects of the impending separation and divorce upon the physical and emotional status of their child. They may request guidance about revealing the arrangements to the child. The pediatrician should advise the parents of the child's need for reliability and predictability in the custody arrangements and should emphasize the need for regularity in the visitations with the absent parent. Encouraging parental cooperation on behalf of the child's interests, the pediatrician should dissuade the parents from using the child as a pawn in the marital strife.

By considering primarily the child's needs and feelings, the pediatrician acts as the child's advocate. If a child's basic physical or emotional disturbance appears to be based on problems of family relations, the pediatrician will need to bring out these issues in an attempt to relieve the stresses placed upon the child. Pediatricians should be aware of the effects of marital discord and divorce upon the physical health of children and should attempt to identify the causes before instituting therapy.

A young child may be brought by a parent, or an older child may come directly, to the pediatrician to discuss problems with physical, behavioral, emotional, social, or developmental manifestations. A pediatrician who does not feel comfortable working with the child's presenting complaints or who feels consultation is needed should assist the family to accept a referral to an appropriate community resource, such as a family counseling service. However, divorce itself is not a reason for a child to be in therapy; the need is less likely if the custodial parent is effective, if the absent parent maintains a good relationship with the child, and if the hostilities between the parents are minimal or cease soon after the divorce.

The pediatrician's goal in working with children of divorce is to maximize the children's adjustment in the critical period following the separation, when most children are very vulnerable and struggling with feelings of being abandoned. Later, the pediatrician can help the children accept the reality of the divorce and give up their hopes of reconciliation between their parents.

42 Incest

by Richard M. Sarles

Incest occurs far more often than is generally believed. It seldom occurs in emotionally sound families and usually represents a serious breakdown of normal individual and family functioning. It is of interest, however, that in certain rural areas of our country incestuous behavior is not looked upon with great disdain and thus the family pathology is often not as severe.

Incest is defined as a sexual act occurring between two persons so closely related that marriage is prohibited by law. This definition is broadened in many areas to include adopted children and stepchildren. A sexual act generally means an overt action by one partner with a sexual intent ranging from physical fondling to genital contact and/or intercourse. Although this definition technically includes prepubertal sex play between siblings, clear-cut evidence of genital sexual intent is usually lacking and curiosity remains as the motivating force in this preadolescent age group.

In normal psychological development children about the age of 4 to 6½ years show strong attachments to the parent of the opposite sex and competitive feelings toward the parent of the same sex. These feelings when recognized by parents are often considered as a cute and nonthreatening passing phase. This stage of psychological development, called the Oedipal period, generally recurs in early adolescence. At this time, however, sexual feelings are present, owing, in part, to the hormonal changes of puberty. Thus, psychologically the stage for potential incestuous relationships exists. Sexual thoughts about one's parents are very frightening and are generally pushed out of conscious awareness. Sexual thoughts between brothers and sisters are not uncommon and are apparently less threatening. Normally, the adolescent transfers those feelings and thoughts to members of the opposite sex outside the family. In addition, the parents resist any seductive behavior on the part of their children and suppress their own incestuous feelings. However, in the emotionally troubled family the normal sociocultural taboo breaks down, allowing incestuous relationships to take place.

Incest is one of the few taboos found in almost every culture, yet its occurrence is amply recorded throughout history. Estimates of the incidence of incest range from 1.1 cases per million population to 4 percent of an unselected psychiatric patient population. The figures are generally considered to reflect a grossly low estimate by those professionals currently in clinical practice and those interested in the area of sexual abuse. These figures may be influenced by the physician's lack of awareness of the problem of incest or a reluctance to become involved in a difficult psychosocial issue. It also may reflect the families' need to keep secret the incestuous relationship due to the sociocultural prohibitions.

Father-daughter incest is most frequently reported and studied. There are indications, however, that brother-sister incestuous relationships are far more common, but do not come to the attention of the authorities. A birth rate of twice the number of infants from brother-sister relationships as from father-daughter incestuous unions seems to add credence to this assumption. Mother-son incest is rare. It is so uncommon, and the taboo so great, that when it does occur it usually represents severe psychopathology or psychosis in one or both partners.

A striking feature of many incestuous relationships is that the affair is often common knowledge to many family members. Such a relationship may exist for several years and even be passed from oldest to youngest daughter. Yet seldom does the problem of incest become overtly visible to the physician. In contrast to child abuse cases, in incest there are no visible physical signs which could alert relatives, neighbors, friends, or school authorities, and furthermore the parents seldom seek help and, in fact, condone and keep secret the incestuous behavior. The relationship often becomes known when an event extraneous to the incest causes the daugher or a sibling to use the incestuous relationship as a weapon to achieve revenge or power or when signs of depression appear in the girl. Increasing awareness of social taboos and the consolidation of personal values (a superego) during adolescence lead to feelings of guilt and depression in some of these girls.

Often the teenager will develop symptoms of irritability, fatigue, change in appetite, sleep disturbances, and school difficulties. These are often the signs of depression in children and adolescents. Suicidal behavior, even the most superficial gesture, should be taken as a serious warning sign that the more adaptive coping mechanisms of the adolescent are weakening.

Conversion symptoms are relatively common in adolescents. They are generally felt to be means of communicating some underlying conflict or an expression of a symbolic wish or fear. Clues are often hidden in the organ system chosen for the conversion symptom, although this does not occur in all cases. For instance, symptoms in the genitourinary system may be specific for conflicts in a sexual area, and chest pains (breast pain) in the female may also indicate sexual concerns.

The primary care physician should consider incestuous relationships when formulating a differential diagnosis in cases of suspected conversion symptoms, depression, or suicidal behavior. The recognition that incest is far more common than we suspect may allow physicians to pursue investigation of possible incest as they would a case of venereal disease, alcoholism, or delinquency.

Questions pertaining to age of menarche, regularity of menstrual periods, contraception, and sexual experiences are commonly asked when acquiring a medical history from a teenage girl. In conjunction with these questions the physician could ask whether her brother, father, or other close relative has ever made sexual advances toward her. This particular question often evokes indignation or protest from the teenager. It is helpful to reply that incestuous behavior is far more common than generally realized and that adolescents involved in such relationships are often troubled but unable to seek help or talk about their feelings. This honest answer usually conveys interest to the adolescent and a willingness of the professional to investigate and discuss any and all issues.

The openness and comfort on the part of the primary care physician generally helps the patient involved in an incestuous relationship feel more at ease and less guilty. It also makes the teenager aware that a helping professional suspects the problem and is not "shocked" or frightened away. If the physician is unwilling to discuss (or unaware of) the problem, the adolescent may interpret the avoidance as a sign that the subject is so taboo that even professionals cannot talk about it. This avoidance inadvertently reinforces the invest taboo and leaves the teenager with no opportunity for relief and help.

In most cases of incest the primary care physician should seek consultation with those professionals interested in behavioral issues of childhood and adolescence, such as child psychiatrists, child psychologists, behavioral pediatricians, and social workers. In many states cases of incest are considered sexual abuse and are incorporated with child abuse under protective services for children. Therefore, primary care physicians should be aware of the laws in their state. The consultant should be expected to perform a thorough psychosocial evaluation of the family and the involved child and recommend an appropriate treatment plan.

Treatment is usually difficult. Removal of the father or the girl from the home provides only temporary relief. Incarceration of the father offers little hope of rehabilitation for the father and may deprive the family of financial support. Group or individual psychotherapy for the girl may help to reduce feelings of guilt and shame and refocus her sexual behavior toward more appropriate partners outside the home. Direct supportive counseling for the mother often has a powerful effect in restructuring the family in that it helps the mother set up appropriate limits and boundaries for herself, her husband, and her daughters.

The long-term prognosis for girls involved in incestuous relationships is unclear. The primary care physician is often the first professional to become aware of the incest problem and can provide long-term follow-up and liaison to the consultants during the primary care of the family.

43 | Adoption

by Marshall D. Schechter

History

The most effective and universal method of providing parents for parentless children and for providing children for childless couples has been adoption. Generally in most countries of the world (until as late as the 1930s), common law governed the practice of adoption and the rights of the child, the biological parents, and the adoptive parents. In many countries it was only recently that the adopted child could partake in the estate of the adoptive parents on the same basis as children born to the parents. In the 1940s and 1950s social agencies in the United States (besides of course looking for personal, social, and economic stability) insisted that the adoptive father be no older than 42 and the adoptive mother no older than 38. However, with increased use of birth control methods, legalization of abortion, and many unwed mothers electing to keep their children, shifts have occurred in adoption practice. Currently there is a marked push for adoption of the older child and the handicapped child and for interracial adoption (since these children represent the preponderant adoptive pool), and adoptions are being legalized for older parents and single female and male adopters. Recognizing that good parenting is not a function of a family's financial status, a number of foresighted agencies have arranged monetary subsidies to maintain economically depressed homes. There is *no* question that adoption is the most satisfactory way of caring for parentless children, particularly in contrast to the orphanages still in existence in many areas of the world. Attesting to the lasting quality of adoption as a societal institution are the personal histories of many, including Sargon of Babylon (circa 2500 B.C.) and Moses, the lawgiver of the Israelites. In contrast to past customs, it is now felt that every child should have the opportunity for family living and that in this country, adoption practice should have as its prime function the well-being of the child.

Practice

This presentation will deal only with those children placed with nonrelatives, or extrafamilial adoptees. When children have one remaining parent with whom they stay and adoption proceedings occur to legalize the relationship to a new parent through marriage—an intrafamilial adoption—those children have to overcome the loss of attachment to the lost (separated, deceased) parent, but at least they still have one stable object tie. About one-half of all recorded adoptions in the United States are of the intrafamilial type.

Generally there are three major participants involved in an extrafamilial adoption procedure: the child, the biological parents, and the adoptive parents. Incidental to the proceedings are social agencies, the courts, attorneys, physicians, and the extended families of the adults directly involved.

About 90 percent of the children placed for an extrafamilial adoption are from out-of-wedlock pregnancies, and therefore one major participant is often a single woman unsupported by the putative father or her own family. She frequently carries the stigma of her out-of-wedlock pregnancy in the same fashion as detailed in Hawthorne's *Scarlet Letter*, and the child so born is the inheritor of the mother's "sins."

The emotional stresses during the pregnancy and immediately postnatally are extraordinarily intense. Pressures from within herself and from outside individuals to consider adoptive placement are very evident, and the time to consider alternative options is slight. One of the major values of a social agency involvement at this time is to provide adequate counseling of the biological mother and to secure a proper surrender agreement if her decision is for adoptive placement. Although there is no evidence that independent adoptions have greater problems attendant than agency-arranged adoptions, legal battles over custody are less frequent in the latter circumstance. There is currently little built into the adoption procedures to provide the biological mother (or the putative father) with any opportunity to work through her feelings about giving up her child and to clarify for her in any sense how this child ultimately develops.

Couples (or now single individuals) applying to agencies for adoption face varying degrees or types of investigations. The major objective is to assess the capability of the prospective adoptive parents to provide adequate and competent parenting for the healthy (physical and emotional) development of the child. Unfortunately, predictive capabilities by any means are limited, and therefore determinations of parenting adequacy can be at best only cross-sectional at the time of the adoption proceedings and usually represent primarily an opinion as to the capability of the adoptive applicants to care for an infant.

Problems of adoptive parents are complex indeed: They are generally older than couples having their first biologic child (10.5 years versus 2.5 years after marriage); they have had to modify their own body image and recognize and accept their lack of fertility; and they have often undergone major physical examinations, and when these have proved negative, it has been suggested to them that unconsciously they did not want to conceive. Furthermore, they do not have the same familial supports as biological parents or the awareness of fetal development during the 9 months of a pregnancy; they are dependent upon judgments of others to have a child, which generally is a private decision between husband and wife; they are subject to criticism and advice from others as to how to raise "someone else's child"; they need to tell the child at some time that he or she was delivered of a different parent; they must live with the unresolved questions about the genealogical background of the child; and they may have the potentially anxiety-producing experience of

seeing their adopted child go in search of the biologic parents.

The infant available for adoption faces a number of hurdles, including inadequate and delayed prenatal care; undue maternal stresses related to the mother's and society's attitudes about out-of-wedlock pregnancies; the separation from the biologic parent and placement for varying periods of time in a foster situation until ultimately settling into the adoptive home; and the possible problems of fitting in with a family whose circadian rhythms might be quite divergent from the child's. The older adoptive child needs to deal with the losses of the past, integrate into a new setting, form new attachments with the adoptive parents, and in cases of interracial adoptions, resolve problems of identification. All adopted children must also settle the questions about their genealogical and genetic heritage and often face difficult doubts about why they were given up in the first place.

The laws of the states vary in a number of respects. All of them, however, call for sealing the original birth certificate and reissuing a new one with the adoptive parents' name on it, and all give adoptive parents the right to return the child to the agency if a congenital or undetected defect is discovered anywhere from 2 to 5 years after adoption. Some states require little or no waiting period between placement and finalization of adoption, while other states make it a necessity for a year to pass with constant social work supervision. A few states will permit adoptions only through recognized adoption agencies, but most states allow independent as well as agency adoptions. In states where independent adoptions are acceptable, attorneys and physicians involved must be particularly cautious about getting surrender papers from the biological mother. In all cases there needs to be a thorough investigation of the child's genetic background.

Areas of Concern

Infant psychological testing has proved equivocal at best. Therefore, despite some of the vaunted claims, matching child to parents other than in the most general terms is difficult. This is especially a problem since the genetic basis for schizophrenia as worked out by Kety and Rosenthal on monozygotic twins placed for adoption emphasizes the need to be far more careful in the discovery of the background of the biological parents. Also, it would be of help for the adoptive family and the adoptee to know of other familial diseases.

There is evidence that adoptees may be more represented in psychiatric clinics and practices than their percentage in the general population would suggest. There appears to be an excessive degree of aggressive and sexual acting out, and some workers have felt that there is an increase in minimal cerebral dysfunction with consequent learning disabilities in adopted children.

When and what to tell the child about being adopted has been debated for a considerable time. There is no doubt that children could react negatively to this information if they understood fully its meaning and if they were told at an age when their ties to their adopted parents were especially shaky. Because of the concern that children may hear of their adoptive status from someone outside the family, adoption agencies worldwide have advocated telling the child early and often about being adopted. This has been likened to the allergist theories of giving sufficient frequent small doses of the toxic substance so that when the full exposure occurred, anaphylactic shock would not ensue. Most of the time this information is shared when the child is so young that the words are often meaningless. As an extreme example, one social worker, as she handed a 5-day-old infant to its adoptive mother, told the mother to include the word "adopted" as early as possible, suggesting that the new mother rock the child to sleep saying, "Go to sleep my darling *adopted* baby." As with other words in any language, the meaning is more often derived from the affect present when the word is said; thus the interpretation of the meaning of the word "adopted" can shift and change according to the child's knowledge and experience at different ages. For instance, a 7-year-old girl who had heard the word all her life but had never before asked its meaning began to mourn for her mommy who "borned her." This same girl when 15 years of age was uncomfortable with the word "adopted" because at that time it represented to her out-of-wedlock birth.

Adolescence is a time when the fantasy of being adopted is ubiquitous. In most people this fantasy serves the purpose of helping teenagers separate more easily psychologically from their parents, but the basic identifications and familial connections are reconstituted later. In the adoptee, however, there is indeed another set of parents with whom a connection has been interrupted but who represent a very real but unknown family tie. The question of where they belong serves as a fantasy base (particularly in those adopted shortly after birth) from which an active search sometimes then occurs. This is painful to the adoptive parents, who fear the loss of love of the child they have reared. It is especially difficult for the adoptee who has to overcome the legal hurdles of the sealed birth certificate, and the probable change in the last name of their biological mother even if they can find the original birth certificate. The biological parents most often have psychologically "sealed over" the event of giving up their child and developed a life-style which precludes the adoptee from reentry. A number of recent books, television plays, and newspaper articles have presented poignant views of the problems encountered by each of the participants to the adoption procedure.

Suggested Solutions

The American Medical Association's handbook on mental retardation lists being born out of wedlock within the group of conditions leading to high-risk infants. Some of these difficulties could perhaps be ameliorated if proper prenatal care was sought very early in the pregnancy. The physician should be a force in the community to help change societal attitudes to permit the acceptance of this most human condition rather than continuing to condemn and isolate the woman who is pregnant out of wedlock. Many school systems are now allowing school-age pregnant (married and unmarried) women to continue in their regular neighborhood schools to finish their education.

Although the economic stability of adoptive homes should be considered, as should other factors of major importance, consideration should be given to monetarily helping particularly loving and capable parents to adopt children even if they might not at the time of placement pass a financial test. There needs to occur a decrease in the length of time from application for adoption until placement of a child. Interracial adoption should be sponsored if adequate homes (supported psychologically and economically) within the ethnic background of the child cannot be found.

Adoption agencies should be encouraged to give

continued help to the adoption participants up through the adult years of the adoptee. A registry (as operative in California in 1976) for adoptees who wish to find their biological parents and for biological parents who wish to find their child placed for adoption should be established, allowing in this fashion a mutual neutral exchange and protecting all the parties simultaneously. Some countries have passed laws requiring the birth certificate to be automatically opened when the adoptee is 18 years of age. This might be a solution here in this country, but one must think about the rights of the biological and adoptive parents as well. The registry concept might be a more reasonable approach. Adoptees have the right to know something of their heritage, including their ethnic, religious, socioeconomic, and educational background. They also deserve to know of any familial illness to which they or their own children could be subject. The telling of being adopted is best done during the latency phase of development (6 to 10 years of age), during which time psychological conflict states are generally least likely to occur.

Studies should be undertaken with adoptees who do not present psychiatric symptoms to help us understand better how to handle this "experimental group" in our society. From self reports it appears that even those individuals who did not have primary or overwhelming psychiatric illnesses still felt their lives were markedly different because they were adopted. It is not a failure of adoptive parenting if adoptees look for their biological parents, nor is it a sign of deeply hidden conflicts if they do not. Adoptees, like all people, are unique and special, and they should have the opportunity to search and find, if they so desire, their genealogical roots.

Families frequently turn to the physician for help in understanding the child's conflicts within the framework of the developmental stage the child is in. Therefore the pediatrician can be of inestimable help in diagnosing behavioral and emotional problems and giving advice, often in a primary preventative fashion, regarding the handling of the adoptee's specific developmental tasks. This would include the timing and methods of telling of adoption since each child's needs are so individual. More particularly, the physician can help the adoptive parents deal with feelings about their lack of fecundity and can help the adoptive child deal with feelings about having been given up for adoption. This capacity to bring parents and child together at an emotional level can serve as a most powerful base to ameliorate problems.

44 | Foster Care

by Oscar C. Stine

Foster care is the child welfare service which provides substitute living arrangements for children whose natural families cannot carry out their child-rearing responsibilities and which provides services to rehabilitate families. The complex system of foster care comprises foster family care, institutional care, and children's group homes and shelters. In 1976, an estimated 450,000 children in the United States received foster care services; nearly four-fifths of these children were living in foster family homes in their communities.

Historically, the 1930 White House Conference on Children and Youth established the principle of family care for homeless children. The conference adopted a "Children's Charter" which declared that every child is entitled to a home, and the love and security provided by a home. Child welfare agencies began actively to seek adoptive parents for orphans and foster parents for the temporarily homeless.

Over the years, however, foster care has changed radically. Conceived as a service to meet the basic needs of temporarily displaced children, the foster care system is now confronted with handling the complex emotional and physical problems of the children entrusted to its care. Today nearly half of the children in foster care have been placed there because of parental neglect, abuse, or exploitation. Among other reasons for placements are situational crises, child behavior problems, physical and mental handicaps, psychiatric and physical illnesses of parents and children, marital difficulties, socioeconomic problems, illegitimacy, and abandonment.

Although out-of-home care may be handled informally by the parents, child placement usually is arranged by public or private child welfare agencies delegated by state law to provide these services for children and their families. Children enter foster care either through application by a parent or guardian to a child placement agency or subsequent to removal from their parents' custody by court order.

Alternative Planning to Foster Placement

A primary goal of all child welfare services is to preserve and strengthen the integrity of the parent-child relationship. Therefore, prior to making the crucial decision to separate children from their natural families, every effort should be made to provide services to enable children to be cared for in their own homes. Community resources, including day care, homemaker and caretaker services, financial assistance, protective services, and health and mental health services, should be made available to meet identifiable needs and problems of the children and their families. For example, if a mother needs hospitalization and has no one to care for her children, the children may be placed in one or more foster family homes or in a children's shelter until the mother is able to resume her parenting responsibilities. In more enlightened communities, the newest resource for families is caretaker service. Available 24 hours a day, the caretaker is trained to meet the needs of children within their own homes. Thus, the children must cope with the absence of their mother, but are not forced to adjust to new living arrangements.

Types of Foster Care

Alternative forms of foster care have evolved: foster family homes, group homes, shelters, and institutions. The selection of a specific type of foster care should be based on a psychosocial assessment of the child and the family situation, the reasons necessitating placement, and the agency's plan for services to provide stability of care for the child.

In a family-centered society, the closest approximation to the nuclear family environment is a foster family home. Implicit is a belief that children must experience continuity and stability in their relationship to their natural parents or, alternatively, to foster parents in order to achieve healthy emotional and physical growth. Because of a reluctance to care for the more "difficult" children, special foster family homes are being recruited for infants and handicapped children, emotionally disturbed youngsters, mentally retarded children, teenagers, and minority-group children.

Group home care in the community uniquely combines aspects of family life and group living. Small, selected groups of children and youth live with the child care staff. Some children, especially teenagers, find more security in the routine of well-ordered group care than with an isolated foster family.

Other children who cannot meet the demands and expectations of family living may be better served by institutional care. The physical facilities provide the security of a stable living arrangement. The institutional program offers the possibility of creating a therapeutic environment by coordinating the child's daily living situation, education, and clinical services. For children whose behavior cannot be tolerated in a family or community or whose problems cannot be treated while living in a family situation, the placement of choice may be the small institution with sufficient qualified personnel to give the children individual attention.

Children's shelters usually provide short-term care. Among the services offered by shelters are immediate protection and care for neglected and abused children; interim care for children, especially sibling-groups, displaced from their families during a crisis situation; and interim care for children who cannot remain in their homes during their wait for other foster placements. Specialized shelters provide comprehensive psychosocial evaluations of children and their families to facilitate appropriate disposition planning. In some communities, shelters provide respite care for families with the responsibilities of caring for children handicapped with physical disabilities, emotional problems, and mental retardation. Successful shelters usually are small with a trained child care staff and adequate appropriations to meet the children's needs.

The Dynamics of Foster Care

The decision that brings children into foster care breaks whatever continuity they have experienced with their own parents, no matter how tenuous that relationship may have been. However, when a child's emotional or physical well-being is believed to be in jeopardy, or when efforts to provide care in the home have been unsuccessful, separation of the child from the parents is justified. This crucial decision of the court places the child in the custody of the local child welfare agency. The decision for child placement should not be an end in itself, but a planned intervention to encourage change in the family situation.

Foster care services have the dual purpose of providing care to meet the needs of the displaced children and treating the social and emotional problems of the children and their parents that precipitated the out-of-home placement. To meet these objectives, the foster care agency must work in collaboration with the foster parents and child care personnel in group homes and institutions and with the multidisciplinary professionals—physician, psychologist, social worker, teacher, lawyer—involved in the efforts to rehabilitate the family.

The emphasis in foster care should be on the early identification of the children for whom restoration of custody to their parents is a realistic goal. Planning and case management should focus on stabilizing and strengthening the family by offering casework services to help change the parents' behavior and attitudes that impair their ability to nurture and protect their children. The rehabilitative plan should specify the services to be provided by the child welfare agency, supplemented by appropriate community resources, and detail the requisite improvements to be made by the natural parents within a specific time period. Most of the children who will leave foster care to return to their parents' care will do so within the first year after placement.

In child placement, complex new relationships demand major adjustments for the displaced children, members of the biological family, and members of the foster family. It is the responsibility of the foster care worker to sensitively facilitate these adjustments.

The Foster Parents

There is more to foster parenting than providing temporary care for displaced children. The uniqueness and complexity of foster parenthood require adjustments in the foster parents' lives to juggle three tasks simultaneously: fulfilling the needs of the new children in their families, maintaining a cooperative and coordinated relationship with the foster care agency, and establishing a working relationship with the biological parents.

Prospective foster parents undergo an investigation of their family lives by the child welfare agency. Ideally, the foster parents must demonstrate their ability to provide an understanding and nurturing environment for needy children and their willingness to relinquish the children upon the agency's request. Realistically, the incentives to accept the challenge of foster family care range from philanthropic to egoistic motives.

Without training and supervision, and altruistic motivation, the attitudes and actions of the foster parents may not provide a rehabilitative experience to meet the children's needs. Foster parents often feel frustrated and overwhelmed in their efforts to help the children entrusted to their care. Although they want the children to feel secure and content in their new homes, the foster parents may not know how to form meaningful relationships. They often feel threatened by the possibility of rejection and the reality of relinquishment. They may try to establish the parent-child bond through control and posessiveness. When the children do not meet their expectations, the foster parents may use subtle or overt threats of abandonment to enforce their compliance. When the foster parents experience feelings of failure in their parenting efforts, they may link the children's problematic behavior to their biological past and disown any responsibility for it. Although essential to a satisfactory adjustment to placement, foster parents vary in their willingness and ability to deal realistically with the children's past.

An ongoing relationship between the children and their biological parents must be maintained whenever the children are expected to return to their parents' care. The presence of the biological parents often complicates the foster parents' attempts to help the children and to cooperate with the agency. The children's behavior and functioning may worsen temporarily as a result of the parents' visits. This may result from the children's unrealistic comparison of and attempt to manipulate the foster parents and natural parents.

It is difficult for most foster parents to feel comfortable with the parents who have emotionally or physically abused and neglected their children. However, the foster parents can be helped to understand that frequently the biological parents' problems with rearing their children originated in their own traumatic childhood experiences and that they are repeating similar destructive child-rearing practices with their own children. Having unmet dependency needs, the parents need nurturing themselves by adults before they can give appropriate care and protection to their children. Foster parents at least have the opportunity to serve as a model for effective parenting.

Because foster care workers often are overburdened with heavy case loads, new modes of involvement of foster parents in the child welfare system have established the partnership concept. Working in close cooperation with the foster care worker and other professionals, the foster parents are involved in assessing the children's needs and problems and in carrying out the recommended therapeutic interventions in the home. Child welfare agencies are providing formal training and on-going supervision for the foster parents in a concerted effort to upgrade foster family care to the status of a professional child care service.

The Children in Placement

Separation from their natural parents is a traumatic experience for the children. Usually confused about the reasons necessitating the placement, they feel guilty about unknown transgressions and unloved and abandoned by their families. Perceiving themselves as unwanted children, they feel ashamed and angry to be placed in the care of strangers.

Overwhelmed by feelings of despair and loneliness, children respond to the separation in a manner that is analogous to a mourning experience. They must work through these feelings to resolve their grief before they can risk forming new relationships.

The new family environment poses threats to the children's identity and adaptations to everyday living. Fearing further abandonment, the children feel forced to change their behavior and attitudes to meet the expectations of the foster parents, who now have the power to give or withhold affection and care. Engulfed in confusion over identity, searching for a sense of belonging, and experiencing conflicts of loyalty, the children test out every aspect of the new situation to learn guidelines for their behavior and boundaries for their new relationships.

The quality of the children's relationships with their biological parents affects their response to accepting new attachments. If the children have experienced past nurturing relationships and have been helped to handle their feelings about the separation, they may risk forming new relationships with empathetic adults.

However, if the past parenting experiences have been tenuous and conflictual, the children may respond with distrust, indifference, and withdrawal or show overt hostility and rebelliousness in protesting a situation thrust upon them. Although the children desperately want relief from their suffering and the security of a nurturing environment, they establish emotional barriers to defend against the possibility of further rejection and loss.

Children who have difficulties in forming new attachments have the greatest need for continuing contacts with their natural parents. Parental visitations arouse the often repressed feelings about separation and help the children deal with their grief, protect their family ties until they can establish new relationships, and give them opportunities to view and compare realistically their relationships with all the adults in their lives.

Children experiencing serious attachment difficulties require intensive rehabilitative services, including psychotherapy, to help in their adjustment to foster placement. However, if the child does not develop healthy relationships with the foster family and neighborhood peers during professional intervention, the agency may use the observation of the professional to evaluate the foster care plan. The out-of-home placement may not be in the children's

best interests, and other arrangements for child care must be devised.

The Natural Parents

Although there are many stressful life situations for which child placement is the appropriate intervention, most parents experience feelings of failure, inadequacy, helplessness, guilt, and shame whenever this action takes place. These overwhelming feelings are present regardless of the reasons necessitating foster care and reflect society's stigma attached to abdicating the parenting role. The parents may be victimized by criticism and withdraw from adult contacts.

Separated from their children, the parents must cope with feelings of depression accompanying their loss. They experience anxiety that their children will not be returned to their care when they feel ready to resume their parenting responsibilities. Also, they fear that their children will reject them and not wish to return to their own home. The parents may experience the loss of other meaningful relationships, such as the breakup of the marriage, after the children have entered placement.

The natural parents often are shown far less attention than the children and the foster parents by the foster care workers. One explanation for the neglect of the natural parents in the foster care triad is the lack of agency commitment to the goal of restoration of the children to their parents' care.

Realistically, establishing working relationships with the natural parents may be difficult. There may be a multiplicity of complex problems requiring interdisciplinary action: health problems, psychological disorders, marital difficulties, unemployment, and financial problems. The parents may be fearful of exposing themselves to professionals and reticent to make the recommended changes in their behavior and attitudes. Even if they are willing to accept professional help, the community resources may not be available to provide the intensive rehabilitative services needed by the parents to make the requisite improvements within a specific time period.

Without firm agency commitment to require the parents to achieve the level of functioning deemed necessary for the return of their children or, alternatively, to press for termination of parental custody, the foster care workers are reluctant to make decisions and thus risk trapping the children in unplanned long-term placements.

Health Care of Foster Children

The problems associated with foster care frequently are brought to the attention of the physician. The majority of displaced children will experience some emotional, behavioral, developmental, or physical manifestations. With an understanding of the ramifications of child placement, the physician can help the children cope with their feelings and make adjustments to the changes in their lives.

All displaced children respond to the separation from their natural parents, irrespective of the quality of the relationship, with an experience analogous to mourning. In response to their loss, the children's feelings are expressed in anger and protest, deep despair, and helplessness. To successfully work through their feelings of grief, the children need an emotionally accepting atmosphere which allows them to freely express their feelings. With empathetic understanding by adults, the children may be able to adjust to their new environment in a brief period of time and begin to risk making new attachments. However, failure to complete the mourning process may have serious immediate and future consequences on the children's functioning. The unresolved grief feelings may be expressed in maladaptive behaviors, may exacerbate reactions to future losses, and may adversely affect the ability to form meaningful relationships.

Children's response to separation is related to their age and stage of development. Young children may experience the loss of previously achieved developmental milestones. They may lose control over toilet training, show speech difficulties, and develop eating and sleeping problems. Outgoing and independent youngsters may become whining, clinging, and demanding. Some children may regress to the more serious withdrawal behaviors, such as mutism and autism.

Older children react with a spectrum of responses including distrust, indifference, withdrawal, and overt hostility. Angry with the adults manipulating their lives and fearing further rejection, they struggle against a sense of helplessness and hopelessness. They may provoke unwary adults to reach out to relieve their suffering only to instigate an argument to show their power to reject. They may protest by rebelliousness in the home and acting-out behavior in the community. School problems, such as poor academic performance, disobedience, day-dreaming, and truancy, may emerge or worsen.

Children placed outside their parental homes have great difficulty coping with the negative feelings aroused by their new status of foster children. They feel stigmatized, and unfortunately, this feeling may be reinforced by their teachers, the parents of friends, and other adults in their lives. They feel ashamed to be rejected and abandoned by their parents; these feelings lower their self-esteem and make them more vulnerable to stress. They lose their self-confidence and face daily living with heightened anxieties and fears.

Frequently, the children feel guilty that they are responsible, for unknown reasons, for their "misfortune" and view the placement as punishment. Apart from their families, they feel that their identity is threatened and fear annihilation. They are caught up in conflicts over loyalty and belonging to two families. They often develop an idealized view of their natural parents and are unable to gain a realistic perspective without continuing contacts.

Unable to cope with their feelings and adjust to the placement, the children may resort to a variety of maladaptive behaviors. They may insulate themselves against further rejection by remaining aloof. They may deny their own identity and develop a pseudoidentity tailored to their foster parents' expectations. They may withdraw to an earlier state of dependency in order to hold on to their family ties. They may become depressed, run away, or commit self-destructive acts.

Although some children enter foster care due to situational crises and parental incapabilities, the majority enter because of abuse, neglect, physical and mental handicaps, and behavior problems. Children's responses to forming new attachments during their placements depend upon their past parenting experiences. Some children may so idealize their families that they reject any surrogate parents. Other children, afraid of further abandonment, are unable to form trusting relationships. Abused and neglected children, who have had conflictual, inconsistent, and unpredictable parenting, may continue to independently meet their own needs. Some deprived children may accept nurturing as a new experience in their lives. When the relationships with the natural parents have been satisfying, the children may form new attachments with the anticipation that they too will be fulfilling.

The physician has the opportunity to become the foster children's confidant, adviser, and advocate. Reassured that the physician is an accepting and understanding listener who will protect their privacy, children may be able to verbalize their anxieties, fears, and feelings. By helping foster children understand that they are not totally responsible for the separation, the physician may be able to put the placement in the proper perspective and relieve the children's guilt feelings; preschool children fantasize their power over happenings in their lives and need reassurance about the events necessitating the placement. Foster children need to discuss how their new living situation affects their lives. With the physician's assistance, the children may be better able to handle their ambivalent feelings toward their natural parents and their foster parents. As a trusted adviser, the physician has the opportunity to help the children understand how their feelings affect their behavior and how to change maladaptive behavior, and thus facilitate the children's adjustment to the realities of the placement situation. However, the physician has the responsibility to investigate the children's complaints about misunderstandings and maltreatment. Acting as the children's advocate, the physician must insist that the agency reevaluate the foster placement to determine whether the children's needs are being met and rights are being protected.

The physician offers valuable services to foster parents by helping them understand the children's specific needs and problems, and establish more optimal conditions for their emotional development. The physician's understanding and empathy may be crucial to assisting the foster parents in providing nurturance to children frequently damaged by their past relationships and resistive to adjusting to new living arrangements.

The natural parents may consult the physician prior to making the decision to place their children. The physician's knowledge and evaluation of the family situation may be very important in the decision making. Some parents may need support to be able to follow through with the best planning for the children. If the children are placed, either voluntarily or by court order, the physician should help the parents handle their feelings of depression, guilt, and shame, resulting from a sense of failure.

The physician offering care to foster children needs an understanding of the local child welfare agency which is responsible for arranging and paying for the children's medical care. Foster care workers need to work closely with the physician to meet the health needs of the children. The primary care physician who does not feel adequate to handle some of the presenting emotional and behavior problems should help the agency worker with the necessary referral to a community mental health facility.

The Foster Care Crisis

The foster care system in our nation is in the midst of a growing crisis. Foster care services have focused primarily on providing substitute living arrangements for children rather than emphasizing supportive and supplemental services to rehabilitate families and reduce the need for child placements. Broad circumstances are crippling the agencies' efforts: a rising child population with an increasing number of children in need of foster care, an increasing number of family breakdowns, a severe shortage of professional social workers in the child welfare field, a grave shortage of qualified foster parents, an overcrowding in residential facilities, a lack of appropriations for essential community services, and a strong resistance in communities to accepting foster children and meeting their needs.

Accompanying the increased use of foster care services are the accelerated costs of providing that care. In 1976, the cost of providing 1 year of foster care for a child in New York City ranged from $5000 to $13,000, depending upon the type of placement. The least costly substitute living arrangement is the foster family home. Unfortunately, state subsidies to foster parents tend to be uniformly low and often do not cover the actual outlays to support the children. To ease the shortage of qualified foster family homes, it is recommended that, in addition to increasing the subsidies, a salary be given to foster mothers. Providing a salary would be consistent with the trend to make the foster parents partners with the child welfare agency.

Partially as a result of an ineffective system, the number of children in foster care annually has increased while the number of adoptive placements has been declining. It is estimated that 50 to 80 percent of the children have been caught in the revolving door of foster care, spending year after year of their childhoods shunted from one foster home to another, or waiting hopelessly in institutions. For these children, temporary foster care has become a permanent way of life.

There are at least three somewhat distinct groups of children who become the long-term-care case load of a foster care agency. One group is formed by those who come into foster care as teenagers. A second group includes severely mentally or physically handicapped children who are usually unadoptable. The third, less distinct group of children are those who have drifted into a situation of long-term care but are at a "point of no return" to their biological families.

Frequently, this long-term care has been an outcome of drifting into out-of-home placements without the benefit of purposeful planning consistent with the goal of providing maximum stability of care for each child in foster care. Decision making which is time-limited and goal-directed would counter the present unplanned drift of children in placement. Child welfare agencies must decide within a definite time period that the children will be returned to their own parents or be freed from parental custody and placed for adoption through court action. In instances in which neither of these alternatives is possible, a plan for permanent foster care should be developed and legally formalized with the foster parents who will be providing the continuing care.

Profound questions of political and moral philosophy surround the parents' rights–child's rights dilemma and the issues of the proper relationship of children to their family and the family to the state. The pendulum now seems to be swinging more in the direction of the rights of children, and in the context of foster care, this change emerges as an increased concern that children have the opportunity for stable parental relationships.

45 | Legal Issues in Child Health Care

by Adele D. Hofmann

The law is much more than a thorny, cumbersome, and sometimes irritating set of rules and regulations which we must all obey lest we risk being hauled into court. Rather, the law should be seen as a definition of individual rights, interpersonal relationships, and mutual responsibilities in the service of fairness and social order. As such it offers significant potential for enhancing the physician's therapeutic armamentarium in the fullest sense.

The purpose of this section is to provide a rational basis for understanding some of the specific legal concerns in providing health care to the young, both within the confines of the medical transaction itself and in advocating for patient's rights in other spheres. Omitting adoption, foster care, and child abuse, which are dealt with elsewhere in this text, those issues will be addressed which are either commonly encountered or set forth as significant principles in the delivery of health care to children and adolescents.

It is essential to keep in mind that answers to legal questions are rarely simple or straightforward. Laws governing the same matter may differ markedly from state to state. Moreover, a particular statute may be vague or ambiguous, rendering interpretation difficult. Past court decisions, governmental agency guidelines, rulings by such authorities as state attorneys general, constitutional considerations, and even common and customary practice—all may also affect what the law in fact may be. It can be difficult, at times, for health care professionals, used to seeking truth through a shared and collaborative effort, to grasp this adversarial and multifaceted nature of the law. The assistance of an attorney should always be sought when the course to be taken is not clear.

Definitions

The Right to Treatment

Recent years have seen a growing commitment to the concept that every individual is just as entitled to health care as to food and shelter. There is, however, no specific legislative or constitutional endowment to this effect covering all citizens, and it reflects an ethical and social principle rather than statutory requirement.

On the other hand, some persons under certain circumstances have gained the legal right to treatment, a precedent that bears promise of future extension to others. Where states or the federal government have enacted special health care systems such as Medicaid and Medicare, these must be made available to all eligible recipients under the equal protection clause of the Fourteenth Amendment. These latter contraints primarily apply to public institutions, and it can be deemed illegal for them to refuse treatment to anyone entitled to these insurance programs.

The private sector, however, is not quite so bound and is generally free to elect whether to care for a given patient or not. Thus private hospitals have usually been accorded the right to refuse to perform abortions while public ones have not. Despite this freedom, certain limitations obtain. First, physicians or private facilities deciding not to treat persons seeking their services bear an obligation to make a referral to another resource. Second, a physician who has already initiated care and wishes to terminate an established relationship must give the patient sufficient notice in order to secure other services without jeopardy to his or her health.

In another instance, a number of recent court challenges have developed over the right to treatment in the area of noncriminal confinement (for example, juveniles, the mentally retarded, the emotionally disturbed, and sexual psychopaths). Some have been successful, others not. The United States Supreme Court has recently ruled that a nondangerous emotionally disturbed patient cannot be retained in custodial care without treatment and must be discharged if he can survive safely in freedom (*O'Connor v. Donaldson*, 1975); but it did not go so far as to *require* treatment per se.

The Right to Privacy

The Supreme Court has affirmed a constitutional right to privacy under the Fourteenth Amendment. First applied to health care in *Griswold v. Connecticut* (1965), the ruling stated that no state could interfere with a woman's privacy in obtaining contraception from her physician. This ruling is also applicable to most aspects of the patient-doctor relationship.

Nor can physicians breach a patient's privacy. No information can be revealed without the patient's (or parent's) permission. These restrictions do not apply to information exchange among professionals directly involved in providing the service in question; there may be free discussion of the patient's case among physicians, nurses, social workers, medical students, and any others who are part of the overall health care team. But information may not be conveyed outside this team without proper patient (parent) authorization. This includes such third parties as other health care providers, insurance companies, schools, camps, employers, social agencies, police, or lawyers. Also, one may be liable for the unwitting revelation of confidential information in the course of casual gossip or through overheard professional conversations in hospital elevators, corridors, or other public places.

However, the concept of privacy is not absolute, and exceptions do exist. First, data of importance to the patient's life or health may be revealed to others without consent in an emergency. Second, laws in most states require the reporting of certain diseases as well as births, deaths, and other such vital statistics. Third, a court order, summons, or subpoena must be responded to. These latter requirements may be qualified to some extent by statutes governing privileged communications. Some states, but not all, have such provisions. Just what information may be withheld needs to be determined in each jurisdiction, for laws governing immunity from forced disclosure of confidential medical matters are far from being as all-encompassing as they are for the lawyer-client or priest-confessional relationship.

Less clear-cut are the physician's obligations to disclose information about a patient which could result in harm to the public. In general, it is the physician's duty to advise appropriate authorities of such matters as, for example, an adolescent's uncontrolled epilepsy in connection with obtaining a driver's license or seeking a job where a seizure would place others at risk. These are diagnostic facts which bear a well-defined potential for significant injury to others. Other parallels can be easily drawn. Considerably greater confusion exists (and no simple answer can be given) where the potential hazard is more conjectural; for example, a patient's verbalized wish to assault another person. Information obtained about past and already committed illegal acts such as a youth's involvement with illicit drugs or petty theft is generally privileged and need not be volunteered. On the other hand, if the confidence is of a more serious nature, such as homicide, bombing, or arson (as may sometimes be revealed in the course of caring for delinquent or leftist youths), whether the patient's right to privilege supersedes public interest is much less clear. Once again, legal counsel should be obtained when in doubt.

Informed Consent

It is an established legal principle that patients have a right to know both the relative benefits and risks of any treatment they are to receive and to give a free and voluntary consent thereto. Just what constitutes an informed consent and just how much information is required to give it are matters of wide debate. Probably there is no such thing as a *fully* informed consent. No patient can ever entirely appreciate all possible risk-benefit combinations and permutations. Nor can patients be expected to make wholly rational decisions about their own fate free of distorting anxiety and past experiences. Nonetheless, patients have the right to be advised of all significant potential consequences to proposed therapies in terms they can readily understand; and it is still their choice whether to proceed or not.

Only when it can be proved to the court's satisfaction that a patient is mentally incompetent to decide for himself or herself will the court order treatment against a patient's wishes. Thus in one Mid-
western state it was recently ruled that an emotionally disturbed woman could be given transfusions
despite her refused consent, but a mature high school
boy in New Jersey was given the right to decide for
himself to play football with but one kidney in spite
of medical recommendations and school prohibitions
to the contrary.

Because the issue of what constitutes a valid informed consent is so nebulous and ill-defined,
physicians are always open to challenge. They will
afford themselves and their patients the best protection if they make their explanations as comprehensive as possible and duly note this in the patient's
record. Further support will be provided by the presence of an objective auditor witness—an outside person who has no vested interest or participatory role
in the case, but sits in on these transactions as an
unprejudiced observer.

Assault and Battery

The law generally views health care as a contractual
agreement between the physician and patient. In the
absence of such an agreement any touching of the
patient is unauthorized and constitutes assault and
battery. Negligence is not at issue, though often they
go hand in hand. But, it would be very difficult for a
patient to successfully pursue an assault charge to its
conclusion without coexisting negligence; that is, if
the patient suffered no injury and was clearly benefited by the services received, the assault charge
would not be practical to bring to the court.

Parents generally contract for the care of their
child, and the treatment of a minor in the absence of
parental permission falls under the tort of assault.
But, as we shall discuss under *Minor's Consent*, this is
far from an absolute matter. Not only is the law
changing rapidly in this area, but it never was what
it seemed to be.

Negligence

Improper treatment and unjustifiable errors in medical management (either by commission or omission)
which result in injury to the patient constitute negligence. Established national standards of practice

within the physician's specialty determine the norm
against which the quality and competency of rendered care is measured. Of course, there is always
considerable debate over just what these standards
are, and unless an obvious mistake has been made,
the case often hinges on just this point. For better or
worse, medical audit and peer review systems offer
prospects for more effectively defining these matters
than heretofore.

The issue of negligence is further blurred by the
inherent conflict between the public's growing expectation of guaranteed good results and the greater
risks of modern medical technology. Redress for
alleged injury is increasingly being sought on the
basis of an unsatisfactory therapeutic outcome without regard to the physician's competence. The complexity of these matters has assumed national promi-
nence in recent years consequent to skyrocketing
malpractice claims and insurance costs.

Statutes of Limitations

Most litigational matters are subject to specified
time limits after which charges may no longer be
brought before the courts. Statutes of limitations define this period. Upon their expiration, an individual
is no longer at risk of liability for an allegedly illegal
act. These laws are quite variable, depending not
only on the particular state but also on the nature of
the charge itself.

Statutes of limitations may also differ in terms of
when they begin to run. In medical care, they can
start either at the time an alleged injury *occurred* or
at the time it was *discovered* (for example, the date
when surgery was carried out or the date when it was
found out that a sponge or instrument was inadvertently left behind).

Until recently, statutes of limitations did not even
begin to run for children until they were legal adults,
regardless of other matters. Physicians caring for the
young could be at risk for negligence or assault for as
long as 25 years. Although this was still widely the
case in 1976, current revisions of malpractice codes
are beginning to reduce this lengthy period of potential liability for a minor's care to no more than around
7 years. It is anticipated that this trend will continue.

While of obvious benefit to physicians, this direction raises a significant constitutional issue for children. If persons are forever deprived of the chance to

pursue their own cases and must solely rely on others to act on their behalf, does this violate their right to equal protection? If statutes of limitations for children run out before majority, this may be the case, as minors will be denied the opportunity to seek their own redress upon assumption of adulthood. Whether this is or is not constitutionally permissible remains to be seen.

Consent for Children

Parent-Child Relationships

There is probably no single legal dilemma in pediatrics wich causes greater difficulty than the issue of consent. Understanding the respective rights and responsibilities of parents and their minor offspring under the law is fundamental. All else is contingent upon this definition.

With the limited exceptions of some recent and notable shifts in matters of custody and the medical care of adolescents, it has long been held that individuals who have not yet reached majority have no legally valid voice of their own. Their interests must be represented by parents or legal guardians, who are responsible for their nurture and support and possess wide controlling rights over their physical and emotional welfare and religious and moral upbringing.

At the same time, parents must act in the child's best interests as defined by a wide variety of protective laws. Their offspring must comply with compulsory school attendance requirements, child labor restrictions, juvenile law, and the like. Nor can parents behave in a neglectful or abusive manner or encourage their child to commit illegal acts. In such instances the courts may relieve them of custody and vest this in another. Parents's rights over their children are not absolute and are constrained by broad social dictates designed to protect the young from exploitation and harm.

Parental Consent

Consent for the medical care of children generally must be obtained from one or both parents or the legal guardian. Ideally this should be in writing. When this is not possible and the situation is urgent,

a two-way telephone call with an auditor witness on an extension or an exchange of telegrams usually will suffice until more formal arrangements can be made.

It is, however, impractical and unnecessary to obtain written consent for every medical contact, and this is customarily omitted in the course of routine, low-risk, nonsurgical care. There is an implied consent when the parent volitionally brings the child to the doctor's office, administers prescribed medication, and pays the bills. However, the physician still bears a responsibility to assure that even this tacit consent is properly informed.

When a child is living with relatives other than parents, it cannot be assumed that they automatically also possess the legal right to consent. Unless the courts have specifically granted the relatives full guardianship rights, parental consent usually is still required. When this is not possible, even if the parents are ill, their whereabouts are unknown, or they have disavowed responsibility, legal advice should be sought on how to proceed. It may be necessary to obtain a court order.

Children in institutions and foster homes sometimes pose similar problems. While foster parents, social agencies, or juvenile detention facilities are charged with the child's custody, they are not always empowered to consent to medical care. This matter should be clarified in each instance. Fortunately most agencies are cognizant of their own procedural requirements in this regard. But in many instances the consent of parents will be necessary. This can pose significant difficulties when the parents' whereabouts are unknown or they are unresponsive to communications, and one may need to ask the court to assume temporary guardianship for the purpose of consent.

The "Co-consent" of Children

Although not yet legislated or even widely practiced, it is still a wise and therapeutically constructive step to obtain the consent of the older child or adolescent as well as that of the parents. Tentative United States Department of Health, Education, and Welfare guidelines relative to research require the consent of minors of 7 years or more if they are to be subjects of human investigation. The author holds that this should apply to all aspects of health care as well, but beginning at the more developmentally appropriate age of about 12 with the initiation of abstract (formal) thought. Recent directions in the law endowing minors with the right to consent to their own health care when capable of understanding the issues involved offer direction here as well and support the concept of obtaining at least an adolescent's co-consent.

Consent Refusal

A classic dilemma is encountered when parental religious beliefs prohibit their acquiescence to the use of blood transfusions in their child. Consistent with the principles governing parent-child relationships under the law, the courts have regularly overridden parental objections and ordered the provision of all necessary therapies in these and similar circumstances. The child's right to the preservation of life and health are paramount. In such situations, physicians will usually be able to treat a child even if parents refuse, but this will require the permission of the courts. A court order can usually be promptly obtained. Any judge is empowered to act at any time, although the exact procedure to be followed may differ from one locale to another. Hospital counsel is usually familiar with these steps.

The problem may be much more complex when an older child or adolescent also holds the parents' religious views and concurs in their treatment refusal. It is unlikely that the courts would uphold a minor's right to refuse treatment if this meant risk of death, and would be most apt to order a transfusion against the child's will. The law generally views its role as protecting children not only from outside harm, but also from their own improvident acts. But the law is not the sole consideration here. There are far-reaching ethical and psychological implications in coercively imposing an unwanted treatment upon anyone who is old enough to intelligently weigh the issues involved, minor or adult. In this instance it is far better to resolve the dilemma without recourse to the courts.

In another circumstance, parents may refuse consent for life-saving surgical procedures on their profoundly defective newborn child. Whether the courts would or would not agree to withholding the correction of intestinal obstruction in a baby with Down's syndrome, for example, is far from resolved. In taking guidance from the recent case of Karen Anne Quinlan, the New Jersey Supreme Court ruled

that respirator support could be terminated for a 22-year-old comatose woman if her father, as legal guardian, deemed this would have been her own will. Critical to the decision, however, was the expert medical opinion that Karen would never be able to emerge from her coma to a "cognitive, sapient state" and that the parents had no motives of their own.

It would be difficult to take such a definitive stance in the instance of a defective newborn whose potential for a "cognitive, sapient state" is unpredictable and where parental motives in avoiding anguish for themselves and siblings might well exist. While the Karen Anne Quinlan case may have direction for the older hopelessly brain-injured child, prudent legal advice would have to recommend in the instance of newborns that the physician not accede to parental wishes, but rather seek a court order mandating treatment.

But it is also true that decisions in both directions are being implemented. This is a most difficult and unresolved gray area which intermingles many sometimes conflicting aspects of ethics, human rights, and the law.

Minor's Consent

The general rule of requiring parental consent for the treatment of all minors is not absolute. There is a rapidly expanding body of law which allows ever larger numbers of adolescents to obtain medical services on their own. First is the widespread pragmatic and categorical statutory response to those minors who will harmfully delay care for such matters as venereal disease and pregnancy when parental consent is a prerequisite. Second is changing definitions of partial and total emancipation. Third is the growing body of United States Supreme Court decisions bestowing constitutional rights on minor children and youth. These measures collectively contribute to the widening acceptance of the view that majority is not the sole determiner of an individual's ability to consent to health care.

The Mature Minor Doctrine

The preceding directions have combined into the relatively new concept called the "Mature Minor Doctrine," that body of statutory, case, and constitutional law which can be invoked in defense of treating minors on their own consent when it is evident that patients are sufficiently mature to understand the nature and consequences of the proposed treatment and that this treatment is for their benefit. Indeed such a defense has probably always existed and, to the author's knowledge, no physician has ever been found liable for damages for treating a minor over the age of 15 years for any purpose or for providing contraceptive service to an adolescent of any age. But it is certainly true that doctors have not been singularly reassured by this statement and still look to statutory direction in quite specific and concrete terms. A considerable legislative outpouring has been the result. Although matters are highly variable from state to state and will need to be specifically determined for each jurisdiction, the following cite the general trends.

Emancipation

Certain categories of minors have been widely granted the right to obtain health care as if an adult. These include minors away from home with parental permission and earning their own living through bona-fide employment; minors who are parents (both for themselves and their child); married minors; minors in the armed services; and minors who, though living at home, are employed and contributing substantially to their own support.

Some states, such as California, Minnesota, and Colorado, have enacted health care consent statutes emancipating minors who are simply living away from home and managing their own financial affairs. Responding to the problem of runaways and alienated youth, these laws are effective even in the absence of parental concurrence or an independent source of income; nor is the duration of separation a factor. A minimum age may or may not obtain.

Other statutes specify a particular age when a minor is entitled to consent to all health care regardless of living circumstances. In most instances this parallels the lowered voting age, or 18 years. But in some, the age of consent is even less. For example, in Alabama one need be but 14 years of age or but 15 in Oregon and Colorado.

Venereal Disease

Every state now has specific laws allowing minors to obtain services for the prevention or treatment of venereal disease on their own. Some do stipulate a minimum age, usually between 12 and 14 years, but more often there is no such restriction. In several, notably Hawaii and Nebraska, parents are to be advised after the fact if venereal disease is indeed found. It is dubious whether this provision is often observed, for to do so would invalidate the law's intent. Few youngsters would seek such services if they knew their parents would find out later on.

Pregnancy

A number of states permit the rendering of confidential services to minors for the diagnosis and treatment of pregnancy. Moreover, even where no such enabling laws exist, the benefits of early prenatal care are so overriding and the mature minor concept so relevant that a doctor who initiates treatment of a pregnant minor with a view toward helping her involve her parents undoubtedly bears little legal risk.

Contraception

Minors also may obtain contraceptive services on their own in many states. This right may be denoted in specific laws or implicit in those which provide for "services related to pregnancy" or "the prevention, diagnosis, and treatment of pregnancy"; both phrases are commonly used.

HEW guidelines pertaining to the allocation of federal family planning funds are also applicable in that they prohibit discrimination based on age or marital status. The courts have widely ruled that contraceptive services must be made available to all minors who are actual or potential welfare recipients even where state laws are not so permissive. This is not always true, however. A 1975 ruling by the Kansas attorney general stated that all persons under 18 are uniformly ineligible for contraceptive services under this state's present laws.

Common and customary practice also finds many physicians rendering confidential family planning services to minors on their own consent even in the absence of specific enabling state laws, and none has been found liable for damages for such actions to date, as far as the author can discern.

Abortion

Following the Supreme Court's decision in *Roe and Doe* (1972), it was widely debated as to whether laws providing for minors to consent to their own care relative to the "diagnosis and treatment of pregnancy" did or did not include abortion. While some held that this procedure should indeed be viewed as a form of treatment of pregnancy, conservatism has been the rule, and in actual practice abortions are rarely performed under these pregnancy laws. In only a few states, such as California and Hawaii, are there specific statutes enabling minors to consent to abortions on their own.

Further constraints have been imposed since this time in state laws governing the performance of abortions. A number have included provisions specifically requiring parental consent for persons under 18 years of age. But in six out of seven subsequent challenges, the courts have ruled that this requirement is unconstitutional and in violation of a minor's right to both privacy and equal protection. Many of these decisions also comment on the capacity and overriding interests of young women who are pregnant to determine their own fates, even though still minors. In 1976 the Supreme Court invalidated statutory parental consent requirements, holding that this impermissably provided for a third party veto over a matter that *Roe and Doe* had determined to be solely between a patient, even if a minor, and her physician. The Court, however, did not go so far as to rule on a minor's right to privacy per se and did imply it would accede to some form of special protections for this group (*Danforth v. Planned Parenthood of Missouri*).

Tangentially, there has been little question in the mind of the courts as to whose interests are paramount when intrafamily conflict exists over the resolution of a teenager's pregnancy. Recent decisions at the state level have well established that parents cannot force a minor to have an abortion against her will; nor can they require her to carry to term if she wishes to terminate the pregnancy.

Drug Abuse and Mental Health Services

Only a few states have specific laws permitting minors to obtain services for drug and alcohol abuse or emotional problems on their own consent, although allowing drug-abusing teenagers some degree of confidentiality in this manner has been a common and customary practice throughout the country. Here again, as in pregnancy, the benefits of early treatment for drug abuse and mental problems

are sufficiently clear and the concepts of the mature minor doctrine sufficiently applicable when youths seek out professional help on their own as to suggest that there is probably minimal risk in instituting therapy on the minor's own consent while working toward achieving parental involvement.

Related Issues

The vast majority of these "minor's consent to health care" laws are enabling rather than compelling. There is probably minimal risk of being liable for breach of contract or violation of privacy if the physician deems it in the minor's best interest to notify parents and proceeds to do so, even if against the minor's will. Indeed, some statutes specifically provide for this option.

The question of who pays is also raised frequently. As consent for treatment is equivalent to a contract which in turn involves an obligation to pay for services rendered and as parents are not generally held responsible for contracts made by their minor offspring, it can be reasoned that adolescents consenting to their own health care are also liable for its costs. Here, too, some statutes include this specific provision. Pragmatically one answers this problem in the same manner as for any patient with limited economic resources, regardless of age. Unfortunately, unless they are already Medicaid recipients under Aid to Dependent Children, it is likely that minors will be able to obtain health insurance on their own.

Emergency Care

There is no question but that a physician may treat a child or minor adolescent without parental consent in an emergency. Some states provide for some other adult to act *in loco parentis* until the minor's own parents can be reached. But many do not have such requirements, and the patient can be treated on the basis of the physician's judgment alone.

The dilemma here is to define just what constitutes an emergency. Many physicians take a narrow view and consider only those who are in immediate danger of losing life or limb to qualify. But it is probable that legislatures have always intended a somewhat broader interpretation which would include less dire but still serious health risks as well as pain and suffering. But because matters have been so ambiguous and these laws so cautiously applied, many states are redrafting their emergency statutes for children. Wording is highly variable, but in essence they permit the rendering of emergency services to minors when any delay in care would increase the risk to the minor's "life or *health*." Again, ambiguity reigns in that the definition of "health" can be as elusive and enigmatic as it is for "emergency." But certainly something more than purely life and limb saving is implied. Some lawyers advocating for minors' rights have argued that these new statutes cover the provision of contraception in averting the greater physical and emotional hazards of pregnancy. But not all would agree, and these laws have rarely been implemented in such expansive terms.

Although the threat of malpractice in modern times is indeed compelling, this author still holds that excessive and unnecessary conservatism has been the general rule. Once again it should be noted that, as far as can be determined, no physician has been found liable for damages for treating a minor over 15 years of age without parental consent. Moreover, suits involving patients under this age have largely been successful only when negligent surgery, adverse drug reactions, and human experimentation have been involved. In further defense of this position, one can also pose an equally valid argument on the opposite side: that a minor has as much right to receive beneficial treatment as does an adult and that withholding it in an urgent situation is even more culpable than failing to obtain parental consent. But it is a fact that charges of alleged injury are much more apt to be levied when a definite procedure has been carried out than when harm accrues because nothing was done.

Rape

Management of the child or adolescent who is the victim of rape or other types of sexual assault involves both proper medical management and the meeting of legal obligations. The following guidelines are based on recent (1970) recommendations of the American College of Obstetricians and Gynecologists:

1 It is the physician's duty to report both alleged and suspected rape in children and adolescents to police or child welfare authorities. This is required under either rape or child abuse laws or both. In some states a physician may not examine a patient until a police surgeon or other authorized medical personnel has seen her first. This should be determined before proceeding.

2 A thorough and complete history is essential. This should include the time, place, and circumstances of the event in the patient's own words. All data and observations may be important pieces of evidence.

3 Examination of minors generally requires parental consent unless an emergency exists. (This author would also exempt the patient who is qualified to consent to her own care by virtue of maturity or emancipation.) All findings should be carefully recorded and photographs obtained where this would helpfully document the patient's condition.

4 The following specimens should be obtained: swabs of the vaginal pool and any suspicious secretions about the vulva for chemical analysis and antigen typing of semen, wet mounts of material from the fornix and vulva for motile sperm, and a culture for *Neisseria gonococcus*.

5 All clothing, photographs, and any other potential evidence should be properly identified and retained for the police or court subpoena.

6 Protection against disease, pregnancy, and psychic trauma should be promptly instituted. This includes the standard treatment for exposure to syphillis and gonorrhea, a short course of high-dose estrogens to block implantation of a fertilized ovum, and a period of frequent visits for emotional counseling and support.

Statutory Rape

All states have laws which stipulate that a minor female below a certain age is incapable of consenting to sexual intercourse, no matter how willing a partner she may be. Any male who has coitus with such a girl is considered to have committed the crime of statutory rape. The age range governing statutory rape is highly variable from state to state; a girl need be but 8 years old in Delaware and 13 in Tennessee to legally consent to sexual intercourse and relieve her partner of liability for this charge. But most states assign an age of somewhere between 16 and 18 years.

Physicians are not generally required to report instances of statutory rape, and these laws are regularly overlooked unless a girl or her parents specifically elect to press charges. Indeed, if these statutes were to be widely enforced, it is safe to say that somewhere around one-third of the entire adolescent population would be involved according to current estimates of teenage sexual behavior.

Sterilization

Sterilization of mentally defective young people used to be an acceptable practice and was even mandated by law in more than 20 states. But in 1973, with the revelation that parental consent was not always informed and that the subject's own interests were often poorly protected, serious questions were raised over this policy. At the heart of the matter is much more than the issue of proper consent, but rather whether anyone can impose sterilization upon a mentally incompetent person at all.

Currently, compulsory sterilization laws are no longer operative. Pending further study, interim HEW guidelines prohibit the use of federal funds for the purposes of sterilizing anyone under 21 years of age. Recent court rulings have also regularly refused the requests of parents to authorize sterilizations of mentally retarded teenage girls and boys.

In the present climate it is recommended that physicians not carry out sterilization of minors until future governmental guidelines provide clear direction or in the unlikely event that a court order can be obtained. Alternate methods of preventing pregnancy and managing menstrual hygiene will have to be found.

The Child as a Donor

There is a universal prohibition on a minor serving as a donor for blood or organs unless there is no alternative for saving the life of the intended recipient. This set of conditions usually only obtains in instances of skin, bone marrow, or kidney transplants between identical twins or between siblings where an advantageous tissue match is not possible through any other pairing. In these circumstances the courts have generally allowed this procedure to be carried out, but only if both the parents and child donor fully concur and the effect on the latter has been fully explored and adjudged not to be hazardous emotionally or physically. Thus the use of a minor donor is within therapeutic considerations when all else has failed for the recipient. But the permission of the court should be obtained, particularly for major transplant procedures. Health care providers have not always sought out the court's concurrence in instances of marrow transplants, considering this a relatively harmless procedure with no long-range consequences. Technically they are at legal risk, but for all practical purposes this is minimal.

Research

Evidences of possible exploitation of captive groups, hidden coercion, and grossly unethical experiments have raised a hue and cry around the issue of informed consent in human investigation. Standards for the performance of research in minors are currently evolving with this point in mind. At the present time it is probably safe to say that no barriers exist to studies which do not compromise the application of accepted medical practice. Nor would there be serious contest to the trial of new therapies which bear promise of benefiting the patient beyond that which can be afforded by established methods. But infinite controversy exists over such protocols as double-blind studies where the specific best interests of the individual minor are subtended to the goals of the project itself.

A general rule is emerging to the effect that neither minors nor their parents are competent to consent to any research that, although of profound potential benefit to others, holds possible risk for the child. Very careful scrutiny is essential in drawing up protocols to assure that subjects who are minors are afforded all due protection and that their own well-being will not be compromised. Medical school committees on human investigation should be looked to for help.

When children are to be the subjects of research, informed consent is necessary—no matter how trivial or innocuous their participation may be. This covers the performance of any tests or collection of specimens which would not ordinarily be done as a part of care itself. Also included is the use of data from the patient's record when there is any possibility that the child could be identified, as in the use of a case history; but one is *not* under such strictures when these data are collected and presented in a coded and unidentifiable form and no risk of injury or invasion of privacy exists.

When consent is indicated, tentative HEW guidelines for all research performed in institutions receiving federal funds (regardless of the source of funding for the project itself) require that this be obtained from both the parent and the minor if he or she is 7 or more years of age. This may be waived for the latter only when the knowledge needed to give an informed consent could act to the patient's detriment (for example, some would so view telling children that they have leukemia in order to secure their consent to try out a new drug). Minors who are orphans or whose parents are otherwise unavailable to give consent may not be active participants in human investigation.

Confidentiality in the Health Care Record

The perils posed by computer technology to individual privacy have been widely heralded in recent times. Virtually every diagnosis now transmitted to third parties such as insurance companies or various state and federal registries bears the potential for being stored indefinitely in some form of data bank, retrievable by a variety of persons at any time unbeknownst to patients or their families. Children have singularly vested interests in this matter, as health information stored during these early years may affect their lives for many decades and may influence such matters as future schooling, employment, and insurability. Another significant point is that when consent to information release is obtained this can hardly be called informed. Few patients or parents see the health care record itself or know precisely what information will be sent on. A last dilemma rests in the records of adolescents which may well contain highly confidential information of their own; yet it is the parents, and not the minor youth, who consent to information release, and the young person rarely has the opportunity to protect his or her own interests on matters about which the parents may not even know.

Health care professionals bear serious responsibility in ensuring that the privacy interests of children and adolescents are duly protected. This requires careful attention to just what information is written in the chart, what terms are used, and what data are forwarded on to others. Parents and maturer children and youth should be fully advised as to the nature of the information to be released and the possible future implications before they give their con-

sent. Protecting the specific confidential interest of adolescents from parents is important as well. Parents and minors should also be informed of their new right of access to records under recently enacted federal privacy laws (see above).

The Federal Privacy Act of 1974

This law entitles all citizens to know whether they are or are not listed in the files of any federal agency or any nonfederal agency receiving federal funds. Further, if they are so listed, they have the right to see their files and seek expungement or correction of erroneous data. Special qualifications obtain to medical records in that persons cannot gain access to their own specific diagnoses, but may have this information sent on to a representative of their choice, such as a family physician. It is up to the latter to interpret these data to the individual.

HEW guidelines pertaining to medical records of minors, issued in 1975, provide that minors may request and gain notification of or access to their medical records (through a designate) without parental representation or concurrence. In the instance of a parent making such a request about his or her child, the agency must observe a number of procedural steps protecting the minor's privacy rights. First, the record cannot be sent directly to the parent but only to a designated health professional. Second, this intermediary is to be advised to carefully consider the minor's privacy interests in determining just how much to reveal to parents. Third, the agency itself cannot reveal to parents whether a file on their minor child does or does not exist, only that *if* it exists it has been forwarded to the designated health professional. Last, the agency is also directed to make every reasonable effort to notify minors of their parents' requests.

Similar but less well-defined and more ambiguous constraints exist in relation to a minor's privacy in matters of alcohol and drug abuse. This federal concern for citizens' privacy and for protecting them from the unwarranted and hidden storage of personal data or their abuse bears firm promise of being extended to the private sector as well.

Patients' Access to Their Own Medical Records

There is a growing challenge to the widespread practice of never allowing patients to read their own medical charts. Several suits have recently overturned this convention, resulting in patients directly obtaining their own records for review. New and valid arguments are being put forth in support of this concept, holding that the health record is really a part of the patient and belongs to the patient rather than to the hospital or physician. While not broadly recognized at the present time, this is a trend that may well expand. Therefore, it is recommended that doctors begin to consider how the health care record can be constructed so that it may be fully shared with the patient (or parents) and to look at how confidential entries of either parent or adolescent can be protected one from the other.

Advocacy

Comprehensive pediatric health care gives equal weight and attention to the biological, emotional, and social needs of the child or adolescent. While biological and emotional needs are primarily met within the health care system itself, social needs often require the recruitment of resources from the community and its various agencies and institutions. But these may not always be responsive. The concept of advocacy as a tool of the medical professions plays its greatest role here.

Advocacy for children is the process of seeking accountability from others when they have been derelict in meeting their responsibility as mandated by human rights, social conscience, or law. The advocate needs to know the locus of power and how to bring pressure to bear on behalf of children in order to secure those rights and services that are the children's due. The advocate speaks for children or adolescents and represents their interests when they are unable to do so themselves; this is most of the time. Minors are often regarded as nonpersons under the law or, at the most, as beneficial recipients of that which others unilaterally decide are in their best interests. Parents are usually their own child's best advocates. But this is not always true; they simply may not be knowledgeable in the ways of demanding accountability, or sometimes their interests may be discordant with those of the child.

Pediatricians are in a particularly strong position to serve as child advocates. Not only are they knowledgeable about children's needs, but the power and authority that others often bestow upon physicians should never be underestimated and can be a potent force. (A note of caution: This power should be seen for the somewhat idealized image that it really is and not be interpreted as a "false passport" for going beyond what one is really competent to do.)

The law is an important lever in childhood advocacy, for it defines the nature and scope of minors' rights both as juveniles entitled to certain protections and as citizens under the Constitution. Space does not permit the exploration of all these issues. Some have already been pointed out, but particular focus will now be given to schools, employment, and the juvenile justice system—all matters that have had an incalculable impact on the life of the young.

Schools

Compulsory Attendance

School attendance laws derive from the last century, when many children worked long and arduous hours in industry. Enacted in parallel with child labor laws, compulsory school requirements were intended to ensure that youngsters obtained a minimum education in preparation for adult life. In most states children must go to school between the ages of 7 and 16. Reciprocally, education must be equally available for all. This equal protection right can be used to advantage in obtaining educational services for the handicapped and disadvantaged who might otherwise be ignored.

Constitutional Rights

Schools have also been the arena for testing minors' constitutional rights. In the Supreme Court's most heralded case, *Brown v. Board of Education* (1955), the right of equal protection was extended to compulsory education and served as the foundation for racial desegregation. The Supreme Court has also affirmed the following: schools may not abridge a student's freedom of speech (*Tinker v. Des Moines Independent School District, 1969*); students are entitled to due process in matters of suspension and cannot be suspended without a hearing (*Goss v. Lopez, 1975*); schools cannot interfere with an individual's right to free exercise of religion and cannot force attendance upon those whose religious beliefs are in conflict with this requirement, as it is for Amish youth (*Wisconsin v. Yoder, 1972*). Nor can schools incorporate religious observances within their curricula or impose patriotic practices upon students against their will (*West Virginia v. Barnette, 1968*). But the court upholds the right of educational institutions to discipline students through corporal punishment (*Baker v. Owens,* 1975), and this remains the only place where one individual can legally inflict a physical blow upon another, albeit governed by a number of due process safeguards.

A variety of other constitutional rights has been taken up at the state level, such as a pregnant girl's right to remain in school, the right of students to determine their own dress and hair length, or the right against unwarranted search and seizure of locker and desk contents. Decisions at this level have been quite variable, and no clear trend has emerged. When at issue, the rights of students in each jurisdiction will need to be determined.

The Family Privacy and Education Act of 1974

The problem of confidentiality and school records came to a head with the revelation of widespread violations of even the most basic privacy rights. Not only was information from school records frequently released indiscriminately, but the data were also often erroneous, pejorative, and misapplied. The Family Privacy and Education Act of 1974 provides that parents of students under 18 years of age attending educational institutions receiving federal funds may view their child's educational records on request and seek expungement or correction of false or inaccurate entries. No information can be released outside of the school setting without proper parental authorization. This right devolves on students themselves once they become 18.

It has not yet been established whether medical communications between doctors and schools about a student are covered by this law. They probably are if they influence the child's placement or educational program in any way. The possibility of parental review should be kept in mind when drafting any document which will be sent on to a school. Proper consent for release of information from or to schools also should be obtained.

Labor

Children under the age of 14 years may not be employed except under highly limited circumstances. They may babysit, hold a paper route, shine shoes, and perform other such traditional childhood labors,

but these may not interfere with school attendance. Additional exceptions exist for children performing seasonal farm labor, allowing migrant minors and those living in a number of agricultural states to work in the fields for more extended periods of time.

An adolescent between approximately 14 and 16 years (depending on the state) can seek more extensive employment. But this may not be more than a certain number of hours during the school year and may not be in hazardous industries. A child's welfare is further protected by requirements of working papers signifying the school's and parents' approval.

Once young people reach age 17 and are released from compulsory school attendance requirements, they may work full time and do not need working papers, but they are still prohibited from employment in dangerous industries. All protections cease when the young person reaches age 18.

Juvenile Justice

Definitions

A variety of labels may be attached to young people in the juvenile justice system, and just what these mean can be confusing. While there is some variation from state to state the following terms are most commonly used:

Juvenile Delinquent This is an individual of or below a certain age—usually 16 years—who has committed an illegal act which would be punishable under criminal law if performed by an adult. Children under 7 years of age are exempt, being deemed innocent at law and not criminally responsible for anything they do. Upon adjudication, juvenile offenders may be simply returned to parental custody subject to probationary supervision, or they may be placed with an agency, or they may be remanded to state training schools for variable periods of time extending from months to years. Their case need not invariably be heard under the juvenile court. In some jurisdictions the judge may exercise discretion and remand the youth to the criminal courts if deemed warranted by the circumstances of the crime.

Person (Child, Minor, Juvenile) in Need of Supervision Known by the mnemonics PINS, CHINS, MINS, and JINS, these youngsters are also below a certain age, usually less than 17 years, and have committed what are called status offenses, or acts which would not be crimes were they adults. This covers such matters as truancy, running away, staying out late, or otherwise being "willfully disobedient." These youngsters also may be subject to probationary supervision or to placement in some facility outside their home for the purpose of "rehabilitation" and helping them return to the path of rectitude.

Youthful Offender Youths between 17 and 21 who are accused of crimes may be subject to either criminal or juvenile proceedings at the discretion of the court. When handed over to the latter, young persons are designated youthful offenders and entitled to all the rehabilitative and secret protections of the juvenile process routinely accorded those of younger years. They must, however, give up their right to a jury trial, which would have been theirs under criminal law.

Neglected Child Here charges are not levied against the child but against the parents, who are held not to have provided the minor with proper care or to have inflicted outright abuse. No onus falls on the child. Parents are not generally subject to punitive damages but rather to constraints upon their parental role. They may be placed under the supervision of the courts through the aegis of a social agency, or the child may be removed from parental custody entirely and placed in foster care. Simple neglect charges are generally not applicable after the child reaches 16, but laws covering children for abuse may extend throughout minority, or until 18 years. Although neglected and abused adolescents are covered under these provisions, they frequently respond to their deprivations by some form of acting out and end up on the wrong end of a PINS charge instead. Parents who physically abuse their teenage offspring often escape blame, managing to hide behind their "right" to use corporal punishment in disciplining a "wayward" minor.

Juvenile Court Proceedings

The basic theory behind juvenile justice is that a child who commits an illegal, antisocial, or improvident act should not be punished as an adult but rather given the opportunity for rehabilitation and should not suffer the stigma associated with public trial or having a criminal record. In its ideal, juvenile proceedings are secret and protective hearings for the benefit of the child in contrast to the adversarial and punitive nature of criminal processes.

The goals of the juvenile justice system are laudable indeed. But they have not been realized. State training schools and state farms have rarely been much more than penal institutions for the young, rather than sources of rehabilitation and genuine help. Efforts at keeping juvenile proceedings secret have failed, and PINS youngsters quickly become labeled troublemakers. Nor is this system always fair. In many instances juvenile delinquents are given terms in state training schools which deprive them of their liberty for infinitely longer times than would be true for adults for the same offense. Status offenders can be incarcerated for years for acts which are not criminal at all. On the other hand, in some jurisdictions youths committing major crimes can be detained only for short periods of time (up to 18 months in New York) and are quickly returned to the community, even if homicide is involved. Many receive no "rehabilitation" at all, and for the majority of repeated offenders the juvenile court system is as but a revolving door.

The solution to this problem is far from clear. Few genuinely rehabilitative resources exist, and the courts often have no alternatives but to send these youngsters to unconstructive state facilities or to turn them back on the streets. Court dockets are incredibly jammed, and unrealistic demands are placed upon juvenile judges. Nor are there any minimal national standards setting the qualifications or training requirements of those who work with juveniles, from probation officers to the judges themselves. The need to look for other solutions is urgent indeed.

Constitutional Rights

Until recently, juvenile court proceedings regularly denied minors due process under the Bill of Rights. This has now changed. In *In re Gault* (1967) the United States Supreme Court ruled that minors were indeed entitled to such protections. And in this and several subsequent cases, juveniles have now come to be accorded nearly all such measures except trial by jury and the right to bail. While admitting to the profound problems of juvenile justice today, the Court still did not wish to eliminate the ideal prospect of secret, rehabilitative hearings. It held that the adversarial processes of a jury trial would deprive minors of this more benevolent approach. And the bail and appeal system would unwarrantedly delay the institution of help.

Incarcerated Youth and Health Care

It is important in the cause of advocacy to point out that children and adolescents in detention facilities awaiting disposition or those serving sentences in state training schools are often the recipients of grossly inadequate medical care and allied health services. Assuredly it is the minimum responsibility of health professionals to remedy this defect.

Court-ordered Examinations

It is well within the province of the courts to order the physical or mental evaluation of a juvenile. Generally this is carried out through public institutions. The health facility is obligated to respond to this order and submit a report on its findings. The examining physician may also be called upon to testify, and the record is certainly subject to subpoena. Thus all observations should be carefully noted and the history recorded in the patient's own words. No judgments beyond the diagnostic assessment and therapeutic recommendations should be made on the chart, and conjectural or confidential information is best left out. Further, patients and their families should be advised in advance that the usual protections of privacy and confidentiality cannot be observed in this instance.

Concluding Points

Using the Law

In considering recourse to the courts in the cause of child advocacy, it is essential that all possible consequences be anticipated and carefully weighed before taking this step. Once legal action is set in motion, it can be difficult to stop and the outcome is not always predictable. While one might expect that a judge would rule in a certain way, this is not always the case and a quite different result may be achieved. One must also consider the impact of court proceedings upon the child and upon the viability of the patient-parent-doctor relationship. One might,

for instance, wish to achieve foster placement for the 14-year-old daughter of alcoholic parents. But if she is truant and acting out in protest, she may well be charged as a person in need of supervision and become so labeled. At the same time the judge may simply admonish the parents without instituting any real change, as viable alternatives to the girl's remaining at home are few and far between. All that may be accomplished are parental wrath and alienation from the health care facility for getting them embroiled with the law and the loss of any opportunity to intervene further on the minor's behalf. This is not to imply that the courts should not be used. Quite the contrary, for this is a most important and potent force. But forethought and careful planning are essential, and this is not a move to be embarked upon impulsively.

Seeking Legal Advice

In determining one's own professional liability and the patient's true rights, hospital and malpractice lawyers invariably take a conservative view. While this is most understandable, a much more flexible position is usually possible without accruing any real increase in potential risk. While the author certainly recommends prudence, one can often overdo caution to the genuine detriment of the patient. This is particularly true for those children and adolescents whose interests conflict with those of the parent or whose families are incapable of adequately meeting their needs. When seeking information on minor patients' rights and on how far a professional may justifiably go, the physician may find that other sources are more helpful. Some of these are state attorneys general (on interpreting state laws and governmental guidelines), the American Civil Liberties Union and its branches (on constitutional rights issues), Planned Parenthood offices (on contraception, pregnancy, and abortion), the Legal Aid Society (on court-related matters), local consumer rights and community law groups, community law and family law departments in law schools, the new departments of law and medicine that are emerging in some universities, and appropriate committees of local bar associations.

46 | A Developmental Approach to Behavior Problems

by T. Berry Brazelton, David M. Snyder, and Michael W. Yogman

Introduction

Every encounter between pediatrician and child is an opportunity for developmental assessment. The continuous, long-term relationship the pediatrician maintains with the child and the family offers data about physiologic and behavioral functioning under a variety of circumstances. When questions arise concerning the normality of a child's behavior, this data base gives the primary health provider a diagnostic and therapeutic edge which a consultant can duplicate only with much time and effort.

The spectrum of behaviors about which parents become concerned is broad indeed. Its range encompasses:

1 Nonproblems, the concerns based on simple misinformation, requiring support and corrective information only

2 Normal but frequently "problematic behaviors" to the parents, such as negativism in the second year

3 Long-standing, relatively fixed "behavior problems," such as continued, too-frequent night waking in 2-year-olds

4 Clearly pathologic behavior based on psychopathology or organicity, such as that seen in an autistic child or a child with lead encephalopathy or major psychiatric deviance which is essentially irreversible

This presentation will take a conceptual approach to the assessment of reversible behavior problems as opposed to the more irreversible ones. The emphasis will be on the center of the spectrum—problem behaviors and behavior problems. These represent both the majority of parental concerns brought to pediatricians' attention and some of the most taxing diagnostic entities in behavioral pediatrics. This section will show how a conceptual approach based on normal development can be applied to these everyday problems in an office practice.

In pediatric practice, the diagnosis of a behavior problem may not be possible in a single encounter. The rush to "make a diagnosis" on the first visit may well be inappropriate. It takes time to assess the dimensions of parental concern as well as the meaning of the behavior to the child. An early diagnosis may miss the appropriate dimensions of each of these. It can lead to extensive diagnostic studies or to referrals which not only may be unnecessary and costly, but may actually make the diagnosis and treatment more elusive by reinforcing parental concerns. This pursuit of a physical diagnosis often will divert the parents from approaching the child's problem. Frequently, the true nature and severity of the behavior problem emerge only as we observe the parents' responsiveness to counseling or the child's reaction to altered parental approaches. This does not imply an interminable diagnostic phase. Rather, it reflects the fact that, in managing behavior problems, diagnosis and treatment often proceed in parallel, the diagnostic hypotheses suggesting counseling approaches, the family's response to these generating more precise diagnostic formulations, and so forth.

Etiology

Behavior problems arise in the course of growing up as a consequence of the normal stresses of coping with new adjustments. These problems must be viewed as part of the "coping process," "the steps through which the child comes to terms with a challenge" (Murphy) and successfully masters the difficulties inherent in learning about oneself and about the environment. The coping process may be modified by genetic, biological, and environmental factors but is always present and needs to be assessed even in those infrequent instances when severe underlying pathology, such as brain damage, autism, or parental psychopathology, is present. The progression from a limited problem behavior to a more global behavior problem and occasionally even to severe psychopathology depends heavily on how effectively the parent-child unit supports this coping process.

In those few instances when problems are becoming more severe, the parents often show excessive concern about the child's symptom rather than the underlying reason. The symptom may in fact be adaptive and represent a coping response to the stress of growing up or to illness or to somatic defect. Most often, the presenting symptom has had its beginning long before, and the parental concerns have reinforced a chain of *behavior→concern→problem behavior→increasing concern→increasing behavior problem*. To understand the etiology and achieve any change in this ever-increasing chain, a pediatrician must understand each link in its development.

Evaluation

The most valuable clinical tool the pediatrician can use to assess developmental behavior in children is observation of the behavior of all participants as they interact with each other. Clinical judgments about parents and children made at every encounter are based on the physician's observational skills. While formal tests of the child's intellectual and emotional functioning can structure these observations and more clearly articulate clinical judgments, tests can never entirely replace careful observation.

When parents make us, as pediatric observers, feel angry or depressed as they describe a problem, this becomes an important measure of the parent's own depth of reactions to the child and the behavior problem. Are these feelings representative of their feelings about their conflicts with the child? Why are they generating parallel feelings in us as we observe them? Observations of moments of intense emotion may provide the best clue to the depth of underlying issues. For example, when a mother brightens and becomes animated as she talks about her child's negativism, the pediatrician can be certain that she enjoys it and can identify with it in her toddler and that it will not create a serious problem for either mother or child. Similarly, when a young father begins to hold on grimly to his contention that his 5-year-old son's enuresis is punishable, the depth of tension and frustration created in us becomes our best measure of his inability to react appropriately to this symptom in the boy and indicates there is a "fixed" problem area between them.

In most instances pediatricians must begin by "listening with a third ear" or observing the behavior and documenting their own reactions to understand clearly what parents mean as they present their children's problem behaviors. As one attempts to gather the necessary information about a disturbing behavior, such as when it was first noted, the circumstances in which it occurs, how the parents react to it, and how the child responds to their reactions, one should be most alert to behavioral signs of deeper concerns. These deeper, often unconsciously controlled concerns are usually the real reasons the parents seek help. Parents are often reluctant to initiate discussion of their fears regarding brain damage, mental retardation, or psychological pathology in the child, and expressed concerns may really cover up their worries about these issues. These underlying concerns may not be expressed on the first visit. To the degree that they are, they signify that the parents feel the pediatrician is taking them seriously and can be trusted to accept their feelings without censure. Establishing this alliance with the pediatrician is certainly the first step toward solution of the problem they are having with their child.

Evaluation of the Parents

In general, a child's behavior becomes problematic because it does not conform to parental expectations.

Evaluation of the parents should start with the assumption that they are concerned about this dichotomy and proceed with specification of the worrisome behavior and how it deviates from their expectations. Insofar as the parents are the focus of attention, we are interested in:

1 How realistic their expectations are

2 How rigid they are in their expectations

3 Whether the child violates these expectations in a narrow or broad area of functioning

4 Whether the violation means abnormality or "badness" in the child or their own failure in parenting

It is also important to determine the etiology of their expectations, for example, from their own past experiences in growing up, their experiences with their older children, the comments of grandparents, and their cultural expectations.

Parents come to the pediatrician feeling guilty, inadequate, often isolated from their children, and defensive about the difficulties they are having. These feelings, which are invariably an impediment to problem solving, may well be the tragic result of our cultural biases which blame parents for everything "wrong" with their children. These feelings commonly give rise to questions about the impact of medications taken during pregnancy, genetic factors, and their own child-rearing style as it affects the child's behavior. In some cases, of course, these concerns are realistic. In others, the overconcern can be a symptom and measure of the degree of severity of the problem. However, in all cases this concern and guilt interfere with the parents' relationship with their child and need to be brought out and examined in a positive and supportive manner. This entails accepting the parents' concern, validating their right to get help, and above all, feeding back to them a perception of their own basic competence and of their child's strengths, along with an assessment of the child's problem.

Occasionally, signs of markedly unrealistic expectations, such as attributing adult goals to an infant or small child, may come to the surface. Significant parental thought disorders may become apparent. Not infrequently, a parent's own needs and concerns about his or her marriage or about another child may turn out to be the underlying motive for the visit. In any case, the degree to which the parents are conscious of their feelings about their child and his or her problematic behavior, and the ease with which they can express them, can tell us much about the kind of treatment approach that is most likely to work.

If the office assessment of the child shows him or her as markedly discrepant from the parents' description, or if their level of concern seems out of proportion to the problem they report, an undiscovered parental concern should be suspected. However, two alternative hypotheses should also be considered. These are:

1 That the behavior observed by the physician is, in fact, not typical of the child

2 That the discrepancy represents a real distortion of the child's behavior by the parents

In the case of significant parental psychopathology, pediatricians may first sense that their observations do not parallel the expressed complaints. Then they may realize that they cannot reach the parents to help them with their reaction to the child. This, then, may suggest that the primary problem is outside the realm of pediatrics altogether. Even in such situations, the manner in which the pediatrician has talked to the parents about their feelings can have a significant influence on their accepting referral to a source of psychiatric help. If they have learned that a candid expression of their concerns and feelings is met with acceptance and understanding, rather than censure or disinterest, it will be considerably easier for them to make use of psychiatric consultation in this area.

Evaluation of the Child

In evaluating a child's behavior at any one time, we must take into account:

1 How inborn individual temperament influences the child's behavior (either overreactivity or underreactivity)

2 Whether the symptom is one that is appropriate to the child's age

3 How the child's reactions to all stress help one see either adaptive strengths or inadequate coping mechanisms

4 The degree to which the symptom has influenced broad areas of a child's function (with the family, peers, in school, etc.)

5 The duration of the symptom as a sign of "fixation"; if the child has not changed over time, one should worry, and if the symptom has increased in severity, this fact becomes even more ominous

In practice, one evaluates a problem on all five levels simultaneously, but separate discussion may clarify the importance of each level.

Temperament as a Background for a Symptom An understanding of infant temperament is helpful in assessing the child's contribution to common problems such as crying, feeding, sleeping disorders, temper tantrums, and poor weight gain. Children vary in the rhythmicity of repetitive biologic functions. These include sleep-awake cycles, appetite, and elimination. Parental interviews (Carey) enable a pediatrician to assess a child's temperamental profile in vital areas of function (activity, intensity, mood, adaptability, rhythmicity, threshold, distractibility, persistence, and approach-withdrawal) as suggested by the longitudinal studies of Thomas, Chess, and Birch. Knowledge of patterns of individual differences such as that of the "temperamentally difficult" (high intensity, low adaptability, low threshold) child help a pediatrician to understand the child's intrinsic contributions to a sleep problem, and this understanding can help the parent in turn to manage this "difficult yet still normal" child.

Age-Appropriateness of Behavior A given behavior has different meanings in children of each age. While this is obvious in the case of motor milestones, it is equally true for behavior problems. Temper tantrums, nightmares, phobias, stuttering, and other types of behavior are regularly seen at certain ages, and usually pass without consequence. For example, temper tantrums in an 18-month-old are an appropriate indicator of the child's growing sense of independence. A tantrum of similar intensity at 4 years of age deserves exploration for an answer as to why the child's striving for autonomy does not take a more mature form. By being aware of the individual temperamental and maturational differences, a pediatrician not only can better evaluate problems when they arise, but can also use this information preventively to understand the child as an individual and,

by sharing this information with the parents, establish an alliance to optimize the child's development.

The Child's Pattern for Coping with Stresses Since the pressures of growing up are a part of everyday life, children's behavioral problems must always be evaluated in the context of how they handle these stresses as well as others that confront them. A pediatrician can note whether the behavioral symptoms in question provide a way for the child to cope better with the pressures of his or her environment. For example, thumb sucking and holding onto a bottle or blanket or beloved toy through the stressful second and third years seem to be healthy solutions to stress. Unless the parents' concern about such a "lovey" makes it nonadaptive, one should see such behavior as a source of strength for the child and reinforce the parents to see it as such. Assessing a child with a stress model allows one to generalize and view the child's underlying resources available to cope with any challenging situation.

A psychological instrument such as the Denver Developmental Assessment can be easily administered in the pediatrician's office, and it may be viewed as just such a stress. Such an assessment can become a way to evaluate the child's "level" of development as well as reaction to the stress of being tested. Then this becomes a way to attend to the child's responses to the stress of testing and how the child is likely to cope with other stresses of life. In other words, we are given an opportunity to see how a child approaches any given problem or item rather than merely whether the test is passed or failed. When a 14-month-old boy turns to his mother to seek help when he is asked to stack blocks, this not only tells us about the child's response to the stress of the test, but also tells us something about the strength of his attachment to his mother and something about his level of autonomy.

The idea of identifying a child's mechanisms for coping is part of the broader principle of being able to list the child's individual strengths, as well as problems in a "problem list." When asked to stack blocks, a 2-year-old may take great delight in knocking them over rather than stacking them. Negativism is a healthy sign of the toddler's growing independence and should not be overlooked.

Influence on Other Areas of Function In determining the significance of any problem to a child, it is crucial to determine how isolated and discrete the problem is. A 4-year-old's bed-wetting at night may represent a discrete delay in maturation, while the same symptom in a 6-year-old may interfere with peer relations (for example, an inability to spend the night at a friend's house). As children grow and attempt to identify with their peers, such a symptom becomes a real source of anxiety about their own adequacy. This anxiety can begin to interfere with all areas of function. They may begin to show signs of deficit in school performance and in their self-esteem in general. In a small child and in the area of feeding, the problem may range from a discrete attempt to control choices, such as refusing vegetables—a transient, self-limited problem—to a more global feeding disturbance, such as a refusal to eat any solid food. When the problem is no longer confined to the feeding area and involves other areas of adjustment such as sleep and toilet problems, this suggests an even more global impairment in the parent-child relationship. The degree to which a problem is a clinically significant one is commonly reflected by the number of functional areas in the child's life which are affected.

Determining the degree to which any symptom affects the child's overall level of function not only has diagnostic implications but also is helpful in managing the problem. A therapeutic plan should account for and support the child's achievements and successful areas while attempting to improve any weaknesses.

Chronicity of Symptom Since development implies change over time, any symptom that becomes chronic is worrisome. Crying, for instance, reaches a developmental peak between 3 and 6 weeks and tapers off by the age of 3 months. When a 6-month-old presents with the persistent problem of "colicky" crying, that child requires evaluation and intervention. Thus, the degree of fixation in a behavior becomes a measure of the degree of problem.

Finally, behavioral symptoms that become inflexible should arouse even more concern. If appropriate 2-year-old negativism is replaced by intense temper tantrums with persistent head banging whenever children do not get their way, this constrained, inflexible behavior pattern is a sign of such children's need for therapeutic attention to their relationship with their parents.

Delaying a diagnostic decision while collecting

observations at several visits allows a pediatrician to assess the inflexibility of any symptom by observing the parents' and child's responses to various therapeutic suggestions. While an assessment of the parents' concerns, as well as the five areas of child behavior described aid the pediatrician, no evaluation is complete without the same kind of observation of the parent-child interaction.

Evaluation of Interaction

A pediatrician should not only evaluate parent and child separately, but also evaluate the interaction of parent and child over time. The essence of parent-child interaction may be seen in the mutual requests for attention and responses by parents with their children. Pediatricians should record observations of these interactions. They can distinguish the mother who sensitively shapes and shows her child how to achieve a task from one who either angrily shoves the child to a task or is completely unavailable to the child. Similarly, pediatricians can distinguish between the child who explores the surrounding environment, using a parent as a secure base, and the child whose interaction with a parent is either minimal or provocative. Value judgments should never substitute for repeated careful observations that attempt to understand the interaction of parent and child on its own terms and in its own culture.

Management

The therapeutic first step may be for the physician to try a simple suggestion. If the parent cannot establish a working relationship with the pediatrician and misuses the suggestion so that the behavioral problem becomes worse or reinforced, this becomes a measure of the depth of the parent's inability to accept help and of the need for more intensive therapy for any solution of the problem. Pediatricians tend to blame themselves when a helping relationship cannot be established instead of recognizing the diagnostic implications of the parents' inability to let down their defenses and to join in a therapeutic effort to help the child.

Pediatric management of childhood behavior problems usually requires seeing parent and child together. By using the child's behavior as a way of communicating with parents and pointing out the child's behavior and their response to it, the pediatrician can help parents to see their children as individuals with strengths as well as weaknesses. For instance, when parents understand and accept their toddler's negativism as a striving for independence, they can pursue the goal of allowing the child the opportunity to work out negative struggles and to define his or her own capacities and limits. In this way, the pediatrician forms an alliance with parents that supports them in their concern, but gives them a goal which enables them to work together at finding adaptive parental responses to help the child.

A pediatrician who no longer feels able to understand or help a family should consider referral to a psychiatrist or social worker who is trained to work with more difficult parents. Because of the nature of the problem and the nature of their relationships with families, pediatricians should approach such referrals even more sympathetically than they might a referral to another physician. The parents' need for defenses against facing the fact that they have a family problem must be respected. The pediatrician may have to see a family several times to gain a clear idea of what kind of referral they will accept and to outline the questions that should be answered. The pediatrician must remain the primary caretaker for the family and continue to support them after therapy is instituted. The pediatrician should remain involved in the assessment. In addition, the pediatrician must clearly understand the consultant's assessment of the problem, for the pediatrician will most often be left to carry out the consultant's treatment and management recommendations after the diagnostic and/or therapeutic interval has terminated.

Pediatric management of behavior problems and active fostering of normal development can be among the most challenging and rewarding aspects of pediatric practice. They need not be especially time consuming, but they do require a knowledge of normal development as a dynamic process and concerned attention in understanding parents' reports and in observing both children and parents' behavior.

47 | Negativistic Behavior

by Sandra R. Leichtman

Parents usually try to provide care which they feel is in the best interest of their children. Yet, in the process of psychological growth and development, the child often displays many behaviors which appear to directly oppose the parents' attempts at care giving. Thus, not infrequently the pediatrician will hear a perplexed parent complain that a child refuses to eat, resists the attempts of the grandmother to play with her or him, is stubborn, or appears to be deliberately trying to get the parents angry.

The reasons for these negativistic acts and the ways in which they are manifested vary according to the developmental stage of the child. Accordingly, the ability of the pediatrician to help a parent understand and manage a child's behavior is dependent on the knowledge of the normal patterns of psychological development.

Early Infancy

Young infants are not aware of their own existence as being separate and independent from that of the mother. For approximately the first 2 months of life, the infant's focus is almost entirely on body needs for sleep, sustenance, physical contact, and relief from discomfort. From approximately 2 to 8 months of age, the mother and infant become mutually dependent on each other for gratification. It is during this period that infants come to view their needs as being satisfied by a force outside of their own bodies. The close intimacy and mutual regulation of mother and infant obscure the separate existences of the two. Instead the mother and infant interact as if they are part of a single system.

Resistance to Feeding

During this period of mutual dependency, a mother might complain of being distressed by the infant's refusing to suck, turning away from the nipple, or generally resisting being fed. Not infrequently, a mother might attribute these behaviors to willful acts of the infant denoting rejection of her. Since the infant does not yet perceive self and mother as separate beings, this resistance to feeding cannot be realistically considered as rejection of the mother. Rather, the infant is probably reacting to specific aspects of the feeding situation, for example, a dislike of a new taste, satiation, or a tense posture assumed by the mother.

Occasionally a situation will arise in which the mother's concern with rejection may lead her to try to force the infant to accept her ministrations, resulting in recurring frustrations for both mother and infant. The primary care health professional can intervene in this unfortunate pattern by helping to relieve the mother's uncertainty and tension. Following examination of the baby, the mother can be reassured that the infant is healthy and well-nurtured. The physician can instruct the mother in ways to hold the baby which may be more comfortable for both mother and infant. Possibly, an adjustment in the feeding schedule might also be suggested. Finally, it is not unusual for a mother to be angry at the almost insatiable demands which the infant places on her for her time and energy. The physician should let the mother express her feelings and encourage her to let others temporarily tend the infant, thus giving her respite from the sometimes exhausting tasks of infant care-taking.

Late Infancy

During the latter half of the first year of life and extending to approximately 18 months of age, significant cognitive, social, and physical developments occur which have important consequences for the infant's becoming increasingly independent. Concommitantly, these developments contribute to the infant's showing new resistant behaviors which the parent may view as being negativistic.

Stranger Anxiety

In early infancy the infant is able to perceive many separate impressions of the mother through their mutual interactions. While recent data suggest that during this period the infant may be able to distinguish between mother and nonmother, it is generally acknowledged that not until late infancy does the infant's increasing ability to remember these consistent impressions permit piecing them together to form a stable concept of the person who has been ministering to his or her needs, the mother. In addition, the mother's touch, smell, and appearance become associated with comfort and pleasure. The mother is now viewed as a special person who is quite separate from the infant.

Whereas previously the response to others was based on how they met the infant's needs, now the mother's presence is seen as being in itself satisfying. When she leaves, the infant is upset. When strangers appear, the infant cries. Before the infant would gleefully accept the keys offered by a friendly relative, but now will accept this offering only if the mother is present. This period of protestation when faced by a person other than the infant's mother is termed *stranger anxiety*.

This change in the infant's behavior may appear puzzling to the mother. The primary care health professional can help the parent by explaining that it is not abnormal for an infant at this age to become attached to the mother and dependent on her for reassurance. Consequently, the infant becomes fearful and wary in the presence of strangers. The mother should be counseled to avoid separations from the infant during this period. Should the infant need hospitalization, "rooming-in" or frequent and prolonged visiting is advisable. If the mother is employed, she should be encouraged to provide the infant with a consistent substitute caretaker.

Since the pediatrician is not exempt from the infant's negative reactions to persons other than the mother, examination may prove very difficult during this period. Thus, it is suggested that the mother be in close proximity to the infant during examination.

Resistance to Parental Interference

Physical development during late infancy results in infants being able to move about on their own accord and to successfully reach for, grasp, and let go of objects of various sizes. For example, with respect to locomotion the infant progresses through stages of sitting alone, creeping, pulling up to a standing position, standing alone, and eventually walking without support.

These developments, combined with the infant's delight in learning about objects in the environment, compulsive desire to repeat new actions until they are mastered, and difficulty in relinquishing enjoyable activities, often lead to conflicts between the mother and infant. Typical problem areas involve eating, sleeping, and dressing. For example, the infant's movement to the upright position often interferes with the mother's ease in dressing the child. With respect to feeding, the infant's great interest in the touch, smell, and feel of the food, desire to manipulate the spoon, and joy in watching objects disappear when released from the hand can lead to battles around feeding. Through anticipatory guidance the physician can help the parent avoid frustration at having to clean up most of the child's planned meal from off the floor by advising the mother to purchase a highchair which has a large tray with upturned edges. Once confronted with the complaint of a feeding problem, physicians can use their knowledge of this early period of independence to recommend ways of dealing with the difficulty. The mother can, for instance, be counseled to give the child another spoon to hold during feedings. It also might be suggested that the baby's food be cut into small pieces for finger feeding. Finally, the mother can be encouraged to permit infant's to attempt to use the spoon themselves until their curiosity is sated.

The infant's resistance to going to bed at this stage is related to the difficulty in separating from the mother and the joys of an environment that is in the process of being discovered. To help both mother and infant deal with this nighttime separation, the physician can suggest that the mother remain with the infant a few minutes at bedtime in order to reassure the infant of her presence. During the daytime, games such as peek-a-boo can be used to help the infant learn to master temporary separation. Finally, prior to bedtime the infant should be engaged in soothing rather than stimulating activities.

Breath Holding

Since language development in infancy is limited, displeasure is often shown through physical actions. A behavior which causes considerable consternation for parents is that of breath holding. When angered or frustrated, the infant may cry vigorously, sometimes hold his or her breath until cyanotic, and even lose consciousness. Occasionally convulsive movements may be noted. Typically, breath-holding spells begin after 6 months of age and peak around 1 year. These spells may show a history of family incidence.

The pediatrician can allay the parents' fears that the child may stop breathing permanently through the assurance that these spells are self-limiting and that no harmful effects are anticipated. If the spells are frequent, they may be a symptom of impaired child-parent interaction. The parents may need the pediatrician's assistance in determining what circumstances may be triggering the breath-holding spells so that they are better able to adjust to the needs of the infant. Unless there are signs of a seizure disorder, anticonvulsants should not be prescribed.

Early Preschool Years

The period in which negativistic behavior is most prominent occurs between the ages of 18 and 30 months and is frequently referred to as the "terrible twos." Physical and cognitive maturation during this period permits the child to run about without the physical support of the mother and to use language to express needs. These developments enable toddlers to move toward still greater independence and autonomy from the mother. In doing so, however, they openly oppose parental aid, insisting on doing things themselves, even when they are not able to master these attempted tasks. Toddlers also frequently refuse to comply with parental suggestions and demands, although these appear to be in their best interests. These behaviors, which oppose the will of others, are used by young children to establish their autonomy.

Opposition to Parental Control

In contrast to the resistant behaviors displayed in early infancy, the negativistic behavior of toddlers is motivated to challenge parental control. It is as if children work toward defining themselves through this oppositionalism. For the parent, this behavior is often viewed as perplexing, frustrating, and provocative.

The physician can help the parent constructively adapt to this difficult stage by discussing the meaning of the negativistic behavior, offering support, and suggesting management techniques. By interpreting the oppositionalism as an important aspect of the child's developing autonomy, the parent may come to accept the temporary clash of wills as an adaptive challenge to authority and not as a personal attack. The parents can be supported in their expressions of anger and despair which are natural reactions to the child's provocative behaviors. They can also be reassured that negativistic behavior is a normal developmental stage which subsides as toddlers feel more secure in their autonomous functioning.

With respect to specific management techniques, it is important for the parent to be consistent in discipline. While parents should not interfere with the child's attempts to master difficult tasks, they should let the child know that their assistance is available if and when the child is ready to accept help. Finally, exaggerated parental distress should be avoided since this will often exacerbate the oppositionalism.

Temper Tantrums

Sometimes when angered by not having their way or frustrated at their own limitations, children may throw themselves on the floor, flail and scream, proclaim that they are unloved, and hold their breath. These tantrums, which usually last only a few minutes, are often best handled by ignoring the outbursts (unless the child is engaged in destructive behavior which must, of course, be stopped), offering nurturance after the tantrum has ended, and helping the child learn to express feelings through words. Temper tantrums usually subside by age 4.

School Years

During the late preschool period the child learns to identify with the parents and adopts their standards of acceptable behaviors. Thus by school age negativistic feelings are usually expressed through verbal rather than physical means. At times, however, fear of persons in authority (such as parents or teachers) or overdependence may inhibit the child from directly expressing negative feelings. The child may then take recourse in nondirect passive behaviors which serve to provoke the persons in authority. Some of these "passive-aggressive" behaviors observed in school-age children include dawdling, excessive yawning, procrastination, and pouting.

These behaviors are displayed by most school-age children at some time, usually in reaction to specific situations. When the pressure of the situation is relieved, the passive-aggressive behaviors frequently disappear. However, if the child develops a fixed pattern in which aggressive or hostile feelings are typically expressed in a passive manner, the physician should consider this behavior as symptomatic of disturbed parent-child relationships and refer the family for a psychological or psychiatric evaluation.

Scholastic Underachievement

One way in which a school-age child may indirectly show opposition to parental control is through academic underachievement. Often this occurs when parents impose their own standards for academic excellence on the child. While the expectations may not be unrealistic in relation to the child's ability, the parental insistence on meeting their standards can lead to considerable resistance. Typically, this negativistic response takes the form of progressive falling in grades through each report card marking period until the last, at which time the student manages to marginally pass the grade. Teacher reports might indicate that the child does not appear to listen in class, refuses to contribute to class discussions, is slow to begin assignments, and rarely completes the homework.

The physician can successfully intervene by eliciting the parents' cooperation in relieving the academic pressure. For example, the physician can suggest to the parents that they make the child responsible for completing all school assignments. When the schoolwork is no longer viewed as an area of conflict between parents and child, the child will often respond by showing rapid and marked improvement in grades.

Adolescence

The adolescent is faced with the task of preparation for assumption of adult roles and responsibilities. Thus, as was the case with the early preschooler, the adolescent actively strives for increased autonomy and independence from parents.

In early adolescence, opposing parental wishes becomes a way of pulling away from dependence on adults. Thus the openly defiant and negativistic behavior associated with the "terrible twos" often reappears, but again represents a passing phase of adaptation. Following this initial oppositionalism, adolescents begin to turn to peers to help them explore values which are to become important to them as individuals and which will help them form a sense of identity.

The physician who directly confronts an early adolescent with the negativistic nature of his or her behavior is likely to encounter increased resistance, sulkiness, and canceled appointments. A more appropriate approach to alleviating the family problems created by the adolescent's rebellion is for the physician to help the parents in setting reasonable limits on the adolescent's behavior, respecting the adolescent's need for privacy, and providing support and guidance when requested.

The adolescent lacking in peer relationships will probably benefit from the counseling and support of the pediatrician. Adolescents whose rebellion takes the form of behaviors which are injurious to themselves or others should be referred for mental health consultation.

48 | Colic

by Edwin A. Sumpter

Colic is paroxysmal crying lasting several hours a day in an otherwise healthy child. For purposes of a comparative clinical study, Wessel more precisely defines colic as continuous crying for 3 h or more during 3 or more days of the week. Symptoms appear during the first weeks of life, intensify about the fourth to sixth week, and gradually diminish by the third to fourth month. In the classical syndrome infants with colic tend to have a low threshold of response to external stimuli, a high activity level which increases with age as the crying increases, unpredictability of biological rhythms, and a crankiness or negativity of mood.

The incidence of colic is difficult to estimate because of this vagueness of definition. In Wessel's study 48 of 98 babies were considered fussy. Of these, 25 were "seriously fussy," meaning their symptoms lasted for more than 3 weeks and required medication. Brazelton's diary study of crying patterns in normal infants revealed a median of $2\frac{3}{4}$ h of crying per day at 6 weeks of age. Many of these would have qualified as having colic by Wessel's criteria.

To the physician in practice, colic is that amount of fussing which drives the family to seek relief. Parental anxiety and tolerance obviously influence which cases come to the physician's attention, but it is not at all clear to what degree these factors are actually etiologic. The most mature and stable of parents may feel concern and frustration. Their need for a warmly responsive infant is not being fulfilled, and their increasing tension is not lost on this easily stimulated child, who may become even more agitated in response to their frantic efforts to quiet the infant. The entire process may be alleviated or further escalated by the quality of the physician's response to the family's sometimes desperate requests for help.

The cause of colic is unknown. A small percentage of cases can definitely be related to milk allergy. Low progesterone levels, "congenital hypertonicity," physiological immaturity of the intestinal tract, parental tension, even some terrifying primordial memory have been cited, but without reproducible data. There is no consistent correlation with the order of birth, race, socioeconomic status, age or emotional health of parents, or whether the infant is breast- or bottle-fed. Thus, colic appears to be the result of poorly understood environmental and intrinsic factors, among which is the very individual repertory of responses with which the child is endowed.

It is not as helpful for the physician to think in the accustomed terms of diagnosis-treatment-cure as in terms of a family with a normal child facing one of the stresses of child rearing. Skillful medical management must be educational as well as immediately helpful. The educational process can best begin before the symptoms appear, at the prenatal and newborn hospital visits. With some experience, the physician may be able to identify some parents whose anxieties and expectations predispose them to making ineffectual responses to a difficult baby. The nursery observation that an infant is hyperresponsive may further alert the physician to possible difficulty. In such cases more than the usual discussion of emotional and developmental aspects of child rearing is indicated, including tactics helpful in handling a particularly fussy baby.

Especially in the case of a first child, an office visit at 2 to 3 weeks of age allows the physician to see how the family and the baby are adjusting to each other and provides a further opportunity to offer guidance. These anticipatory efforts may lessen its impact, but colic will still occur. The first contact with the physician is most often at the time when the parents are at the zenith of their frustration, usually in the evening when the telephone call is least welcome. Though a few reassuring words and suggestions may help for the moment, it is advisable to make plans to see the infant within the next day or two, preferably with both parents in attendance.

The history should include a detailed account of a day, including amount, intensity, and pattern of crying; elimination, feeding, and sleep-wake rhythms; and reactions to external stimuli. Maternal diet in the nursing infant or formula content and preparation should be examined. It is important to determine whether factors other than the baby are creating tension in the home, such as health, economic, marital, or in-law problems. How the crying baby is handled may in itself be a contributing factor to the colic. A careful account and demonstration by the parents of their usual manner of response is important.

The physical examination must be conspicuously thorough. The physician must be satisfied that the infant is thriving, has no nutritional or anatomical explanation for the symptoms, and no evidence of intermittent intestinal obstruction or other surgically correctable abnormality.

Involving parents in the actual assessment of historical and physical examination data gives them an opportunity to correct misinterpretations by the physician and reinforces the therapeutically important fact that their problem is taken seriously and respectfully. They need reassurance that their baby is healthy and that the fussing represents no threat to the infant's well-being. They should understand the individuality of infants' temperamental characteristics, the wide spectrum of normal crying patterns, and the likely course and duration of colic. Concern, frustration, and anger are acceptable and inevitable parental feelings. Though they subtly may feed back to the infant, they are basically the result, not the cause, of the problem. The already present feelings of guilt and ineptitude do not need further reinforcing by physician criticism, implied or direct. "All babies cry, you know," and "You're too tense," are examples of unhelpful, if not counterproductive, comments.

Cow's milk allergy is an infrequent but undeniable cause of colic, and it is thus justifiable to remove cow's milk from the infant's diet in favor of a soybean formula for a trial period of a full week, since any formula change may cause an unexplained improvement in symptoms for a shorter period of time.

Handling the infant in a calm and nonstimulating manner should be demonstrated. There are no psychological or dental contraindications to using a pacifier, and it may be helpful in temporarily quieting some infants, as may a warm water bottle, humming, and gentle rhythmic motion.

Phenobarbital in one of the liquid forms may be given in doses of 4 to 6 mg/kg per day in four divided doses, 15 to 30 min before feeding. The use of a sedative for only a week or two may return order and confidence to the household even though the colic may persist. In severe cases, medication may be required for several weeks, but there should be trial withdrawals during this period. Occasionally an intractable case in an emotionally deteriorating household may require temporary hospitalization or the use of an analgesic such as elixir of meperidine in doses sufficient to bring relief (2 to 6 mg/kg per day given P.O. every 4 to 6 h).

Thoroughness and sensitivity in the initial visit bolster the parents' self-confidence and thus minimize their dependence upon the physician. However, the physician must continue to play an active and available counseling role. Colic is the kind of challenge which may cause underlying psychopathology or marital discord to surface. Alertness to the need for family counseling or psychiatric consultation is part of the physician's obligation.

49 | Self-Stimulating Behaviors

by Richard M. Sarles and Alice B. Heisler

Self-stimulating behaviors such as head banging, head rolling, rocking, thumb sucking, and habits of hair pulling, nail biting, and masturbation are issues of concern for both parents and primary care practitioners. In general, these behaviors are usually self-limited to the preschool period. As such, these habits do not generally signify psychological maladjustment and thus often require little intervention other than reassurance for the parents and the recommendation for adequate stimulation of the child.

Head Banging and Rocking Behavior

Head banging is rhythmical movements of the head against a solid object, such as the crib mattress or occasionally the headboard itself, and is often associated with rocking of the head or the entire body. It is most commonly observed at bedtime or at times of fatigue and stress, and may vary in duration from several minutes to hours. It has been noted that head banging often continues even when the child is asleep. The age of onset shows wide variability, and is most commonly witnessed during the preschool years. The reported incidence of head banging or rocking behavior varies between 3 to 10 percent in a private pediatric population, with a male-female ratio of approximately 2 to 4:1. There is occasionally a positive family history of such behavior, but only 20 percent of siblings of rockers exhibit similar or other rhythmical patterns disturbances.

Various theories have been developed in an attempt to understand these self-limited, but often disturbing, behaviors. Rocking is thought to be a soothing, pleasurable experience every infant encounters in utero and from the neonatal period onward. The seeking of pleasure from movement is repeated throughout life from early childhood rocking in the mother's arms, to childhood jump-rope games, to the playground swing, to dancing in adulthood. Individual constitutional patterns in childhood account for a wide variability in the amount of stimulation any particular child may require. However, in certain children, such as those who are deaf, blind, emotionally disturbed, or severely mentally retarded, marked rhythmical movements may be commonly found. In these cases, the movements probably represent a compensatory reaction to make up for the lack of, or the inability to integrate, stimuli. In addition, the normal child who is inactive due to physical illness generally shows a need for motor release often manifested in bed rocking or other rhythmic body movements which generally disappear once normal mobility is restored to the child.

Physical and neurologic findings in these children are predominantly within normal limits, and EEG studies have been generally nonrevealing. It appears that these behaviors are linked to maturational patterns and closely correlate with teething and other transitions of growth and development, perhaps as a mechanism of tension release. Although psychosocial growth and development are apparently not disturbed and studies indicate no connection of rocking behavior with parental divorce or separation, the question of adequate stimulation for the child in the presence of family turmoil and stress should be investigated.

Treatment is generally directed toward assuring the parents that head banging cannot cause brain injuries or disorder and that such children show no adverse residual in later life and, in fact, are usually well coordinated and completely normal. Padding the crib and securing the bed to prevent rolling may be helpful during the limited rocking behavior. Sedation in the form of diphenhydramine may prove effective, but psychotropic medication is generally unnecessary. Consultation with a child psychiatrist or psychologist is indicated if the head-banging or rocking behavior persists beyond the age of 3. In the child who shows a lack of social interaction, or a preoccupation with self or with self-stimulatory behavior such as overt, compulsive masturbation, consultation may also be indicated.

Thumb Sucking and Nail Biting

Thumb sucking is an almost universal occurrence in infancy during the early oral stage of development. Infants put virtually every object in the mouth until parents place restrictions on certain objects because of considerations of safety.

The pleasurable sensations associated with the double tactile experience of sucking and being sucked, and the feelings of security and comfort which this evokes, tend to reinforce this type of behavior. Many families substitute rubber pacifiers as a more socially acceptable means of oral pleasure, and children themselves often spontaneously suck their security blankets, a doll, or a stuffed animal. Thumb sucking usually occurs during times of stress and at bedtime. Social and family pressures generally limit thumb sucking to the preschool years; however, the habit may persist into adolescence. The incidence of thumb sucking is not known, but it is estimated that approximately 30 to 40 percent of all children engage in finger sucking during the preschool years, and 20 percent continue past the age of 6.

Nail biting is an extension or permutation of the habit of thumb sucking. Some consider this behavior a form of more overt aggression directed toward one's self; others would define nail biting as a variation of thumb sucking since this behavior is also typically seen during times of stress. It is estimated that 40 percent of all children over the age of 6 bite their nails at some time or other, and 20 percent of college students continue as nail biters. Thus nail biting, in contrast to thumb sucking, often continues throughout childhood and into adulthood. There appears to be a family history in most cases, but this habit is so common that such an apparent association may be of no significance. There does not appear to

be any correlation with the number of children in the family, the birth order, the type of feeding or type of feeding schedule, or the age or race of the parents. However, there is a significant association with the time of weaning, in that the later the weaning takes place, the less likely the chance of thumb sucking.

Thumb sucking, nail biting, and cuticle biting or picking generate an increase in the incidence of digital cutaneous infections and an increase in the probability of dental malocclusion. The probability of malocclusion in thumb suckers appears directly related to the age of cessation of the habit. Thus, those children who cease the habit only after 6 years of age generally manifest malocclusion to some degree when seen at 12 years of age.

An underlying cause of tension should always be investigated, but often simple behavior reinforcement therapy is sufficient to alleviate these habits. The parents should be advised to avoid punishment, threats, or anger. Encouragement in the place of restrictions is helpful in engaging children in their own programs to decrease or eliminate these behaviors. Bitter-tasting commercial preparations applied to the fingers may be used as a reminder for the child but are generally inadequate unless supplemented by consistent positive behavioral reinforcement. This reinforcement-reward should be of the child's choosing and may be extra television privileges, dessert, or some other special treat. Weekly visits to the physician for the first month of treatment are important to further reinforce the change in behavior. Hypnosis is another treatment modality which is often quite successful and poses no dangers. Psychotropic medications are of little value. If these habits are linked to other signs of emotional distress, referral to specialists in behavioral disorders is warranted.

Hair Pulling and Twisting

This is an extremely uncommon form of self-stimulating behavior and is often indicative of severe psychological stress upon the child. The obvious cosmetic damage often results in ridicule by peers and shame for the child. The possibility of a formation of a hair ball, or trichobezoar, in the stomach if the child ingests the hair is a serious problem often resulting in hospitalization for surgical removal of the hair ball.

Treatment is usually indicated and varies from initial behavior modification techniques such as a positive reinforcement-reward system to the wearing of a cap. Local irritation from a primary dermatological condition rarely is the cause of disorder, but should be investigated. Hypnosis and/or psychotherapy may be required in many of these cases.

Special Problems in Disturbed Children

A broad spectrum of self-stimulating behaviors may be seen in the severely retarded or emotionally disturbed child. The behaviors, including body twirling or spinning and hand or arm flapping, characteristically are seen in cases of infantile autism or childhood schizophrenia. Excessive rocking behavior is common in the severely retarded and emotionally disturbed child. In addition, severe self-mutilating behaviors such as compulsive self-biting, severe head banging, and skin gouging may be occasionally seen in these disorders, but are more characteristic of certain metabolic-genetic disorders such as the Lesch-Nyhan syndrome and the Cornelia de Lange syndrome.

It is felt that these behaviors are part of a symptom complex in a severe disorder, quite in contrast to the generally isolated behavior previously discussed in normal children. The etiology is generally linked to the basic disorder, and may also reflect the lack of, or disordered integration of, sensory stimuli.

All these cases require treatment for the basic disorder and generally demand specialized treatment modalities beyond the scope and expertise of the primary care physician. Institutionalization is often required, and methods of treatment include aversive behavior modification techniques, arm and neck restraints, head helmets, major tranquilizers, and psychotherapeutic programs.

Masturbation

Masturbatory activity in children is a common occurrence which often leads to great concern of parents. Masturbatory activity may vary from direct manual genital stimulation to movement of the thighs against each other. Rhythmical swaying or thrusting motions of the child while straddling a hobby horse, pillow, stuffed animal, or other objects are other common methods of masturbation in children. Infants and children are capable of a physiological orgastic response similar to that experienced by the adult, except for the absence of ejaculation in the male child. Recognition of this fact was demonstrated in the common practice in Europe about the turn of the century of masturbating an irritable child to induce relaxation and sleep. Occasionally, this orgastic response has been incorrectly thought to represent a convulsive disorder in the preschool child.

Masturbatory activity is generally initiated as a response to the learned pleasure associated with touching of the genitalia first experienced in infancy as normal children explore their own bodies. Masturbation will continue as a lifelong pleasurable experience unless suppressed by parents or other adults. It is important for the practitioner to counsel parents concerning masturbatory practices and emphasize that masturbation is a normal, nondamaging healthy practice which helps children derive pleasure from their own bodies. Myths must be dispelled concerning the belief that masturbation may cause mental retardation, physical deformity, blindness, poor physical and mental health, facial pimples, hair on the palms of the hand, homosexuality, and sexual perversions. Parents should be aware of the normality and almost universal occurrence of masturbation in children, and they should be encouraged not to punish or shame the child. If parents observe masturbatory activity in their child, they may want to suggest to the child the inappropriateness of manipulation of the genitalia in public places or in front of others and inform the child that certain practices such as toileting and masturbation are best carried out in private.

A thorough physical examination is helpful to exclude local genital irritation, monilial infection, or pinworms, although these problems are rarely the causative agents for masturbation. Compulsive, overt masturbation in children and adolescents may lead to social isolation and may signify a deeper emotional problem. Consultation with a specialist in behavioral disorders of children and adolescents is indicated if the practitioner suspects that the masturbatory activity is excessive, compulsive, or overt, or may indicate the presence of a more complicated, troublesome emotional problem.

The practitioner should be aware that even with the current trend of our society toward sexual openness and enlightenment, myths and feelings concerning masturbation are often deep-seated and still persist. Thus, counseling and teaching by the practitioner may be met with covert or overt resistance by parents or school authorities. The practitioner should be prepared to educate those responsible for the growth and development of children.

50 | Fecal Soiling and Retention

by Richard M. Sarles

The act of defecation is a normal biological function governed by both various reflex actions and familial-cultural customs. The bowel pattern of the infant is totally under the influence of biologic reflex; it is usually not until the end of the second year of life, in our Western culture, that the child is asked to control the passage of stools for certain times and places. During the phase of development which is variously labeled as the anal stage, the stage of autonomy, or the negativistic stage, the child focuses on issues of controls and develops a pattern of giving up or retaining the bowel movements which the mother or her surrogate seems to value.

The majority of children become toilet-trained around the age of 3 years. However, some children, including those successfully and those unsuccessfully trained, may at times retain their stools for prolonged periods of time or pass them at inappropriate times or places, such as in their underclothes at school, in dresser drawers, or in closets.

The major disorders associated with abnormal bowel patterns are fecal soiling (encopresis), fecal retention, and psychogenic megacolon. These disorders may appear singly or together, and are generally considered to be of a nonorganic etiology.

Fecal Soiling

Fecal soiling generally refers to the repeated passage of feces in places other than the toilet, by children over the age of 4, in whom no organic dysfunction or illness is present. This behavior usually leads to repulsion, frustration, and anger in the child's parents, teasing and isolation by peers, and even denial of admission to or dismissal from kindergarten or elementary school. Although this disorder is generally described as the involuntary passage of stools, the nature of the soiling in closets or dresser drawers seems to indicate a voluntary process in many of these children.

Those cases in which toilet training was never successful are labeled *primary encopresis*, whereas those cases in which training was successful but soiling developed at a later age are termed *secondary encopresis*. Primary encopresis often has been attributed to families socioeconomically impoverished and in which there is a general laxity about cleanliness and an acceptance of poor bowel habits. Primary encopresis may also be found, however, in middle- and upper-class families with rigid, obsessive-compulsive life-styles. Secondary encopresis is considered to be a manifestation of psychological regression in response to a variety of stresses which may include the birth of a sibling, a death in the family, a separation in the family, or a threatened move. School phobia rarely presents as fecal soiling, but it should be considered in instances where the child is sent home from school because of the encopresis.

Fecal Retention

Fecal retention represents the withholding of feces, in contrast to the inappropriate expulsion by the encopretic child. One may also classify this disorder as primary or secondary depending upon the time of onset of symptoms. Physical causes are rare, although anal fissures may develop with the periodic passage of fecal material of enormous diameter. The psychological aspects of the control battle between mother and child are often dramatic. A child screaming with pain in response to a distended rectosigmoid colon while holding the legs tightly scissored to prevent the passage of feces presents a vivid example of the magnitude of this struggle. Often fecal retention is recognized in the older child only by the associated findings of fecal soiling due to leakage of watery stool around the large fecal plug in the rectum (paradoxical diarrhea.)

Megacolon

The combination of fecal retention and fecal soiling may be associated with the development of megacolon. This psychogenic megacolon is differentiated from the congenital aganglionic megacolon (Hirschsprung's disease) by its later onset of symptoms, periodic voluminous stools, excessive feces in the rectum, and the absence of a narrowed aganglionic segment of rectum or rectosigmoid colon shown by barium fluoroscopy or biopsy. In addition, fecal soiling is the major complaint in psychogenic megacolon and rare in Hirschsprung's disease.

Etiology

Since encopresis, fecal retention, and psychogenic megacolon are closely interrelated as bowel habit disturbances, family dynamics and individual personality patterns are similar and overlapping. While many authors place special emphasis on the nature and timing of bowel training as the causative mechanisms for the various disorders of bowel functioning, the success or failure of bowel training is dependent on a multiplicity of factors and cannot be attributed to a single event, style of toilet training, or single personality characteristic of the mother, father, child, or family. Nevertheless, persistent bowel disorders present certain specific characteristics of the child's personality, familial factors, and possible organic dysfunctions

In general, the incidence of encopresis is low, with approximately 0.7 to 1 percent of first grade boys showing symptoms. It is about one-tenth as common as enuresis, but in contrast to enuresis, there is no family tendency and it rarely occurs at night. Male-female ratio is approximately 4:1, and there appears to be an increased incidence of hyperactivity and reading disability in these boys. Indications of family strife and a higher than normal divorce and separa-

tion rate are found. In general, there is no correlation with intellectual functioning, except for a higher incidence of encopresis in the severely retarded. Encopresis may also be seen in severely regressed psychotic states. However, diseases associated with disorders of the bowels such as cystic fibrosis, lactose intolerance, regional ileitis, or ulcerative colitis rarely lead to encopresis or fecal retention.

The boys are variously described as having poor peer relationships and spending a great deal of time in solitary pursuits such as watching television. They are often neat, obedient, and compliant, but occasionally obstinate in a passive-aggressive manner, concealing their hostility and aggression through fecal soiling and retention. Some of the boys describe feelings of loneliness and rejection, but are unable to directly express their resentment.

The mothers of these children often are incapable of showing any warmth or feeling. They are often rigid, overorganized, compulsive, dominating, and frustrated in their roles as wife and mother. Depression is a common finding. Their encopretic child generally creates feelings of anger and defeat in these mothers due to their own preoccupation with cleanliness and bowel habits.

The fathers present a characteristic picture of a lack of involvement with the family. Absences from the home due to travel or business are common. Even when not absent from the home, these fathers are frequently emotionally and socially withdrawn; this effectively isolates them from their children and wives. Some of the fathers seem to be unwilling to accept a masculine role and passively seek a "substitute mother" in their wives.

The primary care physician should always consider the interaction of psychological and physical factors in the diagnosis and treatment of any illness. This is especially true when dealing with disorders of bowel patterns. A complete physical examination should be performed and appropriate laboratory diagnostic studies done prior to initiating any treatment plan.

Management

Treatment should be directed toward establishing normal bowel patterns and normalizing family and interpersonal dynamics. The physician should explain to the family how disorders of bowel habits may be a manifestation of emotional difficulties and should enlist the parents' cooperation in any treatment plan. It is usually important to reassure both parents that in cases of fecal retention, retained feces will not harm the child due to toxic by-products of the stool. The initial procedure in the regulation of bowel habits may require the use of stool softeners and mineral oil, in addition to alterations of diet to include natural laxatives and food roughage. Enemas should be avoided, but if absolutely necessary the rationale for their use should be thoroughly explained to the child. It is often wise to administer the enemas in the physician's office rather than at the home in order to avoid further conflict of bowel training between mother and child. Laxative medication should not be used, and there does not appear to be any rationale for the use of tranquilizers or other psychotropic medications.

The competitive struggle between mother and child over bowel habits must be interrupted. A simple behavior modification system using a weekly calendar often helps the child assume control. Gold stars or other rewards are given for each nonsoiled day. The record should then be brought to the physician each week by the child during a regular scheduled appointment. During this time the physician should spend individual time counseling both the child and the parents.

Satisfactory results are often achieved by such counseling and by involving the father to a greater degree with the child and family. The treatment outcome also appears to be related to the ability of the mother to reduce her overconcern and overcontrolling nature. Equally important, however, is the physician's skill in dealing with emotional problems and the ability not to take over the mother's role and her need to control the child's bowel habits. That is, the physician must recognize that the child's bowel dysfunction is symptomatic of emotional stress and that the fecal soiling or retention will be given up by the child only as the family problems are relieved.

The primary care physician may desire a consultation in the psychological evaluation and management of such cases. Referrals to professionals trained in behavioral issues of childhood and adolescence such as child psychiatrists, child psychologists, and behavioral pediatricians can be indicated. The consultant should be expected to evaluate the child and family, investigating all the areas previously mentioned in this section, and recommend to the primary care physician an appropriate treatment plan. One such treatment model could be a consultative approach wherein the consultant provides guidance to the primary care physician in the psychological management of the case. Another approach to treatment could be a collaborative model with the consultant treating the individual and family psychological problems, while working closely with the primary care physician in the management of physical problems.

Summary

Fecal soiling, fecal retention, and psychogenic megacolon are the major disorders associated with abnormal bowel habits. The etiology of these disorders is usually nonorganic but rather a reaction to some psychological stress or family dysfunction. Diagnostic evaluation includes a complete history and physical examination with special emphasis on individual and family functioning. Treatment should be directed toward normalizing bowel habits in the child and easing the mother's overcontrolling nature and involving the father to a greater degree with the family. The primary care physician may manage these cases alone or with consultation from other professionals interested in behavioral issues.

51 | Enuresis

by Michael Cohen

For the primary care provider, the evaluation and management of an enuretic child is a frequent and demanding task. An initial consideration of established factual information and etiologic factors will allow for the development of a reasonable, efficient, and successful approach to a wetting child and to the child's family.

Enuresis is defined as involuntary discharge of urine, though it is often used to mean wetting during nighttime sleep (*nocturnal enuresis*). Daytime wetting is termed *diurnal enuresis*. The diagnosis of enuresis should be reserved for wetting beyond the age of 5 in girls and 6 in boys, the sex-related age differences reflecting developmental variations.

Nocturnal enuresis exists in approximately 15 percent of all 5-year-olds, 7 percent of 8-year-olds, and 3 percent of 12-year-olds. Lower socioeconomic groups, families with lower educational levels, and institutionalized populations have a higher reported prevalence of enuresis. Males predominate at all ages within all enuretic populations, with the differential being greater in older children. Somewhat less than 10 percent of all enuretics also have daytime wetting. Diurnal enuresis occurs alone rather infrequently.

Primary enuresis exists when a child has never achieved consistent dryness. A child with *secondary enuresis* is generally considered to have had a period of dryness of at least 3 to 6 months and is commonly referred to as a "relapser" or an "onset enuretic." Among enuretic children, secondary enuresis generally increases with age, with over half of all enuretics being onset type by age 12. Approximately 25 percent of children will have some relapse bedwetting after a period of initial dryness. This form of secondary enuresis is often self-limiting and may occur only at times of illness or emotional stress.

The strong familial aspect of enuresis is well established. In approximately 70 percent of the families with an enuretic child, the symptom will occur in more than one member. In 40 percent of the families, at least one parent had nocturnal enuresis.

Etiology

Enuresis must be considered multifactorial in etiology. Developmental "delays," organic disorders, and psychological factors have all been emphasized as causes of enuresis. (See Sec. 52 for discussion of enuresis as a dyssomnia.) Although definitive proof is lacking, many believe that a delay in adequate neuromuscular bladder control is the major etiologic factor in enuretic children evaluated and managed in their setting. This view is supported by (1) the primary nature of most enuresis, (2) the common familial pattern, (3) the common history of frequency of voiding and urgency to void as a manifestation of a small functional bladder capacity, and (4) the high incidence of spontaneous remission (or developmental maturation). Proponents of this theory would argue that the persistence of enuresis after neuromuscular maturation is based on the psychological effects of the child's interaction with significant individuals in his or her environment.

Organic explanations have focused primarily in the genitourinary and nervous systems. Obstructive lesions of the distal outflow tract, such as posterior urethral valves, have received particular attention as both a cause of urinary tract infections and as an independent cause of enuresis. A current urinary tract infection or the history of previous infections may be causal factors in enuresis. However, in a primary setting, only about 3 to 4 percent of enuretic youngsters will demonstrate significant urologic pathology. Nervous system dysfunction may be associated with enuresis, either through lumbosacral disorders which affect bladder innervation or as a reflection of global mental retardation. While true myelodysplastic disorders may affect bladder function, the radiologic finding of spina bifida occulta has not been shown to be casually related to enuresis. Diabetes mellitus, diabetes insipidus, sickle cell anemia and trait, food allergies, and ingestion of foods or medications with diuretic actions have all been implicated as infrequent causes of enuresis.

Psychological functioning may relate to enuresis at two levels. The enuresis may be only one aspect of a child's general difficulty in behavioral adaptation, or it may be an isolated symptom in a child whose behavioral functioning is otherwise adequate. "Problem" children, as defined by behavioral questionnaires, interviews, and observations make up a small percentage of an enuretic population. There is no justification in presuming psychopathology based on the mere presence of enuresis. As an isolated phenomenon, enuresis, not uncommonly, may be determined by poor or deficient learning of a habit pattern during toilet training. Resistance to initial training efforts, despite the nature of the techniques utilized, appears to be a critical factor.

The evaluation process should be considered as the initial phase of therapy. The positive therapeutic value of a complete evaluation which satisfies the concerns and expectation of the enuretic child and the child's family is well documented. Potential parental guilt, associated with management failures, can be alleviated by a brief explanation of the multifactorial origin of the condition and the common difficulties in management.

History

An estimate of the severity of the enuresis should be determined and expressed as the number of wet nights per week or month (for example, 4/7, 16/20). Quantitation of the enuresis allows for a relatively accurate demonstration of a trend and the effect of intervention. A delineation of the type of enuresis (primary versus secondary, and nocturnal versus diurnal) should be established. The effect of environmental factors on the severity of the symptoms should be explored. Parental management techniques should be discussed, beginning with a history of initial toilet-training efforts. The age and response of the child, the attitudes and approach of the parents, and the results of such efforts are important information. The child's perception of family and peer response to the difficulty should be elicited. An impression as to whether the enuresis is limiting age-appropriate activity should be obtained.

Past medical history will reveal any perinatal difficulties that may have led to neurologic trauma. The weight and gestation of the patient can alter developmental expectations. The review of systems should focus on the genitourinary and nervous systems. Delays in perceptual-motor or communication skills might coexist with a delay in bladder control. In addition to frequency and urgency of urination and symptoms of urinary tract infection, dribbling after and between micturition and dysuria have been found to be more common in enuretic children. Approximately 1 in 10 enuretics will also be encopretic. This association is firmly established and may reflect an underlying deficiency in toilet-training efforts or organic pathology.

Physical Examination

A full examination is essential. Renal disease may be reflected in poor growth or elevated blood pressure. Examination of the genitalia should be complete and sensitive to the feelings of a developing youngster or teenager. A search for major and minor anomalies should be followed by an observation of micturition. Anomalies, including undescended testes, underdeveloped scrotum, epispadias, phimosis and abnormalities in the urethral meatus in males, and location and characteristics of the urethral meatus in females should be observed, since they may be associated with internal anomalies. Abnormalities in the quality (size, velocity, and so forth) of the urinary stream, inability to initiate or stop micturition, dysuria, and dribbling should be noted.

A neurological examination may reveal lower spinal vertebral dysfunction which reflects bladder innervation abnormalities. Gait, muscular strength and tone, deep tendon reflexes, sensory responses, and rectal sphincter tone therefore should be examined.

Laboratory

A urinalysis provides valuable information about a wide range of organic disorders that may be associated with enuresis, including diabetes insipidus, psychogenic water drinking, diabetes mellitus, urinary tract infection, and various forms of renal pathology, such as nephrotic syndrome with proteinuria. Beyond the urinalysis and urine culture, the indication for further evaluation remains quite controversial. In a primary care setting, radiologic studies such as an intravenous pyelogram (IVP) and a voiding cystourethrogram (VCG) are indicated only when there exists significant historical or examination evidence of urological pathology. If these procedures are indeed indicated, the child must be adequately prepared in a manner that will minimize the psychological trauma. The nature of this preparation will depend on the age, sex, and developmental maturity of the child. A measurement of functional bladder capacity should be obtained if bladder training is the proposed form of treatment. Unless there is a strong suspicion of an undiagnosed seizure disorder, the presence of enuresis does not warrant an EEG.

At the conclusion of this type of evaluation, the vast majority of enuretics with significant organic and psychopathology will have been discovered. When their needs exceed the expertise of the primary care physician, these patients should be referred to the appropriate specialist. The remaining group, which constitutes the vast majority of enuretics, will present a picture consistent with a basic developmental delay in bladder control with associated psychological factors. This population is best managed by the clinician who is most familiar with the child and the child's family and environment.

Management

An air of optimism is realistic and may have immeasurable therapeutic value. A positive clinical response to the process of evaluation and intervention has often been labeled a *placebo effect*. The benefit of a carefully planned approach has been documented and should be considered a therapeutic response, not the result of a placebo. Optimism is supported by reports of an annual spontaneous cure rate of approximately 15 percent, after age 5. Optimism can also be cultivated by uncovering a history of parental enuresis.

The active participation of the child will enhance the efficacy of any specific mode of therapy and should be solicited. Such active involvement will also decrease the chances of struggle between child and parents and will promote the child's responsibility for the symptoms.

Reassurance may be the specific therapy for younger children or for children developing transient secondary enuresis in response to environmental stress. When parents feel compelled to do something active while waiting for a remission, various simple measures have been recommended. These suggestions include limiting fluid intake, emptying the bladder at bedtime, or taking the child to the bathroom during the night. If these suggestions are made, it should be with the realization that while they may decrease the symptoms somewhat, they have not been shown to hasten a remission. These tactics may also initiate or aggravate a struggle between parent and child.

Supportive counseling may be required as the sole mode of therapy or as an adjunct to other specific regimens. The goals of counseling could include (1) parental understanding of the multifactorial nature of enuresis, (2) parental acceptance of the child and the symptoms in a manner that allows them to provide maximum emotional support, (3) acceptance by the child of the symptom with an appreciation of "individual differences" that many children demonstrate in other areas of functioning, and (4) appreciation by the patient that he or she can have some control over the enuresis. The requirement for counseling depends on the age of the child, the child's general developmental and behavioral pattern, the family's experience with enuresis, the coexistence of emotional problems, intrafamily communication patterns, and the response to the initial management efforts.

If the enuresis is deterring the child's social, emotional, or cognitive development, a specific modality of therapy beyond reassurance and supportive counseling is indicated. Since there has not been a consistently superior modality, the clinician's experience, enthusiasm, and comfort should dictate the choice of method. Drug therapy, conditioning devices, and bladder training have been shown to be effective by various clinicians.

Pharmacologic agents with anticholinergic or sympathomimetic properties have been used in enuresis. The mechanism of action is thought to be either a direct relaxation effect on the bladder detrusor muscle or an effect on the central nervous system as an antidepressant or stimulant. Imipramine and oxybutyrin are the most commonly used of these agents. It is generally given $\frac{1}{2}$ to 1 h before bedtime, with no proven advantage to multiple daily doses. The initial imipramine dose is 25 mg for children under 12, and 50 mg for older children. The maximum recommended dose is 75 mg. The child should be asked to maintain a diary of success. At the first follow-up visit the drug dosage can be altered and positive feedback can be supplied to the youngster. Once a successful therapeutic response is achieved, the child should be maintained on the medication for approximately 3 months. At the end of this period, a gradual discontinuation of the drug will decrease the likelihood of a relapse. Tapering to once every other night and then every third night should be accomplished over a period of 4 to 6 weeks. The maximum psychological benefit of dryness on nondrug nights can be supplied by emphasizing and praising the child's newly developed bladder control which *will* be sustained without medication. The most common adverse effects are nervousness, sleep disorder, and mild gastrointestinal withdrawal symptoms of nausea, headache, and malaise. The triad of coma, convulsions, and cardiac disturbances occurs with imipramine poisoning in small children, and it may be fatal. Safety precautions in families with younger sibs is warranted.

Enuresis conditioning instruments involve a moisture-sensitive mattress device connected to an alarm which provides auditory stimulation to wake the child upon initiation of wetting. Because the temporal relationship between the wetting episode and the alarm is critical for effective conditioning, a fairly refined instrument with adequate sensitivity is required. Although primary enuretics respond more successfully, the success rate does not relate to the severity of the enuresis. Treatment failures are usually caused by (1) parental and patient resistance, (2) failure of the child to wake, or (3) mechanical difficulties with apparatus. The major complication of the device is a perineum or buttock rash. This side effect has been minimized by eliminating metal foil electrodes. Relapses are common, but dryness is attained more quickly and often permanently with a second course.

Bladder-training therapy is based on the observation that many children with enuresis have a de-

creased functional bladder capacity. The goal of this training is to transform a functionally infantile bladder into one with adult volume and coordination capabilities. The procedure involves the active participation of the child in holding the urine as long as possible once a day for several months. Increasing urine volumes and dry nights are recorded on a calendar which serves as a reinforcement for the child. The clinician must be cautious that the discomfort caused by urine retention does not discourage the participation of the youngster and create a struggle with the parents.

Treatment Failures and Relapses

The experienced clinician will attest to the fact that relapses and treatment failures are relatively frequent with all modes of therapy. A modality of therapy should not be considered a failure until it has been tried for at least 4 to 6 weeks. A failure of one type of therapy might dictate the addition of another mode. If combination therapy fails, the practitioner may have to indicate to the child and the family that the neuromuscular bladder control mechanisms are still too immature and that the symptoms must be tolerated for several more months, when the treatment can be reinstituted. Reassurance of physical and mental normality must accompany this message. However, if any new information concerning organic or psychopathology becomes apparent, further evaluation might be indicated. For example, a treatment failure could be due to noncompliance, which reflects either an underlying family interactional pattern which precludes the necessary empathy and understanding, or emotional needs of family members that require persistence of the symptom. Appropriate investigation of this aspect of the situation should be undertaken by the primary care clinician or a mental health associate. Psychiatric consultation may be indicated when the child demonstrates a significant maladaptive behavior pattern.

Relapses after the discontinuation of successful treatment can be handled by explaining to patients that the nervous system–bladder control mechanism is developing but is not fully mature yet and that a few more months of specific therapy will be required. The previously successful mode of therapy is then reinstituted. This approach allows for maintenance of an optimistic posture and, if necessary, the use of several courses of therapy.

52 | Nightmares and Other Sleep Disturbances

by Thomas F. Anders

Problems associated with sleep affect almost all children during the course of development. They span the gamut from an occasional awakening following a frightening nightmare to severe and intractable insomnia. Within the spectrum are included such disturbances as fear of the dark, difficulty in falling asleep, night waking, sleepwalking, sleep talking, and night terrors. Some persist into adulthood. Although we spend approximately one-third of our lives asleep, it is surprising how scant are the hard data on normal sleep behaviors. Only during the last 20 years, with the introduction of polygraphic recording techniques, have we been able to investigate physiological and behavioral activities during sleep. Actual incidence figures and diagnostic criteria for sleep disorders and sleep disturbances are only now being delineated.

As a general introduction to sleep state physiology and sleep cycles, a brief review is warranted. The initial observations of "active," rapid eye movement (REM) sleep states and "quiet," nonrapid eye movement (NREM) sleep states were made in 1924 by two Czech scientists, Denisova and Figurin. Unfortunately, their publication in Russian and lack of supportive polygraphic evidence precluded widespread recognition of their findings. Since the introduction of polygraphic techniques for studying sleep, it is well established that sleep is not a unitary state of physiologic restitution but rather two cycling states of differing physiologic function and activity.

A description of the *adult* sleep cycle provides an introduction to an understanding of developing sleep patterns in the infant and young child. Four states of electroencephalographic activity during adult sleep have been described by Dement and Kleitman: stage I is typified by low-voltage, fast activity; stage II, by the presence of sleep spindles[1] and K complexes[2] against a low-voltage background; and stages III and IV, by varying degrees of slow, high-voltage, delta-wave activity.[3]

REM sleep is defined by the occurence of a stage I EEG pattern in association with binocularly synchronous rapid eye movements, the suppression of muscle tone as recorded from the chin electromyogram, and accelerated, irregular respiratory and heart rates. NREM sleep lacks rapid eye movements and is accompanied by the presence of tonic muscle activity recorded from the chin electromyogram, a stage II, III, or IV EEG pattern, and slowed, regular cardiac and respiratory rates. Alternating REM and NREM sleep states represent two distinct patterns of neurophysiologic organization: the REM state is highly activated; the NREM state is basal and highly regulated. They follow each other in a periodic fashion, and together, they make up the sleep cycle.

While active-REM sleep periods of infants are qualitatively similar to REM periods of adults, three important quantitative differences have been described: whereas adults spend 20 percent of a night's sleep in active-REM sleep, sleeping full-term neonates, recorded for a 4-h interfeeding sleep period or for an entire 24-h period, spend 50 percent of their

---

[1] Sleep spindles are defined as EEG activity of 12 to 14 Hz, of at least 0.5 s duration, occurring in runs of greater than 6.

[2] K complexes are defined as EEG wave forms having a well-delineated negative sharp wave which is immediately followed by a positive component. The total duration of the complex should exceed 0.5 s. The K complex is generally maximal over vertex regions.

[3] Delta activity is defined as waves of 2 cycles per second or slower which have amplitudes greater than 75 μV from peak to peak.

Table 52-1

Comparison between Infant and Adult Sleep Patterns

	Infant	Adult
Ratio of REM to NREM	50:50	20:80
Periodicity of sleep states	50- to 60-min REM-NREM cycle	90- to 100-min REM-NREM cycle
Sleep onset state	REM sleep onset	NREM sleep onset
Temporal organization of sleep states	REM-NREM cycles equally throughout sleep period	NREM, stages III and IV, predominant in first third of night; REM state predominant in last third of night
Maturation of EEG patterns	Low-voltage, fast EEG pattern	K complexes
	High-voltage, slow EEG pattern	Delta waves
	1 NREM EEG stage	4 NREM EEG stages
Concordance of sleep measures (organization of sleep states)	Poor	Good

total sleep time in this state. The proportionate amount of time spent in active-REM sleep diminishes as the infant becomes older and as central nervous system maturation progresses. Secondly, infants frequently enter sleep through an initial active-REM period, in contrast to adults, who enter their first REM period 90 min after sleep onset. And, thirdly, active-REM periods emerge more frequently in infants than REM periods in adults, so that the infant's sleep cycle is shorter than the adult's. Active-REM periods recur every 50 to 60 min during infancy, rather than every 90 to 100 min, as reported in adults. The staging of quiet-NREM sleep by EEG criteria into four distinct NREM sleep stages becomes possible only after the second 6 months of life. The differences between sleep patterns in infants and adults are outlined in Table 52-1.

Pathologies of Sleep

A sleep disorders clinic, using modern techniques of polysomnography to record multiple physiologic parameters during a night of sleep, is rapidly becoming an important entity in the diagnostic assessment of sleep disturbances. Unfortunately, at present, less than 20 such clinics exist in the United States, and most of them focus on adult disorders of sleep.

For ease of description, clinical sleep disturbances may be divided into four major categories: those in which sleep is shortened (the insomnias), those in which sleep is disturbed by episodic events (the dyssomnias: sleepwalking, bed-wetting, nightmares, night terrors), those in which sleep is affected secondarily by illness, and, finally, those in which sleep during the 24 h is lengthened (the hypersomnias).

In this presentation, the focus is on stage IV NREM dyssomnias—the sleep disorders characterized by episodic events which interrupt sleep. The insomnias have not been a significant problem during childhood. The hypersomnias, including narcolepsy and the sleep apnea syndrome, do occur in children but are rare.

An idealized version of a night's sleep is portrayed in Fig. 52-1. It serves as a useful guide for locating the dyssomnias and sleep disturbances that are described below. An arbitrary distinction between primary sleep disorders and secondary sleep disturbances has been made. Primary sleep disorders refer to those which have related pathophysiologic findings evident from polysomnographic studies. Secondary sleep disorders, much more common in childhood, refer to developmental disturbances or psychological conflicts affecting sleep but not associated with polysomnographic changes.

Primary Sleep Disorders—The NREM Dyssomnias

The primary NREM dyssomnias include pavor nocturnus, or night terrors; somnambulism, or sleep-

Figure 52-1 An idealized all-night sleep state histogram. The various disorders and disturbances of sleep are depicted at their usual point of occurrence.

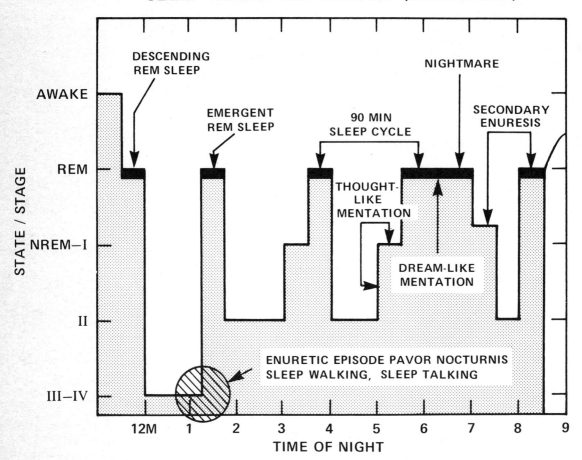

SLEEP—WAKE HISTOGRAM (IDEALIZED)

walking; somniloquy, or sleep talking; and stage IV sleep-related enuresis. Prior to sleep laboratory diagnosis, many children suffering from these disorders were referred to the child psychiatrist. Current evidence suggests, however, that these disorders reflect central nervous system immaturity. They have certain features in common: several of the disorders may occur in the same person; often there is a positive family history for the disorders; they are paroxysmal in nature and are characterized by nonresponsiveness to the environment, automatic appearance to actions, and retrograde amnesia for the episode the following morning. Finally, they all make their appearance at a particular point in the sleep cycle, as indicated in Fig. 52-1. Most younger children "outgrow" the symptoms as neurophysiologic maturation proceeds. In adolescents and adults, however, when these disturbances persist, secondary psychological conflcts frequently complicate the clinical picture. Although specific medications are available for disabling symptomatology, reassuring support to the family and child, blended with an optimistic and patient attitude, generally suffices. Medications should be prescribed only when the symptoms are so severe that they affect waking behavior, particularly school performance, peer interaction, and family relationships. Rarely, temporal lobe seizures may mimic these disorders, but adequate study in a sleep laboratory readily differentiates epileptic disorders from sleep disorders.

Pavor Nocturnus

Pavor nocturnus, or night terrors, is found with greatest frequency in children 3 to 8 years of age. In some infants, symptoms may begin infrequently during the second half of the first year of life, and a small group of children continue to have severe night terror attacks into adulthood.

Night terrors must be differentiated from the more common nightmare or anxiety dream. Nightmares are associated with vivid visual imagery. They occur during REM sleep, and the child is fully aroused following the episode. Recall for the content of the nightmare is excellent. In pavor nocturnus, approximately 90 to 100 min after going to sleep, the child suddenly sits upright in bed and screams. Tachypnea, tachycardia, and other signs of autonomic activation are apparent. The child is usually inconsolable for 5 to 30 min, then finally relaxes and returns to sleep. If the child arouses, dream recall is fragmentary. Retrograde amnesia for the attack is present the following morning. Not infrequently, attacks occur after stressful and/or especially fatiguing daytime activities. The diagnosis can be made most often from the history alone. An attack occurring during the latter third of the night with vivid recall is unlikely to be pavor nocturnus (see Fig. 52-1), but rather a nightmare or a spontaneous awakening. Most night terror episodes in young children occur so infrequently that medication is not indicated. For severe cases, however, the drug of choice is diazepam.

Somnambulism and Somniloquy

Somnambulism and somniloquy present most commonly during the school-age years. According to Kales and Kales, 15 percent of all children between the ages of 5 and 12 have walked in their sleep at least once. Persistent sleepwalking occurs in 1 to 6 percent of the population, afflicting more males than females, and is often associated with nocturnal enuresis. A typical somnambulistic episode consists of the following behavioral sequence: a body movement during stage IV NREM sleep is followed by the subject's abruptly sitting upright in bed. Although the eyes are open, they appear glassy and "unseeing."

Movements are clumsy, and efforts to communicate with the sleepwalker usually elicit mumbled and slurred speech with monosyllabic answers. The total duration of the episode may range from 10 to 30 s when sitting in bed to 5 to 30 min, or more, when actual walking occurs. There is amnesia for the event upon awakening in the morning. Severe sleepwalkers may have episodes 1 to 4 times weekly. The episode occurs most often at the transition point from stage IV NREM sleep to the first REM period. If individuals with a predilection for somnambulism or somniloquy are aroused during stage IV NREM sleep, a walking or talking episode may be precipitated. In contrast, no such response is obtained from nonaffected controls.

Several myths about sleepwalking and sleep talking need to be laid to rest. Sleepwalkers are not acting out dreams and in control of purposeful actions. Sleepwalkers are in danger. They frequently hurt themselves and must be protected from self-injury by securing the environment. Likewise, somniloquists do not reveal their deepest secrets while sleep talking. Their utterances are most often incomprehensible or monosyllabic. Meaningful speech and purposeful walking during sleep suggest psychological dissociative disorders rather than primary physiological NREM dyssomnia symptomatology. Again, as in night terrors, temporal lobe epilepsy must be ruled out. This is so particularly in adults.

As central nervous system maturation progresses, somnambulistic episodes usually diminish and disappear spontaneously. For severe, intractable cases, diazepam has been used successfully.

NREM Stage IV Sleep-related Enuresis

Enuresis should not be considered a syndrome, but rather a symptom of a disorder. By careful history, one should determine whether the enuretic symptom has been present from birth (primary) or has occurred after a period of successful training (secondary), whether it is confined to nighttime or occurs during the daytime as well, and whether organic factors are present. In addition, an attempt should be made to localize the episode to a time of night and point in the sleep cycle. Most commonly, sleep-related enuresis is primary, and occurs only at night and especially during the first third of the sleep period at the transition point from stage IV NREM sleep to REM sleep. Stage IV NREM sleep-related enuresis is probably the most common NREM dyssomnia of childhood. Broughton has defined "an enuretic episode" which generally occurs 1 to 3 h after sleep onset as the child shifts from NREM stage IV sleep to the first REM period. The sleep state change is often associated with a body movement and increased muscle tone, followed by tachycardia, tachypnea, erection in males, and decreased skin resistance. Micturition occurs 30 s to 4 min after the start of the episode in a moment of relative quiet. Immediately following micturition, children are difficult to awaken and, when aroused, indicate they have not dreamed. There is amnesia for the event. Broughton has demonstrated that enuretics with this disorder have higher resting intravesical pressures, especially during stage IV NREM sleep, have more frequent and spontaneous bladder contractions during stage IV NREM sleep, and have secondary contractions in response to naturally and artificially occurring increases in pressure in contrast to nonenuretic controls whose bladder functions and capacities are normal.

For children with severe NREM stage IV sleep-related enuresis, imipramine has proved to be effective. It is unclear whether its efficacy is due primarily to its anticholinergic properties affecting bladder tone or to its stimulant effect on sleep stage pattern. A flexible dosage and slow withdrawal schedule are recommended. (See Sec. 51 for a more complete discussion of enuresis.)

Secondary Sleep Disturbances— The Psychological and Developmental Disturbances of Sleep

The disorders to be described in this section are characterized by normal polysomnography. Nevertheless, they may be a source of psychological suffering for the child and confict within the family. Virtually all parents anticipate sleep disturbances in their children. These secondary sleep disturbances are much more common than those described previously. They often reflect normal phases of development and have been loosely labeled as "insomnias" and "nightmares." By far the majority are transient and, though a source of irritation and concern, are inconsequential. Sometimes, when overwhelming and/or persistent, they may be indicators of more serious psychopathology. Medication, by and large, is not indicated, though the short-term use of chloral hydrate has been advocated to promote peace and quiet in the family and prevent the sleep disturbance from becoming ingrained by "positive" reinforcement. Understanding the source of a child's anxiety, the parental concerns, and the current family situation is most often sufficient to enable the pediatrician to provide supportive guidance until the disturbance subsides.

Secondary sleep disturbances may occur from the imminent approach of bedtime to the time of awakening. Nagera has extensively reviewed these disturbances and classified them according to the most common age of appearance. This system of classification affords optimal understanding of the disturbance within the context of the child's developmental stage.

The First Year of Life

During the first year of life, sleeping through the night ("settling") and night awakenings are the primary concerns of the family. In England, a comprehensive investigation of sleep patterns of infants during the first year of life reported that 70 percent of babies slept through the night, or settled, by 3 months of age. Another 13 percent had settled by 6 months of age; 10 percent never slept through the night without interruption. Once settling had occurred, night waking recurred in 50 percent of the infants during the second half of the first year of life. Environmental factors, such as changed sleeping arrangements, separations, minor trauma, and new family members, were reported to be associated with night waking after settling had occurred, though these factors did not seem to affect the age of initial settling.

The Second Year of Life

The problems of separation and object permanence confront the immature ego of the 2-year-old child. Lacking the capacity to differentiate between absence and total disappearance of an object, the child attempts to hold on to important ties to avoid the fear of loss. A prevalent disturbance of this age, therefore, is reluctance to go to sleep. Substitute objects, such as teddy bears or blankets, often tide the child over difficult separations. By the end of the second year, with the acquisition of language and the development of a sense of object permanence, these difficulties often disappear.

Since children of this age are also easily overexcited

and frightened by daytime experiences, nightmares also make their appearance in this age group. Nightmares, also called "bad dreams" and "anxiety dreams," occur during REM sleep. Most often, the dream reports represent reenactments of daytime experiences, though the characters are frequently animals or monsters. Since the child, at this age, has difficulty distinguishing between dreams and reality, fear of going to sleep may be a prominent feature of children with nightmares.

The Third to the Fifth Years of Life

It is rare to find a child in this age group who is not experiencing some difficulty over sleep, whether it be tardiness in falling asleep, nightmares, projective fears of ghosts and wild animals, fear of the dark, inability to sleep alone, or ritualistic presleep behaviors. These disturbances are usually associated with daytime frightening or otherwise conflictual experiences. They are most often transient and responsive to minimal environmental manipulation. If refractive, on the other hand, the sleep disturbance may represent one symptom of a more profound psychological conflict. In such cases, they reflect most often the child's inability to enter into the widening world of social relationships. Family counseling or individual psychotherapy may be indicated.

The Use of the Sleep Laboratory in the Differential Diagnosis of Sleep Disorders and Sleep Disturbances

More and more, polysomnography in a sleep disorders clinic has been useful in diagnosing sleep-related pathology. The following case report is exemplary:

R, a 7-year-old boy, was referred because of night wakening occurring several times a night, 4 to 5 times a week. These attacks started approximately 1 h after falling asleep and were associated with disorientation, confusion, and screaming. Amnesia followed the event in the morning. Frequently, second and third attacks occurred later in the night. Sometimes these attacks were associated with sleepwalking episodes. Complete physical and neurological examinations, including two EEGs, were unremarkable. A variety of medications, including Dilantin, Valium, Dalmane, Tofranil, and barbiturates, typically were successful for short periods of time, but then the symptomatology worsened once again.

The sleep disorders clinic work-up revealed a complex disturbance. Continuous all-night polysomnography and time-lapse video monitoring were carried out. Approximately 65 min after sleep onset, during the midst of stage IV NREM sleep, R sat up glassy-eyed and began screaming. He appeared in obvious distress and was inconsolable. After about 5 min, he lay back in his bed and returned to sleep. At 3:30 A.M., some 6.5 h after sleep onset, R again aroused and began to cry out. This arousal was from stage I NREM sleep. The arousal followed a body movement and was characterized by a waking EEG pattern. For the next 10 min, R remained awake with eyes closed, sobbing and crying out. Finally, he returned to sleep, covered over by a sheet and curled up in a fetal position. Approximately 1 h later, another attack, resembling the latter, occurred. The character of the first attack was markedly different from that of the later attacks. In the first attack, R seemed disoriented and confused, whereas in the later ones, he awakened and appeared depressed and anxious. Thus, it was apparent from our video monitoring and our polysomnographic recording that we were dealing with two distinct types of sleep disturbance; night terror attacks and night waking episodes. While the various medications had been effective in suppressing the night terror attacks, secondary sleep disturbances repeatedly broke through.

We recommended that since R's anxiety was excessive and inhibiting, family counseling and psychotherapy be instituted. We felt that the secondary sleep disturbance was more important than the night terror attacks and suggested, therefore, that medications be withheld. Six months after evaluation, the family situation has improved, and the nighttime disturbances have significantly diminished without medication.

53 | Tics

by J. G. Kavanaugh, Jr. and Åke Mattsson

Tics are sudden, involuntary, repetitive, seemingly meaningless movements of a striated muscle. While any part of the body may be involved, the face and neck are common sites of occurrence. Tics can present as single actions such as blushing, grimacing, clearing the throat, and jerking the shoulders. Combinations of movements also occur, and one variety can be replaced by another. The old term "habit spasm" for this condition reflects earlier concerns with "bad" habits as well as the lack of clarity regarding the degree of voluntary as opposed to involuntary origin of the movements.

Tics need to be differentiated from the movements of Syndenham's chorea, which are less regular in occurrence and of greater amplitude; the other characteristics of this disease aid in the differentiation. Repetitive movement patterns of infancy such as spasmus nutans, head banging, and bed rocking do not meet the diagnostic criteria of a tic; they are not involuntary but rather self-stimulating solutions to emotional stresses. Also to be excluded are the excessive but voluntary movements of active "squirmy" children who express impatience or frustration through body movements.

Tics are seldom seen before the age of 6 years, after which they are increasingly common, with the peak incidence in the preadolescence years. The 6- to 7-year-old child's consolidation of development of a strict conscience partly explains the common occurrence in this age group. Tics in young adolescents are a symptomatic response to the increasing peer and societal demands that accompany physical and sexual maturing.

The concept of a tic as involuntary, and seemingly meaningless, is important for understanding its etiology and rationale of therapeutic approaches. A tic is a child's response to psychological stress of sufficient duration and intensity to cause a state of emotional tension, yet a stress which the child cannot resolve in the real world. Children naturally act and express with their bodies; active and impulsive movements precede reflection and reasoning. All the component parts of abnormal movement patterns, such as tics, are inherent in the structure and function of the body. The abnormality of the tic is its repetitiveness, lack of meaning, and involuntary nature. All these qualities, all that can be observed, form but a part of an emotional conflict which signals psychological stress within the child. The stresses lie below consciousness and usually are an enigma for the child and the family.

In some cases, it is possible to understand the genesis of the tic as a partial solution of a psychological confict, for example, blinking as alternatively looking and not looking at some forbidden yet enticing subject, and head shaking as visibly showing the observers the negation of unacceptable dangerous feelings and thoughts. In most situations, however, such causal relationships are not evident because the symbolic meaning is too obscure or several separate movements have coalesced into a general pattern. Fortunately, it is neither necessary nor desirable to focus therapeutic efforts specifically on the tic.

Tics are seldom seen as solitary symptoms in otherwise healthy and normally developing children. A careful history will tend to elicit further examples of disturbed behavior, such as enuresis, thumb sucking, sleeping disturbances, learning problems, and difficulty with peers. The tic, however, often becomes the symptom that causes the greatest concern due to its visibility and its tendency to irritate the other family members. Usually children with tics show little concern about them as they are seemingly unaware of them unless someone calls them to their attention. Frequently, though, they harbor angry feelings at their environment for all the misguided effort that has been extended to help, or to force, them to control their involuntary movements. Such efforts may include making children watch themselves in a mirror as well as ceaseless verbal exhortation.

As emotional conflicts are the etiological factor behind the various presentation of tics seen in individual cases, the relief of such conflict is the therapeutic goal. Primary care givers are in an advantageous role for initiating such an effort. They, more than any specialist, follow children as they progress through the developmental stages and will be aware of their personality strengths and weaknesses. Having dealt with prior minor sicknesses and traumas, primary care physicians will become aware of those events and situations that children have experienced as threatening or dangerous.

Of added value to the physician in assessing the situation will be an understanding of the interaction among significant family members. Events that cause stress for the whole family often find their expressions through the family's most vulnerable member. That such a member so often proves to be a child is related to children's limited ability to conceptualize and understand emotional problems; further, when troubled by such problems children are limited in the way they can express to the world their troubled feelings.

Guided by an appreciation of the uniqueness and individuality of the family, the primary care giver initiates therapeutic work in two areas. First, the family concerns about the tic are acknowledged and a direct, nontechnical explanation of the etiological factors is offered. The child is usually included in such a meeting, which should emphasize that the tic is beyond voluntary control and that the family should try to stop focusing all their concerns and efforts on its elimination.

With a mutual agreement that the tic behavior will no longer be the center of attention, the care giver moves to the second phase of intervention. This involves identification of the broader areas of emotional stress and problems of the family and the child, and recommendations for dealing with them. Whether the child is also included in these discussions is an individual matter and relates both to the child's age and maturity and to the nature of the problem. A school problem involving an older child would in most cases best be discussed with the child and family together; marital discord affecting a young child would often not be so discussed. A rigid formula in communicating with the family is not the aim, but rather the establishment of a mood that will enhance the sharing of explanations and advice. The majority of tics, especially those identified early and in patients already known to the care giver, can be effectively managed in a primary care setting.

Those situations in which drugs might be useful in the total management of a case are similar to those covered in Sec. 54.

Considerations of consultation with a specialist such as a child psychiatrist or a child psychologist would be appropriate when (1) the family is clearly unable to shift the focus from excessive concern with the tic to a suggested broader view of the functioning of the child and the family or (2) there is no change or a progression of symptomatology despite the therapeutic efforts that have been mobilized.

A rare, but important, variety of tic was first identified in 1885 when Gilles de la Tourette reported a special syndrome in which patients from an early age showed uncoordinated movements, vocal noises, and echolalia (imitative repetition of another's speech). While slightly over half of these reported cases (five of nine) in addition exhibited coprolalia (involuntary use of vulgar and/or obscene words), this was not initially required for the diagnosis. Incidence and prevalence figures are uncertain; if the presence of coprolalia is made a diagnostic criterion for Gilles de la Tourette's disease, there is a substantial reduction in the number of suspected cases in a condition quite rare by any criteria. In reported series, over 50 percent of the cases had their onset by age 7, and over 90 percent by age 11; there is a male preponderance (4:1).

Early diagnosis of this condition is made difficult since the initial symptom is usually a single tic, indistinguishable in presentation and onset from the more usual variety. The progression of the symptoms with the appearance of involuntary vocalizations and a spread of the tic aid in establishing the diagnosis; coprolalia, when present, is pathognomonic. Haloperidol, the drug of choice, in many instances affords dramatic symptom relief.

54 | Phobias

by J. G. Kavanaugh, Jr. and Åke Mattsson

Phobia is fear, to an extreme degree, of objects or events in the natural environment which are not in reality dangerous to the individual and which would not be of concern to most people. While adults do show phobic reactions, phobias are predominantly an event of early childhood. Indeed, their common occurrence during this period has continued to challenge theoreticians of child development and psychopathology, as therapeutic successes are reported from varying treatment methods based on quite different theoretical ideas about etiology. An extensive literature dates its origins to Sigmund Freud's 1909 case report "Little Hans," which describes an animal phobia in a 5-year-old boy.

Practical as well as theoretical issues are involved in the effort to differentiate phobic responses from the universal fears of early childhood. Every neonate displays fearfulness; initially, such a response will be elicited by nonspecific sensory disturbances of high intensity and sudden onset: for example, loud noises, extreme levels of illumination, rapid movements with seeming loss of support. Such responses are related to the new challenges experienced by the infant just beginning its adaptation to an environment that, in contrast to the more evenly regulated intrauterine life, is experienced as changeable and unpredictable even without extreme variations.

As infants mature, they gain in ability to discriminate sensory impressions and to direct their locomotion. Early in the first year, they begin to recognize and integrate sensations which give increasing predictability and meaning to the unending stimulation to which they are subjected. Relating in a general way to the stages of intellectual (cognitive) development is a generally predictable sequence of fears, but not

phobias. By 8 or 9 months of age, children have formed an early mental representation of their principle care giver, a person so necessary to them that even temporary substitution of someone different is responded to as a threat; this strong negative emotional reaction to unfamiliar persons is predictable enough to have acquired the designation of "stranger anxiety." The 2- to-3-year-old moves in a physically wider world, filled with an increasing array of objects, animate and inanimate. The common animal fears of this period are in part related to the ubiquity of pets, with their noisy and unpredictable behavior. For many children concern about the dark, with its strange-appearing shapes and often unidentifiable noises, heightens their other fears and even becomes a specific fear in itself. Children 7 to 9 years of age have sufficient intellectual powers, combined with a degree of worldly awareness, to comprehend death as a permanent condition which also can happen to them. This new awareness can be experienced as transient strong fears of death and dying. Any of the mentioned fears of childhood may become intensified if the child is aware that they also are major concerns of some close family member.

In contrast to these rather predictable fears, childhood phobias present with two major distinguishing characteristics: first, the seeming incongruity of the object or situation evoking a response and, second, the normality of the child's behavior when the phobic situation can be avoided. Unlike the child exhibiting a tic or showing multiple problems in daily living, the phobic child who is spared confrontation with the "chosen" stimulus is not markedly different from an unaffected peer. Indeed, many observers comment on the phobic child's brightness, pleasantness, and sociability. Such comments indicate the many areas of normal personality functioning which will be available for use in therapeutic approaches to the problem; in addition, these areas of normal function make clear the degree to which the symptom is central to the child's mastery of "unconscious" threat and how the phobic solution enables the child to function in other areas.

The primary care giver need not be overly concerned with differing theories of personality predisposition and causation in cases of phobia; the clinical picture underlying varying theoretical formulations is similar and the history elicited is usually straightforward and pathognomonic (school phobia alone presents sufficient variation to warrant separate consideration; see Sec. 28).

In the usual case, the parents will describe a situation in which a child without previous behavioral problems suddenly shows an intense fear, for example, of a particular animal, of the toilet, or an illness, or of being dirty. At times, there may have been a recent disturbance referable to these fears. The family has often tried reassurance and encouragement. The child's concerns may have widened with the result that more animals are being feared, or previous activities away from home are being avoided, or the sleep pattern may have become disrupted. The child's continued adequate performance in areas not affected by the phobia seems puzzling to the family. At best the child can offer only sketchy explanations of these fears and often none at all.

In trying to more completely understand this behavioral constellation, the primary care giver may find the differing theories less than helpful. Since, however, therapeutic approaches will be shaped by the therapist's theory of what has "gone wrong" with the child's functioning, a brief mention of two major schools of thought is necessary. The traditional psychodynamic explanation postulates that the child develops internal mental conflict, most often related to sexual and aggressive themes. A solution to this painful state is reached by the unconscious displacement of negative feelings onto a specific object. This object becomes the repository of the conflicting impulses and affects with which the child was previously engaged. The child now is able to reduce his or her anxiety by avoiding its designated "source." Psychotherapeutic efforts based on this model work to uncover the linkages of the child's initial conflicted state to the avoided object and, in addition,

to help the child master the underlying threatening emotion.

The other major school of thought is often referred to by the general term of "behaviorism." Its continuing relation to learning theory underlies the concept of a phobia as an example of maladaptive learning which can be corrected by various forms of behavior therapy. An originally fearful situation is assumed to have been reinforced by repeated avoidance, thereby increasing its impact (as possibly corrective positive experiences are phobically avoided). The phenomenon of generalization is used to explain the progression of fears to include additional objects with qualities similar to the original stimulus. Behavior therapy more often uses techniques of direct suggestion and in addition creates special situations for relearning.

Once a phobia is identified, a consultation with a child psychiatrist or child psychologist may be helpful in assessing the severity of the symptom and a prognosis. Many phobias of childhood are minor disrupters of day-to-day living and respond well to brief interventions. Consultation may also be helpful in clarifying the extent of parental involvement in the onset and perpetuation of the symptomatology.

Brief use of sedative or tranquilizing drugs is often indicated in situations of major disruption of the child's functioning, especially those with target symptoms that involve bedtime behaviors or sleep.

Diphenhydramine (Benadryl®) is quite effective as a sleep medication for children up to the age of puberty. Those as young as 1 or 2 years will readily accept the flavored syrup. It is also an effective mild tranquilizer for anxious and hyperactive children up to ages 10 or 11.

Chloral hydrate is an equally safe and effective hypnotic.

Diazepam (Valium) can be used with anxious preadolescent and adolescent patients.

Drugs are most effective as part of the overall management of acute situations when their use is directed toward specific symptoms and for limited time periods.

Specific details of dosage, side effects, potentiations, as well as any special precautions with young patients, should be reviewed in a current package insert or PDR.

School phobia is a complex issue for the primary care giver. Theoretically, it differs from the typical phobias covered above in that the major symptom, school refusal, is often a form of separation anxiety in which the child's basic motivation is to remain at home with the parenting figure, often the mother. Such separation anxiety is often shared, and the parents' concern about the separation is as strong as the child's. Hence, the parent-child dyad is quite likely to be the focus for treatment. School attendance is a legal requirement and often compels the therapist to deal not only with the family and child, but also with school personnel and, in some cases, juvenile court authorities.

In summary, phobias in childhood are of common occurrence and are not difficult to diagnose when adequate history is obtained. The majority of phobic children are spared other behavior symptoms, and their many personality strengths make them good candidates for therapeutic interventions, which should be initiated as early as the condition is identified.

55 | Lying and Stealing

by Gregory Prazar

Acts of lying and stealing by children often evoke strong emotional reactions from parents. Truthfulness and respect for property are two highly valued mores espoused by our society, even though adults frequently violate their own moral codes. It is not widely understood that lying and stealing can represent a spectrum of psychopathology, from a common transient developmental phenomenon to an ominous indication of severe psychiatric disturbance. Too frequently both parents and professionals overreact to symptoms of lying and stealing before analyzing all the relevant information. It is the responsibility of the primary care physician to inquire about symptoms of lying and stealing during regular routine visits, and to help families comprehend the importance of these symptoms if they do occur. To adequately identify and manage these problems, it is necessary to obtain as complete a history as possible from parents and child, encompassing aspects of the home environment (patterns of child rearing, child's interaction with siblings and parents), peer relationships, and school performance.

Lying

When lying by children is presented as a problem to the physician, either directly by parents or indirectly from questions asked by the physician during a regular visit, it is important that several aspects of the child's functioning be considered before definitive action is taken. Features of the child's life to be considered include the individual's maturational level; the influence of family, peers, and school; and, above all, the situation in which lying occurs.

The child's chronologic age and developmental level greatly influence the extent to which lying should be evaluated. Children under 3 years of age are beginning to establish independence from parents. For them, the differentiation between what Stone and Church refer to as "private self and public self" is tenuous. Children at this age have no concept of deception and therefore do not intentionally lie. Experimentation with concepts of language often is interpreted as lying by adults. The toddler, attempting to understand presence and absence of individuals, may tell the father that "mommy is not here" when she may indeed be in the next room. Emotionally painful situations are avoided by all children, especially by toddlers under 3 years of age. To maintain a pleasurable existence, the child may pretend to be hurt in order to be cuddled. The child, whose moral code is immature, thinks nothing of denying a misdeed, since admission might bring painful consequences.

The mental life of the preschool child (3 to 7 years) is one filled with fantasy. According to Stone and Church, 20 to 50 percent of this age group create imaginary companions, pets, or situations. The imaginary companion is usually a helpful, empathetic playmate, although he or she may appear as a disciplinarian for the child. By serving as a surrogate friend, the imaginary companion helps the child to adapt to new social situations. By serving as a disciplinarian, the imaginary companion helps the child to develop a sense of right and wrong. The imaginary companion usually has a very short life span, generally dying of "old age" by the time the child is 5 to 7 years old. For the preschooler, fantasy and reality are frequently not well delineated. This is evidenced by the existence of imaginary companions and also by the child's love for fairy tales. A 4- to

5-year-old unabashedly tells tall tales, although will, when encouraged, admit to creating a make-believe situation. By the age of 6 or 7 years, children are aware of the morality of lying and stealing. Although they are quick to accuse peers of cheating and lying, they continue to cheat seemingly guiltlessly in game situations.

During the ages of 6 to 12 years the child understands the concept of lying and its moral implications. However, lying may continue in an attempt to test adult-imposed moral codes. Children may admit to lying but have a myriad of rationalizations for their behavior. Rules are more important at this age than is winning, so cheating is less important and therefore more infrequent. "Half-beliefs" become a part of the child's life; children become believers of superstitions, from the danger of walking under a ladder to the inevitable orthopedic complications for mothers whose children step on sidewalk cracks. Half-beliefs may extend into adulthood. They are heavily invested with emotion. Their level of acceptance by the individual is inversely proportional to the individual's level of intellectual development.

Aside from developmental issues, external influences (family, school, peers) affect the incidence of lying in children. Parents may unconsciously encourage their children to lie if expectations for the children exceed their ability to fulfill them, and if truthfulness is not valued by the parents (that is, if parents frequently tell lies). Parents who overestimate their child's capabilities and academic endeavors frequently find that their child lies about grades received. Parents who tell "white lies" to protect the feelings of others, or for personal gain, fail to realize that young children cannot discern the moral issues involved in lying. Parents demanding to know why their son hit his younger sister, or why the child broke the cookie jar, are not aware that the child often cannot explain his behaviors to himself, much less to them. When interrogated, the confused child in desperation lies. According to Ginott, "awkward lies" are told to avoid "embarrassing confessions," and confessions which the child knows from experience parents do not want to hear. For example, after hitting his younger sister, the child knows that the parent does not want to hear that the sister was hit because she is disliked by the child. Parents want to believe that their children love each other and find it difficult to accept verbalizations to the contrary.

The child receiving inconsistent discipline, experiencing little positive reinforcement from parents, and living in an inflexible, demanding environment is often the child who lies.

Physicians can aid parents in dealing with childhood lying in several ways. First, by apprising parents of normal behavior during maturational stages, the physician helps the parents more easily understand why their 5-year-old makes up stories or why their 7-year-old cheats at games. Secondly, by helping parents become aware of their importance as role models for their child, the physician effectively guides the parents in verbalizing to their child the importance of truthfulness. Third, when specific problems arise, the physician, by utilizing a gentle and nonpunitive counseling approach, encourages parents to be as tactful and nonthreatening with the child as possible. For example, Spock believes the child who spends much time with imaginary companions may need more age-appropriate friends or may be indirectly asking for more parental involvement in play activities. It is vital that parents are made cognizant of their importance as a role model for the child, and of the child's need for reasonable and clear expectations. Similarly, physicians must understand that they are role models for the parents whom they counsel. The physician who assumes a flexible, constructive, nonthreatening approach to problems raised by parents, and who has been honest in past relationships with the family, is more likely to experience success in counseling.

Lying becomes a symptom of more severe psychopathology under several circumstances. If other behaviors concomitantly exist (such as firesetting, cruelty to animals, enuresis, sleep disturbances, hyperactivity, phobias), there is a much greater likelihood of severe psychiatric disturbance. Similarly, if lying or fantasizing becomes a predominant behavior for children, more ominous behavior disturbances must be suspected, such as chronically poor self-esteem, endogenous depression, and sociopathic behavior. Children with few friends and limited interest in group activities often suffer from low self-esteem and depression. Children who lie for material gain and in an apparent guiltless manner may be displaying early signs of sociopathic behavior. If these symptoms are present, and if attempts at counseling fail to dissipate lying behavior, a referral to a psychiatrically sophisticated professional should seriously be considered.

Stealing

Stealing often represents a much more worrisome symptom to parents than does lying because the former more often involves situations outside of the home, represents a much more serious societal taboo, and more directly affects other people. Indeed, especially during school years, stealing can be an ominous sign of psychiatric disturbance. However, it may also represent conformity to peer pressure and consequently a transient phenomenon.

Children 3 years of age and under take things because they want them and have an immature sense of "mine" and "not mine," a concept related to their beginning struggle for independence from parents. Slowly they develop a conception of their own bodies (or property) and that of their parents. By age 3, children have a firmer sense of what belongs to them. They become possessive of their things and jealous of those of others, although they have only a tenuous grasp of the property rights of others.

Between 3 and 7 years of age, as they begin to develop peer relationships, children become more respectful of property rights. However, they frequently give away their own possessions without realizing it and have not yet developed a concept of one thing being more valuable than many things. Therefore, 25 hoarded pennies may be treasured much more than one piece of paper currency.

The school-age child has a much more sophisticated sense of property rights, although not yet completely mature. Consequently, an 8-year-old may pick up loose change from a table in an unsupervised situation. However, after age 9 respect for property should be well integrated into the child. Children who steal at this age or beyond are motivated by one or more of several factors. They may steal in a group, especially during adolescence, to conform to peer pressure. They may suffer from poor self-esteem because they feel unloved by parents or because they have difficulty making friends. Therefore they may steal to buy friendship and achieve peer acceptance, and to display to themselves and to their parents that they are acceptable because they can succeed in at least one activity. Stealing as a mechanism to improve self-esteem is especially common with adolescents, who are concomitantly attempting to separate from parents and to establish satisfactory same-sex and heterosexual relationships. If adolescents feel a failure in both tasks, they frequently steal.

Families exert an important influence with respect to childhood stealing. If parents stole as children, they are more likely to assume a permissive role to intrafamilial stealing. Their reactions to extrafamilial stealing may be extremely punitive, since their child's stealing will unfavorably reflect upon them as parents. This value discrepancy between intrafamilial and extrafamilial acts is easily recognized by the child, whose resentment frequently precipitates intensified stealing. Parents giving little attention, affection, or approval to their child potentiate poor self-esteem which may result in stealing behavior, as the child attempts to attract attention and approval. Punishment may be ineffective, since the child may rationalize that, as Fraiberg states, "any ensuing punishment will cancel the crime."

Management of stealing, as in management of lying, requires an empathetic, but firm, approach by both physician and parents. Parents should be advised to deal with the specific incident in a forthright manner. The child over 3 should be confronted with the evidence but should not suffer interrogative techniques (for example, "I believe you took $5 from my wallet," rather than, "Why did you take $5 from my wallet?"). Immediate restitution of the stolen item is extremely important. If the article has been taken from a friend, the child should return it. If the article has been stolen from a store, the parent should accompany the child to the store and explain to the manager in a tactful manner that the child took an item without paying for it and now wants to return it. The parents should voice their disapproval of stealing to the child, but should also reinforce their belief in the child's basic integrity. A child who has stolen usually has poor self-esteem; punitive measures serve to damage self-concept further and embue in the child the parent's mistrust.

Several specific questions should come to mind when the child steals, since the answers may aid in management. Is the child receiving a reasonable allowance? If not, the child may feel the need to resort to stealing in order to obtain spending money. Are there unrealistic academic pressures on the child? As previously stated, children who feel they cannot fulfill academic expectations of parents frequently steal to at least transiently display their success in one activity. Is the child having difficulty making friends? Stealing often occurs in situations where the child feels that peer group acceptance can be achieved by offering peers stolen material goods. In cases of group stealing, are alternative community facilities available to occupy extracurricular hours? Although structured community activities may not obliterate all acts of group stealing, they may be helpful in discouraging such acts by offering alternative activities to adolescents.

Stealing assumes more ominous connotations in several situations. As in lying, if other behavioral disturbances coexist, a more psychiatrically sophisticated approach may be necessary. A child who steals without guilt, who compulsively steals (kleptomania), or who seemingly steals in a setting in which apprehension is inevitable may have very serious emotional problems. Frequently, these are children who received little or inconsistent love and security as infants. They will progress to delinquent and ultimately criminal life-styles without psychiatric intervention. Unfortunately, psychic damage to these children is often irreparable by the time psychiatric referral is finally made.

Referral Criteria

Effective referral to psychiatrists for problems of lying and stealing requires several things of referring physicians. Families should be informed of the possible need for referral when the physician first suspects the potential for significant psychopathology. As in managing less severe cases, it is vital that the referring physician be empathetic and nonpunitive in the explanation given to parents. The physician should make sure that the parents do not think their child is "crazy" because he or she is being referred to a psychiatrist. The parents should also know that referral does not sever the physician's relationship with the family. Continued communication by the referring physician, both with the family and with the psychiatrist, often solidifies recommendations made to parents by the psychiatrist and encourages compliance with recommendations. It is beneficial if the physician can personally introduce the family to the psychiatrist. In general, a team approach between referring doctor and specialist increases efficacy of the treatment plan.

Symptoms of lying and stealing in childhood usually cause concern both to parents and to physicians and also create much worry to the child who is involved. The seriousness of these behavioral traits is dependent upon many factors: age of the child; circumstances which precipitate the trait; psychosocial adjustment of the child in school, with peers, and at home; and reaction of parents to the symptoms. The physician's approach to the problem greatly influences whether the symptoms disappear or intensify. In dealing with problems of lying and stealing, it is important for the physician to secure a complete history, to carefully explain to the parents and the patient the significance of the trait, and to ensure regular follow-up for the problem. If referral to psychologically trained professionals becomes necessary, the physician is obligated to prepare the family for the referral, to maintain communication with the consultant, and to offer the family emotional support before and after the consultation occurs. In most cases, lying and stealing represent transient developmental behavior problems which resolve if an empathetic approach is utilized by parents and physician. However, the symptoms are not to be ignored in the hopeful belief that the child "will grow out of it" and "that all children lie and steal."

56 | Depression in Childhood

by Åke Mattsson

Depression consists of a disturbance of mood or emotional state in which the person is faced with feelings of sadness, loneliness, helplessness, and lowered self-esteem. It should be emphasized, however, that depressive states in preschoolers and young school-age children often go unrecognized because young children cannot tolerate painful negative affects for long and are not very able to verbalize and share them with their environment. They tend to ward off such feelings by a variety of behavioral disturbances which often include overactivity and somatic complaints. The primary care giver, alert to the occurrence of depression in young children, may only glimpse a child's sad, despairing mood amid the behavioral irregularities. Without proper identification and treatment, childhood depression may result in major psychopathology and interference with social and academic progress.

Like any illness of childhood, depressive disorders should be evaluated from a combined biological and psychosocial viewpoint. Biological predisposing factors relate to the child's family history, constitution, vulnerability, and maturation. These factors interact with the social environment and with stressful events of an emotionally taxing and depriving nature. Within such a framework, childhood depression, similar to adolescent and adult depression, can be viewed as a disorder of coping and adaptation which usually occurs in a home environment characterized by disturbed parent-child interaction. Whether overt or hidden behind a variety of behavioral disturbances, the child's depressive mood usually has a negative influence on family, peers, and teachers.

Depression in Infants

In infants up to about 18 months of age, depressive syndromes do occur, characterized by a disturbance of affective interaction with the environment and by physiologic abnormalities. *Infantile depression* may be viewed as one type of *disorder of attachment* to a primary care taker resulting from severe deprivation of mothering. Attachment disorders show varying degrees of severity. On one extreme are those infants abruptly deprived of their mothers or those raised in an orphanagelike setting, providing no consistent mothering figure. These children often show the picture of *anaclitic depression*, with a sad or emotionless facial expression, little motor activity, and an unresponsive, apathetic state. Physiologic disturbances usually appear in the form of anorexia, vomiting, marasmus, and skin disorders. Life-threatening in the past, these conditions often carry with them the high risk of retarded growth and mental development unless substitute mothering is provided.

Less drastic manifestations of attachment-deprivation syndromes are seen in infants who show a *failure to thrive,* despite otherwise normal physical findings, and in young children with *psychosocial growth retardation* (or dwarfism). The inadequate parenting of these children usually has taken place in homes characterized by chronic emotional and financial deprivation. Their retarded growth and psychosocial development frequently is accompanied by a peculiar depressed or bland affective state. They show little spontaneity in their interactions and often strike the observer as "frozen, little people."

In terms of *management* of failure-to-thrive, deprived infants, and psychosocially retarded children, parental counseling and community services to the families have shown little success in enhancing the children's development. Recognizing that in a majority of these situations the family and social pathology defies remedies, the physician in charge usually has to recommend early and prolonged foster placement to initiate and maintain more normal physical and mental growth.

Depression in Preschool Children

Toddlers and preschool children can be expected to show *acute transient depressive reactions* in the form of healthy grief reactions to the loss of a close family member, a friend, or even a pet. They appear genuinely sad, frequently cry, and talk about missing the absent or deceased loved one. They may also experience fluctuating physical symptoms, often of a regressive nature, such as bed-wetting, sleep disturbance with nightmares, and feeding problems. The display of true sorrowful emotions in a grieving preschooler usually is short-lived and recurrent. As mentioned before, young children cannot tolerate such painful states for long. Furthermore, their immature cognitive development makes them unable to comprehend both the finality and inevitability of death and the permanence of separation from a closer person. They "deny" the reality of the calamity and cannot yet anticipate a substitute for the dead or absent person. Many fantasized expectations of the return of a deceased parent or a friend take on a quality of reality and often alternate with moments of mournful despair and the beginning realization that death means something very different from separation.

Bereaved preschoolers become very sensitive to implied new losses of their key persons. Regressive whining, clinging, and all kinds of manipulative acts bespeak their strong fears of being left alone and of feeling helpless and seemingly unloved.

In comparison with acute depressive reactions among preschoolers, persistent states of depression in this age group are not common. If not alleviated, however, such early depressive disorders tend to jeopardize the child's adjustment to school and herald problems of both learning and socialization. *Chronically depressed preschool children* usually appear sad, uninterested, and inhibited in age-appropriate activities. They often show a low frustration tolerance with intense aggressive outbursts and periods of restless irritability. A variety of somatic symptoms and complaints may accompany the mood disorder, for example, fatigue, headaches, nausea, abdominal pain, diarrhea, and enuresis. The early history of such children may not always include an actual loss or death of a significant person but marked evidence of inconsistent, depriving, or neglectful parenting. Their poor sense of trust in adults is accompanied by an insecure self-image and low self-esteem. Having experienced much rejection, punishment, and debasement, they fear failures and rebuffs. Such children often will cover up their negative affective state by aggressive provocative behavior, by daring pursuits, or by clowning. Such a child might be the forerunner of a tormenting grade school bully or an early antisocial child with no overt depressive signs.

Depression of Midchildhood

Turning to the depressions of midchildhood, ages 6 to about 12, three clinical syndromes warrant attention: *acute depressive reactions* (often grief reactions), *chronic depressive states*, and *masked depressive reactions* (at times referred to as "depressive equivalents"). Despite their differences in symptomatology, duration, and prognosis, they share certain clinical features related to the school-age child's strides in cognitive and social development. Around age 7 to 8 children begin to conceptualize time and spatial relationships in a more adult manner. This includes the cognizance of death as a permanent condition which also can happen to them. Because of these gains in "existential" awareness and their mental consolidation of a strict conscience, bereaved school-age children tend to grieve and mourn in an adultlike fashion with associated feelings of guilt and painful self-reproaches toward the lost loved person. Rarely, though, do we see such neurotic depressive (grief) reactions lead to deeply despairing, suicidal behavior in preadolescent children.

The outlined developmental achievement of school-age children explains the intensity and pervasiveness of *acute and chronic depressions* in this age group compared with the younger one. Their etiological factors and clinical characteristics, however, remain similar to those described for acute and chronic depressive disorders among preschoolers.

The *masked depressions* of midchildhood, commonly seen in child psychiatric settings, may elude the primary care physician and the child's family and school for quite some time. Persistent somatic complaints and symptoms in school-age children without explainable organic abnormality should arouse the suspicion of an underlying depressive condition in which children successfully hide from themselves and the environment their sadness, helplessness, and guilt. In addition to the physical symptoms, of which headaches, abdominal pain, fatigue, anorexia, nausea, and sleep problems are most common, a host of behavioral disturbances may be "used" to ward off the intolerable depressive affects and loss of self-esteem. Frequent coverups for painful feelings of despair and sadness are overeating, clowning, manic-like hyperactivity alternating with complaints of boredom and fatigue, drop in school performance and difficulty in concentrating, belligerence, a tendency to bravado, occasional running away, and delinquent acts. These depressive equivalents tend to impair the child's social and academic progress. Many of the etiologic factors behind masked depressions are similar to those found among children with chronic depression (who often *do* betray their negative mood). These factors include exposure to prolonged socioparental deprivation and divorce conflicts; being a major caretaker of a sick family member; suffering from a serious physical illness, defect, or learning disability; or experiencing exploitation by delinquent peers or asocial adults.

The adult types of serious depressive disorder, such as manic-depressive illness and psychotic depressive reaction, are rarely seen before adolescence. A small number of depressed prepubertal children, however, show prolonged, deep states of hopelessness, withdrawal, and delusional, self-deprecatory thinking. These tormented patients, whose family situation seems to provide little if any emotional support, frequently come to view suicide as the only way of gaining relief. Indeed, some of them do carry out self-destructive acts, but fortunately these occurrences are rare.

Prevention and Management

In the area of *prevention and management* of childhood depression, primary care physicians hold a strategic position. Together with other health care workers they can identify those mother-infant situations that pose great risks for attachment disorders and early biopsychosocial retardation due to a variety of perinatal vulnerability factors.

A significant proportion of the acute and prolonged depressive states among toddlers and older children cannot be prevented—they represent adaptations to the inevitable sorrows and misfortunes of childhood and prepare the youngster for the successful mastering of future personal crises. Yet, the practitioner can greatly assist the family of a grieving, unhappy child in understanding the reasons for the depressive condition and promoting the child's recovery. Reactions to the temporary absence or permanent loss through death or divorce of significant family members constitute the major reason for childhood depression. Based upon knowledge of the child's developmental stage, the physician can counsel and educate the child's caretakers about the psychological impact of the loss on the child, about the child's style of defending against the painful feelings, and about means of opening communication at home concerning the loss and its effects. The role of the practitioner is ideally the same for the other common sources of depressive states in children, such as physical illness and handicaps, major moves, and academic or social failures.

Drug therapy is seldom indicated for childhood depression. The few studies that have suggested that antidepressants might alleviate depressive symptoms in preadolescents are inconclusive due to methodological deficiencies such as short follow-up periods and lack of control groups and double-blind placebo techniques. Furthermore, these drugs have not received official recommendation for use in depressed patients below age 12. Their utilization, therefore, is rarely indicated.

Many children with chronic and masked depressive reactions do not respond favorably to pediatric counseling and parental support. Their prolonged impaired social and academic functioning calls for referral to a child psychiatrist or clinical psychologist. A period of psychotherapy with children and their families often is found necessary to help such children gradually uncover the sad, helpless, and lonely state from which they so unremittingly have protected themselves.

57 Childhood Fire Setting

by William F. Gayton

Introduction

The extent of the problem of fire setting in children is unclear. Available estimates obtained from child psychiatric populations suggest a prevalence rate of 2 to 3 percent. The number referred to physicians is also reported to be small. Recent reports suggest that these figures may be underestimates. When parents at a child guidance clinic were asked to fill out a symptom checklist on the child being referred for help, 15 percent checked the item "sets fires." When 300 adults from the general population were asked, "If you had a child who repeatedly set fires, what would you do?" only 54 percent responded in a way that would have led to appropriate professional referral. Moreover, only 15 percent indicated they would seek help from a physician.

These findings suggest that fire setting in children may be more prevalent than is believed and that parents are confused as to what is an appropriate referral source. Physicians would seem to be in an ideal position to help with both of these matters. Relating to parents in such a way as to convey an interest in their children's social/emotional development, as well as their physical well-being, would provide parents with an opportunity to discuss behavioral problems such as fire setting. Early detection of childhood fire setting is especially important in view of the potential and life-threatening danger to the rest of the family and community. A willingness on the part of the physician to routinely screen for such problems would facilitate early recognition. Physicians also have an excellent opportunity to help with the confusion concerning an appropriate referral source. It appears that a significant percentage of parents and physicians are unsure how to respond to a child who sets fires. Physicians willing to concern themselves with behavioral problems of their patients are in an excellent position to prevent the inappropriate parental responses that do occur, such as burning children to teach them a lesson or calling the police to give them a good scare.

Etiology

Early psychoanalytic theoretical speculations emphasized the relationship between fire setting and sexual problems. Fire setting was thought to result from parental prohibitions against masturbation and was viewed as a substitute activity for masturbatory behavior. Direct study of childhood fire setters has suggested a more diverse picture. In particular, the aggressive elements of fire setting have received emphasis. Fire setting is viewed as a means by which children retaliate against those aspects of the environment which have rejected them. Recent writers have also emphasized the multidetermined aspects of the behavior. While noting that in some instances fire setting may be a manifestation of sexual problems, they also point out its frequent association with impulse control problems and in some cases with severe emotional disturbance including psychotic conditions. Failure to find a typical personality profile with childhood fire setters is consistent with this view.

Severe family dysfunctioning is mentioned with regularity in studies of childhood fire setters. A high incidence of parental psychopathology is noted, including alcoholism and psychosis. Varying degrees of child abuse and father absence are also present.

In this context, fire setting is most likely an aggressive response to situational frustration, and the physician will need to approach the problem in terms of the total family. An exclusive focus on what's wrong with the child will not lead to an effective resolution of the problem.

A high incidence of academic difficulties is reported. Available estimates suggest that underachievement is present in roughly 75 percent of the cases. These difficulties may be the result of the personality disturbance associated with the fire-setting behavior. On the other hand, the possibility that fire setting is a way of handling the frustration stemming from school failure should also be considered. The physician needs to be alert to the presence of an undetected learning disability.

There have been several attempts to include fire setting in children as part of a symptom triad (along with enuresis and cruelty to animals) predictive of later violent behavior. The evidence for such a relationship is based on either clinical case studies or retrospective data gathered from adjudicated adult individuals being evaluated for the court. Such studies have considerable methodological deficiencies, and further evidence is clearly needed before fire setting in children can be used as a predictor of adult violent behavior. In this context, it should be noted that no long-term follow-up studies of childhood fire setters are available, and it is unclear whether fire setting is a self-limiting symptom or whether it carries more serious prognostic implications.

The dynamics of fire setting in children would therefore appear to be multifaceted. Physicians will need to approach the problem without preconceived notions about the meaning of the behavior. Each child will require an individual approach based on the idea that fire setting may mean different things for different children.

Management

Approaches to management will depend on the physician's assessment of the seriousness of the problem. Key factors include the age of the child and the frequency of the behavior in the past. Although young children (4 to 6 years) may set fires for purposes of experimentation, fire setting in the older child usually reflects more serious psychiatric disturbance. The frequency of previous episodes is directly related to seriousness, and a history of repetitive fire setting is an especially poor prognostic sign. Although fires set by younger children are usually spotted early and extinguished quickly, serious consequences may occur. One investigator found that in 33 children who had been associated with the death of another person, death was caused by fires in 6 cases and in 8 of the remaining 27 children compulsive fire setting was present.

In cases where the behavior seems to be related to novelty and curiosity, the following steps are recommended. Discuss with the parents the necessity for reality controls. For example, encourage them not to leave the child at home unsupervised or provide the child with easy access to matches. They should communicate clearly to their child that playing with fire is inappropriate, and a full discussion of the dangers of such behavior should be included. Discuss with the parents the necessity for rewarding children when they engage in behavior which is incompatible with fire setting, such as returning matches they have found without lighting them.

Active attempts should be made to discourage the parents from trying to help children get over their fascination with fire by allowing them to light fires in their presence. Frequently, the parents will assign the child the job of lighting the dinner candles or their cigarettes in hopes this will reduce the child's interest in fire. The problem with this approach is that children are not able to make the discriminations necessary between permissible and nonpermissible opportunities to light matches. Parents should also be warned about the dangers of overreacting, in terms of either excessive alarm or punitiveness. These reactions may paradoxically increase the frequency of the behavior by suggesting to the child that this is an especially effective way of retaliating against the parents.

For more serious cases of childhood fire setting, the parent will first have to be introduced to the idea that the fire setting is part of a broader pattern of disturbance. Discussing with the parent other aspects of the child's behavior and illustrating how such behavior fits a broader symptom picture will be necessary. The parents need to recognize that serious cases of childhood fire setting are often an attempt to communicate distress. The possibility that the incidents are a response to environmental frustration, including family dysfunctioning, needs to be discussed. This ought to be done in a nonblaming manner with an emphasis on doing something to help the child. At this point, referral to a mental health professional is appropriate. Because of the potential danger associated with childhood fire setting, direct contact between the physician and the consultant is recommended. The physician will need to emphasize the seriousness of the problem and the need for quick attention. After referral has been made, the physician should make a routine call to the family to ensure that the referral has been followed through.

In extreme cases, the possibility of hospitalization will have to be discussed with the parents. This will be necessary in cases where children appear to be out of control and where the parents are unable to manage the situation. Such a drastic measure as hospitalization is necessary in order to help children reestablish controls over their behavior. It may help to emphasize to parents that clinical experience suggests that the fire setting behavior typically terminates soon after hospitalization.

58 | Child Abuse and Child Neglect

by Eli H. Newberger, James N. Hyde, Jr., Joanne C. Holter, and Alvin A. Rosenfeld

The abuse and neglect of children are complex and disturbing problems. Many physicians and nurses find it difficult to approach these problems with the same logic and order with which they approach other complex child developmental and familial problems. The distress associated with thinking about child abuse can be expressed in denial, where, failing to consider the possibility of maltreatment, physicians and others may limit their activities only to treating the child's injuries. When child abuse or neglect is suspected, uncertainty or worry about how to handle the family may lead the clinician to ignore his or her legal responsibility to report the case findings to the mandated protective agency. If the case is reported, a continuing obligation to the child and the family may not be acknowledged; one may assume that case management responsibility is safely passed to a child welfare agency.

In excellent child health practice, child abuse can be seen as a problem of distressed parenting behavior and as a symptom of family crisis. This view leads to a pediatric approach of continuing involvement and support of parents and child. Even after the diagnosis of suspected child abuse or neglect is made, there is no simple solution. Successful case management requires the coordinated efforts of professionals from several disciplines. Prevention of child abuse and neglect involves addressing cultural traditions, social values, and economic realities which may exert a deleterious impact on a family's ability to protect its offspring.

What Is Child Abuse?

In 1961, Kempe and his colleagues coined the term the "battered child syndrome." They drew attention to the most severe form of child abuse. The physical injuries most frequently include fractures, soft tissue injuries, burns, hematomas, welts, internal injuries, bruises, and contusions. One should be particularly alert to multiple injuries, a history of repeated injuries, and untreated old injuries. Physical abuse is felt by many authorities to be the most severe manifestation in a spectrum of disturbances involving a family's ability to nurture and protect a child, the special qualities of that child, and an environment which stresses the parent-child relationship.

In 1974, Congress passed the Child Abuse Prevention and Treatment Act, Public Law 93-247, which defines child abuse and neglect as "the physical or mental injury, sexual abuse, negligent treatment, or maltreatment of a child under the age of eighteen by a person who is responsible for the child's welfare under circumstances which indicate that the child's health and welfare is harmed or threatened thereby." The definition suggests that child abuse and neglect can take many forms.

Physical neglect defies exact definition but may include the failure to provide the child with the essentials of life, such as food, clothing, shelter, care and supervision, and protection from harm. Its manifestations may be seen in children with symptoms of malnutrition, "failure to thrive," and medical and dental neglect.

The maltreatment need not be willful, but this is not to say that a parent's anger, expressed actively or passively toward a child, is not primary in many child abuse and neglect cases. Abusing and neglecting parents may have excessive and premature expectations of their children and believe in the value of physical punishment to correct undesirable behavior. Often the angry feelings, of which the child's condition is a symptomatic expression, appear to derive from the violent circumstances or deprivation of the parent's own upbringing, and they may reflect a deep disappointment that the child has not been able to meet the parent's own dependency needs.

Phases in Management of Child Abuse and Neglect

The goals in the diagnosis and management of child abuse and neglect include exploring possible causal factors, assessing the family's capacity to protect and nurture the child(ren), and identifying the appropriate helping services to strengthen the family's functioning.

The phases in the management of child abuse and neglect are summarized in Table 58-1.

In child abuse and neglect, the diagnostic assessment involves the taking of an adequate medical-

Table 58-1
Phases in Management of Child Abuse and Neglect

Phases in Management	Primary Considerations	Interventions to Protect the Child and Help the Family
Diagnostic assessment: Medical history Physical examination Skeletal survey Laboratory tests	Are the physical findings at variance with the history?	Provide more comprehensive medical workup
	Is child abuse or neglect suspected?	Inform the parents of the suspicions and the physician's responsibility to protect the child
Photographs	What is the legal responsibility regarding suspected child abuse?	Make a report to the mandated agency
	Is the home safe for the child?	Continue the evaluation on an out-patient basis
	Is the child "at risk"?	Hospitalize the child for protection and further evaluation
Consultations for evaluation of family dynamics and child development	What is needed to make the home safe for the child's return?	Arrange for multidisciplinary conferencing for disposition planning
Rehabilitation program:	What resources will meet the needs of the child and the family?	
Health needs		Arrange for primary health care and appropriate treatment for the child and family.
Physical, social and environmental needs		Mobilize community resources, such as child care, homemaker service, foster home placement
Follow-up planning:	Who will monitor the health and community services to the child and the family?	
Medical care Social work services Nursing services Other services		Provide coordination and integration of the helping resources

social history and completing a physical examination, including an assessment of the child's development. If the physical findings are at variance with the given history, a more comprehensive medical work-up, including a skeletal survey and laboratory tests, may be deemed appropriate. If child abuse is suspected, photographs are often taken of the child's injuries. This is not always necessary, however, and may be contraindicated if it will appear to the family as part of an interrogatory and alienating approach to their problems with their child.

The physician has the dual responsibility to give the necessary emergency treatment and protection to the child and to attend to the parent's distress. It is important to emphasize to the parent the child's need for treatment and protection, which may include admission to a hospital, and to demonstrate a concern and ability to help the parent through the crisis. No direct or indirect attempt should be made to elicit a confession from the parent. Such maneuvers hamper the gathering of vital information and the fostering of a helpful professional relationship. Interviewing the parent can be a difficult and vexing task for medical personnel, who may be overwhelmed with angry feelings toward abusing and neglectful parents. It is important to keep in mind that these parents may themselves have been abused or neglected as children and may be following much the same pattern in rearing their own offspring.

Because of the complexity of abuse and neglect, and the need to address may causal factors, professionals in several disciplines must work together to give the family services appropriate to their needs. Social workers and nurses play vital roles in evaluating the family's functioning, the parent-child interactions, the child's physical and psychological development, the parent's expectations of the child, the parent's own experiences in childhood, and the home environment. A psychiatric consultation may offer a clearer understanding of family dynamics.

This information is vital to answering the question: Is the home safe for the child? If the child is believed to be "at risk," protection through hospitalization may be vital for diagnostic assessment as well as for protective shelter; or temporary foster home placement may be arranged through a child protective agency.

In explaining the physician's legal obligation to report suspected child abuse under the state law, compassion and honesty will help to allay the parent's anxiety. The parent needs to know what specific actions will result from the physician's report to the child protective agency.

Implications of Child Abuse Reporting Statutes for Clinical Practice

An accepted tenet of child abuse management tells professionals to be compassionate and to convey to parents their interest in helping to maintain the integrity of the family unit. On the other hand, child abuse reporting laws force us to make judgments about families which we and the family may feel are onerous and heavily value-laden. Additionally, the perceived effect of reporting is to bring to bear a quasilegal mechanism which, while nonpunitive in theory, may be the opposite in practice. In some states, parents may be jailed as a result of the mandated case report.

Professionals may thus be torn between their legal responsibility to report and their clinical judgment which may suggest that reporting itself may jeopardize the opportunity to develop a satisfactory treatment program for the family. Often this conflict is expressed in reticence to inform families that they are being reported, or reluctance and even frank refusal to report cases of abuse and neglect.

While there are no clear-cut rules which resolve this conflict definitively, two simple guidelines make it easier for the mandated professional to come to terms with legal responsibility and clinical judgment:

1 The family must be told that a report is being filed. Much of the apprehension which may surround the receipt of this information can be alleviated by explaining to the family what the reporting process is and is not; it does not necessarily mean that the child will be taken away or that a court hearing will be held. The reporting process can best be presented to the family as a referral of the family for services, and an explicit acknowledgment that they have a serious problem in protecting their child, which others, including the reporting practitioner, can help to solve.

2 The mandated professional can explain to the family that the report represents an obligation that the practitioner is bound by law to fulfill.

Often, rather than reacting in a hostile manner, families will greet the news with relief. The reporting process may secure help which they have been seeking for a long time. They may be relieved that the concerns about their parenting abilities are finally out in the open where they can be dealt with in a straightforward manner.

While such an approach to child abuse reporting may palliate the anxiety of the professional and the family, it does not remove the real, inherent labeling and stigmatizing aspects of the reporting process as it exists in most states today. Unfortunately, this is a problem that cannot be alleviated simply by a revision of reporting itself; it is rather an aspect of our society's perception of child abuse and the abusing parent. So long as child abuse is viewed as a form of radically deviant behavior, and as a symptom of pathology and sickness in others, the stigmatizing process will continue. All who are concerned with the prevention and treatment of child abuse have, therefore, a responsibility to demythologize the problem: to recognize that the potential to act in ways which we identify as deviant is in all of us. Until attitudes and policies change toward troubled families, whose children may bear physical signs of their distress, we shall have to work within the prevailing legal framework and to assure to the extent possible that children and families are helped—not harmed—by it.

All state statutes abrogate privileged communication when it involves a case of known or suspected child abuse. In reporting to mandated state agencies, the reporter should identify the facts as they are known; hearsay and secondary source information can be labeled as such. Most states have provisions in their statutes for central registers, which may become repositories for information both founded and unfounded, depending on the expungement provisions of the individual statutes. Who has access to this information is left up to the individual states, and it is well to remember that information that is submitted in such reports may be used at some later date to raise the issue of competency of a family or the risk to a child.

The principle on which most prevailing statutes are built is that services should be made available to families in which child abuse has been reported as a problem. It is incumbent upon the professional reporting a suspected case to continue involvement in management to assure that appropriate help will be given and that the family will not "fall between the cracks" of the service structure.

Case Management

A report of suspected child abuse or neglect is assigned to a protective agency worker for an investigation of the allegations, determination of the family's needs, and provision of appropriate services. The first issue to be settled is whether the child can safely remain in the parental home. The decision making involves answering the following questions: Are the child and family in need of protective services? Is there a need for immediate action? Should the child be placed in protective custody? Should the child be removed from the parental home? Is court involvement necessary?

If the initial investigation indicates a need for protecting the child, the investigating worker has three immediate alternatives, depending upon the severity of the case: the child can be hospitalized; the child can remain at home under protective supervision and with supportive services to the parents; or the child can be removed to an emergency shelter or other temporary facility. If the child's safety is in question and the parents refuse voluntary placement of the child, the case is frequently referred to the juvenile court.

In the past, the protective agency's activities often involved removing the child victim from the hazardous home situation. The book *Beyond the Best Interests of the Child* emphasizes the need for choosing the "least detrimental alternative" in decision making in child protection; this concept suggests that the impact on the child's development must be considered in any decision affecting the family. Studies have shown that foster home and institutional placements often result in long-term damaging effects on the children and their families. Therefore, a child should be separated from the family only after the evaluation of the family situation reveals that the child's risk of reinjury is great and that time is needed to activate the necessary supportive services for the troubled family.

There are divergent opinions regarding the hospitalizing of children whose conditions do not medically indicate admission. The American Academy of Pediatrics Committee on the Infant and Preschool Child advocates hospitalization as a means for providing the necessary time and resources for complete diagnostic evaluation; in addition, until a more thorough evaluation is made, the hospitalized child is protected. Every hospital should formulate a policy concerning the admission of suspected abused or neglected children. Whatever policy is adopted, it should be coordinated with the local child protective agency. Some state statutes allow physicians or hospital administrators to admit a child to a hospital without the parent's consent; this action requires a court order which may be obtained by telephone and justified on the next court day. However, if the parents are treated with sensitivity and honesty, most physicians should not find it difficult to convince the parents of the need to hospitalize their child.

Helping abused or neglected children and their families requires the coordinated efforts of many professionals. A single situation may involve protective agency and hospital social workers, pediatricians, a psychiatrist, a psychologist, public health nurses, a juvenile court judge, lawyers, and a number of other professionals. It is vitally important that medical personnel invest the necessary time and energy to assist the protective agency worker in working out a disposition plan for the child and the family. The physician's responsibilities may involve attending several multidisciplinary conferences; making requests for supportive services, such as day care, counseling, and homemaker services; and working with the parents to engender a relationship of confidence and trust, which will enable them to accept the recommended professional services. This takes time, patience, persistence, and a capacity to deal with ambiguous data in situations of conflict and crisis. It is never easy.

The help and advice of consultants from various disciplines can be an invaluable asset to decision making. Nevertheless, the ultimate responsibility for the protection of the child and the rehabilitation of the family rests with the protective agency, or in some jurisdictions with the juvenile court. The medical professional must acknowledge that he or she must work with, but cannot control, the decisions or professional actions of child welfare colleagues. A supportive and gracious demeanor and responsive attitude can foster communication in the individual case and sustain relationships for future interdisciplinary work.

After investigating and evaluating the family, the protective agency worker's role is often that of facilitator. Once the needs of the family have been determined, the worker must locate the appropriate community resources (such as day care and mental health services) and prepare the family for referral to them. In order to help strengthen family life and prevent further maltreatment, the worker must have access to various counseling and concrete services designed to modify the specific psychological and environmental conditions that lead parents to abuse and neglect their children.

In handling abusive and neglectful situations, intervention is more effective if the dynamics of the abusive pattern are understood. It has been found that the parents themselves have often experienced very traumatic experiences, frequently involving abuse or neglect, in childhood. In essence, they may be rearing their own children in a similar fashion. Abusive parents often demand performance from their children that is clearly beyond the ability of the children and ignore the children's own needs, limited abilities, and helplessness. Abused children are often perceived as being different from siblings and other children; they fail to respond in the expected manner or possibly are different, for example, retarded or hyperactive. Crises, stemming from personal, social, economic, and environmental stresses, play a crucial role in the life of the family and are often the precipitators of an abusive act.

There probably is no universal pattern underlying neglectful actions involving children. However, neglectful behavior appears to be a parental response to internal and external stresses; the parents also are themselves often victims of misfortune.

Because of the parents' personality traits (immaturity, excessive dependence, distrustfulness, social isolation, and poor self-esteem are seen frequently in practice) and their failure to seek out or respond appropriately to offers of help, many professionals conclude that abusive and neglectful parents are unmotivated and untreatable. Despite their initial resistance to professional intervention, it is recognized that a majority of the parents genuinely want assistance and can be helped to modify destructive child-rearing practices.

The sequelae of abusive and neglectful actions may result in immediate and long-term effects on the children's physical, neurological, cognitive, and emotional functioning. Steele, Martin, Kempe, and others have emphasized that abnormal child-rearing experiences may predispose these children to act out their angry feelings in becoming abusive parents, or by committing antisocial acts, such as delinquency and adult crime, later in life. In the interest of helping these children in their subsequent growth and development, professionals can break the generational cycle of abuse and neglect.

Family rehabilitative services may include medical and dental care; 24-h comprehensive emergency services; public health nurse visitations; psychiatric care; individual or family counseling; group therapy; self-help group support; day care, crisis nursery or babysitting services; family planning; homemaker service; parent aides; short- or long-term placement; financial assistance; job counseling and training; employment; advocacy for more adequate housing; and transportation.

Providing and coordinating the necessary services specific to each family is a function beyond the capability of any one professional, discipline, or agency. However, the interdisciplinary nature of case management frequently proves to be a problem because of the lack of effective communication among the professionals. It is well to keep in mind Abraham Maslow's warning that if the only tool you have is a hammer, you treat every problem as if it were a nail.

Interdisciplinary and Interinstitutional Issues

Primary professionals involved in the management of child abuse and neglect are physicians and nurses, social workers, and lawyers and judges. Table 58-2 presents a conceptual model of three levels of action for each discipline and the interdisciplinary relationship at each level.

Social Policy

All the states have passed legislation requiring the reporting of suspected child abuse to public authorities. In the early statutes, physicians were given the primary responsibility to report suspected physical abuse to the protective service agency. The focus has since been broadened to include other child-caring professionals, but physicians in hospitals and private practices continue to play the central role in identifying, diagnosing, and reporting child abuse.

Early state child abuse legislation was viewed as a tool to identify abuse at the earliest possible time and as a means of strengthening child protective services. But if laws requiring protective services are to be effective, appropriations to support the expansion of these services are essential. Many services to children and families depend upon a combination of federal, state, and local appropriations. These appropriations currently lag far behind the level needed to create good service programs and staff them with the number and quality of personnel required to make the services effective. If protective service agencies and workers are unable to respond adequately to reports of suspected abuse or neglect, they lose the confidence of physicians and other reporting professionals and of the troubled families. Families stop asking for help.

Table 58-2
Interdisciplinary and Interinstitutional Issues

| Level of Action | Disciplines | | |
	Medical	Social Work	Legal/Judicial
Social policy	Entitlement for health services	Appropriations for protective services and staff	Child abuse legislation: mandate for reporting by child-caring professionals
Institutional practice	Hospital policies and procedures on child abuse and neglect; orientation to family; roles of nurses and social workers; physicians' and nurses' skills and practices.	Agency orientation: specialized service programs; orientation to treatment; capacity to involve other disciplines	Judicial response: differing courts' policies: legal representation for victim, parents, and agency; tendency to keep child with family or to separate family members
Individual case management	Identification, diagnosis, and reporting of suspected cases; continuing health care	Family evaluation and treatment	Possible court action, with or without placement of child in foster home care, requiring social and other services to family

Professionals stop filing reports except in the most blatant abuse cases. Early identification and intervention are lost.

The problem does not lie principally in the way protective services are conceived in the legislation. The gap is between what the programs are authorized by law to do and the appropriation of funds to carry out the programs. At each level—federal, state, and local—appropriations fall short of recognized service needs. Until there is a commitment to a social policy that assumes responsibility for assuring every community adequate protective services, the needs of abused and neglected children and their families will not be met.

Institutional Practice

Frequently physicians have not had training and clinical experience in prevention and treatment of child abuse and neglect, in evaluating nonmedical family problems, and in planning appropriate long-range family rehabilitation with multidisciplinary professionals. Not understanding the orientation and practice of social workers, lawyers, judges and members of other nonmedical professions, physicians may be uncomfortable working in interdisciplinary management of abuse cases.

Child abuse imposes many stresses and strains upon medical personnel. Decision making is enhanced in hospital settings by written policy and procedural steps in handling suspected child abuse and neglect cases and by available consultative services. Physicians in private practice may be at a disadvantage in working with these troubled families if they do not have easy access to consultants and to colleagues for emotional support. Physicians are reluctant to report abuse based on suspicions and may delay reporting until more substantial evidence is available. When reporting leads to court involvement, physicians often lack the skill and experience to present testimony in the best interests of the child and family.

When physicians do become involved in child abuse and neglect cases, they may become discouraged by the gaps in community resources. However, few physicians see themselves as agents for bringing about social change, and many avoid becoming involved in solving community problems.

By tradition, training, and experience, child protection has been the responsibility of the social work profession. This specialized child welfare service is delegated by law to offer help to any child considered or found to be neglected, abused, or exploited. The protective agency has an obligation to explore, study, and evaluate the facts of suspected abuse and neglect cases and to provide appropriate services until the family situation has been stabilized and the potential hazard to the physical or emotional well-being of the child is lessened or eliminated. Too often the agency is prevented from fulfilling its role by ineffective programs, inadequately trained and limited staff, insufficient funding, and a lack of essential community resources. It is a startling fact that no state has developed community child protective programs adequate in size to meet the service needs of all reported cases of abuse and neglect.

To cope with the acute and complex problems presented in child abuse and neglect cases, an effective child protective program must recognize the necessity for comprehensive staff development and sufficient staff to allow each worker a manageable case load of approximately 20 to 25 active cases. Although an important aspect of protective services involves the application of basic social work knowledge and skills, an interdisciplinary approach to case management is imperative. Cooperation and coordination among social work, medical, and legal/judicial resources are vital.

Judicial proceedings may be necessary to provide care and protection for the child and modify parental behavior or circumstances affecting the welfare of the child. Too few provisions have been made to protect the legal and constitutional rights of children and their parents. Parents have the right to counsel in a suspected abuse or neglect proceeding. Of special concern is counsel for the child. Recently, provision for the appointment of a *guardian ad litem* to protect the child's interests has been made statutorily possible in some jurisdictions.

When court action is planned, the protective agency worker and other professionals qualifying as expert witnesses should have legal counsel readily available for advice and assistance in preparation of the facts and in presentation of testimony to the court. Unfortunately, because legal assistance is often lacking, professionals are reluctant to use the authority of the court as a community resource to rehabilitate the family. Instead, they reserve court involvement for family situations deemed hopeless after social service intervention and expect separation of the child from the family and punishment for the parents.

Individual Case Management

Identification, diagnosis, and reporting of child abuse are critically important, but they cannot, by themselves, assure that children will be protected. These initial activities must be correlated with effective services to abused children and their families. Physicians should be aware that the protective service system has as its major function the coordination of acute care services. When the roles of the professionals involved from the several disciplines are defined, a serious gap in services may be found: no professional or agency has assumed the responsibility for the provision and coordination of long-term therapeutic intervention. Health workers can become child advocates and prime movers for the development of multidisciplinary child abuse and neglect programs within their communities.

Realities and Dilemmas for Health Professionals

While much of recent literature on child abuse and neglect has focused on clinical aspects of diagnosis, intervention, and treatment, little attention has been given to the impact of the orientation of institutions, and the professionals who staff them, on clinical practice. The actual incidence of child abuse and neglect continues to be debated, with annual estimates cited from 200,000 to 4.5 million cases. A great number of the reported cases originate from hospital settings. However, pediatricians and other child health providers are aware of many cases of suspected abuse and neglect which they do not report to the child protective agency.

The evolution of child health practice has contributed to the persistent denial of child abuse and neglect. Social and behavioral determinants of illness are still frequently ignored, and treatment modalities are often unknown or lacking. The result has been that children who present physical consequences of these complex causal processes are treated symptomatically.

Although it is quite unlikely that the conceptual and philosophical orientation of the practice of medicine will change dramatically overnight, there are, nonetheless, several important and abiding realities of child abuse and neglect cases that are particularly noteworthy for health care professionals to consider during the diagnostic and treatment process.

First, *child abuse is a symptom of family dysfunction resulting from complex causal processes*. Frequently, physicians view child abuse and neglect cases in terms of the presenting symptomatology (for example, fractures, bruises, burns, and failure to thrive) and give little attention to the underlying causes of family dysfunction. Traditionally, the training of physicians and other health personnel has focused rather narrowly on the biological aspects of the etiology of disease and only recently has begun to acknowledge the importance of the environmental and social determinants of illness. The complexities of managing child abuse and neglect cases overwhelm many physicians. Access to a competent, multidisciplinary team can both expedite getting help for the victims and their families and provide valuable support and consultation to the physicians.

Second, *child abuse and neglect occur in all cultural, social, and economic strata of society*. When the professional staff is socially, culturally, and economically discrepant from the patient population, there is the danger that behavior may be interpreted in a culturally biased fashion, that strengths in families may be seen as weaknesses, or that a child's illness may be characterized by a more value-laden diagnostic label than would happen in a similar situation involving a child from the same social background as the professional staff (for example, "child abuse" versus "accident," and "neglect" versus "failure to thrive").

Third, *child abuse cases arouse overwhelming emotional reactions which may interfere with the objectivity and sound judgment of the involved professionals*. Often the professionals are not consciously aware of these aroused feelings. The accessibility for consultation of others who are not directly involved in the management of a particular case, but who are sensitive and competent to deal with both technical and human aspects of case management, provides the professionals with a mechanism for dealing with these feelings and not permitting them to surface in a way which might be detrimental to the management of the case.

Fourth, *the initial assessment in child abuse and neglect cases frequently is oriented toward the diagnosis of adult psychopathology*. The physician's orientation to abuse and neglect situations may be to search for psychopathology in the suspected perpetrators. Several studies demonstrate a small percentage of abusive adults to be seriously mentally ill. A more productive approach would be to concentrate on the family's potential to respond to helpful services. Successful intervention builds on the family's strengths and uses community resources to enhance the family's functioning.

Fifth, *child abuse and neglect are not monolithic entities.* Child abuse and neglect are complex problems with medical, social, psychological, and legal components. After the diagnostic assessment is completed, there are no simple solutions or cures. Therefore, the outcome in case management cannot be predicted with certainty. However, it is recognized that many abusive and neglectful parents genuinely want professional help to become more nurturing, protecting parents and to stabilize their family situations. A compassionate and understanding response from the helping professionals is essential to the parents' coming to terms with their problems and responsibilities in protecting their offspring.

Sixth, *in child abuse and neglect situations, family rehabilitation usually requires prolonged involvement.* These situations can be especially distressing for professionals who are accustomed to an efficient diagnostic and treatment process: defining the etiology of the illness; operating on its causes, either with drug therapy or surgical intervention; and finally waiting a short period of time for the therapeutic outcome. Child abuse and neglect cases almost never follow this pattern, although the rewards of successful treatment can be no less gratifying.

Seventh, *the door to the physician's office, or to the entrance to the hospital emergency room, is perceived by many people as the only portal of entry into the human service system.* At a time when the availability of services and resources to assist families with life crises is diminishing, and as social and economic stresses seem ever more to be threatening the integrity of the family unit, it is little wonder that medical personnel are hearing cries for help from patients and their parents. Isolated families may have nowhere else to turn. If we are not sufficiently cognizant of this new role which has been thrust upon us, we may force parents to package their problems in ways that they know will demand attention. All too frequently, we can look retrospectively in the medical chart of a child who has been identified as abused or neglected only to find that the parents brought the child in frequently in the past complaining of vague or undetectable symptoms. One can only speculate about the number of such cases that might have been prevented had time been taken to find out why the family sought help at that time.

Eighth, *the severity of a child's presenting symptoms may bear no relationship to the prospect for the successful management of the family's problems.* The symptoms with which the child presents are not always an accurate reflection of the nature and extent of family dysfunction. In fact, chronicity may be a more important factor in estimating prognosis: long-term patterns of behavior may have lasting and profound implications for both the child and the family. Here again, the importance of the early recognition of family distress is underscored.

Ninth and last, *child abuse and neglect cases necessarily bring health professionals in contact with other disciplines whose professional orientation, training and skills, and methods of practice may be unfamiliar.* Medical personnel must respect and acknowledge the opinions and orientations of those in other professions whose actions and recommendations are formed by different underlying principles and assumptions. Coordinated interdisciplinary management is essential to successful intervention in child abuse.

Primary and Secondary Prevention

It is unlikely that child abuse and neglect can be eradicated without changes in attitudes and priorities in society. The acceptance of violence in our culture is undoubtedly a factor in the complex causality of child abuse. Poverty and unemployment play important primary roles.

There are definite actions that physicians and other health professionals can take toward the goal of prevention. The identification of abusive or neglectful families generally occurs when the child is brought for treatment of an injury or condition. Awareness of the indicators of maltreatment, such as the differential diagnoses between childhood accidents and physical abuse, should lead not only to reporting of suspected abuse, but to "reaching out" to the troubled families to prevent repeated incidents of abuse or neglect.

Any professional who has contact with parents and parents-to-be must be sensitive to their knowledge of child growth and development, their preparedness to cope with the role and responsibility of parenthood, and problems that may influence their ability to handle their children. Personality factors that may influence the parents' ability to nurture and protect their children may include immaturity, excessive dependence, aggressiveness, alcohol and other drug abuse, emotional instability, and mental disturbance.

Several studies indicate that a significant number of

maltreated children are low-birth-weight infants. The traditional hospital practice which separates mothers and infants can thwart the parents' development of positive feelings for the children. The "special" children—premature, handicapped, multiple-birth, unhealthy, unplanned and unwanted—seem from available data to run a higher risk of maltreatment than "normal" children. Preventive efforts can include the provision of educational and supportive services to the families who have "special" children.

In many abusive and neglectful families, crises are frequent, and isolation limits parents' ways of coping with stress. Services and facilities to reach out and help vulnerable families should be available in the community. If parents are aware that such services— 24-h hot lines, self-help groups, crisis nurseries or day care, emergency shelters, and family crisis centers—are available to any family in need, they may refer themselves before their children become the unwitting victims of their frustration and anger.

Poverty is recognized as an aggravating influence on families with the potential to maltreat their children. The environmental and social stresses are more serious, and the opportunities for occasional relief from child-caring responsibilities are fewer. It is possible for a concerned professional community to make the delivery of services to the victims of poverty less chaotic, more reliable, more supportive to personal dignity and self-esteem, and thus more protective to children. We can work, furthermore, for the development of social policies which make for more equitable access to the goods and resources of society.

Prevention of abuse and neglect requires the support of family life. During regular office or clinic visits, the physician can ask the parents gently probing questions: Are you having any particular problems with your children? When there are problems, do you have someone to help you? Do you share the responsibility of child care? How do you feel about your children? What were your experiences in childhood? Is there something which I or someone else can do to help? Sympathetic questioning will show concern for the parents and help detect problems that the parents might not otherwise reveal. With knowledge of the family's problems and needs, and with the basis of an excellent professional relationship, an effective referral can be made for appropriate community services.

Parents' abilities to nurture and protect their children can be fostered by an effective health care system and by other services and programs which support family life and help people manage personal crises more effectively. Health professionals can, by stimulating coordinated action, help make the community a more favorable environment for supporting child health and growth.

59 | Sexual Misuse of Children

by Alvin A. Rosenfeld

In the late 1960s child abuse laws in many states were broadened to include sexual abuse. Since that time, protective care agencies have been perplexed and disturbed by the increasing numbers of cases reported to them. Children reported to these agencies range in age from infants to adolescents. The sexual activities reported include rape, molestation, and confrontation by an exhibitionist.

Rape may be defined as a crime of having sexual intercourse with a woman or girl forcibly and without her consent. Rape is a physical abuse (not a sexual one) with sex as the "weapon." In contrast to the violence experienced by raped older children, most prepubertal children having physical contact with the adult are involved in genital activities that can be termed *immature gratification;* these behaviors consist of looking, touching, feeling, or kissing and do not involve intercourse. Adolescents are involved more often in actual intercourse.

Child abuse statutes have based the conceptualization of *sexual abuse* upon the understanding of both physical abuse and rape. In this conceptualization, sexual relationships between adults and children are seen as interactions between victims and perpetrators, with one party imposing his will upon the other. Thus, the child, like a rape victim, is thought of as being forced into sexual activities either by physical force or through irresistible deception and manipulation by the adult. The adult is seen both as fully responsible and as morally repugnant.

This approach is appropriate for rape cases and necessary in a legal context where culpability must rest with the adult. However, it reflects psychological reality of the adult-child relationship for only a portion of the cases. It portrays inaccurately a most important subgroup of sexual abuse cases which come to professional attention: those in which the child has in some way participated in the activity. The importance of this subgroup appears to be that in it we find the greatest psychiatric morbidity. Because the inappropriate sexual activities between children and adults are so varied, Brant and Tisza coined the term "sexual misuse" as a more accurate description of the spectrum. They defined it as "exposure of a child within a given social-cultural context to sexual stimulation inappropriate for the child's age and level of development." This term seems more useful from a psychological perspective since it also includes sexual seductiveness by a parent. In these cases, while there is often no contact between the parent and the child, there can be associated symptoms, such as enuresis or nightmares.

Professionals have been debating for years whether, or to what extent, children who are sexually involved with adults desire or participate in the activity. Some have argued that the child be considered the innocent victim of the troubled and deranged adult. Others have objected that this idea is naïve. They have argued that these children seem to desire the sexual activity. In the past, some authors suggested that these children had some inborn defect which makes them more desirous of early sexual contact. More recent writers contend that these children seek out sexual contact as a means of obtaining nurturance in an environment that seems emotionally depriving. While there is probably some truth in each position, it remains exceedingly difficult to assess *whether and to what extent a child participated in a sexual activity with an adult.* It is also hard to understand to what extent a child can give "informed consent" in the face of a request from a respected, admired, or loved adult.

Accidental and Participant Victims

Weiss and his coworkers attempted to resolve this apparent difference of opinion by delineating two types of sexual involvement between adults and children, *accidental* and *participant*. In the accidental involvement, children were the unwary victims of a truly abusive situation, while in the participant involvement, children seemed to be active participants or initiators of a relationship with an adult. Although participant victims were far more common in Weiss's sample, subsequent research seems to indicate that this is an artifact of the types of cases reported. Thus, participant victims seem to come to the attention of authorities more commonly, while accidental cases, which seem in fact to be far more frequent, do not usually come to professional attention.

Accidental victims are usually approached by an exhibitionist or fondled by a stranger on a single occasion. Since these children are aware that the parent is available as a protective adult, they usually tell a parent of the event immediately after it occurs. If the parents are capable of psychologically supporting the child, they will discuss the event with the child and reassure him or her. Under these circumstances, long-term psychologic sequelae are unlikely.

Participant victims are often involved over long periods of time with a person they are well acquainted with. There are several possible reasons why the parent is rarely informed of the relationship. At times, the child has learned that the parent does not wish to know and if informed, will accuse the child of fabrication. In other cases, the child has become aware that the parent's ability to be protective is impaired. This may come about because of a lack of commitment and concern about one's children, as a result of debilitating depression, through preoccupation with personal matters, or because of dyssocial patterns of child rearing. *Clinical experience suggests that in a large proportion of cases the parents' impaired ability is associated in an as yet unclear way with the fact that the same-sex parent had a similar sexual experience in the formative years, often when that parent was the identical age as the child is when first sexually involved with an adult.*

Participant Victims of Incest

Participant victims seem to fall into two major subgroups, victims of incest and molested children. In some families, a child is actually raped on one occasion by a parent or person who stands in the psychological position of parent. Like other cases of actual rape, these should not be considered sexual misuses. They are physical abuses and should be handled accordingly. In most cases of incest, however, either the charge is not rape or the accusation that a rape took place does not fit the facts, since the "rape" turns out to be a relationship which has lasted for years. These children are often active participants in the relationship.

Children who participate in incest over long periods of time seem to come from grossly dysfunctional families. While this is immediately obvious in some cases, it may take several interviews to appreciate in others. Incest is now thought of as a *symptom* of defective family functioning. Generational boundaries which support distinct social and psychological roles for parents and children have been obliterated. Thus, in father-daughter incest, the mother has often abrogated the duties appropriate to her role (cooking, cleaning, rearing the younger children) to one daughter. Both parents have often experienced multiple losses, both actual and psychological, early in life. The parental marriage is often strife-torn. While the parents are usually sexually estranged, the fathers in some cases of father-daughter incest maintain that adultery is more reprehensible than incest. In addition, while adultery threatens to break up the family, incest may serve a tension-reducing function which keeps the family intact. To quote Lustig, "The family members appear uniformly frightened of family dissolution, and the function of incest to the family unit as a whole appears to be its preservation as an ongoing system."

Incest must be viewed as a relationship between at least three people: the two participants and the nonparticipating parent. The nonparticipating parent often denies any knowledge of the incest, and may even act as the martyred victim. This denial often represents an attempt of the parent to preserve self-respect since the clinical material often suggests that the parent was fully aware of the incestuous relationship. Even when the nonparticipating parent is aware of the relationship, she may not intervene since she fears the loss of her husband's income through incarceration more than she fears the social disapproval of incest. On occasion, the mother is relieved to be freed of her coital "chores."

In most cases, the child becomes aware that the nonparticipating parent will not serve as a protective adult. Therefore, the adult participant can often easily intimidate the child into silence. In other cases, however, the child may not see the incest in a negative way. In a setting of emotional deprivation, the incestuous relationship may provide the child with a sense of attention and warmth, albeit in a very inappropriate fashion. The positive aspects of some children's experience of participant relationships and their sense of responsibility for the involvement makes them reluctant to report the relationship even in the absence of threats. Though incest is a sexual activity, its psychological meaning is usually more elementary, embodying a search for the safety, comfort, and nurturance of the good protective parent that neither parents nor children ever had. In this way, sexuality is used as a substitute for nonsexual intimacy, the pleasure in spending time together.

Molested Participant Victims

Some children who are molested by someone other than an immediate relative participate in the activity. These children often have same-sexed parents who were misused in an almost identical fashion at the same age. There is often significant parental disagreement in these families, particularly over sexual matters. Furthermore, the children are in some way included in, or privy to, the parental sexual discord. In some cases, the disagreement may be manifested in arguments between the parents about proper ways to educate children about sexuality. This can result in the child getting two conflicting messages about appropriate sexual behavior. In other families, the children frequently witness parental arguments about whether one or another sexual activity will be performed. Whether through overstimulation, seduction, or excessive warnings about the evils of sexuality, both parents may inadvertently focus the young child's attention on sexuality and foster an excessive curiosity, confusion, or excitement that culminates in inappropriate sexual activity.

Management

General Principles

There is no typical presentation of sexual misuse since it may represent many forms of behavior. Because parents may try to hide the misuse out of a sense of shame or from allegiance to another family member, only a careful history and a willingness to ask about

and *to hear about* sexual involvements of a child will lead to a complete understanding of the situation in these cases.

The symptoms and signs of actual sexual misuse are often vague or nonspecific. The more obvious presenting complaints in young children are often of a genital nature, such as injuries, irritations, or venereal disease. Compulsive masturbation in a young child may also indicate misuse, though it can also be a sign of central nervous system pathology or a poor parent-child relationship in the absence of sexual misuse. In other children, the presentation may be less obvious and masked in difficulties with friends or studies, symptoms of school difficulties, isolation from peers, stealing, or running away. Conversion reactions, especially abdominal pains, chest (breast) pains, and headaches are also common.

At times, the presenting complaint will be of a sexual molestation. It must be remembered that while many of these accusations are true, some turn out either to be false or to be an accusation of the wrong person. In these cases, the clinician may find that while the accusations are untrue, they may indicate that children are confused about their own emerging sexuality or are frightened that other family members are having difficulty controlling their sexuality. Thus, while allegations may lack factual validity, they usually indicate psychological concerns about sexuality that warrant careful investigation.

Cases of sexual misuse arouse a multiplicity of strong feelings, ranging from outrage to titillation over the details of the events. Because these feelings are uncomfortable, a professional staff can begin to act in unfortunate ways. A clinician may deny that misuse is occurring in order to avoid facing unpleasant realities. In this way, repeated vaginal rashes in a 6-year-old may be described as "nonspecific" with the etiology "unknown." In other cases, when a clear-cut case of long-term participant misuse is seen, the staff begins to cry rape and to act in an alarmed, outraged fashion. In these cases, a careful assessment may not be done because of the staff's intense moral indignation. A conscientious staff often has a personal, natural protective attitude toward children. It can be very difficult to face the reality that the child participated in and perhaps enjoyed the sexual misuse. Sometimes, out of anxiety, the clinician may quickly pass the case on to a psychiatrist, psychologist, or social worker before completing a careful assessment.

The proper approach in all cases of sexual misuse is to remain calm and thoughtful. All family members should be interviewed, and each should have an opportunity to see the evaluator separately. It is the primary clinician's job to ascertain the realities of the situation. Since the families are often suspicious, frightened, or embarrassed, it is important to let them know that the clinician is there to help. An interrogatory style of interviewing usually alienates the family and creates resistance to professional intervention. In speaking to the misused child, the evaluator should use terms the child is familiar with.

It is important to discover whether the child is an accidental or participant victim, since in the former case, assuring the parents will usually enable them to support the child and thus avoid long-term ill effects. Since all the parents are usually guilty about their failure to prevent the misuse, the presence of guilt does not help separate the two types of relationships. Clues to the accidental or participant involvement of the child are provided by the answers to the following questions: (1) Was the relationship prolonged? (2) Has the child been involved with more than one adult? (3) Did the child accept gifts or remuneration? (4) Did the child know the adult? (5) Did the child tell the parent of the event immediately? Finally, the clinician should make a judgment about the parents' ability to be protective and supportive to the child.

Accidental Victims While supportive parents can ameliorate the effects of molestation, not all parents have that capacity. In accidental cases, if parents overreact or try to deal with their guilt feelings by vociferous attempts to punish or attack the offending adult, the results can be unfortunate. As Lewis and Sarrell have stated, "The child observes the reaction of rage in the parents and develops a revulsion against all future sexual feelings and experience."

The primary physician should try to help the parents be more rational in their reaction. If the parents appear to have insufficient personal resources to deal with the situation, they should be referred for crisis intervention.

Participant Victims The participant cases present a different set of problems. It is often difficult to understand why a case is being brought to professional attention after so many years. Often, as the child becomes pubertal, the adolescent sees the rela-

tionship in the context of the intense sexual stirrings of that age. This new, *sexual* perception of the relationship may lead the adolescent to end it. In other cases, the adolescent becomes aware of the social condemnation of incest, feels ashamed, and stops the relationship. An adolescent who is striving to form a sexual relationship with a peer may call in the authorities because an incestuous one stands in the way. In still other cases, the relationship may be reported by the child as a way of punishing a parent for some other matter totally unrelated to the sexual relationship.

While most primary clinicians are concerned with the child, *it is important to remember that once a relationship is detected and reported, the participating parent can become suicidal or psychotic.* The physician should be alert to this possibility.

If appropriate mental health resources are available, all participant cases should, after initial evaluation, be referred to a clinician expert in evaluating and treating misused children and their families. Many states require that sexual abuse be reported to appropriate authorities. When this is done, the evaluator should determine whether therapeutic intervention promises to improve the situation significantly so that incarceration of the offender is not necessary in incest cases. When the offender is not a parent, it is important to assess whether the adult represents a threat to *other* young children. This information will help the agency and court decide what action to take.

Prosecution is invariably traumatic to children, though the trauma can be reduced in some localities by having the child testify in the judges' chambers, rather than in an open courtroom. In prosecuted cases, children are often required to tell their story over and over again and may be subjected to strenuous cross-examination. Forty percent of cases are dismissed outright. If prosecution is planned, therefore, it is imperative that the child be prepared and supported through this trying experience.

The long-term effects of participant relationships are difficult to ascertain. In both the incestuous and the molested type, it seems likely that the outcome depends more on the general quality of interpersonal relationships in the family than upon any other factor. Thus, if there is a good relationship between the parent and the child with real communication, the outcome will undoubtedly be better than in a situation where parent and child are unable to or do not communicate.

60 | Childhood Psychosis

by Irving B. Weiner

Psychotic disorders are serious impairments of personality functioning characterized by disorganized and illogical thinking, distorted perceptions of reality, inappropriate ways of relating to people, and poor control over feelings and impulses. Psychoses sometimes occur with gross brain syndromes caused by trauma or intoxication, in which case they are referred to as *organic psychoses. Functional psychoses,* which are far more common, arise independently of demonstrable organic pathology, usually as the result of an unfavorable interaction between psychological stress and some constitutional disposition or vulnerability to psychotic breakdown.

The nature of the stresses that precipitate a psychosis and the form it takes vary considerably with the age of the individual. Although there is no clear consensus on how the functional psychoses of childhood should be classified, it is useful to distinguish among the following three patterns of disturbance: *infantile autism,* which begins at or soon after birth and interferes with normal psychological development from the earliest days of life; *childhood schizophrenia,* which begins between 2 and 12 years of age and represents a breakdown or regression in psychological functioning following some period of normal development; and *adolescent schizophrenia,* which begins following puberty and is continuous with adult forms of the disorder.

Infantile Autism

The primary characteristic of infantile autism is a lack of relatedness to people. Autistic children are indifferent and unresponsive to social overtures. As infants they do not clamor for attention, they do not enjoy being picked up, and they do not cuddle or cling when someone holds them. They rarely look or smile directly at other people, and they seem happiest when left alone.

For these reasons, mothers of autistic children have usually not found pleasure in their maternal efforts: "It was like taking care of an object; he never seemed to know or care whether I was around, and I never got any feeling of warmth from him." Nevertheless, because physical development proceeds normally in autistic infants, their serious psychological problems are often unnoticed initially or attributed to their being "placid" or "reserved" babies.

Between 2 and 5 years of age, however, these children begin to display a number of unmistakable behavioral peculiarities. Most prominent in this regard are (1) a need to preserve sameness, which makes them intolerant of any change in their environment, such as moving around the furniture in their bedroom, and leads them into many strange ritualistic behaviors, such as sitting for hours turning a radio on and off, without listening to it; and (2) marked speech abnormalities, consisting either of failure to develop any communicative speech or of speech that is hard to understand because of peculiar diction and syntax.

Infantile autism is fortunately a rare condition, with an incidence estimated at 2 per 10,000 live births. It is nevertheless noteworthy for the devastating handicap it imposes on psychological development from birth on, despite normal physical development, and for its serious long-term consequences. Some autistic children improve spontaneously and others respond favorably to specialized and intensive treatment programs. The general prognosis for the condition is poor, however. Substantial improvement can be expected in no more than 25 percent of cases. The majority of autistic children do not improve, and one-half of them require residential placement by the end of adolescence.

Childhood Schizophrenia

Childhood schizophrenia may begin as early as the preschool years (ages 2 to 5), following an unremarkable infancy, in which case it is reflected in many of the same symptoms seen in infantile autism: ritualistic, repetitive behaviors and intolerance for change in the environment; strange, incomprehensible speech patterns or even a total loss of previously established language skills; excessive, diminished, or unpredictable responses to sensory stimulation; a poor grasp of bodily integrity or even of identity as being a distinct person; bodily rigidity and strange posturing; aloofness from people and tendencies to treat people as if they were inanimate objects; and periods of unaccountably severe anxiety and violent temper tantrums.

During the grade school years schizophrenic children are additionally likely to develop delusions or hallucinations that detach them even further from reality and from appropriate relationships to people. Common among these symptoms are unrealistic fears about other children being "out to get them," bizarre fantasies about possessing special powers, and the conviction of being a machine or some kind of animal rather than a person. As an index of the frequency of these and other symptoms of serious personality breakdown, childhood schizophrenia is diagnosed in 10 percent of 2- to 12-year-olds seen in psychiatric clinics and hospitals.

The distinction between childhood schizophrenia and infantile autism is based not only on differences in age of onset but also on differences in course and prognosis. Autistic children who do not improve tend eventually to develop primary features of mental retardation, epilepsy, or aphasia. In contrast, approximately 90 percent of schizophrenic children subsequently present evidence of adult schizophrenia. However, the social prognosis for childhood schizophrenia is generally less grim than for infantile autism. With proper treatment a moderately good social adjustment during adolescence can be expected for about one-third of schizophrenic children, and another one-third will usually be able to make some kind of marginal social adaptation outside of an institution. The remaining one-third, however, face the prospect of more or less permanent residential care.

Adolescent Schizophrenia

Adolescent schizophrenia, unlike infantile autism and childhood schizophrenia, is neither a rare condition nor a condition so marked by grossly deviant behavior as to make its diagnosis obvious. Adult schizophrenia, which accounts for one-quarter of all hospital beds and half of the mental health beds in the United States, most commonly has its beginnings during the teenage years. This means that pediatricians who care for adolescents will see an appreciable number of young people in whom various kinds of apparently minor behavior problems constitute in fact the early stages of schizophrenic disorder. Regarding the magnitude of the problem, recent data indicate that 22 percent of 12- to 18-year-old psychiatric patients have either an overt or an emerging schizophrenic condition.

The adolescent behavior problems from which schizophrenia emerges usually involve either *withdrawal* or *storminess*. Withdrawn adolescents keep to themselves, avoiding activities that would bring them into contact with people and having few interests in common with others. They express little or no emotion, and they may appear apathetic and unenthused about life. Stormy adolescents, in contrast, exercise little control over their emotions or actions. They consequently tend to be in constant difficulty with their parents, peers, and teachers over behavior that others find unpredictable, inconsiderate, or outlandish. Neither withdrawal nor storminess is by itself diagnostic of schizophrenia, and both can occur in the context of numerous other behavior disorders. However, either pattern appearing in adolescence, especially if it represents a marked change from a youngster's childhood behavior, should alert the clinician to the possibility of incipient schizophrenia.

Generally speaking, the older people are when they develop a functional psychosis, the better their prospects are for improvement and recovery. Conversely, the earlier in life people break down in response to stress, the greater their probable constitutional disposition or vulnerability to psychosis. Hence the prognosis in adolescent schizophrenia is usually less guarded than in cases of childhood schizophrenia. However, because untreated schizophrenia is a progressively debilitating disorder, positive outcome in the individual case is significantly influenced by how soon the disorder is recognized and how promptly appropriate treatment is instituted.

61 | Health Care Delivery to Adolescents

by Sandra R. Leichtman and Stanford B. Friedman

Adolescence refers to that period of physical and psychosocial growth which marks the transition from childhood to adulthood. The beginning of adolescence is characterized by the onset of puberty and the psychological reaction to these developmental changes; the end of adolescence is marked by preparedness for and opportunity to assume an adult role in society. Throughout the adolescent period the interaction of physical and psychosocial factors creates unique problems and challenges for adolescents, their parents, and their physicians.

With the onset of pubescence adolescents experience many changes in physical and sexual growth and maturation which may be confusing to them. Among the concerns of adolescents are whether they are "normal" and maturing at a rate similar to that of other adolescents. In their attempts to psychologically adjust to these body changes, adolescents should know that they can turn to their physicians for professional help regarding normal or abnormal issues of growth and development. Many relatively "minor" problems, such as acne, may be of great concern to body-conscious adolescents. It is important that physicians anticipate adolescents' concerns and encourage the asking of questions which adolescents may be reluctant to pose lest they appear naïve or for fear of the physician's response.

Adolescents often react to the difficult developmental process of breaking away from dependence on parents by purposely opposing adult requests, deriding parental standards, and imprudently flouting adult privileges. Not infrequently adolescents will transfer feelings related to parental authority onto the physician, producing challenging and often frustrating doctor-patient relationships. Concern with being controlled, for example, can lead adolescents to refuse medical recommendations or to counter suggestions with arguments which may appear illogical or unreasonable to the physician. On the other hand, adolescents may actively seek the counsel of physicians because they are viewed as possessing wisdom by virtue of being adult authorities outside of the direct parent-child relationship. In either case, the physician needs to be able to encourage and respect the adolescent's wish to act as an independent individual, while at the same time recognizing that the adolescent usually still requires adult guidance and control.

Another potential difficulty in providing medical services to adolescents involves the physician's attitudes toward adolescent behavior, especially in the area of sexuality. Included among the common sexual concerns of adolescents are fears of homosexuality and fantasied consequences of masturbation. Any adolescent involved in or contemplating intimate heterosexual relationships should be able to turn to the physician for advice regarding such issues as birth control, pregnancy, and venereal disease. It is critical that the physician's own personal beliefs regarding adolescent sexuality do not interfere with the ability to provide medical counseling and treatment in a manner which will be most helpful to the adolescent and consistent with the adolescent's value system. The adolescent does not seek out the physician for a sermon.

Finally, the transitional nature of the adolescent period creates complications with respect to adolescent problems and to the question of who should treat the adolescent. The lack of synchronization of the physical and psychosocial changes which characterize the adolescent age group results in the adolescent being neither child nor adult, but unevenly sharing attributes of both. For example, while the adolescent may resemble the adult with respect to biological aspects of sexual maturity, psychological immaturity can impede prudent judgment, resulting in such problems as venereal disease and pregnancy. Thus, the physician wishing to manage adolescent problems needs to be relatively comfortable with the dual and changing nature of the adolescent.

Whose Province Is the Adolescent?

Some pediatricians and pediatric clinics refuse to see a patient over 12 years of age, claiming the onset of pubescence marks the end of childhood and thus of pediatric practice. Other pediatricians and clinics consider the ages of 16 or 18, or on rare occasions even older, as the upper limits for appropriate clientele. On the other hand, an internist may refuse to see adolescents due to discomfort in dealing with their psychological "immaturity" and the nature of their problems. A common lament of parents of adolescents is that they cannot find appropriate medical care for the adolescents.

With respect to psychosocial issues of adolescence, primary care physicians are in the advantageous position of having already developed relationships with the adolescent and the parents. In addition, these physicians are aware of the adolescent's history of physical and emotional development. However, some pediatricians may be uncomfortable about providing the education and counseling required by the adolescent patient struggling with adjustment problems, and they may feel ill-prepared to deal with issues of adolescent sexuality, including gynecological examinations. Adolescents also challenge the physician with such problems as drug use, truancy, running away from home, a wide range of "acting out" behaviors such as delinquency and vandalism, and frequent refusal to follow medical advice. A potential difficulty for both the pediatrician and family practitioner involves avoiding aligning oneself with the patient against the parent or vice versa; this difficulty is heightened by issues of confidentiality. The adolescent may be reluctant to confide in the physician because of the latter's previous identification as an advocate for the parent.

For the adolescent, the advantages of continuing with the pediatrician or family practitioner include the past establishment of a trusting relationship and the avoidance of having to expose one's body and intimate problems to a strange person—the potential new physician. However, an adolescent may view seeing a pediatrician as being childish and may thus wish to change to a doctor who treats adults or who specializes in the problems of adolescence.

Since the middle or late adolescent is physically more like an adult than a child, the medical training of the internist is appropriate for management of this adolescent's medical concerns. However, the internist may have little training (or patience) in managing the special psychological characteristics of this age group.

In response to the demands made by adolescents on health care delivery and the unique psychosocial characteristics of adolescent health care, the subspeciality of adolescent medicine has developed. Since the founding of the first nationally recognized adolescent clinic in Boston by Dr. J. Roswell Gallagher in 1951, there has been a rapid proliferation of adolescent facilities and an increasing number of fellowship programs for training specialists in adolescent medicine. The adolescent specialist offers the advantages of advanced knowledge regarding specific adolescent disorders, as well as training in the interaction of physical development, disease, and the psychological issues of adolescence. A potential difficulty is that the adolescent has to form a new relationship with the adolescent specialist, and then later as an adult form still another relationship with an internist or family physician.

Whether specialist or generalist, the major consideration in whether or not to treat adolescents must be the physician's interest and comfort in dealing with the complicated interactions of physical development, disease, and the psychosocial status of this age group. Since adolescents have unique characteristics, advanced training in adolescent medicine through fellowships, postgraduate workshops, or symposiums is recommended for physicians wishing to provide optimal medical care to this age group.

Where Should Adolescent Medical Services Be Delivered?

Outpatient Facilities

If the pediatrician wishes to continue with patients through adolescence, alterations in the office or clinic may be needed to respect the adolescent's need not to be treated as a child. The adolescent is likely to feel infantilized if made to wait in an office replete with crying infants, murals of Walt Disney characters; and children's books, toys, and furniture. To provide more hospitable surroundings for the adolescent, part of the waiting room may be arranged around a reading area containing material appropriate for adolescents. Suggestions include magazines on sports, pop music, and fashion and booklets on teenage health issues. In addition, some pediatricians may consider arranging for specific office hours and days devoted solely to their teenage patients.

Many hospitals maintain adolescent clinics with facilities structured and operated in a manner well articulated with the psychosocial needs of the adolescent. Certain adult outpatient clinics, particularly obstetrics and gynecology, are becoming increasingly aware of the specialized needs of the adolescent and have set aside specific hours in which only adolescent patients are seen.

A relatively recent movement in providing outpatient health care services to hard-to-reach adolescents is the establishment of "free clinics." The physical facilities range from store-front clinics to small moving vans which park in areas where runaway or disaffected adolescents tend to congregate. Generally, the population served by these clinics consists of adolescents outside the mainstream of society and/or youngsters fearful of consulting their usual physicians because they wish to keep their problems from their parents.

Inpatient Facilities

Hospital confinement can be a particularly distressing situation for both the adolescent and the hospital staff. Constraints imposed by medical treatment and by hospital regulations seriously interfere with the adolescent's quest for freedom and motor activity. Also, the need for hospitalization may be interpreted by the adolescent as "proof" that his or her body is not normal. The reactions of the adolescent to being hospitalized, including anger, rebellion, and depressive symptomatology, often create serious management problems for the physicians and ward personnel.

Generally, hospitals set relatively firm policies with respect to age of admission for pediatric and adult inpatient units. These arbitrary, and often inflexible, demarcations can impede optimal patient care for adolescents. It is as inappropriate to hospitalize a preg-

nant 15-year-old on a pediatric ward as to admit a physically and psychologically immature 13-year-old to an adult ward. Some hospitals have adolescent inpatient wards or have designated sections of the pediatric wards for adolescents. These units provide the benefits of a staff interested in adolescents and trained to support and to counsel them, as well as manage their medical and surgical problems. Often ward facilities are available for games (pool, table tennis), music, and adolescent discussion groups. Adolescent inpatient units require a high staff-to-patient ratio to adequately care for the complexities and difficult behavior problems so typical of such facilities.

While the adolescent unit is uniquely prepared to treat the total patient, difficulties arise with respect to the medical aspects of patient care. Characteristically, multiple medical and surgical subspecialties (orthopedic surgery, neurosurgery, chemotherapy, opthalmology) admit to an adolescent unit. However, a comprehensive patient-care approach is not always appreciated by subspecialty staff, who would prefer to admit adolescent patients to their own specialty-oriented wards. This difference in orientation frequently creates major friction among services and challenges the best efforts of resolution through communication at all levels. Other potential difficulties for specialists when adolescent patients are segregated include duplication of expensive equipment and complications in rounding schedules. An adolescent ward therefore presents an administrative challenge which, if not met, can actually deter optimal hospital care to teenagers.

How Are Services Delivered?

General Approach

As stated, adolescents generally wish to be approached as independent individuals with many, if not all, of the rights and privileges of adults. However, from the vantage point of adults, adolescents often seem reluctant to assume the associated responsibilities. In truth, adolescents are neither children nor adults and should not be expected to behave as either. They should be encouraged to make their own appointments (and cancel them when appropriate) and assume as much of their medical care as judged appropriate by the health team. It is important, however, to consider the psychological and social "age" of the adolescent, as well as the chronological age. This is especially true of teenagers with chronic illness, who may enter adolescence with many handicaps—both physical and psychological. The latter may include a history of poor school performance, parental overprotection, and difficulties with peer relations.

There is no agreement on how best to manage the adolescent patient with regard to the parents. Some physicians tend to relate primarily with the adolescent; others work primarily through the parents. Of most importance is to define the ground rules to all concerned and to always allow some opportunity to see the adolescent alone and the parents alone. The adolescent's confidentiality should be protected, but it is also desirable to let the parents—who ultimately are responsible for their child's welfare—know whether satisfactory progress is being made. These issues are often easier to resolve in medical and surgical cases than when managing problems related to such teenage difficulties as pregnancy, venereal disease, or drug abuse.

The rights of adolescents to seek medical advice and help are discussed in detail elsewhere in this text (see Sec. 45). Suffice it to say that increasingly adolescents in most states are being given the right to obtain medical attention without parental consent *or* knowledge. This legal right, however, does *not* contradict the general tenet that teenagers, especially the younger ones, are best helped if at some point their parents are involved. The matter of confidentiality is always relative, and balance must be struck between preserving the teenager's right to medical care and privacy and the parents' obligation in our society to be responsible for their children. In the area of confidentiality, physicians should never promise more than they wish to deliver—an adolescent boy threatening suicide should not be told his parents will remain uninformed!

Management of Referrals

Even the specialist with advanced training in the physical and psychosocial development of the adolescent often will find it necessary to refer a patient for medical or psychological consultation. As with all referrals, the primary care physician can play a key role in helping the parents and the adolescent select the best possible consultation or specialist to manage a particular medical problem. Such consultation should be arranged with the care most physicians use

in selecting medical care for their own family members.

The family should be advised as to why the consultation or referral is desirable and informed of the options available. In cases of serious disease or trauma, the primary care physician should introduce the family to the specialist who will be assuming the major medical responsibility. In any event, the primary care physician has a major role in "translating" specialty medicine to both the teenager and the family.

Referral for emergency psychiatric consultation should be made when an adolescent presents with an acute psychiatric episode, such as repeated drug intoxication, serious threats of injury to self or others, or depressive symptoms characterized by suicidal ideation or behavior. For reasons of expediency and legality it is usually essential that the adolescent's parent or guardian be involved in the emergency referral process.

There will be times, other than emergency situations, when the primary care physician believes a referral is needed for psychological, psychiatric, or social reasons. Often adolescents are not "ready" to seek psychiatric or psychological help, or they view such treatment as a sign that they are "crazy." Thus, it is important that before making the referral, the physician set up a special appointment with the adolescent, and often the family, to determine whether the patient is willing to seek such help and to discuss ways in which mental health consultation or treatment will be beneficial. The adolescent's strengths, as well as problem areas, should be included in the discussion. In order to be assured of appropriate referral resources, it is useful for the physician to establish relations with at least a few mental health professionals working with adolescents in the community. Adolescents will often feel relief through the knowledge that the physician is acquainted with and has realistic confidence in the person or resource to whom they are to be referred.

Time/Cost Dimension

As a youngster reaches puberty, the physician wishing to carry the patient through adolescence may find it useful to set up an appointment in order to discuss the many physical changes which will be occurring and to encourage the adolescent to ask questions regarding physical or psychosocial issues for which he or she wishes education or guidance. Although the physician may have been following the patient for a number of years, this "special" appointment is in many ways comparable to an initial visit and should be charged accordingly. Before this appointment is set up, it is important that the adolescent and the family be informed of the nature of the visit, the anticipated time involvement, and the charges.

For the physician who offers counseling services to the adolescent, fees should be apportioned according to the amount of time involved. Primary care physicians are often reluctant to charge appropriately for their time, feeling that for the same money the family could have "real psychiatric help." What is underestimated is the resulting effectiveness and *efficiency* of the primary care physician's "knowing" the family.

There are, of course, situations in which charging according to time commitment may not be appropriate. For example, when parents refuse to support the troubled adolescent's seeking of counseling, the physician may wish to set up a special rate which the adolescent is able to pay. The matter of charging adolescents, in view of changing laws giving adolescents the right to medical care, is an issue that is still far from resolved.

62 | Psychosocial Development of Adolescents

by Sandra R. Leichtman

No single physical, psychological, intellectual, scholastic, legal, or chronological criterion can adequately describe the complex phenomenon of adolescence. Rather, an adequate definition of adolescence needs to consider the interactions of specific biological and psychological developmental processes within the context of a particular social environment. This integrated framework provides a comprehensive and meaningful approach to providing services for the adolescent.

For a youth to be considered an adolescent, the physical changes of puberty need to be accompanied by some perception by the individual of these changes. Thus, it is not the physical aspects of pubescence per se which mark the onset of adolescence, but rather the psychological reaction of an individual to the bodily changes characteristic of this age. The chronological equivalent is approximately 11 to 13 years, with males generally entering the adolescent period about a year or two later than females.

While the onset of adolescence is defined by psychophysical criteria, the termination of adolescence is primarily determined by psychosocial criteria. Specifically, the end of adolescence is marked by preparedness for and opportunity to assume an adult role in society. The psychosocial tasks which the adolescent needs to accomplish in preparing for adulthood include gaining independence from parents, forming intimate sexual relationships, delineating educational and occupational goals, and establishing a positive and consistent sense of identity which is congruent with societal norms. The chronological ages at which these tasks are accomplished are strongly influenced by social and cultural factors. An individual planning for an occupation requiring a graduate degree may need to prolong dependence on parents for financial support and possibly postpone interpersonal commitments. Another individual from a family with limited financial resources may need to become self-sufficient at the completion of high school education or even earlier. In the former case, adolescence may be considered to extend into the early twenties or beyond; in the latter case, adulthood may be reached as early as 16 years of age.

As a stage of development, adolescence is frequently described as a time of storm and stress characterized by psychological upheaval and pathological behaviors. Thoughts, feelings, and behaviors which would be considered deviant in an adult or child are dismissed as being a normal part of the developmental process of breaking away from dependence on adults and adjusting to a changing body image. This picture of adolescence as being a time of intense turmoil is based largely on the conceptualizations of psychotherapists working with a select group of adolescents needing help for emotional problems. Popular fiction, as for example, *The Catcher in the Rye*, reinforces this image. Studies of more representative populations of adolescents, however, have failed to support this view. While during the early and middle stages of adolescence there is often temporary withdrawal, as well as increased defiance, adolescents in general cope remarkably well with the developmental stresses. In addition, the incidence of psychopathology in adolescence does not differ significantly from that in adults. When an adolescent presents with moderate or severe emotional difficulties, these complaints should be considered as potential signs of psychopathology, rather than as normal patterns of adaptation.

A second common portrayal of the adolescent emphasizes a generation gap between parents and youth. The adolescent is considered to be disenchanted with parental standards and behavior, distrustful of adult authority, and antagonistic to the values of the general society. Feeling alienated from the world of adults, the adolescent becomes a member of a peer subculture which creates its own sets of standards to govern behavior. Support for this view of a generational conflict is seen in the many verbal battles between adolescents and their parents, particularly in the early and middle stages of adolescence. A great number of these arguments, however, are focused on relatively superficial issues, as for example, length of hair or use of the family car. In general, there is usually some degree of mutual respect between adolescents and parents, as well as a shared basic value system. Intense intergenerational conflict is often indicative of disturbed parent-child relationships and is almost always rooted in difficulties occurring prior to adolescence.

With respect to the existence of an adolescent subculture, young adolescents do show strong conformity to peer-group pressures and norms. Again, it is usually superficial issues (for example, standards of dress and interests in particular popular singers) which govern the adolescent's behavior in a manner which may be disagreeable to parents. Usually, adolescents tend to gravitate to peer groups which share the general value systems of their parents. Adolescent participants in civil rights movements, for example, are often from families which hold "liberal" political views.

Early Adolescence

Physical Development

Psychologically, the time of greatest difficulty for adolescents and their families may be the early stage of adolescence, as the adolescent first attempts to understand and adjust to the body changes of pubescence and to gain independence from adults.

Both male and female adolescents are concerned about whether their bodies are normal and physically attractive and whether their ultimate height and weight will be within acceptable limits. While parents, schools, books, and commercially prepared pamphlets usually provide the most accurate and reliable sources of information regarding normal physical and sexual growth and development, it is frequently the less accurate processes such as discussions and comparisons with peers which are most influential to the adolescent. Close friends may pore over books and pamphlets together, sharing intimate thoughts and feelings about anticipated body changes. Locker rooms provide opportunities for comparing one's body with those of peers. In attempts to learn about the opposite sex, adult magazines, for example *Playboy* and *Playgirl*, are frequently secreted and studied.

Despite the formal and informal preparation, the actual occurrence of a specific physical event is often frightening and confusing to the adolescent. The onset of menses may be associated with temporary withdrawal from interpersonal relationships, secretiveness, and rigid compliance to hygienic suggestions (such as showering every day during menstruation). While prior to her first period, the young adolescent female may have been proudly telling her friends of the anticipated event, when menstruation actually occurs, it is usually the mother who is turned to for reassurance, and friends are expected to surmise that this change has occurred. Boys may react similarly with respect to their first nocturnal emission.

Psychological reactions to pubescent changes also may include those emotional reactions produced, at least in part, by physiological processes. Hormonal fluctuations during different stages of the menstrual cycle, for example, have been implicated in mood changes. Many women experience premenstrual tension characterized by feelings of anxiety, depression, lability of affect, and irritability. For the young adolescent female unaware of the relationship between her menstrual cycle and moods, these feelings are particularly difficult to understand. Additionally, premenstrual complications such as bloating, cramps, and skin eruptions all may potentially contribute to feelings of lowered self-esteem.

An important psychophysiological adjustment for the young adolescent male involves his concerns around control of sexual and aggressive impulses which are probably related, in part, to the marked increase in testosterone at pubescence. As with the female, the young adolescent male may temporarily withdraw from interpersonal relationships or become increasingly rebellious in attempts to adjust to the physiological changes.

Masturbation, which usually lacks the sanction of parents, often concerns adolescents. Although 90 percent of male adolescents are reported to masturbate, for many adolescents this activity remains fraught with guilt and fantasied negative consequences. Considering masturbation as aberrant behavior, the adolescent may be reluctant to talk about the existence of this secret activity with parents or peers. In light of the adolescent's strong negative feelings regarding masturbation, it is often helpful for the physician to bring up the subject in a nonjudgmental matter-of-fact manner, noting that this is a normal behavior. This approach can avoid both the intrusiveness and the potential embarrassment of direct questioning about a sensitive area, as well as maintain the adolescent's need for privacy.

Since the female growth spurt precedes that of males by almost 2 years, there is a period of time during early adolescence when females are taller than males of the same age. The situation may create concerns for both sexes regarding questions of ultimate height, with males feeling small and insecure and females fearing they will always tower over males. By middle adolescence, around 15 years of age, males and females are approximately of equal height. Generally, females reach their ultimate height by age 17 or 18, but males may continue to grow for several more years.

Normal variation in maturation is particularly marked in adolescents. Although early or late maturation often has negligible effects on ultimate physical development, the psychological consequences may be critical during adolescence and may continue through adulthood.

For adolescent males, prestige and popularity are linked with masculine physical attributes, including strength and athletic prowess. The late-maturing male, at a distinct disadvantage with respect to these attributes, is often plagued by feelings of social and sexual inadequacy. Peers, who are themselves insecure with regard to the normality of their own bodies, may reinforce these feelings by teasing the late maturer.

Since the negative self-concept which the late-maturing male may develop during this time often persists through adulthood, it is important that the physician be aware of the potential psychological difficulties. The physician should support the late maturer, acknowledging that although he is slow to develop, his body is not abnormal and he will eventually develop into a physically and sexually mature man.

In contrast, the early-maturing male is likely to be viewed by peers as popular, attractive, and self-assertive. He is at an advantage with respect to athletic competition, as well as social relationships. He may feel more confident than his male counterparts in entering into heterosexual interactions, since he is closer to the same development level as his female classmates.

For females, the effects of early or late maturation are less consistent and less pervasive. There is again a tendency for the early maturer to be in a more advantageous position than the late maturer, who must continue to worry whether she will grow up to womanhood. There are, however, disadvantages to early maturation, including premature pressure for dating by older males and teasing by physically immature males or females uncomfortable with their own developmental status.

Psychosocial Development

In early adolescence the developmental task of gaining eventual independence from parents begins. For the young adolescent, this process is complicated by the reality factors of needing to rely on parents for financial and emotional support, as well as for guidance on control of sexual and aggressive impulses.

Typically, the adolescent will challenge parental authority on relatively minor issues, such as clothing styles or refusal to baby-sit for younger siblings. Since these challenges represent assertions of autonomy, however, they are often presented in a forceful, emotional, and seemingly uncompromising manner. Behaviors characteristically displayed by young children—such as pouting, yelling, crying, and slamming doors—are not uncommon adolescent responses to not getting one's way. An adolescent's own parents are almost always viewed as less reasonable than the parents of peers.

The early adolescent's conflict over independence creates a dilemma for both parents and adolescents. The adolescent will resent the parent's offering of help with homework, yet blame poor grades on parent's "refusal" to help. When a dating curfew is imposed, the adolescent will be openly angry at this sign of lack of parental trust, yet at another, unspoken, level may be grateful for this external control.

The adolescent's conflict with parents extends to other adults who hold authority, particularly teachers. In contrast, some adults who are outside of the authoritarian role are idolized and emulated by adolescents. A camp counselor, for example, may become a strong and meaningful identification figure for the adolescent.

Peer relationships, particularly close same-sex friendships, are extremely important in the psychosocial development of early adolescents. The functions of peer relationships during this time are numerous. They include providing feedback regarding normality, extending emotional support in the struggle for independence, offering companionship for shared activities, and presenting models of age-appropriate behavior. Rejection by peers will often increase the young adolescent's preoccupation with self, leading to even more withdrawal and reinforcing feelings of being different.

The psychosocial development of young adolescents affects medical care in a number of ways. First, the physician is not infrequently presented with psychological and interpersonal problems which are directly related to psychosocial developmental issues. The physician may be requested, for example, to serve as ombudsman in the chronic disagreements between adolescents and their parents. The physician who chooses to assume this counseling role must listen to and support both sides in working toward compromises. One useful method of disentangling problems and permitting both adolescent and parents to save face is through preparing a contractual agreement. Since providing this type of counseling involves a time commitment considerably greater than that required for a strictly medical visit, charges should be apportioned accordingly.

Secondly, psychosocial conflicts and issues related to illness can interact in a manner which is detrimental to medical care. The adolescent's resistance to adult authority, for example, may be exhibited in refusing to comply with the physician's recommendations. Asthmatic adolescents may use the threat of attacks to win concessions from parents. Diabetic adolescents may flagrantly deny dependence on insulin or refuse to follow medical procedures, since to comply might signify proof to them that they are different from their peers.

Such behaviors are seen frequently in the practices of physicians who work with adolescents, and no doubt contribute to the reluctance of many physicians to treat this age group. To be of maximal benefit to the ill adolescent, it is important that the physician avoid becoming entangled in the "battle of wills" typical of adolescent interactions with adults at this stage. Instead, the physician should work toward helping the adolescent recognize the self-defeating nature of such behavior and encourage the adolescent to as-

sume major responsibility for caring for the illness. At the same time, the physician should permit the adolescent to express feelings of despair and anger at being ill. Providing emotional support may be particularly important, since the adolescent may not share these negative feelings with peers for fear of bringing attention to his or her abnormal body.

Yet, the adolescent's readiness to be both supported and influenced by peers can be used constructively in helping the adolescent adjust to illness or prepare for medical procedures. Before the adolescent has elective surgery, for example, it is beneficial to arrange a meeting with peers who are already undergoing the procedure. Introducing adolescent patients with chronic illnesses to each other provides them with the opportunity to offer mutual emotional support without needing to feel uniquely different or inferior.

Middle Adolescence

Physical Development

Physical growth in middle adolescence occurs at a slower rate than in early adolescence and manifests itself in more acceptable body proportions. Torso growth and shoulder girth increase so that the once clumsy adolescent no longer appears to be "all arms and legs." The male growth spurt results in the male catching up and surpassing the female in height, reducing the fears of both sexes regarding ultimate height. In addition, the female becomes capable of conception and the male of impregnation.

The development of more attractive body proportions and the establishment of adult sexual maturity decreases adolescents' questions of whether they are normal, and if and when they will grow to be so. With greater strength and agility, their participation in sports becomes more rewarding and provides an acceptable way to cope with aggressive feelings. Chronically ill adolescents, while often denied this direct physical outlet, can be encouraged to participate in other competitive ventures, for example, chess, rifle marksmanship, or debating.

Psychosocial Development

In middle adolescence the decreased preoccupation with body changes permits greater emotional investment in interpersonal relationships. Friendships involving both sexes become increasingly important in the exploration of who one is and what one wants to become. Thoughts and feelings are shared at an intimate level which extends beyond mere confidences. Within the context of close friendships, the mid-adolescent demonstrates remarkable ability to look objectively at oneself and to offer and accept constructive suggestions for change.

Since adolescents learn about themselves according to how peers relate and respond to them, rejection by peers can create a painfully negative self-concept and seriously limit the opportunity to learn socially adaptive behaviors. A friendless adolescent, for example, may become involved in promiscuous sexual activity in a desperate attempt to form close relationships and feel desired by others. The result of this behavior is often further exclusion by peers.

The process of becoming more comfortable with the opposite sex usually begins with the heterosexual group interactions provided through social cliques and extracurricular activities. Initial dating, which may be in part instigated by social pressure, is usually fraught with anxiety and may be relieved only through discussions with same-sex peers before and after dates. During this early stage, dating may be sporadic and based more on social ritual than emotional involvement. With increased experience, anxiety subsides and heterosexual relationships become more meaningful, leading to the expression of intimate feelings integrated with sexual exploration.

Handicapped adolescents are often at a disadvantage in the development of heterosexual relationships. Cliques which assign prestige according to physical attractiveness and athletic prowess do not readily extend themselves to adolescents who lack these qualities. Initial dating patterns, based more on superficial standards than emotional involvements, tend to exclude the handicapped adolescent. Thus, despite assurances of normal sexual development, the handicapped adolescent is likely to feel sexually inadequate.

The physician should provide a comfortable setting, without interruptions, to encourage the adolescent to express questions and feelings about sexual behavior, including issues related to sexual intercourse and contraception. The tendency to use one's own past adolescent experiences and current values must be resisted by the physician, who also must be *knowledgeable* about adolescent sexual behavior from the psychological, social, and cultural points of view. Yet,

this approach must be tempered with respect for the privacy of the adolescent who wishes not "to share all," and probing questions may quite appropriately be resented.

The middle adolescent's increased sense of independence is reinforced by the legal sanction of a driver's license. Physically handicapped or chronically ill adolescents, however, may be denied this important rite of passage. Epileptic adolescents, for example, are often not permitted to obtain a license unless they have been free of seizures for periods ranging from 6 months to 4 years.

The automobile serves several other functions in addition to being a symbol of freedom. Among these are means of finding privacy for heterosexual explorations and increasing the range of friendships. The automobile is also used imprudently by many adolescents who assume the privilege of driving without the attendant responsibilities. Displays of bravado, as well as general feelings of invulnerability to injury, result in many accidental injuries and deaths. Accident-related deaths are the leading cause of mortality for adolescent males, with motor vehicle accidents accounting for more deaths than all other causes of accidents combined.

The adolescent's relationships to larger societal institutions, for example, schools, also change in middle adolescence. In large high schools, academic tracks are selected to prepare the student for vocations or college requirements. Adolescents planning to go to college may spend considerable time and effort in perusing college catalogs and rehearsing for pre-admission interviews.

Academic achievement is strongly related to parental aspirations, socioeconomic status, and intellectual ability. In the adolescent's planning for the future, parental influences are generally greater than peer influences, although parents and peers often hold similar values. School dropouts, with the possible exception of those who need to support families, usually show a history of poor academic achievement, low aspirations, and negative self-images, problems which existed prior to leaving school. While not expected to provide educational or vocational guidance, the physician can assist the potential dropout through referral to other professionals who can help the adolescent explore alternative plans, such as those offered through work-study programs, "free" schools, or vocational training institutes. Social workers, public health nurses, educational and vocational specialists, and psychologists are particularly helpful referral sources. Occasionally, continuation of school may not, in fact, be advantageous to the adolescent.

Vocational plans are in a state of transition during middle adolescence. The glamorous and exciting fantasy choices of childhood and the decisions based on areas of interest of early adolescence are gradually replaced by more realistic aspirations. Experience in work situations is made possible in middle adolescence through the issuance of work permits. While many adolescents welcome the opportunity to earn money and demonstrate responsibility, the number of job openings may be severely limited. Adolescents, particularly those from the lower socioeconomic groupings, are frequently the first to be laid off in times of high unemployment. This situation is one likely to reinforce cynicism regarding achievement of the "American dream."

Late Adolescence

Physical Development

Adult height and contour are essentially complete by late adolescence, as are secondary sexual characteristics. Physical and sexual immaturity is of particular concern to the older adolescent, even though the "delay" in development may still be well within normal limits and reflect no endocrine or other physical problem. The physician should nevertheless acknowledge the developmental status of such adolescents, as a common fear is that the physician is unaware of the growth delay and therefore has "missed something." Discussion of the adolescent's physical development is an opportunity for the physician to offer counseling if further help and advice are desired.

Psychosocial Development

In late adolescence, the psychosocial adaptations of the early and middle adolescent periods are integrated and consolidated in a manner which produces a stable and consistent sense of self. Additionally, society provides the opportunity for the realization of economic self-sufficiency, which in turn promotes independence from parents and emotional commitments to potential marriage partners. The convergence of these social and psychological factors con-

tributes to the establishment of a firm and positive identity which is congruent with societal norms.

As late adolescents become more certain of their identity and more invested in forming intimate heterosexual relationships, their interpersonal relations become increasingly similar to those of adults. The emotional support provided by peers becomes less important, and large social cliques and extended same-sex friendships are replaced by groups of couples. In contrast to adults, however, late adolescents maintain rather strict age segregation, rarely forming close reciprocal social relations with individuals who are not within their age range.

Parents are generally viewed by the late adolescent in a relatively realistic and balanced manner. The idealized parental image of the child and the hypercritical attitude of the early adolescent are no longer evidenced. Instead, the late adolescent is able to accept parental shortcomings and to recognize that parents themselves face many difficult situations, including, for instance, planning for the care of elderly grandparents and worrying about financial concerns. Late adolescents also become increasingly aware of how like their parents they are, discovering anew shared interests and values.

The late adolescent is in the position either to directly seek employment which will provide economic self-sufficiency or to pursue advanced professional training. In the former situation the adolescent is able to assume an adult role at an earlier age than in the latter case. When advanced education is required for occupational goals, adolescence is often prolonged because of the financial dependence on parents. The achievement of many adolescent psychosocial tasks is, however, still possible with respect to the formation of intimate heterosexual relationships (although marriage may be postponed), attainment of emotional independence from parents, and establishment of a positive and consistent self-image.

Chronically ill adolescents encounter many problems in their attempts to master adolescent psychosocial tasks and to enter into adult roles. In addition to the limitations presented by the illness per se, other restrictions are imposed by potential employers and college admission boards. There is often reluctance to accept a chronically ill individual because of concerns about potentially high absenteeism, possibilities of attacks while at work or school, and presumed emotional difficulties assumed to be associated with chronic illness. When presented with a choice between a normal adolescent and an equally talented handicapped adolescent, the employer or admission counselor is likely to favor the former.

It is important for the physician to be aware of the educational and occupational barriers which the adolescent is likely to encounter. If a chronically ill adolescent is applying to college, for example, the physician should offer to write a letter to the admission board which emphasizes the adolescent's ability to function effectively. The physician also can be instrumental in securing financial assistance for vocational training through referral to the Department of Vocational Rehabilitation for the state in which the adolescent resides.

Chronically ill adolescents also face difficulties in the establishment of a positive and consistent sense of identity. Feelings of being different, attributable both to the illness itself and to the negative reactions of peers to the handicapped adolescent, strongly contribute to lowered self-esteem. Overprotection by parents can seriously interfere with autonomous functioning. Staying at home while peers are on dates can raise doubts regarding sexual adequacy.

While it is important for the physician to assist the adolescent in recognizing limitations imposed by the illness so as to provide for appropriate educational and occupation planning, it is equally critical that the physician help the adolescent recognize and develop special assets, including social, personal, scholastic, and artistic skills. The physician can help the chronically ill adolescent and the parents to achieve the goal of having the adolescent incorporate the illness into his or her self-concept so that a near normal life with respect to psychological, social, and even occupational functioning may become possible.

63 | The Secular and Cultural Influences on Growth and Development

by Thomas E. Cone, Jr.

At first glance the concept that growth and development have secular, that is, long-term, and cultural dimensions may seem unlikely. However, it is now a well-known phenomenon in human biology that, at least during the past century, children from widely different parts of the world have been maturing earlier and earlier and becoming larger and larger at each age. And if one defines culture as the totality of socially transmitted behavior patterns, beliefs, institutions, and all other products of human work and thought characteristic of a population, it becomes self-evident why cultural influences exert profound influences on growth and development. Dietary preferences and taboos and how infants and children are cared for, housed, and treated when ill will surely affect the child's growth and development.

Secular Accelerative Trends

Children in the United States and in Western Europe are not only growing taller in successive generations but also reaching biologic maturity at an earlier age. This secular acceleration of statural size and biologic maturation has been evident during the past century, and until 1976 there was no published evidence that these accelerative trends were slowing down. From the results of a recent study by Zacharias et al. it now appears that middle-class American girls are no longer reaching sexual maturity at a younger and younger age. For example, in this study menarche was found to be occurring at an average age of 12.8 years, which is about the same age as it was occurring in the late 1940s.

Also, a recent government report (1976), published by the National Center for Health Statistics (NCHS), analyzing data on more than 20,000 American children from infancy through adolescence, concluded that the trend toward ever-bigger American children had either ceased or nearly ceased; this was the "most dramatic and significant finding" of its study.

Figures from this report show that the stature of Americans increased steadily, decade by decade, during most of the last century. According to the NCHS figures, the average height of adults today is slightly more than 5 ft 9 in for men and 5 ft 4 in for women: gains of about 4 in in the last 100 years. The average height of a recruit during the Revolutionary War was almost 5 ft 6 in, and there was little change between 1776 and 1876.

An appreciation of these biologic variables is of importance for all who are interested in the dynamics of human growth and development as well as for the clinician concerned with the routine health evaluation of children and adolescents. It also is reasonable to assume that the continuous lowering of the age of adolescence, at least during the past century, would have sociologic as well as medical impact.

357

Secular Acceleration in Height

This acceleration in the rate of growth probably started about a century ago. In 1876, Roberts stated that the average factory child in England at the age of 9 years weighed as much as one of 10 years had in 1833 and that there had been comparable gains in children at all ages of childhood beyond infancy during this period of 43 years. Kiil's review of the growth in stature of Norwegian men during the past 200 years would also suggest that the present accelerative phase began about 1830 to 1840.

The first real effort to measure growing children in the United States was performed by Henry P. Bowditch in 1877. The secular trend for boys and girls in the United States is shown in Fig. 63-1. This figure compares the median heights of Boston schoolchildren measured by Bowditch in 1877 with those living in the same city and of similar ancestry measured by Stuart and his associates during the years 1930 to 1956. One should realize that in comparing Bowditch's measurements with those of Stuart's group we are contrasting the former investigator's cross-sectional data with the longitudinal studies of the latter workers.

However, merely for the depiction of secular trends the use of these two different types of growth data would seem justifiable.

Further evidence that this is a real accelerative growth trend rather than a juggling of unrelated samples and comparisons comes from many American colleges and universities. In general, these data have been obtained from the entrance physical examinations of students and indicate the secular change which has taken place in this segment of the American population. By comparing year after year the dimensions of students of the same age, it is apparent that their height has been gradually increasing. For example, in 1885, the average freshman at Yale College was 5 ft 7½ in tall and weighed 136 lb; only 4.5 percent of that group was more than 6 ft tall. By 1957, the Yale freshman on average was 3 in taller and was 20 lb heavier; moreover 29 percent of this group exceeded 6 ft in height.

This accelerative growth trend is not a New Haven phenomenon alone. Similar information regarding increases in height and weight are available from entrance records of students at Amherst (going back to

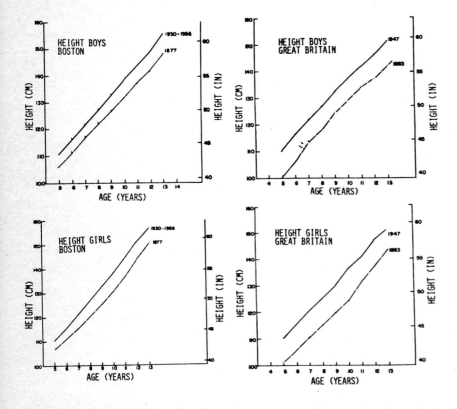

Figure 63-1 Increase in mean stature of boys and girls in Boston measured in 1877 and during the years 1930 to 1956. Secular trend in height of boys and girls in Great Britain measured in 1883 and 1947.

1861) and the universities of Kansas, Cincinnati, Wisconsin, and Washington. Nor is it confined to men: Data from Vassar, Smith, and Newcomb Colleges and from Stanford University reveal that young college girls in the 1950s were about 1 in taller and 10 lb heavier than their predecessors at the turn of the last century.

The reasons for this secular change in growth are not certain. Better nutrition, the improvement of the standard of living, the control of many of the serious diseases of childhood, and the ever-widening dissemination of information concerning proper health habits must all play a role. However, if the actual cause be nutritional, it must be some dietary change considerably more subtle than a simple increase in calories. Furthermore, there is evidence that the accelerative trend antedated the era of scientific medicine.

The effect of race is impossible at most ages to disentangle from the effects of nutritional and socioeconomic circumstances. For example, Greulich has shown that Japanese born and reared in California were significantly taller and heavier than their age peers in Japan. This disparity of growth has become less marked as the standard of living in Japan continues to improve.

The difference in the size of children 50 to 100 years ago and today reflects both the acceleration of the maturing process and the greater mature adult height; children are now taller at each age, and also their eventual adult heights are greater. Analysis of the extent to which the latter factor is involved is somewhat complicated by observing that maximal height some 50 years ago was probably not reached until the age of about 26, but now, in high socioeconomic groups in Western Europe and in America, is reached at about 18 to 19 years of age in boys and 16 to 17 in girls.

Secular Trend of Age of Menarche

If the acceleration of statural size appears surprising, the hastening of biologic maturation, using the age of menarche as an index, is even more so. The acceleration appears to be real, though admittedly data obtained by the recollective method are always suspect: probit analysis (percentage menstruating at each age) is less liable to error.

Tanner, more than any other current writer, has stressed the continuous trend over the last 100 years toward the earlier occurrence of puberty in children. This trend is dramatically shown in Fig. 63-2, which indicates the changes in the average ages of menarche from 1840 to 1960 in a number of countries. During

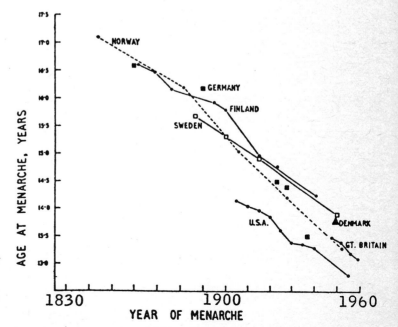

Figure 63-2 Secular trend in age of menarche from 1830 to 1960. *(From J. M. Tanner, Growth at Adolescence, 2d ed., Springfield, Ill., Charles C Thomas, 1962. Courtesy of Blackwell Scientific Publications.)*

this period, it would appear that the age of menarche has been decreasing by about 3 to 4 months per decade. Tanner has recently remarked that there are some signs that the trend shown in Fig. 30-2 has stopped. For example, in Oslo there has been virtually no change between 1952 and 1970, and in London very little between 1959 and 1970. The first study of the age of menarche in the United States done by Bowditch in 1877 gave an average age of 14¾ years. Between that date and the present there has been a speeding up of the average age of menarche by at least 20 months or about 2 months per decade until about the late 1940s, at which time the age of menarche began to level off.

This change in menarcheal age, which is observed in many countries and races, may be regarded as only one phase of the general worldwide quickening in the physical development of human beings. It is an interesting corollary of this quickening that as the menarche occurs earlier, the menopause comes at a later period in a woman's life.

A provocative hypothesis to explain the acceleration of the age at menarche has recently been offered by Frisch and Revelle. Their hypothesis is that a critical body weight (metabolic size) triggers menarche. According to Frisch, recent and historical evidence indicates that the mean weight at menarche of Caucasian girls has been about 47 kg for over a century.

This hypothesis is supported by a recent study by Frisch in which the mean weights at menarche of 30 undernourished girls and 30 well-nourished controls did not differ, although the undernourished girls attained menarche 2 years later than the well-nourished girls, and at a significantly greater height. Frisch's explanation of earlier menarche is simply that children now are bigger sooner and girls, thus,

reach the mean critical weight, 47 kg, more quickly. She hypothesizes also that the secular trend should end when the weight of children of successive cohorts remains the same, because of the attainment of maximal nutrition and child care. However, the report of Zacharias et al. casts some doubt about the reliability of Frisch's hypothesis that menarche occurs at a critical body weight.

The accelerative growth trend yields still another illustration of the necessity of judging adolescents on the basis of biologic rather than chronologic age. Furthermore, when growing up is hastened, adolescents' earlier biologic maturation has sociologic and psychologic implications. Heterosexual behavior and pregnancy become more likely at an earlier chronologic age, the biologic soundness of such offspring presents a problem, and these adolescents themselves face emotional adjustments which are comparatively difficult to face at a period of development when their psychologic maturity is not commensurate with their biologic maturity.

Not the least of their problems—and ours—is the diminished *time* provided adolescents whose biologic maturity comes early. It is only after puberty that their intellectual development reaches a stage which permits them to conceptualize at an abstract level (to "think about thinking") and so to give meaningful attention to their own identity. At this time, if their capacities are not to be stunted and their idealism thwarted, they need freedom from pressure and hurry—a psychologic moratorium as Mead has called it. When adolescents are hurried into the business and responsibilities of the workaday world—whether by early maturation or by poverty—we and they can inadvertently be robbed of their potentialities.

64 | The Short Boy and the Tall Girl

by Christopher H. Hodgman

Shortness in boys or tallness in girls is often acknowledged first in early adolescence, at a time when differences are hardest to tolerate, the body image is normally uncertain, and independence and separate identity are not yet achieved. For many adolescents, appearance is the single factor most important for popularity, boys often wishing to be taller, girls shorter.

Excessive or inadequate height in teenagers may lead to a variety of maladaptive behaviors because it accentuates discontinuities between chronological, physiological, and emotional development. As early adolescents, youngsters of unusual size are often dependent, socially immature, negativistic, and rebellious. Since most problems of unusual size are inherited, at least in societies where nutrition is adequate, parents may have experienced similar problems themselves and may overidentify with or overprotect their children. The association of height with the publicized complications of chromosomal aberrations, whether relevant to their teenager or not, may frighten them. In turn, parental worry may upset an otherwise competent youngster.

The physician often feels much pressure from patient and parents for a solution. The medical evaluation should be undertaken quickly to lessen anxiety. It will usually reveal no physical problem for which medication would be necessary. Instead, the appropriate help will consist of ongoing emotional support. The physician must state the problem for the patient and family, eliciting and acknowledging their unhappiness and worry about the future. Facts may need repeated explanation until they are assimilated. Accompanying conditions—for example, acne or obesity—should be treated energetically. Finally, any assets the teenager can emphasize should be encouraged. Such support will require repeated visits, which the patient's own doctor can best offer. However, if the teenager is particularly distressed or symptomatic, psychiatric consultation should not await hoped-for changes at maturity.

The Short Boy

Shortness in our society is seen as undesirable for both sexes, but especially for males in whom height and masculinity are equated. Most boys seen for shortness are either constitutionally (hereditarily) short or late developers whose skeletal age is a year or more behind their chronological age. Longitudinal studies disclose that shorter, later-maturing boys are less well-adjusted, have a poor self-concept, and do less well socially, athletically, and academically, sometimes carrying these patterns into adulthood.

A thorough medical history is required, including developmental data and a growth curve from birth. Musculoskeletal, renal, gastrointestinal, neurological, and endocrine pathology all need to be considered, but can usually be fairly rapidly excluded. A careful growth history from parents and relatives may reveal familial patterns of delayed growth or unsuspected shortness in forebears. Healthy short boys must be distinguished from those whose growth curves are erratic or suddenly lowered, suggesting illness. Child abuse, mental retardation, or bizarre dietary habits may be discovered in reviewing the teenager's emotional and social adjustment. The school may supply useful information.

The physical examination should include accurate recording of height and the careful staging of pubertal development, as well as exclusion of other illnesses and assessment of overall health. Facial asymmetry, eyelid ptosis, or dysmorphology of the external ear or the palmar creases may be noted. The meticulousness of the examination can be therapeutic in itself.

Laboratory evaluation in cases without evident pathology should be limited to urinalysis, a complete blood count and sedimentation rate, and a competent hand-wrist bone age to assist in predicting ultimate height by the Bayley-Pinneau tables. Other diagnostic procedures should be done only if indicated by the preliminary evaluation.

Treatment of the healthy short boy is preventive, for emotional rather than somatic complications. In constitutional shortness, when heredity, bone age, and physical development suggest little potential for more growth, the physician's first task, as noted previously, is to help the parents and boy deal with their frustration and unhappiness. In particular, a short father may need much support himself to be able to help his son. The boy needs a response that matches his chronological age rather than his size, rewarding strengths and abilities rather than emphasizing only shortness. Establishing the diagnosis is thus only the first phase of treatment for constitutional shortness.

In the developmentally delayed boy, distress over sexual immaturity as much as or even more than concern about height may lead parents or teenager to seek early use of androgens. Because androgens can diminish ultimate height by premature epiphyseal closure, consultation by an endocrinologist familiar with adolescent growth problems is indicated before induction of pubertal changes and growth, and for careful assessment of dosage and subsequent bone age maturation. With or without androgenic therapy, those boys who are particularly unhappy or symptomatic with respect to their height and development may benefit by psychiatric support.

The Tall Girl

The young adolescent girl who is taller than her classmates often feels awkward, different, and unattractive. Her opinion of herself is often poor, and her relationships with her parents are frequently dependent and strained. Her posture may be poor to minimize her height and breast contours.

The history should include the girl's growth curve from infancy, her history of pubertal changes, and a careful medical history to exclude such entities as acromegaly, gigantism, or Marfan's syndrome. The family history will probably indicate parents of above-average height; the menarcheal age for mother and female relatives may help predict the girl's menarche if it has not occurred. Her emotional adjustment and stability should be considered with respect to future care. The parents' response is also important to assess. They may see their tall daughter as older than she is and fear accelerated social maturity or premature sexual activity.

The physical examination should include careful measurement of height to follow the growth pattern, as well as accurate staging and recording of sexual maturation to aid in predicting future growth. Most pathological conditions causing excessive growth are excluded by careful physical examination.

Laboratory evaluation is usually limited to urinalysis, complete blood count and sedimentation rate, and a competent hand-wrist bone age.

In many instances it is possible to predict that the girl will not end up excessively tall. If the menarche has occurred, most girls will grow no more than 3 or 4 in. Use of bone age, family history, and sexual maturational evidence can further refine this prediction.

If a height of 6 ft or more can be anticipated, or if the girl and her family cannot be dissuaded from somatic intervention, referral to an endocrinologist for estrogen therapy may be indicated. Since undesirable long-term effects cannot presently be ruled out, such treatment should not be undertaken lightly. Estrogenic closure of the epiphyses may diminish ultimate height if used several years before the adolescent growth spurt would naturally occur. The family and the patient need to know that once estrogen is begun, it must be continued for several years until epiphyseal closure and that it will entail early menarche, possible menorrhagia, and areolar pigmentation; studies suggest that most girls handle these consequences well.

The usual tall girl does not require somatic treatment but does need sympathy, time, and an opportunity to express her worries about the future. Most tall girls learn to be comfortable with their appearance over time, particularly when other teenagers, including later-developing boys, catch up to their heights. There is even some evidence that for such girls early growth and maturation are associated with positive social and even academic performance in later years. If a tall girl is unusually distressed, referral for psychotherapy may be indicated as part of the continuing support of patient and parents by the primary physician.

65 | Adolescent Sexual Behavior

by Sharon B. Satterfield

The onset of puberty is generally defined as menarche in the female and ejaculatory competence in the male. Puberty occurs 1 to 2 years earlier for the female, a biological fact which partially explains the custom of girls dating males who are older. The adolescent experiences a rapidly changing body and sexual desires, often in the context of ignorance, insecurity, and multiple cultural taboos against sexual expression.

The most important influence upon adolescent sexual behavior is probably the early communication about sex from the family. In the first 2 years of life, the children are initiated into the nonverbal communications among family members and toward themselves. In our society caressing forms of touching quickly diminish after age 6, only to reappear in adolescence as "petting." Adolescents with sexual problems commonly associate the lack of affectionate touching between family members to their later discomfort with sexuality. The ability to engage in nongenital forms of caressing is also an important positive prognostic factor in the treatment of sexual dysfunction.

As children explore their own bodies, they assimilate reactions of family members toward masturbation, nudity, and "dirty words." These reactions constitute a significant source of sex education and contribute to the formation of attitudes about sexuality and body image as an adolescent. Having viewed one's genitalia as "dirty" or shameful does not help develop a positive body image or ease in accepting the changes of puberty.

In addition to the early family years, a profound influence upon adolescent sexual behavior comes from the attitudes and behavior exhibited by peers. Sexual myths are common, and most myths are communicated by peers. Ford and Beach categorized our society as sexually repressive compared with most modern and ancient civilizations, since we prohibit communication about sex as well as sexual behavior itself. Since many adults equate providing information about sex with condoning sexual behavior, it is not unusual that sexual myths persist. A common example of such misinformation is the persistent belief that masturbation will cause insanity or retardation. Sexual ignorance correlates with a higher risk of pregnancy and venereal disease, and the most sexually active teenagers are often the least informed.

There is no doubt that sexual attitudes have changed dramatically in the twentieth century. One has only to compare the material in novels, films, and television to determine that the United States has experienced an increasing tolerance toward explicit sexuality. The effect of changing attitudes upon the sexual behavior of adolescents, however, is less clear.

Early Adolescence

Psychoanalysts have characterized preadolescence and early adolescence as a period of developmental "bisexuality" in which the individual engages in friendships almost exclusively with members of the same sex but later develops a heterosexual orientation. In girls, this period is characterized by crushes on female teachers. Boys often participate in group forms of exposure, as in seeing who has the largest penis. Particularly in males, there are likely to exist actual homosexual liaisons which are not characteristic of adult homosexuality, but may produce concern about being homosexual.

Young adolescents are likely to be concerned about their dreams and fantasies. Many, at some time, feel guilt at being preoccupied with sexuality or are concerned that they might be homosexual as a result of close friendships. It is often important that they be reassured by a professional that their thoughts and feelings are normal and that fantasies are likely to provoke a genital response.

Pubertal anomalies may create severe disruption in normal psychosexual development. If puberty is precocious, frequently the adolescent is expected by adults and peers to act older than his or her chronological age. When puberty is delayed, an arrest of psychosocial development is likely to occur. If the anomaly is physically evident, the adolescent may withdraw from peers in embarrassment. Teenagers who suffer from chronic disability or disease often feel that they will never be attractive to peers. Adolescents' perceptions of their bodies should be explored so that they can realize that their "problem" may be normal, as when the right scrotum hangs lower than the left or when there is a discrepancy between the size of the breasts. Sex education, particularly from health professionals, is crucial during these periods. Talking with an understanding adult or with responsible peers may alleviate a great deal of anxiety.

Although masturbation occurs almost universally in the adolescent male, there is widespread fear, ignorance, and guilt associated with the practice. According to Sorenson, males are more likely to masturbate than females and at a younger age. Only about one-third of adolescent girls report masturbating. This does not necessarily represent a biological difference between the sexes but the fact that female adolescents are more likely to be discouraged in sexual experimentation by societal pressures and that women tend to be less genitally focused in their sexuality. Masturbation has been suggested by sex therapists, not only as a healthy alternative for the teenager who does not wish to have intercourse, but, particularly for women, as an important component in the development of normal orgastic response.

Middle and Late Adolescence

As teenagers reach midadolescence, they naturally separate gradually from family influence in their search for identity. At this time, the peer group exerts increasing influence, often to the dismay of parents. This is also a time when many health professionals feel less able to influence the adolescent.

The peer group of an adolescent determines, to a great extent, the individual's sexual behavior. It must be remembered, however, that this influence is exerted upon a framework molded by many years of attitudes developed at home and in society at large. It is not uncommon to see teenagers following their parents past behavior. Where a girl's mother might have married at 16, the daughter might have a monogamous relationship involving intercourse with a boyfriend at the same age. Dating patterns are particularly dependent upon peer norms and usually begin with group parties before pairing off occurs. However, in some communities, adolescents experience a great deal of pressure from adults to conform to premature dating patterns in order to fulfill the parents' social expectations.

The adolescent usually follows a fairly predictable series of behavior: dating, kissing, deep kissing, breast stimulation over clothes, breast stimulation under clothes, genital apposition, and sexual intercourse. There is wide variability among individual teenagers as to how far or how fast they progress on this scale.

Since adolescents have proved a difficult population to sample, it is difficult to estimate how many adolescents have engaged in sexual intercourse. Kinsey, in 1953, reported that one-third of all single females had had intercourse by age 25, less than 10 percent by age 17. Zelnick and Kantner, in 1972, reported that 46.1 percent of single females have had intercourse by age 19 and that the age varies somewhat by socioeconomic class. Sorenson, in 1973, reported that 52 percent of all adolescents and 45 percent of single females have engaged in intercourse by age 19.

In clinical interviews with adolescents, it appears that the double standard is diminished, that "love" is not as frequently a prerequisite for a sexual relationship, and that, indeed, some young women are ashamed of their virginity. On the other hand, many adolescents profess to hold to their parents' beliefs that premarital sex is wrong.

Adolescents feel free to try a wider variety of lifestyles than in previous generations. Some older adolescents choose to live together with or without a sexual relationship. Communal living offers an alternative to the extended family. Having children without marriage or having marriage without children are also options open to increasing numbers of young adults. Sorenson reports that 72 percent of all adolescents agree that two people should not have to get married to live together. It remains to be seen whether our society will expand its options or return to a nuclear family (see Sec. 37).

Adolescents give many reasons for becoming involved in sexual relationships. For some, sex has become a means of communicating, a step toward a relationship rather than the result. They justify this form of behavior on the basis that sex is "natural," whereas verbal communication is more painful and frustrating. For many, sex represents the communicating of a level of trust or caring within a relationship.

Many other adolescents feel that sex for physical pleasure alone is acceptable. They see sex for love, sex for reproduction, and sex for pleasure as being different but all worthy motivations. Some adolescents view their sexual behavior as part of a constant search for new experiences. This may represent a healthy index of maturity, or it may result from frustration in the compulsive search for excitement that often accompanies depression. Adolescents may use sex as an escape from loneliness or other pressures. Many report that peers influence their behavior considerably. Possibly the most difficult adolescents for the professional are those who use sex as a challenge to parents or what they perceive as an unresponsive society. Sexual behavior is often the signal to adults that communication has broken down in other areas. Much of sexual behavior is still determined by the relationship in which one is involved. Sex as reward or punishment is not uncommon and is often related to communication patterns learned earlier in life, particularly from the parents.

Biologically, sexual behavior is linked to reproduction. Traditionally our culture, with a strong double standard, has supported the notion that woman's drives and reproductive function have to be linked. "Liberated" adolescents, both male and female, now refuse to accept this doctrine without question. The "unisex movement" produced teenagers of both sexes that not only dress alike but share tasks once stereotyped by sex. Dating appears to be oriented toward getting to know one another rather than acquiring a mate.

Pregnancy

Sexual behavior of adolescence cannot be discussed without alluding to the incidence of teenage pregnancy and venereal disease. While the overall birth-

rate has been dropping in America, the number of teenage mothers has risen, their ages decreasing. Teenage mothers create enormous social problems because emotionally they are rarely prepared to cope with the demands of a child, the pregnancy interrupts their education, and it may result in estrangement from family or friends.

In many cases, adolescents deny the possibility that they are fertile. Often they are embarrassed about seeking contraceptive advice because of the risk that their parents might find out. Others are reluctant to use a contraceptive because it interferes with spontaneity, the "naturalness" of the act, or because they do not wish to admit to themselves or their partner that they really wished or planned to have intercourse. However, in many cases young people refuse contraception because they wish to, or have unconscious desires to, conceive. Many troubled, lonely teenagers believe that having a baby will finally provide them with someone who will love them.

Often, if her mother was a teenage mother and many of her peers have babies, a young girl responds to societal pressures to become pregnant. It is common in some instances for a grandmother to actually encourage the pregnancy, overtly or covertly. Some adolescents, both male and female, feel insecure in their sexual identity and need to prove to themselves or others that they are capable of producing a child.

Promiscuity

"Promiscuity" is a term frequently used lightly by adults toward adolescents, often merely to indicate that an adolescent is sexually active. However, if defined as indiscriminate or compulsive sexual intercourse with several partners, the term is usually directed toward females. Promiscuous behavior is frequently a sign of underlying emotional problems in the adolescent or the result of severe family conflict and discord.

The capacity for intimacy is acquired gradually and often with a certain amount of trial and error on the part of the adolescent. Disappointment over a relationship is common and can be a constructive learning experience for the adolescent, if it does not lead to a compulsive form of sexual activity. Serial monogamy, that is, extended, meaningful relationships without the commitment of marriage, is increasingly common in late adolescence.

Venereal disease is obviously a consequence of sexual behavior, often of promiscuity, and is reaching epidemic proportions. Little can be done to eradicate the problem unless the motivation for the behavior is understood.

Homosexuality

Homosexuality is an uncomfortable issue for many adolescents, parents, and professionals. The question of the normality of homosexuality is currently being debated in the United States. Many adolescents are deeply ashamed of homosexual urges. It is important to distinguish between transient homosexual behavior and the adoption of a homosexual life-style. Kinsey described homosexuality as a continuum, not an "either-or" phenomenon. It is important for the adolescent to understand that it is natural to have homosexual urges. One should discover one's place on the continuum, rather than feel pushed to either extreme, where one is unable to have meaningful relationships with the members of one sex. It is also important to distinguish between feelings and urges and the necessity to act upon them.

Kinsey reported that approximately 60 percent of males had experienced homosexual activity before puberty and that 37 percent of males had at least one homosexual encounter leading to orgasm; only 13 percent of females reported a homosexual experience. Since 2 to 4 percent of the adult male population practice exclusive homosexuality, it becomes obvious that this transient experimentation does not invariably lead to a homosexual life-style. Sorenson, on the other hand, reports that only 11 percent of boys and 6 percent of girls have one or more homosexual experiences, and he points out the discrepancies among various studies. Clinicians indicate that teenage girls are currently more likely to experiment with homosexual liaisons of a transient manner than in the past.

We understand little about the etiology of homosexuality except that it is becoming increasingly evident that true homosexuality is dynamically determined before adolescence. A popular theory implicates the domineering mother combined with a weak or absent father. Professionals must confront their own judgments of whether it is a deviant state which should be "cured." In fact, homosexual behavior in late adolescence can rarely be discouraged. If this is attempted, the adolescent is usually made to feel more guilty and ashamed than before. Adoles-

cents who are unsure or unhappy with their sexual identity can be helped considerably by counseling. The severely emotionally disturbed adolescent may present homosexuality as a symptom of total identity confusion. This problem must be distinguished from the adolescent who is otherwise functioning adequately.

Sexual Dysfunction

Adolescents may seek professional advice about sexual questions or problems but usually go to community agencies such as Planned Parenthood, to peer counseling services in schools, or to neighborhood clinics rather than to pediatricians or family doctors. They often seek approval for behavior or advice on relationships. The judgmental adult will turn them away quickly. Reassurance about the normality of a situational disturbance such as erectile failure may prevent severe dysfunction in the adult.

The question "What is normal?" will be debated in medical circles for many years. The answer "Whatever occurs between consenting adults" is a popular response but not applicable to most adolescents. The behavior of each adolescent must be put in the context of other measurements of maturity. The extent of the behavior, how publicly it occurs, and the degree of impulsivity involved are useful indicators. For instance, a certain amount of voyeurism occurs in all adolescents, but not to the extent of habitually invading the privacy of others. Sadistic behavior to the harm of another, either psychologically or physically, should be an indication for psychiatric intervention. Exhibitionism in groups is a common phenomenon in adolescence, but not in a public one-to-one relationship, particularly with an unwilling observer.

Sexual dysfunction is reported by adolescents, and in many dysfunctional adults etiological factors include traumatic events during adolescence such as fear of discovery, ridicule by a partner, pressure to perform fast, or severe moralistic prohibitions. Kaplan distinguishes between immediate causes of sexual dysfunction usually arising from the current relationship or environment of the couple, and the remote deeper causes which individuals carry with them from an earlier stage in life. Immediate causes of dysfunction include sexual ignorance, fear of failure, demand for performance by the partner, an excessive need to please the partner, intellectual defenses against erotic feelings, and communication failures. Deeper causes include intrapsychic conflicts or severe cultural constriction.

Common forms of dysfunction in the male are premature ejaculation and erectile dysfunction. Retarded ejaculation, though once considered rare, is common in its mild form. These dysfunctions may all occur in the adolescent, and except for the traumatically induced, the cause is rarely organic.

Members of both sexes may report concern about a "low sex drive." They should be advised that this is an individual phenomenon dependent upon multiple factors, particularly the state of the particular relationship. Low sexual drive, "tension," orgastic dysfunction, and vaginismus are all present among adolescent females, although there are no data to determine the incidence. Vaginismus, although seemingly less common, may be diagnosed early in adolescence if one is alert for the girl who is unable to insert a tampon or whose vaginal muscles spasmodically contract upon pelvic exam. It also may occur secondary to a painful case of vaginitis.

Sexual abuse, both rape and incest, are increasingly reported. In many cities, more than 50 percent of reported victims are children and adolescents. The professional must deal with victims of abuse in a gentle, supportive manner, being particularly aware of the reactions of their families. Parents, particularly fathers, may feel guilty. It is common for the victim and her family to have delayed emotional reactions months or years later. Often, secondary sexual dysfunction in the woman or her partner is subsequently reported.

Conclusion

Teenagers require a thorough sex history carefully integrated into the routine history and examination, particularly when they present with vague complaints or questions about the genitourinary system. The interviewer should emphasize questions designed to elicit attitudes rather than experiences. Thus, asking what one thinks of abortion usually elicits attitudes, and *also* the adolescent's sexual experiences. The interviewer should be nonjudgmental and empathetic and, most of all, assure confidentiality.

Adolescence is a time of physiological and emotional lability when the individual must integrate a rapidly changing body to form a stable identity, including the ability to relate to others. Emerging sexuality is a significant factor in obtaining this identity and is influenced by society in general, by the family, and by the individual's particular peer group.

66 The Teenage Parent

by Elizabeth R. McAnarney and Barbara N. Adams

In recent years, teenagers giving birth to infants have contributed significantly to the population of the United States. In 1974, out of approximately 3,160,000 births to all age groups, 608,000 children were born to women less than 19 years of age. Since 1961, with the exceptions of 1969 and 1970, the birthrate has decreased. Between 1960 and 1973, births to mothers less than 16 years old rose by 80 percent from approximately 26,000 to 48,000, and by 25 percent from 163,000 to 204,000 to mothers 16 and 17 years old. The majority of teenagers still bear children within wedlock. In 1971, there were 424 births per 1000 married women between the ages of 15 and 19 years and 22.5 births per 1000 unmarried women between the ages of 15 and 19 years. Even though the number of births to teenagers is reaching a plateau, adolescent pregnancy and childbearing are still major health concerns.

Adolescents mature (see Sec. 63) and are sexually active earlier than their counterparts in previous generations. The mean age of menarche is between 12.6 and 12.9 years of age, and an estimated 40 to 50 percent of never-married females have had intercourse at least once by age 19. Despite their sexual activity, most teenagers do not use contraception. Abortion has become an increasingly popular option for some adolescents, and in 1973, approximately one-third of all the legal abortions recorded in the United States were performed on women 20 years of age or less. Even though contraception and abortion are available, many adolescents choose to have children. Teenagers become pregnant for many reasons. The circumstances are unique for each individual and usually result from several contributing factors.

Some adolescents are depressed (see Sec. 68), and pregnancy is an attempt to resolve their sadness. Acute, reactive depression may result from the loss of a loved one—parent, grandparent, or caring relative—through death, separation, or divorce. The teenager may get pregnant in an attempt to create another individual that can be loved.

The girl in the following vignette became pregnant and expected her newborn to provide her with the affection her mother once did.

Joan was a 15-year-old girl who was 4 months pregnant when she sought medical care. She was separated from her mother at 10 years of age, when she was placed in a foster home. When Joan was 14½ years old, her mother died. Following her mother's death, she had been dating a 19-year-old man and deliberately became pregnant. She told the doctors about her depression following her mother's death and her need to have this baby.

Chronic, unresolved depression may precede the pregnancy by several years. A series of problems beginning in childhood—such as poor school attendance, running away, suicidal behaviors, or drug overdoses—may be antecedents to pregnancy. Pregnancy may thus represent the girl's chronic inability to resolve her sadness.

The adolescent in the following example had made multiple attempts to resolve her depression. Pregnancy occurred following several other problems—poor school record, running away, excessive use of alcohol, and a suicidal gesture.

Mary was a 13-year-old girl living with her widowed mother and her two older siblings. Mary had a chronic history of withdrawn behavior and absenteeism from school. At 12 years of age, she had run away and was seen in the emergency department twice, once with acute alcohol ingestion and again for a suicidal gesture. On the last emergency department visit, she was described as a depressed teenager, who stated that she had been sad ever since her father died 7 years before. She then became pregnant, but said that she had not sought care until her sixth month as it took too much energy to get to the hospital.

Groups of teenage girls may become pregnant at the same time. Teenagers have a strong need to be similar to their friends. Peer pressure to become pregnant may originate from the same-sex group or from heterosexual friends. Adolescent males may discourage the use of contraception and abortion by their female partners and actively encourage them to become pregnant to prove their masculinity.

Pregnancy and parenthood may represent positive accomplishments for teenagers who have experienced few successes in their lives. Some pregnant teenagers have had problems in school or with the law. Having a baby represents tangible evidence of one's sexuality and success as a female. Additionally, teenage peer approval is frequently given a girl who has had a baby, when she may have been previously excluded from peer groups.

Some family members encourage their adolescents to become pregnant, either through direct approval of their teenager's sexual activity or by indirect encouragement. In the following vignette, Susan's mother wanted the child, and thus Susan became pregnant and gave her mother the baby she could not have.

Susan was a 14-year-old girl who was 3 months pregnant when initially seen. Her mother had undergone a hysterectomy for endometrial carcinoma 1 year before Susan conceived. Her mother frequently said that she would like to have had more children and regretted that she never would. On hearing of Susan's pregnancy, her mother was pleased and immediately began making plans for rearing the baby within the family as one of Susan's siblings.

Some teenagers become pregnant as a direct confrontation of parental authority. Independence is one of the major developmental tasks of adolescence.

Some teenage girls think that the only way to gain their independence from their family is through pregnancy. This motivation was probably more common when a girl's options for obtaining independence were more limited than today. However, some adolescents wanting to force separation from an overprotective or hostile home environment may still use pregnancy as a means to that end.

Once pregnant, adolescents, particularly the very young, are at greater medical and psychosocial risk than are women in their twenties. Their children are also at more risk for neonatal problems. The young teenage mother has a higher incidence of pregnancy-related hypertension and pelvic inlet contraction. Earlier studies citing increased incidence of toxemia, anemia, and weight gain among young mothers were poorly controlled for race and socioeconomic status and thus are in question. As with the obstetric studies, some pediatric studies have also been poorly controlled and thus are being challenged. Yet, major psychosocial problems may remain for both the young mother and her child.

School success for pregnant adolescent girls has often been minimal prior to conception. In most states, laws have changed and now allow pregnant teenagers to remain in their own school or one of their choice. However, some girls drop out on their own accord. The uneducated adolescent will then have difficulty gaining employment in today's competitive work world. Marriage, as an immediate solution to her problems, is fraught with difficulties. An estimated one out of two teenage marriages ends in divorce. Thus uneducated, the young mother may remain dependent on welfare for extended periods of time.

Once pregnant, teenagers are at high risk of repeating pregnancy during their adolescence. Adolescents who have multiple pregnancies may never finish their education, never get off public assistance, or never change their life-styles. The morbidity and mortality of subsequent children born to teenage mothers are greater than those of their first-borns.

The major thrust of the nearly 250 specialized programs for pregnant adolescents has been toward educating teenagers to options other than immediate repeat pregnancy by providing medical and psychosocial services in one program. The repeat pregnancy rate, uncorrected for marital status, 2½ years after the initial deliveries, was 24 percent for a group of adolescents receiving health care in a specialized program, the Rochester Adolescent Maternity Project (RAMP), in Rochester, New York. The repeat pregnancy rate for adolescents delivered during a similar time period for a matched group of teenagers cared for in an obstetrics clinic where there were few psychosocial services but similar medical care in the same community was 43 percent. Studies of the Young Mother's Program (YMP) in New Haven, Connecticut, concluded that participation in a special program may delay immediate repeat adolescent pregnancy, but may not prevent the second conception.

The primary care professional can help the pregnant adolescent by confirming the pregnancy; by discussing the alternatives of (1) keeping the pregnancy and the child, (2) keeping the pregnancy and giving the baby up for adoption, or (3) having an abortion; and by counseling her during the pre- and postpartum periods if specialized services are not available. Following the disposition of the pregnancy, the physician can teach the teenager about her sexuality and contraception and prescribe birth control.

Diagnosis

The diagnosis of pregnancy poses problems for both the adolescent and the health provider that usually do not occur with adults. Teenagers often are hesitant to seek help and may not know where it is available. Once at the doctor's office, they frequently are fearful of discussing their concerns about pregnancy. Pregnant girls present to the primary care professional's office in several ways. Some say they may be pregnant. Others complain of somatic symptoms, such as headaches or abdominal or joint pains, when their real concern is of being pregnant. Every teenage girl whose reason for seeking care is unclear should be asked when she had her last menstrual period.

Confirmation of pregnancy is clearly within the primary care physician's or nurse practitioner's roles. The medical history of the pregnant girl should include information about the father of the baby. Pregnancy as a result of an incestuous relationship, particularly among the very young, should be considered. Physical evaluation always includes a pelvic examination. Urine screening for pregnancy can be done by slide test; when using Gravindex, there may be a negative result prior to 42 days past the last menstrual period. Some adolescents do not know when they had their last menstrual period, so using dates exclu-

sively can be hazardous. Therefore, it may be necessary to follow the teenager and repeat the urine test until pregnancy can be diagnosed or excluded.

Disposition

The primary care provider, especially one who knows the girl and her family, is in an ideal position to raise issues about the disposition of the pregnancy and discuss them fully with the young patient. She should be asked about how she plans to tell her boyfriend and her family about the pregnancy, and she should be informed that the options of the disposition of the pregnancy are abortion, adoption, or keeping the baby. Marriage as a possibility should be raised, and her future educational and vocational plans should be discussed. Present and future finances of personal and health care should also be considered with the young patient. The primary care physician can assist immediately with issues directly related to the pregnancy.

Parents should be informed of the pregnancy if the girl still lives at home, is less than 18 years old in most states, carries her baby to term, or has an abortion. The family often provides needed emotional support for the pregnant teenager. The earlier the parents are told of their daughter's pregnancy, the longer the professional will have to work with the entire family. Adolescents may feel more comfortable informing their parents about the pregnancy in the presence of a supportive professional than telling them alone at home. Young expectant fathers, long neglected from the consideration of health care workers, should know about the pregnancy and should be included in the decision-making process.

The primary care physician can discuss alternatives and assist the teenager as she makes her own decision about the pregnancy. The alternatives the adolescent has are to keep the pregnancy and the baby, continue the pregnancy and give the baby up for adoption, or have an abortion. The doctor must be aware of the developmental age of the teenager, as younger adolescents may only be able to discuss issues of immediate importance, while older girls may be more capable of thinking about the future. Professionals must be ever-conscious of their own feelings about sex and pregnancy in teenagers and should attempt to present the alternatives in the most objective manner possible. The ultimate decision about what to do is the patient's, except in situations where this is clearly not indicated, such as the very young adolescent or the retarded teenager.

Despite the appearance that the adolescent has made her final choice about the pregnancy, discussion about her decision-making process should be initiated by the professional. Is it her decision to keep the pregnancy or have an abortion, or is she being forced into it by her family? Does she know about abortion? If so, what does she know? If she continues the pregnancy, does she understand the need for health care during the prepartum period, labor, and delivery? Does she want to keep the child or place it for adoption? Has she considered her own developmental needs as an adolescent? What does she know about child care? Gentle exploration of these issues will help the adolescent clarify her choice. The physician may want to see the teenager and her family and/or her boyfriend together for some of these discussions.

The primary care doctor should expedite referral to an obstetrical program if the adolescent chooses abortion. Delay in this referral may result in the performance of a saline abortion, rather than the more benign procedure of a suction abortion.

Girls who continue the pregnancy may be referred by the physician for obstetrical care to an adolescent maternity project, the office of a private obstetrician, or an obstetrical clinic. The future role of the primary care professional will depend upon where the teenager goes for obstetrical care. Adolescent maternity projects usually combine medical and psychosocial services in one setting and are based on the premise that teenagers, particularly the very young, experience more medical and psychosocial problems than older women. If she receives care in such a comprehensive setting, the role of the primary care doctor or nurse practitioner may cease and resume only in providing of pediatric services to the newborn infant.

Other sources of obstetric care are private obstetricians' offices and obstetrical clinics. A major deficiency in most of these settings is the lack of psychosocial services. If the adolescent receives medical care in one of these sites, then the primary care doctor or nurse practitioner should arrange for those supplementary services necessary for comprehensive care.

Counseling

The primary care professional might choose to do individual and/or group counseling in the office. Individual counseling might concentrate on the discussion of immediate issues such as pregnancy, labor, childbirth, and sexuality as well as future considerations—the young parent's education, vocation, and care of the expected infant. The physician may have to seek information from the local school and the local department of social services in order to be of optimal help.

Groups can provide an effective method of communication and education for teenagers. If there are two or more pregnant adolescents in one practice and the health professional is knowledgeable about group process, a group can be started. Groups have the advantage of providing peer support and help in the developmental tasks of adolescence such as independence, identity, and peer associations. An unstructured format for groups is optimum since it allows the adolescents to choose their own content, reflecting issues important to the pregnant girls at any point in time. "Significant others," such as young husbands or boyfriends, can be included.

The Adolescent Father

Most of the focus during pregnancy is on the girl, at times to the exclusion of the adolescent father. In the past, it has been argued that young fathers, as a group, have not complied with special programs that provided care for their partner's pregnancy. Even though it is true that male teenagers may find it difficult to understand why they should attend medical facilities when they are not ill, this represents only one explanation for their lack of attendance. Adolescent maternity projects which have initiated programs for young fathers frequently are located in settings, such as hospitals or schools, that may be threatening environments to teenagers. If such programs were placed in the neighborhoods or nonthreatening surroundings such as drop-in centers or teenage males' social sites, such efforts might prove more successful.

Adolescent fathers wanting to be present at the birth of their baby should be offered the opportunity to attend preparatory sessions. They often comply well to such educational programs, even when they are located in hospitals. Following the birth, the young father may continue his interest and involvement with the baby, independent from his relationship with the mother. Lack of success in programs for adolescent fathers may be an issue of failure of professionals to understand teenagers' developmental needs in program planning, rather than noncompliance and lack of interest on the part of the young fathers. Preparation for fatherhood might be considered as part of individual or group work.

Postpartum Care

Adolescent girls, once pregnant, are at high risk to repeat pregnancy during their adolescence. A major goal in the care of the teenager during pregnancy is preparation for responsible family planning. Ideally, responsibility for contraception following the first pregnancy should be shared by both male and female partners.

Remaining nonpregnant is difficult for some adolescents. Those factors present before and contributing to the first conception may still be unresolved. In addition, contraceptive usage is difficult for teenagers. Family planning facilities are often not readily accessible, offer too little anonymity, and are too costly for adolescents. Even when birth control methods are prescribed, teenagers often use foam, condoms, or diaphragms irregularly or improperly and are unable to follow a regular pill-taking regimen.

Parenting

Teenage parents face multiple problems. Although often experienced in babysitting, teenagers are not prepared for the reality of round-the-clock child care. Adolescents may expect complacent babies who eat and sleep with regularity, and they may become disillusioned easily when the child demands far more time and effort than they were prepared to give.

Young parents frequently live with their own parents or other family members, and observing the efficiency with which these relatives care for the child adds to their own lack of confidence. The adolescent's reaction may be to give up parenting and to relinquish this task to other caretakers in her home. The child, in turn, becomes confused and has difficulty forming a bond with his or her own parents and may even not identify them as the actual parents. Simple teaching about child care and role modeling by the professional can help the young parent. Home visits are an effective way to observe the teenage mother with her baby and to help her in the care of her infant.

Many teenagers expect their baby to immediately fulfill their own needs for love and are disappointed when they do not see the infant responding as they had expected. For example, a teenager may think her crying baby will be immediately comforted by being picked up. When the infant does not respond as she anticipated, she can easily feel rejected by the infant and unloved by her own child. However, with time and the patience of the health care team, teenagers can learn about the needs of infants and the variety of responses that can be made to meet the needs.

Mixed feelings about motherhood are appropriate for teenagers. They want to be good mothers and genuinely love their children, but they also want to be engaged in normal teenage activities. It is important for the professional to keep in mind the necessity for each teenager to gain knowledge and expertise to fulfill her role as a parent, and also to move through the adolescent period in concert with her peers. Often families will need help in effecting an appropriate balance for the young mother between her duties as a parent and her peer, school, and social activities.

67 | Rape

by Richard M. Sarles

Rape is a form of violent physical assault and not primarily a sexual act. The reported incidence of rape, like that of other violent crimes, has increased in the recent past. Figures from the Federal Bureau of Investigation show an increase of 121 percent in reported cases of rape between 1960 and 1970. Many localities have reported rape to be the fastest-growing type of violent crime in their communities. Since 30 to 50 percent of all rape victims are between the ages of 15 and 22, it seems likely that the primary care physician may be called upon to provide care for the unfortunate child or adolescent victim of a rape attack.

The physician must be sensitive to the interaction of emotional, social, and physical factors. The feelings evoked by a case of rape on the patient, family, staff, and legal authorities require particular interpersonal tact and sensitivity coupled with careful and complete medical-legal care.

Medical-Legal Aspects

The victim of an alleged rape should be considered a medical and psychological emergency. A physical assault nearly always results in physical injury and psychological trauma. The special significance of sexual assault, with the invasion and violation of parts of the body given special rights of privacy by society, creates the need for efficient, empathetic, sensitive emergency medical and emotional care. Adolescent rape victims, with the particular concerns of body image, self-image, and sexual identity normal to this age, demand even greater understanding and awareness on the part of the staff in order to preserve their dignity and privacy. Although medical facilities available to the rape victim will vary greatly among large urban medical centers, suburban private practitioners' offices, community hospitals, and rural practitioners' offices, some general guidelines can be outlined for most cases.

Upon arrival at the medical facility the adolescent should be taken immediately from the waiting room to a private examining room by a female nurse who should advise the teenager and her parents regarding all procedures necessary for the evaluation of a case of alleged rape. A consent form must be obtained for the examination, the collection of specimens, and the release of any information to law enforcement authorities. The nurse should prepare the adolescent both physically and psychologically for the physical examination and remain with her until the examination is completed. If the police accompany the adolescent, they should be asked to wait in a waiting room apart from the adolescent and other patients, if possible, until the entire examination and collection of all medical and legal data are completed.

The primary care physician should perform a complete history and physical examination, keeping in mind that it is the physician's responsibility to acquire evidence that may be used in legal proceedings to support the victim's charges or support the defense of the accused. However, the physician must remember that rape is not a medical diagnosis and therefore the physician is not expected to render a legal opinion. A careful history should include a verbatim description of the alleged attack and the current physical and emotional state of the patient. The time of the attack and the exact time of the examination should be noted. The gynecological history should include the age of menarche, regularity of menses, date of last menstruation, and parity. These questions may help the physician when offering counseling to the teenage victim concerning medication to prevent pregnancy. It is also important to indicate if the teenager has bathed, showered, douched, changed clothes, voided, or defecated since the attack, as this may materially alter the collection and validity of evidence.

The general physical examination is best carried out by the primary care physician following the cephalocaudal approach of examining the ears, nose, throat, chest, heart, and abdomen to help relieve anxiety and a specific focus on the genital area. All contusions, bruises, and lacerations anywhere on the body should be carefully noted, and sketches or pictures may be valuable. An estimation of the stage of sexual development should be made.

Many hospitals and group practices follow a specific protocol for the management of the rape victim; they usually recommend the gynecological exam be performed by an experienced specialist in gynecology. In this case the primary care physician should introduce the consultant to the patient and should remain with her during the exam, if possible. In those circumstances where gynecological consultation is not readily available, the primary care physician should be aware that certain medical-legal issues dictate a standardized examination.

A detailed description of the genital area should include (1) the presence or absence of lacerations, scratches, bruises, petechiae, hematomas, or erythema; (2) the nature of the introitus and the appearance of the hymen; (3) the presence or absence of a mucoid exudate in the vagina; and (4) the presence or absence of menstrual flow. Speculum examination should not be performed on the young or virginal adolescent. Satisfactory collection of material does not require a speculum or bimanual exam but may be carried out by using soft-tipped cotton applicator sticks and a small medicine dropper. Materials to be obtained are (1) a small amount of vaginal fluid from the posterior fornix for acid phosphatase determination (for seminal fluid) and a saline wet mount to detect the presence and motility of sperm; (2) a cervical culture for *Neisseria gonorrhea*; and (3) a serological test for syphilis. It should be recognized that a positive culture for *N. gonorrhea* and a positive serological test for syphilis only indicate that the patient had these diseases at the time of the rape. A more detailed collection of data such as fingernail scrapings, pubic hair combings, vaginal secretions for ABO semen typing, and the collection of any loose hair or dried blood on the victim is recommended by some writers, but this practice varies widely with localities. All data and evidence must be carefully labeled and documented and should never be left unattended or stored in unlocked containers. When turned over to other authorities they must be carefully receipted.

Emotional Aspects

The immediate emotional reactions to rape are generally those of shock, disbelief, rage, fear, and embarrassment. Feelings of being "used," "dirty," and "violated" are common. These feelings may be intensified by the parents' or the girl's feelings that she may have contributed to bringing on the attack.

Within the first several weeks following the attack, psychosomatic complaints, especially gynecological, genitourinary, and gastrointestinal, are common. Fears of being harmed by the accused or his friends and harassment by siblings and friends often result in isolation, withdrawal, and school phobia. Social isolation and withdrawal is often compounded by the termination of a relationship with a steady boyfriend. Sexual fears and concerns are common in both sexually experienced and virginal adolescents, and may be manifested in signs of psychosocial regression such as the lack of personal hygiene and the wearing of sloppy clothes in order to appear less attractive and desirable. It is rare for the teenage rape victim to become sexually promiscuous or suicidal or to turn to the use or abuse of drugs or alcohol unless there was a previous history of psychosocial difficulties.

Treatment

The medical treatment includes the acute care and repair of any injury; inquiry concerning current tetanus immunization, especially if the skin has been broken or if the rape took place in a contaminated area, such as an alley or old house; and recommendation for prevention of pregnancy and venereal disease. Diethylstilbestrol, 25 mg twice a day for 5 days is the usual recommended therapy for prevention of pregnancy. However, the low incidence of pregnancy from rape (7 percent), the side effects of severe nausea and vomiting, and the possible carcinogenic effects make the use of this medication highly controversial. Prophylaxis recommended for gonorrhea is 1 g of oral probenecid followed by 4.8 million units of procaine penicillin intramuscularly. If the patient is allergic to penicillin, then tetracycline hydrochloride is acceptable given in the dose of 1.5 g initially followed by 0.5 g four times a day for 4 days. It should be noted, however, that the efficacy of prophylaxis for gonorrhea is also open to question.

Treatment of emotional issues usually center on crisis intervention and supportive counseling. The greatest help the adolescent rape victim can have is the support and understanding of her parents. Therefore, the primary care physician must make a special effort to work closely with them. The parents need to be able to express their own feelings of rage toward the accused and to talk about their own guilt over not providing total protection for their child. Parents need to be reassured that their daughter is not "ruined" or "dirty" and that in the majority of cases of rape the girl does not foster or bring about the rape herself.

In the normal process of exploring and experimenting in interpersonal relationships, many females behave in a coy or seductive fashion. Adolescent rape victims often wonder if their behavior was too seductive or if it was seductive at all; they often fear that they may have invited or brought on the rape themselves. The sensitive physician should reassure the teenager that in the majority of cases the girl does not bring about the rape herself. In addition, it should be emphasized that seductive behavior by a female is not a license for a male to engage in physical or sexual assault and is never an excuse for rape.

Many of the same issues and concerns described for the girl and her parents may be experienced by the girl's boyfriend, fiancé, or husband. Reactions such as rage toward the assaulter, revulsion or withdrawal from the girl, or conversely, hypersexual behavior toward her may be demonstrated by the male. Suggestions as to how she may inform her boyfriend of the attack and the recommendation of an individual or a joint counseling session with him can be very supportive and helpful to the teenage girl.

The adolescent should be encouraged to discuss her anger, rage, fear, and embarrassment. The physician who is aware of the normal psychosocial developmental tasks of adolescents will recognize that the violent assault of rape may interrupt the teenager's normal drives for independence and disrupt the process of the formation of sexual and self identities and intimacy with the opposite sex. Although psychi-atric help is not usually necessary for the rape victim, excessive or prolonged psychosomatic complaints, school phobia, isolation, and depression warrant referral.

Follow-Up

The primary care physician should be responsible for follow-up care. Repeat cultures for *N. gonorrhea* and a serological test for syphilis should be repeated in 6 weeks. At this time the adjustment of the adolescent can be discussed with her and her parents.

The physician should be sensitive to the violent intrusion rape causes in the physical and psychological life of the adolescent. Active medical treatment and care for the emotional needs of the teenager are the responsibility of the primary care physician.

Rape of Teenage Males

The rape of the teenage male in noninstitutional settings is extremely uncommon. Only anecdotal reports are to be found in the literature, and no general statements can be made concerning the immediate or long-term effects of such attacks. The relative power of most teenage males, compared with that of the female, may enable the male to resist such attacks, accounting for the paucity of reported cases. In addition, the homosexual nature of such an attack may lessen the likelihood of the teenage victim reporting the rape. Conversely, the homosexual nature of the act of anal penetration may dissuade males from actually attacking other males except in institutional settings where such behavior is often condoned, or at least tolerated, and is not viewed as homosexual but rationalized as a form of normal sexual expression while in confinement. It is important to note, however, that such attacks in institutions have the same underlying dynamic as noninstitutional female rape, that is, the fusion of sexual and aggressive feelings to conquer and to degrade the victim.

If a teenage male victim of rape is seen by the primary care physician, the same tact and sensitivity shown to the female rape victim and her family must be afforded to the male. The medical-legal aspects remain the same for both sexes, and virtually all the issues discussed concerning the medical and psychological management and treatment of the female may be applied to the male victim with minor variations.

68 | Adolescent Depression and Suicide

by Åke Mattsson

One behavioral hallmark of adolescents is their fluctuations in mood, from peaks of elation and self-confidence to depths of depression and self-doubt. The primary care giver often has to evaluate whether a sad, despairing mood in a teenager is an age-appropriate, adaptive, depressive response to a loss or disappointment or whether it implies a serious depressive illness with possible suicidal tendencies.

Developmental Aspects

Because depressive mood swings are part of normal adolescence and must be distinguished from psychopathology, it is helpful to recapitulate briefly the biological and psychosocial development of adolescence. The physiological changes of puberty, including growth spurt and maturation of sexual organs and functions, are accompanied by a rise in sexual and aggressive drives as well as many anxious (hypochondriacal) concerns about the condition of the changing body. In the psychosocial area, the adolescent is struggling to attain emotional independence and a sense of identity in a society that often prolongs dependence on family and educational systems. The breaking away from the key persons of childhood usually arouses sad, lonely feelings, like being a stranger amidst one's family. The first experiences of being in love often result in painful disappointments.

In terms of cognitive development, the teenager has reached the phase of formal or abstract (adult) operational thinking. This implies the ability to be introspective, think, and reason about one's thinking and mental constructions. Adolescents overevaluate their emotional experiences and often maintain that no one can understand how they "feel." Another cognitive gain is the ability to construct ideals and ideal persons that usually prove disappointing because of their abstract, unrealistic qualities. Finally, adolescents' egocentric preoccupation with their own inner life is paralleled by their belief that others are as concerned about their appearance and behavior as they are. These cognitive changes help to explain the vulnerability of teenagers to open or implied remarks about them and their proneness to self-critical, introspective, depressed moods as well as conceited, hostile attitudes toward alleged adversaries.

Clinical Manifestations of Depression

Normal depressive mood swings in adolescence impress the observer as short-lived depressive states where youngsters have a sullen or sad appearance, are irritable and prone to angry or crying outbursts, and tend to keep to themselves or a friend. Seldom is there interference with sleeping, eating, and other basic functions. Again, these depressive mood swings are inevitable and adaptive as teenagers are loosening their ties with the family and also experiencing keenly felt disappointments involving peers, idolized adults, ideals, and beliefs.

A second group of depressive adolescent states, also inevitable and usually adaptive, includes the *acute depressive reactions.* These usually occur as healthy, transient grief responses to the loss through death or separation of a family member, friend, or teacher. Mournful, longing feelings preoccupy the youngster, whose daily functioning may suffer for weeks or months.

Some adolescents never work through their grief, but become increasingly depressed and incapable of their normal social and work performance. Their condition represents the third major type of adolescent depression, classified as a *neurotic depressive disorder* (or depressive neurosis). This state is clearly maladaptive and, if untreated, may proceed to paralyze the patient's willpower and wish to live. The *common signs and symptoms of adolescent depressive disorder* are the following: a persistent sad mood with feelings of hopelessness and helplessness; self-incriminating and guilty remarks often related to a deceased or lost person; loss of initiative and motivation; indecisiveness and poor concentration; withdrawal from family and peers; drop in academic and vocational performance; diminished appetite and physical activity; insomnia and other sleep disturbances; and preoccupation with life and death issues, often including suicidal ideation.

A fourth depressive condition, the *masked depressions* of adolescence, can be viewed as a subgroup of the neurotic depressive disorder. Some teenagers cannot tolerate their painful feelings of mournful despair and helplessness for very long and try to deny and mask them with a variety of physical and behavioral problems. The masked depressions may elude the primary care physician and the adolescent's family for quite some time, especially when they present as persistent, yet vague somatic complaints and malfunctioning without explainable organic abnormality. Other common disturbances (depressive equivalents) "used" to ward off intolerable sad and lonely feelings include the following: overeating; restless hyperactivity often alternating with bored inactivity; defiant, belligerent attitudes; school truancy; running away from home; reckless exhibitionistic acts at times ending in "accidental" self-destruction; bouts of alcohol and drug abuse; sexual escapades; and delinquent acts.

Psychotic depressive disorders represent the fifth type of adolescent depression. They occur rarely (less than 0.5 percent of large adolescent psychiatric samples, compared with 8 to 10 percent for schizophrenia) but carry a serious prognosis due to the common suicidal intention of the patients. In addition to the already mentioned depressive symptomatology, the psychotic, depressed youngster shows impaired reality testing, confusion and thought distortion, and often delusions of guilt or of hypochondriasis.

The prognosis for a psychotic depression becomes more ominous when there are no precipitating environmental events, when there is a positive family history of depressive illness, and when the patient has suffered from previous, severe depressive episodes at times alternating with periods of excitable, hyperenergetic, or manic behavior. (This type of serious depressive illness is sometimes referred to as "endogenous" or manic-depressive, in contrast to the "exogenous," neurotic one, assumed to have environmental precipitants.) It should be stressed, however, that many psychotic depressions clearly have originated from neurotic or masked depressive disorders that have gone unrecognized or have been treated less than optimally.

The differential diagnosis and management of adolescent depressive disorders will be discussed following the section on suicidal behavior.

Suicidal Behavior

A majority of normal adolescents will at least give fleeting consideration to ending life or being dead during some of their depressive mood swings. Similar thoughts may also occur during the mourning of a lost beloved person, without any intention of teenagers to actually harm themselves.

In contrast, genuine suicidal behavior denotes psychopathology which is characterized by a preoccupation with thoughts of destroying oneself or by actual suicidal acts. It is appropriate to discuss adolescent suicide in relation to the broader topic of depression in adolescence because depressive states with feelings of despair and hopelessness are central etiologic factors in most suicidal behavior among teenagers.

The suicidal rate among children below age 14 is low in this country—less than 1 death per 200,000 per year. In ages 15 to 19, the rate acutely rises to at least 10 deaths per 100,000 individuals. In this age group, suicide ranks as the third leading cause of death, following accidents and malignant neoplasms. In terms of completed adolescent suicides, boys outnumber girls by 3 to 1, while the ratio is the reverse for nonsuccessful suicidal attempts: 3 girls to 1 boy. The estimated ratio of attempted suicides to actual suicides is at least 50:1. Among actual suicides, males tend to choose highly lethal, violent means of self-destruction, such as firearms and explosives, with little margin for survival. Methods used by females usually are less lethal, such as poisoning, especially overdosage of drugs, which may provide time for rescue. It must be stressed that official suicidal statistics are highly unreliable since suicidal deaths are commonly reported falsely as "accidental" and a number of traffic deaths probably represent acts of self-destructive behavior, especially among young males.

Most studies on suicidal behavior among adolescents demonstrate much evidence of chronic childhood and family problems, a period of escalation of emotional conflicts associated with entering adolescence, and a final stage of days and weeks preceding the suicidal attempt characterized by a dissolution of the youngster's few remaining meaningful relationships, often through the loss of a close relative or friend. The adolescent becomes isolated, prone to contemplating death as an end to a painful state of loneliness. Severe depression and suicidal intention seldom occur out of the clear blue sky except in some rare instances of acute adolescent psychotic disorders, such as schizophrenia and psychedelic drug intoxication, where delusional beliefs or marked (identity) confusion may prompt self-destructive behavior.

A large number of suicidal adolescents have for at least a month shown "warning signs" of their depressed state: withdrawal, loss of initiative, drop in school performance, complaints of loneliness and sadness, crying episodes, appetite and sleep disturbance, and verbalization of suicidal thoughts. The "masked" or hidden signs of depression, already described, should also alert the teacher, parent, or primary care giver that a teenager may be experiencing mounting inner tension, sense of hopelessness, and loss of self-esteem, for which death is seen as the only means of relief.

Among the clinical subgroups of adolescent self-destructive behavior, long-standing depressive states constitute a major one. Youngsters in such states often have sustained death of or desertion by a parent or a close friend, and at times several such losses. A pervasive state of loneliness and despair is characteristic, at times mixed with guilt reactions toward the lost person and a view of death as a possibility for rejoining the deceased or for "rebirth." Obviously, these states represent neurotic depressive disorders with a serious prognosis and a high risk for repeated self-destructive behavior as long as the underlying depressive state remains unaltered.

A second major group of suicidal adolescents are expressing their "final cry for help," having lived under overwhelming external stress for a long time. Major family disruption, material scarcity, and physical illness are common burdens to these youngsters, who usually respond favorably to crisis intervention aimed at improving their external life situation.

A third common group of suicidal adolescents is made up of angry, revengeful teenagers desperately attempting to alter their thwarting and hostile environment. In contrast to the two previous subgroups, the manipulative suicidal adolescent tends to be a girl with no history of previous attempts, usually only mildly depressed, and without any long-standing wish to die. Her intention is to gain attention, to scare, and to get back at someone. The phrase "manipulative suicidal gesture," however, carries a risky implication that the desperate behavior requires less careful psychiatric attention than that of the neurotically depressed adolescent. This is far from true; actually many of these angry, rebellious teenagers require longer follow-up than the previous groups and often repeat their suicidal behavior.

The fourth group comprises the smallest number of self-destructive adolescents: those suffering from delusions of guilt and self-accusation and who are preoccupied with thoughts of self-annihilation as part of a psychotic depressive reaction or an acute schizophrenic disorder. Often, these patients spend much time daydreaming and have withdrawn from peers and family.

Differential Diagnosis and Management of Adolescent Depression and Suicidal Behavior

The primary care physician evaluating a depressed, perhaps also suicidal adolescent must assess the depth of the youngster's depression and the risk of the adolescent trying to harm himself or herself. This requires separate interviews with the adolescent and the essential family members (usually the parents), during which the physician inquires about the youngster's medical history, individual and family adjustment, school performance, and peer relationships. The physician should try to elucidate (1) possible recent events that have precipitated the depressive disorder, such as loss of loved ones through death or separation, academic setbacks, and physical illness in the patient or a close family member; (2) any evidence of long-standing family, school, or peer problems; (3) the possibility of organic brain syndrome due to central nervous system disease; (4) any history of drug abuse; (5) the possibility of a psychotic process of depressive or schizophrenic nature with cognitive impairment, preoccupation with feelings of guilt and worthlessness, delusions, or hallucinations; (6) the presence or absence of the common signs of depression, including a sad, despairing, hopeless mood; self-accusatory remarks; loss of motivation; indecisiveness and poor concentration; withdrawal from family and peers; diminished appetite; sleep disturbance; and any suicidal preoccupation or actual attempts; and (7) any evidence of depression masked by signs of restless hyperactivity, marked irritability, running away from home, reckless driving and other dangerous physical acts, and heavy alcohol and drug consumption.

The primary care giver should openly discuss the possibility of a depressive condition with adolescent patients and always inquire whether they have had any thoughts of harming themselves. Most depressed teenagers feel relieved to find that their physician understands their painful and sad state and that it is a condition common to many youngsters.

The evaluation of a depressed teenager obviously includes a complete physical examination and any laboratory tests that are indicated. A school report often is of great help in complementing the family's observations of the youngster's change in behavior and academic performance.

At the conclusion of the evaluation, the primary care physician may decide to counsel the adolescent and the parents provided the following conditions exist: (1) the depressive condition is an exaggerated but normal form of depressive adolescent mood swing or an acute depressive reaction precipitated by clearly identifiable personal losses or frustrations; (2) the adolescent, the parents, and the physician all understand the major reasons for the depressive state and feel reasonably certain that the patient is not contemplating suicide or planning to engage in highly risk-filled behavior such as running away or driving while intoxicated; (3) there is no evidence of a long-standing neurotic depressive disorder (depressive neurosis) or a psychotic disorder, and the home and school environments are cooperative and willing to make recommended changes and support the patient's counseling sessions. These sessions, usually weekly to start out with, first aim at

gaining the teenager's trust in the primary care giver, who then can help the patient to further explore and understand the reasons for his or her sad and helpless feelings and other complaints. The emphasis should be on their "normality" and adaptive nature and on the patient's strengths and hopeful future.

A prompt psychiatric referral should be made if the primary care physician has doubts about his or her ability or lacks the desire to undertake such counseling or finds the adolescent severely depressed, psychotic, or suicidal. It then becomes the psychiatrist's responsibility to assess the seriousness of the self-destructive ideation or attempt and to decide on hospitalization or following the youngster on an outpatient basis. Obviously, any need for emergency medical care of a suicidal teenager calls for admission and subsequent psychiatric evaluation.

It also should be the psychiatrist's task to evaluate the indications for antidepressant or antianxiety drug therapy in adolescent depressive disorders. In some cases of neurotic depression and in most instances of psychotic depression, psychopharmaca are helpful adjuvants to the other therapeutic interventions with the depressed teenager. The optimal and safe usage of these potent drugs requires considerable treatment experience with disturbed adolescents. Therefore, the administration of antidepressant and antianxiety pharmaca (especially the tricyclics and the phenothiazines) to a child or adolescent should be shared with a psychiatrist.

In a situation of psychiatric referral, the primary care giver can provide assistance in the evaluation of the depressed adolescent due to a knowledge about the youngster's social and medical history and ability to cope with stressful situations. The primary care giver also helps the family to gain confidence in the psychiatrist and often provides follow-up with the adolescent after the psychiatrist has terminated evaluation or treatment.

Not only can the primary care physician prevent adolescent suicidal acts by prompt recognition of serious depressive states and suicidal potentials among teenagers; equally important is the physician's common role as an "identifier" of the various types of depression seen in adolescents, from the normal depressive mood swings to the rare psychotic depressions. Most adolescent depressive states are transient, usually adaptive, preparing the youngster for successful mastery of the inevitable losses and disappointments of adult life. The physician counselor

assumes the role of an empathetic listener and sup-
porter, who often takes an active, directive role in both
explaining the reasons for the depressive condition
and charting new courses for the patient and the
family. Together, the health professional and the
adolescent often find that most depressive states are
normative, self-limited crises with good potentials to
promote the young person's psychological and social
growth and the attainment of self-reliance and beginning independence.

69 Anorexia Nervosa

by Robert A. Hoekelman and Stephen Munson

Anorexia nervosa is a condition characterized by extreme weight loss without demonstrable organic cause. It occurs with greatest frequency in preadolescent and adolescent females, but is also seen in males (less than 10 percent of cases) and in postadolescent females. Its incidence and prevalence are unknown. Most clinicians believe both have increased during the past decade, perhaps due to societal influences or to increased recognition of the condition by primary care physicians. Parents also have become increasingly aware of anorexia nervosa because of extensive publicity in the lay press.

Clinical Picture

There is little problem in recognition of anorexia nervosa when it presents in its classic form. Table 69-1 lists the characteristics that occur with amazing regularity in these patients.

Voluntary dieting with marked weight loss may be precipitated, seemingly, by a casual remark by a classmate or member of the family referring to the patient's body proportions. This, then, is interpreted

Table 69-1
Characteristics of Anorexia Nervosa

Voluntary dieting
Marked weight loss (20–40%)
Ritualistic exercising
Preoccupation with food
Amenorrhea
Unrealistic self-perception
Sense of helplessness
Withdrawal and depression
Bradycardia and hypotension

as a reference to obesity although overweight as an initial condition is usually not present except in the eye of the patient. The German term for anorexia nervosa is *Pubertätmagersucht—magersucht* being "the pursuit of thinness." Bruch believes that patients with anorexia nervosa are not anorexic, but invoke tremendous willpower in limiting food intake while having hunger sensations which may be quite intense. Often there is temporary loss of this control and patients will become bulimic and gorge themselves. Such "excesses" are short-lived and are countered by self-induced vomiting and a new resolve to lose more and more weight. The patient may rationalize her restriction of food intake on the basis of reduced appetite, nausea, or recurrent abdominal discomfort while eating. Alternation between bulimia and food refusal often marks the prodromal period before persistent refusal to eat results in significant, prolonged weight loss. A loss of 20 percent of initial body weight is considered acceptable for making the diagnosis of anorexia nervosa, particularly in those patients who were at or less than expected weight for age and height at onset.

Although they adamantly refuse an adequate diet, patients with anorexia nervosa are preoccupied with all aspects of nutrition, taking great pleasure in preparing and serving to others the food they deny themselves. Often the girl with anorexia nervosa takes over the entire food preparation activities for her family, showing particular interest in baking cakes, pies, cookies, and other high-caloric treats. The patient never eats these, but persistently proffers them to members of her family and others. When hospitalized, patients with anorexia nervosa often occupy themselves with helping to serve food trays to other patients. A career in dietetics or some occupation which involves food handling is the ambition of many.

Patients with anorexia nervosa frequently display an intense interest in physical activity. This includes elaborate, repetitive, ritualistic exercise programs which expend a surprising amount of energy considering the degree of cachexia present. These are individual rather than group activities and include calisthenics, jogging, and walking long distances. When confined to the hospital, patients are often found running in place in their rooms or walking incessantly up and down the corridors.

Patients with anorexia nervosa usually deny the malignant course of their food restriction and misperceive the extent of their cachexia. They hide their thinness from others by never allowing themselves to be seen undressed and by often wearing bulky turtleneck sweaters and oversized pants. They persistently insist that they are not underweight and that, if anything, they need to become thinner. In many cases the pursuit of thinness gives the patient an enjoyable sense of mastery over her body. This is in contrast to the general sense of helplessness and lack of autonomous self-control experienced in most other aspects of her life. In less typical cases, the patient acknowledges the extent of her thinness and relies on her helplessness to rationalize her continued refusal to eat and gain weight.

As the disease progresses and marked weight loss is accomplished, patients with anorexia nervosa become withdrawn and depressed. This is enhanced by expressed parental concerns over the patient's thinness and attempts to make the patient eat and gain weight.

Amenorrhea is common in anorexia nervosa although the cause is unknown. Starvation itself may result in amenorrhea, but amenorrhea may precede weight loss in anorexia nervosa patients and may persist long after the weight lost has been regained—sometimes for years.

Since amenorrhea ordinarily results from pituitary, ovarian, or endometrial dysfunction, investigators have looked to these origins to explain amenorrhea in anorexia nervosa. They have found that there are normal amounts of follicle-stimulating hormone (FSH) and decreased amounts of luteinizing hormone (LH) in the plasma of most patients with anorexia nervosa, that estrogen production is diminished, that endometrial biopsy shows no proliferation or secretory changes, and that the cyclic administration of exogenous estrogens produces menstruation.

It is postulated that there is a selective interruption in the stimulatory pathways from the hypothalamus to the anterior pituitary gland which prevents full production of LH and that this, in turn, results in amenorrhea. The cause of the diminished stimulation is unknown. No lesion has ever been demonstrated in the hypothalamus, and since the process is reversible, one is led to postulate an inorganic etiology.

Amenorrhea on a presumed psychogenic basis is not peculiar to patients with anorexia nervosa. It has also been observed in women who leave home (immigrants, nuns, college students, and nurses in training); in women whose husbands go to war or on long sea voyages; in women confined to prison; in women who fear pregnancy; in women who have lost a loved one (it is common in mothers of victims of sudden infant death syndrome); in women who, themselves, have come close to death; and in debutants.

Other symptoms and physical signs that occur in anorexia nervosa, particularly in advanced stages, include weakness; fatigue; bradycardia; hypotension, hypothermia; constipation; cold, blue, erythematous hands and feet with dry, cracked skin; loss of scalp hair; growth of lanugolike hair on the arms, legs, and trunk; minimal development of secondary sexual characteristics; and absent libido. Figure 69-1 demonstrates the appearance of a 15-year-old patient with advanced anorexia nervosa.

Psychosocial Aspects

The syndrome of anorexia nervosa occurs in patients with a variety of psychiatric diagnoses. Dally reports that the majority of patients fall into three groups: those with hysterical, those with obsessional, and those with a mixture of schizoid and neurotic characteristics. Despite their generally withdrawn and sad appearance, these patients are seldom psychotically depressed or overtly schizophrenic.

Traditionally, psychoanalytic investigation of this disorder has focused on the importance of sexuality in its etiology. Frightening sexual fantasies, including those of oral impregnation, were found to play a role in this choice of symptoms in both girls and boys. However, these fantasies are by no means present in all or even most of the patients experiencing this disorder.

Figure 69-1 Advanced anorexia nervosa in a 15-year-old girl.

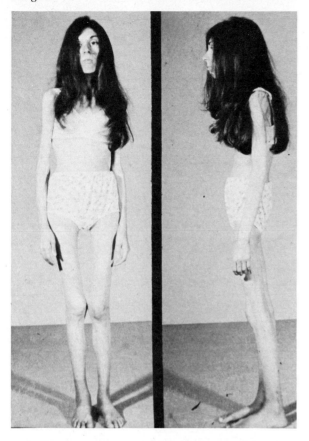

Most recent psychoanalytic literature has focused on the etiologic significance of early and continuing effects of parent-child interaction. The parents of patients with anorexia nervosa are often successful, work-ethic-oriented and concerned about their social image. In most cases there seems to be an element of parental, particularly maternal, overinvolvement and inappropriate control of the child's behavior. In the most severe cases, the children surrender their own wishes to those of the parents from an early age, appearing compliant and surprisingly trouble-free during such generally troublesome periods as the "terrible two's." To the extent that the parents encourage school achievement and the pursuit of age-appropriate goals, these children perform well and are supported by school and peer groups until preadolescence. However, during this period, they are deprived of important experiences in dealing with

problems autonomously. At puberty, social and physical developmental pressure toward autonomy becomes increasingly strong. Lack of previous autonomous experience becomes depressingly apparent, and a struggle ensues between the desire to maintain the previous mode of perfect obedience and the pressure to adapt to appropriate developmental demands.

Food restriction helps resolve the struggle in several ways. First, food refusal is a direct statement of defiance to overprotective and controlling parents in a culture in which food is valued as a gift of love. Second, starvation prevents growth and the further development of secondary sexual characteristics, which are a reminder of adult autonomy and frightening sexuality. Third, the degree of self-control necessary for the syndrome to persist provides a sense of mastery in the face of intense feelings of helplessness and weakness.

It is probable that the severity and persistence of this syndrome are directly related to the extent of parent-child overinvolvement from which the adolescent is struggling to extricate herself.

Minuchin and his group have studied the families of anorexia nervosa patients and have described several characteristics which are usually present. First, these families display an unusual degree of overprotectiveness among all family members. Second, they are remarkably unable to resolve conflict. Third, family members are abnormally involved or enmeshed in each other's personal lives. Finally, these family patterns are rigidly repeated regardless of their developmental appropriateness. To the extent that everyone is involved in everyone else's affairs, parental conflict is shared among the children. Minuchin's group has hypothesized that the self-starvation of anorectics serves as a means of detouring parental concern away from their own persistently unresolved conflict. Thus, the anorectic's food refusal serves yet another purpose—the maintenance of family stability.

Differential Diagnosis

The primary care physician must be convinced that there are not other diseases that are producing the observed clinical picture of anorexia nervosa. Endocrine dysfunction, central nervous system disease, malabsorption syndromes, malignancy, and chronic infections must be included in the differential diagnosis.

Hypopituitarism has many of the features of anorexia nervosa, including cachexia, amenorrhea, generalized hypometabolic state, and decreased excretion of urinary 17-ketosteroids. In the previously normally developed and functioning individual who develops hypopituitarism, one must consider chronic epidemic encephalitis in which the hypothalamus is destroyed. A supracellular cyst arising from the remnants of the craniopharyngeal duct may also mimic anorexia nervosa. However, each of these entities is extremely rare. Tumors of the hypothalamic region usually produce symptoms of hyperpituitarism with sexual precocity and gigantism.

In anorexia nervosa, normal bone age, normal or elevated serum growth hormone levels, lack of arrest of linear growth, presence of circulating gonadotrophins and thyroid-stimulating hormone (TSH), plus a positive response to the Metopirone test, rule out panhypopituitarism.

Primary ovarian dysfunction can be ruled out in cases of anorexia nervosa by the prior development of secondary sexual characteristics and menarche, by absence of elevated levels of serum FSH, and by determination of circulating estrogens which are present though diminished.

A normal response to exogenous ACTH in anorexia nervosa patients rules out adrenal insufficiency, and normal thyroid function tests rule out hyperthyroidism.

Malabsorption syndromes causing such severe weight loss are almost always associated with steatorrhea, bloating, and hypoproteinuria. It is of interest to note that chronic regional enteritis is found with greater frequency in patients with anorexia nervosa than in the general population. The reason for this is not understood, but is generally believed that the regional enteritis contributes little to the clinical picture that patients with anorexia nervosa present.

Malignancies and chronic infections such as tuberculosis, pyelonephritis, and abscesses are almost always associated with specific signs, symptoms, and abnormalities in routine laboratory determinations not found in anorexia nervosa.

The number of diagnostic tests utilized in ruling out other disease entities will vary with the point in the course of the disease when the physician is consulted and with his or her degree of astuteness in recognizing anorexia nervosa as a diagnostic possibility. In only rare instances will any of the diseases discussed here deserve serious consideration in the differential diagnosis.

The clinician should have no difficulty in making the diagnosis of anorexia nervosa when it is seen in its classical form. Nor is there any problem in convincing parents to accept referral for psychiatric treatment or even hospitalization for initial management when their child is so ill. The real difficulty lies in making the diagnosis before the situation becomes dire and, at that point, convincing the parents that intensive treatment is necessary to reverse the process.

The role of the primary care physician in the management of anorexia nervosa, then, is to first ascertain the diagnosis and rule out other disease processes and, second, to ensure that treatment of the patient and her family in conjunction with a psychiatrist is instituted.

Treatment

The management of anorexia nervosa has two goals—effecting weight gain and improving the patient's autonomy, effectiveness, and self-esteem. Adequate management of the psychiatric aspects of this condition must proceed from what we know of the factors involved in its etiology and maintenance. It is not sufficient and, indeed, it may be dangerous to enforce weight-gaining programs alone. Questions concerning the patient's identity must be resolved encouraging appropriate self-determination based on a clear answer to the question, "Who am I?" In addition, the family must be encouraged to face and resolve its conflicts appropriately while releasing its oppressive control over its adolescent children. Such psychotherapy is a difficult task, and these patients should be referred to experienced therapists.

The primary care physician and the psychiatrist need to work in concert, with the former directing the weight-gaining aspect of treatment and the latter the psychotherapy. They must agree upon their therapeutic plan and communicate frequently throughout the course of treatment. The two roles, which must be thoroughly understood by the patient and the patient's family, are essential since neither therapist can successfully accomplish both aspects of treatment simultaneously. The full cooperation of the parents in instituting the treatment plan must be enlisted. This is usually assured if they are fully informed of the rationale for therapy and the consequences of noncompliance. It is essential, also, that the patient understand that the parents have pledged their full cooperation so that attempts by the patient to influence them against continuation of therapy are minimized.

In less severe cases where symptoms have been present no more than a year, treatment can usually be successfully accomplished on an ambulatory basis. However, hospitalization for initial therapy is necessary in most instances. This establishes the seriousness of the diagnosis in the minds of the patient and the parents, indicates their commitment to deal with the situation forthrightly, enables rapid confirmation of the diagnosis, and provides a controlled environment in which both aspects of therapy can be quickly instituted. An adolescent inpatient unit is an ideal setting for treatment, but a general pediatric unit is also adequate. In either situation, the entire staff must be apprised of the treatment plan since they will contribute significantly to its success.

Weight gain is effected with behavioral modification built upon a baseline of complete deprivation. Positive reinforcement with rewards for gains is utilized rather than negative reinforcement with punishment for losses or failure to gain. It is of utmost importance to resolve at the outset the issue of control. The physician must be clearly "in charge" and must handle all negotiations with the patient concerning food, weight, and privileges. Staff and, when the patient is treated at home, the parents must be kept informed of the negotiations in detail, but they must be freed from decision making and therefore of the manipulative methods the patient invariably attempts to use to set one caretaker against the other.

The whole issue of control is best resolved with a written contract negotiated with the patient by the physician. This is simply a document in which the specific weights the patient must attain in order to gain specific privileges are stated. Figure 69-2 shows a typical in-hospital contract. The regime starts by establishing the complete deprivation baseline with the removal of all personal and social privileges— essentially the patient is placed in a room by herself and is restricted to her bed without even being allowed the use of the bathroom. The levels at which privileges are rewarded are chosen with a sense of humaneness (bathroom privileges are restored early)

and with ascertainment beforehand of those privileges that mean the most to the patient (books and homework, having visitors, going home, and the ultimate reward of discharge). For instance, in the contract shown, the use of television was not negotiated since the patient did not enjoy watching television. Weight loss, which rarely occurs on this regime, is dealt with by allowing only the privileges designated for that particular weight level. In essence, this results in loss of a privilege or privileges and as such is a form of punishment or negative reinforcement. Should there be no weight gain or extremely slow weight gain, again a rare occurrence, the contract needs to be renegotiated. The use of dire forms of negative reinforcement, such as tube feeding, which may produce severe psychologic trauma should be avoided and resorted to only as a lifesaving measure and with maximum support to the patient by the attending psychiatrist.

The patient is allowed free selection of food and may eat as much as or little as she wishes whenever she wishes. This relieves everyone of becoming involved in struggles over the quantity of food eaten. The only end point of concern is the weight attained. The patient soon learns that she must eat in order to gain. The discharge weight is chosen as one that is reasonable for the patient's age and height (less than two standard deviations below the mean), that is acceptable to her in terms of her own compromised perceptions, and that is attainable within a relatively brief period of hospitalization (2 to 3 weeks).

Following discharge from the hospital, a simple contract is arranged. If the patient falls below the discharge weight, as determined at weekly visits, she is readmitted without any privileges whatsoever, and remains hospitalized on these terms until that weight is again attained.

Figure 69-3 shows a weight-gaining contract for a patient treated on an ambulatory basis. It carries the threat of hospitalization (again, negative reinforcement). Interspersed in the privileges to be gained are certain significant ones to the patient (return to school, eating with the family, and the ultimate reward of being allowed to cook).

The actual negotiation of the contract is usually one-sided, with little input or objection to the terms by the patient even though ample opportunity for this is provided. The signing of the contract by the patient and the physician provides a symbolism of agreement to the terms. Although this may seem

<u>Weight Gain Contract for Sylvia Smith</u>

On 9/7/77 all social and personal privileges will be
removed to be returned individually when specific weights
are attained as detailed here. Sylvia will be allowed
to eat as much and as often as she wishes as the work
schedules of the hospital personnel allow. She shall
be allowed to choose whatever foods are available in
the hospital. These may be supplemented with foods
from home.

<u>Weight to be Obtained</u>	<u>Privilege Obtained</u>
68 lbs. (starting weight)	Bed Rest in Hospital Gown
69 lbs.	Use of the Bathroom
71 lbs.	Use of the Shower
73 lbs.	May be Out of Bed in Room
75 lbs.	May Make or Receive Telephone Calls
77 lbs.	Parents May Visit
79 lbs.	May Have Reading Materials
81 lbs.	Doors to Room May be Closed
83 lbs.	May Have Writing Materials
86 lbs.	May be Out of Room
89 lbs.	May Use Activities Room
91 lbs.	May Have Visitors Other than Parents
93 lbs.	May Leave Hospital for an Afternoon or Evening
95 lbs.	May Go Home Overnight
98 lbs.	May Go Home Over Weekend
101 lbs.	May be Discharged

Should Sylvia's weight fall below a previously attained
level, the privilege indicated for that level will be
removed until that level is again reached. The terms of
this contract are fully binding except that, if after any
four consecutive days no weight is gained, those terms
will be renegotiated.

Sylvia Smith
Sylvia Smith

William John
William John, M. D.

Figure 69-2 Weight gain contract for
a hospitalized patient with anorexia
nervosa.

very contrived, the patients comply with great seriousness and ceremony.

One observed phenomenon in the regaining period in some patients is the appearance of edema
restricted to the feet, ankles, and lower legs. The
serum protein concentrations are normal in these
patients. The edema is probably due to dependency
(they rarely lie down) and to a reduced circulation
time.

Prognosis

Follow-up studies on patients with anorexia nervosa
present differing pictures of its severity and implications for future adjustment. Because of historical confusion about diagnosis and the utilization of different
treatment regimens, comparisons of reported results

are not easily made. However, a few conclusions can
be drawn. First, it seems clear that a small but significant number of these patients die of the complications of their self-induced starvation. The rate
varies between 7 and 15 percent in large series reported, but more recent experience would indicate
that the mortality from anorexia nervosa is considerably less than this.

Weight gain with behavioral modification is successful in the vast majority of cases, and maintenance of that gain, under continued surveillance, is
equally successful despite bizarre eating habits. In
fact, that maintenance, almost to the exact ounce
required, is accomplished with incredible accuracy
by some patients. Over time, approximately 50 percent of patients experience low weight or marked
swings between over- and underweight. Menstrual
irregularities occur in a similar proportion of pa-

<u>Weight Gain Contract for Marie Green</u>

On 10/5/77 the privileges listed below shall be removed and returned when the specific weights shown
are attained.

<u>Weight to be Attained</u>	<u>Privileges to be Returned</u>
74 lbs. (starting weight)	
75 lbs.	Out of Doors
76 lbs.	Reading
77 lbs.	School
78 lbs.	Shopping
79 lbs.	After School Activities
80 lbs.	Eating with Family
82 lbs.	Exercising
84 lbs.	Sending and Receiving Mail
86 lbs.	Television
88 lbs.	Cooking

Should Marie's weight fall below a previously attained
level, the privilege indicated for that level will be
removed until that level is again reached. Hospitalization will be necessary if Marie's weight falls below
70 pounds or if she should fail to reach 80 pounds within
two weeks.

Figure 69-3 Weight gain contract for a patient with anorexia nervosa treated on an ambulatory basis.

Marie Green

Joan Land, M. D.

tients, and many require cyclic estrogen therapy for institution of menses and maintenance of regular cycles.

The overall psychological, social, and sexual adjustment experienced by these patients is unknown, but many do lead apparently normal lives with successful careers, appropriate intrafamilial relationships, and adequate libido and sexual performance. However, others are incapacitated in these respects throughout their lives. It is safe to say that the prognosis is best for those patients who are diagnosed and treated early in the course of their illness. Those patients who are most inclined to do poorly are those whose psychopathology was most severe at the time of the anorexia nervosa episode. Predominantly hysterical personality traits seem to predict a better outcome than schizoid or obsessive-compulsive traits.

70 | Runaway Children

by William M. Schmidt

Running away is one kind of reaction by a child during adolescent development to stresses in family and society. It has been estimated that a million children, more than half girls, run away annually. In certain situations the act of running away may be constructive, but whether this is true or not in an individual case, the runaway status itself is one of hazard to which the physician's attention must be directed.

Street existence if at all prolonged usually involves grossly inadequate personal hygiene, casual sleeping arrangements, poor diet, and frequently drug and alcohol abuse. Skin infections, parasitic infestations, sexually transmitted diseases, and unwanted pregnancies are often problems which cause the runaway to look for medical care. Respiratory infections and gastroenteric disorders are frequent. The dental condition of children who have been on the street a long time is poor. Minor trauma is common, and the risk of more serious trauma exists because of accidents, and of injury inflicted upon young girls and boys who become victims. Occasional reports of murders of runaway children gain momentary public notice, while the more common problems of most runaways are not given the sustained attention they should have.

The variety of situations from which runaway children come and the individual differences they display preclude a routine approach to their care. A complete history and thorough examination, although desirable, is seldom appropriate or even feasible at the first encounter. The runaway child is one who is hurting, in a psychologic sense, and often physically as well. The child may be angry, confused, or depressed. The act of running away is a punishable offense in some states, and the child may be aware of this and therefore especially frightened, the more so if drug violations are also involved. The physician's first concern should go to questions of comfort in relation to illness or injury, painful or worrisome symptoms, and anxiety. If the first encounter is friendly, helpful, and reassuring, more complete care may follow a little later or in a subsequent encounter.

Community programs offer the best chance of stabilizing the runaway child's status, effecting either an early return to the family or, if that is not possible, an alternative which is safe and suitable until definitive arrangements can be worked out and prove to be acceptable.

Traditional children's and family social agencies, public and private, continue to have a part in providing care for runaway children as one of the services in their programs. Among them, Traveler's Aid, with local organizations throughout the country, will provide help so far as it is able or refer to sources to meet needs beyond its scope. In larger cities family service associations and children's agencies are equipped to offer counseling, referral, and to some extent other services. One source of information about such agencies could be a hospital social service department. Another channel is an information and referral service under the aegis of a federation of community agencies, such as United Way.

In many cities newer organizations have been formed which are capable of making their services immediately available and perhaps of giving greater assurance to a young person who fears, with or without reason, arrest and forced return to the family from which he or she has run away. These newer agencies which can respond to the crisis situation provide outreach programs with street-workers, temporary shelter care, short-term small-group runaway houses, and child and family counseling. These primary services must be backed up with well-planned medical care, clear-cut arrangements for medical and psychiatric consultation, and referral as needed to hospitals, clinics, and health centers. Referral and reporting procedures designed to assure proper care should also protect the child from violation of confidentiality.

The newer agencies may usually be reached through the same channels as the more traditional organizations. In addition, they may be found in the phone book under such a listing as "hot line" if their organizational name is not known. Operation Peace of Mind in Houston, Texas, takes calls free of charge (800-231-6946) from young persons who want messages sent to their parents and also provides referral information if requested. Calls from parents are also accepted, but, of course, this is only rarely a resource for helping them to locate their children. The National Runaway Switchboard in Chicago (800-621-4000) also may be called free of charge and is prepared to give information on available services. Both the Houston and Chicago programs were in operation in mid-1979. Operation Peace of Mind reported that it was receiving 1200 to 1400 calls a week.

More than half of the runaways in a Massachusetts study were from 13 to 15 years old. A model act for consent of minors has been drafted by the Committee on Youth of the American Academy of Pediatrics. The Society for Adolescent Medicine has also published a draft model act. Social agencies which provide services for unattached minors will be able to supply information on the current status of state laws governing consent of minors for medical care. If the law of a state is unduly restrictive, inappropriately limiting needed medical care, its amendment should be sought. The model acts provide good bases for working out desirable amendments.

The same considerations apply to other legislation which may be an impediment to appropriate care. For example, until recently, one state's law provided a penalty of a $500 fine, a year in prison, or both for a person convicted of offering shelter for a night to a runaway without parental consent (harboring a minor). To meet a runaway child's immediate needs, to calm severe anxieties, and to work out an acceptable arrangement for notification of parents, if not for an early return of the child, time is needed—time and the safety of a sheltered environment. Therefore, the law should authorize a grace period of 48 to 72 h before mandatory notification of parents.

From the limited follow-up information available it appears that some children who have returned home and remained there report that their runaway episode was a "good" experience. Others, of course, recall difficulties. If underlying problems of child and family in the home of a returned runaway are unchanged, it must be assumed that there is a continuing risk of running away or of other difficulties. In a Massachusetts series of 357 runaway children for whom information could be obtained, 55 percent had histories of previous runaway episodes. Consideration should be given to this. It may be possible to work out arrangements for the child to live temporarily out of his or her home, where a certain amount of independence can be assured in a framework of sensible order and supervision.

Community programs for runaway children are not always available, nor are all community programs able to provide a complete range of services. In recent years reductions in public and private funding of social services have further restricted programs for runaway children. The physician treating a runaway child can only try to make the best use of the existing agencies. When these are inadequate, the physician can join with others in urging more generous and more nearly adequate support for community programs for children who are without the protecting care of their own families.

71 | Drug, Alcohol, and Tobacco Abuse

by S. Kenneth Schonberg,
Michael I. Cohen, and
Iris F. Litt

During the past decade drug abuse became a pediatric concern when this behavior, previously in the main confined to adults, spread to adolescents and older children. Although the character of illicit drug use is constantly changing with the evolution of new patterns of usage, treating the somatic consequences of substance abuse has become a part of ambulatory and inpatient pediatric practice.

Traditionally, drug-related illnesses have been discussed either by outlining the physiologic consequences associated with the abuse of a particular substance or by reviewing the effects of abuse upon different organ systems. However, such approaches are at variance with the usual presentation for care of most teenage drug abusers. The adolescent seldom seeks care because of a particular drug habit or the impairment of a specific body organ, but rather because of a symptom complex which has mandated medical attention. In this respect, teenage drug abusers are not unlike other patients where the etiology and extent of pathology require a comprehensive analysis of all the differential possibilities. If drug abuse, with either one or several agents, is not considered along with other possible etiologic factors to explain the presenting symptoms, the physician may miss an opportunity for meaningful therapeutic intervention. Therefore, in keeping with the more usual method by which such adolescent patients come to medical attention, drug-abuse-related illnesses will be discussed as they initially appear to the primary care health professional.

The Medical History

Inquiries as to the extent of drug involvement should be made of every teenager presenting for a periodic health examination. Such questioning should be a natural adjunct to the assessment of other psychosocial indicators, including academic progress, sexual behavior, family and peer relationships, and recreational interests. An accurate drug history can be obtained only in an atmosphere of confidentiality and privacy, with parents excluded from the interview process. In the proper setting, positive responses should be expected from the majority of teenagers when questioned regarding the use of alcohol, cigarettes, and marijuana. The teenager should be questioned on not only the specific type of drug used, but also the extent of use, the setting in which use occurs, and the degree of social, educational, and vocational disruption attributable to the drug abuse behavior. The information gathered from such questioning is necessary for a proper appraisal of the need for further intervention. In large part obtaining such information will depend upon the physician's ability to respond to positive answers without alarm or dismay.

Although over 80 percent of adolescents will have tried alcohol before graduating from high school, with a third of these reporting weekly use, teenagers will seldom volunteer information on the extent of their alcohol use unless questioned directly. The medical complications of chronic alcoholism, though severe, do not appear until after adolescence. The pediatrician's task is to identify those teenagers who are experiencing psychosocial disruption with alcohol being a factor or are at greatest risk of becoming alcoholic adults. The youngster who is doing poorly in school, is having difficulty with peer relationships, or is involved in delinquent behavior, and is concurrently drinking, is not difficult to identify as one in need of special attention.

The teenager who has not experienced academic or social failure but whose drinking goes beyond experimentation or occasional use represents a more difficult dispositional problem. Although no specific criteria can be used to determine who is at greatest risk of future difficulty, a history of alcoholism in a parent or widespread alcohol abuse within the teenager's peer group are factors which have been associated with a poor prognosis. Even for this high-risk group, no specific therapy may be indicated beyond the need for periodic reevaluation of the situation. For most teenagers the current history of alcohol use should be noted, quantitated, and used as a reference point by which to evaluate information obtained during subsequent visits.

Although fewer teenagers use tobacco than alcohol, more than 50 percent of high schoolers do smoke at least occasionally. The long-range cardiac, pulmonary, and carcinogenic consequences of cigarette smoking have been well publicized, and this information has not escaped the teenage population. The pediatrician has little to add in the way of warning that has not already been proffered by the schools and the press. It would seem negligent, however, when taking a medical history not to inquire regarding the adolescent's smoking habits and offer counsel on those health issues regarding tobacco that have more immediate relevance to the life of the teenager. The adverse effect of smoking on pulmonary function may make an impact on the adolescent with athletic aspirations. The pregnant teenager concerned with the welfare of her unborn baby may alter her smoking habits when informed of the possible association between tobacco and low birth weight and neonatal mortality. Adolescents with a respiratory illness, particularly asthma, must be apprised of the immediate effects of smoking upon their day-to-day health. All these issues lend themselves to discussion in the give and take of the personal history interview.

It is most common that a teenager's marijuana smoking will be appreciated only through the taking of a drug use history. Only rarely will a teenager present because of an acute intoxication secondary to marijuana smoking or will a family seek medical attention specifically for a "marijuana problem" in their teenager. Although recent years have seen a reduction in the panic associated with the discovery of an adolescent's use of marijuana, the physician's role remains to place the teenager's use of this intoxicant in proper perspective so that an appropriate assessment of the need for further intervention can be made. The primary consideration in the evaluation of the "pot"-abusing teenager is whether or not the use of this intoxicant is but a symptom of more serious underlying psychopathology. In this regard, the marijuana smoker is not unlike the adolescent drinker.

The physiologic changes which are produced by marijuana smoking are in the main benign, are rarely of a degree requiring medical attention, and are peripheral to the more important behavioral issues of intoxicant use by adolescents. However, the frequency with which teenagers and their parents raise questions about the medical side effects of marijuana smoking makes an understanding of these physiologic effects relevant to the counseling role of the physician.

The marijuana smoker experiences both tachycardia and a transient low-grade elevation of systolic and diastolic blood pressure. Neither of these cardiac consequences is of clinical significance. Sore throats and bronchitis are frequent sequelae to marijuana smoking, and the teenager may seek treatment for those illnesses. A potential long-term pulmonary consequence in the chronic abuser is carcinoma of the lungs. Bronchial biopsies of marijuana smokers with clinical diagnoses of chronic bronchitis revealed lesions characteristic of the early stages of cancer. Other evidence suggesting carcinogenic potential includes the demonstration that marijuana tar induces tumors when painted on the skin of mice.

A number of possible endocrine effects of marijuana have been reported in males with histories of prolonged and frequent use of marijuana. They include depression of testosterone levels in the blood, diminished sperm counts, impaired sexual function, and gynecomastia. With the exception of gynecomastia, which may require surgical intervention, associated clinical problems of impotence and infertility should respond to abstinence from marijuana. The long-term effects of these endocrine imbalances on the developing adolescent are as yet unclear.

The acute behavioral effects of marijuana seldom bring a teenager to medical attention except as a consequence of trauma sustained while intoxicated. The marijuana "high" causes, in addition to elation, a loss of critical judgment, distortions in time perception, impairment of recent memory, and poor performance on divided attention tasks, such as driving. The infrequency with which marijuana intoxication is directly linked with trauma is probably related to the lack of specific signs of abuse and the absence of a readily available method for the detection of marijuana metabolites in body fluids. An occasional patient will present with an acute adverse reaction to marijuana manifested as a toxic psychosis with depression or panic. Both the symptoms and the treatment of these reactions are similar to those noted for hallucinogen abuse. Controversy still exists as to whether prolonged and permanent personality changes observed in marijuana smokers are secondary or coincidental to the abuse of this intoxicant.

A history of marijuana smoking, alcohol consumption, or the abuse of any drug by an adolescent should be used as an indication for further exploration into the possibility of underlying psychopathology. Frequently, the psychosocial problems which initiate drug-taking behavior are of greater clinical importance than the specific medical complications of abuse.

The Physical Examination

The teenager who is heavily involved in drug abuse is more likely to come to medical attention with a specific illness secondary to abuse rather than through a routine physical examination. However, few adolescents abuse drugs without some concern over the potential somatic consequences of their behavior, and they may seek the reassurance of a "check-up" to prove to themselves that all is well. In such circumstances the teenager may deny a history of drug abuse even when questioned directly so as not to prejudice the results of the examination. The physician must be alert to those physical findings which are either pathognomonic of or associated with illicit substance abuse.

The abuser of either marijuana or amphetamines may have an accelerated pulse rate, the latter drugs also being associated with weight loss and closely mimicking the presentation of hyperthyroidism. Pinpoint pupils unresponsive to light are characteristic of opiate abuse. Barbiturates usually produce sluggish pupillary responses, but we have observed pinpoint pupils in many teenagers using only barbiturates. Conjunctivitis and irritation or ulceration of the nasal mucosa may be found in the teenager abusing drugs by inhalation. Glue "sniffers," marijuana smokers, and "snorters" of heroin or cocaine are likely to manifest these findings.

The majority of the specific physical signs of drug abuse are to be found on the skin and are associated with the subcutaneous or intravenous abuse of opiates and, less commonly, barbiturates. Subcutaneous fat necrosis, similar to that seen in diabetics receiving insulin therapy, is quite common in teenagers who are injecting heroin under their skin ("skin popping"). Cutaneous scars ("tracks") following the course of superficial veins will be found in any teenager with a prolonged history of injecting drugs intravenously. They are caused by either chronic inflammation secondary to repeated injections or the deposition of carbonaceous material from needles which were briefly flamed in an attempt at sterilization. The teenager will frequently disguise these tracks by covering them with a self-administered tattoo applied with a needle and india ink. Any tattoo, placed by an amateur or professional, and found in the antecubital fossa should be examined closely for tracks or needle marks. Plastic surgery for the removal of tracks and tattoos should be offered to the patient, as these stigmata often interfere with later employability and thereby compromise rehabilitative efforts.

Laboratory Testing

The teenager who is clinically well will occasionally demonstrate abnormalities of laboratory tests which raise suspicion as to covert drug usage. Although neither anemia nor total peripheral white blood cell count abnormalities are associated with substance abuse, peripheral eosinophilia may be found in up to a third of heroin users. The majority of these teenagers will have no evidence of parasites, asthma, or allergy. The etiology of this eosinophilia is unknown.

The routine urinalysis yields no findings specific to drug abuse with the rare exception of mild proteinuria in association with serum glutamic pyruvic transaminase elevations which have been noted in heroin-abusing adolescents. These teenagers show evidence of focal glomerulonephritis when evaluated by renal biopsy.

A biologic false positive serologic test for syphilis, as evidenced by a weakly reactive VDRL test which cannot be confirmed by other specific testing, may be found in approximately 10 percent of heroin users. Although these false positive test results may occur in any teenager with active liver disease, they have been observed in heroin abusers without evidence of hepatic dysfunction.

Although assessment of liver function is not commonly performed as a part of the usual laboratory evaluation in teenagers, it represents the most fruitful screening test for unsuspected opiate abuse and the most common source of chemical abnormality in the known heroin user. Nearly 40 percent of clinically well adolescents with a history of heroin abuse will have serum elevations of glutamic pyruvic transaminase and glutamic oxaloacetic transaminase. Other indicators of hepatic function are usually normal, including serum bilirubin and alkaline phosphatase. The transaminase abnormalities may persist for months or years after heroin abuse has been interrupted and are not associated with signs or symptoms of hepatic dysfunction. Liver biopsies performed in adolescents with enzyme abnormalities documented over a period of 4 months or longer revealed histologic evidence of chronic persistent hepatitis. The long-term prognosis for teenagers with this disease process is as yet unclear. No specific therapy seems indicated or effective at this time.

Dermatologic Presentations

The cutaneous infections associated with adolescent drug abuse are among the most commonly encountered somatic disturbances faced by the young patient but often never reach prompt medical attention. The abuser uses neglect or self-medication as a routine approach to these problems. It is only when these lesions represent a significant threat that medical attention is sought, and even then the young addict usually withholds any voluntary admission of his or her life-style.

Both the intravenous ("mainlining") and subcutaneous routes of drug administration are characterized by the lack of sterile technique. Skin abscesses and cellulitis are common-place among teenage abusers, albeit often ignored. When these conditions do come to medical attention, they must be regarded with a high index of suspicion that the patient is a drug abuser. The presence of needle marks will confirm drug abuse as an etiologic factor.

Localized pain is the most frequent presenting symptom of skin abscesses, with *Staphylococcus aureus* being the most common organism. Fever and leucocytosis are relatively uncommon, and regional adenopathy may or may not be present. Treatment involves incision and drainage and the administration of an appropriate antibiotic as determined by isolation of the causative organism by culture.

Skin abscesses and superficial skin ulcers are potential sites for the growth of clostridium organisms, and tetanus has been reported in adult heroin addicts. A similar incidence of tetanus in teenagers has not been encountered and is probably related to residual protection from childhood immunizations. The administration of tetanus toxoid booster should, nevertheless, be considered.

Superficial thrombophlebitis, particularly of the upper extremities, is common among drug-abusing teenagers and represents a cause of both localized symptoms and systemic infection. Treatment includes local soaks and systemic antibiotic therapy. Anticoagulation is not a necessary part of the treatment for superficial phlebitis.

Fever of Unknown Origin— Systemic Infection

The teenager presenting to the clinician with a site of systemic infection or a fever of unknown origin may require, depending on the specific complaint, cultures, a white blood count, a urinalysis, an electrocardiogram, and a chest x-ray. In the course of this evaluation it should be remembered that intravenous drug abuse may be an etiologic factor in the development of the infectious process. The direct injection of bacteria into the bloodstream during intravenous drug administration and septic embolization from a site of superficial thrombophlebitis will give rise to the hematogenous dissemination of infection to the heart, brain, osseous structures, and less commonly, other organs.

Endocarditis in the drug abuser may affect either

the right or left side of the heart. Right-sided endocarditis is associated with few, if any, systemic signs and almost always affects a previously undamaged tricuspid valve; *S. aureus* is the most frequently encountered organism. Left-sided endocarditis may involve either normal or previously damaged mitral or aortic valves and is usually associated with systemic evidence of infection. Streptococcus is the most frequently encountered organism, and fungal infections with candida have been reported. The teenager with endocarditis must be hospitalized and treated with intravenous antibiotics as determined by isolation of the causative organism.

Central nervous system infection may be secondary to endocarditis or be a primary manifestation of drug-related septicemia. Brain abscess is rare during adolescence, and this diagnosis should suggest the possibility of intravenous drug abuse. Multiple microabscesses are a more frequent finding than a single large abscess, and there may be an absence of focal neurologic signs. As the only manifestation of this illness may be fever or a personality change, lumbar puncture, electroencephalography, and transaxial computerized tomography may be required to reach the correct diagnosis. *S. aureus* is the most frequent organism encountered. The same organism has been associated with the increased frequency of osteomyelitis encountered among intravenous drug abusers. The treatment and prognosis for central nervous system infection and osteomyelitis is the same as in the nonuser of drugs.

Both pneumonia and tuberculosis are reported with increased frequency in adult heroin addicts; however, these findings have not been noted in teenage abusers in any unusual proportions. Hence pulmonary infection in itself cannot be viewed as pointing toward underlying drug abuse.

The inadvertent injection of starch and talc used as fillers from medicinal preparations designed solely for oral use may lead to pulmonary angiothrombosis and granulomatosis. Although pulmonary hypertension and cor pulmonale can be the eventual consequences of this process, it would be unusual for these problems to become clinically apparent during adolescence. Nevertheless, the examination of teenagers manifesting unexplained respiratory compromise should include an evaluation for these conditions and the possibility of intravenous drug abuse as well as the usual cultures, chest x-ray, and tuberculosis skin testing.

Salpingitis, Amenorrhea, and Infertility: Gynecologic Presentations

The female adolescent drug abuser who comes to medical attention because of a gynecological problem will primarily present because of symptoms related to gonococcal salpingitis. The findings of abdominal pain, cramps, vaginal discharge, fever, and leucocytosis are identical in the drug abuser and nonuser. However, the increase in sexual activity often required as a source of revenue to support a drug habit puts these adolescents at particular risk of contracting a gonococcal infection. We recommend that all such patients with acute salpingitis be hospitalized for appropriate antibiotic therapy.

Although amenorrhea is a common finding among female adolescent heroin abusers, they seldom seek medical attention for this complaint. We suspect that adolescent girls, without regularly established menstrual cycles, are more susceptible to this disorder than are older women heroin addicts. As anovulation often accompanies the amenorrhea, these girls experience no increase in pregnancies despite their promiscuity. Menses, ovulation, and fertility usually return to normal within a few months to a year after cessation of heroin abuse, and contraceptive advice must be part of the rehabilitation of these patients.

Abdominal Pain

There are many physiologic and psychosomatic illnesses which produce abdominal pain in teenagers, and among them are a variety of illicit-drug-related conditions. Constipation is almost universal among opiate abusers and at the extreme will cause symptoms indicative of intestinal obstruction. Hemorrhoids, otherwise extremely uncommon during adolescence, may result and give rise to rectal bleeding. Constipation responds rapidly to interruption of opiate abuse. Although constipation is one of the more benign complaints, it represents the most common presentation of the young methadone-maintained patient.

An increased incidence of peptic ulcer disease has been reported in adult narcotic addicts; however, no such increase has been noted in the adolescent. When ulcer disease or any other cause of acute abdominal pain does occur, the discomfort may be falsely attributed by the addict to withdrawal symptomatology and is quickly self-treated with further opiate abuse. Having thus masked the symptoms of possible intra-abdominal pathology, the teenager may not come to medical attention until perforation of a hollow viscus has occurred. Similarly, the physician faced with a patient experiencing opiate withdrawal must be cautious not to overlook other serious illness by attributing all symptoms to the abstinence syndrome.

Severe abdominal pain, anorexia, vomiting, and gastrointestinal hemorrhage may accompany a rather large and acute ingestion of alcohol. Although the chronic medical complications of alcoholism, such as cirrhosis, are not found in teenagers, acute gastritis and acute pancreatitis may accompany the consumption of a large quantity of alcohol. The pain of acute gastritis will subside without specific medication beyond occasional use of antacids. However, persistent bleeding will require more vigorous therapy with iced saline lavage, increased and regular antacid therapy, and specific diagnostic studies to delineate the origin of the hemorrhage.

In addition to severe abdominal pain and profuse vomiting, acute pancreatitis will be accompanied by elevations of serum amylase and lipase. Occasionally, an elevation in the 12- or 24-h urinary excretion of amylase is present and helps to confirm the clinical impression when serum concentrations are found to be normal.

In most instances, the addict with abdominal pain should be hospitalized for evaluation. Although the majority of such problems do not require specialty consultation, it is only through the close observation and testing available on an inpatient basis that a definitive diagnosis can be made.

Jaundice

In evaluating the teenager who presents with jaundice, one must consider the possibility of drug abuse as an etiologic factor. Acute viral hepatitis accounts for the majority of hospitalizations among intravenous opiate abusers. Although primarily associated with the "mainlining" of heroin, hepatitis has also been reported in intravenous abusers of other substances, including barbiturates and amphetamines. The inhalation of cleaning fluid, an abuse practiced most commonly by younger adolescents, can cause an acute toxic hepatitis with a similar clinical picture.

The symptoms, signs, and serologic abnormalities found in such a patient will not differ from those of the non-drug user with acute hepatitis. Symptoms

will include right upper quadrant tenderness, anorexia, nausea, juandice, and hepatomegaly. Elevations of serum transaminases and hyperbilirubinemia are expected, while hepatitis B surface antigen is present in over one-fourth of patients. The assessment of such a jaundiced teenager should include a prothrombin time, as it has been our experience that prolongations of greater than 19 s, with a control of 12 s, may be an indication of impending hepatic encephalopathy. Transaminase elevations are of little value in predicting this untoward development. Other indications of early hepatic encephalopathy are changes in sensorium and behavior. In the drug-using teenager, belligerence and lack of cooperation are often incorrectly attributed to a withdrawal syndrome or an underlying personality disturbance, rather than encephalopathy. This error in judgment is thus further compounded by inappropriately treating the patient with sedative medications. The administration of sedatives to such a patient with acute compromise of liver function may very well precipitate coma.

Dehydration or evidence of impending hepatic encephalopathy is an indication for hospitalization in any teenager. However, we believe the drug-abusing teenager with hepatitis should be hospitalized more readily than the non-drug user with a similar clinical picture. Indications particularly pertinent to the drug user include the increased likelihood of a noncompliant patient and a home situation less able to render supportive care. Additionally, the physician may use the hospitalization as an opportunity for intervention in the drug-abuse problem itself.

Changes in Sensorium: Intoxication, Acute Psychosis, Lethargy, and Coma

The teenager presenting with apparent intoxication, disorientation, lethargy, or coma represents a complex diagnostic and therapeutic problem. Even when head trauma, diabetic acidosis, hypoglycemia, encephalitis, and other causes of coma and confusion can be excluded, and the diagnosis of intoxication is clear, the specific causative drug must be determined. Information from the patient, the family, or friends may provide a ready answer; however, such information may be unavailable or unreliable.

Although the overwhelming majority of mild intoxications never come to medical attention, an occasional youngster may be brought to care because of being "high." A wide variety of substances are capable of producing a "high," including inhaled airplane glue or cleaning fluid, marijuana, alcohol, and cocaine. Teenagers who exhibit euphoria or minimal disorientation require only that they be protected against self-injury. At an appropriate time after sensorium has cleared, inquiries should be made as to the nature, frequency, and pattern of episodes of intoxication so as to determine the need, if any, for further psychosocial intervention.

Teenagers with severe alcohol intoxication can usually be distinguished by their distinctive aroma and, except in instances of extremely large or mixed ingestions, are not at serious physiologic risk. Treatment need only be supportive with protection against the aspiration of vomitus and observation for the development of either respiratory depression or the intestinal complications of a large alcohol ingestion, including acute gastritis and pancreatitis. Even in those instances where the teenager is not at risk, a brief hospitalization while the teenager regains sobriety may be preferable to the immediate discharge of an intoxicated adolescent into the care of distraught parents.

The adolescent who comes to medical attention as a result of an acute psychosis is most often suffering from an hallucinogenic ingestion or "bad trip." A wide variety of compounds are capable of producing hallucinations, including lysergic acid diethylamide (LSD), peyote (mescaline), and occasionally marijuana or hashish. Hallucinations may recur weeks or months after the ingestion of LSD as part of a "flashback" phenomenon. In addition, the ingestion of large doses of amphetamines may precipitate an hallucinatory state marked by paranoia and aggression. A similar psychotic episode may follow abrupt cessation of amphetamine abuse. Accompanying hallucinations, which are almost always visual, the teenager will often have dilated pupils, hyperreflexia, hyperthermia, and tachycardia.

Identification of the specific hallucinogen which has been abused is extremely difficult and of little therapeutic value. Even when the substance is known, the adolescent seldom has accurate knowledge of its exact concentration, as these compounds are frequently adulterated and misrepresented by the seller. Appropriate toxicologic testing of body fluids or confiscated drug samples is not readily available to most clinicians and hospitals.

Regardless of the hallucinogen abused, treatment is nonspecific and directed at allaying anxiety and preventing the patient from injury to self or others. The teenager should be brought to a quiet, nonthreatening environment. Most emergency rooms are inappropriate for this need. Verbal contact should be established and maintained, with frequent reassurance that the hallucinogenic experience is temporary and drug-related. If at all possible, physical restraints should be avoided as they are certain to increase anxiety and panic in the already frightened adolescent.

Sedatives should be administered only if verbal contact does not successfully control behavior or cannot be maintained because of limitations of time or staff. Any sedation administered will further compromise sensorium and may thereby increase the severity of hallucinations. All the medications most commonly utilized carry other additional risks. There is a potential danger in the administration of phenothiazines, as hallucinogens are often adulterated with anticholinergics and this combination of drugs may precipitate circulatory collapse. Haloperidol in a dose of 2 to 5 mg intramuscularly may be administered to control the agitation of an acute drug-related psychosis. This dose may be repeated as soon as 1 h later if severe symptoms persist or recur, although the frequency with which extrapyrimidal reactions have been associated with this drug mandates that the dosage be kept to a minimum when it is utilized at all.

In most instances, teenagers presenting with acute drug-related psychosis should be hospitalized. These adolescents may have brief periods of lucidity and then relapse into hallucinations. It is difficult to determine with certainty that the teenager has fully recovered without an opportunity to observe behavior over at least a few hours. In addition, there is always a question as to whether the drug ingestion unmasked a preexistent psychosis rather than simply precipitating psychotic behavior in an otherwise healthy individual. The answer to that question is best gained through an opportunity to observe and evaluate the adolescent on an inpatient basis.

The adolescent with an opiate or barbiturate "overdose" will have evidence of respiratory depression, constricted or sluggish pupils, and lethargy or coma. In such a patient with respiratory depression precipitated by an unknown agent, naloxone will have both diagnostic and therapeutic potential. Although it is of no therapeutic benefit in the teenager with sedative "overdose," it is free of the respiratory depressant effects common to earlier narcotic antagonists and therefore can be used without fear of accentuating respiratory compromise in the nonopiate intoxication. Naloxone is also useful in propoxyphene ingestions. Failure of the teenager to respond to an initial dose of 0.01 mg/kg of naloxone given intravenously would indicate that the symptoms were not due to an opiate. Pupillary dilatation, an improved level of consciousness, and an increase in the respiratory rate in response to the administration of naloxone would highly suggest that a narcotic produced the syndrome. The presence of recent evidence of intravenous drug abuse would also support the diagnosis of opiate overdose. Pulmonary edema and hypoxemia may occur in the teenager with an opiate "overdose" and require intubation, assisted ventilation, and administration of oxygen under positive pressure. Even the adolescent who responds dramatically to naloxone alone will require hospitalization for continuing observation, as the antidotal action persists for only a few hours and relapse with respiratory depression may occur. This is a particular hazard in the patient with a methadone "overdose," as its duration of action is between 24 and 48 h. If relapse does occur, repeated administration of naloxone in a standard dose of 0.4 mg should be offered as necessary.

As previously noted, the teenager with a sedative intoxication will present a clinical picture not dissimilar to that seen with opiate overdose. The patient with a barbiturate overdose will have pinpoint or slowly reactive pupils unresponsive to naloxone, whereas a glutethimide overdose will yield widely dilated pupils. In either case, treatment is in the main supportive. Gastric lavage should be performed with care and in those instances where the teenager is comatose or severely depressed only after the insertion of a cuffed endotracheal tube to prevent aspiration pneumonia. The respiratory rate and arterial blood gases must be monitored and mechanical ventilation instituted at the first sign of ventilatory failure. Intravenous fluids should be administered to assure a high urine output. Analeptics have no role in the treatment of sedative overdose, and although hemodialysis may be effective, it seldom is necessary as the supportive measures noted above are usually adequate.

Hospitalization for observation is almost always indicated for the teenager presenting with a drug intoxication even if emergency room treatment negates all immediate medical risks. Each situation must be carefully evaluated for the possibility of suicidal intent, as it is unusual for experienced adolescent drug users to inadvertently exceed their known drug tolerances. Even in those instances where self-destruction was not a motivation, the occurrence of an "overdose" may signal the loss of ability to control one's own drug-abuse behavior. The teenager should not be released from care until a meaningful effort has been made to minimize future risk.

Abstinence Syndromes

The involuntary hospitalization of the addicted teenager requires treatment to prevent the discomfort and danger inherent in a withdrawal syndrome. At times, drug withdrawal will not be imposed upon the adolescent, but rather, some life crises will provide the motivation for voluntary detoxification. In either case, adolescents are often ambivalent regarding their abstinence and will require careful and meticulous attention to their symptoms lest they become disruptive of the hospital setting or interrupt their attempts at freedom from addiction.

A teenager must abuse narcotics daily for weeks to months before becoming at risk of developing an opiate withdrawal syndrome. Within 12 h after the last dose of heroin, and 36 h after the last dose of methadone, the addicted adolescent should begin experiencing a progression of symptoms which will include yawning, gooseflesh, lacrimation, restlessness, dilated pupils, muscle cramps, diarrhea, and tachycardia. Insomnia may be severe during the first week of withdrawal and persist to some degree for up to a month after drug abstinence.

Most teenagers who report less than daily heroin usage are not physiologically addicted but rather are psychologically habituated. Nevertheless, they will be quite fearful that they will become ill if their opiate supply is interrupted. Most often these teenagers will require no specific therapy beyond reassurance that relief for discomfort will be offered if symptoms appear. The adolescent who manifests symptoms and signs of opiate abstinence may be treated in a variety of ways. Methadone may be offered in a dose of approximately 40 mg per day orally and then withdrawn slowly at a rate of 5 mg every 1 to 2 days over 1 to 2 weeks. An alternative therapy is to administer 10 mg diazepam every 4 to 6 h. This medication may be offered intramuscularly or by mouth. Better results can be anticipated if the intramuscular route is utilized at least initially, since the adolescent addict has greater faith in the efficacy of needle-administered drugs.

Diazepam will relieve most symptoms with the exception of diarrhea and insomnia. If diarrhea is persistent or severe, it can be treated with diphenoxylate hydrochloride. No satisfactory treatment for the insomnia associated with opiate withdrawal is available, and the addiction-prone adolescent must be cautioned against self-medication with barbiturates in a search for sleep. Diazepam will need to be continued for 4 to 7 days after the last dose of opiate, the longer treatment being reserved for methadone addiction and the shorter course for heroin addiction.

Unlike opiate-addicted adolescents, barbiturate addicts are at grave risk of a life-threatening withdrawal syndrome if their sedative dosage is abruptly discontinued. They will develop restlessness, postural hypotension, and seizures in rapid succession and usually within 36 h of their last dose. Occasionally, a teenager will not come to medical attention until after a seizure has occurred and may then require large doses of anticonvulsants to prevent further convulsions. The teenager presenting for voluntary detoxification before seizures have occurred should be offered phenobarbital as a substitute for the abused sedative on a weight-for-weight basis. This will require an estimation by the physician of the total daily abused dose, which should then be divided into four parts and administered every 6 h. The daily dose of phenobarbital should then be reduced slowly to zero at a rate of 120 mg per day. As this method of detoxification is reliant upon the accuracy of the original estimate of daily abuse gained from the addict, it is extremely difficult to make an accurate judgment as to the appropriate initial dose of phenobarbital. If too much medication is offered, the teenager is at risk of iatrogenically induced barbiturate overdose and coma. If too little phenobarbital is given, convulsions may ensue. To be confident that an adequate dose has been administered, it is often necessary to induce mild barbiturate toxicity, with nystagmus, ataxia, and dysarthria, but stopping short of respiratory depression and coma. Treatment within this narrow therapeutic range requires careful observation of the adolescent, particularly during the first few days. As the teenager may well become somnolent during the initial stages of treatment because the starting dose of sedative is set a bit too high, there may develop a concomitant interruption of oral intake. Therefore intravenous fluids should be administered routinely and intake and output carefully monitored.

The high incidence of convulsions during barbiturate withdrawal and the need for frequent reevaluation and adjustment of therapy mandate in-hospital treatment of this abstinence syndrome. In many instances the guidance of a neurologist or a physician with expertise in addictive illnesses may be necessary.

The management of the opiate abstinence syndrome can be accomplished on an ambulatory or an inpatient basis and does not require specialty consultation. In general, greater success can be anticipated with hospitalization, as this both physically separates the addicted teenager from a supply of illicit narcotics and offers the continuous support and reassurance that may be required.

Conclusion

Whether the adolescent voluntarily presents for treatment of a drug abuse problem, is compelled to seek medical attention because of a drug- or alcohol-related illness, or is discovered to be using drugs and/or alcohol during a routine evaluation, the physician is in an advantageous position to intercede beyond the confines of treating somatic illness. The illegality and stigma of drug abuse often prevent the teenager from seeking help from the clergy, educators, and particularly family members. Protected by federal guidelines which ensure the confidentiality of the doctor-patient relationship in drug abuse treatment, the pediatrician who uses a nonjudgmental sympathetic approach to these teenagers may be able to establish trust, gather sufficient information, and make a knowledgeable judgment as to the need for further intervention. Such information must include not only the history of past and present drug or alcohol abuse, but also the nature of peer and family relationships, the extent of involvement with law enforcement authorities, the degree of educational or vocational disruption, and the adolescent's own interpretation of the need for subsequent therapy. Often the extent of substance abuse and related disruption is so minimal as to require no further action beyond the counsel of the physician. At the other extreme are teenagers with severe psychopathology who are in obvious need of psychiatric care. A variety of other therapeutic modalities, not all of which may be present in a given community, are available for the treatment of substance-abusing teenagers. Group or individual counseling may be indicated for the verbal teenager with less than severe drug involvement but with some evidence of psychosocial disruption. Group residences are available for adolescents coming from nonsupportive home settings. They usually offer counseling and a place to stay while teenagers continue their education or employment. Therapeutic communities are appropriate for more deeply drug-involved teenagers. These residences are most often operated on a communal basis and staffed by former addicts with or without professional support. The retention rate for teenagers within these programs is poor and may reflect the adolescent's inability to tolerate the rigors of relative incarceration and abrasive therapy.

Methadone maintenance treatment programs may be appropriate for the older teenager who is opiate-addicted. This treatment modality substitutes a synthetic narcotic, methadone, for the abused opiate. A single daily oral dose of methadone can both prevent narcotic craving and block the euphoric effect of subsequently administered heroin. With the need to obtain illegal opiates interrupted, the adolescent is now free to take advantage of supportive services and make an effort toward restructuring his or her life. Therapy is aimed toward eventually withdrawing methadone treatment and preparing the patient for a drug-free existence. Unfortunately, although many adolescents do well while remaining in treatment, evidence to date indicates a high incidence of subsequent drug abuse and significant morbidity and mortality after discharge from these programs.

Often limitations of time for adequate psychosocial evaluation or lack of familiarity with available therapeutic resources will prevent the practitioner from reaching a meaningful long-term disposition. In these instances, referrals need be made to other professionals or agencies with expertise and interest in the field of teenage drug and alcohol abuse. In this regard, substance abuse does not differ from other behavioral problems where specific therapeutic recommendations must sometimes await an evaluation not available in the pediatrician's office.

72 | Conversion Reactions

by Gregory Prazar and Stanford B. Friedman

Definition, Incidence, and Etiology

The amalgamation of emotions and physical symptomatology in patients challenges the primary physician to formulate priorities in history-taking, diagnosis, and management. Some somatic complaints, such as headaches, nausea, and vomiting, can be a direct result of emotional upsets. Indeed, anxiety frequently is associated with palpitations, sweating, and tremulousness; depression frequently is manifested by symptoms of fatigue and weakness. Other somatic complaints reflect organic disorders, such as peptic ulcer or migraine headaches, which may be precipitated by emotional turmoil. Still other physical problems are attributed to conversion symptoms. This entry will be the focus of this discussion.

Conversion reactions represent a form of communication of the uncomfortable, or as Engel writes, "a psychic mechanism whereby an idea, fantasy, or wish is *expressed* in bodily rather than in verbal terms and is *experienced* by the patient as a physical symptom rather than as a mental symptom." The idea or wish is psychologically threatening to the individual or unacceptable for the individual to express directly. A conversion symptom serves as a form of decompression so that unpleasant affects associated with the acknowledgment of the wish are dissipated through use of a somatic symptom. Because the wish is completely unconscious, the patient in no way relates any psychological stigmata to the somatic complaint. As Hollender states, "The conversion symptom is a code which conceals the message from the sender as well as from the receiver."

To understand why a wish or thought is represented by a bodily symptom, it is necessary to explore patterns of everyday behavior, and of infant develop-ment. Body activity (that is, gestures) is used to express ideas during verbal interaction. Common conversational phrases frequently allude, in a metaphorical manner, to the intermixing of emotion and body functioning. "I'm fed up" and "He gives me a pain in the neck" are two such examples. Developmentally, the infant expresses feelings and communicates through visible behavior long before spoken language becomes the dominant mode of communication. Furthermore, the infant explores and learns about the environment, including the people in it, by using the body as an investigative tool (for example, placing new objects in the mouth) and as a means of making contact.

Any bodily process that can be perceived by the individual can serve as the focus for conversion symptoms. Similarly, somatic symptoms of relatives or close friends can also serve as the source for a patient's complaint. It is the patient's *interpretation* of the observed person's symptom that provides a model for the somatic complaint. When the symptom is adapted from one observed in another person, that person frequently is one who evokes strong feelings in the patient. Experiencing guilt about feelings or impulses toward the other, the patient may assume the other person's symptom as a form of self-punishment while at the same time psychologically expressing the forbidden wish.

All body systems may be invoked in conversion symptomatology. The sensory system is frequently involved (for example, parasthesia, anesthesia, diffuse pain), although typically symptoms do not follow innervation of cutaneous nerves. Motor system involvement can be represented by extremity paralysis, tremors, or weakness. Hyperventilation and dizziness are two other frequent conversion symptoms, as are nausea and vomiting, and visual problems.

Although studies have been done with respect to incidence rates of certain individual somatic complaints, specific overall incidence rates for conversion symptoms in children and adolescents are not known. Available data suggest an incidence rate of between 5 and 13 percent. Conversion symptoms may appear to be more common in adolescents than in children because the former more often present with somatic complaints of an alarming nature, such as chest pains and fainting spells, whereas children frequently suffer from more indolent complaints, such as sporadic abdominal pains. Conversion symptoms are 2 to 3 times more common in females than in males, and may appear as early as 7 to 8 years of age. There appears to be no correlation between occurrence of conversion symptoms and socioeconomic status, although less sophisticated patients more often present with bizarre and physiologically unexplainable symptoms. Conversion symptoms, especially in adolescents, may occur as a mass phenomenon. For example, groups of teenage girls who faint at rock concerts in the presence of a rock star idol are displaying a conversion symptom.

Although conversion symptoms have no organic basis by themselves, biochemical or physiological changes can occur as a consequence of a conversion reaction. These are referred to as *conversion complications*. They include such changes as muscle atrophy secondary to long-standing paralysis and respiratory alkalosis secondary to acute hyperventilation. It is important to differentiate conversion complications from psychophysiologically mediated lesions, such as peptic ulcers, in which physiological processes concomitant with emotions contribute to altered activity of an *involuntary* bodily function.

Interview Techniques

Since symptoms due to conversion and somatic processes can easily be confused, the evaluation of any patient with a somatic complaint should always take into consideration the diagnostic possibility of a conversion symptom. Concomitant attention to personal history (family functioning, school performance, peer relationships) and physical functioning demonstrates to the patient and to the family that the physician appreciates without prejudice the importance of all elements that may be contributing to ill health. Respect for the importance of the emotional-physical interaction is thereby suggested, so that this concept will not be a foreign one if later presented to the family in a diagnostic framework. Such an approach also contributes to the physician's understanding, as Engel states, "of those personal, family, and social circumstances which are most relevant to the understanding of the illness and the care of the patient," whether the ultimate diagnosis is conversion or not.

Open, nondirective questioning ("Tell me how that felt," as opposed to "Did it feel like a stabbing pain?") during history-taking more often elicits the patient's association of feelings with somatic complaints. This may be an important diagnostic clue in conversion symptoms. When patients spontaneously volunteer information concerning life events, they should be encouraged to offer more such data. However, the physician should not overtly suggest a cause-and-effect relationship between emotion and physical symptoms unless patients themselves consider that possibility. In fact, because conversion symptoms are unconscious, patients will fail to see any association and indeed may be alienated by such an interpretation. In summary, interviews with all patients should be open-ended, and should encompass social, personal, and physical history. Gentle encouragement to talk about life events along with physical functioning most often helps patients volunteer personal feelings or significant life events associated with somatic complaints.

Diagnostic Criteria for Conversion Symptoms

The conversion symptom has a specific, but unconscious symbolic meaning to the patient. In other words, the conversion symptom is often related to the unconscious wish, and the physical impairment serves to prevent acting out of the wish. For example, the adolescent male with a hand paralysis may have anxieties about masturbating. The physician treating children and adolescents may not always be aware of the symbolic meaning of the symptom. Indeed, the concept that conversion symptoms have a symbolic meaning to the patient was formulated only after a series of these patients had undergone extensive psychotherapy. Although it may be intellectually rewarding for the physician to be cognizant of the presence of a symbolic meaning, ignorance of the *specific* symbolism does not prevent adequate treatment of the patient.

Patients with conversion symptoms frequently display characteristic patterns of behavior, sometimes designated as those of the "hysterical personality." Such characteristics include egocentricity, labile emotional states (quick shifts from sadness to elation, and from anger to passivity), dramatic, attention-seeking behavior, and sexual provocativeness (displayed in gestures and in mannerisms of dress). Patients with such characteristics tend also to be demanding and to display an air of "pseudomaturity," and present strong dependency in personal interactions. However, personal relationships are rarely truly intimate or satisfying. Although many aspects of the hysterical personality are seen in adolescent patients with conversion symptoms, such characteristics also are demonstrable in adolescents free of such symptoms. Therefore, hysterical behavior traits in adolescents are not synonymous with conversion symptoms, and in isolation are not indicative of psychopathology.

The manner in which the patient with a conversion symptom describes the problem is frequently distinctive. The account is graphic and frequently bizarre, and often dramatized. A pain may be described as "thousands of burning needles thrust into my leg," or as "a giant spike being driven into my chest." Patients are suggestible, so that any symptom description alluded to by the physician may be readily adopted and thereafter reported as such, thus the importance of a nondirective interview approach.

As previously described, conversion symptoms are unconsciously adopted in an attempt to reduce unpleasant affects, especially anxiety, depression, and guilt. Therefore, although patients may describe incapacitating pain, they often affect an air of unconcern. Psychiatrists refer to this as *"la belle indifference."* "Primary gain" refers to the extent to which the conversion symptom diminishes the unpleasant affect and communicates symbolically for the patient the forbidden wish. Patients with conversion reactions often are stubborn in their conviction that the symptom is due to organic causes. This reflects denial of the underlying emotional problem. On the other hand, insistence, especially by an adolescent, that a symptom is psychological in origin may indicate denial of a physical problem. Therefore, with adolescent patients the differential between conversion symptoms and physical disease cannot rest purely on the patient's emotional response.

Conversion symptoms not only effect a primary gain for the patient but also serve to aid in coping with the environment. In this respect, the conversion symptom achieves a "secondary gain" for the patient. For example, the patient with a conversion symptom defending against homosexual thoughts may be excused from attending school, where anxiety may have been intensified. Limitations imposed by the symptom may be in contradiction to the patient's *verbalized* wishes to participate in activities, but nevertheless remove the patient from potentially threatening social interactions. Interference with daily activities also provides a secondary gain to the patient in that attention and, frequently, expressions of love are attracted from parents or significant others. This situation may be quite resistant to change, not only because the symptom is continually reinforced but also because the symptom meets psychological needs of the *parents*. In effect, the symptom may provide the parents with a reason for nurturing or infantilizing their child. Consequently, the patient and the entire family may fall into a vicious cycle of dependence upon the symptom.

Demonstration of secondary gain does not assure a diagnosis of conversion. To an extent all illness is involved with some secondary gain. The bedridden patient must accept increased attention in order to cope with physical confinement. Therefore a degree of secondary gain is necessary for adequate adaptation to a physical disability. However, in the case of a conversion symptom, secondary gain not only intensifies symptoms but may be associated with further occurrence of somatic complaints. Since perpetuation of secondary gain is dependent upon concern from others, a conversion symptom is more readily exhibited in the presence of those individuals meaningful to the patient.

Children and adolescents who develop conversion symptoms are often overprotected and become extremely dependent upon parents. Daily familial communication may have been heavily invested in somatic complaints, the child recognizing how often activities may have been canceled because of a father's headaches or a mother's cramps. Therefore the patient's symptom may conform to the unspoken interactional rules of the family. The patient's problem is thus indirectly reinforced by the family, who may even assume an air of indifference with respect to the symptoms.

Precipitation of a conversion symptom may be related to specific stress events. Changes in school, final exams, new social experiences, and/or parental conflict are examples of life events which may induce a conversion symptom. However, because the association between conflict and conversion symptomatology is unconscious to the patient, history will be helpful only if details concerning daily activities are elicited by the interviewer.

Symptom selection is based upon the patient's unconscious remembrance of bodily function or upon the patient's understanding of symptoms in others. The conversion patient's symptom may appear quite dissimilar to that displayed by the other since it is the patient's *perception* of disease which governs symptom display. Parents and relatives frequently misinform children and adolescents about disease entities, fearing that the truth would be too frightening for the youngsters. However, such misinformation may actually potentiate the child's fantasies and result in presentation of a symptom quite different from the actual one experienced by the individual serving as the model.

Choice of symptom also may be based on a previous physical illness suffered by the patient. Thus, patients with a past history of seizures may present a history of atypical, and physiologically unexplainable, seizures after many years of adequate medical control. Unfortunately these patients often receive only a complete physiologic work-up for seizures. The physician assumes, despite the atypical history, that the diagnosis rests in "where the money is"—or was—in the past.

Since the somatic complaint expressed by the patient is based upon a "model symptom," a physical disease often is mimicked. Most children and adolescents are medically unsophisticated. Close scrutiny of symptom history and description often reveals anatomical and physiological discrepancies. The child or adolescent presenting with a "stocking anesthesia" (an anesthesia confined to a specific extremity area without relationship to cutaneous nerve innervation) demonstrates an example of such symptom inaccuracy. It is based upon the patient's concept of his or her body, not on anatomical principles.

A thorough history may not only elicit symptom inconsistencies in the present illness, but may also reveal a past record of unexplainable or recurrent bouts of illness associated with life events. A past history of chronic abdominal pain occurring only on school days, a history of somatic complaints associated with stressful social events, or documentation of abdominal surgery with equivocal findings should raise suspicion that the patient's presenting problem may represent conversion.

A list of the diagnostic criteria for conversion symptoms appears in Table 72-1. No one diagnostic criterion can serve as confirmatory, and each patient with a conversion symptom may not display every criteria listed. However, the diagnosis of a conversion symptom cannot be made solely on the basis of negative physical and laboratory findings. It is not a diagnosis of exclusion.

Differential Diagnosis of Other Psychosomatic Disorders

Other psychosomatic disorders may at times be confused with conversion symptoms. Patients exhibiting *hypochondriasis*, a frequent entity especially in adolescents, view their symptoms with extreme concern. There is none of the apparent indifference seen in patients with conversion symptoms. Patients with conversion symptoms frequently seem relieved when an organic etiology is entertained. Patients with hypochondriasis become more concerned if an organic diagnosis is suggested, since they suspect and fear serious or fatal disease. However, neither type of patient is reassured more than transiently by being informed they have *no* disease.

Malingering is rarely seen in children or adolescents.

Table 72-1

Criteria for Diagnosis of Conversion Symptoms

The symptom has symbolic meaning to the patient.
Conversion symptoms are more common in individuals with an hysterical personality.
The patient reports symptoms in a characteristic style.
The patient shows an apparent lack of concern about symptoms (*la belle indifférence*).
The symptom reduces the patient's anxiety (primary gain).
The symptom helps the patient cope with the environment (secondary gain).
Health issues and symptoms are frequently used in family communication.
The symptoms occur at times of stress.
The symptom has a model.
The patient frequently has a medical history of past unexplained symptoms.
The history and physical findings are inconsistent with anatomical and physiological concepts.

It is a phenomenon more commonly associated with patients in institutionalized settings where immediate advantages are obtained with illness. It may even be regarded as an appropriate means of avoiding threatening or unpleasant circumstances. Attempts to feign illness are often naïve, especially in younger children. Malingerers exhibit, as Engels states, "an intense need to be nurtured or to suffer." Many appear to be accident-prone, and readily submit to painful procedures. They are also aloof and hostile to the physician, so that discovery of their deception can be forestalled. In contrast, patients with conversion symptoms are often appropriately fearful of procedures and appear charming and garrulous when in the presence of a physician. A common bond between malingering and conversion is represented in familial reaction to illness. In both situations unconscious parental psychological needs may cause parents to unwittingly support the child's symptoms.

Somatic delusions represent an indication of psychosis and are not frequently confused with conversion symptoms. Other signs of severe mental illness are usually present (inability to relate to peers, visual or auditory hallucinations, stereotypic behaviors). Furthermore, the symptoms described are sometimes intermittent and are frequently *extremely* bizarre. For example, the patient with somatic delusions may verbalize his conviction that his heart is shriveling up or that there is something wrong with the blood running from his head to his leg.

Psychophysiologic symptoms may occur when conversion symptoms have failed to dissipate anxiety. Thus, continuing anxiety activates biologic systems (especially the autonomic nervous system) resulting in such physiologic changes as tachycardia, hyperperistalsis and vasoconstriction. Patient cognizance of these changes is manifested by symptoms of palpitations, diarrhea, and sweating. In this situation, the symptom itself has no original symbolic meaning, and results from a reaction to *actual* body changes. Therefore, psychophysiologic symptoms can occur when conversion symptoms have failed. Similarly, conversion symptoms can replace psychophysiological symptoms.

Care of the Patient with Conversion Symptoms

Conversion symptoms are virtually always initially seen and eventually managed by pediatricians or other primary care providers. Families see this as appropriate since the presenting aspect of the crisis is "physical." They typically will accept a diagnosis of conversion only from a "professional" they consider to be an expert in physical disease. Nevertheless, with cases of suspected conversion, interviewing acumen and sensitivity to the patient's feelings are paramount. The initial interaction between the physician and the patient will be crucial in determining the degree of success achieved in dealing with a conversion symptom. In essence, care of the patient begins before a definitive diagnosis is made.

The physician should consider with the patient and the family that the etiology of any disorder involves both physical and emotional factors. As Schmitt states, the family should be told that "everyone's body has a certain physical way of responding to emotional stress"; similarly, every individual has an emotional response to a physical stress. Simple examples should be given (for example, most people have experienced that headaches are often intensified when one is upset). If the physician communicates an appreciation of the role of emotions in physical disease, the family may more readily volunteer information about psychosocial functioning. Furthermore, an eventual diagnosis involving emotional aspects may be more acceptable, since the family has been prepared for the possibility. Focusing only on an organic diagnosis intimates to the parents that psychological involvement is "unlikely, unimportant, and improbable." Turning to psychological issues after all physical tests prove unremarkable implies to parents that this tack was chosen as a "last resort" because the physician was inadequate to ascertain an organic cause. A concurrent physical-psychological approach not only prepares the physician to approach the problem with psychotherapeutic intent, but may also save the family time and money since multiple laboratory tests frequently may be avoided.

After the evaluation has been completed, the physician must synthesize a treatment plan. Although patients with conversion symptoms are suggestible, reassurance that the symptom will "go away" rarely is effective and makes no inroads into a psychological investigation of the symptom. Indeed, suggesting that the symptom will persist may give time to work out a therapeutic relationship with the patient and sometimes has a paradoxical effect. Similarly, placebo medication is usually ineffective and raises questions of medical ethics. If medication does prove helpful in alleviating a symptom, results will be evanescent. Because medication does not relieve the underlying conflict responsible for the symptom, eventually another symptom may appear. Patients with conversion symptoms definitely require some form of psychotherapy. The primary physician must decide who will provide this service.

Frequently primary care physicians—pediatricians, internists, general practitioners, or family physicians—are extremely reluctant to follow patients with conversion symptoms. Motives for this reluctance include lack of interest in dealing with psychiatric problems, minimal intellectual understanding of conversion symptoms, lack of appropriate training in psychiatry or adolescent medicine, and the economic problems involved in providing time-consuming psychiatric services in a system designed for acute medical care.

If the patient is to be referred, a decision must be made concerning referral sources. Referral possibilities for patients include private psychiatrists, child psychiatry clinics (usually located in university hospitals or in association with a community mental health center), and community social support agencies. Private psychiatrists trained in dealing with children and adolescents are limited in number and are prohibitively expensive for many families. Child psychiatry clinics and community mental health centers are much less expensive (usually providing service on a sliding-scale fee) but are limited in personnel, frequently have long waiting lists, and are often unable to provide long-term counseling. Furthermore, geographic distribution of clinics presents a problem since often patients cannot be seen in a specific clinic unless they live in a certain "catchment" area. Social service agencies vary in their policy concerning acceptance of patients with conversion reactions. Since these agencies rarely have medically trained help, they are extremely reluctant to become involved with patients manifesting somatic complaints.

Lack of availability of appropriate referral sources may make it most efficacious for the primary physician to follow the patient. Such a management decision may be of great benefit to the patient and the family, especially if the physician has established a comfortable relationship with the family. With respect to evaluative procedures, many physicians have found it helpful to schedule several 30- to 45-min sessions in order to establish rapport and to obtain a complete medical, familial, and psychosocial history

from the patient and the family. If the patient is an adolescent, two 45-min sessions should be devoted to seeing the patient without parents. One 45-min appointment usually suffices to talk separately with the parents. Seeing the adolescent before talking with the parents often reinforces to the patient that the physician is his or her doctor and not someone who is primarily interested in parental opinions. With younger patients, the physician may want to spend more evaluative time with parents.

The physician's common sense should dictate when further organic tests will be futile. This may be difficult if parents are averse to accepting a psychological diagnosis and therefore feel a need for further diagnostic tests. It can be helpful to meet with parents to reinforce that they are doing the best they can for their child and to offer them emotional support. An exploration of what other diagnoses the parents have considered is also helpful, as is an inquiry into their fears concerning results of further diagnostic tests. This approach frequently dissipates parental anxiety and allows progression to psychotherapeutic counseling.

After the initial sessions have been completed, follow-up appointments with the patient can be scheduled in 20- to 30-min blocks every 1 to 2 months. More frequent visits may be necessary if the symptom interferes with school attendance, peer relationships, and familial functioning. During sessions with the patient, verbalized somatic complaints should be minimized by the physician. The patient should be encouraged to talk about life events (school, friends, family, dating). It will be necessary to reinforce that the patient's pain is real, but that frequently being upset can intensify or even cause the pain. The physician also needs to meet with parents, although not as regularly. In sessions with parents, (1) the reality of the patient's pain should be reinforced so that misconceptions that the pain is "all in his head" or "faked" are dispelled; (2) the parents' reaction to the patient's progress and complaints should be assessed; and (3) the parents should receive emotional support to bolster their self-concept as parents. Most families appreciate the extra time spent by the physician with them, and consequently comply with the increased associated costs of longer appointments.

The physician needs to have realistic goals in dealing with these patients. Complete disappearance of symptoms seldom occurs. However, patients may acquire increased coping skills so that the symptom interferes minimally with their daily functioning and so that dependency on secondary gain is decreased. The physician's role may be crucial (1) in discouraging "doctor shopping" by the family in order to find a physical diagnosis, (2) in forestalling expensive and unnecessary laboratory tests, and (3) in preventing unnecessary surgery.

Referral to psychiatrically trained professionals becomes necessary if symptoms persist despite intervention or if symptoms continue to interfere with the patient's daily activities or functioning. Patients and their families will most readily accept referral if the possibility is mentioned early in treatment sessions, if the physician helps the family understand that seeing a psychiatrically trained person does not connote "craziness," and if the physician maintains contact with the family after the referral.

The prognosis for patients with conversion reactions is not known. In a report of 74 children with psychogenic pain, R. Friedman found that a large number of patients were noted as improved after several years, whether intervention took place or not. Patients with conversion symptoms may indeed have an encouraging future. The symptom may be "transitory, related to environmental stress, or to a developmental crisis, and may be amenable to therapeutic intervention." On the other hand, there is a group of patients whose childhood or adolescent conversion symptoms mark the beginning of a life-long career of conversion illness.

Conclusion

Conversion reactions represent an emotionally charged issue, not only for the patient but also for the physician, since patients displaying such symptoms frequently elicit from their physicians a wide range of emotions. The physician's emotional response may reveal the frustration experienced in dealing with such difficult patients. All patients presenting with somatic complaints have feelings about their symptoms. An evaluation of any somatic complaint should involve inquiry into aspects of the patient's family, school performance, and peer relationships. A better understanding of the patient's baseline emotional functioning can be achieved in this way. The physician must communicate to the parents, and to the patient, that it is acceptable to have feelings about somatic complaints. Both family and patient may be much more accepting of primary emotional involvement if permission for feelings is given early in the physician-patient interaction. The diagnosis of a conversion reaction should *never* be one of exclusion and should follow specific diagnostic criteria.

Care of the patient following diagnosis requires regular visits with the patient, with the understanding that palliation of the symptom may be the best that can be achieved. When the physician feels uncomfortable in handling a patient with a conversion reaction, or when ongoing follow-up appears to have made no progress in diminution of the symptom, referral to a psychiatrically trained professional should be undertaken. However, referral should not end the physician's contact with the patient, since ongoing physician interest may improve patient compliance with the referral source. The patient with a conversion symptom will not outgrow the symptom and will not permanently respond to placebo medication. Such patients severely tax the primary physician's diagnostic and therapeutic acumen. However, the physician who respects the involvement of emotions with somatic complaints can serve a vital role in helping patients with conversion symptoms cope with their disorder.

73 Childhood Accidents

by Howard C. Mofenson and Joseph Greensher

CASUALTIES, CAUSES, AND CURES

This chapter will update the challenge laid down to pediatricians by Dietrich in 1954, that "accident prevention in childhood is your problem, too." In the past, accidents have been regarded as product-related or behavioral problems rather than a public health problem. As will be evident from the National Safety Council statistics cited below, the casualty count in both lives lost and maimed is significant enough to warrant the concerted action of primary care physicians. There has been considerable progress made in understanding the environmental situations and circumstances contributing to the occurrence of accidents. A better knowledge of the causal factors will give a more rational approach toward the solution of this problem.

The first organized effort to secure information on product-related injuries in children began with the establishment of the Accident Prevention Committee of the American Academy of Pediatrics in 1952. This has been the basis for continued activities in cooperation with many other organizations, manufacturers, and government to improve the safety of products and has resulted in safety education, identification of environmental hazards, voluntary compliance, and legislation of safety standards.

The Casualties

Accidents are the leading cause of death among all persons aged 1 to 38. The 1974 accident death total was approximately 105,000. Disabling injuries numbered about 11 million, including 380,000 resulting in some degree of permanent impairment. Accident costs amounted to about $43.3 billion.

It is estimated that 40,000 to 50,000 children are permanently injured each year, and a minimum of 1 million seek medical care because of injuries from accidents. Accurate statistics gathering is hampered by the practice of only listing those accidents which cause high fatalities. The accidents which produce fatalities are not necessarily the producers of a large number of nonfatal injuries.

Accidents account for more deaths in the age group 1 through 14 than the next six most common reported causes: cancer, congenital anomalies, pneumonia, heart disease, homicide, and stroke. Although no accurate statistics are available, child abuse represents a significant cause of death in children. Accidental injury has in the past 2 decades become the leading cause of death in children. This can be attributed indirectly to the medical profession, and in no small part to pediatricians, whose work in public health, medical practice, and research in many of the formerly fatal diseases has sharply reduced their incidence and consequences. It is through this decline in other causes of death that accidents have achieved this distinction. In 1920, only one in every twenty children who died, died of accidental injury, but by 1970, the figures rose to one in every three children, and one of every eight hospital beds was filled with an accident victim.

The statistical breakdown for the various types of accidents will be presented below under their individual discussions.

The Causes

The word "accidents" has proved a barrier to eluci- dating their causes. This word implies that they are "bad breaks" or "acts of God" not understandable in terms of the usual causes of disease, and people often attribute their avoidance to "sheer luck" or "a mira- cle." The terms *injury* and *injury control* would be preferable.

Three facets are involved in accidents that warrant investigation: The host (who is affected), the agent (what object is the direct cause), and the environ- ment (where and when did it happen).

The importance of *the host* as a factor in the causa- tion of accidents is evident from the difference in incidence at various ages. The preschool child is endangered by poisonings, the school-age child by drowning and firearm accidents. The immobile child under 1 year of age faces different hazards when he becomes a toddler. These factors are im- portant in planning prevention. Some children are more susceptible, and boys are generally more prone to accidents. The male death rate from accidents is twice that of the female with two exceptions. The female death rate exceeds that of the male in non- pedestrian motor vehicle accident deaths in children under 3 years of age and in deaths from fires in chil- dren 3 to 10 years of age. A child who has had a poi- soning episode is more likely to have a second than is a matched control.

The identification of *agents* involved has allowed some measures to be taken for prevention, for exam- ple, flammable fabrics and refrigerator door entrap- ment, but it will prove impossible to control acci- dents completely by abolition of the agent.

The physical and social *environment* play an im- portant role in causing accidents. It is the setting in which the host and agent interact. Time of year, time of day, illness, relocation, and frequent accidents in other members of the family have all been found to be factors which are associated with the occurrence of accidents.

A Boston study showed that there was additional stress present when accidents occurred. The stressful situations found included:

1 Hunger or fatigue. Accidents occurred more frequently during the hour before a scheduled meal, the late afternoon, or before bedtime. Ma- ternal tension is probably an important factor at these times.

2 Hyperactivity.

3 Illness, pregnancy, or menstruation of the mother. A study in England showed women more likely to have auto accidents during days of pre- menstrual tension. This has not been proved in childhood accidents, but research data suggest that a strong correlation exists.

4 Recent substitution in the caretaker of the child.

5 Illness or death of other family members.

6 A tense relationship between parents.

7 Sudden changes in environment such as occur in relocating or at vacation time.

8 Maternal preoccupation, rushed, or too busy. Saturday was found to be the worst accident day, with 3 to 6 P.M. the worst hours.

Another study has suggested that childhood acci- dents were recurring symptoms of maladjustment to environment or family. Poor housing, marital dis- harmony, and physical or mental ill health were found to be present in a significant number of these cases.

Using poisoning as a model of childhood acci- dents, it was found that repetitive poisoning was not related to environmental hazards or lack of super- vision, but rather to marital tension and a tense and distant atmosphere.

An understanding of various concepts which have been used in accident literature and research is essential.

Accident proneness implies a diagnosis of preexist- ing personality characteristics that predispose an individual to accidents. This implication tends to exclude further investigation of the environment. The concept of accident proneness is now skeptically regarded by research workers.

Accident repetitiveness is an observed pattern of behavior which lasts for varying periods of time.

Accident liability views the individual and his rela- tionship to his environment. In childhood this im- plies that not only the child, but the family and the environment are involved in accidents. Liability re- sults not only from personality characteristics but also from many other factors, such as exposure to hazards; sensory, motor, and neural functioning; ca- pacity to make judgments; degree of experience and training; and exposure to social and other stresses.

Behavior characteristics have been found which increase exposure to accident liability or reduce a child's ability to cope with hazards. Most of these features are present at 1 year of age and may be useful in identifying the child at risk.

The child with increased exposure is very active, daring, excessively curious, and happy-go-lucky; mimics the behavior of older people; and has exaggerated oral tendencies.

The child with reduced ability to cope with hazards is high-strung, hot-headed, stubborn, easily irritated or frustrated; careless in play; lacks self-control; aggressive; and has poor concentration or attention ability.

Family life-style has also been found to be a factor in accidents. Men with dull jobs appear to have a greater need for instant gratification. They seek recreational thrills and surround themselves with more dangerous devices. The children in these families have been noted to have more accidents.

Hospitalization requiring separation of infants from parents has been correlated (but not proved) with an increase in the incidence of childhood accidents as well as child abuse.

Child abuse or neglect may be a significant cause of accidents (estimates vary from 10 to 50 percent).

Any child with two or more significant accidents in a 12-month period needs an in-depth investigation of the circumstances.

The Cures

In 1970 Sobel stated that if we were to make any progress in accident prevention we must broaden our perspective to include a consideration of parental mental health and capacity to provide a milieu in which the child's needs are met.

It is not unreasonable to believe that a profile of the family and child at risk can be developed to aid in identification of the individuals in need of behavior modification and other techniques to reduce accidents.

The physician can gain insight into potential problems by obtaining a history of the family which includes parental occupation, education, income; attitude toward the children and each other; the use of medication, alcohol, tobacco; TV-watching time; and past auto accidents. A clue to the family life-style may be indicated by the family recreational activities and hobbies.

Medical personnel can attempt to gain insight into

parent-child rapport. An observation made by David Levy can be useful. He found that when something complimentary was said about a baby while the mother was holding it, the average mother would look down at the baby. If she failed to do this, there was often a lack of good rapport. Observations of the way the parent stands beside the infant on the examining table may also indicate an awareness of the baby's safety and comfort.

Parents, particularly the mothers, should be made aware of the danger signals and take extra precautions during times of additional stress, simplifying family life and doing only those things necessary to maintain health and comfort.

Until the social scientists can give us more accurate tools we must continue to seek out the agents most responsible and remove or modify these, along with continuing to educate the parents and children on accident prevention, using our present knowledge.

THE VICTIMS

The stages of childhood development can serve as a guide for the indicated accident-prevention immunization. A Boston study found a lack of understanding of developmental expectations to be present in 87 percent of the parents whose children had accidents. The physician should understand and be able to give a general view of the developmental stages, their common hazards, and the precautions that can be taken to prevent the typical accidents.

The Infant from Birth to 4 Months

These infants can *wiggle* and *squirm* but are completely helpless. There is a need for instruction in proper bathing to prevent drowning and burns, falls, aspiration hazards, crib safety, and the dangers of filmy plastics, pillows, and harnesses. Proper automotive restraints and flame retardant garments should be purchased and used.

The Infant from 4 to 7 Months

These infants are *awakening, learning* to reach, to roll over, and to sit. The parents need advice on infant furniture and toy safety. The crib or playpen is the safest area for this age group.

The Infant from 7 Months to 1 Year

These *mobile infants* have an increasing danger from falls as they begin to crawl, stand, and walk. Parents must be made aware that, as these children pull themselves erect, they pull everything down. There is danger from hanging table cloths, hot foods on the stove, dangling electric cords, empty sockets, unguarded staircases, and reachable dangerous household products and medicines. Flame-retardant clothing and proper automotive restraints are essential.

The infant under 1 year of age needs 100 percent protection. The major accidents to be prevented are mechanical suffocation, ingestion or inhalation of food or foreign objects, motor vehicle injuries, fire and burn injuries, and falls. Mechanical suffocation has been listed as the leading cause of death in this age group, but this category is suspect as it may also include cases of sudden infant death syndrome and infection.

The Toddler Age 1 to 2 Years

This *curious investigator* should alert parents to open doors, windows, and drawers. The toddler's climbing ability is excellent; they like to play in water, take everything apart, can stoop and recover, can mimic behavior of adults and older children, can push and pull, lift and carry, and have no sense of danger.

Parents must be alerted to thermal and electrical hazards and the perils of water. Safe toys should be purchased and play supervised. Syrup of Ipecac should be available in the home for emergency treatment of ingestions.

The safest area for this age group is the playpen with free periods of supervised house roaming.

The 2- to 3-year-old Child

This *hurrying child* is lightening fast and runs much of the time. The same precautions as for the toddler must still be continued.

The 3- to 5-year-old Child

Children of this age are *teachable* and should be taught their full name, traffic safety, obedience, and responsibility. Children at this age begin to develop skills, can throw objects, ride a tricycle, climb trees, and explore the neighborhood. Parents should supervise the areas where the children play and remove dangerous hazards. The children should not be relied upon to protect themselves; supervised play is advised until the age of 5 years.

The major accidents to be prevented in the age group 1 to 5 are motor vehicle injuries, fire and burn injuries, drowning, and poisoning.

The 5- to 9-year-old Child

"Daring and *adventurous"* characterize this age group. The children are often part of a group and will "try anything." They should be taught water safety, bicycle safety, and fire and burn prevention. Appropriate care should be taken if firearms are in the home. Care of pets and animal-bite prevention can be taught.

At age 6, 90 percent of their safety will be their own responsibility.

The 10- to 14-year-old

Strenuous physical activity marks this age group. Supervised recreational facilities should be available. Good examples should be set in preparation for automobile driving.

The major accidents in this age group are motor vehicle, fire, burn, and firearm injuries, and drowning.

REFERENCES

Mental Health of the Young: An Overview

Erikson, E. H.: *Childhood and Society,* 2d ed., New York: Norton, 1963.

Piaget, J.: *The Origins of Intelligence in Children,* New York: Norton, 1963.

Richmond, J. B.: Child development: A basic science for pediatrics, *Pediatrics,* 39:649–658, 1967.

Richmond, J. B.: An idea whose time has arrived, *Pediatr. Clin. North Am.,* 22:517–523, 1975.

Thomas, A., Chess, S., and Birch, H.: *Temperament and Behavior Disorders in Children*, New York: New York University Press, 1968.

Changing Patterns of Family Structure

Aries, P.: *Centuries of Childhood*, New York: Random House, Vintage Books, 1962, p. 128.

Goode, W. J.: *After Divorce*, New York: Free Press, 1957, p. 3.

Goode, W.: *World Revolution and Family Patterns*, New York: Free Press, 1963.

Goode, W. J.: *Introduction to the Contemporary American Family*, a New York Times Book, Chicago: Quadrangle Books, 1971, p. 28.

Lederer, W., and Jackson, D.: *The Mirages of Marriage*, New York: Norton, 1968.

Rubin, Z., and Peplau, L. A.: Who believes in a just World? *J. Social Issues*, **31**:65, 1975.

Skolnick, A.: *The Intimate Environment*, Boston: Little, Brown, 1973.

Skolnick, A., and Skolnick, J.: *Intimacy, Family and Society*, Boston: Little, Brown, 1974.

Employed Mothers

Hoffman, L. W., and Nye, F. I.: *Working Mothers*, San Francisco: Jossey-Bass, 1974.

Howell, M. C.: Effects of maternal employment on the child, *Pediatrics*, **52**:327, 1973.

Howell, M. C.: Employed mothers and their families, *Pediatrics*, **52**:252, 1973.

Howell, M. C.: *Helping Ourselves: Families and the Human Network*, Boston: Beacon Press, 1975.

Women Workers Today, U.S. Women's Bureau, 1976.

Day Care and Preschool Programs

American Academy of Pediatrics, Committee on Infant and Preschool Child: *Recommendations for Day Care Centers for Infants and Children*, Evanston, Ill., 1973.

Bronfenbrenner, U.: "Is Early Intervention Effective?" in *A Report on Longitudinal Evaluations of Preschool Programs*, Vol. II, U.S. Office of Human Development, 1974.

Bronfenbrenner, U.: Appendix A, "Research on the Effects of Day Care on Child Development," in Advisory Committee on Child Development of the National Research Council, *Toward a National Policy for Children and Families*, Washington, D.C.: National Academy of Sciences, 1976.

Bronfenbrenner, U.: "Who Cares for America's Children?" in V. C. Vaughan, III, and T. B. Brazelton (eds.), *The Family—Can It Be Saved?* Chicago: Year Book, 1976, 3–32.

Cohen, D. J.: *Day Care: 3. Serving Preschool Children*, U.S. Office of Child Development, 1974.

Fein, G., and Stewart, O. D.: *Day Care in Context*, New York: Wiley, 1973.

Richmond, J. B.: Disadvantaged children: what have they compelled us to learn? *Yale J. Biol. Med.*, **43**:127–144, December 1970.

Richmond, J. B., Zigler, E., and Stipek, D.: *Head Start: The First Decade*, U.S. Office of Child Development, 1977.

Rutter, M.: Parent-child-separation: psychological effects on the children, *J. Child Psychol. Psychiatr.*, **12** (4): 233–261, 1971.

Marital Discord and Divorce

Addeo, E. G.: *Inside Divorce: Is It What You Really Want?* Radnor, Pa.: Chilton, 1975.

Despert, J. L.: *Children of Divorce*, New York: Doubleday, 1962.

Freed, D. J., and Foster, H. H.: The shuffled child and divorce court, *Trial*, May/June 1974.

Goldstein, J., Freud, A., and Solnit, A. J.: *Beyond the Best Interests of the Child*, New York: Free Press, 1973.

Goode, W. J.: *Women in Divorce*, New York: Macmillan, 1969.

Hetherington, E. M., and Parke, R. D.: "The Aftermath of Divorce," in *Readings in Child Psychology: A Contemporary Viewpoint*, New York: McGraw-Hill, 1977.

Incest

Sarles, R. M.: Incest, *Pediatr. Clin. North Am.*, **22**:633–642, 1975.

Weinberg, S. K.: *Incest Behavior*, New York: Citadel Press, 1955.

Adoption

Goldstein, J., Freud, A., and Solnit, A. J.: *Beyond the Best Interests of the Child*, New York: Free Press, 1973.

"Mental Retardation," in *A Handbook for the Primary Physician*, American Medical Association, 1965.

Schechter, M. D.: "About Adoptive Parents," in E. J. Anthony and T. Benedeck (eds.), *Parenthood: Its Psychology and Psychopathology*, Boston: Little, Brown, 1970.

Schechter, M. D., and Holter, F. R.: Adopted children in their adoptive families, *Pediatr. Clin. North Am.*, **22**:653–661, 1975.

Sirosky, A. D., Baran, A., and Pannor, R.: Identity conflicts in adoptees, *Am. J. Orthopsychiatry*, **45**:18–27, 1975.

Foster Care

Felker, E.: *Foster Parenting Young Children: Guidelines for a Foster Parent*, New York: Child Welfare League of America, 1974.

Jaffee, B., and Kline, D.: *New Payment Patterns and the Foster Parent Role*, New York: Child Welfare League of America, 1970.

Moss, S., and Moss, M.: Surrogate mother-child relationships, *Am. J. Ortho-psychiatry*, **45**:382–390, April 1975.

Shyne, A.: *The Need for Foster Care*, New York: Child Welfare League of America, 1969.

Wiltse, K.: Decision making needs in foster care; Jones, M. A.: Reducing foster care through services to families; Pike, V.: permanent planning for foster children; Stone, H.: introduction to foster parenting: a new curriculum, *Children Today*, U.S. Department of Health, Education, and Welfare Publication 77-30014, vol. 5, no. 6, November-December 1976.

Legal Issues in Child Health Care

American Academy of Pediatrics, Task Force on Medical Liability: *An Introduction to Medical Liability for Pediatricians*, Evanston, Ill.: American Academy of Pediatrics, 1975.

American College of Obstetricians and Gynecologists: *Suspected Rape*, Technical Bulletin no. 14, July, 1970.

Cooke, R. E.: The role of ethics in pediatrics, *Am. J. Dis. Child*, **129**:1157, 1975.

Curran, W. J.: Confidentiality and the prediction of dangerousness in psychiatry, *N. Eng. J. Med.*, **293**:285, 1975.

Curran, W. J., and Beecher, H. K.: Experimentation in children: A reexamination of legal ethical principles, *J.A.M.A.*, **10**:77, 1969.

Duff, R. S., and Campbell, A. G. M.: Moral and ethical dilemmas in the special-care nursery, *N. Eng. J. Med.*, **289**:890, 1973.

Fletcher, J.: Abortion, euthanasia, and care of defective newborns, *N. Eng. J. Med.*, **292**:75, 1975.

Hofmann, A. D.: Is confidentiality in health care records a pediatric concern? *Pediatrics*, **57**:170, 1976.

Hoffman, A. D., and Pilpel, H. F.: The legal rights of minors, *Pediatr. Clin. North Am.*, **20**:989, 1973.

Levine, A., with Cary, E., and Divoky, D.: *The Rights of Students: The Basic ACLU Guide to a Student's Rights*, New York: Avon, 1973.

Levine, M. D., Camitta, B. B., Nathan, D., and Curran, W. J.: The medical ethics of bone marrow transplantation in childhood, *J. Pediatr.*, **86**:145, 1975.

Paul, E. W.: The sterilization of mentally retarded persons: The issues and conflicts, *Family Planning/Population Reporter*, **3**:96 1974.

Paul, E. W., Pilpel, H. F., and Wechsler, N. F.: Pregnancy, teen-agers and the law; 1976, *Family Planning Perspectives*, **8**:16, 1976.

Polier, J. W.: The child and the law: Contemporary situations in juvenile justice, *Am. J. Public Health*, **63**:386–392, 1973.

The rights of children, Parts I & II, *Harvard Educational Rev.*, **43**:481–704, 1973; **44**:1–196, 1974.

Shaw, A.: Dilemmas of "informed consent" in children, *N. Eng. J. Med.*, **289**:885, 1973.

Stone, A. A.: Overview. The right to treatment—comments on the law and its impact, *Am. J. Psychiatr.*, **132**:1125, 1975.

U.S. Department of Health, Education, and Welfare: Privacy act of 1974; Implementation, *Federal Register*, **40**:47406, Oct. 8, 1975.

U.S. Department of Health, Education, and Welfare: Privacy rights of parents and students; Implementation, *Federal Register*, **40**:1208, Jan. 6, 1975; **41**:9062, Mar. 2, 1976.

Zuckerman, R. J.: Abortion and contraception: A minor's constitutional right to privacy, *Family Planning/Population Reporter*, **4**:114, 1975.

A Developmental Approach to Behavior Problems

Balint, M.: *The Doctor, His Patient and the Illness*, New York: International Universities Press, 1972.

Carey, W. B.: A simplified method for measuring infant temperament, *J. Pediatr.*, **77**:188–194, 1970.

Erikson, E.: *Childhood and Society*, New York: Norton, 1950.

Frankenburg, W. K. et al.: Revised Denver Developmental Screening Test, *J. Pediatr.*, **79**:988, 1971.

Lewis, M.: *Clinical Aspects of Child Development*, Philadelphia: Lea and Febiger, 1971.

Murphy, L.: *The Widening World of Childhood*, New York: Basic Books, 1962.

Murphy, L., and Moriarty, A.: *Vulnerability, Coping, and Growth*, New Haven: Yale University Press, 1976.

Thomas, A., Chess, S., and Birch, H.: *Temperament and Behavior Disorders in Children*, New York: New York University Press, 1968.

Negativistic Behavior

Fraiberg, S. H.: *The Magic Years*, New York: Scribner, 1959.

Levy, D.: "Oppositional Syndromes and Oppositional Behavior," in P. H. Hoch and J. Zubin (eds.), *Psychopathology of Childhood*, New York: Grune & Stratton, 1955.

Lewis, M.: *Clinical Aspects of Child Development*, Philadelphia: Lea & Febiger, 1971.

Senn, M. J. E., and Solnit, A. J.: *Problems in Child Behavior and Development*, Philadelphia: Lea & Febiger, 1968.

Colic

Brazelton, R. B.: Crying in infancy, *Pediatrics*, **29**:579–588, 1962.

Sumpter, E. A.: Behavior problems in early childhood, *Pediatr. Clin. North Am.*, **22**:663–672, 1975.

Thomas, A., Chess, S., and Birch, H. G.: *Temperament and Behavior Disorders in Children*, New York: New York University Press, 1968.

Wessel, M. A., Cobb, J. C., Jackson, E. B., Harris, Jr., G. S., and Detwiler, A. C.: Paroxysmal fussing in infancy, sometimes called "colic," *Pediatrics*, **14**:421–434, 1954.

Self-Stimulating Behavior

Fletcher, B.: Etiology of fingersucking: Review of literature, *J. Dent. Child.*, **42**:293–298, 1975.

Green, A.: Self-mutilation in schizophrenic children, *Arch. Gen. Psychiatry*, **17**:234–244, 1967.

Kravitz, H., Rosenthal, V., Teplitz, A., Murphy, J., and Lesser, R.: A study of head-banding in infants and children, *Dis. Nerv. Syst.*, **21**:203–208, 1960.

Lourie, R.: The role of rhythmic patterns in childhood, *Am. J. Psychiatry*, **105**:653–660, 1949.

Smolev, S. R.: Use of operant techniques for the modification of self-injurious behavior, *Am. J. Ment. Defic.*, **76**:295–305, 1971.

Fecal Soiling and Retention

Hoag, J. M., Norris, N. G., Himeno, E. T., and Jacobs, J.: The encopretic child and his family, *J. Am. Acad. Child Psychiatry*, **10**:242–256, 1971.

Levine, M. D., and Bakow, H.: Children and encopresis, *Pediatrics*, **58**:845–852, 1976.

Richmond, J. B., Eddy, E. J., and Garrard, S. D.: The syndrome of fecal soiling and megacolon, *Am. J. Orthopsychiatry*, **24**:391–401, 1954.

Enuresis

Brazelton, R. B.: A child oriented approach to toilet training, *Pediatrics*, **29**:121, 1962.

Cohen, M.: Enuresis, *Pediatr. Clin. North Am.*, **24**:545, August 1975.

Marshall, S., et al.: Enuresis: An analysis of various therapeutic approaches, *Pediatrics*, **52**(6):813–817, December 1973.

Poussaint, A. F., et al.: A controlled study of imipramine (Tofranil), *J. Pediatr.*, **67**:283, August 1965.

Starfield, B.: Enuresis: Its pathogenesis and management, *Clin. Pediatr.*, **11**:343–350, June 1972.

Werry, J. A.: The conditioning treatment of enuresis, *Am. J. Psychiatry*, 123–226, August 1966.

Nightmares and Other Sleep Disturbances

Broughton, R.: Sleep disorders: Disorders of arousal? *Science*, **159**:1070–1078, 1968.

Guilleminault, C., and Anders, T.: The pathophysiology of sleep disorders in pediatrics. II. Sleep disorders in children, *Adv. Pediatr.*, **22**:151–174, 1976.

Kales, A., and Kales, J.: Sleep disorders: Recent findings in the diagnosis and treatment of disturbed sleep, *N. Engl. J. Med.*, **290**:487–499, 1974.

Nagera, H.: Sleep and its disturbances approached developmentally, *Psychoanal. Study Child*, **21**:393, 1966.

Tics

Kanner, L.: *Child Psychiatry*, 4th ed., Springfield, Ill.: Charles C Thomas, 1972, chap. XXXII, "The Muscular System."

Mahler, M. S.: A psychoanalytic evaluation of tic in psychopathology of children, *Psychoanal. Study Child*, **3**:279–310, 1949.

Shapiro, A. K., Shapiro, E., and Wayne, H. L.: The symptomatology and diagnosis of Gilles de la Tourette's syndrome, *J. Am. Acad. Child Psychiatry*, **12**:702–723, 1973.

Woodrow, K. M.: Gilles de la Tourette's Disease—A review, *Am. J. Psychiatry*, **131**:1000–1003, 1974.

Phobias

Anthony, E. J.: "Psychoneurotic Disorders," in A. M. Freedman and H. I. Kaplan (eds.), *Comprehensive Textbook of Psychiatry*, Baltimore: Williams & Wilkins 1975, vol. 2.

Freud, S.: "Analysis of a Phobia in a Five Year Old Boy," *Standard Edition*, London: Hogarth, 1955, vol. 10, pp. 5–149.

Schmitt, B. D.: School phobia—the great imitator: A pediatrician's viewpoint, *Pediatrics*, **48**:433–441, 1971.

Lying and Stealing

Clemmens, R. L., and Kenny, T. J.: *Behavioral Pediatrics and Child Development*, Baltimore: Williams & Wilkins, 1975.

Fraiberg, S. H.: *The Magic Years*, New York: Scribner, 1959.

Ilg, F. L., and Ames, L. B.: *Child Behavior*, New York: Harper & Row, 1955.

Spock, B.: *Baby and Child Care*, New York: Pocket Books, 1971.

Depression in Childhood

Cytryn, L., and McKnew, D. H.: Proposed classification of childhood depression, *Am. J. Psychiatry*, **129**:149–155, 1972.

McDermott, J. F.: Divorce and its psychiatric sequelae in children, *Arch. Gen. Psychiatry*, **23**:421–427, 1970.

Malmquist, C. P.: Depressions in child and adolescence, *N. Engl. J. Med.*, **284**:887–893, 955–961, 1971.

Pearce, J.: Depressive disorder in childhood, *J. Child Psychol. Psychiat.*, **18**:79–82, 1977.

Powell, G. F., Brasel, J. A., and Blizzard, R. M.: Emotional deprivation and growth retardation simulating idiopathic hypopituitarism, *N. Engl. J. Med.*, **276**:1271–1283, 1967.

Spitz, R. A.: Anaclitic depression, *Psychoanal. Study Child*, **2**:313–342, 1946.

Childhood Fire Setting

Heath, A. H., Gayton, W. F., and Hardesty, V. A.: Childhood firesetting: A review of the literature, *Can. Psychiatr. Assoc. J.*, in press.

Kaufman, I., Henis, L. W., and Reiser, D. E.: A re-evaluation of the psychodynamics of fire setting, *Am. J. Orthopsychiatry*, **22**:63–72, 1961.

Nurcombe, B.: Children who set fires, *Med. J. Aust.*, **1**:579–584, 1964.

Rothstein, F.: Explorations of ego structures of firesetting children, *Arch. Gen. Psychiatry*, **9**:246–253, 1963.

Vandersall, J. A., and Wiener, J. M.: Children who set fires, *Arch. Gen. Psychiatry*, **22**:63–71, 1970.

Yarnell, H.: Firesetting in children, *Am. J. Orthopsychiatry*, **10**:262–286, 1970.

Child Abuse and Child Neglect

Ebeling, N. B., and Hill, D. A. (eds.): *Child Abuse: Intervention and Treatment*, Acton, Mass.: Publishing Sciences Group, 1975.

Gil, D. G.: *Violence against Children*, Cambridge, Mass.: Harvard, 1970.

Goldstein, J., Freud, A., and Solnit, A.: *Beyond the Best Interests of the Child*, New York: Free Press, 1973.

Helfer, R. E., and Kempe, C. H. (eds.): *The Battered Child*, 2d ed., Chicago: University of Chicago Press, 1975.

Helfer, R. E., and Kempe, C. H. (eds.): *Child Abuse and Neglect: The Family and Community*, Cambridge, Mass.: Ballinger, 1976.

Kempe C. H, and Helfer, R. E. (eds.): *Helping the Battered Child and His Family*, Philadelphia: Lippincott, 1972.

Martin, H. (ed.): *The Abused Child: A Multidisciplinary Approach to Development Issues and Treatment*, Cambridge, Mass.: Ballinger, 1976.

Walters, D.: *Physical and Sexual Abuse of Children: Causes and Treatment*, Bloomington, Ind.: Indiana University Press, 1975.

Sexual Misuse of Children

Brant, R. S. T., and Tisza, V. B.: The sexually misused child, *Am. J. Orthopsychiatry*, **47**:80–90, 1977.

Burgess, A. W., and Holmstrom, L. L.: Rape and trauma syndrome, *Am. J. Psychiatry*, **131**:981–986, 1974.

Lewis, M., and Sarrell, M.: Some psychological aspects of seduction, incest and rape in childhood, *J. Am. Acad. Child Psychiatry*, **8**:609–619, 1969.

Lustig, N., Dresser, J. W., Spellman, S. W., and Murray, T. B.: Incest, *Arch. Gen. Psychiatry*, **14**:31–40, 1966.

Rosenfeld, A. A., Nadelson, C., Krieger, M. J., and Backman, J.: Incest and sexual abuse of children, *J. Am. Acad. Child Psychiatry*, **16**:334–346, 1977.

Sarles, R. M.: Incest, *Pediatr. Clin. North Am.*, **22**(3):633–642, 1975.

Weiss, J., Rogers, E., Darwin, M. R., and Dutton, C. E.: *Psychiatr. Q.*, **29**:1–27, 1955.

Childhood Psychosis

Ekstein, R.: "Functional Psychoses in Children: Clinical Features and Treatment," in A. M. Freedman, H. I. Kaplan, and B. J. Sadock (eds.), *Comprehensive Textbook of Psychiatry*, 2d ed., Baltimore: Williams & Wilkins, 1975, pp. 2189–2200.

Goldfarb, W.: "Childhood Psychosis," in P. H. Mussen (ed.), *Carmichael's Manual of Child Psychology*, 3d ed., New York: Wiley, 1970, vol. 2, pp. 765–830.

Miller, R. T.: Childhood schizophrenia: A review of selected literature, *Int. J. Mental Health*, **3**:3–46, 1974.

Rimland, B.: "Infantile Autism: Status and Research," in A. Davids (ed.), *Child Personality and Psychopathology: Current Topics*, New York: Wiley, 1974, vol. 1, pp. 137–167.

Weiner, I. B.: *Psychological Disturbance in Adolescence*, New York: Wiley, 1970, chap 4, "Schizophrenia."

Weiner, I. B., and Del Gaudio, A. C.: Psychopathology in adolescence: An epidemiological study, *Arch. Gen. Psychiatry*, **33**:187–193, 1976.

Health Care Delivery to Adolescents

Gallagher, J. R., Heald, F. P., and Garell, D. C. (eds.): *Medical Care of the Adolescent*, 3d ed., New York: Appleton-Century-Crofts, 1976.

Kalogerakis, M. G. (ed): *The Emotionally Troubled Adolescent and the Family Physician*, Springfield, Ill.: Charles C Thomas, 1973.

Psychosocial Development of Adolescents

Conger, J. J.: *Adolescence and Youth*, New York: Harper & Row, 1973.

Erickson, E. H.: *Identity: Youth and Crisis*, New York: Norton, 1968.

Offer, D.: *The Psychological World of the Teen-Ager: A Study of Normal Adolescence*, New York: Basic Books, 1969.

Semmens, J. P., and Krantz, K. E. (eds.): *The Adolescent Experience: A Counseling Guide to Social and Sexual Behavior*, New York: Macmillan, 1970.

Weiner, I. B.: *Psychological Disturbance in Adolescence*, New York: Wiley, 1970.

Whisnant, L.: A study of attitudes toward menarche in white middle-class American adolescent girls, *Am. J. Psychiatry*, **132**:809, 1975.

The Secular and Cultural Influences on Growth and Development

Bowditch, H. P.: *Eighth Annual Report, State Board of Health*, Boston: Wright, 1877.

Cone, T. E., Jr.: Secular acceleration of height and biologic maturation in children during the past century, *J. Pediatr.*, **59**:736, 1961.

Frisch, R. E.: "Critical Weight and Menarche: Initiation of the Adolescent

Growth Spurt, and Control of Puberty," in M. M. Grumbach, G. D. Grave, and F. E. Mayer (eds.), *Control of Onset of Puberty*, New York: Wiley, 1974.

Hathaway, M. L., and Foard, E. D.: *Heights and Weights of Adults in the United States*, Human Nutrition Research Division, Agricultural Research Service, U.S. Department of Agriculture, Home Economics Research Report 10, 1960.

Tanner, J. M.: *Growth at Adolescence*, 2d ed., Springfield, Ill.: Charles C Thomas, 1962.

The Short Boy and the Tall Girl

Bayley, N., and Pinneau, S. R.: Tables for predicting adult height from skeletal age, revised for use with the Greulich-Pyle hand standards, *J. Pediatr.*, **40**:423, 1952.

Gallagher, J. R.: "Short and Tall Stature in Otherwise Normal Adolescents: Management of the Medical and Psychological Problems," in L. I. Garnder (ed.): *Endocrine and Genetic Diseases of Childhood*, Philadelphia: Saunders, 1969.

Mussen, P. H., Conger, J. J., and Kayan, J.: *Child Development and Personality*, New York: Harper & Row, 1963, chap. 13, "Adolescence."

Tanner, J. M.: Sequence, tempo and individual variation in the growth and development of boys and girls aged twelve to sixteen, *Daedalus*, **100**:907, 1971.

Wettenhall, H. N. B.: "Growth Problems," in J. R. Gallagher, F. P. Heald, and D. C. Garell (eds.): *Medical Care of the Adolescent*, 3d ed., New York: Appleton-Century-Crofts, 1976.

Adolescent Sexual Behavior

Ford, C. F., and Beach, F. A.: *Patterns of Sexual Behavior*, New York: Harper & Row, 1951.

Kaplan, H. S.: *The New Sex Therapy*, New York: Brunner/Mazel, 1974.

Kinsey, A. C., Pomeroy, W. B., and Martin, C. E.: *Sexual Behavior in the Human Male*, Philadelphia: Saunders, 1948.

Kinsey, A. C., Pomeroy, W. B., Martin, C. E., and Gebhard, P. H.: *Sexual Behavior in the Human Female*, Philadelphia: Saunders, 1953.

Schofield, M.: *The Sexual Behavior of Young People*, Gretna, La.: Pelican Books, 1968.

Sorenson, R. C.: *Adolescent Sexuality in Contemporary America*, New York: World, 1973.

Zelnick, M., and Kantner, J.: The probability of premarital intercourse, *Soc. Sci. Res.*, **1**:335, 1972.

The Teenage Parent

Duenhoelter, J. R., Jimenez, J., and Baumann, G.: Pregnancy performance of patients under 15 years of age, *Obstet. Gynecol.*, **46**:49, 1975.

Klerman, L. V., and Jekel, J. F.: *School-Age Mothers: Problems, Programs, and Policy*, Hamden, Conn.: Shoe String Press, 1973.

McAnarney, E. R.: Adolescent pregnancy: A pediatric concern?, *Clin. Pediatr.*, **14:**19, 1975.

Sarrel, P., and Davis, C.: The young unwed primipara: A study of 100 cases with a 5 year follow-up, *Am. J. Obstet. Gynecol.*, **95:**722, 1966.

Stickle, G., and Ma, P.: Pregnancy in adolescents: Scope of the problem, *Contemporary Ob-Gyn*, **5:**85–91, 1975.

Rape

Brugess, A. W., and Holstrom, L. L.: Rape trauma syndrome, *Am. J. Psychiatry*, **131:**981, 1974.

Davis, A. J.: "Sexual Assaults in the Philadelphia Prison System and Sheriff's Vans," in A. Shiloh (ed.): *Studies in Human Sexual Behavior: The American Scene*, Springfield, Ill.: Charles C Thomas, 1970, pp. 330–340.

Hilberman, E.: *The Rape Victim*, American Psychiatric Association, 1976.

Sutherland, S., and Scherl, D. J.: Patterns of response among victims of rape, *Am. J. Orthopsychiatry*, **40:**503, 1970.

U.S. Federal Bureau of Investigation: *Uniform Crime Reports of the United States*, 1970.

Adolescent Depression and Suicide

Finch, S. M., and Poznanski, E. O.: *Adolescent Suicide*, Springfield, Ill.: Charles C Thomas, 1971.

Malmquist, C. P.: Depressions in childhood and adolescence, *N. Engl. J. Med.*, **284:**887, 1971.

Mattsson, A., Seese, L. R., and Hawkins, J. W.: Suicidal behavior as a child psychiatric emergency, *Arch. Gen. Psychiatry*, **20:**100, 1969.

Morrison, G. C. (ed.): *Emergencies in Child Psychiatry: Emotional Crises of Children, Youth and Their Families*, Springfield, Ill.: Charles C Thomas, 1975.

Schneer, H. I., Perlstein, A., and Brozovsky, M.: Hospitalized suicidal adolescents: Two generations, *J. Am. Acad. Child Psychiatry*, **14:**268, 1975.

Anorexia Nervosa

Bruch, H.: *Eating Disorders: Obesity, Anorexia Nervosa and the Person Within*, New York: Basic Books, 1973; London: Routledge, 1974.

Bruch, H.: Perils of behavior modification in treatment of anorexia nervosa, *J.A.M.A.*, **230:**1419, 1974.

Dally, P.: *Anorexia Nervosa*, New York: Grune & Stratton, 1969.

Minuchin, S., Baker, L., Rossman, B., et al.: A conceptual model of psychosomatic illness in children, *Arch. Gen. Psychiatry*, **32:**1031, 1975.

Runaway Children

American Academy of Pediatrics, Committee on Youth: A model act providing for consent of minors for health services, *Pediatrics*, **51**:293, 1973.

Howell, M. C., Emmons, E. B., and Frank, C. A.: Reminiscenses of runaway adolescents, *Am. J. Orthopsychiatry*, **42**:840, 1973.

Saltonstall, M. B.: *Runaways and Street Children in Massachusetts*, Boston: Massachusetts Committee for Children and Youth, February 1973.

U.S. Senate, Committee on the Judiciary, 92d Congress, Subcommittee to Investigate Juvenile Delinquency: *Runaway Youth*, Washington, D.C. 1972.

Walker, D. K.: *Runaway Youth: An Annotated Bibliography and Literature Overview*, Office of Social Services and Human Development, Office of the Assistant Secretary of Planning and Evaluation, U.S. Department of Health, Education, and Welfare, May 1975.

Drug, Alcohol, and Tobacco Abuse

American Academy of Pediatrics, Committee on Environmental Hazards: Effects of cigarette-smoking on the fetus and child, *Pediatrics*, **57**:411, 1976.

Banks, T., Fletcher, R., and Ali, N.: Infective endocarditis in heroin addicts, *Am. J. Med.*, **55**:444, 1973.

Buchner, L., Cimino, J., Raybin, H., and Stewart, B.: Naloxone reversal of methadone poisoning, *N.Y.S. J. Med.*, **72**:2305, 1972.

Hadden, J., Johnson, K., Smith, S., et al.: Acute barbiturate intoxication, *J.A.M.A.*, **209**:893, 1969.

Litt, I. F., and Cohen, M. I.: The drug-using adolescent as a pediatric patient, *J. Pediatr.*, **77**:195, 1970.

Litt, I. F., Cohen, M. I., Schonberg, S. K., et al.: Liver disease in the drug-using adolescent, *J. Pediatr.*, **81**:238, 1972.

Maugh, T. H.: Marihuana: The grass may no longer be greener, *Science*, **185**:683, 1974.

Richter, R. W., and Pearson, J.: "Heroin Addiction-related Neurologic Disorders," in R. Richter (ed.): *Medical Aspects of Drug Abuse*, Hagerstown, Md.: Harper & Row, 1975.

Sellers, E. M., and Kalant, H.: Drug therapy: Alcohol intoxication and withdrawal, *N. Engl. J. Med.*, **294**:757, 1976.

Smith, D. E., and Wesson, D. R.: Phenobarbital technique for treatment of barbiturate dependence, *Arch. Gen. Psychiatry*, **24**:56, 1971.

Solursh, L., and Clement, W.: Hallucinogenic drug abuse: Manifestations and management, *Can. Med. Assoc. J.*, **98**:407, 1968.

Weil, A. T., Zinberg, N. E., and Nelson, J. M.: Clinical and psychological effects of marijuana in man, *Science*, **162**:1234, 1968.

Conversion Reactions

Apley, J.: *The Child with Abdominal Pains*, Oxford, England: Blackwell Scientific Publications, 1959.

Chodoff, P., and Lyons, H.: Hysteria: The hysterical personality and "hysterical" conversion, *Am. J. Psychiatry,* **114:**734, 1958.

Engel, G. L.: "Conversion Symptoms," in C. M. MacBryde and R. S. Blacklow (eds.): *Signs and Symptoms: Applied Physiology and Clinical Interpretation,* Philadelphia: Lippincott, 1970.

Friedman, R.: Some characteristics of children with "psychogenic" pain, observations on prognosis and management, *Clin. Pediatr.,* **11:**331, 1972.

Friedman, S. B.: Conversion symptoms in adolescents, *Pediatr. Clin. North Am.,* **20:**873, 1973.

Oster, J.: Recurrent abdominal pain, headache and limb pains in children and adolescents, *Pediatrics,* **50:**429, 1972.

Schmitt, B. D.: School phobia—the great imitator: A pediatrician's viewpoint, *Pediatrics,* **48:**433, 1971.

Childhood Accidents

Dietrich, H. F.: Accident prevention in childhood is your problem, too, *Pediatr. Clin. North Am.,* November, 1954, p. 759.

Haddon, W., Jr., et al.: *Accident Research Methods and Approaches,* New York: Harper & Row, 1964.

Klein, D.: The influence of societal values on rates of death and injury, *J. Safety Res.,* **3:**1, 1971.

Matheny, A. P., et al.: Assessment of children's behavioral characteristics: A tool in accident prevention, *Clin. Pediatr.,* **11:**437, 1972.

Sobel, R.: The psychiatric implications of accidental poisoning in childhood, *Pediatr. Clin. North Am.,* **17:**653, 1970.

Index